Research Anthology on Big Data Analytics, Architectures, and Applications

Information Resources Management Association
USA

Volume I

Published in the United States of America by
IGI Global
Engineering Science Reference (an imprint of IGI Global)
701 E. Chocolate Avenue
Hershey PA, USA 17033
Tel: 717-533-8845
Fax: 717-533-8661
E-mail: cust@igi-global.com
Web site: http://www.igi-global.com

Library of Congress Cataloging-in-Publication Data

Names: Information Resources Management Association, editor.
Title: Research anthology on big data analytics, architectures, and
  applications / Information Resources Management Association, editor.
Description: Hershey, PA : Engineering Science Reference, an imprint of IGI
  Global, [2022] | Includes bibliographical references and index. |
  Contents: Overview of big data and its visualization / Richard S.
  Segall, Arkansas State University, USA, Gao Niu, Bryant University, USA
  -- Big data analytics and visualization of performance of stock exchange
  companies based on balanced scorecard indicators / Iman Raeesi Vanani,
  Allameh Tabataba'i University, Iran, Maziar Shiraj Kheiri, Allameh
  Tabataba'i University, Iran. | Summary: "This complete reference source
  on big data analytics that offers the latest, innovative architectures
  and frameworks, as well as explores a variety of applications within
  various industries offering an international perspective on a variety of
  topics such as advertising curricula, driven supply chain, and smart
  cities"-- Provided by publisher.
Identifiers: LCCN 2021039213 (print) | LCCN 2021039214 (ebook) | ISBN
  9781668436622 (h/c) | ISBN 9781668436639 (eisbn)
Subjects: LCSH: Big data. | Quantitative research.
Classification: LCC QA76.9.B45 .R437 2022 (print) | LCC QA76.9.B45
  (ebook) | DDC 005.7--dc23/eng/20211019
LC record available at https://lccn.loc.gov/2021039213
LC ebook record available at https://lccn.loc.gov/2021039214

British Cataloguing in Publication Data
A Cataloguing in Publication record for this book is available from the British Library.

The views expressed in this book are those of the authors, but not necessarily of the publisher.

For electronic access to this publication, please contact: eresources@igi-global.com.

List of Contributors

Table of Contents

Section 2
Development and Design Methodologies

Volume II

Section 3
Tools and Technologies

Section 4
Utilization and Applications

Volume IV

Section 5
Organizational and Social Implications

Section 7
Critical Issues and Challenges

Preface

Society is now completely driven by data with many industries relying on data to conduct business or basic functions within the organization. With the efficiencies that big data bring to all institutions, data are continuously being collected and analyzed. However, data sets may be too complex for traditional data processing, and therefore, different strategies must evolve to solve the issue. For managers, data management can be particularly overwhelming as businesses sift through information and determine how to utilize it. Thus, investigating the current architectures and applications of data analytics is integral for achieving efficient and productive processes. The field of big data works as a valuable tool for many different industries.

Staying informed of the most up-to-date research trends and findings is of the utmost importance. That is why IGI Global is pleased to offer this four-volume reference collection of reprinted IGI Global book chapters and journal articles that have been handpicked by senior editorial staff. This collection will shed light on critical issues related to the trends, techniques, and uses of various applications by providing both broad and detailed perspectives on cutting-edge theories and developments. This collection is designed to act as a single reference source on conceptual, methodological, technical, and managerial issues, as well as to provide insight into emerging trends and future opportunities within the field.

The *Research Anthology on Big Data Analytics, Architectures, and Applications* is organized into seven distinct sections that provide comprehensive coverage of important topics. The sections are:

1. Fundamental Concepts and Theories;
2. Development and Design Methodologies;
3. Tools and Technologies;
4. Utilization and Applications;
5. Organizational and Social Implications;
6. Managerial Impact; and
7. Critical Issues and Challenges.

The following paragraphs provide a summary of what to expect from this invaluable reference tool.

Section 1, "Fundamental Concepts and Theories," serves as a foundation for this extensive reference tool by addressing crucial theories essential to understanding the concepts and uses of big data in multidisciplinary settings. Opening this reference book is the chapter "Understanding Big Data" by Profs. Naciye Güliz Uğur and Aykut Hamit Turan of Sakarya University, Turkey, which defines big data basically and provides an overview of big data in terms of status, organizational effects (technology, healthcare, education, etc.), implementation challenges, and big data projects. This first section ends with the chapter "A Brief Survey on Big Data in Healthcare" by Prof. Ebru Aydindag Bayrak of Istanbul University-Cerrahpaşa, Turkey and Prof. Pinar Kirci of Bursa Uludağ University, Turkey, which presents a brief introduction to big data and big data analytics and their roles in the healthcare system.

Section 2, "Development and Design Methodologies," presents in-depth coverage of the design and development of big data architectures for their use in different applications. This section starts with "Big Data Analytics and Models" by Prof. Ferdi Sönmez of Istanbul Arel University, Turkey; Prof. Ziya Nazım Perdahçı of Mimar Sinan Fine Arts University, Turkey; and Prof. Mehmet Nafiz Aydın of Kadir Has University, Turkey, which explores big data analytics as a comprehensive technique for processing large amounts of data to uncover insights. This section ends with the chapter "Big Data Analytics and Visualization for Food Health Status Determination Using Bigmart Data" by Profs. Sumit Arun Hirve and Pradeep Reddy C. H. of VIT-AP University, India, which elaborates on pre-processing a commercial market dataset using the R tool and its packages for information and visual analytics.

Section 3, "Tools and Technologies," explores the various tools and technologies used in the implementation of big data analytics for various uses. This section begins with "Big Data and Advance Analytics: Architecture, Techniques, Applications, and Challenges" by Prof. Surabhi Verma of National Institute of Industrial Engineering, Mumbai, India, which investigates the characteristics of big data, processes of data management, advance analytic techniques, applications across sectors, and issues that are related to their effective implementation and management within broader context of big data analytics. This section ends with the chapter "Big Data for Satellite Image Processing: Analytics, Tools, Modeling, and Challenges" by Prof. P. Swarnalatha of Vellore Institute of Technology, Vellore, India and Prof. Prabu Sevugan of VIT University, India, which presents an introduction to the basics in big data including architecture, modeling, and the tools used.

Section 4, "Utilization and Applications," describes how big data is used and applied in diverse industries for various technologies and applications. The opening chapter in this section, "An Analysis of Big Data Analytics," by Profs. Vijander Singh, Amit Kumar Bairwa and Deepak Sinwar of Manipal University Jaipur, India, explains that the immense measure of organized, unstructured, and semi-organized information is produced each second around the cyber world, which should be managed efficiently. This section ends with the chapter "Computational and Data Mining Perspectives on HIV/AIDS in Big Data Era: Opportunities, Challenges, and Future Directions" by Prof. Ali Al Mazari of Alfaisal University, Saudi Arabia, which provides a review on the computational and data mining perspectives on HIV/AIDS in big data era.

Section 5, "Organizational and Social Implications," includes chapters discussing the ways in which big data impacts society and shows the ways in which big data is used in different industries and how this impacts business. The chapter "Big Data and IoT Applications in Real Life Environment" by Prof. Anjali Chaudhary of Noida International University, India and Pradeep Tomar of Gautam Buddha University, India, discusses various applications of big data and IoT in detail and discusses how both the technologies are affecting our daily life and how it can make things better. This section ends with the chapter "Cloud Computing Big Data Adoption Impacts on Teaching and Learning in Higher Education: A Systematic Review" by Prof Fahad Nasser Alhazmi of King Abdulaziz University, Saudi Arabia, which evaluates and assesses the impact of big data and cloud computing in higher education.

Section 6, "Managerial Impact," presents coverage of academic and research perspectives on the way big data analytics affects management in the workplace. Starting this section is "Big Data Technologies and Management" by Profs. Jayashree K. and Abirami R. of Rajalakshmi Engineering College, India, which discusses the background of big data. It also discusses the various application of big data in detail. This section ends with the chapter "Exploring Big Data Analytic Approaches to Cancer Blog Text Analysis" by Prof. Viju Raghupathi of Koppelman School of Business, Brooklyn College of the City University of New York, Brooklyn, USA and Profs. Yilu Zhou and Wullianallur Raghupathi of Gabelli School of Business, Fordham University, New York, USA, which establishes an exploratory approach to involving big data analytics methods in developing text analytics applications for the analysis of cancer blogs.

Section 7, "Critical Issues and Challenges," highlights current problems within the field and offers solutions for future improvement. Opening this final section is the chapter "A Survey on Comparison of Performance Analysis on a Cloud-Based Big Data Framework" by Profs. Krishan Tuli and Amanpreet Kaur of Chandigarh University, India and Prof. Meenakshi Sharma of Galgotias University, India, which discusses the survey on the performance of the big data framework based on a cloud from various endeavors which assists ventures to pick a suitable framework for their work and get a desired outcome. This section ends with the chapter "How Big Data Transforms Manufacturing Industry: A Review Paper" by Profs. Victor I. C. Chang and Wanxuan Lin of Xi'an Jiaotong-Liverpool University, Suzhou, China, which defines what big data means for the manufacturing industry. It explains four advantages about big data analytics and their benefits to manufacturing.

Although the primary organization of the contents in this multi-volume work is based on its seven sections, offering a progression of coverage of the important concepts, methodologies, technologies, applications, social issues, and emerging trends, the reader can also identify specific contents by utilizing the extensive indexing system listed at the end of each volume. As a comprehensive collection of research on the latest findings related to big data, the *Research Anthology on Big Data Analytics, Architectures, and Applications* provides data scientists, data analysts, computer engineers, software engineers, technologists, government officials, managers, CEOs, professors, graduate students, researchers, and academicians with a complete understanding of the application and impact of big data. Given the vast number of issues concerning usage, failure, success, strategies, and applications of big data in modern technologies and processes, the *Research Anthology on Big Data Analytics, Architectures, and Applications* encompasses the most pertinent research on its uses and impact on global institutions.

Section 1
Fundamental Concepts and Theories

Chapter 1
Understanding Big Data

Naciye Güliz Uğur
iD https://orcid.org/0000-0003-2364-5445
Sakarya University, Turkey

Aykut Hamit Turan
Sakarya University, Turkey

ABSTRACT

In today's world, it is necessary to use data or information available in a wise manner to make effective business decisions and define better objectives. If the information available is not utilized to its full extent, organizations might lose their reputation and position in this competitive world. However, data needs to be processed appropriately to gain constructive insights from it, and the heterogeneous nature of this data makes this increasingly more complex and time-consuming. The ever-increasing growth of data generated is far more than human processing capabilities and thus computing methods need to be automated to scale effectively. This chapter defines Big Data basically and provides an overview of Big Data in terms of current status, organizational effects (technology, health care, education, etc.), implementation challenges and Big Data projects. This research adopted literature review as methodology and refined valuable information through current journals, books, magazines and blogs.

INTRODUCTION

Big data has been one of the major areas of focus in the field of data management. Big data provides the business solutions which help the organizations making their decisions. Current growing value for the data helps organizations innovate quickly the optimum usage of data and keep up the edge (Lukoinova and Rubin, 2014).

Implementation of methodologies should be in context with a technology base that is growing to be a moving target. The main technology behind fostering the rate of innovation in big data platforms and solutions is the open source technology development and delivery model. Organizations face challenges with evolving business needs and technologies, organizations hold the flexibility for the platforms, solu-

DOI: 10.4018/978-1-6684-3662-2.ch001

tions, and evolving their capabilities so that they derive value and positive insights from their big data investments (Nimmagadda and Dreher, 2013).

According to the latest Worldwide Semiannual Big Data and Analytics Spending Guide from International Data Corporation (IDC), worldwide revenues for big data and business analytics (BDA) will grow from $130.1 billion in 2016 to more than $203 billion in 2020 (IDC, 2015).

Figure 1. Market predictions on big data (USD Billion)
Source: IDC (2015)

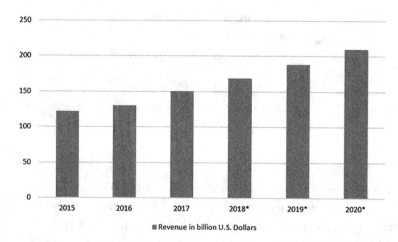

Organizations which handle the big data and implement its methodologies are expected to make 40% more profits than regular software industry does in the current scenario. The increasing value for big data makes it easier to predict the gains for the organization in the future. Organizations currently lack the human resource and talent which can give them the best big data engineering experience and help them grow.

The era of big data has established a new path for exploring data in newer forms and finding different ways to handle the data on a large scale. Although processing and maintaining a large data is a challenge, big data challenges have given the scope to find a solution for these challenges and implement them for a better data environment (Chen et al., 2013). Big data has been into existence since the 1990s and data integration has been one of the major challenges since then. Data Integration in large: Challenges of Reuse, a research paper which was published in 1994 signifies the existence of big data from 1990s.

This chapter defines Big Data basically and provides an overview of Big Data in terms of current status, organizational effects (technology, health care, education etc.), implementation challenges and Big Data projects. This research adopted literature review as methodology and refined valuable information through current journals, books, magazines and blogs.

BACKGROUND

Evolution of large data sets from major industries is termed as big data in the field of data science. The first large-scale methods for metadata creation and analysis (an arrangement of clay tablets revealing data about livestock) has been linked to the Sumerian people, active in the early Bronze Age (Erikson, 1950). Similarly, card catalogs, and other information methods used in libraries (Lee, Clarke and Perti, 2015), are forerunners to the large-scale digitized metadata collections of today, as they too were technologies used for gathering and storing facts about data in comprehensive and systematized ways (Lee, Clarke and Perti, 2015). The rise in digital technology is leading to the overflow of data (Gog et al., 2015), which constantly requires more updated and faster data storage systems (Sookhak, Gani, Khan, and Buyya, 2017). The recognition of data excess started as early as the 1930s but was not actually named Big Data until the mid-1990s by John Mashey (Kitchin and McArdle, 2016). The sudden increase in the U.S. population, the dispensing of social security numbers, and the wide-ranging increase of knowledge (research) required more detailed and organized record-keeping (Gandomi and Haider, 2015).

Big data can be classified as the large volumes of data-sets with a higher complexity level. Gandomi and Haider (2015), IDC, IBM, Gartner, and many others have contributed with an excellent summary regarding Big Data characteristics. Clearly, size is the first characteristic that comes to mind considering the question "what is big data?" (Gandomi and Haider 2015). Following that, the Three V's have emerged as a common framework to describe big data (Chen, Chiang, and Storey, 2012; Kwon, Lee, and Shin, 2014): Volume, Variety, and Velocity. There have been more additions: IBM, White (2012) introduced Veracity – the fourth V, SAS introduced Variability and Complexity, the fifth V and Oracle introduced Value as the sixth V. While these are commonly used today there are possibilities with further enhancements more may be added or defined further contextually. There is even the possibility of having "smarts" added to this volume of data as well. There are questions about the usefulness and life of the data as well.

The concept of big data has been described as "a phenomenon defined by the rapid acceleration in the expanding volume of high velocity, complex, and diverse types of data. Big Data is often defined along three dimensions -- volume, velocity, and variety" (TechAmerica Foundation, 2012, p. 7). Many authors will refer to those three characteristics as the 3V's. Others define big data as "datasets whose size is beyond the ability of typical database software tools to capture, store, manage, and analyze" (MGI, 2012, p. 3).

Despite big data 3V's characteristics - volume, velocity. and variety, some authors write about multiple fourth V's such as variability, vulnerability, veracity, and value. The fundamental definition is not affected by many V's, but all together they do provide a better understanding of different aspects of big data (Seddon and Curie, 2017). It is anticipated that volume of data will increase 44 times by 2020; velocity will increase as data is brought in from every imaginable device, and variety will increase due to a greater diversity in the data being collected. (Fernandes, O'Connor, and Weaver, 2012).

In order to define Big Data, we look at the definitions for each of the 5 Vs below as they seem to characterize Big Data broadly:

- *Volume* - Volume is the large data-sets that represent big data. Volume makes a huge difference for an organization as the huge data is what they require to make business decisions.
- *Variety* - This represents the different types of data available, such as text, numbers, images, videos, documents, spreadsheets, etc. This signifies the category or type of data something belongs to. The big data comes from different sources which makes it very unpredictable and consists of different forms which are ideally unstructured, structured and semi-structured. The unstructured data has the log files, HTML tags. Structured data consists of the relational database data which is represented in tables. Semi-structured data consists of XML files and data from other text files.

- *Velocity* - Velocity represents the speed of data at which it is transmitted and received from the source and destination. Velocity plays a crucial role in data management as the process flows in the business are highly impacted by the speed of data transfer.
- *Veracity* - Veracity represents the uncertainty of the data as it comes from an untrusted source and needs more optimization. Veracity ideally is characterized by raw data.
- *Value* - Value represents the revenue and market value gained by an organization using the big data. Value is measured in terms of revenue and business's success with their clients using the tools for generating the value for data.

Figure 2. 5V's of big data

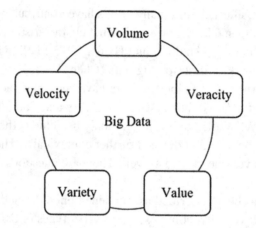

The five v's of big data impact the scope, time, and budget for any project which deals with big data (Yin and Kaynak, 2015). The opportunity cost, ambiguity, and collection ability play a role in authenticity/reliability of the data, the inconsistencies behind gathering and gaining the data and the value derived and implementation costs from the data.

In summary, having gone through the definitions that exist in literature today and having looked at characteristics to date, we are still not close to agreeing on the definition of the term, Big Data.

CURRENT STATUS

IT departments do not measure the growth of Big Data by the number of records that are in storage but by the amount of space required to store the records (Kitchin, and McArdle, 2016). To illustrate this point Abbasi, Sarker, and Chiang (2016) noted this space now consists of "Gigabytes, Terabytes, Exabytes, and Petabytes" (p. 5) versus previous traditionally records based number approaches to data management. As well as the expanding data size, the monetary value of Big Data also increases with a very high rate. The global big data market size was valued at USD 25.67 billion in 2015 and is expected to witness a significant growth over the forecast period (Grand View Research, 2016).

Figure 3. Big data market by service (USD million)
Source: Grand View Research (2016)

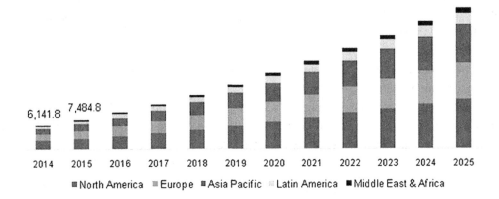

This widespread growth pattern stems from many different sources such as social networking sites, wired and wireless broadband access, and the widespread use of search engine sites (Hashem, et al., 2015). Additional non-interactive devices are also filling storage such as radio frequency identification (RFID) and sensors associated with the Internet of Things (IoT) (Reimsbach-Kounatze, 2015). Expanding market also affects software markets. Big Data market is shared by analytics, database, visualization and distribution tools, and software. Database related products are the main driver of the commercial transactions.

Figure 4. Big data market share by software (USD million)
Source: Grand View Research (2016)

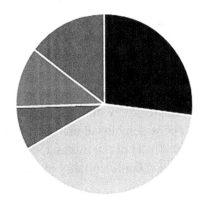

This growth is so rapid that both practitioners and academics are trying to keep up with newer and faster analytics and statistics (Gandomi and Haider, 2015). Since the majority of Big Data is unstructured (approximately 95%), the data is harder to process (Gandomi and Haider, 2015). While IoT and Big Data analytics appear to have incredible potential for converting various businesses, many academics and industry experts are struggling to comprehend these ideas and capture the business value in joining

IOT and big data analytics (Riggins and Wamba, 2015). In addition, very few academic studies exist assessing the real potential of IoT and Big Data analytics (Riggins and Wamba, 2015). However, as noted previously, there are many different projects underway to resolve the difficulty of converting raw data into information and then into knowledge.

In recent years, the explosive growth of data has been observed in numerous industries like e-commerce, health, social networks, etc. Access to preferred data in such massive datasets necessitates sophisticated and effective gathering methods. In the past, special algorithms have served as common descriptors for numerous tasks including image cataloging and recovery (Ahmad et al., 2018). The algorithms perform extremely well when equated to hand-crafted queries and filters. However, these algorithms are typically high dimensional, necessitating a lot of memory and CPU for indexing and gathering. For extremely large datasets, use of these high dimensional algorithms in raw usage becomes infeasible (Ahmad et al., 2018).

Boone, Skipper, and Hazen (2017) conducted a study to Increase request for receptive, cost effectual, and maintainable procedures that necessitated service parts deliberation and acceptance of new industry models and resolutions that cover the complete life-cycle of merchandises. Many organizations are looking to big data information. Though service parts supervisors have long trusted examination and optimization, big data information is thought to be more incorporating and thus particularly capable. Hereafter, big data and its associated uses are suggested as a means of refining service parts supervision practices. More precisely, information gathered from consultations with service parts supervisors is used to build a basis describing the encounters of service parts supervision. This background then aids as the foundation for big data connected suggestions for overcoming the emphasized encounters. Thus, the examination answers the demand for service parts supervision connected backgrounds while developing a starting point for suggestions for supervisorial thought and intellectual examination (Boone et al., 2017).

The advance of Big Data that of personal data, in particular, dispersed in numerous data sources presents huge opportunities and understandings for companies to discover and influence the importance of linked and assimilated data. However, privacy fears impede distribution or trading data for connection across diverse organizations (Vatsalan et al., 2017). Privacy-preserving record linkage (PPRL) purposes to address this situation by recognizing and joining records that match to the identical real-world individual across numerous data sources stored by diverse parties without revealing any sensitive data about these individuals (Boyd et al., 2017). PPRL is progressively being required in numerous practical application areas. Instances include public health, observation of crime, deception exposure, and national security. Big Data and PPRL creates numerous challenges, with the three main ones being (a) scalability to several large data warehouses, due to their considerable volume and the movement of data within Big Data solutions, (b) attaining high quality and effects of the link in the occurrence of variety and veracity of Big Data, and (c) maintaining discretion and confidentiality of the individuals represented in Big Data pools (Vatsalan et al., (2017).

IT departments have encountered several new skills due to Big Data, including how to gather, allocate, accumulate, clean, examine, filter, examine, portion, protect, and envision data (Purdam, 2016). Considering the problem of accumulating and saving big data, an array of new systems emerged in recent years to handle these kinds of big data encounters (Gudivada, BaezaYates, and Raghavan, 2015). Big Data computational analysis is considered an important aspect to be further enhanced to intensify the operational margin of both public and private initiatives and signifies the next frontier for their modernization, competition, and throughput (Esposito et al., 2015). Big Data is typically formed in different sectors of private and public organizations, often physically distributed throughout the world, and are categorized by a large size and variety (Rajan, 2015). Therefore, there is a solid need for strategies handling larger and faster amounts of data in settings characterized by multifaceted event processing programs and multiple mixed sources, dealing with the numerous issues related to resourcefully gathering, examining, and distributing them in a fully controlled manner (Esposito et al., 2015). This necessity leads to newer, faster, and better software (Kim et al., 2016).

Developing and running software creates large quantities of raw data about the development process and the end user usage. This information can be turned into creative perception with the assistance of skilled data scientists (Kim et al., 2016). Unfortunately, data scientists with the skills to analyze these very large data-sets are difficult to come by (Hilbert, 2016). Data scientist comes in many different forms such as Insight Providers, Modeling Specialists, Platform Builders, Polymaths, and Team Leaders (Kim et al., 2016).

Many "big data" and "fast data" analysis methods such as Hadoop, Spark, and Storm have come from the Apache foundation (Dimopoulos, Krintz, and Wolski, 2016). These programs are used by analysts to implement a variety of applications for query support, data mining, machine learning, real-time stream analysis, statistical analysis, and image processing (Dimopoulos, Krintz, and Wolski, 2016). Another software platform named R is a free, prevailing, open source software platform with widespread statistical computing and graphics abilities (Xu, et al., 2016). Due to its advanced expressiveness and many domain explicit packages, R has become the 'lingua franca' for many parts of data analysis, acquiring power from community-developed packages (Xu et al., 2016).

With the extremely rapid growth of information and intricacy of systems; artificial intelligence, rapid machine learning, and computational intelligence methods are highly required. Many predictable computational intelligence methods face constraints in learning such as intensive human involvement in addition to connection time. However, effective learning algorithms offer different yet significant benefits including rapid learning, ease of execution, and minimal human involvement. The need for competent and fast execution of machine learning methods in big data and dynamic changing methods poses many research encounters (Sun et al., 2017). Big Data, from an industry point of view, is leading the way to newer and better methods of doing business (Shin and Choi, 2015). The common view, in most industries, is that growth of Big Data, though difficult now, will achieve a status that is manageable and thus controllable in the future (Kitchin and Lauriault, 2015). German officials and scientist believe this so strongly that they are referring to Big Data as the Fourth Industrial Revolution and calling it "Industrie 4.0" (Yin and Kaynak, 2015). Akter and Wamba (2016) used the phrase "the next frontier for innovation, competition, and productivity." Industries such as retail, are utilizing Radiofrequency Identification (RFID) marked merchandises to develop marketing campaigns based on the movement of merchandise (Cao, Chychyla, and Stewart, 2015).

ORGANIZATIONAL EFFECTS

Akter and Wamba (2016) stated the definition of Big Data is more than merely larger storage or the gathering of data from social media sites with millions of members. Bigness is an indication of scalability issues in one or more extents — the four Vs of variety, velocity, veracity, and volume (Abbasi, Sarker, and Chiang, 2016). Big data is an inaccuracy, suggesting that bigness is a fundamental characteristic of a dataset. Rather, Big Data defines the association between a dataset and its usage framework (Akter and Wamba, 2016). A dataset is too large for a specific use when it is computationally not feasible to convert the data using traditional or outdated software tools (George et al., 2016). With the immense amounts of data currently available, businesses in nearly every industry are focusing on manipulating data for the competitive benefit (He et al., 2015). A key challenge for IT researchers and IT experts alike is that data growth rate is exceeding the ability to maintain the required hardware and necessary software to manage the high volume of data (Saltz, 2015). Simply stating, analyzing "data in motion" creates new encounters because the anticipated patterns and perceptions are moving targets, and this is not the situation for static data (Abbasi, Sarker, and Chiang, 2016). Junque de Fortuny et al. (2013) noted the growth rate is approximately 50% annually or doubling every two years.

Gobble (2013) and Manyika et al., (2011) identify big data as the next big thing in innovation and the next frontier for innovation, competition, and productivity, respectively. Strawn (2012) called it the fourth paradigm of science. Furthermore, McAfee and Brynjolfsson (2012) appropriately categorized their article on Big Data as a management revolution similar to what Ann Keller et al., (2012) termed Big Data as bringing a revolution in science and technology.

The emergence of new technologies, new processes, threats, regulations and thought leadership all affect the organization more than ever. Organizations which handle the big data and implement its methodologies are expected to make 40% more profits than regular software industry in the current scenario. The increasing value for big data makes it easier to predict the gains for the organization in the future. Organizations currently lack the human resource and talent which can give them the best big data engineering experience and help them grow.

Technology is now being established that is able to process enormous amounts of organized and unorganized data from various causes and sources. This information is often denoted to as big data, and opens new areas of study and uses that will have a growing impact in all parts of society (Marvin et al., 2017). Big Data and its velocity are being applied in the food safety area and acknowledged several encouraging trends particularly the speed by which the information is being transmitted. In numerous parts of the world, governments encourage the publication on the Internet of all information produced in publicly financed research projects. This program opens new chances for interested parties dealing with food safety to report issues which were not conceivable before. The use of mobile phones as exposure devices for food safety and the communication of social media as early caution of food safety situations are a few instances of the new improvements that are conceivable due to Big Data (Marvin et al., 2017).

Big data will also offer new potentials for research by allowing access to linked data, medical information, and social media. The total extent of information, however, does not remove and may even intensify systematic inaccuracy. Therefore, procedures addressing systematic error, scientific knowledge, and underlying theories are more significant than ever to confirm that the indicator is apparent behind the noise (Ehrenstein et al., 2017).

The era of big data has established a new path for exploring data in newer forms and finding different ways to handle the data on a large scale. Although processing and maintaining a large data is a challenge, big data challenges have given the scope to find a solution for these challenges and implement them for a better data environment (Du, 2013). Big data has been into existence since the 1990s and ways to success have been one of the major mysteries since then. Data Integration in large: Challenges of Reuse, a research paper which was published in 1994 signifies the existence of big data challenges from the 1990s.

Technology

Netflix analyzes millions of real-time data points that its viewers create, thus helping the firm determine if a pilot will become a successful show (Xu et al., 2015). Facebook hosts over 500 terabytes of data every day – including uploaded photos, likes and users' posts (Provost and Fawcett, 2013). Google alone contributed roughly $54 billion to the US economy in 2009 (Labrinidis and Jagadish, 2012). Akamai Technologies Inc, a leading global Content Delivery Network provider collects and analyzes petabytes of data every day to help its customer base with cloud performance and security initiatives. Amazon, another e-commerce/technology company, utilizes its various data points to ensure personalized experiences for its client base.

Machine learning (ML) is constantly releasing its influence in a wide collection of applications. It has been pressed to the front in current years somewhat owing to the arrival of Big Data and its velocity. ML procedures have never been better guaranteed while tested by Big Data. Big Data empowers ML procedures to expose more fine-grained configurations and make more opportune and precise forecasts than ever before; yet it creates major tests to ML such as model scalability and distributed computing (Zhou et al., 2017). The framework of Big Data is balanced on ML which follows the stages of preprocessing, knowledge, and assessment. In addition, the framework is also comprised of four other components, namely big data, consumer, realm, and method (Zhou et al., 2017).

Healthcare

Burg (2014) argued that Big Data can enable a better and transparent healthcare system. Allouche (2014) identified cost saving and unnecessary procedure reducing capabilities from Big Data. Tormay (2015), identifies pharmaceutical RandD as the engine that fuels the pharmaceutical industry. He claims this engine has been declining in productivity over the last 20 years with increasing costs, demands for better standard care, and concomitant productivity challenges. He believes that data, specifically the fast and voluminous nature along with technological advances will help revitalize this engine. Furthermore, Groves et al. (2013) document the innovations identified because of Big Data projects. Another organization, Intel, announced its Collaborative Cancel Cloud in August of 2015 to enable diagnosing of cancer patients based on their specific genome sequencing and tailor a precision treatment plan for them all based on the concept of Big Data.

Education

Erwin (2015) insists students to be more literate in their abilities to use data. He argues that there is a growing call for students to develop data literacy. His theory is more of a project-based learning where students solve real-world problems with data that is provided to them will enable them to build skills and be able to meet the current demands of business. Similarly, Rijmenam (2014) reasoned changes in the education systems by using Big Data to change the way that students and teachers interact. A more practical example, Gwinnett, in suburban Atlanta, Georgia, is the 14th largest school system in the United States, has 23,000 employees and transports more people every school day than the locally based carrier, Delta Air Lines. All that activity generates information, more and more of it captured digitally and in 2002, as the school system's leaders continued seeking fresh educational solutions, they began to explore how analytics could help how all that information could be investigated for patterns, relationships, dependencies, and predictors.

Public Sector (Government)

Gamage (2016), in his article, examines the opportunities presented by effectively harnessing big data in the public-sector context. He talks about the impact of Big Data and how it will play an important role in the future. Furthermore, he also outlines key challenges to be addressed to adapt and realize the benefits of Big Data in the public sector. Similarly, another article, stemming from SAP's partnership within the Middle East governments, documents high level of Big Data production, consumption and the need to train public sector to be successful at these opportunities.

Miscellaneous

The Big Data Strategy framework in Servitization as proposed by Opresnik and Taisch (2014) is focusing on new revenue streams and decreasing product-service costs in manufacturing. An optimization model for green supply chain management based on Big Data proposed by Zhao et al. (2017) is a scheme that minimizes the inherent risk of hazardous materials, associated carbon emissions and economic cost. The Cebr (Center of Economics and Business Research) (2012) has anticipated that the benefits of big data innovation opportunities would contribute £24 billion to the UK economy between 2012 and 2017. These opportunities are described to be identifying hidden patterns, better decision making, improving business processes and developing new business models (Halaweh and Massry 2015). There are many more examples of such initiatives and values across industries that organizations are realizing and going back to the accumulation of data is reaching out to every industry and organization across geographies.

IMPLEMENTATION CHALLENGES

The growth in big data comes along with unstructured data which dominates the data mainly. Therefore, organizations tend to find new methods for handling the unstructured data in large volumes. Organizations implement technologies like Hadoop to handle this data, currently as Hadoop is the only big data tool currently in the market. Hadoop is an open source currently being provided by two organizations Hortonworks and Cloudera. However, some of the tools in Hadoop are not available in the services provided by Cloudera. Big data tools are used individually for different tasks based on the requirement. Some of the big data tools are MapReduce, Yarn, Pig, Hive (Seay et al., 2014).

Another important aspect of big data is the integration services and the storage. Big data integration services include the tools which are used to integrate the data from different sources to gain meaningful insights. Big data integration plays a major role as it provides the organization with necessary data which stands as a base to make the business decisions. KARMA and Talend stand as the best data integration tools currently in the market and Talend has been used by Groupon, one of the largest e-commerce organizations. The different data jobs from different sources were implemented using Talend which gave them good profits on a whole.

The storage of big data has been another important aspect, where the data is generated every second. A load of huge data chunks has to be managed efficiently in order to make use of this data. The storage servers and third-party storage providers bridge the gap between big data and storage. But securing this data is much important for organizations. Accordingly, they tend to use different security measures to prevent the data breach (Ives et al., 1999).

Menon and Hegde (2015) wrote that the indication of the growth of knowledge as an approaching storage and retrieval problem came in 1944 when Fremont Rider, a Wesleyan University librarian, estimated that university libraries in America were doubling in size every sixteen years. Given this growth rate, Rider estimated that in 2040 the Yale Library would contain approximately 200,000,000 volumes, stretching over 6,000 miles of shelves and requiring a cataloging staff of over six thousand people to maintain. While the development of knowledge was generally considered good for humanity, it was leading to a major storage and retrieval situation for libraries (Menon and Hegde, 2015). As the amount of data continued to multiply in the ensuing decades, organizations began to design, comprehend, and execute centralized computing methods that would allow them to automate their inventory systems (Erikson, 1950). As these methods began to mature across organizations and develop within enterprises, organizations began to apply the analysis of the data to avail themselves with solutions and insight that would allow them to make improved business judgments i.e., business intelligence (Wang, 2016).

Wixom et al. (2014) believed that with business intelligence continuing to grow rapidly, the challenge of management and storage quickly became a real issue within IT departments. To offer more functionality, digital storage had to become more cost-effective (Chang, and Wills, 2016). This challenge led to the advent of Business Intelligence (BI) platforms (Wang, 2016). As these BI platforms continue to develop, the data gathered enabled and will enable companies, scientific and medical researchers, our national defense and intelligence organizations, and other organizations to create innovative breakthroughs (Wixom et al., 2014).

At the same time as it problematized data overflow, the Big Data industry was also involved in spreading the myths such as, methodological issues no longer mattered, Big Data provided a comprehensive and unbiased source of data on which to base decisions about data, and in hyping the promises of Big Data sets (Kimble and Milolidakis, 2015). Like Wes Nichols (2013), co-founder and CEO of MarketShare, a predictive-analytics company based in Los Angeles, many market researchers placed a great amount of confidence in the usability of large datasets that concurrently produced and analyzed data. In the past, associating sales data with a few dozen isolated advertising variables used to be acceptable (Oh and Min, 2015). However, many of the world's biggest companies are now deploying analytics 2.0 (Jobs, Aukers, and Gilfoil, 2015), a set of practices that compute through terabytes of data and hundreds of variables in real time to define how well advertising touch points interact (Fesenmaier et al., 2016). This resulted in 10 to 30 percent improvements in marketing performance.

Instead of data storage and integration issues, big data visualization has also been one of the major challenges for organizations. Therefore, they tend to build data samples to build on the tools for data visualization. Visualizations help to understand the data better than its original form. Visual analytics can be integrated with big data to understand and implement the data for a better business.

Some of the data visualization challenges identified is given by:

Meeting the need for speed: Many organizations use data for their business growth. And this data comes from numerous sources. Organizations tend to use different methods to keep this data organized to derive the insights. Few of these methods are discussed below:

- Visualization of data which helps them to perform the analysis more efficiently.
- As the challenge grows with more granularity constraints, some of the organizations are using parallel processing hardware units to grab the large crunch of data at once. This helps them to perform data optimization quickly.
- Grid computing has been another approach to grab a large amount of data in smaller units of time.

Understanding the data: Getting a meaningful insight from the data is a huge task as the data comes from different sources. For an instance, data coming from a social networking site, where it is important to know the user from whom the data is gathered from. Implementation of visual analytics without the proper context can prove useless for organizations. Expertise at domain level is very much needed in this case as the analytics team needs to be aware of the data sources and the understanding of consumers' data usage and interpretation.

Addressing data quality: Although the data is collected and processed quickly to serve the purpose, it is very likely that a data which has no context is of no value to the consumer. To address this challenge, organizations need to have an information management team to analyze the data and assure that the data is clean. Visualizing this analyzed data can be of a huge value and source of information for organizations and the consumers.

Displaying meaningful results: Graphical representation of huge data is a common challenge faced by organizations. For an instance, consider the data from a huge retail business. When the stock-keeping unit (SKU) data which has more than a billion plots, it's difficult to have a look at each plot and speculate. Therefore, data needs to be split into clusters and the small data is to be separated from the big ones to derive the insights.

Dealing with outliers: Big data can be represented in the form of tables and sets as well, but this would be a challenge to viewers. The efficient way of displaying the big data would be by implementing the visual analytics and represent the data in the form of graphs and charts. This would make it easier for the viewers to understand and spot the growth.

On a whole, data visualization plays a key role in big data as this is the main source of information for organizations. The simpler the form of representation is, the simpler would be the analysis and derivations from this data.

Organizations face many challenges with big data in terms of storage, visualization or integration, therefore they look for new solutions and tools which can handle the big data efficiently. This clearly states that big data is the new challenge which needs more research for its development.

SOLUTIONS AND RECOMMENDATIONS

In today's world, it is necessary to use the data or information available in a wise manner to make effective business decisions and define better objectives (Laudon and Laudon, 2016). If the information available is not utilized to its full extent, organizations might lose their reputation and position in this competitive world. However, data needs to be processed appropriately to gain constructive insights from it, and the heterogeneous nature of this data makes this increasingly more complex and time-consuming (Ang and Teo, 2000). The ever-increasing growth of data generated is far more than human processing capabilities and thus computing methods need to be automated to scale effectively (Das et al., 2015).

Variety, velocity, and volume were identified as three key attributes of Big Data by Laney in 2001. Many authors and business specialists modify these attributes. In 2012, IBM added a fourth dimension to this called veracity. Ebner et al. (2014) define Big Data as "a phenomenon characterized by an ongoing increase in volume, variety, velocity, and veracity of data that requires advanced techniques and technologies to capture, store, distribute, manage, and analyze these data." Big Data helps to unlock potentials of different fields like predictive modeling, data integration, network analysis, natural language processing, etc. Thus, Big Data technologies have huge economic potential that should be harnessed by executives in a proper manner. Questions related to the IT infrastructure, capturing crucial information, analytical requirements, etc. should be asked by the executives to determine the way in which way Big Data solution needs to be handled.

In recent times, the research on Big Data has been always concentrated toward creating better algorithms and designing robust data models (Saltz and Shamshurin, 2016). However, not much work has been done regarding finding out the best methodology for executing such projects (Ahangama and Poo, 2015) (Saltz, 2015). The exploratory nature of Big Data projects demands a more specific methodology that can handle the uncertain business requirements of such projects (Saltz, 2015). According to a survey carried out by Kelly and Kaskade (2013), "300 companies reported that 55% of Big Data projects don't get completed and others fall short of their objectives." The reasons for such project failure can be identified at the beginning of the project or can be reduced at a later stage by some coordination methodology (Saltz, 2015).

A well-defined Big Data analysis project methodology would help to address different issues like roles and responsibilities of team members, project stakeholders, expected project outcome, relevant data architecture or infrastructure, approaches for validation of results, etc. (Saltz, 2015). It might be a notion that there is no need for such a methodology to be defined since; Big Data projects are often open-ended in nature. Agile methodology can be used for such projects instead. The sheer goal of finding the "value in data" is not enough. There needs to be communication between the team regarding the next steps (Saltz, 2015).

Different process methodologies have been defined in other domains. The Software Development Life Cycle (SDLC) is used in the software development domain. Optimizing business processes is used in the operations research domain, while statistical analysis is used in quantitative research. Big Data projects do not always fall specifically in these categories, although they might be similar to them. Software projects have less focus on the data aspect. A large number of extract-transform-load (ETL) processes need to be performed. Determining the relevant data sources is a crucial task in Big Data projects. This step is not a part of the SDLC. Kaisler et al. (2013) found out that "trend analysis may not require the precision that traditional database (DB) systems provide." This shows that acceptable levels of data quality depend in most cases on data usage (Kaisler et al., 2013). Even if any software methodology was to be applied to Big Data projects, it would be difficult to determine which software methodology to use since different alternatives like waterfall or agile are in practice. Business Intelligence is another domain that deals with making effective business decisions by scrutinizing the data available. A business intelligence system that can react to unanticipated requirements also needs to be developed (Krawatzeck, Dinter, and Thi, 2015). Thus, any combined BI methodology cannot suffice a Big Data project thoroughly.

Goodwin (2011) noted that poor communication is a factor due to which 75% of corporate business intelligence projects face failure. Thus, Team Effectiveness is an essential aspect of any Big Data project. Hackman (1987) proposed a model that focuses on different factors from input to output. It is one of the most widely used models. While continuous improvement is one of the criteria in Hackman's model, a vital factor is measuring the team's performance. The model created by DeLone and McLean (1992) is based on system creation, usage, and consequences of use.

FUTURE RESEARCH DIRECTIONS

Further along the path of this chapter, there are several potential extensions and challenging directions to be explored regarding Big Data. New systems and solutions have been proposed in Big Data systems. Big Data's relation and integration with Industry 4.0, Artificial Intelligence and emerging Business Intelligence projects are brand new research areas, including different industry diversities. Researchers can examine how Big Data rules emerging technology trends.

CONCLUSION

Data is growing at a rate we never imagined. Large volumes of digital data are generated at a rapid rate by sources like social media sites, mobile phones, sensors, web servers, multimedia, medical devices and satellites, leading to a data explosion. The importance of capturing this data and creating value out of it has become more important than ever in every sector of the world economy. While the potential of creating meaningful insights out of big data in various domains like Business, Health Care, Public Sector Administration, Retail and Manufacturing are being studied, data science related technologies are expanding to capture, store and analyze big data efficiently.

This chapter clearly observed the various opportunities being explored, examined and extracted for the betterment and effectiveness of organizations across the different industries that have successful Big Data projects. Also Big Data is basically defined and an overview of Big Data is provided in terms of current status, organizational effects (technology, health care, education etc.), implementation challenges and Big Data projects. The main purpose of this research was to build on the current diverse literature around Big Data by contributing discussion and data that allow common agreement on definition, characteristics, and factors that influence successful Big Data projects. The research questions being investigated are based on the argument establishing Big Data be used as a tool for the organization by which to develop and create enterprise-wide efficiencies.

REFERENCES

Abbasi, A., Sarker, S., & Chiang, R. H. (2016). Big data research in information systems: Toward an inclusive research agenda. *Journal of the Association for Information Systems, 17*(2), I–XXXII. doi:10.17705/1jais.00423

Ahangama, S., & Poo, C. C. D. (2015). Improving health analytic process through project, communication and knowledge management.

Ahmad, J., Muhammad, K., Lloret, J., & Baik, S. W. (2018). Efficient Conversion of Deep Features to Compact Binary Codes using Fourier Decomposition for Multimedia Big Data. *IEEE Transactions on Industrial Informatics, 14*(7), 3205–3215. doi:10.1109/TII.2018.2800163

Akter, S., & Wamba, S. F. (2016). Big data analytics in E-commerce: A systematic review and agenda for future research. *Electronic Markets, 26*(2), 173–194. doi:10.100712525-016-0219-0

Allouche, G. (2014). *How Big Data can Save Health Care*. Innovation Excellence. Retrieved from [REMOVED HYPERLINK FIELD]http://www.innovationexcellence.com/blog/2014/11/14/how-big-data-can-save-health-care/

Ang, J., & Teo, T. S. (2000). Management issues in data warehousing: Insights from the Housing and Development Board. *Decision Support Systems, 29*(1), 11–20. doi:10.1016/S0167-9236(99)00085-8

Boone, C. A., Skipper, J. B., & Hazen, B. T. (2017). A framework for investigating the role of big data in service parts management. *Journal of Cleaner Production, 153*, 687–691. doi:10.1016/j.jclepro.2016.09.201

Boyd, J., Ferrante, A., Brown, A., Randall, S., & Semmens, J. (2017). Implementing privacy-preserving record linkage: Welcome to the real world. *International Journal of Population Data Science, 1*(1). doi:10.23889/ijpds.v1i1.153

Burg, N. (2014). How Big Data Will Help Save Healthcare. *Forbes Magazine, 10*.

Cao, M., Chychyla, R., & Stewart, T. (2015). Big Data analytics in financial statement Audits. *Accounting Horizons, 29*(2), 423–429. doi:10.2308/acch-51068

Cebr. (2012). *The Value of Big Data and the Internet of Things to the UK Economy*. Retrieved from https://www.sas.com/content/dam/SAS/en_gb/doc/analystreport/cebr-value-of-big-data.pdf

Chen, H., Chiang, R. H., & Storey, V. C. (2012). Business intelligence and analytics: From big data to big impact. *Management Information Systems Quarterly, 36*(4), 1165–1188. doi:10.2307/41703503

Chen, J., Chen, Y., Du, X., Li, C., Lu, J., Zhao, S., & Zhou, X. (2013). Big data challenge: A data management perspective. *Frontiers of Computer Science, 7*(2), 157–164. doi:10.100711704-013-3903-7

Das, M., Cui, R., Campbell, D. R., Agrawal, G., & Ramnath, R. (2015). Towards methods for systematic research on big data. *Proceedings of the 2015 IEEE International Conference on Big Data* (pp. 2072-2081). IEEE. 10.1109/BigData.2015.7363989

Dimopoulos, S., Krintz, C., & Wolski, R. (2016). Big data framework interference in restricted private cloud settings. *Proceedings of the 2016 IEEE International Conference on Big Data* (pp. 335-340). IEEE. 10.1109/BigData.2016.7840620

Du, Z. (2013). Inconsistencies in big data: Cognitive Informatics & Cognitive Computing (ICCI* CC), 2013. *Proceedings of the 12th IEEE International Conference. IEEE.*

Ebner, K., Buhnen, T., & Urbach, N. (2014, January). Think big with Big Data: Identifying suitable Big Data strategies in corporate environments. *Proceedings of the 2014 47th Hawaii International Conference on System Sciences (HICSS)* (pp. 3748-3757). IEEE.

Ehrenstein, V., Nielsen, H., Pedersen, A. B., Johnsen, S. P., & Pedersen, L. (2017). Clinical epidemiology in the era of big data: New opportunities, familiar challenges. *Clinical Epidemiology, 9*, 245–250. doi:10.2147/CLEP.S129779 PMID:28490904

Erikson, E. H. E. (1950). *Childhood and society*. New York: Norton.

Erwin, R. (2015). Data literacy: Real-world learning through problem-solving with data sets. *American Secondary Education*, *43*(2), 18–26.

Esposito, C., Ficco, M., Palmieri, F., & Castiglione, A. (2015). A knowledge-based platform for Big Data analytics based on publish/subscribe services and stream processing. *Knowledge-Based Systems*, *79*, 3–17. doi:10.1016/j.knosys.2014.05.003

Fernandes, L. M., O'Connor, M., & Weaver, V. (2012). Big data, bigger outcomes. *Journal of American Health Information Management Association*, *83*(10), 38–43. PMID:23061351

Fesenmaier, D. R., Kuflik, T., & Neidhardt, J. (2016). Rectour 2016: workshop on recommenders in tourism. *Proceedings of the 10th ACM Conference on Recommender systems* (pp. 417-418). ACM.

Gamage, P. (2016). New development: Leveraging 'big data' analytics in the public sector. *Public Money & Management*, *36*(5), 385–390. doi:10.1080/09540962.2016.1194087

Gandomi, A., & Haider, M. (2015). Beyond the hype: Big data concepts, methods, and analytics. *International Journal of Information Management*, *35*(2), 137–144. doi:10.1016/j.ijinfomgt.2014.10.007

George, G., Osinga, E. C., Lavie, D., & Scott, B. A. (2016). Big data and data science methods for management research.

Gobble, M. M. (2013). Creating change. *Research Technology Management*, *56*(5), 62–66. doi:10.5437/08956308X5605005

Goodwin, K. (2011). *Designing for the digital age: How to create human-centered products and services.* John Wiley & Sons.

Grand View Research. (2016). *Big Data Market Size, Share Forecast, Industry Research Report, 2025.* Retrieved from https://www.grandviewresearch.com/industry-analysis/big-data-industry?utm_source=Pressrelease&utm_medium=referral&utm_campaign=abnewswire_05oct&utm_content=content

Groves, P., Kayyali, B., Knott, D., & Van Kuiken, S. (2013). The 'big data' revolution in healthcare. *The McKinsey Quarterly*, *2*(3).

Gudivada, V. N., Baeza-Yates, R. A., & Raghavan, V. V. (2015). Big Data: Promises and Problems. *IEEE Computer*, *48*(3), 20–23. doi:10.1109/MC.2015.62

Hackman, J. R. (1987). The design of work teams. In J.W. Lorsch (Ed.), Handbook of organizational behavior (pp. 315-342). Englewood Cliffs, NJ: Prentice-Hall.

Halaweh, M., & Massry, A. E. (2015). Conceptual model for successful implementation of big data in organizations. *Journal of International Technology and Information Management*, *24*(2), 2.

Hashem, I. A. T., Yaqoob, I., Anuar, N. B., Mokhtar, S., Gani, A., & Khan, S. U. (2015). The rise of "big data" on cloud computing: Review and open research issues. *Information Systems*, *47*, 98–115. doi:10.1016/j.is.2014.07.006

He, W., Shen, J., Tian, X., Li, Y., Akula, V., Yan, G., & Tao, R. (2015). Gaining competitive intelligence from social media data: Evidence from two largest retail chains in the world. *Industrial Management & Data Systems*, *115*(9), 1622–1636. doi:10.1108/IMDS-03-2015-0098

Hilbert, M. (2016). Big data for development: A review of promises and challenges. *Development Policy Review*, *34*(1), 135–174. doi:10.1111/dpr.12142

IDC. (2015). *Double-Digit Growth Forecast for the Worldwide Big Data and Business Analytics Market Through 2020 Led by Banking and Manufacturing Investments, According to IDC.* Retrieved from https://www.idc.com/url.do?url=/includes/pdf_download.jsp?containerId=prUS41826116&position=51

Ives, Z. G., Florescu, D., Friedman, M., Levy, A., & Weld, D. S. (1999, June). An adaptive query execution system for data integration. *SIGMOD Record*, *28*(2), 299–310. doi:10.1145/304181.304209

Jobs, C. G., Aukers, S. M., & Gilfoil, D. M. (2015). The impact of big data on your firms marketing communications: A framework for understanding the emerging marketing analytics industry. *Academy of Marketing Studies Journal*, *19*(2).

Junqué de Fortuny, E., Martens, D., & Provost, F. (2013). Predictive modeling with big data: Is bigger really better? *Big Data*, *1*(4), 215–226. doi:10.1089/big.2013.0037 PMID:27447254

Kaislcr, S., Armour, F., Espinosa, J. A., & Money, W. (2013). Big data: Issues and challenges moving forward. *Proceedings of the 2013 46th Hawaii international conference on System sciences (HICSS)* (pp. 995-1004). IEEE.

Keller, S. A., Koonin, S. E., & Shipp, S. (2012). Big data and city living–what can it do for us? *Significance*, *9*(4), 4–7. doi:10.1111/j.1740-9713.2012.00583.x

Kelly, J., & Kaskade, J. (2013). CIOS & Big Data what your IT team wants you to know. Retrieved from http://blog.infochimps.com/2013/01/24/cios-big-data

Kim, M., Zimmermann, T., DeLine, R., & Begel, A. (2016). The emerging role of data scientists on software development teams. *Proceedings of the 38th International Conference on Software Engineering* (pp. 96-107). ACM. 10.1145/2884781.2884783

Kimble, C., & Milolidakis, G. (2015). Big data and business intelligence: Debunking the myths. *Global Business and Organizational Excellence*, *35*(1), 23–34. doi:10.1002/joe.21642

Kitchin, R., Lauriault, T. P., & McArdle, G. (2015). Knowing and governing cities through urban indicators, city benchmarking and real-time dashboards. *Regional Studies. Regional Science*, *2*(1), 6–28.

Kitchin, R., & McArdle, G. (2016). What makes Big Data, Big Data? Exploring the ontological characteristics of 26 datasets. *Big Data & Society*, *3*(1).

Krawatzeck, R., Dinter, B., & Thi, D. A. P. (2015, January). How to make business intelligence agile: The Agile BI actions catalog. *Proceedings of the 2015 48th Hawaii International Conference on System Sciences (HICSS)* (pp. 4762-4771). IEEE.

Kwon, O., Lee, N., & Shin, B. (2014). Data quality management, data usage experience and acquisition intention of big data analytics. *International Journal of Information Management, 34*(3), 387–394. doi:10.1016/j.ijinfomgt.2014.02.002

Labrinidis, A., & Jagadish, H. V. (2012). Challenges and opportunities with big data. *Proceedings of the VLDB Endowment International Conference on Very Large Data Bases, 5*(12), 2032–2033. doi:10.14778/2367502.2367572

Laudon, K. C., & Laudon, J. P. (2016). *Management information system*. Pearson Education India.

Lee, J. H., Clarke, R. I., & Perti, A. (2015). Empirical evaluation of metadata for video games and interactive media. *Journal of the Association for Information Science and Technology, 66*(12), 2609–2625. doi:10.1002/asi.23357

Manyika, J., Chui, M., Brown, B., Bughin, J., Dobbs, R., Roxburgh, C., & Byers, A. H. (2011). *Big data: The next frontier for innovation, competition, and productivity*. McKinsey Global Institute.

Marvin, H. J., Janssen, E. M., Bouzembrak, Y., Hendriksen, P. J., & Staats, M. (2017). Big data in food safety: An overview. *Critical Reviews in Food Science and Nutrition, 57*(11), 2286–2295. doi:10.1080/10408398.2016.1257481 PMID:27819478

McAfee, A., & Brynjolfsson, E. (2012). Big Data: The Management Revolution. *Harvard Business Review, 90*(10), 60-66. PMID:23074865

Menon, S. P., & Hegde, N. P. (2015, January). A survey of tools and applications in big data. *Proceedings of the 2015 IEEE 9th International Conference on Intelligent Systems and Control (ISCO)* (pp. 1-7). IEEE. 10.1109/ISCO.2015.7282364

MGI. (2012). *Big Data: The next frontier for innovation, competition, and productivity*. Retrieved from https://www.mckinsey.com/~/media/McKinsey/Business%20Functions/McKinsey%20Digital/Our%20Insights/Big%20data%20The%20next%20frontier%20for%20innovation/MGI_big_data_exec_summary.ashx

Nichols, W. (2013). Advertising Analytics 2.0. *Harvard Business Review, 91*(3), 60–68. PMID:23593768

Nimmagadda, S. L., & Dreher, H. V. (2013). Big-data integration methodologies for effective management and data mining of petroleum digital ecosystems. *Proceedings of the 2013 7th IEEE International Conference on Digital Ecosystems and Technologies (DEST)* (pp. 148-153). IEEE. 10.1109/DEST.2013.6611345

Oh, Y. K., & Min, J. (2015). The mediating role of popularity rank on the relationship between advertising and in-app purchase sales in mobile application market. *Journal of Applied Business Research, 31*(4), 1311. doi:10.19030/jabr.v31i4.9318

Opresnik, D., & Taisch, M. (2015). The value of big data in servitization. *International Journal of Production Economics, 165*, 174–184. doi:10.1016/j.ijpe.2014.12.036

Provost, F., & Fawcett, T. (2013). Data science and its relationship to big data and data-driven decision making. *Big Data, 1*(1), 51–59. doi:10.1089/big.2013.1508 PMID:27447038

Purdam, K. (2016). Task-based learning approaches for supporting the development of social science researchers' critical data skills. *International Journal of Social Research Methodology, 19*(2), 257–267. doi:10.1080/13645579.2015.1102453

Rajan, K. (2015). Materials informatics: The materials "gene" and big data. *Annual Review of Materials Research, 45*(1), 153–169. doi:10.1146/annurev-matsci-070214-021132

Reimsbach-Kounatze, C. (2015). *"The Proliferation of "Big Data" and Implications for Official Statistics and Statistical Agencies: A Preliminary Analysis", OECD Digital Economy Papers, No. 245.* Paris: OECD Publishing. doi:10.1787/5js7t9wqzvg8-

Riggins, F. J., & Wamba, S. F. (2015). Research directions on the adoption, usage, and impact of the internet of things through the use of big data analytics. *Proceedings of the 2015 48th Hawaii International Conference on System Sciences (HICSS)* (pp. 1531-1540). IEEE. 10.1109/HICSS.2015.186

Rijmenam, M. (2014). *Think bigger: Developing a successful big data strategy for your business.* Amacom.

Rubin, V., & Lukoianova, T. (2013). Veracity roadmap: Is big data objective, truthful and credible? *Advances in Classification Research Online, 24*(1), 4. doi:10.7152/acro.v24i1.14671

Saltz, J. S. (2015). The need for new processes, methodologies and tools to support big data teams and improve big data project effectiveness. *Proceedings of the 2015 IEEE International Conference on Big Data (Big Data)* (pp. 2066-2071). IEEE. 10.1109/BigData.2015.7363988

Saltz, J. S., & Shamshurin, I. (2016). Big data team process methodologies: A literature review and the identification of key factors for a project's success. *Proceedings of the 2016 IEEE International Conference on Big Data (Big Data)* (pp. 2872-2879). IEEE. 10.1109/BigData.2016.7840936

Seay, C., Agrawal, R., Kadadi, A., & Barel, Y. (2015, April). Using hadoop on the mainframe: A big solution for the challenges of big data. *Proceedings of the 2015 12th International Conference on Information Technology-New Generations (ITNG)* (pp. 765-769). IEEE. 10.1109/ITNG.2015.135

Seddon, J. J., & Currie, W. L. (2017). A model for unpacking big data analytics in high-frequency trading. *Journal of Business Research, 70,* 300–307. doi:10.1016/j.jbusres.2016.08.003

Shin, D. H., & Choi, M. J. (2015). Ecological views of big data: Perspectives and issues. *Telematics and Informatics, 32*(2), 311–320. doi:10.1016/j.tele.2014.09.006

Sookhak, M., Gani, A., Khan, M. K., & Buyya, R. (2017). Dynamic remote data auditing for securing big data storage in cloud computing. *Information Sciences, 380,* 101–116. doi:10.1016/j.ins.2015.09.004

Sun, F., Huang, G. B., Wu, Q. J., Song, S., & Wunsch, D. C. II. (2017). Efficient and rapid machine learning algorithms for big data and dynamic varying systems. *IEEE Transactions on Systems, Man, and Cybernetics. Systems, 47*(10), 2625–2626. doi:10.1109/TSMC.2017.2741558

TechAmerica Foundation. (2012). *Demystifying Big Data: A practical guide to transforming the business of government.* Retrieved from http://www.techamerica.org/Docs/fileManager.cfm?f=techamerica-bigdatareport-final.pdf

Tormay, P. (2015). Big data in pharmaceutical R&D: Creating a sustainable R&D engine. *Pharmaceutical Medicine*, *29*(2), 87–92. doi:10.100740290-015-0090-x PMID:25878506

Vatsalan, D., Sehili, Z., Christen, P., & Rahm, E. (2017). Privacy-preserving record linkage for big data: Current approaches and research challenges. In *Handbook of Big Data Technologies* (pp. 851–895). Cham: Springer. doi:10.1007/978-3-319-49340-4_25

Wang, C. H. (2016). A novel approach to conduct the importance-satisfaction analysis for acquiring typical user groups in business-intelligence systems. *Computers in Human Behavior*, *54*, 673–681. doi:10.1016/j.chb.2015.08.014

White, T. (2012). *Hadoop: The definitive guide*. O'Reilly Media, Inc.

Wixom, B., Ariyachandra, T., Douglas, D. E., Goul, M., Gupta, B., Iyer, L. S., . . . Turetken, O. (2014). The current state of business intelligence in academia: The arrival of big data. CAIS, 34, 1.

Xu, W., Huang, R., Zhang, H., El-Khamra, Y., & Walling, D. (2016). Empowering R with high performance computing resources for big data analytics. In *Conquering Big Data with High Performance Computing* (pp. 191–217). Cham: Springer. doi:10.1007/978-3-319-33742-5_9

Xu, Z., Liu, Y., Mei, L., Hu, C., & Chen, L. (2015). Semantic based representing and organizing surveillance big data using video structural description technology. *Journal of Systems and Software*, *102*, 217–225. doi:10.1016/j.jss.2014.07.024

Yin, S., & Kaynak, O. (2015). Big data for modern industry: Challenges and trends [point of view]. *Proceedings of the IEEE*, *103*(2), 143–146. doi:10.1109/JPROC.2015.2388958

Zhao, R., Liu, Y., Zhang, N., & Huang, T. (2017). An optimization model for green supply chain management by using a big data analytic approach. *Journal of Cleaner Production*, *142*, 1085–1097. doi:10.1016/j.jclepro.2016.03.006

Zhou, L., Pan, S., Wang, J., & Vasilakos, A. V. (2017). Machine learning on big data: Opportunities and challenges. *Neurocomputing*, *237*, 350–361. doi:10.1016/j.neucom.2017.01.026

ADDITIONAL READING

Abbasi, A., Sarker, S., & Chiang, R. H. (2016). Big data research in information systems: Toward an inclusive research agenda. *Journal of the Association for Information Systems*, *17*(2), I–XXXII. doi:10.17705/1jais.00423

Akter, S., & Wamba, S. F. (2016). Big data analytics in E-commerce: A systematic review and agenda for future research. *Electronic Markets*, *26*(2), 173–194. doi:10.100712525-016-0219-0

Chen, H., Chiang, R. H., & Storey, V. C. (2012). Business intelligence and analytics: From big data to big impact. *Management Information Systems Quarterly*, *36*(4), 1165–1188. doi:10.2307/41703503

Fernandes, L. M., O'Connor, M., & Weaver, V. (2012). Big data, bigger outcomes. *Journal of American Health Information Management Association*, *83*(10), 38–43. PMID:23061351

Jobs, C. G., Aukers, S. M., & Gilfoil, D. M. (2015). The impact of big data on your firms marketing communications: A framework for understanding the emerging marketing analytics industry. *Academy of Marketing Studies Journal*, *19*(2).

Kimble, C., & Milolidakis, G. (2015). Big data and business intelligence: Debunking the myths. *Global Business and Organizational Excellence*, *35*(1), 23–34. doi:10.1002/joe.21642

Saltz, J. S., & Shamshurin, I. (2016). Big data team process methodologies: A literature review and the identification of key factors for a project's success. *Proceedings of the 2016 IEEE International Conference on Big Data (Big Data)* (pp. 2872-2879). IEEE. 10.1109/BigData.2016.7840936

Yin, S., & Kaynak, O. (2015). Big data for modern industry: Challenges and trends [point of view]. *Proceedings of the IEEE*, *103*(2), 143–146. doi:10.1109/JPROC.2015.2388958

KEY TERMS AND DEFINITIONS

Big Data: The large volumes of data-sets with a higher complexity level.

Value: Value represents the revenue and market value gained by an organization using the big data.

Variety: This represents the different types of data available, such as text, numbers, images, videos, documents, spreadsheets, etc.

Velocity: Velocity represents the speed of data at which it is transmitted and received from the source and destination.

Veracity: Veracity represents the uncertainty of the data as it comes from an untrusted source and needs more optimization.

Volume: Volume is the large data-sets that represent big data.

This research was previously published in Big Data Analytics for Sustainable Computing; pages 1-29, copyright year 2020 by Engineering Science Reference (an imprint of IGI Global).

Chapter 2
Overview of Big Data and Its Visualization

Richard S. Segall
Arkansas State University, USA

Gao Niu
Bryant University, USA

ABSTRACT

Big Data is data sets that are so voluminous and complex that traditional data processing application software are inadequate to deal with them. This chapter discusses what Big Data is and its characteristics, and how this information revolution of Big Data is transforming our lives and the new technology and methodologies that have been developed to process data of these huge dimensionalities. This chapter discusses the components of the Big Data stack interface, categories of Big Data analytics software and platforms, descriptions of the top 20 Big Data analytics software. Big Data visualization techniques are discussed with real data from fatality analysis reporting system (FARS) managed by National Highway Traffic Safety Administration (NHTSA) of the United States Department of Transportation. Big Data web-based visualization software are discussed that are both JavaScript-based and user-interface-based. This chapter also discusses the challenges and opportunities of using Big Data and presents a flow diagram of the 30 chapters within this handbook.

WHAT IS BIG DATA?

Big Data is defined as collections of datasets whose volume, velocity or variety is so large that it is difficult to store, manage, process, and analyze the data using traditional databases and data processing tools (Bahga & Madisetti, 2016). According to an estimate by IBM, 2.5 quintillion bytes of data is created every day, and that 90% of the data in the world today has been created in the last two years alone (IBM, 2017).

DOI: 10.4018/978-1-6684-3662-2.ch002

In 2012, United States (US) government committed $200 million in "Big Data" research and development investment (The White House, 2012). Big Data application is estimated worth $300 billion dollars for the US health care industry, and $250 billion euros for the Europe's public section administration (Manyika, Chui, Brown, Bughin, Dobbs, & Roxburgh, 2011). So what is Big Data? The numerical definition of Big Data is evolving with the development of the technology. A dynamic definition is that data which exceeds the capacity of commonly used hardware and software tools to capture, store and analyze within a tolerable elapsed time is considered as Big Data (Franks, 2012). Clegg (2017) authored a book on how the information revolution of Big Data is transforming our lives.

According to Marr (2016), Big Data in practice includes such as for Walmart: How Big Data is used to drive supermarket performance, Netflix: How Netflix used Big Data to Give us the programs we want, Rolls-Royce: How Big Data is used to drive success in manufacturing, and Facebook: How Facebook uses Big Data to make customer service more personal. Table 1 below list other multifaceted applications of Big Data as authored as individual chapters of Marr (2016) of how forty-five successful companies used Big Data to deliver extraordinary results.

Table 1. Successful applications of Big Data analytics by organizations and companies around the world

Organization/Company	Big Data Application
Amazon	How predictive analysis is used to get a 360-view of customers
Caesar's	Big Data at the Casino
Dickey's Barbecue Pit	How Big Data is used to gain performance insights into one of America's most successful restaurant chains
Experian	Using Big Data to make lending decisions and to crack down on identify fraud.
Fitbit	Big Data in the fitness arena
John Deere	How Big Data can be applied on farms
LinkedIn	How Big Data is used to fuel social media success
Ralph Lauren	Big Data in the fashion industry
Tera Seismic	Using Big Data to predict earthquakes
Transport for London	How Big Data is used to improve and manage public transportation in London, UK.
Twitter	How Twitter is used and IBM deliver customer insights from Big Data
Uber	How Big Data is at the center of Uber's Transportation Business
US Olympic Women's Cycling Team	How Big Data Analytics is used to optimize athletes performance
Walt Disney Parks and Resorts	How Big Data is Transforming our Family Holidays
ZSL and London Zoo	Big Data in the zoo and to protect animals

[Derived from book by Marr (2016).]

Characteristics of Big Data

The Big Data concept is formed due to the rapid development of computer technology. There is tremendous amount of data being generated and analyzed every day. The concept describes how this large amount data has been utilized to benefit the society. It is not just large amount data, instead, it is an ad-hoc definition of how the data is being collected, processed and distributed. There are some commonly accepted characteristics of Big Data, such as volume, velocity and variety. (Russom, 2011).

- Volume represents the size of the data. For example, number of observations, number of variables, number of files etc. Most of the personal and working computers equipped with hard drives and memories with gigabyte (GB) level or terabyte (TB) level, and thus TB is considered as the minimum threshold of Big Data volume as of 2017. However, "big" as of today will not be "big" as of tomorrow due to the rapid growth of the data storage and processing technology.
- Velocity represents the speed or frequency of the data been generated and streamed into the database. Big Data often involves high velocity. For example, Facebook has more than 10 million photos uploaded every hour (Mayer-Schönberger & Cukier, 2013).
- Variety represents the data comes from various sources and in various formats. Data is not collected by handwritten notebook anymore, it comes from social network, smart phones, trading platforms, machines and others. When you browse your Facebook or drive with dongle in your car that records your driving behavior, it will contributes to the generation of the Big Data. The data is also in different format such as continuous or discrete, longitudinal or time series, and different computer science or communication languages. The data could also be structured or unstructured. If the data is stored in various format such as dates, numbers and texts and has no predefined format, it is considered as unstructured data.
- 3V of Big Data is then extended into a 5V characteristics which includes value and veracity. (Ishwarappa & Anuradha, 2015).
- Value represents the data needs to have potential useful information for future study. It cost human and technology resources for companies and institutions to maintain a Big Data database. You can't say you are working with Big Data unless there is potential value from it.
- Veracity represents the accuracy of the data. It is almost impossible for all of the data to be 100% accurate when dealing with Big Data, but the accuracy level is still a critical aspect to check with. A data sources full with incorrect information will only mislead the conclusions drawn from the study.

Data Measurement

Volume is a significant aspect of Big Data, this sections describes the data measurement and computing power evolvement. The following chart is the data measurement computer system utilized. The smallest unit of the data measurement is bit which stores values 0 or 1. The reason a Byte is 8 bits is because combination of 8 binary data will allow the system to generate 256 (2^8) unique values which is sufficient amount of variety to include all of the commonly used letter, number and symbols according to American Standard Code for Information Interchange (ASCII).

1,024 was selected so that data is compatible with decimal number system, however kilobyte is not exactly 1,000 bytes due to the binary storage and data processing mechanism of computer. However, it is common to see the measurement equivalency is represented by 1,000. For example, you purchased a commercial made personal computer with hard drive labeled with 250GB storage, but when you clicked "My computer" icon, it shows 10GB free out of 232.83GB, this is because 250,000,000,000 B = 232.83 * 1,073,741,824 B = 232.83 GB.

Figure 1. Big Data characteristics (Designed by Niu, November, 2017)

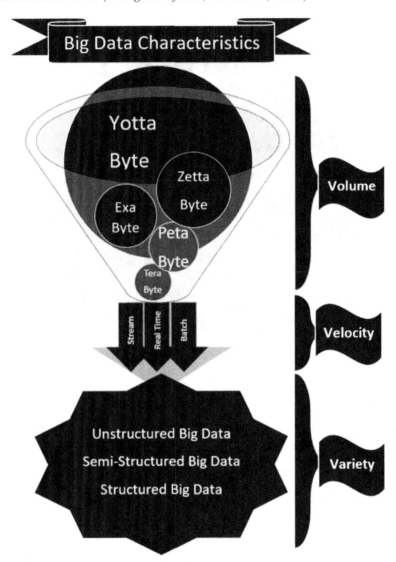

With the basic understanding of what is the data measurement, the following will establish how much information each of the data measurement unit stores:

- 1 Megabyte stores information equivalent to a medium sized novel; (Indiana University, 2013)
- 1 Terabyte stores information equivalent to all of the books in a large library; (Indiana University, 2013)
- 1 Petabyte stores information equivalent to 13.3 years of high-definition video, or all of the content in the U.S. library of congress (Johnston, 2012)
- 2.5 Exabyte data generated each day in 2012. There more data generated and stored each second across internet than 20 years ago (McAfee & Brynjolfsson, 2012)
- 1.2 Zettabyte is the annual run rate for global Internet Protocol (IP) traffic in 2016 (Cisco, 2015)

Figure 2. 5V of characteristics (Designed by Niu, November, 2017)

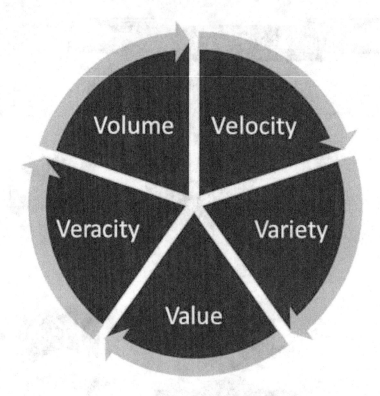

Big Data concept has been developed rapidly, it is dynamic, what was considered as Big Data 20 years ago is not anymore in today's computing power.

BIG DATA TECHNOLOGY

In the past, companies had been writing big checks to database venders such as Oracle, Microsoft and IBM. After 2000, Google started to encounter a problem that the data they collected were so large that no single database vender will be able to store and process their data anymore, and hence the need for Big Data technology evolved as well as Big Data Analytics. An entire book on the technology of hands-on approaches to Big Data has been published by Bahga and Madisetti (2016). Below are a few of the tools and frameworks for "batch processing" of Big Data.

MapReduce

MapReduce is a parallel processing model and programming concept that was initially developed by Google to solve the Big Data issue. It divides the dataset into smaller clusters, maps the clusters into different computers or servers for processing, and then aggregates the information for the results. MapReduce is a programming model that specifies the computation so that the computation can take advantage of utlizing lots of machines or computers.

There are three phases for MapReduce, map, shuffle and reduce. Map phase breaks down the calculation by different elements of the document such as different format of data, or different dimension of the calculation. Shuffle phase reassigns all of the elements into different computing machine according to the characteristics. Then Reduce phase collects the calculations and aggregates them for resulting. The example provided below is an overly simplified illustration. How to divide the data into different groups or clusters so that the next phase of computation if effective and efficient is a scientific subject.

Table 2. Data measurement

Measurement	Size		
	Exact Measurement	**Exact Measurement**	**Traditional Measurement**
Bit	Binary Data (0 or 1)	Binary Data (0 or 1)	Binary Data (0 or 1)
Byte (B)	8 bits	8 bits or 1 B	8 bits or 1 B
Kilobyte (KB)	1,024 B	1,024	1,000
Megabyte (MB)	1,024 KB	1,048,576	1,000,000
Gigabyte (GB)	1,024 MB	1,073,741,824	1,000,000,000
Terabyte (TB)	1,024 GB	1,099,511,627,776	1,000,000,000,000
Petabyte (PB)	1,024 TB	1,125,899,906,842,620	1,000,000,000,000,000
Exabyte (EB)	1,024 PB	1,152,921,504,606,850,000	1,000,000,000,000,000,000
Zettabyte (ZB)	1,024 EB	1,180,591,620,717,410,000,000	1,000,000,000,000,000,000,000
Yottabyte (YB)	1,024 ZB	1,208,925,819,614,630,000,000,000	1,000,000,000,000,000,000,000,000

(Designed by Niu, November 2017)

Hadoop

Hadoop is an open-source software framework for the storage and distributed batch processing of large datasets on a cluster of machines (Ishwarappa & Anuradha, 2015). It is a leading Big Data technology with Hardoop YARN (Yet Another Resource Negotiator) as the next generation architecture of Hadoop. Hadoop was designed and developed by Doug Cutting and Mike Cafarella in 2005. It is widely used technology, for example, LinkedIn's Hadoop-based analytics predicts "People You May Know" for its over 200 million members (Sumbaly, Kreps, & Shah, 2013).

Hadoop has a Schema on read mechanism when it collects and stores the data. Schema on read means when you transfer data from one location (file) to another, you don't have to specify the data format that needs to be transferred, but when you access the data, you have to specify the format through your extraction code. However, other traditional programming mechanism such as SQL utilizes a concept of Schema of write, which means when you transfer, convert or save the data into a different location, you have to preconfigure the data ahead of time, such as date should be MM/DD/YYYY or MM-DD-YYYY. When you extract the data, all you need to do is to call on the name of the data. Schema on read feature allows the system to process data much more efficiently and be able to process a large amount of data and leave the processing work until later on.

Figure 3. MapReduce mechanism example (Designed by Niu, November 2017)

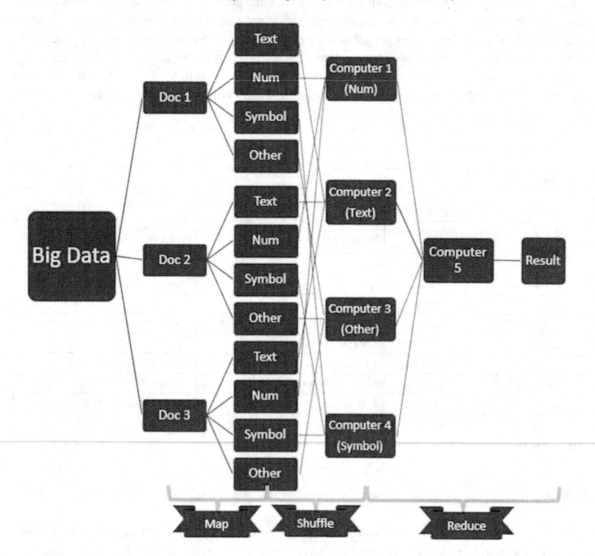

Hadoop stores the data as compressed files. It duplicates the files and distributes them into multiple servers or machines. This is not waste of computer resources, instead due to this feature Hadoop could afford to have fast, secure computation and continuously deliver results to end users. For example, Hadoop stores all of your photos into hundreds of servers. When you search for one of your historical photo, Hadoop commands each computer, also called name note, run a query on one day of the data, such as computer 1 searches all January 1st photos, and computer 2 searches all January 2nd photos etc. In this way, the work has been distributed. It is also very secure, because if one of the stored data is lost due to physical damage to hardware, the complete data is still intact. On the other hand, traditional data warehouse stores data in a well-defined format, with rows, columns, data formats, and unique ID link different format. Speed wise it cannot process significant large amount data, but traditional data warehouse is perfectly fine to handle data which requires high security level such as financial or confidential information. Because if any part of the data is missing, it can be easily detected.

Hadoop is an open-source software which means the original source code is made freely available and may be modified. There are many different modules that are Hadoop related. Table 3 lists a few (The Apache Software Foundation, 2017).

Table 3. Table of Hadoop and its related projects

Apache Hadoop Project	Hadoop-Related Projects		
Hadoop Common	Ambari™	HBase™	Spark™
Hadoop Distributed File System (HDFS™)	Avro™	Hive™	Tez™
Hadoop YARN	Cassandra™	Mahout™	ZooKeeper™
Hadoop MapReduce	Chukwa™	Pig™	

(Designed by Niu, November 2017)

HADOOP-RELATED PROJECTS

The following are concise descriptions of each of the above Hadoop-Related Projects listed in Table 3. The source of these statements except for those as cited otherwise are from Bahga and Madisetti (2016).

Ambari

A completely open-source management platform for provisioning, managing, monitoring and securing Apache Hadoop clusters (Hortonworks, 2017)

Avro

Avro is an Apache project that provides data serialization services.

Cassandra

Cassandra is a scalable, highly available, fault tolerant open-source non-relational database system.

Chukwa

Chukwa is a Hadoop subproject devoted to large-scale log collection and analysis. Chukwa is built on top of the Hadoop Distributed File System (HDFS) and MapReduce framework and inherits Hadoop's scalability and robustness. Chukwa also includes a flexible and powerful toolkit for displaying monitoring and analyzing results, in order to make the best use of this collected data. (Yang, 2015)

HBase

A non-relational distributed database, plus Phoenix that is a high-performance SQL layer for low latency applications.

Hive

Data warehouse system for ad-hoc queries and analyses of large datasets and table and storage management service.

Mahout

Project of the Apache Software Foundation to produce free implementation of distributed or otherwise scalable machine learning algorithms focused primarily in the areas of collaborative filtering, clustering and classification.

Pig

Scripting platform for analyzing large datasets.

Spark

Apache Spark is a fast and general engine for large-scale data processing.

Tez

Tez is the next generation Hadoop Query Processing framework written on top of YARN (Yet Another Resource Negotiator).

ZooKeeper

Centralized service which provides highly reliable distributed coordination.

THE INTERFACE OF COMPONENTS OF BIG DATA STACK

Figure 4 shows the interface of the component of Big Data Stack.

Figure 4. Big Data stack (developed by authors (2017))

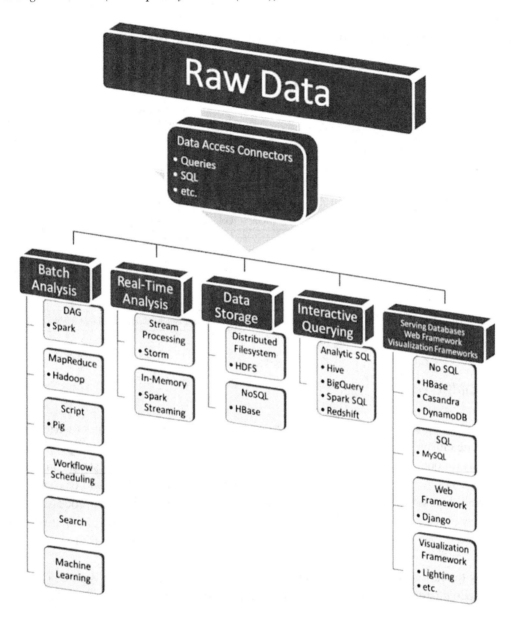

SUPERCOMPUTER

A supercomputer is a computer at the frontline of processing capacity and speed of calculation. Super-computers can be used for Big Data analytics such as quantum physics calculation, weather forecasting, simulations of airplane in wind tunnel or denotation of nuclear weapons. Supercomputers could be grid computing or cluster computing. Grid computing represents the calculation is distributed into a large number of computers. Hadoop has a similar mechanism to the grid computing. Cluster computing represents a large number of processors are in use with a close proximity (Segall, 2013). Previous work by the co-editor and co-author Segall in the area of supercomputing, high performance computing and

Big Data has been published as Segall, Cook and Zhang (2015), Segall and Gupta (2015), and Segall (2016a, 2016b, 2017a, 2017b).

Table 4 presents the top 10 fastest computers in the world as of November 2017.

Table 4. Top 10 fastest computers in the world as of November 2017

Rank	Supercomputer System	Company	Organization	Country
1	Sunway TaihuLight	NRCPC	National Supercomputing Center in Wuxi	China
2	Tianhe-2 (MilkyWay-2)	NUDT	National Supercomputer Center in Guangzhou	China
3	Piz Daint	Cary Inc.	Swiss National Supercomputing Centre (CSCS)	Switzerland
4	Gyoukou	ExaScaler	Japan Agency for Marine-Earth Science and Technology	Japan
5	Titan	Cary Inc.	DOE/SC/Oak Ridge National Laboratory	United States
6	Sequoia	IBM	DOE/NNSA/LLNL	United States
7	Trinity	Cary Inc.	DOE/NNSA/LANL/SNL	United States
8	Cori	Cary Inc.	DOE/SC/LBNL/NERSC	United States
9	Oakforest	Fujitsu	Joint Center for Advanced High Performance Computing	Japan
10	K computer	Fujitsu	RIKEN Advanced Institute for Computational Science (AICS)	Japan

(Designed by Niu, November 2017; adapted from Top 500, 2017)

CLOUD COMPUTING

Cloud computing happens when a task is distributed to a cloud server. Task is not distributed to a specific one or one cluster of computers. Grid computing is when more than one computers are working simultaneously for one task. Normally the task is distributed to a number of processing computers. Cloud server usually could be in a format of grid, but conversely not all grids are a cloud or part of cloud.

One of the benefits of cloud computing is the flexibility of task assignment for processing efficiency. Tasks with low processing requirement could be moved to processors with low computing power, and if the requirement ever increased, cloud server can maintain and distribute the task to one or a group of processors.

According to Gartner's 2017 Magic Quadrant for Cloud Infrastructure as a Service (IaaS), the following table demonstrates the leading providers based on their ability to execute.

BIG DATA ANALYTICS SOFTWARE AND PLATFORMS

Categories of Big Data Analytics software include the following: Data Ingestion, Hadoop Systems, Stream computing, Analytics/Machine Learning, Content Management, Integration, and Data Governance (PredictiveAnalyticsToday, 2017).

The categories shown in Table 6 are used in Table 7: Top 20 Big Data Analytics Software and Platforms that provides each in ranked order with website of each. Descriptions of the features for each of the twenty Big Data software and platform follow.

Table 5. Leading cloud Infrastructure as a Service (IaaS)

Rank	Cloud Provider		Recommended Usage						
			Cloud-Native Application	E-Business Hosting	General Business Application	Enterprise Application	Development Environments	Batch Computing	Internet of Things Application
1	Amazon Web Services		x	x	x	x	x	x	x
2	Microsoft Azure		x		x		x	x	
3	Google Cloud Platform		x					x	
4	Alibaba Cloud		x				x	x	
5	Virtustream					x			
6	IBM Cloud			x	x			x	
7	Rackspace	Public Cloud	x	x			x		
7	Rackspace	Private Cloud	x		x		x		

Source: (designed by Niu, November 2017; adapted from Leong, Bala, Lowery, & Smith, 2017)

Table 6. Categories of Big Data Analytics software

Category of Big Data Analytics Software	Description
Data Integration, Data Management, ELT, and Warehouse	Provides features for effective Data Warehousing and Management for managing data as a valuable resource.
Hadoop System	Provides features for massive storage for any kinds of data with enormous processing power and ability to handle virtually limitless concurrent tasks or jobs.
Stream Computing	Features for pulling in streams of data and streaming it back as a single flow.
Analytics/Machine Learning	Features for advanced analytics and machine learning.
Content Management	Features for comprehensive content life cycle and document management.
Integration	Features for Big Data integration from any source with ease.
Data Governance	Comprehensive Security and Compliance solution to protect the data.

(Derived from PredictiveAnalyticsToday 2017)

1. Talend Open Studio

Software for Data Integration and free to download open-source license tool that fully supports all facets of ETL processes. It provides more than 800 built-in connects than any other ETL solution, thus making it easy to implement connections between diverse database types, file formats, and enterprise solutions (Talend Open Studio, 2017).

2. Aracadia Data

Acadia Data unifies data discovery, visual analytics and business intelligence in a single, integrated platform that runs on Hadoop clusters (Aracadia Data, 2017).

3. Informatica PowerCenter Big Data Edition

Is highly scalable, high performance enterprise data integration software that uses visual environment to build ETL data flows that run on Hadoop. The data flows can be reused and collaborate with other developers and analysts with a common integrated development environment (Informatica PowerCenter Big Data Edition, 2017).

4. GoodData

The GoodData platform includes advanced distribution and product lifecycle management features to automate the process of maintaining one-to-many cloud deployments (Good Data, 2017).

5. Actian Analytics Platform

Features include Vectorized Query Execution, maximizing CPU cache for execution, column-based storage, data compression, positional data trees (PDTs), and storage indices. Actian Analytics Platform runs complex queries against billions of records in just seconds (Actian Analytics Platform, 2017).

Table 7. Top 20 Big Data Analytics software and platforms

Name of Big Data Analytics Software / Platform	Category	Web URL
1. Talend Open Data	ETL Software	https://www.talend.com/?utm_source=PredictiveAnalyticsToday&utm_medium=Review&utm_campaign=PA2.
2. Aracdia Data	Business Intelligence Software	https://www.arcadiadata.com/
3. Informatica	Big Data Software	https://www.informatica.com/products/big-data.html?utm_source=PredictiveAnalyticsToday&utm_medium=Review&utm_campaign=PAT#fbid=2tuRknAh7K4
4. GoodData	Business Intelligence Software	https://www.gooddata.com/?utm_source=PredictiveAnalyticsToday&utm_medium=Review&utm_campaign=PAT
5. Actian Analytics Platform	Dig Data, Big Data Analytics, Predictive Analysis	https://www.actian.com/
6. Attivio Active Intelligence Engine	Big Data Software	https://www.attivio.com/?utm_source=PredictiveAnalyticsToday&utm_medium=Review&utm_campaign=PAT
7. Opera Solutions Signal Hubs	Big Data Software	https://www.operasolutions.com/?utm_source=PredictiveAnalyticsToday&utm_medium=Review&utm_campaign=PAT
8. Datameer	Big Data Analytics Platform	https://www.datameer.com/?utm_source=PredictiveAnalyticsToday&utm_medium=Review&utm_campaign=PAT
9. FICO Big Data Analyzer	Big Data Analytics Platform	http://www.fico.com/en/analytic-cloud
10. Google BigData	Big Data Platform	https://cloud.google.com/solutions/big-data/
11. Wavefront	Big Data Software	https://www.predictiveanalyticstoday.com/wavefront/
12. Oracle Big Data Analytics	Big Data Platform	https://www.oracle.com/big-data/products.html
13. IBM Big Data	Big Data Platform	https://www.ibm.com/analytics/hadoop/big-data-analytics
14. Amdocs Insight	Big Data Platform	https://www.amdocs.com/real-time-data-management
15. Amazon Web Services	Big Data Platform	https://aws.amazon.com/products/#analytics-1
16. Splunk Big Data Analytics	Big Data Platform	https://www.splunk.com/en_us/solutions/solution-areas/big-data.html
17. DataTorrent	Big Data Ingestion Software	https://www.datatorrent.com/?utm_source=PredictiveAnalyticsToday&utm_medium=Review&utm_campaign=PAT
18. Palantir Big Data	Big Data Platform	https://www.palantir.com/products/
19. Cloudera Enterprise Big Data	Big Data Platform	https://www.cloudera.com/products.html
20. HPCC System Big Data	Big Data Platform	https://hpccsystems.com/

(PredictiveAnalyticsToday, 2017)

6. Attivio Active Intelligence Engine

Attivio Active Intelligence Engine is a unified information access platform that brings together structured and unstructured content by integrating and correlating all data and content with no advance data modeling. It provides advanced text analytics, intuitive, Google-like search for business intelligence (BI) and integration with BI and data visualization tools (Attivio Active Intelligence Engin, 2017).

7. Opera Solutions Signal Hubs

The signal hubs employs machine learning and are domain specific collections of signals along with the technology required to continually extract, store, and refresh, and present selected signals and recommended best actions (Opera Solutions Signal Hubs, 2017).

8. Datameer

Datameer is a SaaS Big Data analytics platform that is targeted for department special deployments (Datameer, 2017).

9. FICO Big Data Analyzer

Big Data Analyzer empowers a broad range of users to collaborate, explore data and discover new insights from any type and size of data on Hadoop (FICO Big Data Analyzer, 2017).

10. Google Big Data

Google Big Data is a cloud platform that unifies batch and stream processing that is fully managed with serverless architecture that utilizes Spark and Hadoop (Google Big Data, 2017).

11. Wavefront

Wavefront is a hosted platform for ingesting, storing, visualizing and alerting on metric data. It is based on a stream processing approach invented at Google that allows metric data to be manipulated with unparalleled power (Wavefront, 2017).

12. Oracle Big Data Analytics

Features include SQL Cloud Service, Oracle Big data Discovery, Oracle R Advanced Analytics for Hadoop, Business Intelligence and Data Visualization Cloud Service (Oracle Big Data Analytics, 2017).

13. IBM Big Data

Features include Data Management & Warehouse, Hadoop System, Stream Computing, Content Management, and Information Integration & Governance (IBM Big Data, 2017).

14. Amdocs Insight

Features include Real-Time Analytics, Amdocs Logical Data Model, Modern Data Infrastructure Management, and Analytical Applications Ecosystems (Amdocs Insight, 2017).

15. Amazon Web Service

Features include computing using Amazon Cloud Front, Storage using Amazon S3, database using Amazon Aurora, migration using Database Migration Service, and Amazon Virtual Private Cloud (Amazon Web Service, 2017).

16. Splunk Big Data Analytics

Features include Splunk Analytics for Hadoop, Splunk ODBC and DB Connect, Easy to deploy and use, massively scalable, real0time alerts, and robust security (Splunk Big Data Analytics, 2017).

17. DataTorrent

DataTorrent RTS is proven in production environments to reduce time to market, development costs and operational expenditures for Fortune 100 and leading Internet companies. It provides connectors for technologies such as message busses, SQL and NoSQL databases, flat files, Kafka, Scoop, Flume, and Twitter (DataTorrent, 2017).

18. Palantir Big Data

Features include Data Integration, Iteration and Collaboration, Custom Metric Development, Flexible Modeling, Privacy and Security Controls, and Algorithmic Processing (Palantir Big Data, 2017).

19. Cloudera Enterprise Big Data

Cloudera enterprise Big Data is powered by Apache Hadoop and features include Data Engineering, Analytical and Operational Database, secure without compromise, and easy to manage (Cloudera Enterprise Big Data, 2017).

20. HPCC Systems Big Data

Features include Scalable Automated Linking Technology, Data Refinery Cluster, Rapid Data Delivery Cluster, Seamless Data Integration, Knowledge Engineering Language, and Enterprise Control Language (HPCC Systems Big Data, 2017).

BIG DATA VISUALIZATION

Big Data visualization is different from traditional classical data visualization, because the data has a higher volume, larger variety of data format and high data processing speed. Unlike traditional graphs, Big Data visualization methods focus on high dimensional relationships. The following visualization methods provide better presentation to thoroughly understand the data. The data is extracted from Fatality Analysis Reporting System (FARS) managed by National Highway Traffic Safety Administration (NHTSA) of United States Department of Transportation (DoT).

Figure 5. Example of Treemap graph (Designed by Niu, November 2017)

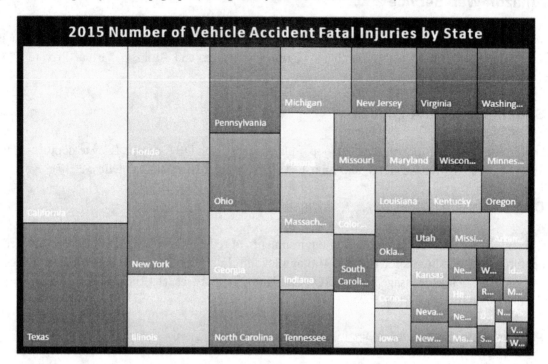

Treemap method uses size and color to demonstrate the data. In the example shown in Figure 5, size represents the population of the state, and the color represents the number of vehicle accident fatal injuries per person. Darker color corresponds to a higher number of fatal injuries per person.

Sunburst method projects out the proportional relationship within each of the variables visually like a sun. In the example shown in Figure 6, the inner circle has higher portion of male which represents the number of fatal injuries mostly happened to males. And within male fatalities, it most likely happened in the state highway. Within the categories of male together with State Highway fatalities in Figure 6, the highest proportion was for "Alcohol Not Involved".

Parallel coordinates method shows the relative relationship. In Figure 7, the number of fatal injuries example, the highest fatal injuries categories (21-30 years old) on country road (1096 fatal injuries) and state highway (2121 fatal injuries) are different. But with the parallel coordinates, the relationship between different categories are demonstrated proportionally.

Circle packing method uses color and circle size to describe the dataset. In the example shown in Figure 8, the color represents the region and size represent the total number of fatal injuries in 2015.

Heat map demonstrates map with coloring algorithm. The example in Figure 9 shows number of fatal injuries by state, color towards black represents higher total number of fatal injuries in 2015, and color towards grey represents lower total number of fatal injuries. Heat map could utilize more than two colors to demonstrate numerical value.

Streamgraph demonstrate time series data in a centered coordinate system. In the example given in Figure 10, four US (United States) regions total number of fatal injuries are aggregated into one wave according to time. And the proportional relationship between each region can be interpreted from this graph.

Figure 6. Example of Sunburst graph (Designed by Niu, November 2017)

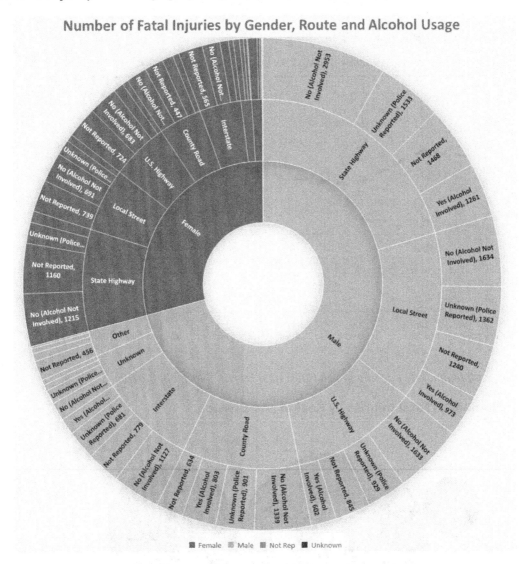

There are also numerous other types of visualization methods that could help with Big Data analysis, such as network analysis, circular network diagram. Method selection depends on data type and logical conclusions that the graph attempted to demonstrate.

Various visualization techniques were designed and implemented to realize the visualization methods. Script based techniques are developed, such as Java, so that programmers and software engineers are able to add interactive charts into their websites or applications conveniently. Some of the techniques are developed with user friendly interface so that Big Data analytics can be performed without coding. The following table includes a list of popular Big Data visualization tools, it categorized the tool as JavaScript based and user interface based techniques.

Figure 7. Example of parallel coordinates graph: Number of fatal injuries by age group and route (Designed by Niu, November 2017)

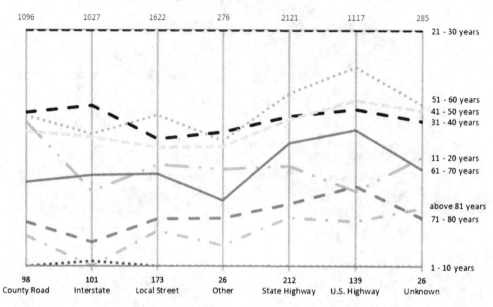

Number of Fatal Injuries by Age Group and Route

Figure 8. Example of circle packing graph (Designed by Niu, November 2017)

Number of Fatal Injuries by Region and Division

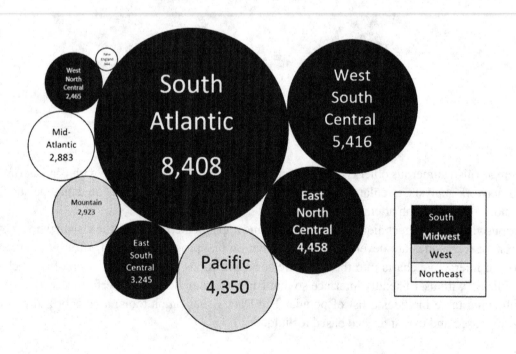

Figure 9. Example of heatmap graph (Designed by Niu, November 2017)

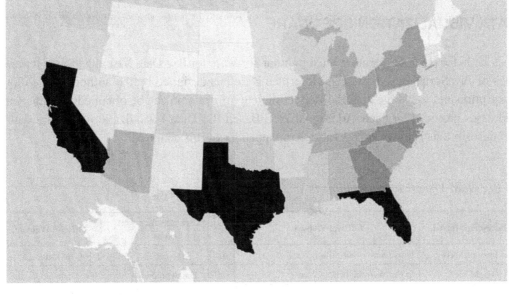

Figure 10. Example of streamgraph graph (Designed by Niu, November 2017)

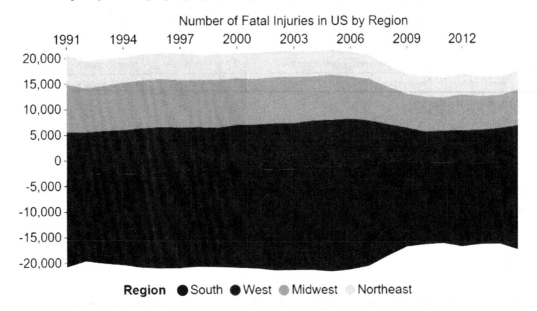

BIG DATA VISUALIZATION FOR TABLETS AND MOBILE DEVICES

Both SAS® Visual Analytics and SAS® Visual Statistics are designed to provide Big Data Analytics for mobile devices and Tablets and is discussed in Segall (2017a, 2017b). SAS® Visual Statistics is one of the modules built within SAS® Visual Analytics. SAS® Notes for classroom teaching are available from

SAS® Institute, Inc. for SAS® Visual Analytics Software as authored by Bell, Hardin and Matthews (2017) and SAS® Visual Statistics as authored by Ravenna, Truxillo and Wells (2017).

BIG DATA VISUALIZATION SOFTWARE

Below is a table for some of the other most popular software for Big Data Visualization software in the categories of JavaScript Based and User Interface Based as designed by the authors, and followed by brief description and web page images. More complete information can be obtained from the web page URL addresses provided for each. Additional Web-Based Big Data Visualization Software with URLs and brief descriptions is provided by Table 9 in Appendix of this chapter.

Table 8. Big Data Visualization techniques

	JavaScript Based	Official Website		UserInterface based	Official Website
1	FusionCharts	https://www.fusioncharts.com/	10	Tableau	https://www.tableau.com/
2	HighCharts	https://www.highcharts.com/	11	Datawrapper	https://www.datawrapper.de/
3	Dygraphs	http://dygraphs.com/	12	Paraview	https://www.paraview.org/
4	Timeline JS	http://dygraphs.com/	13	Infogram	https://infogram.com/
5	Chart JS	http://www.chartjs.org/	14	Plotly	https://plot.ly/
6	D3 JS	https://d3js.org/	15	Qlik	https://www.qlik.com/
7	Leaflet	http://leafletjs.com	16	Sisense	https://www.sisense.com/
8	Google Charts	https://developers.google.com/chart/	17	Visually	https://visual.ly/
9	RawGraphs	http://rawgraphs.io/	18	Gephi	https://gephi.org/

(Designed by Niu, November 2017)

1. Fusion Charts

Fusion charts is a JavaScript based visualization service for web developers. It offers more than 90 chart types and 1400 maps. Service has been categorized as FusionCharts XT, FusionWidgets XT, Power-Charts XT and FusionMaps XT.

2. HighCharts

HighCharts provides JavaScript services to help developers for their visualization needs. It focuses on interactive graphs.

3. Dygraphs

Dygraphs is an open-source and free services. It focuses on handling large datasets, and incorporating interactive functions within graphs. Dygraphs is JavaScript based visualization tool.

4. Timeline JS

Timeline JS is JavaScript free visualization tool that focuses on a timeline graph. It is a web designed tool for web developers to showcase the time line of a story.

5. Chart JS

Chart JS is a HyperText Markup Language 5 (HTML5) based JavaScript visualization tool. It is open-source and free.

6. D3 JS

D3 JS is a JavaScript library that provides visualization solutions. It focuses on the control of the final visual results and be able to provide innovative and interactive graphs.

7. Leaflet

Leaflet is an open-source and JavaScript based visualization tool. It focuses on mobile based interactive maps.

8. Google Charts

Google charts provides interactive visualization solutions by taking user supplied data. It will express the visualization in JavaScript for developer's further utilization.

9. RawGraphs

RawGraphs is an open-source software and allows users generate graphs through the web. It could also generate JavaScript for developers further use. Users has been generated various typical Big Data graphs such as streamgraph, customized treemap etc.

10. Tableau

Tableau is a visualization software focuses business intelligence. It is built with a user friendly interface, users of the software only needs to drag the variable names to generate graphs after input the data. It has a powerful geographical processing function. The use of Tableau Software for university teaching is discussed in Segall (2017a, 2017b). Instructors' resources web pages for Tableau software are provided at Tableau (2017).

11. Datawrapper

Datawrapper is a user interface based visualization tool. The website generates charts and maps. It has a rich map library including various countries option for visualization.

12. Paraview

Paraview is an open-source user interface based visualization tool. The software has visualization functions specifically designed for structural analysis, fluid dynamics, astrophysics and climate science.

13. Infogram

Infogram is a user interface based visualization tool. The software focuses on business intelligence and is able to generate infographics and create business reports based on users' data.

14. Plotly

Plotly is an open-source visualization tool that allows users to create interactive data graphs and share via the web. It also provides consulting services.

15. Qlik

Qlik is a user interface data visualization software. Users only need to drag and click to explore and generate data after uploading. It is a business oriented instead of scientific research oriented Big Data visualization tool.

16. Sisense

Sisense is a user interface data visualization software. The software is designed for various types of business such as Healthcare, Finance, Marketing, Retail and Public Sector.

17. Visually

Visually is a web based data visualization and infographics technique. Data analysts and designers utilize the technology to provide services such as visualization animated videos.

18. Gephi

Gephi is an open-source and free software. It has a powerful network analysis function.

CHALLENGES AND OPPORTUNITIES

Data Quality Challenge

There are challenges when dealing with Big Data. It shows that there are typical issues of missing data, volatility and selectivity with Big Data analysis (Daas, Puts, Buelens & van den Hurk, 2015). Volatility occurs when the data collection phase involves inconsistent process, such as portion of data collected daily, and others collected weekly. Inconsistent data challenges Big Data analytics. Selectivity occurs when data collected is biasedly selective instead of representative. It will challenge the researchers to be able to conduct unbiased statistical analysis to support decision making process.

Privacy Violation

The Internet has generated tremendous amounts of data continuously without explicit permission of users. It raises a question that does the Big Data processor have legal right to collect, analyze or distribute the data and data related products? Social security numbers and birthdates are obvious examples that are related to privacy and security. But other types of data such as medical search records may easily categorize into a grey area and challenges Big Data users to properly comply with regulation.

Hardware and Software

Building a large database is challenging due the high cost of hardware. The current personal or working computer are in the level of GB to process data, but the amount data generated every day are in TB and PB level like social media and financial records. Purchasing and maintaining hardware with sufficient capacity cost significant amount financial and human resources.

Because software is limited by the hardware capacity (Tole, 2013), thus it is also a challenge in the Big Data era. Currently, Hadoop and its related projects are the leading software dealing with Big Data. There will be more software developed to improve the efficiency of Big Data analytics for various sectors of industries.

OPPORTUNITIES FOR BIG DATA

Big Data presents a tremendous potential financially and socially in the future. The value of Big Data has already been recognized by many industries and governments (Benjelloun, Lahcen & Belfkih, 2015). Retailers use Big Data for better marketing and customer services; financial industry analyzes Big Data of business and economic vitals for dynamic decision-making support; health care industry utilize Big Data of patients for more effective treatment and pandemics prediction; and social media is generating massive amount data from its digital material to improve effective communications. With Big Data, weather and climate could be better predicted to help farmers increase production. And politicians can benefit from getting in-time feedback with the help of Big Data.

The subsequent chapters of this Handbook build upon the successful technologies and applications of Big Data. Figure 11 shows the overview and flow of the 30 chapters in this Handbook of Big Data Storage and Visualization Techniques.

ACKNOWLEDGMENT

Dr. Richard Segall needs to acknowledge a 2017 Summer Research Grant awarded by the College of Business of Arkansas State University for completion of this research.

Figure 11. Overview and flow of chapters of Handbook of Big Data Storage and Visualization Techniques edited by Segall and Cook (2018)

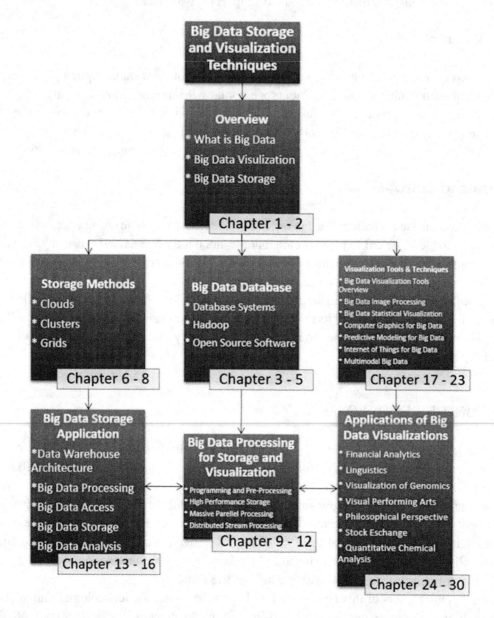

REFERENCES

Actian Analytics Platform. (2017). Retrieved on November 21, 2017 from https://www.predictiveanalyticstoday.com/actian-analytics-platform/

Amazon Web Service. (2017). Retrieved on November 21, 2017 from https://www.predictiveanalyticstoday.com/amazon-web-service/

Amdocs Insight. (2017). Retrieved on November 21, 2017 from https://www.predictiveanalyticstoday. com/amdocs-insight/

Arcadia Data. (2017). Retrieved on November 21, 2017 from https://www.predictiveanalyticstoday. com/arcadia-data/

Attivio Active Intelligence Engine. (2017). Retrieved on November 21, 2017 from https://www.predictiveanalyticstoday.com/attivio-active-intelligence-engine/

Bahga, A., & Madisetti, V. (2016). *Big data science & analytics: A hands-on approach.* Big-Data-Analytics Book Company. Retrieved from www.big-data.analytics.com

Bell, R., Hardin, B., & Matthews, L. (2017). *SAS® Visual Analytics for SAS® 9: Getting Started Course Notes.* Cary, NC: SAS Institute, Inc.

Benjelloun, F. Z., Lahcen, A. A., & Belfkih, S. (2015, March). An overview of big data opportunities, applications and tools. In Intelligent Systems and Computer Vision (ISCV), 2015 (pp. 1-6). IEEE. doi:10.1109/ISACV.2015.7105553

Capterra. (2017). *Big Data Software.* Retrieved November 25, 2017 from https://www.capterra.com/ big-data-software/?utf8=%E2%9C%93&users=&feature%5B4%5D=39433&commit=Filter+Results &sort_options=

Circle Packing Graph. (2017). Retrieved on November 19, 2017 from https://en.wikipedia.org/wiki/ Circle_packing

Cisco. (2017). *The Zettabyte Era: Trends and Analysis.* Retrieved November 23, 2107 from https:// www.cisco.com/c/en/us/solutions/collateral/service-provider/visual-networking-index-vni/vni-hyper-connectivity-wp.html

Clegg, B. (2017). *Big Data: How the information revolution is transforming our lives.* London, UK: Icon Books, Ltd.

Cloudera Enterprise Big Data. (2017). Retrieved on November 21, 2017 from https://www.predictive-analyticstoday.com/cloudera-enterprise-bigdata/

Daas, P. J., Puts, M. J., Buelens, B., & van den Hurk, P. A. (2015). Big data as a source for official statistics. *Journal of Official Statistics, 31*(2), 249. doi:10.1515/jos-2015-0016

Datameer. (2017). Retrieved on November 21, 2017 from https://www.predictiveanalyticstoday.com/ datameer/

DataTorrent. (2017). Retrieved on November 21, 2017 from https://www.predictiveanalyticstoday.com/ datatorrent/

FICO Big Data Analyzer. (2017). Retrieved on November 21, 2017 from https://www.predictiveanalyticstoday.com/fico-big-data-analyzer/

Franks, B. (2012). *Taming the big data tidal wave: Finding opportunities in huge data streams with advanced analytics (Wiley & SAS Business Series).* Hoboken, NJ: John Wiley & Sons. doi:10.1002/9781119204275

GoodData. (2017). Retrieved on November 21, 2017 from https://www.predictiveanalyticstoday.com/gooddata/

Google Big Data. (2017). Retrieved on November 21, 2017 from https://www.predictiveanalyticstoday.com/google-bigdata/

Heatmap. (2017). Retrieved on November 19, 2017 from https://en.wikipedia.org/wiki/Heat_map

Hortonworks. (2017). *Apache Ambari.* Retrieved on November 20, 2017 from https://hortonworks.com/apache/ambari/

HPSS Systems Big Data. (2017). Retrieved on November 21, 2017 from https://www.predictiveanalyticstoday.com/hpcc-systems-big-data/

IBM. (2017). *What is Big Data?* Retrieved on November 20, 2017 from http://www-01.ibm.com/software/in/data/bigdata/

IBM Big Data. (2017). Retrieved on November 21, 2017 from https://www.predictiveanalyticstoday.com/ibm-big-data/

Indiana University. (2013). *What are bits, bytes, and other units of measure for digital information?* Retrieved October 30, 2017 from https://kb.iu.edu/d/ackw

Informatica PowerCenter Big Data Edition. (2017). Retrieved on November 21, 2017 from https://www.predictiveanalyticstoday.com/informatica-powercenter-big-data-edition/

Ishwarappa, D., & Anuradha, J. (2015). A brief introduction on big data 5Vs characteristics and Hadoop Technology. *Procedia Computer Science*, *48*, 319–324. doi:10.1016/j.procs.2015.04.188

Johnston, L. (2012, April 25). *A "Library of Congress" Worth of Data: It's All In How You Define It.* Retrieved October 30, 2017, from https://blogs.loc.gov/thesignal/2012/04/a-library-of-congress-worth-of-data-its-all-in-how-you-define-it/

Le, J. (2016, Aug 18). *The 10 Algorithms Machine Learning Engineers Need to Know.* Retrieved from https://www.kdnuggets.com/2016/08/10-algorithms-machine-learning-engineers.html

Leong, L., Bala, R., Lowery, C., & Smith, D. (2017). *Magic Quadrant for Cloud Infrastructure as a Service, Worldwide.* Retrieved on November 24, 2017 from https://www.gartner.com/doc/reprints?id=1-2G2O5FC&ct=150519

Manyika, J., Chui, M., Brown, B., Bughin, J., Dobbs, R., & Roxburgh, C. (2011). Big data: The next frontier for innovation, competition, and productivity. Washington, DC: McKinsey Global Institute.

Marr, B. (2016). *Big data in practice: How 45 successful companies used big data analytics to deliver extraordinary results.* John Wiley & Sons, Ltd. doi:10.1002/9781119278825

Mayer-Schönberger, V., & Cukier, K. (2013). *Big data: A revolution that will transform how we live, work, and think.* Boston: Houghton Mifflin Harcourt.

McAfee, A., & Brynjolfsson, E. (2012). Big data: The management revolution. *Harvard Business Review*, *90*(10), 61–68. PMID:23074865

National Highway Traffic Safety Administration. (2017). *NCSA Data Resource Website Fatality Analysis Reporting System (FARS) Encyclopedia.* National Center for Statistics and Analysis (NCSA) Motor Vehicle Traffic Crash Data. U.S. Department of Transportation. Retrieved on November 20, 2017 from ftp://ftp.nhtsa.dot.gov/fars/

Opera Solutions Signal Hubs. (2017). Retrieved on November 21, 2017 from https://www.predictive-analyticstoday.com/opera-solutions-signal-hubs/

Oracle Big Data Analytics. (2017). Retrieved on November 21, 2017 from https://www.predictiveanalyticstoday.com/oracle-bigdata-analytics/

Palantir Big Data. (2017). Retrieved on November 21, 2017 from https://www.predictiveanalyticstoday.com/palantir-bigdata/

Ravenna, A., Truxilla, C., & Wells, C. (2017). *SAS® Visual Statistics: Interactive Model Building Course Notes.* Cary, NC: SAS Institute, Inc.

Russom, P. (2011). Big data analytics. *TDWI Best Practices Report, 19,* 40.

Samuel, A. L. (2000). Some studies in machine learning using the game of checkers. *IBM Journal of Research and Development, 44*(1-2), 206-226.

Segall, R. S. (2013). Computational Dimensionalities of Global Supercomputing. *Journal of Systemics, 11*(9), 75–86.

Segall, R. S. (2016). *Invited Plenary Address at International Institute of Informatics and Systemics (IIIS) Conference titled: "Big Data: A Treasure Chest for Interdisciplinary Research".* 20th Multi-conference on Systemics, Cybernetics, and Informatics (WMSCI 2016), Orlando, FL. Retrieved on December 26, 2016 from http://www.iiis.org/ViewVideo2016.asp?id=14

Segall, R. S. (2016). *High Performance Computing and Data Mining in Bioinformatics.* FedEx Institute of Technology, Presentation at 13th Annual Meeting of MidSouth Computational Biology and Bioinformatics Society (MCBIOS), Memphis, TN. Retrieved on June 19, 2017 from http://www.memphis.edu/bioinformatics/announcements/pdfs/mcbios2016.pdf

Segall, R. S. (2017a). *Using Tablets and Mobile Devices for Visual Analytics of Big Data in Bioinformatics.* Presentation at 14th Annual Meeting of MidSouth Computational Biology and Bioinformatics Society (MCBIOS), Little Rock, AR. Retrieved on June 19, 2017 from https://mcbios.org/sites/mcbios.org/files/MCBIOS2017_Program_Book_Final_1_0.pdf

Segall, R. S. (2017b). Technologies for Teaching Big Data Analytics. *Proceedings of 48th Meeting of Southwest Decision Sciences (SWDSI).* Retrieved on June 19, 2017 from http://www.swdsi.org/swdsi2017/SWDSI_2017_CONFERENCE_PROGRAM4.pdf

Segall, R. S., & Cook, J. S. (2014). Data Visualization and Information Quality by Supercomputing. In *Proceedings of the Forty-Fifth Meeting of Southwest Decision Sciences Institute* (SWDSI). Dallas, TX: Academic Press. Retrieved on June 19, 2017 from http://www.swdsi.org/swdsi2014/2014_SWDSI_CFP_MARCH_2014_v7.pdf

Segall, R. S., Cook, J. S., & Zhang, Q. (2015). *Research and Applications in Global Supercomputing*. Hershey, PA: IGI Global Inc. Retrieved on May 19, 2017 from http://www.igi-global.com/book/research-applications-global-supercomputing/118093

Segall, R. S., & Gupta, N. (2015). Overview of Global Supercomputing. In *Research and Applications in Global Supercomputing* (pp. 1-32). Hershey, PA: IGI Global Inc. Retrieved on May 19, 2017 from http://www.igi-global.com/chapter/overview-of-global-supercomputing/124335

Splunk Big Data Analytics. (2017). Retrieved on November 21, 2017 from https://www.predictiveanalyticstoday.com/splunk-bigdata-analytics/

Streamgraph. (2017). Retrieved on November 19, 2017 from https://en.wikipedia.org/wiki/Streamgraph

Sumbaly, R., Kreps, J., & Shah, S. (2013, June). The big data ecosystem at linkedin. In *Proceedings of the 2013 ACM SIGMOD International Conference on Management of Data* (pp. 1125-1134). ACM. 10.1145/2463676.2463707

Sunburst Graph. (2017). Retrieved on November 19, 2017 from https://en.wikipedia.org/wiki/Pie_chart#Ring_chart_.2F_Sunburst_chart_.2F_Multilevel_pie_chart

Sutton, R. S., & Barto, A. G. (1998). Reinforcement learning: An introduction: Vol. 1. *No. 1*. Cambridge, MA: MIT Press.

Tableau Software. (2017). *Tableau Community Instructor's Resource Page*. Retrieved on May 31, 2017 from https://community.tableau.com/community/teachers/overview

Talend Open Studio. (2017). Retrieved on November 21, 2017 from https://www.predictiveanalyticstoday.com/talend-open-studio-for-data-integration/

The Apache Software Foundation. (n.d.). Retrieved October 30, 2017, from http://hadoop.apache.org/

The White House. (2012). *Obama Administration Unveils "Big Data" Initiative: Announces $200 Million in New R&D Investments*. Retrieved October 30, 2017, from https://obamawhitehouse.archives.gov/the-press-office/2015/11/19/release-obama-administration-unveils-big-data-initiative-announces-200

Tibco. (2017). *Parallel Coordinates Plot*. Retrieved on November 19, 2017 from https://docs.tibco.com/pub/spotfire/6.5.2/doc/html/para/para_what_is_a_parallel_coordinate_plot.htm

Timeline of Computer History. (n.d.). Retrieved October 30, 2017, from http://www.computerhistory.org/timeline/computers/

Tole, A. A. (2013). Big data challenges. *Database Systems Journal*, 4(3), 31–40.

Top 500. (2017). *The List November 2017*. Retrieved on November 24, 2017 from Top 500 (2017) https://www.top500.org/lists/2017/11/

Treemap. (2017). Retrieved on November 19, 2017 from https://en.wikipedia.org/wiki/Treemapping

Van Hasselt, H., Guez, A., & Silver, D. (2016, February). *Deep Reinforcement Learning with Double Q-Learning*. AAAI.

Wavefront. (2017). Retrieved on November 21, 2017 from https://www.predictiveanalyticstoday.com/wavefront/

Yang, E. (2015). *Chuckwa. Hadoop Wiki*. Retrieved on November 20, 2017 from https://wiki.apache.org/hadoop/Chukwa

Yottabyte. (2017). Retrieved on November 21, 2017 from https://en.wikipedia.org/wiki/Yottabyte

Zhou, L., Pan, S., Wang, J., & Vasilakos, A. V. (2017). Machine learning on big data: Opportunities and challenges. *Neurocomputing*, *237*, 350–361. doi:10.1016/j.neucom.2017.01.026

KEY TERMS AND DEFINITIONS

Big Data: Data that exceeds the capacity of commonly used hardware and software tools to capture, store, and analyze within a tolerable elapsed time is considered big data. The three main characteristics of big data are volume, variety, and velocity.

Circle Packing Graph: Circle packing is the study of the arrangement of circles (of equal or varying sizes) on a given surface such that no overlapping occurs and so that all circles touch one another (Circle Packing Graph, 2017).

Data Measurement: Unit measurement to indicate the volume of data in modern computer storage devices.

Hadoop: Hadoop is an open-source software framework for the storage and processing of large datasets on a cluster of machines.

Heatmap: A heat map (or heatmap) is a graphical representation of data where the individual values contained in a matrix are represented as colors (Heatmap, 2017).

Machine Learning: A process that gives machine the ability to learn without being explicitly programmed.

MapReduce: A programming algorithm that divides and maps the elements of datasets; then shuffles and distributes to cluster computing powers for big data processing.

Parallel Coordinate Plot: A parallel coordinate plot maps each row in the data table as a line, or profile. Each attribute of a row is represented by a point on the line. This makes parallel coordinate plots similar in appearance to line charts, but the way data is translated into a plot is substantially different (Tibco, 2017).

Schema on Read: Data analysis strategy that new data is transferred to a plan or schema without a predefined format.

Schema on Write: Data analysis strategy that new data is transferred to a structured predefined format.

Streammap: A streamgraph, or stream graph, is a type of stacked area graph which is displaced around a central axis, resulting in a flowing, organic shape. (Streammap, 2017).

This research was previously published in the Handbook of Research on Big Data Storage and Visualization Techniques; pages 1-32, copyright year 2018 by Engineering Science Reference (an imprint of IGI Global).

APPENDIX

Table 9. Additional web-based Big Data Visualization software

Name of Web-Based Big Data Visualization Software	Web URL	Description
1010data	https://1010data.com/	1010data is a leading business intelligence provider (Forrester & Gartner), trusted by over 850 of the world's largest companies.
Alooma	https://www.alooma.com/	Alooma brings all your data sources together into BigQuery, Redshift, Snowflake and more.
AnswerMiner	https://www.answerminer.com/	An amazing and fast data exploration tool with many unique features like relation maps and decision trees.
Arimo	https://arimo.com/	Machine learning algorithms and a powerful big-compute platform, Big Apps multiply the value of your organization's data and people.
Axibase Time Series Database	https://axibase.com/products/ axibase-time-series-database/	ATSD is a distributed NoSQL database designed from the ground up to store and analyze time-series data at scale.
BI on Big Data	http://www.kyvosinsights.com/	Kyvos is revolutionizing analytics with its breakthrough OLAP on Big Data technology.
BillRun	https://billrun.com/	Open-source billing solution, designed for Big Data. On-prem and SaaS, pre- and post-pay.
Cloudera Enterprise	https://www.cloudera.com/ products.html	Cloudera delivers the modern platform for machine learning and analytics optimized for the cloud.
Cogniteev	http://www.cogniteev.com/	Cogniteev is a data access automation platform that enables companies to access and analyze complex data sets.
Datadog Cloud Monitoring	https://www.datadoghq.com/	Datadog is the essential monitoring service for hybrid cloud environments. The platform assists organizations in improving agility, increasing efficiency and providing end-to-end visibility across dynamic or high-scale infrastructures.
DataLux	http://www.vivorbis.com/	Big Data Platform solution with state of the art analytics, data lake, aggregation capabilities, and more.
Datameer	https://www.datameer.com/	Empowers organizations to embark on a data journey that answers a wide range of new, deeper business questions.
DataPlay	https://dataplay.us/	Integrated suite of applications that fully meets your analysis, visualization, and presentation needs in market research.
Domo	https://www.domo.com/	Domo is cloud -based business management platform, and first solution that brings together five products into one elegant platform enabling users to connect, prepare, visualize, engage and optimize their business around data.
Graph DB	https://ontotext.com/	A semantic repository, a NoSQL database system used for storage, querying, and management of structured data.
Ideata Analytics	https://ideata-analytics.com/	Self-service analytics platform to source, clean, analyze, and visualize Big Data at scale using Apache Spark.
IQLECT	http://www.iqlect.com/	Actionable insights with real-time Big Data analytics. Fully converged platform and solutions for organizations of any size.

Name of Web-Based Big Data Visualization Software	Web URL	Description
Looker	https://looker.com/	Looker works the way the web does: browser-based, its unique modeling language lets any employee leverage the work of your best data analysts. Operating 100% in-database, Looker capitalizes on the newest, fastest analytic databases to get real results, in real time. Lookers lightweight open architecture make it easy for developers to quickly and flexibly build, deploy, and iterate custom on data applications.
MicroStrategy Enterprise Analytics	https://www.microstrategy.com/us	A comprehensive enterprise analytics and mobility platform that delivers a full range of analytical and reporting capabilities.
MongoDB	https://www.mongodb.com/	From startups to enterprises, for the modern and the mission-critical
Periscope	https://www.periscopedata.com/	Periscope connects directly to your database and lets you run, visualize, and share analyses on billions of rows of data in seconds.
Phocas Software	https://www.phocassoftware.com/	Phocas Software is an award-winning Business Intelligence software used by companies across numerous industries and around the globe.
Salesforce Analytics Cloud	https://www.salesforce.com/products/einstein-analytics/overview/	For every business user. Explore any combination of data, get answers instantly, and share with your team. From any device, anywhere, faster than ever before. For analysts. Deliver new insights to your business users however, wherever, and whenever they want them.
SEQUEL	http://sequel.jeremyevans.net/	SEQUEL provides easy-to-use data access solutions for IBM and empowers users with quality insight to make key business decisions.
Sisense	https://www.sisense.com/	Sisense provides an end-to-end solution for tackling growing data sets from multiple sources that comes out-of-the-box with the ability to crunch terabytes of data and support thousands of users--all on a single commodity server.

(Created by Co-Editor Jeffrey S. Cook using (Capterra, 2017))

Chapter 3
Introduction of Big Data With Analytics of Big Data

Preeti Bala
Institute of Management Studies, Noida, India

ABSTRACT

This chapter explained big data and how to do the data analytics in big data along with the basics of big data with its common traits. This chapter described technology that is used to handle the big data like, NoSQL, Hadoop, MangoDB, MapReduce, etc. This chapter explained the challenges that we are facing to handle big data and discussed some live projects in big data.

INTRODUCTION

The new word came into the existence "Big Data" is due to the fact that we are creating a huge amount of data every day. The Birth of Big Data can be traced back to 1998 in a silicon graphics slide deck by John Mashey with the title "Big Data and the next Wave of infra Stress." Before analysing challenges and other aspects of big data, let us examine where big data comes from? The big Data comes from us .Its future is at the mercy and whims of our fingertips. Big Data is generated when formerly no digitized processes become digitized.

That is our life is getting digitized; we now use online banking, online shopping .e-learning, emails, and instead of the traditional methods. Big data comes relatively new types of data sources that previously were not mined for. Big data is also turned as devices become more integrated into our everyday lives. Everyone has a mobile phones, camera, laptop, takes pictures and makes videos and then uploads them to social networks, which keeps on adding to the huge bulk of data .we generate lots of big data as we willingly share information with the world through social media in the form of tweets, comments likes and many more. (Bifet, 2013)

The key enables for the growth of big data can be summarised as follows:

1. Increase in storage capacities
2. Increase in processing power

DOI: 10.4018/978-1-6684-3662-2.ch003

3.   Availability of data

Two important trends in the era of Big Data are as follows:

1.   The digitization of virtually "everything ".
2.   Advanced analytics technologies and techniques that enable organization to extract insights from data with high levels of sophistication, speed, and accuracy.

Big Data generated usually share some or all the following features:

1.   Digitally generated –IT will be a digital data
2.   Passively produced –It may be a by product of our interaction with digital services in our day to day life
3.   Automatically collected –There may be some system that collects and stores relevant data generated.
4.   Geographically or temporally trackball- Mobile phone location data or call duration time.
5.   Continuously analysed – Information can be analysed in real time for human well-being.
6.   Doug Laney was the first person who highlighted the three dimensions of big data the three V"S

BIG DATA "THE THREE V'S"

1.   **Volume:** Nowadays data is expanding rapidly to fill up the available space for storage .we are very familiar at the rate at which we copy videos and songs from one mobile to other mobile. Every minute, 72 h of videos are uploaded on you tube. So the data in increasing at a rate of pet byte datasets these days and Exabyte is not farway.
2.   **Variety:** From excel tables and databases, data structure has changed to lose its structure and hundreds of formats such as pure text, photo audio, video, web, GPS data sensor data, relational database s, documents, SMS, pdf, and flash are added to the data set .No one no longer has control over the input data format. No structure can be imposed like in the past to keep control over analysis .As new applications are introduced, new data formats come up.
3.   **Velocity:** In earlier days, companies used to batch process the data when the data were of the same kind .this is now becoming impossible because with the new sources of data such as social and mobile applications, batch processing breaks down .The data is now streamed into the server in real time in a continuous fashion, and the result is only useful if the delay is very short (Ward, 2013).

And while they cover the key attributes of big data, we believe organizations need to consider an important fourth dimension: veracity/variability .Inclusion of the veracity as the fourth Big Data attribute emphasizes the importance of addressing and managing the uncertainty inherent within some type of data.

One more V can also be included along with the 4-V definition of big data to make it complete.

Value:- The economics /business value of different data may vary ;the challenge is in identifying what data is valuable in extracting information out of that .Analyzing huge data sets can reveal stunning insights on consumer preferences and behaviour and can guide in business decision making and drive in revenue.

Figure1. The Dimension of Big Data

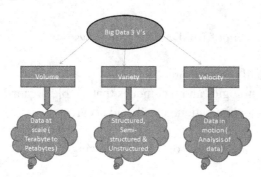

Gartner summarizes this is his definition of Big Data in 2012 as high volume, velocity, and variety information assets that demand cost-effective, innovative forms of information processing for enhanced insight and decision –making .

Value: Another definition by oracle's Lumpkin is: "Big Data has a huge potential impact, but organizations cannot sweep aside existing architectures-for any organization this has to be evolutionary ".

Big Data, like traditional data, needs to be captured, stored, organized and analyzed .Now internet applications are increasing at an unprecedented level, and people and devices are all loosely connected, generating a huge data ocean. Organizations can take data from any source, harness relevant data, and analyze it to help in cost reduction, time –reduction, new and optimized product development, and smarter business decision-making. But the companies are not accustomed to collect information from these sources; nor are they used to deal with such large volumes of unstructured data. So this information available to enterprises is not captured or stored for long-term analysis .because of the hugeness of data volume, many companies do not keep their Big Data, nor do they have cost-effective way to capture and store this data (Peglar, 2012).

Why Collect and Store Terabytes of Data?

Traditionally data warehousing systems typically acquire data from existing relational database. More than 80% of stored corporate data unstructured, data that are not encompassed by a relational database management system such as DB2 and oracle. Unstructured data types that organizations now want to extract information value from include the followings:

1.   Email and other forms of electronic communication
2.   Web based content, including click streams and social media-related content
3.   Digitized studio and video.
4.   Machine generated Data (RFID, GPS, and sensor -generated data. Log files and so on) and the Internet of things.

Big data Analytics is becoming an important tool to improve efficiency and quality of organizations .Many companies today are making mission-critical decisions with only 20% 0f data they have in the company local databases. Beyond that critical data, Non-traditional, less structured data such as weblogs, social media, email, sensors and photographs, could be used for extracting useful information .Now more and more companies are looking to include non-traditional data with their traditional enterprise data for enhancing their business intelligence analysis (Labrinidis, 2012).

Integrating Big Data with traditional data gains a 360 degree view of the latest business patterns. The applications of Big Data analysis can be viewed in the following areas.

1. **Business**: Customer personalization, customer needs.
2. **Technology**: Reduce process time for hours to seconds.
3. **Health**: DNA mining to detect hereditary diseases.
4. **Smart Cities**: Cities with good economic development and high quality of life could be analysed.
5. **Oil and gas**: For providing health and safe drilling, risk management, production optimization and cost management can be done by analysing the huge amount of data generated by sensors.

Telecommunications

Network analytics and optimization from device, sensor, and GPS inputs to enhance social networking and promotion opportunities. These applications will allow people to have better services and better customer experiences and also to be healthier by collecting more accurate and detailed performance information on everything, from product inventories to sick days. This boots performance in each sector .Big data analytics can substantially improve decision making .The companies are using data collection and analysis to conduct controlled experiments to make better management decisions, segmentations of customers, and thereby more precisely tailoring products or services to each narrowed customer groups .The business insights acquired by big data analysis may bring small improvements of 0.5, 1,20r 3 percentage in key performance, but this itself could be considered very worthwhile in many organizations .Big data analytics can also be helpful in after-sales service offering a proactive maintains and also can be used to improve the development of the next generation of products and services . In precise, the big data analytics brings in integrate new information with the traditional corporate data and fit the insight they glean into their existing business processes and operations (Fan, 2013).

In the area of unstructured content, text in particular is being targeted for analysis .Case management , fault management for field services optimization, customer sentiments analysis research optimization, media coverage analysis, and competitor analysis are just a few examples of Big Data analytic applications associated with unstructured content .

BIG DATA ANALYSIS

Big data analytics refers to tool and methodologies that aim to transform massive quantities of raw data into "data about the data "-for analytics purposes. The term "Big data analytics "may be new to us, but data ware housing, data mining, and data base technologies have existed in various forms for years .IT professionals have been working large amounts of data in various industries for years .The only difference is that now the trend has changed .Years ago, we did not analyze email messages, PDF files or videos. Digging and analysing these semi-structured and unstructured data are new concepts. Similarly, wanting to predict the future is not a new concept, but to access and store all the huge data that is created new.

Data as a service can drive in business. Various sources claim that 90% of the data that exists today is only 2-years old .And the data is growing faster .To make raw data useful to users, it must be integrated with various data from the field of finance and sales, with product with marketing with social media, with competitors' data, with demographic data, and more and more .Amazon, which was an online e-commerce product company, is now looked up as a cloud data centre company (Kosinski, 2016).

Amazon playing a significant role in recommendation engine over the years from various open source technologies. We can simply say that big data is a old wine in new bottle.

Similarities between big data and data mining are as follows:

1. Provided analytical means to acquire valuable and actionable insights into behavioural systems to facilitate decision-making or to increase knowledge about a domain of interest.
2. Can be used to explore the elements of a data set and describe their characteristics.
3. The data elements can be used as variables in unsupervised or supervised learning processes in building a model to group individuals across a spectrum of attributes, classifying them according to target attributes, predicted outcomes, or generating forecasts.

Big Data relies on powerful data mining and data statistical l analysis algorithms to detect patterns to detect patterns, trends, and correlations over a vast unstructured data horizon. Once trained, algorithms can help make predictions that can be used to detect anomalies in the form of large deviations from the expected trends or relations in the data .Forward-looking and proactive decision-making requires defining a common framework for information processing.

Figure 2. Big Data Analysis Pipeline

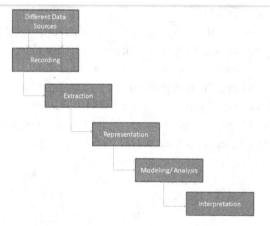

BIG DATA ANALYSIS PIPELINE

Data acquisition and recording: Big data is not generated its own .It should be collected from where it is generated, such as from spreadsheets, text files, and web contents .These large magnitudes of data need to be filtered then stored to the target data warehouse or business intelligence systems .

We can see that data is generated from various sources at the rate could not be completely stored for analysis .Algorithm that can be analyze data at the time of generation should be implemented, and only the required data should be recorded rather the whole data and then sorting out the unwanted (Sun, 2013).

Filtering /Cleaning: This keeps instances and observations of relevance and gets rid of irrelevant pieces of information as we need only those data that make sense during the analysis .Rather, we require an information extraction process that pulls out the required information from the under-lying sources and expresses it in a structured from suitable for analysis.

Integration/aggregation and representation: Data analysis is not just simply locating, identifying, and understanding data. For effective large-scale analysis of data, we require different data structure and semantics to represent the data in a computer –understandable and resolvable format. They may be many ways to store data, but some designs have advantage over the other.

Analysis and Modelling: This involves querying and mining of Big Data .The process of Querying and mining big data is fundamentally different from that of traditional databases as Big data is a often a noisy, dynamic, and heterogeneous untrustworthy set of data. Once the data is ready to be analysed, we can use powerful algorithms and computational tools to dive into the data .A characteristics of these algorithms is their ability to adapt their parameters in response to new streams of data by creating algorithms of their own to take care of parts of the data.

Interpretation: Big Data may not always tell us the truth .For example patients may choose to hide risky behaviour and caregivers may sometimes misdiagnose a condition, patients may also inaccurately recall the name of drug, leading to missing or misleading information in their medical record. There are many possible sources of error: computer systems can have bugs, models almost will be based assumptions the rules can be based on erroneous data. Analyzing these data may give us a wrong output .Ultimately, a decision-maker, provided with the results of analysis has to interrupt these results .These interpretations cannot happen from a vacuum. Usually it involves examining all the assumptions made and retracting the analysis. This is a challenging work because of its complexity (Ye, 2016).

There are two main strategies for dealing with big data: sampling and using distributed systems .Sampling is based on the fact that if the dataset is too large and we cannot use all the examples,

then we can obtain a subset of the examples .The major popular distributed systems used nowadays are based in the Map Reduce framework.

1. **Early warning**: Detecting anomalies in the usage of digital media, fast responses can be developed at the time of crisis.
2. **Real-time Awareness**: Accurate mapping of services needs helps in designing program and policies accordingly.
3. **Real-time feedback**: Ability to predict demand and supply changes

CHALLENGES IN BIG DATA ANALYSIS

Heterogeneity and incompleteness-Heterogeneity is supposed to occur in human-generated data .But the machine analysis algorithm expects a homogeneous data .So prior to data analysis, we need to carefully structure these data .There are also chances for incompleteness. For example, some details of patient may go missing from hospital database; it can be deliverable done by the patient or by his absence of mind. Whatever be the situation, analysis would based on missing data would provide us wrong details. For example, people may not disclose their unemployment status, in that case, the analysis may be skewed since it considers the more employed population mix that exists and hence results in wrong outcomes .this incompleteness may remain even after the data is cleaned and corrected which should be managed during data analysis .Recent works on managing probabilistic data can make through in this area.

Figure 3. Understanding the dynamics of the ecosystems

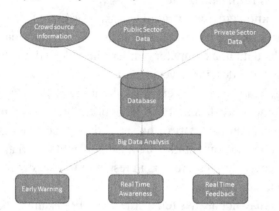

Scale

The size of data to be managed is a challenging issue in Big Data analysis .In earlier days, this challenge was mitigated by developing faster processors, which provide us with the resources needed to cope with increasing volume of data. But the data volume is moving faster than computer and CPU speed .Even though we tried to improve the processing capacity by doubling clock cycle frequency and increasing the number of cores, this could not be in pace with the amount of data increase .Another approach is to work on the output/input systems for improving performance .Even newer storage technologies do not have the same large spread in performance between sequential and random input/output performance .which requires rethinking of how we design storage processing for large data processing systems. These changes in the storage subsystems potentially touch every aspect of data processing, including query processing and scheduling, database design, concurrency control and recovery mechanisms (Shen, 2019).

Timeliness

When the Data volume increases, the time to process these data will also increase .Timeliness is an important performance factor in certain systems; For example, if a fraudulent credit card transaction is suspected, it should be prevented before the transactions gets committed . However, it is not just the processing time that matters when we refer to speed in the context of Big Data. There is an acquisition rate challenges in the process of Big Data collection. Typically it is often necessary to find elements from a large data set that meet a specific repeatedly occurring criterion. Scanning the entire data set to find suitable is obviously imparactical. So to deal with the problem of timeliness, we need to properly index the data set. New indexing Structures are to be designed to support such queries that have response time limits (Peglar, 2012).

Privacy

Privacy of Data is another area of concern in the case of Big Data Analysis .Managing privacy is both a technical and sociological problem that should not be addressed to realize the promises of Big Data. Consider the data received from location-based services ;hiding the user identity alone without hiding the location information would not address the privacy concerns as by tracking the location information, like "a trail of packet crumbs" one could be associated to certain residence or office locations and thereby determine the user's identity. And by analyzing the usage pattern over time .we can also reveal private information such as health issues and religious preferences.

Human Collaboration

Big Data analysis setup needs to handle input from different people who might be geographically separated but have to do a collaborative analysis results. Crowd sourcing websites such as Wikipedia and websites providing product reviews will be greatly benefited if they have a big data analysis framework to check the trustworthiness and true motive of the contributors. Another example is Mturk, the crowdsourced initiative from Amazon, which is based on the quantity of work completed, can make way for an extra"error" element which the tasks are done quickly to get it completed. Heterogeneity, scale factor, timeliness, complexity, and privacy problems with Big Data impede progress at all phases of the pipeline that can create value from Big data .The problems start right away from the data acquisition, what data to keep and what to discard. Much data today is not in a structured format ; for example, tweets and blogs are less structured, converting this to a structured from for analysis .Data analysis is a clear bottleneck in many applications due to the lack of scalability of the underlying algorithms and due to the complexity of the data that needs to be analyzed. The presentation and interpretation of the results by nontechnical domain experts is crucial in extracting actionable knowledge out of it. Moreover, the shortage of skilled people and confusion around what technology platform to use are also inhibitors in the growth of Big Data analysis (Kosinski, 2016).

BIG DATA AND CLOUD: THE CONVERGING TECHNOLOGIES

The question often asked is: what is the relationship between cloud and Big Data? Why are these two entirely different areas brought for discussion together? While Big Data is all about extracting value out of "variety, velocity, and volume "(3V) from the unstructured i formation or assets available, cloud focuses on –demand, elastic, scalable, pay-per-use self –service models.

Traditional tools such as conventional relational databases are suited only to handle large amounts of data as long as that data undergoes a structuring process. Big data is an all-encompassing term coined to represent the huge volumes of unstructured data that many businesses and most large internet companies have to handle today. The analysis of this large volume of data requires on-demand compute power and distributed storage to crunch the 3V data problem, and cloud seamlessly provides this elastic on-demand compute required. Cloud has glorified the "as-a-service" model by hiding the complexity and challenges involved in building a scalable elastic self –services application that could solve at least some problems associated with Big Data (Shen, 2019).

REASON BEHIND USING CLOUD FRAMEWORK TO ANALYZE BIG DATA

Requirement of on-demand computing power for big data analysis: Big data analysis requires great processing capacity, which could be supported only by augmenting internal resources .The cloud option enables companies to use on-demand storage space and computing power via public cloud services for certain analytics initiatives and provide added capacity and scale as needed, thus providing a cost –effective infrastructure.

Hide the complexity and challenges involved: Big Data is a mixture of internal and external data sources .Enterprises keep their most sensitive data in-house .But huge volumes of Big Data generated by third party and public providers may be located externally, such as in a cloud environment . Moving relevant data sources from where they reside, either in internal or public cloud data centres or in edge systems and client devices, does not makes any sense as this simply waters resources .So it is better to do the analysis data from its original location .This reduces the complexity of collecting data and the challenges of security.

To extract value from Big Data: Analytics as services provides users with on demand analytics for optionally scheduling available resources, forecasting demand and act accordingly, identifying rarely accessed data, and so many other applications. Aaas helps customers to pick their required solution as as a service and pay only for their required analysis .Unlike Aaas, the cost incurred in the traditional process is high since the company has to plan its course from the scratch .Whatever be the cloud delivery model, business with varying needs budget can unleash the spirit of Big Data in the cloud environment (Kosinski, 2016).

TOOLS THAT WE USED TO DEAL WITH BIG DATA

Google was the first company to effectively use Big Data. Collected and analysed massive collections of web pages and the relationships between them and created first truly universal search engine, capable of querying and indexing billons of web pages without human intervention. They did not rely on the traditional technologies and relational databases. Engineers at Google created a massively distributed system, consisting of a collection of autonomous computers networked together and distributed system, consisting of a collection of autonomous computers networked together and a distribution middleware, which enables computers to co-ordinate their activities and to share the resources of the entire system, so that users perceive it as a single, integrated computing facility. They could keep the system low cost by using off-the –shelf hardware.

The infrastructure for BIG Data has unique requirements for conducting deep analytics by integrating the components of Big Data platform with the enterprise data. Combining the traditional data set with the big data only will provide the company a clear view of the analysis. In between data acquisition and data analysis, their lies the data organization stage where the NOSQL data bases are frequently used to acquire and store Big Data. These databases are well suited for dynamic data structures and were highly scalable to meet the requirements of BIG Data streams of higher velocity, higher variety, and very high volume .NoSQL databases are often used to collect and store social media data. NOSql Can be abbreviated as not only SQL .Some of the NOSQL databases are HBase, MongoDB,Cassandra and CouchDB.

Data Organization can also be called data integration .The infrastructure required for organizing Big Data must be able to process and manipulate data in the original storage location since moving around data in large volume in wastage of time as well as money. It should support very high throughput to deal with large data processing required to handle large variety of data formats, from unstructured to structured .Apache's HDFS(hadoop distributed file system)is a new technology that allows large data volumes to be organized and processed while keeping the data on the original data storage cluster.

Analysis should be done in distributed environment, where an amount of data will stay where it was originally created and be transparently accessed from data warehouses. The Infrastructure required for the analysis of Big Data must be able to support deeper analytics such as statistical analysis and data mining, on a wider variety of data types stored in diverse systems. MapReduce is a software framework that allows developers to write programs that process massive amounts of unstructured data in parallel across distributed nodes. MapReduce programs run on these distributed HDFS clusters generating and aggregating results on the same cluster .Underthe Mapreduce process, queries are split and distributed across parallel nodes and processed in parallel, which could be called the Map step. The results are then gathered and delivered and that in the reduce step. MapReduce is a programming framework that supports processing a large volume of data on distributed nodes, enabling organizations to get their arms around these vast quantities of unstructured data.

GLIMPSE OF LIVE PROJECTS IN BIG DATA

Stock exchange, online banking, and online purchasing increased the dataflow through computerized systems. They are captured and Stored for inventory monitoring, customer behaviour, and market by the finance and banking sectors .we can also find big sets in the field of life sciences, such as genome sequencing; clinical data and patient data are analyzed and used in science and research. Other areas of research where Big Data is important are astronomy, oceanogstorage, and analysis of these Big Data sets. Companies with solutions to Big Data analytics have been pursuing more progressive ideas, aiming to use Big Data being used today by accessing and analyzing petabytes of information to deliver the response in real time.

Real –time data analyzing streams to identify traffic patterns: The project focuses on analyzing huge volumes of real –time streaming data, both structured and unstructured, to identify the current traffic condition .It also estimates the expected travel duration in the present traffic scenario offering alternate travel routes and eventually helping to improve traffic in a metropolitan area.

1000 genomes project: This is government –initiated project to collect the generic traits of people analyze all human genetic variations, which could be used by researchers studying generic diseases. However research labs lack sufficient storage and computation infrastructure.

Atmospheric radiation measurement climate research facility: It aims to further our understanding of the earth's climate through Big Data.

BioSense 2.0: It is an integrated national public health surveillance system for the early detection and rapid assessment of potential bioterrorism-related illness. The program uses symptomatic data gathered for tracking health problems, such as the recent flu outbreak,in real time as they evolve and gives health professionals the insights they need to prepare best possible responses to such situation. It is also built on collaborative Cloud-hosted database with the aim of making the data instantly accessible to end users across the world (Peglar, 2012).

HURDLE THAT WE ARE FACING TO ANALYZING THE BIG DATA

The most important obstacle is not the technology but the lack of skilled people who can manage large amounts of structured and unstructured data. Having the infrastructure to handle a large volume and variety of data is also an issue, which is now getting mitigated when we started moving to the cloud. Putting our analysis our analysis of BIG Data in a presentable form that is, right data model for the right problem, should get prime importance in Big Data analysis. Choosing the correct database is important since our data analysis would be perfect only when the choice of database is perfect. We can have a wide range of technologies such as graphs databases (Neo4j),document databases (Mongo DB,Couch DB) and column family database (Hbase,Cassandra) (Shen, 2019).

For example for analyzing social networking data, we have to use the column family database and for a blogging system, the database of choice would be document database .Determining which data technology to use is another obstacle in the field of Big Data analysis. Professionals have to be trained so that they can use the new tools and technologies of Big Data and adopt the new environment.

REFERENCES

Bifet, A. (2013). Mining big data in real time. *Informatica (Vilnius), 37*(1).

Fan, W., & Bifet, A. (2013). Mining big data: Current status, and forecast to the future. *SIGKDD Explorations, 14*(2), 1–5. doi:10.1145/2481244.2481246

Kosinski, M., Wang, Y., Lakkaraju, H., & Leskovec, J. (2016). Mining big data to extract patterns and predict real-life outcomes. *Psychological Methods, 21*(4), 493–506. doi:10.1037/met0000105 PMID:27918179

Labrinidis, A., & Jagadish, H. V. (2012). Challenges and opportunities with big data. *Proceedings of the VLDB Endowment International Conference on Very Large Data Bases, 5*(12), 2032–2033. doi:10.14778/2367502.2367572

Peglar, R., & Isilon, E. M. C. (2012). *Introduction to Analytics and Big Data-Hadoop*. Storage Networking Industry Association.

Shen, Z., Wang, X., & Spruit, M. (2019, June). Big Data Framework for Scalable and Efficient Biomedical Literature Mining in the Cloud. In *Proceedings of the 2019 3rd International Conference on Natural Language Processing and Information Retrieval* (pp. 80-86). 10.1145/3342827.3342843

Sun, J., & Reddy, C. K. (2013, August). Big data analytics for healthcare. In *Proceedings of the 19th ACM SIGKDD international conference on Knowledge discovery and data mining* (pp. 1525-1525). ACM.

Ward, J. S., & Barker, A. (2013). *Undefined by data: a survey of big data definitions*. arXiv preprint arXiv:1309.5821

Ye, Z., Tafti, A. P., He, K. Y., Wang, K., & He, M. M. (2016). Sparktext: Biomedical text mining on big data framework. *PLoS One, 11*(9), e0162721. doi:10.1371/journal.pone.0162721 PMID:27685652

KEY TERMS AND DEFINITIONS

Appalachia: A geographic and cultural region of the Mideastern United States. The population in media is portrayed as suspicious, backward, and isolated.

Ethnocentric: A belief that one's own culture is superior to other cultures.

Family-Centricity: The belief that family is central to wellbeing and that family members and family issues take precedence over other aspects of life.

This research was previously published in Advanced Deep Learning Applications in Big Data Analytics; pages 110-125, copyright year 2021 by Engineering Science Reference (an imprint of IGI Global).

APPENDIX

The Institute of Museum and Library Services has collected some interesting statistics indicating that despite the sharp decline in library usage over the last ten years, libraries have actually seen an *increase* in the number of people who come through their doors annually since the beginning of the current recessionary period in 2008. Was this a contradiction, or some kind of error? Table 1 shows the data in question.

Table 2. Visits to public libraries

Year	Per Capita Visit to Public Library	Year	Per Capita Visit to Public Library
1998	4.2	2003	4.6
1999	4.3	2004	4.6
2000	4.3	2005	4.7
2001	4.4	2006	4.8
2002	4.4	2007	5.0

(Data Source: National Center for Education Statistics, 1998-2007)

Chapter 4
Introduction to Big Data and Business Analytics

Dineshkumar Bhagwandas Vaghela
https://orcid.org/0000-0002-4410-9513
Shantilal Shah Government Engineering College, India

ABSTRACT

The term big data has come due to rapid generation of data in various organizations. In big data, the big is the buzzword. Here the data are so large and complex that the traditional database applications are not able to process (i.e., they are inadequate to deal with such volume of data). Usually the big data are described by 5Vs (volume, velocity, variety, variability, veracity). The big data can be structured, semi-structured, or unstructured. Big data analytics is the process to uncover hidden patterns, unknown correlations, predict the future values from large and complex data sets. In this chapter, the following topics will be covered more in detail. History of big data and business analytics, big data analytics technologies and tools, and big data analytics uses and challenges.

INTRODUCTION

The modern technologies generate very complex and unstructured data in very huge amount such as RFID data, web logs, sensors devices, Internet searches, machinery, social networks like Facebook, Twitter and many more, vehicle sensors, portable computers, cell phones, call center records and GPS devices. All these technologies are used in different types of the applications. In sentiment analysis, the sentiments from different sources on specific topic can be collected which are in terms of large volume. The sentiments about the product, movies or any person can be viewed from different official sites or from social media sites such as Twitter, Facebook, Instagram and many more. Politicians and governments often use sentiment analysis to understand how the people feel about themselves and their policies. The Figure 1 shown below represents the sources of Big Data.

The rapid generation of the large volume of data has 5V's characteristics. Here 5V refers Volume, Velocity, Variety, Variability and Veracity. Here 5 V's of big data has been clearly explained in Figure 2.

DOI: 10.4018/978-1-6684-3662-2.ch004

Figure 1. Sources of Big Data

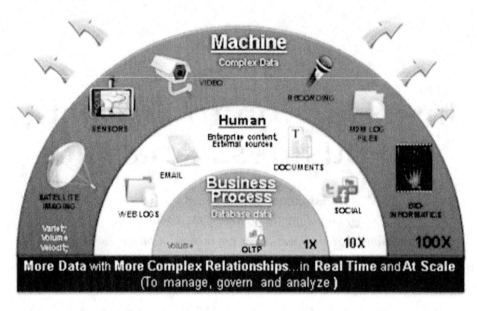

Figure 2. 5 V's of Big Data

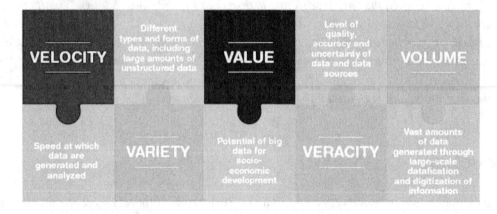

5V's (Volume, Velocity, Variety, Variability, Veracity)

Volume

Volume refers an amount of data generated every unit time. Here the data can be of any form like emails, sensor data, video clips, photos, twitter messages etc. which the people generates and share within the unit time period. These data are in the form of hundreds of Zetta Bytes or Bronto Bytes. It has been noticed that on Facebook approximately 10 billion messages have been sent per day with clicking "like" button 4.5 billion times and upload more than 350 million photos every day (He et al., 2013). The amount of data generated per unit time is exponentially increasing; i.e all the data generated in the world between the beginning of time and 2008, the same amount of data will soon be generated every minute (Chen et al., 2012). This scenario bothers the researchers to store and analyze such a huge volume of data with tradition database technologies. But this problem has been overcome with the help of distributed systems where parts of data are stored at different geographical locations and brought together or processed and combined the results by software.

Velocity

Velocity refers to the speed at which new data is generated and the speed at which data moves around. As we know the social media messages become viral in fraction of seconds, speed of checking the credit card transactions for fraudulent activities, or the trading systems takes milliseconds to take decision to buy or sell shares by analyzing social media networks. This only happens with the big data technologies which allow the users/decision makers to analyze the data without putting them into database like traditional database processing approach.

Variety

Variety refers to the different types of data such as structured, semi structured or unstructured. Traditional data processing technologies use structured data that fits into tables or relational databases. But, at present, 80% of the world's data is semi structured or unstructured, and hence they cannot be easily put into tables. These data are photos, video sequences or social media updates and many more. With big data technology we can now harness differed types of data (structured and unstructured) including messages, social media conversations, photos, sensor data, video or voice recordings and bring them together with more traditional, structured data.

Veracity

Veracity refers to the messiness or trustworthiness of the data. As we know that the data are available in many forms, due to this the quality and accuracy are not controllable. The large volume also makes up for the lack of quality or accuracy. This problem is resolved by the big data and analytics technologies.

Value

This is the most important aspect of Big Data. It is good to have access of big data but it will be useless if it is not turned into correct value. In business, the big data with quality values are helpful for decision making and generating more business after working the analytics on the big data.

HISTORY OF BIG DATA AND BUSINESS ANALYTICS

The emergence of statistics started in year 1663 in London. The scientist John Graunt did first experiment on statistical data analysis. In this he has recorded information about the mortality. After a long time in year 1865, the term "business intelligence" is used by Richard Millar Devens in his Encyclopedia of Commercial and Business Anecdotes, in this he described how the banker Henry Furnese achieved an advantage over competitors by collecting and analyzing information relevant to his business activities in a well structured manner.

The modern data storage has been started in 1926, but in 1928 Fritz Pfleumer, a German-Austrian engineer, invents a method of storing information magnetically on tape. The principles he developed are still in use today, with the vast majority of digital data being stored magnetically on computer hard disks.

The beginning of business intelligence has been started in 1958, IBM researcher Hans Peter Luhn defines Business Intelligence as "the ability to apprehend the interrelationships of presented facts in such a way as to guide action towards a desired goal." (Klipfolio, 2018). In 1962 the first steps are taken towards speech recognition, when IBM engineer William C Dersch presents the Shoebox Machine at the 1962 World Fair. It can interpret numbers and sixteen words spoken in the English language into digital information.

The starting of large data centers begin in 1965, The US Government plans the world's first data center to store 742 million tax returns and 175 million sets of fingerprints on magnetic tape. In 1970 IBM mathematician Edgar F Codd presents his framework for a "relational database". The model provides the framework that many modern data services use today, to store information in a hierarchical format, which can be accessed by anyone who knows what they are looking for (Chan et al., 2013). Prior to this accessing data from a computer's memory banks usually required an expert.

In 1989, the first use of the term Big Data came into picture. In 1991, Computer scientist Tim Berners-Lee announced the birth of what would become the World Wide Web and in 1999 and 2000 the first use of the term "Internet of Things". This word describes increasing the number of online devices and their communication among each other without any human intervention. After that, very first time the scientist Peter Lyman and Hal Varian (2000) attempted to quantify the amount of digital information in the world, and its rate of growth. They concluded: "The world's total yearly production of print, film, optical and magnetic content would require roughly 1.5 billion gigabytes of storage. This is the equivalent of 250 megabytes per person for each man, woman and child on Earth." (Lyman & Varian, 2000).

In 2001, Doug Laney, analyst at Gartner, defined 3 Vs: Volume, Velocity and Variety of Big Data (Laney, 2001). Now these become the common characteristics of Big Data. In this year the term "Software as a Service" came into picture and the concept fundamental today are the industry-standards.

In 2005, Web 2.0 increases data volumes, in this year the concept of "Hadoop"- the open source framework created specifically for storage and analysis of Big Data sets. It is much flexible with unstructured data (voice, video, raw text...etc.) which are increasingly generating and collecting.

In 2008, The world's servers process 9.57 Zetta bytes (9.57 trillion gigabytes) of information which is equivalent to 12 gigabytes of information per person, per day. In International Production and Dissemination of Information, it is estimated that 14.7 Exa bytes of new information are produced this year. In 2014, the rise of the mobile machines – as for the first time, more people are using mobile devices to access digital data, than office or home computers. 88% of business executives surveyed by GE working with Accenture report that big data analytics is a top priority for their business.

Finally we can conclude: Big Data is not a new or isolated phenomenon. Like other key developments in data storage, data processing and the Internet, Big Data is just a further step that will bring change to the way we run business and society. At the same time it will lay the foundations on which many evolutions will be built.

BIG DATA ANALYTICS TECHNOLOGIES AND TOOLS

Big data analytics is the process to uncover hidden patterns, unknown correlations, predict the future values from large and complex data sets. These statistics can be helpful for decision making.

Why is Big Data Analytics Important?

Big data analytics helps organizations to analyze by binding the data and use it to identify new opportunities. This makes smarter moves of business, higher profits, open doors of new and existing business, more efficient operations and making the customers happier. As per the deep literature review big data analytics can be helpful as shown in Figure 3:

1. **Cost reduction:** Big data technologies such as Hadoop and cloud-based analytics bring significant cost advantages when it comes to storing large amounts of data – plus they can identify more efficient ways of doing business;
2. **Faster, better decision making:** With the speed of Hadoop and in-memory analytics, combined with the ability to analyze new sources of data, businesses are able to analyze information immediately – and make decisions based on what they've learned (Wills et al., 2014);
3. **New products and services:** With the ability to gauge customer needs and satisfaction through analytics comes the power to give customers what they want. Davenport points out that with big data analytics, more companies are creating new products to meet customers' needs.

Figure 3. Importance of Big Data analytics

The traditional databases are not well suitable for storing semi-structured or unstructured data types. The traditional databases are most well for structured data types. Moreover to this, the traditional database technologies may not be able to process big data which need to be updated frequently or even continually, for example real-time stock market data, online activities of website visitors or the performance of the mobile applications. These all are the reasons, why big data storage and processing tools need to be understood. The most of the big data are stored in NoSQL databases and processed by Hadoop framework and its tools including:

- **YARN:** A cluster management technology and one of the key features in second-generation Hadoop. It is one of the key features in the second-generation Hadoop 2 version of the Apache Software Foundation's open source distributed processing framework. It is characterized as a large-scale, distributed operating system for big data applications;
- **MapReduce:** A software framework that allows developers to write programs that process massive amounts of unstructured data in parallel across a distributed cluster of processors or standalone computers. The MapReduce algorithm contains two important tasks, namely Map and Reduce. Map takes a set of data and converts it into another set of data, where individual elements are broken down into tuples (key/value pairs);
- **Spark:** An open-source parallel processing framework that enables users to run large-scale data analytics applications across clustered systems;
- **HBase:** A column-oriented key/value data store built to run on top of the Hadoop Distributed File System (HDFS). It is one of the NoSQL database;
- **Hive:** An open-source data warehouse system for querying and analyzing large datasets stored in Hadoop files. It supports summarization and analysis too;
- **Kafka:** A distributed publish-subscribe messaging system designed to replace traditional message brokers. Apache Kafka is an open-source stream processing platform developed by the Apache Software Foundation written in Scala and Java. The project aims to provide a unified, high-throughput, low-latency platform for handling real-time data feeds;
- **Pig:** An open-source technology that offers a high-level mechanism for the parallel programming of MapReduce jobs to be executed on Hadoop clusters.

Usually the big data are processed before it gets stored into a data warehouse or any analytical database for any future processing. In most of the cases, Hadoop and NoSQL databases are primarily used. The incoming streams of raw data are treated as the primary repository and many of the big data analytics users adopt the concept of Hadoop Distributed File System. In such architectures, data can be analyzed directly in a Hadoop cluster or run through a processing engine like Spark. These data are well organized, configured and partitioned properly to acquire good performance on Extract, Transform and Load (ETL) integration jobs and analytical queries.

After pre-processing the data are ready and they can be analyzed with analytical tools of data mining. They generate the patterns and relationships; predictive analytics from the data sets which are helpful for forecasting or future prediction in any application domain. Text mining and statistical analysis software can also be considered good role in big data analytical processing. For both ETL and analytical applications using MapReduce or other way queries can be executed in batch-mode. The programming languages such as Python, R and Scala with the help of SQL or NoSQL can be used for the big data analytical processing.

The Tools Should Meet the Following Criteria

- The tools should run on big data platforms or high performance analytics systems;
- They should use advance analytic algorithms and models;
- They support all type of structured/semi structured/ unstructured data;
- The performance should be scalable and also be easily integrated with other technologies.

The tools must also support the essential characteristics and include integrated algorithms and methods as listed below:

- **Clustering and segmentation:** Which divides a large collection of entities into smaller groups that exhibit some (potentially unanticipated) similarities. An example is analyzing a collection of customers to differentiate smaller segments for targeted marketing;
- **Classification:** Which is a process of organizing data into predefined classes based on attributes that are either pre-selected by an analyst or identified as a result of a clustering model. An example is using the segmentation model to determine into which segment a new customer would be categorized;
- **Regression:** Which is used to discover relationships among a dependent variable and one or more independent variables, and helps determine how the dependent variable's values change in relation to the independent variable values. An example is using geographic location, mean income, average summer temperature and square footage to predict the future value of a property;
- **Association and item set mining:** Which looks for statistically relevant relationships among variables in a large data set. For example, this could help direct call-center representatives to offer specific incentives based on the caller's customer segment, duration of relationship and type of complaint;
- **Similarity and correlation:** Which is used to inform undirected clustering algorithms. Similarity-scoring algorithms can be used to determine the similarity of entities placed in a candidate cluster;
- **Neural networks:** Which are used in undirected analysis for machine learning based on adaptive weighting and approximation.

BIG DATA ANALYTICS USES AND CHALLENGES

The data for big data analytic process are gathered from both external and internal sources of the related application, such as student admission prediction, weather related data, scientific research data or many more. Nowadays the big data are also in use of real-time streaming data to analyze. This data are fed into Hadoop cluster system through Spark streaming module or other open source stream processing engines like Flink and Storm.

In the past, early big data systems were mostly deployed on-premises, particularly in large organizations that were collecting, organizing and analyzing massive amounts of data. But nowadays due to the cloud architecture and the cloud platform vendors like Amazon Web Services (AWS) and Microsoft have made easy for the organizations to store, manage and process their data in cloud using Hadoop clusters. The Hadoop suppliers like Hortonworks and Cloudera supports distribution of the big data framework on the AWS and Microsoft Azure clouds.

Potential pitfalls that can trip up organizations on big data analytics initiatives include a lack of internal analytics skills and the high cost of hiring experienced data scientists and data engineers to fill the gaps. The other pitfalls are like the amount of data that's typically involved, and its variety, can cause data management issues in areas including data quality, consistency and governance; also, data silos can result from the use of different platforms and data stores in a big data architecture. In addition, integrating Hadoop, Spark and other big data tools into a cohesive architecture that meets an organization's big data analytics needs is a challenging proposition for many IT and analytics teams, which have to identify the right mix of technologies and then put the pieces together.

Many of the large companies struggle to figure out that what to do with big data (Watson et al., 2013). It is something a niche technology, without knowing it, some companies find hard way after adopting big data technology without truly knowing what to do with it. The company should consider the following challenges before implementing a Big Data and Analytics solution:

1. **Data Quality:** The organization has various sources from where the data are coming and they need to store in a data warehouse. It's the big challenge when the inconsistent data from disparate sources need to combine at a data warehouse. There are the chances of encountering errors. These inconsistent data, missing data, logic conflicts result in data quality challenges. Poor data quality results in faulty reporting and analytics necessary for optimal decision making;

2. **Understanding Analytics:** There is the need of experts who understand what exactly analysis will be performed. The analytical tools produce the quality reports, but it is that much important to understand the report to make decisions for the future success of the organizations;

3. **Quality Assurance:** The data must be 100% accurate to get 100% quality of the analytical results. The end users use these results to make the best business decisions and it helps for the future success of the business. For this a successful Software Testing Life Cycle (STLC) is required to develop and it will be costly and time intensive process;

4. **Performance:** A Big Data and Analytics solution must also be carefully designed to meet overall performance requirements. While the final product can be customized to fit the performance needs of the organization, the initial overall design must be carefully thought out to provide a stable foundation from which to start. Major customizations are extremely expensive;

5. **Designing the Solution:** In most of the cases it is high level perception that what is required out of a Big Data and Analytical solution. Without knowing this may cause the difficult time and results in miscommunication between the business users and the technicians developing a Big Data & Analytics solution;

6. **User Acceptance:** There are many challenges to overcome to make a Big Data and Analytics solution that is quickly adopted by an organization. Having a comprehensive user training program can ease this hesitation but will require planning and additional resources;

7. **Cost:** The cost is also one of the big challenges for Big Data and its analytic process. It is more expensive one if any organize wants to implement it.

BIG DATA ANALYTICS FOR SENTIMENT ANALYSIS

The data are collected from various sources which later processed with text analytics to mine the opinion. The data are usually collected from the Internet and other sources like social media platforms and stored in various data formats. The big data technology can handle the different sources and formats of both structured and unstructured data. For this one has to need having the setting up a Hadoop cluster and a Hadoop Distributed File System (HDFS) to store the data. An HDFS provides a flexible way of managing big data. The data can be retrieved from different sources with the help of following:

- A Twitter feed
- An RSS feed
- A Mobile Application

Once the data retrieved and combined, the complete sentiment analysis on a single data source is possible using R, Jaql, Pig or Hive Pig and Hive are SQL-like syntax languages that run on the Hadoop platform.

CONCLUSION

The large volume of data which cannot be stored and processed on a single machine can be treated as a big data. These data are generated on very high velocity with different varieties and need to be collected at a single data store and to be preprocessed. Big data tools can provide unbiased insight into generated data from any source or space for proper and accurate decision making and implementation. There are lots of challenges for any organization to store, handle and process the big data. These data mainly based on the opinions of products, person or any other. The opinion can be in the form of sentiments which need to be identified very well using big data tools and technologies.

REFERENCES

Chan, J. O. (2013). An architecture for big data analytics. *Communications of the IIMA*, *13*(2), 1–13.

Chen & Storey. (2012). Business intelligence and analytics: From big data to big impact. *Management Information Systems Quarterly*, *36*(4), 1165–1188.

Fitzgerald. (2014). Training the next generation of business analytics professionals. *MIT Sloan Management Review*.

He, X. J. (2013). The effect of supply chain strategy on quality and U.S. competitiveness. *Communications of the IIMA*, *13*(2), 15–27.

Klipfolio. (2018). *What is business intelligence?* Retrieved from https://www.klipfolio.com/resources/articles/what-is-business-intelligence

Laney, D. (2001). *Application Delivery Strategies.* Retrieved from https://blogs.gartner.com/doug-laney/files/2012/01/ad949-3D-Data-Management-Controlling-Data-Volume-Velocity-and-Variety.pdf

Lyman, P., & Varian, H. R. (2000). *How Much Information?* Retrieved from http://groups.ischool.berkeley.edu/archive/how-much-info/how-much-info.pdf

Watson, H. J., Wixom, B. H., & Ariyachandra, T. (2013). Insights on hiring for BI and analytics. *Business Intelligence Journal, 18*(2), 4–7.

Wills, M. J. (2014). Decisions through data: Analytics in healthcare. *Journal of Healthcare Management, 59*(4), 254–262. doi:10.1097/00115514-201407000-00005 PMID:25154123

Chapter 5
What Is Open Source Software (OSS) and What Is Big Data?

Richard S. Segall
Arkansas State University, USA

ABSTRACT

This chapter discusses what Open Source Software is and its relationship to Big Data and how it differs from other types of software and its software development cycle. Open source software (OSS) is a type of computer software in which source code is released under a license in which the copyright holder grants users the rights to study, change, and distribute the software to anyone and for any purpose. Big Data are data sets that are so voluminous and complex that traditional data processing application software are inadequate to deal with them. Big data can be discrete or a continuous stream data and is accessible using many types of computing devices ranging from supercomputers and personal workstations to mobile devices and tablets. It is discussed how fog computing can be performed with cloud computing for visualization of Big Data. This chapter also presents a summary of additional web-based Big Data visualization software.

INTRODUCTION: HOW OPEN SOURCE SOFTWARE, FREE SOFTWARE, AND FREEWARE DIFFER

Open Source Software (OSS)

Open-Source Software (OSS) is a type of computer software in which source code is released under a license in which the copyright holder grants users the rights to study, change, and distribute the software to anyone and for any purpose. (Wikipedia (2019a))

For software to be considered "Open Source", it must meet ten conditions as defined by the Open Source Initiative (OSI). Of these ten conditions, it's the first three that are really at the core of Open Source and differentiates it from other software. These three conditions are according to the Open Source Initiative (2007):

DOI: 10.4018/978-1-6684-3662-2.ch005

1. **Free Redistribution**: The software can be freely given away or sold.
2. **Source Code**: The source code must either be included or freely obtainable.
3. **Derived Works**: Redistribution of modifications must be allowed.

The other conditions are: (Open Source Initiative (2007))

4. **Integrity of The Author's Source Code**: Licenses may require that modifications are redistributed only as patches.
5. **No Discrimination against Persons or Groups**: no one can be locked out.
6. **No Discrimination against Fields of Endeavor**: commercial users cannot be excluded.
7. **Distribution of License**: The rights attached to the program must apply to all to whom the program is redistributed without the need for execution of an additional license by those parties.
8. **License Must Not Be Specific to a Product**: the program cannot be licensed only as part of a larger distribution.
9. **License Must Not Restrict Other Software**: the license cannot insist that any other software it is distributed with must also be open source.
10. **License Must Be Technology**:Neutral: no click-wrap licenses or other medium-specific ways of accepting the license must be required.

Macaulay (2017) discussed benefits of open source software that are summarized in Figure 1 below.

Figure 1. Benefits of Open Source Software (OSS) (Derived from Macaulay (2017))

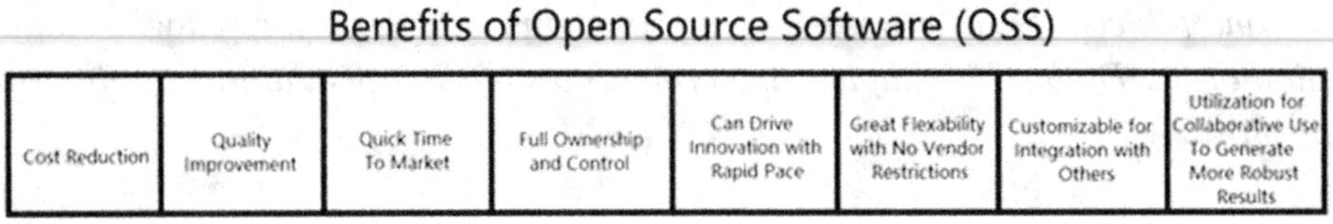

Benefits of Open Source Software (OSS)

Cost Reduction	Quality Improvement	Quick Time To Market	Full Ownership and Control	Can Drive Innovation with Rapid Pace	Great Flexability with No Vendor Restrictions	Customizable for Integration with Others	Utilization for Collaborative Use To Generate More Robust Results

Open Source License

According to Wikipedia (2019f) an open source license is a type of license for computer software and other products that allows the source code, blueprint or design to be used, modified and/or shared under defined terms and conditions. This allows end users and commercial companies to review and modify the source code, blueprint or design for their own customization, curiosity or troubleshooting needs.

Open-source licensed software is mostly available free of charge, though this does not necessarily have to be the case.

Licenses that only permit non-commercial redistribution or modification of the source code for personal use only are not considered generally as open source licenses.

Free Software or Freeware

Unlike the Open Source term, Free Software only has 4 "Freedoms" with its definition and are numbered 0-3 as created by the Free Software Foundation (FSF) (2019a) as follows:

The freedom to run the program for any purpose (Freedom 0)
The freedom to study how the program works and adapt it to your needs (Freedom 1)
The freedom of redistribution of software (Freedom 2)
The freedom to improve the program and release your improvements to the public to benefit the while community. (Freedom 3)

Although not explicitly outlined as a freedom, access to source code is implied with Freedoms 1 and 3. You need to have the source code in order to study or modify it. Figure 2 illustrates the relationship and overlap of these properties of Free Software with Open Source Software and was drawn using Drake (2019) discussion of the difference between free and open source software.

Figure 3 compares the features of freeware versus shareware that illustrates the later has fewer features than the former freeware.

Figure 2. Comparisons of features of Open Source Software (OSS) versus Free Software

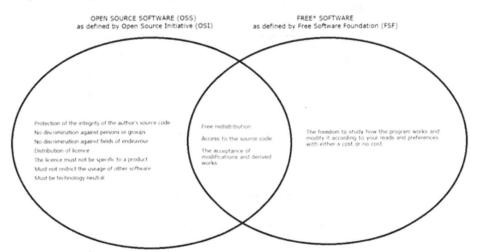

Figure 3. Comparison of the features of Freeware and Shareware

Features of Freeware and Shareware	
Freeware	Shareware
No cost to acquire	Limited Free Trial Period
Normally shared with no source code	
Unable to modify	Probably Limited Features of Full Version
Not Proprietary Protected	

Free Open Source Software (FOSS)

Not all software is free and Free Open Source Software (FOSS) is both free and open. The Free Software Foundation (FSS) (2019b) provides a searchable directory of over 15,000 free software packages.

Free and open-source software (FOSS) is software that can be classified as both free software and open-source software. That is, anyone is freely licensed to use, copy, study, and change the software in any way, and the source code is openly shared so that people are encouraged to voluntarily improve the design of the software. This is in contrast to proprietary software, where the software is under restrictive copyright licensing and the source code is usually hidden from the users. (The Free Software Foundation (FSS) (2019b))

Open Source Software Development Versus Traditional Software Development

The traditional method for software development includes a planning phase, development phase, modification and testing phase before general release followed by potential plans for new releases as needed as shown in Figure 4. The time line for this cycle typically is anywhere form nine months to almost three years.

Figure 4. Traditional software development cycle

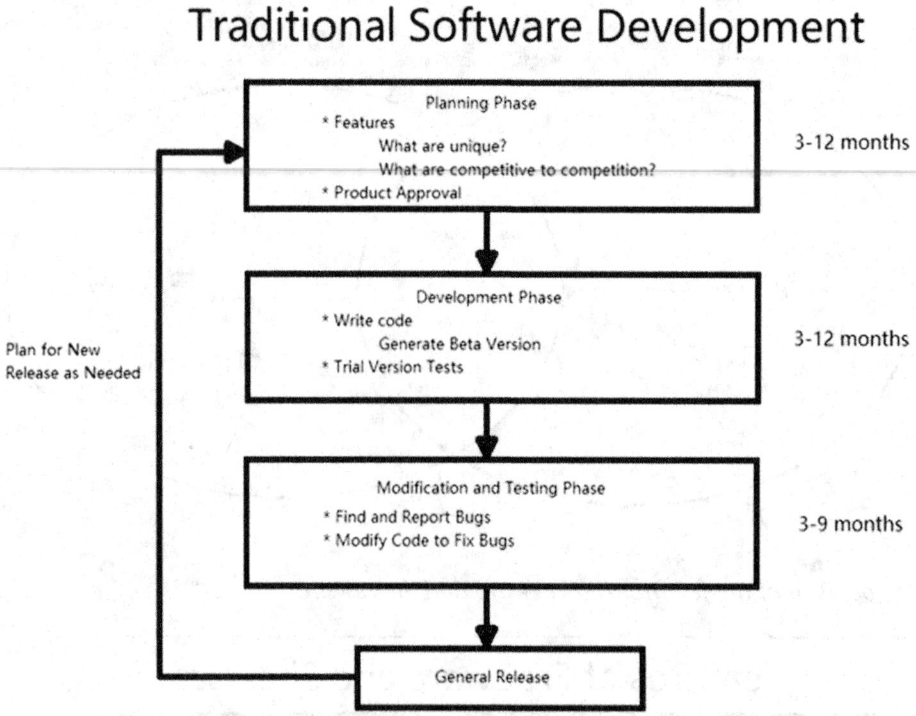

Saini & Kaur (2014) performed an extensive review of open source software development life cycle models, and Mandal et al. (2011) preformed open incremental model for an Open Source Software Development Life Cycle Model 'OSDLC'.

The Open Source Development Life Cycle (OSDLC) as discussed by Linux Foundation (2011), Haddan (2008), and Goldman & Gabriel (2005) entails multiple internal users/developers who each provide improvements to the Open Source Software (OSS) prior to its release to worldwide users/developers. These external users then subsequently provide an additionally enhanced source code for a new release version for potentially additionally improved source code upon feedback from both internal and external users. Figure 5 below illustrates the Open Source Development Cycle.

Figure 5. Open Source Software development cycle

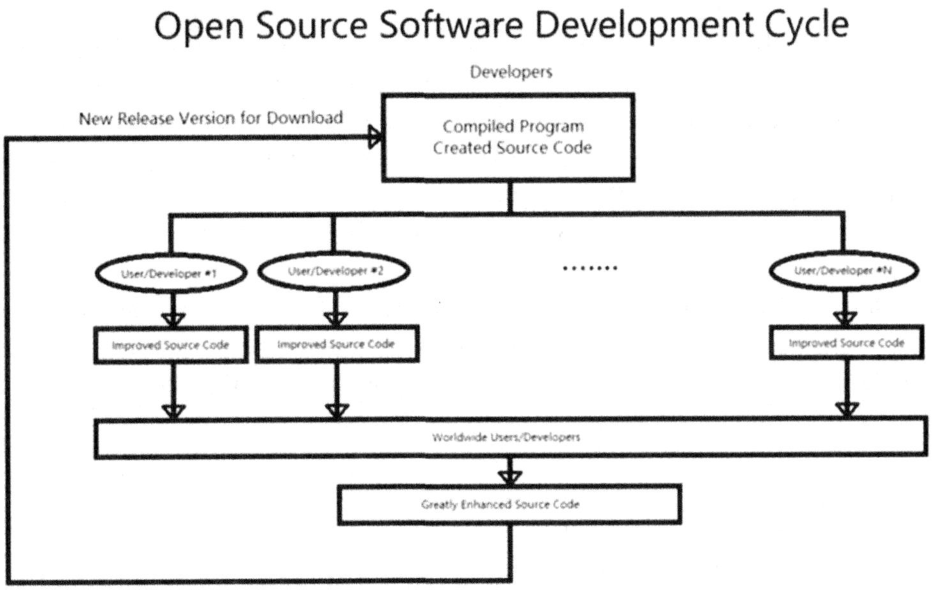

Freeman et al. (2018) discussed several of the best open source software for software development from which the following Table 1 was derived.

Table 1. Open Source Software for software development

Open Source Software Name	Features
Tuffle Framework	Suite of tools to help develop. test, and deploy smart contracts to the Ethereum blockchain.
Blockstack	Set of application development tools for building blockchain-based decentralized applications (dapps) on the Bitcoin blockchain.
Julia	High performance dynamic programming language for numerical computing.
Taucharts	Data-focused JavaScript charting library

INTRODUCTION: WHAT IS BIG DATA?

Big Data is defined as the collections of datasets whose volume, velocity or variety is so large that it is difficult to store, manage, process, and analyze the data using traditional databases and data processing tools. (Bahga & Madisetti, 2016) According to an estimate by IBM, 2.5 quintillion bytes of data is created every day, and that 90% of the data in the world today has been created in the last two years alone. (IBM, 2017)

In 2012, United States (US) government committed $200 million in "Big Data" research and development investment. (The White House, 2012) Big Data application is estimated worth $300 billion dollars for the US health care industry, and $250 billion euros for the Europe's public section administration. (Manyika, Chui, Brown, Bughin, Dobbs, & Roxburgh, 2011) So what is Big Data? The numerical definition of Big Data is evolving with the development of the technology. A dynamic definition is that data that exceeds the capacity of commonly used hardware and software tools to capture, store and analyze within a tolerable elapsed time is considered as Big Data. (Franks, 2012). Clegg (2017) authored a book on how the information revolution of Big Data is transforming our lives.

According to Marr (2016), Big Data in practice includes such as for Walmart: How Big Data is used to drive supermarket performance, Netflix: How Netflix used Big Data to Give us the programs we want, Rolls-Royce: How Big Data is used to drive success in manufacturing, and Facebook: How Facebook uses Big Data to make customer service more personal. Table 2 lists other multifaceted applications of Big Data as authored as individual chapters of Marr (2016) of how forty-five successful companies used Big Data to deliver extraordinary results.

Table 2. Successful applications of Big Data analytics by organizations and companies around the world [Derived from book by Marr (2016).]

ORGANIZATION/COMPANY	BIG DATA APPLICATION
Amazon	How predictive analysis is used to get a 360-view of customers
Caesar's	Big Data at the Casino
Dickey's Barbecue Pit	How Big Data is used to gain performance insights into one of America's most successful restaurant chains
Experian	Using Big Data to make lending decisions and to crack down on identify fraud.
Fitbit	Big Data in the fitness arena
John Deere	How Big Data can be applied on farms
LinkedIn	How Big Data is used to fuel social media success
Ralph Lauren	Big Data in the fashion industry
Tera Seismic	Using Big Data to predict earthquakes
Transport for London	How Big Data is used to improve and manage public transportation in London, UK.
Twitter	How Twitter is used and IBM deliver customer insights from Big Data
Uber	How Big Data is at the center of Uber's Transportation Business
US Olympic Women's Cycling Team	How Big Data Analytics is used to optimize athletes performance
Walt Disney Parks and Resorts	How Big Data is Transforming our Family Holidays
ZSL and London Zoo	Big Data in the zoo and to protect animals

Le (2016) discussed Big Data with machine learning algorithms such as those used by Netflix's to make movie suggestions based on movies you have watched in the past or Amazon's algorithms that recommend books based on books you have bought before. Opportunities and challenges of using machine learning algorithms for Big Data were studied by Zhou et al. (2017).

Previous research in Big Data was presented in Segall & Cook (2018), Segall (2016a) and in the context of supercomputing in Segall (2013), Segall & Cook (2014), Segall, Cook, & Zhang (2015), Segall & Gupta (2015), and Segall (2016b).

CHARACTERISTICS OF BIG DATA

The Big Data concept is formed due to the rapid development of computer technology. There is tremendous amount of data being generated and analyzed every day. The concept describes how this large amount data has been utilized to benefit the society. It is not just large amount data, instead, it is an ad-hoc definition of how the data is being collected, processed and distributed. There are some commonly accepted characteristics of Big Data, such as volume, velocity and variety. (Russom, 2011).

- Volume represents the size of the data. For example, number of observations, number of variables, number of files etc. Because most personal and working computers equipped with hard drives have memories with gigabyte (GB) level or terabyte (TB) capacity, the TB is considered as the minimum threshold of Big Data volume as of 2019. However, "big" as of today will not be "big" as of tomorrow as in Figure 6 due to the rapid growth of the data storage and processing technology.
- Velocity represents the speed or frequency of the data that has been generated and streamed into the database. Big Data often involves high velocity. For example, Facebook has more than 10 million photos uploaded every hour. (Mayer-Schönberger & Cukier, 2013)
- Variety represents the data coming from various sources and in various formats. Data is not collected by handwritten notebook anymore, it comes from social network, smart phones, trading platforms, machines and others. Browsing Facebook or driving a car that records driving behavior, contributes to the current generation of the Big Data. The data is also in different format such as continuous or discrete, longitudinal or time series, and different computer science or communication languages. The data could also be structured or unstructured. If the data is stored in various format such as dates, numbers and texts and has no predefined format, it is considered as unstructured data.

3V of Big Data is then extended into a 5V characteristics which includes value and veracity as shown in Figure 7 and discussed. (Ishwarappa & Anuradha, 2015).

- Value represents the data needing to have potential useful information for future study. It cost human and technology resources for companies and institutions to maintain a Big Data database. It cannot be considered as Big Data unless there is potential value from it.
- Veracity represents the accuracy of the data. It is almost impossible for all of the data to be 100% accurate when dealing with Big Data, but the accuracy level is still a critical aspect to check with. A data sources full with incorrect information will only mislead the conclusions drawn from the study.

Figure 6. Big data characteristics (Designed by Niu, November, 2017)

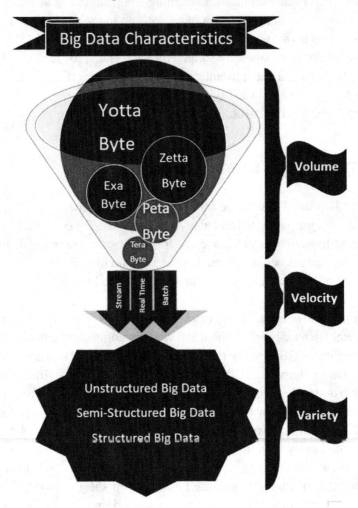

Streaming Versus Real Time Versus Batch

Streaming data is generated and delivered continuously, such as financial trading information, social network and geospatial service (GPS signals). Real time data has tight deadlines that result are guaranteed, such as TV signals are requested, processed and transmitted within time interval such as a minute. Batch data is collected and processed, then transmitted as a package to the client, it has higher latency tolerance.

Streaming and real time data processing consist of individual or micro batches of data with continues and high frequency of transmission between end-points and central data processor. But batch data transmission involves with large portfolio of data and normally involves with latencies in minutes or hours. Figure 8 illustrates a comparison of the generation of streaming, real time, and batch data.

A more thorough description of streaming data is achieved by splitting the Big Data analysis into computation and consumption phases (Psaltis, 2017). The computation phase includes data collection and processing. And consumption phase includes data delivery to users such as clients, smart phone application or clouds. In data computation phase, data collection could be hard real-time systems (i.e.

with absolute deadlines that must be met), soft real-time systems (i.e. need not meet absolute deadlines at all times) or near real-time systems (i.e. meeting deadlines within a time window). In consumption phase, data delivery could be streaming or non-streaming.

For example, YouTube videos could be uploaded with processing time due to regulation compliance process time, the process may take seconds or minutes and defined as near real time computation. However, once the videos are uploaded, it is delivered continuously or called streaming data, since it is delivered to viewers immediately. Figure 9 shows differences between real time and streaming data under different data process phases of data collection and data delivery.

Figure 7. 5V of Characteristics (Designed by Niu, November, 2017)

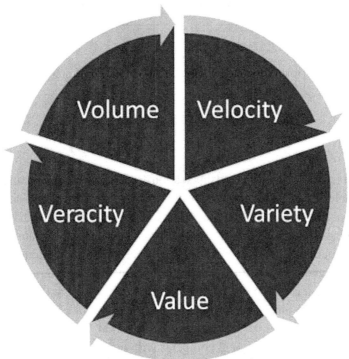

Figure 8. Streaming, real time and batch data comparison (Designed by Niu, March, 2018)

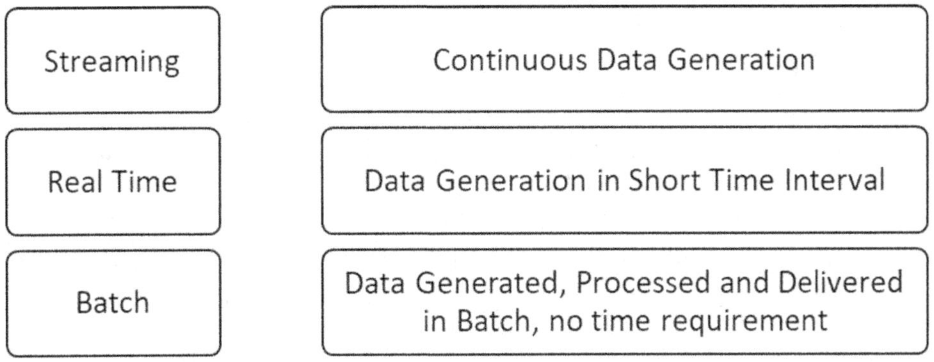

Streaming	Continuous Data Generation
Real Time	Data Generation in Short Time Interval
Batch	Data Generated, Processed and Delivered in Batch, no time requirement

Figure 9. Real time and streaming data under different data process phase (Designed by Niu, March, 2018)

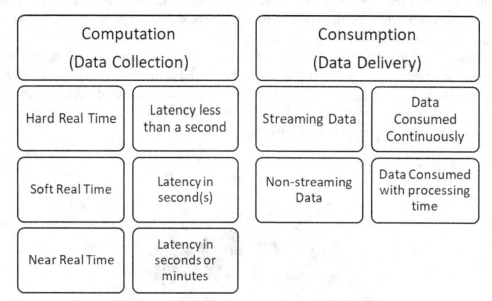

Data Measurement

Volume is a significant aspect of Big Data, and this section describes the data measurement and computing power evolvement. Table 3 shows data measurement as utilized in computer systems. The smallest unit of the data measurement is bit which stores values 0 or 1. One of the reasons to have 1 byte consisting of 8 bits is because combinations of 8 binary data will allow the system to generate 256 (2^8) unique values and this is sufficient amount of variety to include all of the commonly used letter, number and symbols according to American Standard Code for Information Interchange (ASCII).

1,024 was selected so that data is compatible with decimal number system, however kilobyte is not exactly 1,000 bytes due to the binary storage and data processing mechanism of computer. But, it is common to see the measurement equivalency represented by 1,000. For example, if "My computer" icon is clicked for a commercially made personal computer with hard drive labeled with 250GB storage, it would then show a maximum of 232.83GB free space. Because traditionally 250GB represents 250 * 1000 * 1000 * 1000 byte. But for computer, 250G represents 250 * 1024 * 1024 * 1024 byte. Therefore, if a hard drive labeled with 250GB, the computer will only recognize it as

$$232.83GB = \frac{250*1000*1000*1000}{1024*1024*1024}$$

With the basic understanding of what is the data measurement, the following will establish how much information each of the data measurement unit stores:

- 1 Megabyte stores information equivalent to a medium sized novel; (Indiana University, 2013)
- 1 Terabyte stores information equivalent to all of the books in a large library; (Indiana University, 2013)

Table 3. Data measurement (Designed by Niu, November 2017)

Category	Exact Measurement		Traditional Measurement
Bit	Binary Data (0 or 1)	Binary Data (0 or 1)	Binary Data (0 or 1)
Byte (B)	8 bits	8 bits or 1 B	8 bits or 1 B
Kilobyte (KB)	1,024 B	1,024	1,000
Megabyte (MB)	1,024 KB	1,048,576	1,000,000
Gigabyte (GB)	1,024 MB	1,073,741,824	1,000,000,000
Terabyte (TB)	1,024 GB	1,099,511,627,776	1,000,000,000,000
Petabyte (PB)	1,024 TB	1,125,899,906,842,620	1,000,000,000,000,000
Exabyte (EB)	1,024 PB	1,152,921,504,606,850,000	1,000,000,000,000,000,000
Zettabyte (ZB)	1,024 EB	1,180,591,620,717,410,000,000	1,000,000,000,000,000,000,000
Yottabyte (YB)	1,024 ZB	1,208,925,819,614,630,000,000,000	1,000,000,000,000,000,000,000,000

- 1 Petabyte stores information equivalent to 13.3 years of high-definition video, or all of the content in the U.S. library of congress. (Johnston, 2012)
- 2.5 Exabyte data is generated each day in 2012. There more data generated and stored each second across internet than 20 years ago. (McAfee & Brynjolfsson, 2012)
- 1.2 Zettabyte is the annual run rate for global Internet Protocol (IP) traffic in 2016. (Cisco, 2015)

Big Data concepts have been developing rapidly; it is dynamic, what was considered as Big Data 20 years ago is not anymore in today's computing power.

THE INTERFACE OF COMPONENTS OF BIG DATA STACK

Big Data can be utilized in batch analysis, real-time analysis, data storage, interactive querying and serving databases with NoSQL (Not Only Structured Query Language) or SLQ (Structured Query Language), and other methods. Figure 10 below illustrates the interface of these components in a stack of Big Data that is created from raw data that is accessed by many types of connectors such as queries and SQL. This chapter discusses the methods shown in Figure 10 for each of these Big Data stacks.

Figure 10. Big Data stack

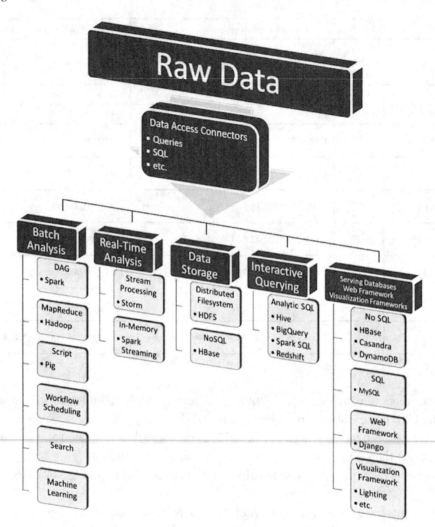

OPEN SOURCE SOFTWARE PLATFORMS FOR CLOUD AND FOG COMPUTING

This section describes the key characteristics of Cloud Computing and Fog Computing. Cloud Computing is a major computing technology currently used to store, process and analyze Big Data. Fog Computing is a supplement to Cloud Computing and it can be performed with Cloud Computing as a mechanism for visualization of Big Data.

What Is Cloud Computing?

Cloud computing happens when a task is distributed to the cloud server. The task is not transmitted to a specific one or one cluster of computers. Grid computing is when more than one computers are working simultaneously for one task. Normally the task is transmitted to a number of processing computers. The cloud server usually could be in a format of grid, but conversely not all grids are a cloud or part of cloud.

One of the benefits of cloud computing is the flexibility of task assignment for processing efficiency. Tasks with low processing requirement could be moved to processors with low computing power, and if the requirement ever increased, cloud server can maintain and distribute the task to one or a group of processors.

According to Gartner's 2017 Magic Quadrant for Cloud Infrastructure as a Service (IaaS) as discussed in Leong et al. (2017), the following Table 4 demonstrates the leading providers based on their ability to execute.

What Is Fog Computing?

Fog Computing is defined in detail in "The National Institute of Standards and Technology (NIST) Definition of Fog Computing" and is the title of NIST Special Publication 800-191 published in August 2017. This "Special Publication" not only includes definition and characteristics of Fog Computing, but also definitions of Fog Node, architectural service types and deployment method, and Mist Computing as "Lightweight Fog Layer". The "Fog Computing Conceptual Model" is the title of NIST Special Publication 500-325 published in March 2018.

The NIST (2017) definition of Fog Computing is the following:

"Fog computing is a horizontal, physical or virtual resource paradigm that resides between smart end devices and traditional cloud or data centers. This paradigm supports vertically-isolated, latency-sensitive applications by providing ubiquitous, scalable, layered, federated, and distributed computing, storage, and network connectivity."

Fog Computing is related with cloud computing. It is extension of the cloud that performs computing before serving the data to the cloud. Fog Computing could reduce cloud computing latency, because limited number of edge devices are communicating with the fog, then fog communicate computing to reduce traffic and latency on the cloud.

Fog Computing also could solve limited cloud bandwidth issue. Because of the layers of fog, data protection mechanism could be enhanced on each fog compared with overly broad protection on cloud. Lastly Fog Computing also could enhance internet connectivity due to its point-knot-source structure compared with point-source, where the point represents the edge device, the knot represents the fog, and the source presents the cloud

Fog is a middleware between Internet of Things (IoT) and cloud as shown by Aazam et al. (2018) within book "Fog Computing and Internet of Things" edited by Rahmani et al. (2018) that shows the range of applications benefiting by Fog Computing as health care, connected wind farms, smart grids, smart traffic light applications, smart homes and factories, and energy conservation.

Books on the subject of Fog Computing that have been recently published by IGI Global include those of Raj and Raman (2018) handbook of research on cloud and Fog Computing infrastructures, Srinivas, Lather and Siddesh (2018) on the rise of Fog Computing in the digital era, and Information Resources Management Association (2019) on breakthroughs in research and practice in Fog Computing.

Ahuja and Deval (2018) indicated that Fog Computing has been proposed by Cisco in early 2014 and that is otherwise known as Edge Computing is the integration of Cloud Computing and IoT. According to Ahuja and Deval (2018), Fog Computing meets the data processing needs of IoT devices that are

Table 4. Leading cloud infrastructure as a service (IaaS) (Designed by Niu, November 2017)

Rank	Cloud Provider		Recommended Usage						
			Cloud-native Application	E-Business Hosting	General Business Application	Enterprise Application	Development Environments	Batch Computing	Internet of Things Application
1	Amazon Web Services		x	x	x	x	x	x	x
2	Microsoft Azure		x		x		x	x	
3	Google Cloud Platform		x					x	
4	Alibaba Cloud		x				x	x	
5	Virtustream					x			
6	IBM Cloud			x	x			x	
7	Rackspace	Public Cloud	x	x			x		
		Private Cloud	x		x		x		

Source: Leong, L., Bala, R., Lowery, C., & Smith, D. (2017)

resource constrained by bringing computation, communication, control and storage closed to the end users, and further indicates that one can think of IoT-Fog-Cloud as being part of a continuum.

Bhardwaj (2018) discussed novel taxonomy to select fog products and challenges faced in fog environments, and presented a review of academic literature work on Fog Computing. Dubey et al. (2015) studied fog computing for enhancing Telehealth Big Data using Fog Data. Yang (2017) studied IoT stream processing and analytics in the fog.

Barik et al. (2018) discussed the emergence of Fog Computing for mining analytics in Big Data from geospatial and medical health applications by proposing and developing a fog computing-based framework named FogLearn. The research of Barik et al. (2018) applied the FogLearn framework by utilizing machine learning for the analysis of pathological feature data that was obtained from smart watches worn by patients with diabetes with location indicated by geographical parameters of a geospatial database.

Fog computing and Edge Computing are similar and had been referred interchangeable. However, there are some difference between the mechanisms. The following section discusses the difference between two computing mechanisms.

What Is Fog Computing Versus Edge Computing?

The difference between Fog Computing and edge computing is where the processing intelligence is placed. Fog Computing's intelligence is placed at the local area network level, and edge computing's intelligence is placed at the end user's appliance level. Both Fog Computing and edge computing are measures of enhancing the efficiency of cloud computing by preprocess the data, instead of replacing the cloud computing. Figure 11 shows the Fog Computing mechanism and Figure 12 shows the edge computing mechanism.

Figure 11. Fog computing mechanism (Designed by Niu, March, 2018)

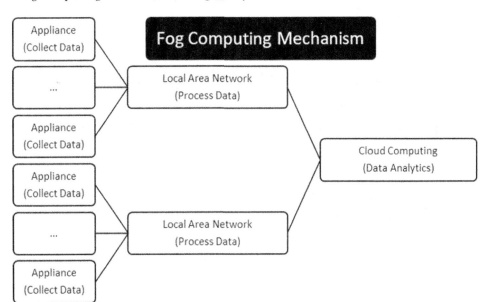

Fog Computing collects endpoints or appliance's generated data in the local area network level. And once the data is collected and processed, then it will be transmitted to the cloud. This intermediate step significantly reduced the latency between the appliances and cloud, thus improved the efficiency. Fog Computing is scalable. Because of its layered processing mechanism, it is easier to down device and procedure with failure.

Edge computing had end gateway at the appliance level. End point generates or collects data, and then at the same time processed the data. For example, smart phone application collects and process health data and then sent the requested data to the cloud for further analysis. Edge gateway also improves cloud efficiency since it processes the information before communicating with cloud which improved the quality of data. It also reduces the points of failure compared with Fog Computing, because each edge gateway works independently.

Figure 12. Edge computing mechanism (Designed by Niu, March, 2018)

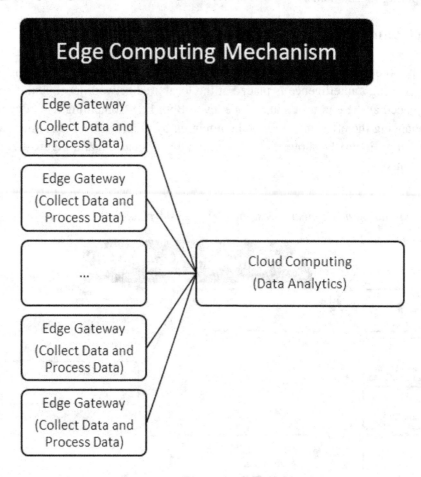

Open Source Software (OSS) for Fog and Cloud Computing

Huang et al. (2013) discussed evaluating open source cloud computing solutions for geosciences. Bellavista and Zanni (2017) studied the feasibility of fog computing deployment based on dcoker containerization over an embeeded microprocessor named RaspberryPi.

Bellavista and Zanni (2017) also extended an open-source framework for IoT application named Kura that is used for building IoT gateways for scalable fog computing.

Pan and McElhannon (2018) discuss the applications of open source platform Cloudlet in their study of future edge cloud and edge computing for IoT.

Barik et al. (2016) used open source compression techniques for reducing the transmission to the cloud in their study that developed a Fog Computing based framework named FogGIS for mining analytics from geospatial data.

Gaurav (2018) presented an in-depth study of iFogSim an open source simulator for Edge Computing, Fog Computing and IoT.

Bruschi et al. (2016) presented an in depth study of Open Volcano an open source software platform for fog computing that provides scalable and virtualized networking technologies able to natively integrate cloud services.

Dianomic (2019) discusses their product FogLAMP that is an open source platform for the Internet of Things (IoT) as the most powerful platform to simplify data management in the fog that can distributed at the Edge to act together provide scalability, elasticity and resilience.

The following is a list and description for some current Fog Computing open source software and platforms:

OpenVolcano

OpenVolcano is an Open Source Software that supports mobile edge and Fog Computing services. StratoV and Caldera are the main control and data plan of architecture components. Data plan of architecture includes data collection, configuration and elaboration. The project was introduced by DROP project and is the lead by the CNIT S3ITI Laboratory. It is a major result of INPUT project. European Commission under the Horizon 2020 program funded the project. (INPUT - In-Network Programmability for next-generation personal cloud service support, 2018 & OpenVolcano, 2018)

FogLAMP

FogLAMP os an open source platform for the Internet of Things (IoT) that uses modular microservices architecture with forwarding to cloud-based services (Dianomic (2019)).

FOG Project

FOG Project is a free open source network computer cloning and management solution that can be used with various versions of Windows. It ties together a few open source tools with a PHP-based web interface. (FOG Project (2019))

iFogSim

IFogSim is an open source simulator for edge computing, fog computing and Internet of Things (IoT). iFogSim evaluates resource management and scheduling policies across edge and cloud resource under different scenarios. (Gaurav (2018))

BIG DATA ANALYTICS SOFTWARE AND PLATFORMS

Categories of Big Data Analytics software that can be used as interfaces for Fog Computing include the following: Data Ingestion, Hadoop Systems, Stream computing, Analytics/Machine Learning, Content Management, Integration, and Data Governance. (PredictiveAnalyticsToday (2018).)

Table 5. Categories of Big Data analytics software (Derived from PredictiveAnalyticsToday (2018).)

CATEGORY OF BIG DATA ANALYTICS SOFTWARE	DESCRIPTION
Data Integration, Data Management, ELT, and Warehouse	Provides features for effective Data Warehousing and Management for managing data as a valuable resource.
Hadoop System	Provides features for massive storage for any kinds of data with enormous processing power and ability to handle virtually limitless concurrent tasks or jobs.
Stream Computing	Features for pulling in streams of data and streaming it back as a single flow.
Analytics/Machine Learning	Features for advanced analytics and machine learning.
Content Management	Features for comprehensive content life cycle and document management.
Integration	Features for Big Data integration from any source with ease.
Data Governance	Comprehensive Security and Compliance solution to protect the data.

The categories in Table 6 "Top 20 Big Data Analytics Software and Platforms" that provides each in ranked order with website of each. Descriptions of the features for each of the twenty Big Data software and platform follows Table 6.

Talend Open Studio

Software for Data Integration is free to download open-source license tool that fully supports all facets of Extract, Transform and Load (ETL) processes. It provides more than 800 built-in connects than any other ETL solution, thus making it easy to implement connections between diverse database types, file formats, and enterprise solutions. (Talend Open Studio, 2018)

Arcadia Data

Arcadia Data unifies data discovery, visual analytics and business intelligence in a single, integrated platform that runs on Hadoop clusters. (Arcadia Data, 2018)

Table 6. Top 20 Big Data analytics software and platforms ((PredictiveAnalyticsToday (2018).)

Name of Big Data Analytics Software / Platform	Category	Web URL
1. Talend Open Data	ETL Software	https://www.talend.com/?utm source=PredictiveAnalyticsToday &utm_medium=Review&utm_campaign=PA2.
2. Arcadia Data	Business Intelligence Software	https://www.arcadiadata.com/
3. Informatica	Big Data Software	https://www.informatica.com/products/big-data.html?utm_sou rce=PredictiveAnalyticsToday&utm_medium=Review&utm_ campaign=PAT#fbid=2tuRknAh7K4
4. GoodData	Business Intelligence Software	https://www.gooddata.com/?utm_source=PredictiveAnalyticsTod ay&utm_medium=Review&utm_campaign=PAT
5. Actian Analytics Platform	Dig Data, Big Data Analytics, Predictive Analysis	https://www.actian.com/
6. Google BigData	Big Data Platform	https://cloud.google.com/solutions/big-data/
7. Wavefront	Big Data Software	https://www.predictiveanalyticstoday.com/wavefront/
8. IBM Big Data	Big Data Platform	https://www.ibm.com/analytics/hadoop/big-data-analytics
9. Attivio Active Intelligence Engine	Big Data Software	https://www.attivio.com/?utm_source=PredictiveAnalyticsToday &utm_medium=Review&utm_campaign=PAT
10. Datameer	Big Data Analytics Platform	https://www.datameer.com/?utm_source=PredictiveAnalyticsTod ay&utm_medium=Review&utm_campaign=PAT
11. Opera Solutions Signal Hubs	Big Data Software	https://www.operasolutions.com/?utm_source=PredictiveAnalytic sToday&utm_medium=Review&utm_campaign=PAT
12. Amazon Web Services	Big Data Platform	https://aws.amazon.com/products/#analytics-1
13. FICO Big Data Analyzer	Big Data Analytics Platform	http://www.fico.com/en/analytic-cloud
14. Cloudera Enterprise Big Data	Big Data Platform	https://www.cloudera.com/products.html
15. DataTorrent	Big Data Ingestion Software	https://www.datatorrent.com/?utm_source=PredictiveAnalyticsTo day&utm_medium=Review&utm_campaign=PAT
16. Palantir Big Data	Big Data Platform	https://www.palantir.com/products/
17. Oracle Big Data Analytics	Big Data Platform	https://www.oracle.com/big-data/products.html
18. Qubole	Big Data Platform	https://www.predictiveanalyticstoday.com/qubole/
19. Syncsort	Big Data Ingestion Software	https://www.predictiveanalyticstoday.com/syncsort/
20. Amdocs Insight	Big Data Platform	https://www.amdocs.com/real-time-data-management

Informatica PowerCenter Big Data Edition

Is highly scalable, high performance enterprise data integration software that uses visual environment to build Extract, Transform and Load (ETL) data flows that run on Hadoop. The data flows can be reused and collaborate with other developers and analysts with a common integrated development environment. (Informatica PowerCenter Big Data Edition, 2018)

GoodData

The GoodData platform includes advanced distribution and product lifecycle management features to automate the process of maintaining one-to-many cloud deployments. (Good Data, 2018)

Actian Analytics Platform

Features include Vectorized Query Execution, maximizing CPU cache for execution, column-based storage, data compression, positional data trees (PDTs), and storage indices. Actian Analytics Platform runs complex queries against billions of records in just seconds. (Actian Analytics Platform, 2018)

Google Big Data

Google Big Data is a cloud platform that unifies batch and stream processing that is fully managed with serverless architecture that utilizes Spark and Hadoop. (Google Big Data, 2018)

Wavefront

Wavefront is a hosted platform for ingesting, storing, visualizing and alerting on metric data. It is based on a stream processing approach invented at Google that allows metric data to be manipulated with unparalleled power. (Wavefront, 2018)

IBM Big Data

Features include Data Management & Warehouse, Hadoop System, Stream Computing, Content Management, and Information Integration & Governance. (IBM Big Data, 2018))

Attivio Active Intelligence Engine

Attivio Active Intelligence Engine is a unified information access platform that brings together structured and unstructured content by integrating and correlating all data and content with no advance data modeling. It provides advanced text analytics, intuitive, Google-like search for business intelligence (BI) and integration with BI and data visualization tools. (Attivio Active Intelligence Engin, 2018)

Datameer

Datameer is a SaaS Big Data analytics platform that is targeted for department special deployments. (Datameer, 2018)

Opera Solutions Signal Hubs

The signal hubs employs machine learning and are domain specific collections of signals along with the technology required to continually extract, store, and refresh, and present selected signals and recommended best actions. (Opera Solutions Signal Hubs, 2018)

Amazon Web Service

Features include computing using Amazon Cloud Front, Storage using Amazon S3, database using Amazon Aurora, migration using Database Migration Service, and Amazon Virtual Private Cloud. (Amazon Web Service, 2018)

FICO Big Data Analyzer

Big Data Analyzer empowers a broad range of users to collaborate, explore data and discover new insights from any type and size of data on Hadoop. (FICO Big Data Analyzer, 2018)

Cloudera Enterprise Big Data

Cloudera enterprise Big Data is powered by Apache Hadoop and features include Data Engineering, Analytical and Operational Database, secure without compromise, and easy to manage. (Cloudera Enterprise Big Data, 2018)

DataTorrent

DataTorrent RTS is proven in production environments to reduce time to market, development costs and operational expenditures for Fortune 100 and leading Internet companies. It provides connectors for technologies such as message busses, SQL and NoSQL databases, flat files, Kafka, Scoop, Flume, and Twitter. (DataTorrent, 2018)

Palantir Big Data

Features include Data Integration, Iteration and Collaboration, Custom Metric Development, Flexible Modeling, Privacy and Security Controls, and Algorithmic Processing. (Palantir Big Data, 2018)

Oracle Big Data Analytics

Features include SQL Cloud Service, Oracle Big data Discovery, Oracle R Advanced Analytics for Hadoop, Business Intelligence and Data Visualization Cloud Service. (Oracle Big Data Analytics, 2018)

Qubole Data Service

Qubole Data Service is a comprehensive autonomous bog data platform that self-optimizes, self-manages, and learns form usage through combinations of heuristics and machine learning. (Qubola, 2018)

Syncsort

Syncsort provides enterprise software that allows organizations to collect, integrate, sort and distribute more data in less time, with fewer resources and lower costs. Syncsort software provides specialized solutions spanning "Big Iron to Big Data," including next gen analytical platforms such as Hadoop, cloud, and Splunk. (Syncort, 2018)

Amdocs Insight

Features include Real-Time Analytics, Amdocs Logical Data Model, Modern Data Infrastructure Management, and Analytical Applications Ecosystems. (Amdocs Insight, 2018)

BIG DATA VISUALIZATION

Once data is transmitted by devices that may or not be connected directly to the cloud by using a fog environment, the problem arises as how to visualize Big Data and what techniques can be used. The following discusses data visualization techniques using Big Data that was extracted from Fatality Analysis Reporting System (FARS) managed by National Highway Traffic Safety Administration (NHTSA) of United States Department of Transportation (DoT). (National Highway Traffic Safety Administration, 2017)

Big Data visualization is different from traditional classical data visualization, because the data has a higher volume, larger variety of data format and high data processing speed. Unlike traditional graphs, Big Data visualization methods focus on high dimensional relationships. The following visualization methods provide better presentation to thoroughly understand the data.

Treemap method uses size and color to demonstrate the data. In Figure 13, size represents the population of the state, and the color represents the number of vehicle accident fatal injuries per person. Darker color corresponds to a higher number of fatal injuries per person.

Figure 13. Example of treemap graph (Designed by Niu, November 2017)

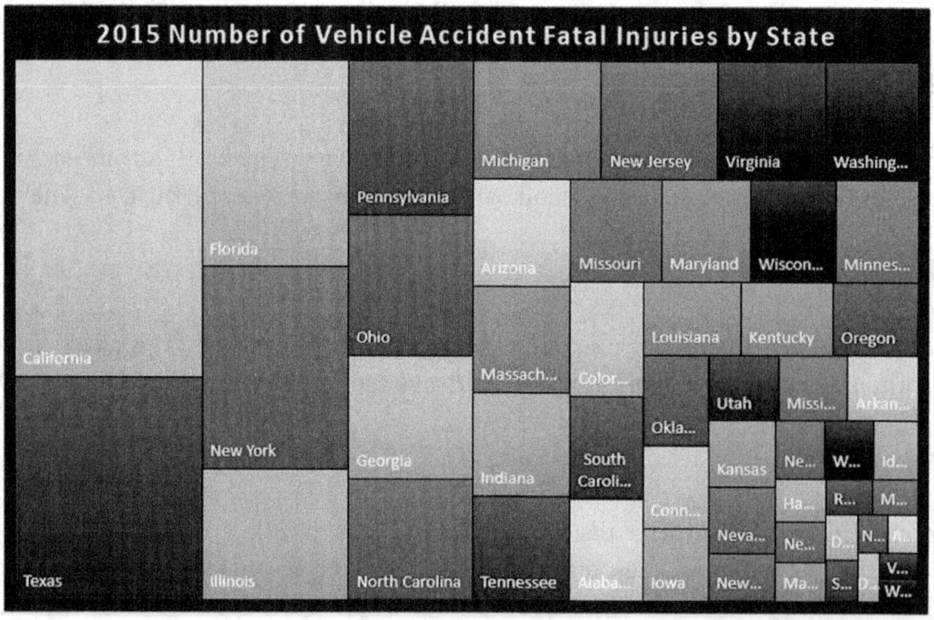

Figure 14. Example of sunburst graph (Designed by Niu, November 2017)

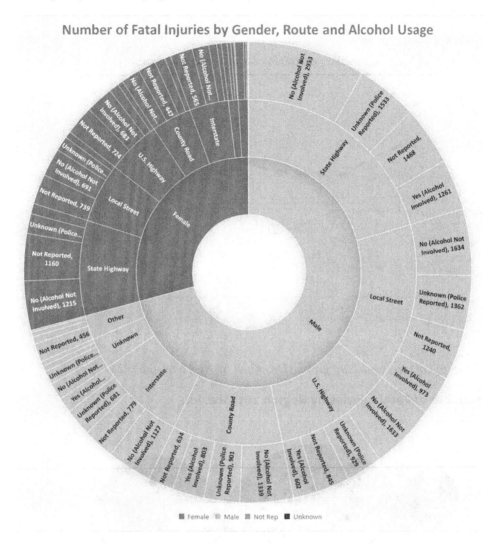

Sunburst graph is a ring chart, also known as a sunburst chart or a multilevel pie chart, is used to visualize hierarchical data, depicted by concentric circles. The circle in the centre represents the root node, with the hierarchy moving outward from the center. (Sunburst graph, 2017).

Sunburst method projects out the proportional relationship within each of the variables visually like a sun. In Figure 10, the inner circle has higher portion of male which represents the number of fatal injuries mostly happened to males. And within male fatalities, it most likely happened in the state highway. Within the categories of male together with State Highway fatalities in Figure 14, the highest proportion was for "Alcohol Not Involved".

Parallel coordinates method shows the relative relationship. In Figure 15, the highest fatal injuries categories (21-30 years old) on country road (1096 fatal injuries) and state highway (2121 fatal injuries) are different. But with the parallel coordinates, the relationship between different categories are demonstrated proportionally.

Figure 15. Example of parallel coordinates graph: number of fatal injuries by age group and route (Designed by Niu, November 2017)

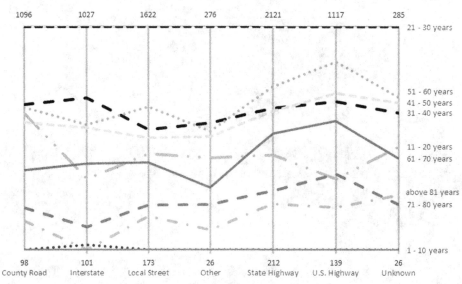

Number of Fatal Injuries by Age Group and Route

Figure 16. Example of circle packing graph (Designed by Niu, November 2017)

Number of Fatal Injuries by Region and Division

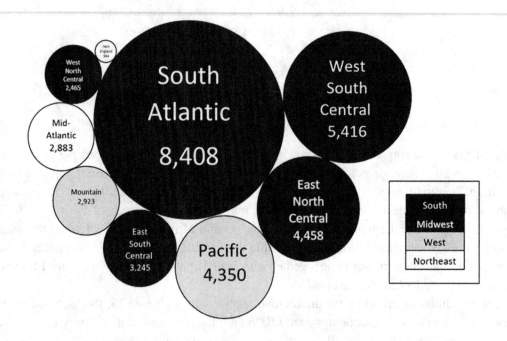

Circle packing method uses color and circle size to describe the dataset. In figure 16, the color represents the region and size represent the total number of fatal injuries in 2015.

Heat map demonstrates map with coloring algorithm. Figure 17 shows number of fatal injuries by state, color towards black represents higher total number of fatal injuries in 2015, and color towards grey represents lower total number of fatal injuries. Heat map could utilize more than two colors to demonstrate numerical value.

Figure 17. Example of heatmap graph (Designed by Niu, November 2017)

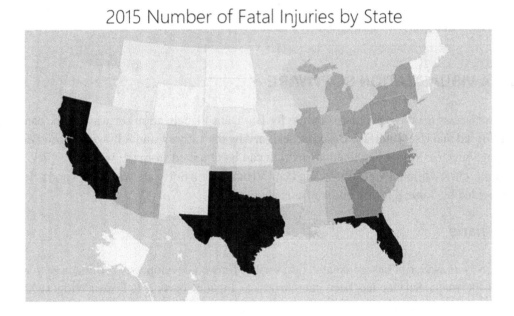

Figure 18. Example of streamgraph graph (Designed by Niu, November 2017)

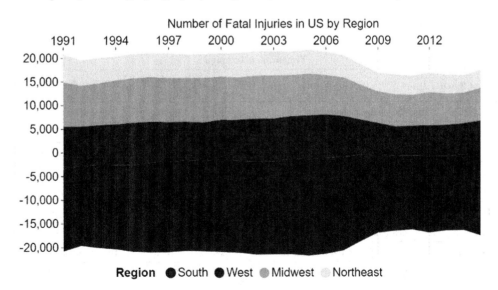

Streamgraph demonstrate time series data in a centered coordinate system. In Figure 18, four US (United States) regions total number of fatal injuries are aggregated into one wave according to time. And the proportional relationship between each region can be interpreted from this graph.

There are also numerous other types of visualization methods that could help with Big Data analysis, such as network analysis, circular network diagram. Method selection depends on data type and logical conclusions that the graph attempted to demonstrate.

Various visualization techniques were designed and implemented to realize the visualization methods. Script based techniques are developed, such as Java, so that programmers and software engineers are able to add interactive charts into their websites or applications conveniently. Some of the techniques are developed with user friendly interface so that Big Data analytics can be performed without coding. The following table includes a list of popular Big Data visualization tools, it categorized the tool as JavaScript based and user interface based techniques.

BIG DATA VISUALIZATION SOFTWARE

Table 7 summarizes the most popular software for Big Data Visualization software in the categories of JavaScript Based and User Interface Based as designed by the authors, and followed by brief description and web page images. More complete information can be obtained from the web page URL addresses provided for each. Additional Web-Based Big Data Visualization Software with URLs and brief descriptions is provided by Table 8 in Appendix of this chapter.

Fusion Charts

Fusion charts is a JavaScript based visualization service for web developers. It offers more than 90 chart types and 1400 maps. Service has been categorized as FusionCharts XT, FusionWidgets XT, Power-Charts XT and FusionMaps XT.

Table 7. Big Data Visualization Techniques (Designed by Niu, November 2017)

Visualization Techniques				
JavaScript Based	**Official Website**	**UserInterface based**	**Official Website**	
1	FusionCharts	https://www.fusioncharts.com/	10	Tableau	https://www.tableau.com/
2	HighCharts	https://www.highcharts.com/	11	Datawrapper	https://www.datawrapper.de/
3	Dygraphs	http://dygraphs.com/	12	Paraview	https://www.paraview.org/
4	Timeline JS	http://dygraphs.com/	13	Infogram	https://infogram.com/
5	Chart JS	http://www.chartjs.org/	14	Plotly	https://plot.ly/
6	D3 JS	https://d3js.org/	15	Qlik	https://www.qlik.com/
7	Leaflet	http://leafletjs.com	16	Sisense	https://www.sisense.com/
8	Google Charts	https://developers.google.com/chart/	17	Visually	https://visual.ly/
9	RawGraphs	http://rawgraphs.io/	18	Gephi	https://gephi.org/

HighCharts

HighCharts provides JavaScript services to help developers for their visualization needs. It focuses on interactive graphs.

Dygraphs

Dygraphs is an open-source and free services. It focuses on handling large datasets, and incorporating interactive functions within graphs. Dygraphs is JavaScript based visualization tool.

Timeline JS

Timeline JS is JavaScript free visualization tool that focuses on a timeline graph. It is a web designed tool for web developers to show the time line of a story.

Chart JS

Chart JS is a HyperText Markup Language 5 (HTML5) based JavaScript visualization tool. It is open-source and free.

D3 JS

D3 JS is a JavaScript library that provides visualization solutions. It focuses on the control of the final visual results and be able to provide innovative and interactive graphs.

Leaflet

Leaflet is an open-source and JavaScript based visualization tool. It focuses on mobile based interactive maps.

Google Charts

Google charts provides interactive visualization solutions by taking user supplied data. It will express the visualization in JavaScript for developer's further utilization.

RawGraphs

RawGraphs is an open-source software that allows users to generate graphs through the web. It can also generate JavaScript for additional use for developers. Users have generated various typical Big Data graphs such as streamgraph, customized treemap etc.

Tableau

Tableau is a visualization software that focuses on business intelligence. It is built with a user-friendly interface, so that users of the software only need to drag the variable names to generate graphs after inputing the data. It has a powerful geographical processing function. Segall (2017a, 2017b) discusses the use of Tableau Software for university teaching. Instructors' resources web pages for Tableau software are provided at Tableau (2017).

Datawrapper

Datawrapper is a user interface based visualization tool. The website generates charts and maps. It has a rich map library including various countries option for visualization.

Paraview

Paraview is an open-source user interface based visualization tool. The software has visualization functions specifically designed for structural analysis, fluid dynamics, astrophysics and climate science.

Infogram

Infogram is a user interface based visualization tool. The software focuses on business intelligence and is able to generate infographics and create business reports based on users' data.

Plotly

Plotly is an open-source visualization tool that allows users to create interactive data graphs and share via the web. It also provides consulting services.

Qlik

Qlik is a user interface data visualization software. Users only need to drag and click to explore and generate data after uploading. It is a business oriented instead of scientific research oriented Big Data visualization tool.

Sisense

Sisense is a user interface data visualization software. The software is designed for various types of business such as Healthcare, Finance, Marketing, Retail and Public Sector.

Visually

Visually is a web based data visualization and infographics technique. Data analysts and designers utilize the technology to provide services such as visualization animated videos.

Gephi

Gephi is an open-source and free software. It has a powerful network analysis function.

BIG DATA VISUALIZATION FOR STREAMING DATA

Big Data visualization for streaming data is inevitably involved with dynamic graph. Most of the commonly used data analytics software are designed to process batch data, such as SAS, R or Excel VBA. Updated versions of these software started to incorporated functions of visualizing dynamic data. However, collecting and processing data in real time is still a challenge for the traditional batch processing software.

The following Figure 19 is an example of visualization of streaming cyber-attack data created by NORSE. Cyber-attack incidents are captured, its origination location, targeting location, types of attack, IP address and other vital information are captured and visualized. The data is streamed out in less than a second, and demonstrates the attacks in a dynamic pattern.

Figure 19. Cyber-attack streaming data visualization example (NORSE, 2018)

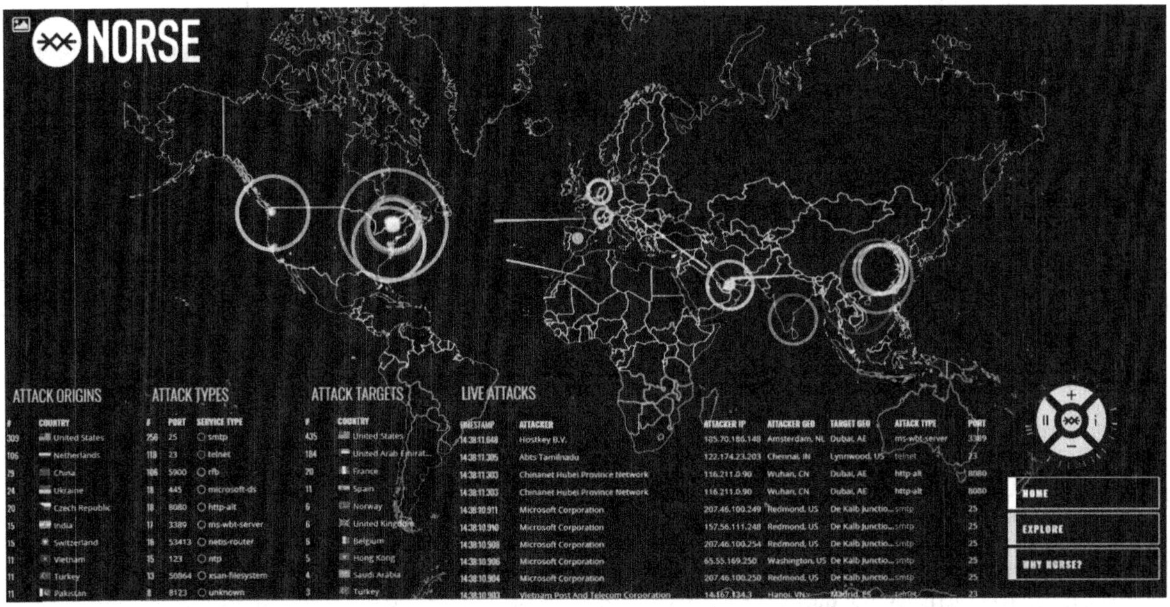

Data stream management for processing high-speed data streams is discussed in depth in Garofalakis et al.(2016) for foundations and basic stream synopses, mining data streams, applications, and system architectures and languages such as the Stanford Data Stream Management System and Sensor network integration with streaming database systems.

Many of the primary software tools used to do large-scale data analysis required by applications such as Internet web search, teleconferencing, geo-location and map services were born in the cloud as discussed by Li & Qiu (2014) in their book titled "Cloud Computing for Data-Intensive Applications".

Li & Qiu (2014) includes titled chapters pertaining to systems and applications of "Cloud Networking to Support Data Intensive Computing", programming models of "Executing Storm Surge Essential Ensembles on PAAS Cloud", and cloud storage "Supporting a Social Media observatory with Customizable Index Structures: Architecture and Performance".

Deshpande (2011) authored a text for data replication for Oracle Streams 11g for design and management for powerful data replication solution. Nabi (2016) authored a book on Pro Spark Streaming for real-time analytics that includes chapters on real-time ETL (Extract Transform Load) and corresponding analytics, discretized streams or DStreams for Real-Time Resilient Distributed Datasets (RDD). Gupta (2016) authored a book on real-time Big Data Analytics for design, process, and analysis of large data sets of complex data in real time. Chapters in Gupta (2016) include that devoted to programming with RDDs and analysis of streaming data using Spark steaming.

Ellis (2014) wrote book on real-time analytics with techniques to analyze and visualize streaming data that has chapters devoted to topics such as designing real-time streaming architectures, data-flow management in streaming analysis, processing streaming data, storing streaming data, delivering streaming metrics, and statistical approximation of streaming data.

Dunning & Friedman (2016) authored a book about streaming architecture for new designs using Apache Kafka and MapR streams. Dunning & Friedman (2016) explained how to recognize opportunities where streaming data may be useful and show how to design streaming architecture for best results in a multi-user system. They also explained why stream-based architectures are helpful to support microservices, and describe particular tools for messaging and streaming analytics that best fit the requirements of a strong stream-based design.

Basek et al. (2017) authored book on stream analytics with Microsoft Azure for real-time data processing for quick insights using Azure Stream Analytics that includes chapters on designing real-time streaming pipelines, developing real-time event processing with Azure streaming, and how to achieve seamless scalability with automation.

Bifet et al. (2017) authored book on machine learning (ML) for data stream with practical examples in Massive Online Analysis (MOA) that is an open-source software framework that allows users to build and run ML and data mining experiments on evolving data streams. Bifet et al. (2017) discusses Big Data stream mining and hands-on introduction to MOA and its Graphical user Interface (GUI).

BIG DATA VISUALIZATION SOFTWARE FOR MOBILE DEVICES AND TABLETS

Fog Computing utilizes mobile devices such as tablets that interface with data in the cloud.

Segall (2017a, 2017b) discusses SAS® Visual Analytics and SAS® Visual Statistics as new software that are designed to provide Big Data Analytics for mobile devices and tablets. Segall (2017a) presents actual classroom experiences using tablets and mobile devices for visual analytics of Big Data in bioinformatics, and Segall (2017b) for technologies for teaching Big Data analytics.

SAS® Visual Statistics is one of the modules built within SAS® Visual Analytics software. Bell, Hardin and Matthews (2017) and Ravenna, Truxillo and Wells (2017) authored two books of SAS® Notes from SAS® Institute for classroom teaching that utilizes Big Data of over 3 million rows of data that can be uploaded from the Teradata University Network (TUN). This Big Data set is for the Insight Toy Company as available from TUN for classroom teaching using mobile devices.

CONCLUSION

This chapter discusses what Open Source Software (OSS) is and what Big Data is and its key characteristics and components that can be used for its visualization using software and platforms. These software and platforms could be those not only created with the sole purpose for Fog Computing but also others for Big Data Visualization that can be implemented into Fog Computing with the Internet of Things (IoT).

This chapter also illustrates how Fog Computing can use Big Data in both its discrete and continuous forms such as data streaming. The chapter also discusses the differences between Fog Computing and Edge computing. Visualization of Big Data is an important issue because of the dimensionalities and velocity of the data that otherwise would be unknown, and the elements of Internet of Things (IoT) with Fog Computing make this possible using the software discussed each with their unique characteristics.

The opportunities for utilization of Open Source Software (OSS) for Big Data and Fog Computing are endless. The applications of Open Source Software to Big Data and its visualization to Fog Computing that connects with the Internet of Things (IoT) is the future for economic growth. Open Source Software is also the mechanism for efficiency and effectiveness of software dissemination to not only individual researchers and entrepreneurs, but also to businesses and large-scale organizations who want to use their software tools for not only personnel computers, but also with tablets and mobile devices.

ACKNOWLEDGMENT

Acknowledgements to Co-Editor Dr. Gao Niu are indicated in several figures of this chapter who converted hand-drawn figures created by the author into computer images as shown.

REFERENCES

Aazam, M., St-Hilaire, M., Lung, C.-H., Lambadaris, I., & Huh, E.-H. (2018). IoT resource estimation challenges and modeling in fog. In *Free and open source software in modern data science and business intelligence*. IGI Global.

Actian Analytics Platform. (2018). Retrieved on May 13, 2018 from https://www.predictiveanalyticstoday.com/actian-analytics-platform/

Ahuja, S. P., & Deval, N. (2018). From Cloud Computing to Fog Computing: Platforms for the Internet of Things (IoT). *International Journal of Fog Computing*, *1*(1), 1–14. doi:10.4018/IJFC.2018010101

Amazon web Service. (2018). Retrieved on May 13, 2018 from https://www.predictiveanalyticstoday.com/amazon-web-service/

Arcadia Data. (2018). Retrieved on May 13, 2018 from https://www.predictiveanalyticstoday.com/arcadia-data/

Attivio Active Intelligence Engine. (2018). Retrieved on May 13, 2018 from https://www.predictiveanalyticstoday.com/attivio-active-intelligence-engine/

Barik, R. K., Dubey, H., Samaddar, A. B., Gupta, R. D., & Ray, P. K. (2016). FogGIS: Fog computing for geospatial big data analytics. Proceedings of 2016 IEEE Uttar Pradesh Section International Conference on Electrical Computer and Electronic Engineering (UPCON). Retrieved May 16, 2019 from https://arxiv.org/ftp/arxiv/papers/1701/1701.02601.pdf

Basak, A., Venkataraman, K., Murphy, R., & Singh, M. (2017). *Stream Analytics with Microsoft Azure.* Birmingham, UK: Packt Publishing Ltd.

Belavista, P., & Zanni, A. (2017) Feasibility of fog computing deployment based on docker containerization over RaspberryPi. ICDCN '17 Proceedings of the 18th International Conference on Distributed Computing and Networking. Retrieved May 16, 2019 from http://delivery.acm.org/10.1145/3010000/3007777/a16-Bellavista.pdf?ip=147.97.138.188&id=3007777&acc=ACTIVE%20SERVICE&key=F82E6B883-64EF649%2EB319B24617D6E2C4%2E4D4702B0C3E38B35%2E4D4702B0C3E38B35&__acm__=1558043198_90653cd3b7954cf3a7cfa60797254435

Bell, R., Hardin, B., & Matthews, L. (2017). *SAS® Visual Analytics for SAS® 9: Getting Started Course Notes.* Cary, NC: SAS Institute, Inc.

Benjelloun, F. Z., Lahcen, A. A., & Belfkih, S. (2015, March). An overview of big data opportunities, applications and tools. In Intelligent Systems and Computer Vision (ISCV), 2015 (pp. 1-6). IEEE. doi:10.1109/ISACV.2015.7105553

Bhardwaj, A. (2018). Novel Taxonomy to Select Fog Products and Challenges Faced to Fog Environments. *International Journal of Fog Computing*, *1*(1), 35–49. doi:10.4018/IJFC.2018010103

Bifet, A., Gavadlda, R., Holmes, G., & Pfahringer, D. (2017). *Machine Learning for Data Streams with Practical Examples in MOA.* Cambridge, MA: The MIT Press.

Brown, J. P. (2017). *Open Source Software: Implementing a Successful OSS Management Practice.* SilverStream Consulting, LLC.

Bruschi, R., Lago, P., Lamanna, G., Lombardo, C., & Mangialardi, S. (2016). Open Volcano: An open-source software platform for fog computing. 2016 28th International Teletraffic Congress- The First International Conference in Networking & Practice, Wurzburg, Germany.

Capterra. (2017). Big Data Software. Retrieved November 25, 2017 from https://www.capterra.com/big-data-software/?utf8=%E2%9C%93&users=&feature%5B4%5D=39433&commit=Filter+Results&sort_options=

Circle Packing Graph. (2017). Retrieved on November 19, 2017 from https://en.wikipedia.org/wiki/Circle_packing

Cisco. (2017). The Zettabyte Era: Trends and Analysis. Retrieved November 23, 2107 from https://www.cisco.com/c/en/us/solutions/collateral/service-provider/visual-networking-index-vni/vni-hyper-connectivity-wp.html

Clegg, B. (2017). *Big Data: How the information revolution is transforming our lives.* London, UK: Icon Books, Ltd.

Cloudera Enterprise Big Data. (2018). Retrieved on May 13, 2018 from https://www.predictiveanalyticstoday.com/cloudera-enterprise-bigdata/

Daas, P. J., Puts, M. J., Buelens, B., & van den Hurk, P. A. (2015). Big data as a source for official statistics. *Journal of Official Statistics*, *31*(2), 249–262. doi:10.1515/jos-2015-0016

Datameer. (2018). Retrieved on May 13, 2018 from https://www.predictiveanalyticstoday.com/datameer/

DataTorrent. (2018). Retrieved on May 13, 2018 from https://www.predictiveanalyticstoday.com/datatorrent/

Deshpande, K. (2011). *Oracle Streams 11g Data Replication*. Oracle Press.

Dianomic. (2019). The most powerful platform to simply data management in the fog. Retrieved May 16, 2019 from http://dianomic.com/platform/

DiBina, C., Cooper, D., & Stone, M. (2006). *Open Source 2.0: The continuing revolution*. O'Reilly Media Inc.

Drake, M. (2017). The Difference between Free and Open-Source Software. Retrieved Mary 22, 2019 from https://www.digitalocean.com/community/tutorials/Free-vs-Open-Source-Software

Dubey, H., Yang, J., Constant, N., Amiri, A. M., Yang, Q., & Makodiva, K. (2015). Article. Proceedings of the ASE Big Data & Social Informatics (ASE BD&SI '15).

Dunning, T., & Friedman, E. (2016). *Streaming Architecture: New Designs using Apache Kafke and MapR Streams*. O'Reilly Media, Inc.

Ellis, B. (2014). *Real-Time Analytics: Techniques to Analyze and Visualize Streaming Data*. John Wiley & Sons, Inc.

Familiar, B., & Barnes, J. (2017). *Business in real-time using Azure IoT and Cortanna Intelligence Suite*. Apress.

FICO Big Data Analyzer. (2018). Retrieved on May 13, 2018 from https://www.predictiveanalyticstoday.com/fico-big-data-analyzer/

Findley, K. (2016). Open source won. So, now what? Wired. Retrieved May 12 from https://www.wired.com/2016/08/open-source-won-now/?GuidesLearnMore

Findley, K. (2019). The WIRED guide to open source software. Retrieved May 12, 2019 from https://www.wired.com/story/wired-guide-open-source-software/

Frampton, M. (2018). *Complete guide to open source big data stack*. Apress.

Franks, B. (2012). Taming the big data tidal wave: Finding opportunities in huge data streams with advanced analytics. Hoboken, NJ: John Wiley & Sons; doi:10.1002/9781119204275.

Free Software Foundation. (2019a). Retrieved May 22, 2019 from https://www.fsf.org/

Free Software Foundation. (2019b). Free Software Resources. Retrieved May 22, 2019 from https://www.fsf.org/resources/

Freeman, J., Heller, M., Wayner, P., & Yegulalp. (2018). The best open source software for software development. InfoWorld. Retrieved May 22, 2019 from https://www.infoworld.com/article/3306453/the-best-open-source-software-for-software-development.html

Garfinkel, S. L. (1993). Is Stallman stalled: One of the greatest programmers alive saw a future where all software was free. Then reality set in. Retrieved May 12, 2019 from https://www.wired.com/1993/01/stallman/?GuidesLearnMore

Garofalakis, M., Gehrke, J., & Rastogi, R. (Eds.). (2016). Data Stream Management: Processing High-Speed Data Streams. Springer-Verlag; doi:10.1007/978-3-540-28608-0.

Gaurav, K. (2018). iFogSim: An open source simulator for Edge Computing, Fog Computing and IoT. Retrieved May 16, 2019 from https://opensourceforu.com/2018/12/ifogsim-an-open-source-simulator-for-edge-computing-fog-computing-and-iot/

Goldman, R., & Gabriel, R. P. (2005). How to do Open-Source Development. Chapter 6 of Innovations Happens Elsewhere. Retrieved May 22, 2019 from https://www.dreamsongs.com/IHE/IHE-54.html#pgfId-956812

GoodData. (2018). Retrieved on May 13, 2018 from https://www.predictiveanalyticstoday.com/gooddata/

Google Big Data. (2018). Retrieved on May 13, 2018 from https://www.predictiveanalyticstoday.com/google-bigdata/

Gupta, S., & Saxena, S. (2016). *Real-Time Big Data Analytics*. Birmingham, UK: Packt Publishing.

Haddan, I. (2008). The Open Source Development Model: Overview, Benefits and Recommendations. Retrieved May 22, 2019 from http://aaaea.org/Al-muhandes/2008/February/open_src_dev_model.htm

Haff, G. (2018). *How open source ate software: Understanding the open source movement and so much more*. Apress.

Hahn, R. W. (2002). *Government policy toward open source software*. Brookings Institute Press.

Hassan, N. A., & Hijazi, R. (2018). *Open source intelligence methods and tools: A practical guide to online intelligence*. Academic Press.

Heatmap. (2017). Retrieved on November 19, 2017 from https://en.wikipedia.org/wiki/Heat_map

Huang, Q., Yang, C., Liu, K., Xia, J., Xu, C., Li, J., ... Li, Z. (2013). Evaluating open-source cloud computing solutions for geosciences. *Computers & Geosciences*, §§§, 5941–5952.

IBM. (2017). What is Big Data? Retrieved on November 20, 2017 from http://www-01.ibm.com/software/in/data/bigdata/

IBM Big Data. (2018). Retrieved on May 13, 2018 from https://www.predictiveanalyticstoday.com/ibm-big-data/

Indiana University. (2013, January 7). What are bits, bytes, and other units of measure for digital information? Retrieved October 30, 2017 from https://kb.iu.edu/d/ackw

Informatica PowerCenter Big Data Edition. (2018). Retrieved on May 13, 2018 from https://www.predictiveanalyticstoday.com/informatica-powercenter-big-data-edition/

INPUT - In-Network Programmability for next-generation personal cloud service support. (2018). Retrieved on March 27, 2018 from http://www.cloudwatchhub.eu/serviceoffers/input-network-programmability-next-generation-personal-cloud-service-support

Janert, P. K. (2011). *Data analysis with open source tools*. O'Reilly Media, Inc.

Johnston, L. (2012, April 25). A "Library of Congress" Worth of Data: It's All In How You Define It. Retrieved October 30, 2017, from https://blogs.loc.gov/thesignal/2012/04/a-library-of-congress-worth-of-data-its-all-in-how-you-define-it/

Koranne, S. (2011). Handbook of open source tools. Springer Science+Media Business, LLC. doi:10.1007/978-1-4419-7719-9

Layton, R., & Watters, P. A. (2016). *Automating open source intelligence: Algorithms for OSINT*. Waltham, MA: Elsevier.

Le, J. (2016, Aug 18). The 10 Algorithms Machine Learning Engineers Need to Know. Retrieved from https://www.kdnuggets.com/2016/08/10-algorithms-machine-learning-engineers.html

Leong, L., Bala, R., Lowery, C., & Smith, D. (2017). Magic Quadrant for Cloud Infrastructure as a Service, Worldwide. Retrieved on November 24, 2017 from https://www.gartner.com/doc/reprints?id=1-2G2O5FC&ct=150519

Li, X., & Qiu, J. (Eds.). (2014). Cloud Computing for Data-Intensive Applications. Springer Science+Business Media. doi:10.1007/978-1-4939-1905-5

Lindberg, V. (2008). *Intellectual property and open source: A practical guide to protecting code*. O'Reilly Media Inc.

Linux. (2011). Understanding the Linux Open Source Development Model. Retrieved May 22, 2019 from http://www.ibrahimatlinux.com/uploads/6/3/9/7/6397792/00.pdf

Liu, X., Dastjerdi, A. V., & Buyya, R. (2016). Stream processing in IoT: Foundations, state-of-the-art, and future directions. In *Internet of Things: Principles and Paradigms*. Morgan Kaufmann.

Mandal, S., Kandar, S., & Ray, P. (2011). Open Incremental Model: A Open Source Software Development Life Cycle Model 'OSDLC'. *International Journal of Computers and Applications, 212*(1), 2473–3327.

Manyika, J., Chui, M., Brown, B., Bughin, J., Dobbs, R., & Roxburgh, C. (2011). *Big data: The next frontier for innovation, competition, and productivity*. Washington, DC: McKinsey Global Institute.

Marr, B. (2016). Big data in practice: How 45 successful companies used big data analytics to deliver extraordinary results. John Wiley & Sons, Ltd. doi:10.1002/9781119278825

Mayer-Schönberger, V., & Cukier, K. (2013). *Big data: A revolution that will transform how we live, work, and think*. Boston: Houghton Mifflin Harcourt.

McAfee, A., & Brynjolfsson, E. (2012). Big data: The management revolution. *Harvard Business Review*, *90*(10), 61–68. PubMed

Metz, C. (2015). Google just open sourced the artificial intelligence engine at the heart of its online empire. Retrieved May 13, 2019 from https://www.wired.com/2015/11/google-open-sources-its-artificial-intelligence-engine/?GuidesLearnMore

Nabi, Z. (2016). Pro Spark Streaming: The Zen of Real-Time Analytics using Apache Spark. Apress. doi:10.1007/978-1-4842-1479-4

National Highway Traffic Safety Administration. (2017). NCSA Data Resource Website Fatality Analysis Reporting System (FARS) Encyclopedia. National Center for Statistics and Analysis (NCSA) Motor Vehicle Traffic Crash Data. U.S. Department of Transportation. Retrieved on November 20, 2017 from ftp://ftp.nhtsa.dot.gov/fars/

National Institute of Standards and Technology. (2017). *The Definition of Fog Computing NIST SP 800-191 Includes NIST SP-500-291*. U.S. Department of Commerce.

National Institute of Standards and Technology. (2018). Fog Computing Conceptual Model NIST SP 500-325 & 500-291. U.S. Department of Commerce. Retrieved from on April 8, 2018. doi:10.6028/NIST.SP.500-325

Superior Attack Intelligence, N. O. R. S. E. (n.d.). Retrieved (Screenshot) on March 19, 2018 from http://map.norsecorp.com/#/helps

Open Source Initiative. (2007). The Open Source Definition. Retrieved on May 22, 2019 from https://opensource.org/osd

Opera Solutions Signal Hubs. (2018). Retrieved on May 13, 2018 from https://www.predictiveanalyticstoday.com/opera-solutions-signal-hubs/

Oracle Big Data Analytics. (2018). Retrieved on May 13, 2018 from https://www.predictiveanalyticstoday.com/oracle-bigdata-analytics/

Palantir Big Data. (2018). Retrieved on May 13, 2018 from https://www.predictiveanalyticstoday.com/palantir-bigdata/

Pan, J., & McElhannon, J. (2018). Future edge cloud and edge computing for Internet of Things applications. IEEE Internet of Things Journal., 5(1), 438–449. doi:10.1109/JIOT.2017.2767608

Predictive Analytics Today. (2018). Top 50 Big Data Platforms and Big Data Analytics Software. Retrieved on May 11, 2018 from https://www.predictiveanalyticstoday.com/bigdata-platforms-bigdata-analytics-software/

Psaltis, A. (2017). *Streaming Data*. Shelter Island, NY: Manning Publications Co.

Qubole. (2018). Retrieved on May 13, 2018 from https://www.predictiveanalyticstoday.com/qubole/

Quora. (2017). What are the Apache Spark concepts around its DAG (Directed Acyclic Graph) execution engine, and its overall architecture? Retrieved on May 10, 2018 from https://www.quora.com/What-are-the-Apache-Spark-concepts-around-its-DAG-Directed-Acyclic-Graph-execution-engine-and-its-overall-architecture

Rahmani, A. M. Liljeberg, Preden, J-S., & Jantsch, A. (Eds.). (2018). Fog Computing in the Internet of Things: Intelligence at the Edge. Springer Nature.

Raj, P., & Raman, A. (2018). Handbook of Research on Cloud and Fog Computing Infrastructures for Data Science. Hershey, PA: IGI Global; doi:10.4018/978-1-5225-5972-6.

Ravenna, A., Truxilla, C., & Wells, C. (2017). *SAS® Visual Statistics: Interactive Model Building Course Notes*. Cary, NC: SAS Institute, Inc.

Russom, P. (2011). Big data analytics. *TDWI Best Practices Report*, *19*, 40.

Sani, M., & Kaur, K. (2014). A review of open source software development life cycle models. *International Journal of Software Engineering and Its Applications*, *8*(3), 417–434. Retrieved from https://www.researchgate.net/publication/289328296_A_review_of_open_source_software_development_life_cycle_models

Segall, R. S. (2013). Computational Dimensionalities of Global Supercomputing. *Journal of Systemics, Cybernetics and Informatics*, *11*(9), 75–86. Retrieved from http://www.iiisci.org/journal/sci/FullText.asp?var=&id=iSA625MW

Segall, R. S. (2016a). Invited Plenary Address at International Institute of Informatics and Systemics (IIIS) Conference titled "Big Data: A Treasure Chest for Interdisciplinary Research". 20th Multi-conference on Systemics, Cybernetics, and Informatics (WMSCI 2016), Orlando, FL. Retrieved on December 26, 2016 from http://www.iiis.org/ViewVideo2016.asp?id=14

Segall, R. S. (2016b). High Performance Computing and Data Mining in Bioinformatics. FedEx Institute of Technology. Presentation at 13th Annual Meeting of MidSouth Computational Biology and Bioinformatics Society (MCBIOS), Memphis, TN. Retrieved on June 19, 2017 from http://www.memphis.edu/bioinformatics/announcements/pdfs/mcbios2016.pdf

Segall, R. S. (2017a). Using Tablets and Mobile Devices for Visual Analytics of Big Data in Bioinformatics. Presentation at 14th Annual Meeting of MidSouth Computational Biology and Bioinformatics Society (MCBIOS), Little Rock, AR. Retrieved on June 19, 2017 from https://mcbios.org/sites/mcbios.org/files/MCBIOS2017_Program_Book_Final_1_0.pdf

Segall, R. S. (2017b). Technologies for Teaching Big Data Analytics. Proceedings of 48th Meeting of Southwest Decision Sciences (SWDSI). Retrieved on June 19, 2017 from http://www.swdsi.org/swdsi2017/SWDSI_2017_CONFERENCE_PROGRAM4.pdf

Segall, R. S., & Cook, J. S. (2014). Data Visualization and Information Quality by Supercomputing. In Proceedings of the Forty-Fifth Meeting of Southwest Decision Sciences Institute (SWDSI). Dallas, TX: Academic Press. Retrieved on June 19, 2017 from http://www.swdsi.org/swdsi2014/2014_SWDSI_CFP_MARCH_2014_v7.pdf

Segall, R. S., & Cook, J. S. (2018). Handbook of Big Data Storage and Visualization Techniques. IGI Global. Retrieved June 2, 2019 from https://www.igi-global.com/book/handbook-research-big-data-storage/179829

Segall, R. S., Cook, J. S., & Niu, G. (2019). Overview of Big Data-Intensive Storage and its Technologies for Cloud and Fog Computing. *International Journal of Fog Computing, 2*(1), 74–119. doi:10.4018/IJFC.2019010104

Segall, R. S., Cook, J. S., & Zhang, Q. (2015). Research and Applications in Global Supercomputing. Hershey, PA: IGI Global Inc. Retrieved on May 19, 2017 from http://www.igi-global.com/book/research-applications-global-supercomputing/118093

Segall, R. S., & Gupta, N. (2015). Overview of Global Supercomputing. In Research and Applications in Global Supercomputing (pp. 1-32). Hershey, PA: IGI Global Inc. Retrieved on May 19, 2017 from http://www.igi-global.com/chapter/overview-of-global-supercomputing/124335

Segall, R. S., & Niu, G. (2018). Big Data and Its Visualization with Fog Computing. *International Journal of Fog Computing, 1*(2), 51–82. doi:10.4018/IJFC.2018070102

Srinivasas, K. G., Lathar, P., & Siddesh, G. M. (2018). *The Rise of Fog Computing in the Digital Era.* Hershey, PA: IGI Global.

Sunburst Graph. (2017). Retrieved on November 19, 2017 from https://en.wikipedia.org/wiki/Pie_chart#Ring_chart_.2F_Sunburst_chart_.2F_Multilevel_pie_chart

Syncsort. (2018). Retrieved on May 13, 2018 from https://www.predictiveanalyticstoday.com/syncsort/

Tableau Software. (2017). Tableau Community Instructor's Resource Page. Retrieved on May 31, 2017 from https://community.tableau.com/community/teachers/overview

Talend Open Studio. (2018). Retrieved on May 13, 2018 from https://www.predictiveanalyticstoday.com/talend-open-studio-for-data-integration/

The Apache Software Foundation. (n.d.). Retrieved October 30, 2017, from http://hadoop.apache.org/

The White House. (2012, March 29). Obama Administration Unveils "Big Data" Initiative: Announces $200 Million in New R&D Investments. Retrieved October 30, 2017, from https://obamawhitehouse.archives.gov/the-press-office/2015/11/19/release-obama-administration-unveils-big-data-initiative-announces-200

ThinkSys. (2017). The Benefits and Challenges of Open Source Software. Retrieved May 22, 2019 from https://www.thinksys.com/development/benefits-and-challenges-open-source-software/

Tibco. (2017). Parallel Coordinates Plot. Retrieved on November 19, 2017 from https://docs.tibco.com/pub/spotfire/6.5.2/doc/html/para/para_what_is_a_parallel_coordinate_plot.htm

Tole, A. A. (2013). Big data challenges. *Database Systems Journal, 4*(3), 31–40.

Tozzi, C. (2018). *For Fun and Profit: A History of the Free and Open Source Software Revolution.* Cambridge, MA: The MIT Press.

Treemap. (2017). Retrieved on November 19, 2017 from https://en.wikipedia.org/wiki/Treemapping

Wavefront. (2018). Retrieved on May 13, 2018 from https://www.predictiveanalyticstoday.com/wavefront/

Wikipedia. (2017). Streamgraph. Retrieved on November 19, 2017 from https://en.wikipedia.org/wiki/Streamgraph

Wikipedia. (2019a). Free and open source software. Retrieved from https://en.wikipedia.org/wiki/Free_and_open-source_software

Wikipedia. (2019b). Freeware. Retrieved from https://en.wikipedia.org/wiki/Freeware

Wikipedia. (2019c). Open Source Software. Retrieved from https://en.wikipedia.org/wiki/Open-source_software

Yang, E. (2015). Chuckwa. Hadoop Wiki. Retrieved on November 20, 2017 from https://wiki.apache.org/hadoop/Chukwa

Yang, S. (2017). IoT stream processing and analytics in the fog. *IEEE Communications Magazine*, *55*(8), 21–27.

Yottabyte. (2017). Retrieved on November 21, 2017 from https://en.wikipedia.org/wiki/Yottabyte

Young, M. (2019). *Software licensing agreement: What you need to know about software licensees*. Internet Attorneys Association, LLC.

Zhou, L., Pan, S., Wang, J., & Vasilakos, A. V. (2017). Machine learning on big data: Opportunities and challenges. *Neurocomputing*, *237*, 350–361. doi:10.1016/j.neucom.2017.01.026

KEY TERMS AND DEFINITIONS

Big Data: Data that exceeds the capacity of commonly used hardware and software tools to capture, store and analyze within a tolerable elapsed time is considered as big data. The three main characteristics of big data are volume, variety, and velocity.

Circle Packing Graph: Circle packing is the study of the arrangement of circles (of equal or varying sizes) on a given surface such that no overlapping occurs and so that all circles touch one another (Circle Packing Graph, 2017).

Data Measurement: Unit measurement to indicate the volume of data in modern computer storage devices.

Free and Open Source Software (FOSS): Software that can be classified as both free software and open source software (Wikipedia, 2019a).

Freeware: Software, most often proprietary, that is distributed at no monetary cost to the end user (Wikipedia, 2019b).

Heatmap: A heat map (or heatmap) is a graphical representation of data where the individual values contained in a matrix are represented as colors (Heatmap, 2017).

Machine Learning: A process that gives machine the ability to learn without being explicitly programmed.

Open Source Software (OSS): A type of computer software in which source code is released under a license in which the copyright holder grants users the rights to study, change, and distribute the software to anyone and for any purpose (Wikipedia, 2019c).

Parallel Coordinate Plot: A parallel coordinate plot maps each row in the data table as a line, or profile. Each attribute of a row is represented by a point on the line. This makes parallel coordinate plots similar in appearance to line charts, but the way data is translated into a plot is substantially different (Tibco, 2017).

Schema on Read: Data analysis strategy that new data is transferred to a plan or schema without a predefined format.

Schema on Write: Data analysis strategy that new data is transferred to a structured predefined format.

Streaming Data: Data that has been originated, collected, processed or delivered time-wise continuously is considered as streaming data.

Streammap: A streamgraph, or stream graph, is a type of stacked area graph, which is displaced around a central axis, resulting in a flowing, organic shape (Streammap, 2017).

Sunburst Chart: A ring chart, also known as a sunburst chart or a multilevel pie chart, is used to visualize hierarchical data, depicted by concentric circles. The circle in the centre represents the root node, with the hierarchy moving outward from the center (Sunburst Graph, 2017).

Treemap: Treemaps display hierarchical (tree-structured) data as a set of nested rectangles. Each branch of the tree is given a rectangle, which is then tiled with smaller rectangles representing sub-branches (Treemap, 2017).

Yottabyte: The yottabyte is a multiple of the unit byte for digital information. The prefix yotta indicates multiplication by the eighth power of 1000 or 1024 in the International System of Units (SI), and therefore one yottabyte is one septillion (one long scale quadrillion) bytes. The unit symbol for the yottabyte is YB. 1 YB = 1000^8 bytes = 1024 bytes = 1000000000000000000000000 bytes = 1000 zettabytes = 1 trillion terabytes (Yottabyte, 2017).

This research was previously published in Open Source Software for Statistical Analysis of Big Data; pages 1-49, copyright year 2020 by Engineering Science Reference (an imprint of IGI Global).

APPENDIX

Table 8. Additional web-based Big Data visualization software (Created by Jeffrey S. Cook, Co-Editor of Handbook of Big Data Storage and Visualization Techniques, IGI Global, 2018 using (Capterra, 2017).)

Name of Web-Based Big Data Visualization Software	Web URL	Description
1010data	https://1010data.com/	1010data is a leading business intelligence provider (Forrester & Gartner), trusted by over 850 of the world's largest companies.
Alooma	https://www.alooma.com/	Alooma brings all data sources together into BigQuery, Redshift, Snowflake and more.
AnswerMiner	https://www.answerminer.com/	An amazing and fast data exploration tool with many unique features like relation maps and decision trees.
Arimo	https://arimo.com/	Machine learning algorithms and a powerful big-compute platform, Big Apps multiply the value of organization's data and people.
Axibase Time Series Database	https://axibase.com/products/axibase-time-series-database/	ATSD is a distributed NoSQL database designed from the ground up to store and analyze time-series data at scale.
BI on Big Data	http://www.kyvosinsights.com/	Kyvos is revolutionizing analytics with its breakthrough OLAP on Big Data technology.
BillRun	https://billrun.com/	Open-source billing solution, designed for Big Data. On-prem and SaaS, pre- and post-pay.
Cloudera Enterprise	https://www.cloudera.com/products.html	Cloudera delivers the modern platform for machine learning and analytics optimized for the cloud.
Cogniteev	http://www.cogniteev.com/	Cogniteev is a data access automation platform that enables companies to access and analyze complex data sets.
Datadog Cloud Monitoring	https://www.datadoghq.com/	Datadog is the essential monitoring service for hybrid cloud environments. The platform assists organizations in improving agility, increasing efficiency and providing end-to-end visibility across dynamic or high-scale infrastructures.
DataLux	http://www.vivorbis.com/	Big Data Platform solution with state of the art analytics, data lake, aggregation capabilities, and more.
Datameer	https://www.datameer.com/	Empowers organizations to embark on a data journey that answers a wide range of new, deeper business questions.
DataPlay	https://dataplay.us/	Integrated suite of applications that fully meets analysis, visualization, and presentation needs in market research.
Domo	https://www.domo.com/	Domo is cloud -based business management platform, and first solution that brings together five products into one elegant platform enabling users to connect, prepare, visualize, engage and optimize their business around data.
Graph DB	https://ontotext.com/	A semantic repository, a NoSQL database system used for storage, querying, and management of structured data.
Ideata Analytics	https://ideata-analytics.com/	Self-service analytics platform to source, clean, analyze, and visualize Big Data at scale using Apache Spark.
IQLECT	http://www.iqlect.com/	Actionable insights with real-time Big Data analytics. Fully converged platform and solutions for organizations of any size.

Name of Web-Based Big Data Visualization Software	Web URL	Description
Looker	https://looker.com/	Looker works the way the web does: browser-based, its unique modeling language lets any employee leverage the work of the best data analysts. Operating 100% in-database, Looker capitalizes on the newest, fastest analytic databases to get real results, in real time. Lookers lightweight open architecture make it easy for developers to quickly and flexibly build, deploy, and iterate custom on data applications.
MicroStrategy Enterprise Analytics	https://www.microstrategy.com/us	A comprehensive enterprise analytics and mobility platform that delivers a full range of analytical and reporting capabilities.
MongoDB	https://www.mongodb.com/	From startups to enterprises, for the modern and the mission-critical
Periscope	https://www.periscopedata.com/	Periscope connects directly to the database and lets users run, visualize, and share analyses on billions of rows of data in seconds.
Phocas Software	https://www.phocassoftware.com/	Phocas Software is an award-winning Business Intelligence software used by companies across numerous industries and around the globe.
Salesforce Analytics Cloud	https://www.salesforce.com/products/einstein-analytics/overview/	For every business user. Explore any combination of data, get answers instantly, and share with others. From any device, anywhere, faster than ever before. For analysts. Deliver new insights to business users however, wherever, and whenever they want them.
SEQUEL	http://sequel.jeremyevans.net/	SEQUEL provides easy-to-use data access solutions for IBM and empowers users with quality insight to make key business decisions.
Sisense	https://www.sisense.com/	Sisense provides an end-to-end solution for tackling growing data sets from multiple sources that comes out-of-the-box with the ability to crunch terabytes of data and support thousands of users--all on a single commodity server.

Chapter 6
Healthcare Big Data:
A Comprehensive Overview

Pijush Kanti Dutta Pramanik
https://orcid.org/0000-0001-9438-9309
National Institute of Technology Durgapur, India

Saurabh Pal
https://orcid.org/0000-0002-9053-4617
Bengal Institute of Technology, India

Moutan Mukhopadhyay
Bengal Institute of Technology, India

ABSTRACT

Big data has unlocked a new opening in healthcare. Thanks to the considerable benefits and opportunities, it has attracted the momentous attention of all the stakeholders in the healthcare industry. This chapter aims to provide an overall but thorough understanding of healthcare big data. The chapter covers the 10 'V's of healthcare big data as well as different healthcare data analytics including predictive and prescriptive analytics. The obvious advantages of implementing big data technologies in healthcare are meticulously described. The application areas and a good number of practical use cases are also discussed. Handling big data always remains a big challenge. The chapter identifies all the possible challenges in realizing the benefits of healthcare big data. The chapter also presents a brief survey of the tools and platforms, architectures, and commercial infrastructures for healthcare big data.

1. INTRODUCTION

Healthcare industry is going through a trailblazing makeover. Due to the significant advancement in digitised and open and pervasive healthcare systems, it is generating a massive amount of data. This healthcare data is truly comparable to the Big Data both in size and nature, hence termed as healthcare Big Data. Though compared to other industries, the healthcare industry has been lagging behind in the

DOI: 10.4018/978-1-6684-3662-2.ch006

adoption of Big Data technologies, the changed medical and clinical landscape has forced the stake-holders to delve into the development quickly. Suddenly, Big Data has become crucial for almost every operational, clinical, and management task (Bresnick, 2017). The healthcare people are now convinced of the benefits of Big Data and persuading themselves to analyse the data for extracting new insights that have given them the access to promising new threads of knowledge which are being transformed into innovative and purposeful actions (Groves et al., 2013).

Several healthcare use cases are well-suited for incorporating Big Data technologies. The healthcare Big Data analytics has opened up many exciting avenues in different healthcare operations including diagnosis and medical care, clinical decision support, population health management etc. (Bresnick, 2017). The success of healthcare Big Data is mostly dependent on the efficient collection and storage of massive quantities of disparate data acquired from diverse sources and also running it through an in-depth analysis (McDonald, 2017). The effective utilization of healthcare Big Data and obtained knowledge through analytical processes has the potential to save a significant amount of money and most importantly, people's lives (Lebied, 2017).

This chapter provides a preliminary and overall understanding of healthcare Big Data. The rest of the chapter is organised as follows. Section 2 discusses the 'big' aspect of the healthcare data including the ten 'V's of healthcare Big Data. It also covers the basics of healthcare Big Data analytics as well as the present healthcare Big Data market. Section 3 identifies several advantages of Big Data in healthcare. Section 4 mentions some application areas while Section 5 lists some specific examples of healthcare Big Data. The associated challenges are discussed in Section 6. Section 7 provides a brief survey of the different platforms and tools, architectures, and practical infrastructure for healthcare Big Data. Section 8 concludes the chapter.

2. BIG HEALTH DATA

2.1. The Data Overload

Back in 2012, a study estimated that healthcare data boast the largest share (30%) in occupying the overall electronic data storage in the world (Brown, 2015). To make the things graver, healthcare data is growing at a rapid pace, in fact seriously rapid. Among the growing digital universe healthcare is one of the fastest growing sectors. A report from the EMC Corporation along with the research firm IDC suggests that the digital healthcare data is growing at 48% per year whereas the growth rate of the overall digital universe 40% per year for the (IDC, 2014). The report estimates that the size of healthcare data will swell to 2,314 Exabytes by 2020 from a figure of 153 Exabytes in 2013 with an annual growth rate of 48%. The report elaborates that if all the digital healthcare data are stored on a stack of tablet computers, the height of the tower, by the year 2020, would cross 82,000 miles scaling from 5,500 miles in 2013 (Leventhal, 2014). The above statistics are sufficient to get a picture of the growth rate of the healthcare data and if this rate is continued, the healthcare data volume will soon reach the zettabyte and yottabyte scale.

2.2. The 'V's of Healthcare Big Data

2.2.1. Volume

The term 'Big' in healthcare Big Data itself certifying that volume of created and accumulated healthcare data is huge. Over the years, it is expected to grow even further. Clinical notes and trial data, lab results, personal medical records, claims data, FDA submissions, medical device data, human genetics and population data, genomics, radiology images, 3D imaging, and biometric sensor readings are the primary information productive contributors in the exponential growth of healthcare data (Bresnick, 2017) (Raghupathi & Raghupathi, 2014).

2.2.2. Velocity

The healthcare data can be generated either by humans or sensors (Crapo, 2017). Traditional healthcare management systems are typically populated by the human-generated (entered by people) data. In that case, the rate at which the data flows into the system can be manageable. But widespread use of IoT and smart medical devices has led to the generation of real-time health data. Newly accumulated data come in constant and rapid flow which makes collecting and storing really challenging. Also, because of real-time health applications, the unified healthcare system's response time is very crucial. Though trying to react to every health data stream may cause the inefficient and uneconomical use of resources. So, it is important to decide which data require immediate action and which can be deferred.

2.2.3. Variety

Healthcare data come from various sources and, hence, in diverse shapes (e.g. structured, unstructured and semi-structured) formats (e.g. plain text, blobs of text, pictures, video, medical image, etc.) and sizes. Data captured at different estranged locations are typically incompatible because of different data structure and semantics. This requires the development of specialized data structures, communication protocols, and storage systems (Crapo, 2017).

2.2.4. Veracity

Veracity represents the quality of the data. Here, data quality includes integrated, trustworthiness, complete, and bias and noise free. Maintaining these qualities in health data is a serious challenge because of the diversity of sources and channels. Obviously, veracity is, probably, the most sensitive issue among the all 'V's in healthcare Big Data.

2.2.5. Validity

Validity represents the accuracy and correctness of data. The validity of data is also measured by how up to date it is and whether it is generated through standard scientific protocols and methods (Bresnick, 2017).

2.2.6. Viability

From the ocean of healthcare data, it is important to identify the relevant data for each use case (Bresnick, 2017). Relevancy of data is required to maintain for achieving desired and accurate outcome through analytical and predictive measures.

2.2.7. Volatility

As mentioned above, the healthcare data are generated and being changed at a rapid rate. Hence, they tend to live short. But the question is how short? How quickly does the data change? It is important to determine how long the data is relevant, how long to store it and the data of which time period should be considered for analysis (Bresnick, 2017).

2.2.8. Vulnerability

It need not be mentioned explicitly that the privacy and security are of utmost importance for healthcare data especially as data are stored in the cloud and travels to different data junctions (for details, refer Section 6).

2.2.9. Visualization

Healthcare data not only need to be correct and accurate, they have to be presented unambiguously, and attractively to the user. Large and complex clinical reports need to be presented in a way that is meaningful and less time-consuming to understand. Proper visualisation helps in finding valuable insights as it reflects the details in an expressive and usable way.

2.2.10. Value

The ultimate purpose of healthcare Big Data analysis is to gain value in the form of better health services. Better governance, better analytics, and smarter decision making are the core factors for creating maximum value out of healthcare data (Bresnick, 2017). For healthcare organisations, Big Data brings value by shifting profit pools towards the right direction by reducing overall cost.

2.3. Healthcare Big Data vs. Healthcare Smart Data

The healthcare Big Data is basically the data which contains the patient's electronic health records (EHRs) and other related medical information. The objective of this is to provide healthcare services based on the past records. Application of analytics and data science on Big Data gives an opportunity to find the rightful insight. Data analytics instead of trying to combine all the available data, target the right data and thus gives the physician the rightful insights. But still, the gap exists between what is demanded and what is stored in Big Data. But it is not necessary that a voluminous data may always reveal the information which is exactly asked for. Similarly, merely Big Data may not provide valuable and precise insights to the physician.

On the other hand, smart data are data which gives rightful information as per the context. It allows physicians to make smart choices like coordinating the treatment of a patient suffering from multiple illnesses, able to diagnose the diseases better and getting a complete picture of the patient based on the family history. For a particular patient's ailment, based on symptoms smart data accurately advices the right medication and predict any future complications. Smart data is the meaningful data that is extracted from the healthcare Big Data based on the type of data, its volume, and validity. (Bresnick, 2016).

Inferring smart data from Big Data need proper planning and implementation. The focus is what the organization need after Big Data is applied to the system. Based on the system requirement it is wise to enrich the Big Data with the appropriate type of valid data in quality and volume. For example, scanning endless PDF, X-rays of fractures, and blood test data would not necessarily help a physician in diagnosing a patient with stomach ailment or why someone is reacting negatively to a certain medication. To have smart data, the Big Data should be enriched with appropriate and correlated data. It is important to understand that what is being collected is what is being delivered (Bresnick, 2016) (Leventhal, 2014).

2.4. Healthcare Big Data Analytics

Healthcare Big Data analytics is expected to change the face of healthcare. The healthcare sector has been a bit hesitant to embrace the Big Data scenario quickly (TF7 Healthcare subgroup, 2016). With most of the healthcare services now slowly coming to Big Data, a whole new paradigm of services that can be provided to patients can be opened.

Till now the whole treatment and caring of the patient are done by the hospital, but with the advent of Big Data, the treatment has become much easier and more focused (Raghupathi & Raghupathi, 2014). Furthermore, the Big Data analytics will significantly bring down the cost of clinical treatment, administration, medication, etc. The healthcare Big Data will enable the physicians, by providing proper insights, to understand where the attention is needed at any given point of time and take care of the patient accordingly.

The healthcare Big Data, if used properly, has the potential to become the guiding force for the physicians to improve the existing healthcare facilities. It will also help to gain more insight into the health of local population so that the suitable health services can be rendered to them (Crapo, 2017).

2.4.1. Descriptive Analytics

In the descriptive analysis, the various events that have occurred in the past are described. Data mining is performed on the aggregated data to get the details about the event that has happened in the past. The descriptive analysis, in a nutshell, can be summarised by a simple question as "What has happened?" (TF7 Healthcare subgroup, 2016).

Descriptive analytics in healthcare provides insight into the origin and the reason for spreading diseases and how long the quarantine periods might need. It can also shed light on which medicines failed and which combination of drugs succeeded? It can also identify the unhealthy lifestyle that leads to the disease and also the measures taken for its cure.

2.4.2. Diagnostic Analytics

Diagnostic analysis is an analytic technique that uses the descriptive analytics details to identify the reason for an event i.e. it tries to identify the various causes due to which a certain event happened in the past. In a nutshell, diagnostic analytics can be said to ask a simple question "Why did it happen?" (TF7 Healthcare subgroup, 2016).

Diagnostic analytics in healthcare can provide insights into the causes of various disease outbreaks, administrative and patient treatment malpractices, etc. It is also helpful in identifying the reasons - why certain diseases remain dormant and when do they become active i.e. conditions required for the pathogens to germinate. Diagnostic analysis deals with finding out the reason behind an event in the past using techniques of data mining, correlation, and data discovery.

2.4.3. Predictive Analytics

Predictive analytics is an advanced analytics technique which uses data mining, machine learning, artificial intelligence, and statistical modelling to predict future events. Predictive analytics in healthcare empower us to follow the saying "prevention is better than cure" in the true sense.

The predictive analytics in healthcare has a great scope as we can predict diseases that will afflict a person based on his/her habits, genetic makeup or history, or based upon the work environment or home environment (Lebied, 2017). This type of analysis can play its role in a larger scale by helping us in judging the health of the population in the future thus allowing us to take proper precautionary measures. Predictive analytics, if used properly, can prevent many future patients from being in a hospital.

2.4.4. Prescriptive Analytics

Prescriptive analytics deals with finding the best course of action for the predicted scenario derived from the predictive analysis. The prescriptive analysis extends the predictive analysis and descriptive analysis to find out what to do with a predicted event. Based on the available predictions, the predictive analysis provides the answer to the question "What should we do?" (TF7 Healthcare subgroup, 2016). It can suggest possible decision-making options that can lead to mitigating risks.

Prescriptive analytics in healthcare can completely change the face of modern healthcare where not only the diagnosis will be done very quickly but also the treatment will be based on the patients' medical history. This will lead to a better treatment in terms of medicine incompatibilities and side-effects.

2.5. The Healthcare Big Data Market

The healthcare industry has gained a massive business value during the last couple of years. Fuelled by the large-scale adoption of EHR by governments, hospitals, and physicians, it is expected to grow to US$18.7 Billion by 2020 ("Revolutionizing the Healthcare Industry with Big Data, Analytics and Visualization", 2015). Whereas the healthcare and medical analytics are expected to grow at a CAGR of 27.1% to reach US$24.55 Billion by 2021 from US$7.39 Billion in 2016 (marketsandmarkets.com, 2016). The whole healthcare market will be changed due to the transformation of the healthcare data from the normal data to the Big Data. Big Data allows for change of so many things in the health industry, for example, it provides better data storage facilities at a low cost and also allows one to work on the data at a low cost. The Health Big Data market is open to various possibilities such as using the analytics power of the Big Data by the pharmaceutical companies to give better drugs at cheaper costs, reducing the administrative loads on the physicians. The healthcare Big Data will allow organisations to meet the consumer demand for affordable medical care. One of the major contributions of the goodies of using Big Data technologies in healthcare is applied to the unprivileged countries/states where there are inadequate doctors and medical facilities.

3. THE BIG DATA ADVANTAGE IN HEALTHCARE

Digitization of data accumulated from patient records, prescriptions, medical imaging, laboratory, pharmacy and insurance results in an enormous amount of data that is known as healthcare Big Data. This enormous amount of data can lead to knowledge traces that would significantly improve the quality of medical and healthcare services. The Big Data analysis would infer meaningful insights that help in making informed decisions, disease surveillance, and other healthcare and medical services. Patients, physicians, healthcare organization, pharmaceutical companies, policymakers and other stakeholders will be suitably benefited from the knowledge inferred. The applications would be individual and people in mass health surveillance; predicting health issues of individuals like calculating the medical complication and risk associated with a patient, the disease advancement/progression of disease; analysis of the particular kind of treatment suitable for the person; analysis of current treatment strategies to detect whether the diagnosis and applied treatment are correct or not, and thus adjusting the treatment plan accordingly. It may inform the patient about their current and future health state which allows them to make better-informed decision. The projection of Big Data application into the current medical and health service is advantageous in scaling the quality and accountability of health services, some of the advantages are discussed below (Raghupathi & Raghupathi, 2014).

3.1. Reducing Healthcare Cost

Today's healthcare system is a disease centred model where based on the symptoms of disease and lab reports, physicians reccomend the treatment procedure. The treatment procedure is quite centred on clinical expertise and medical evidence, further based on treatment results, other alternative treatment options are suggested. The treatment procedures are recursive, time-consuming and costly. Healthcare Big Data with the enormous amount of data on medical cases, treatment patterns, medicines and their effectiveness, genetic data allows for a patient-centred model of treatment. This information allows analysing and diagnosing the patient correctly and further predicting the correct treatment pattern. In another application, Big Data in genetics ensures personalized profiling and hence personalized medicine for patient allowing accurate treatment. Healthcare Big Data infer knowledge do actually reconcile the redundant costly treatment procedure (Srinivasan & Arunasalam, 2013).

3.2. Reducing Hospital Readmissions

The probability of patient returning back within a month after treatment at the hospital are getting high. This incurs cost and resource to hospital. Big Data analytics applied to the patient medical record, history, chart information, and the patient lifestyle record can identify the patients who are at risk of having medical complications and again readmission. Thus, identifying the patients who need additional care would able to reduce the hospital readmissions ("Seven Big Data Examples That Have Improved Healthcare Operations", 2016).

3.3. Optimized Workforce

Hospitals and other health organizations critically face the classical problem of recruiting staffs and scheduling them. For many staff recruited, there will be a risk of under usage of resources while minimizing the numbers can lead to poor customer services. This problem can be overcome by the application of Big Data. Big Data obtain data from various sources can well predict the number of patients that would come on the daily and hourly basis. Further, hospital admission record analysis over a time series of years can get the future trend on the type and number of patient that would be admitted to the hospital. The application of data science for crunching the raw data delivers information that would allow the organization to optimize its workforce based on the future requirements (Lebied, 2017).

3.4. Real-Time Alerting

One of the biggest functional advantages of Big Data is real-time alerting. Big Data incorporated into services in hospital and clinics would analyse the medical records of patients and thereby in real-time provides advice to a physician for prescriptive decision. Further patient's medical and health data collected by wearable devices (Pramanik et al., 2019) are being analysed in the cloud in association to Big Data to feed real-time information of patient current medical issues, future medical ailment, and preventive measures. The patients' data being collected over time would allow the doctors to see the health status of people in society and thereby taking corrective strategy for any deviation observed. The real-time data is also shared by the health organization to react immediately to any disturbing results found in patient monitoring (Lebied, 2017).

3.5. Analysing Electronic Health Records (EHRs)

Analysing the enormous electronic health record would make a physician comprehend the treatment trends, their effects, and side effects. Moreover, the Big Data allows the updated patient data to be shared among doctors for their treatments and, also, medical cases are exchanged among doctors thus reducing duplicate test and redundant treatment procedure ("7 Big Data Use Cases for Healthcare", 2016).

3.6. Analysing Hospital Networks

Analysing hospital care and management data would be useful in administrating critical medical condition case, strategies for reducing postoperative infection and analysing the medicine (antibiotics) and treatment procedure carried out by doctors which found ineffective in a cure. ("7 Big Data Use Cases for Healthcare", 2016)

3.7. Control Data for Public Health Research

Medical and health organizations, hospitals and small clinics produce huge medical data. This is overwhelming data for medical professionals. As most of the data are raw, unstructured and cluttered, probably these data in their direct form are difficult for medical professional and policymakers to suitably use in public health regulations and decision making. There is a gap between what health professionals want and to what data exists. These data without the application of Big Data is of no use. Application of data analytics can regularize and standardize the public health data, filling the existing gap and thus providing information that can be applied in various regulation and research work for providing better care and health services ("7 Big Data Use Cases for Healthcare", 2016).

3.8. More Efficient Medical Practice

Big Data helps in providing effective treatment for the patient. Big Data analytics gives knowledge about the diseases, their symptoms, treatment pattern, and medicine effectiveness in different stages of illness to the physician that would help them for better-informed healthcare practice while treating a patient.

3.9. Using Health Data for Informed Strategic Planning

On the outbreak of diseases or growth in chronic disease rate among the population, Big Data on public health records like immunizations, distribution, and availability of medical services enables to design strategies for public health. Big Data map the required services over a region in comparison to the available services and thus inferring what necessary steps need to be taken for controlling the public health issues (Eastwood, 2013).

3.10 Optimizing Workflows in Healthcare

Hospitals have multiple departments, limited patient admission capacity, limited doctors and staff with varying schedule and varying flow of incoming patients with different need and treatment make healthcare services in the hospital very dynamic. The patient's health issues span multiple factors like involving treatment from different departments and different physicians at different stages of treatment, laboratory tests, and medication. Further, there are cases of medical complication for inappropriate diagnosis and treatment and hospital readmissions. This volatile state demands completely planned and managed workflow ready for an emergency and changing situations. Healthcare data enriched by multiple sources of data such as real-time patient data (patient health status, location etc.), medical records of patients, nursing information, laboratory data and machine status (available, working etc.) helps to identify the current operational state of hospital and thus allow to take informed decision for better healthcare services by best utilization of resources ("TF7 Healthcare subgroup", 2016).

3.11. Better Safety Practices

The patients who underwent surgery are often suspected of postoperative infections. Big Data analytics of electronic medical record can well inform in previous the susceptibility of patients for getting an infection. This ensures preventive measures like intensive postoperative care, pre- and post-operation preventive medication etc. This predictive analysis promotes better patient safety ("Seven Big Data Examples That Have Improved Healthcare Operations", 2016).

3.12. Patient Engagement

Today's one of the healthcare challenges is patient's engagement leading to patient's awareness, retention and proactive care. A huge spending is done on the healthcare segment though even after that, patients are never properly taken care of resulting in bigger health problems. Patients engagement are found in getting insights, communication, personal wellness tracking, medical management, new disease diagnosis, personal history, immunization, health cost planning, social services research and clinical trial participation etc. Patients want to be engaged so that they are aware, engaged and feel confident (Shah, 2016). This further improves patients' satisfaction and experience leading to the better outcome. Patient interactions with physicians, hospital and clinic staff, pharmacy and pharmaceutical company, laboratory and other counselling staff increases one's engagement. Controlled and updated data about the patient helps the service provider to attune the services to patient's need, helping patients to be more engaged in managing their health issues. To realize the situation Big Data has contributed to a bigger extent. Using Big Data insight, healthcare providers can identify the individuals with critical illness or need support in terms of insurance, medical counselling, care and managing their medical cases. These people are informed regularly. Patients are delivered with a personalized message or called. The personalized messages make people aware of their individual journey as a patient. Utilising Big Data technologies, when the patient makes contact with the clinic or hospital for healthcare service, the physician or the hospital staff may already be aware of patient's history, communication preference and their healthcare journey (Disch, 2016).

3.13. Big Data Is Helping to Prevent Unnecessary ER Visits

Many often patients frequently visit multiple hospitals and clinics for the same or different ailment or disease which causes repetitive treatment procedure, discontinuity in treatment and in the worst case, a wrong treatment that leads to critical health jeopardy and wastage of money and time. In this direction, the application of Big Data would help the patient in reducing unnecessary visits to medical and health agencies, further make sure the treatment is on the right course. Big Data allows the updated medical record of patient to be shared in emergency department so that when patient shifts between hospitals/clinics or take a new treatment for ailment, the staff will have the knowledge of patient's medical history, treatment procedures carried out, drug administered and the reports of various lab test that are already done. This definitely eases the patient diagnosis, reducing patient overhead and increasing satisfaction (Lebied, 2017).

4. APPLICATIONS OF HEALTHCARE BIG DATA

4.1. Battling the Flu

Flu is an epidemic which may outbreak at any moment of time with potential to spread across in a short period of time. Every year around the world Flu takes millions of lives. Centres for Disease Control and

Prevention (CDC), an operating component of the Department of Health and Human Services in the USA is fighting against disease and their control and prevention. The CDC receives 700,000 reports of patients with Flu-like symptoms every week. Doctors, hospitals, and laboratories send a large amount of data to CDC. The reports include the where and what kind of treatment was given by the physician. Big Data analytics has been tremendously useful to get scientific insight from the data stored over time. CDC has made the information public through FluView, an application developed and deployed at CDC (Nambiar et al., 2013). FluView reports in real time how the influenza is spreading across, along to that how vaccines and antivirals can aid patients etc. It gives doctors the answers they need to effectively battle the outbreak, such as knowing which vaccine is effective to which virus strains and whether or not antiviral drugs will be effective in recovery.

Other similar applications where Big Data have been used to capture and analyse the data on the pandemic are FluNearYou[1] and GermTracker[2]. FluNearYou asks the person to input data on their symptoms; based on the symptoms the application generates a map that can allow users to prepare themselves and take preventive measures against infection. GermTracker takes the data from social media posts and analyses them for the disease outbreak. The huge data obtained thus gives a view of a pandemic which doctors might have missed.

4.2. Diabetes and Big Data

Diabetes has become a major health problem in the world. Most of the people are diagnosed with type2 diabetes, a condition where the body cannot use insulin effectively. In these cases, Insulin injections are administered to patients to control sugar level in blood. Diabetes can be controlled by monitoring the patient's sugar levels regularly and further administrating insulin based on the situation.

In managing diabetes and the betterment of patient health, Common sensing has pioneered smart insulin pen cap technology called GoCap[3]. GoCap is a data-driven smart cap that fits over the injection needle of a standard insulin pen and measures the volume of insulin in the pen. GoCap records the time, amount and kind of insulin in the logbook and further sends the data through the Internet to mobile devices of doctors and family members. The information is also displayed and recorded in the mobile device application. The GoCap mobile application helps the patients to enter information about their food intake and glucose levels at the different time of day. These accumulated data on patients helps the doctors to provide personalized treatment to patients.

4.3. Fight Cancer

Big Data on cancer treatment is an accumulation of data collected from cancer patients at different stages of treatment like pre-detection, pre-treatment and end stage. These data can effectively be used in cancer prediction for new cases. Using the historical data of patients, the predictive machine learning algorithm can well identify cancer. Flatironhealth has developed an Oncology cloud service called OncoCloud (Flatiron, 2017) which aims to gather data during diagnosis and treatment and further make it available to the researcher for their advanced study. Another example of Big Data in cancer treatment programme is the Cancer Moonshot Programme (Orcutt, 2016). Cancer is triggered by genetic changes and often genome information is required for therapeutic treatment. In this direction, Big Data as a huge data repository provides enough information about human genomics, patients case reports and their background details. The valuable insight which can be obtained from these data would help to identify the genetic changes which had trigger cancer in a patient and the treatment procedure. Big Data which consist of millions of readable and usable samples would allow scientist all over the world to analyse and work on the data. For widespread and new trends of treatment, sharing of data is essential so that the medical researcher can use a large amount of data on treatment plans and recovery of cancer patients.

4.4. Improved Diagnosis and Treatment

In the healthcare industry, Big Data plays a pivotal role. The application of Big Data includes analysis of the disease pattern and predicts outbreaks. Furthermore, it allows public health monitoring and tracking epidemic and helps doctors and medical health policymakers to prevent future outbreaks. Big Data allows the doctor to keep an efficient record of patient's medical history and thereby enable doctors to provide proper healthcare service for their patients. Further, the data insight allows doctors to carry diagnosis and treatment of patient located remotely connected to the Internet. The patient can contact doctors and get the advice within a minute. The enablement of IoT helps to monitor patient and raise real-time alerts. Big Data helps both sick and healthy patients to connect doctors for improved health and treatment.

4.5. Tackling Opioid Abuse

Opioid abuse is often described as a new "epidemic" in the world. More than 15000 patients die every year on painkiller drug medication and several thousand are killed for the drug overdose or wrong usage. Pain medication is a tricky area for physicians; depending on individual person's capacity doctors prohibit prescribing the opioid use above a certain threshold. Ignoring the prescribed medication and their dosages, patients misuse the drug intakes and often uses them wrongly to what is called as drug abuse. The responsibility of reducing and preventing the drug abuse is split between the patient himself and the healthcare system. In America, to stop this, monitoring programs have started. This includes maintaining a centralized database with data analytics and decision-making system which detect prescription abnormalities, track drug dispensing patterns and preventing the patient from taking dangerous amounts of opioid. Electronic Prescription for Controlled Substances (EPCS) (HealtIT.gov, 2016) - a standard practice which has helped to reduce the opioid epidemic by enabling the practitioners to prescribe medicine electronically which can be shared and monitored everywhere.

4.6. Precision Medicine

The EHR is a major source of Big Data, the EHR contains sociodemographic, medical, and genetics treatment details which allows scientists and clinicians to predict more accurately for a patient's ailment and further reasons for precision medicine. The precision medicine model allows appropriate therapeutic and preventive approaches based on patients' genetic makeup, lifestyle, and environmental factors that work effectively for an individual.

Doctors are often misled in case of instantaneous diagnosis (for emergency) and symptomatic treatments. Applying data science and analytics over Big Data, precise information based on the patient context can be obtained. This information would serve in making precise prescriptive decisions.

4.7. Evidence-Based Medicine

Around the world, evidence-based medicine (EBM) is a standard way of medication. Clinical trial on diseases or ailment treatment methods includes rigorous experiments on patients and involves risk. It is often difficult to generalize the clinical trial methods testing and often the positive test result on a small group of people may not work on the outside world.

Big Data helps in EBM to sort out and identify the effective clinical methods applied to real patients. By data mining over practice-based clinical data of actual patients, it is easy to find out which patient has gone under what treatment, how well the treatment has done or has it any side effects. The data can then be analysed at an individual level to create a patient data model, which can be aggregated across the population to infer wider insights into disease prevalence, treatment pattern etc. Clinicians match the symptoms to a larger patient database and identify the accurate disease in a faster and efficient way (Marr, 2016).

4.8. Genomic Analytics

Researchers are getting a fascinating new perspective on human genome due to advancements made in Big Data analytics. Since genes are all about information, Big Data is a perfect fit for genetics. Researchers are able to look more closely at human genes and they are applying Big Data analytics in this issue. A typical human genome contains more than 20,000 genes, simply mapping a genome requires 100 gigabytes of data. Sequencing multiple genomes and tracking gene interactions, multiples the number by many times. Much of the work done with the human genome and Big Data analytics deals closely with health and medicine. One of the pioneering application of genetics and Big Data is creating personalized medicine and new drugs. One's gene analysis could help in finding the inheritable traits that can be passed to the next generation. This is specifically important for people who are susceptible to passing disease like diabetes, anaemia, heart disease, cancer, obesity etc to their child. Big Data analytics helps the researcher in understanding the human genome and they can get a view of future diseases.

4.9. Clinical Operations

Big Data accumulating a large amount of clinical data from various sources can assist staff in clinical operations. It helps in enhancing the operation of healthcare facilities, the quality of clinical trial and research. Clinicians can do the comparative studies on different patient cases in the different area of treatments. Big Data has changed the mindset of researchers from hypothesis-based treatment to the research-based analysis on a large amount of data resulting in accurate treatment method.

4.10. Patient Monitoring

The wide adoption of EHR in hospitals and clinics has enriched Big Data. Big Data provides a deep Clinical knowledge and understanding of disease and illness. For patient monitoring, various sensors are used to screen for patient's vital statistic like blood pressure, heartbeat, respiratory, oxygen in the blood, and sugar level etc. Any change in the data pattern is analysed along with Big Data and further alerts are raised for preventative measures. Big Data having patient's past medical knowledge, analyses the current statistics to predict the future medical complication and ailments.

4.11. Medical Device and Pharma Supply-Chain Management

Proper functioning of hospitals and clinics availability medical devices and pharmaceutical supplies are proper in quantity is of utmost importance. Many hospitals are not implementing the appropriate supply chain strategies, this cost to hospitals in terms of poor quality services. Nonstandard ordering methods and unnecessary product may cause stockpiling similarly also may cause in supply deficiency. The supply chain is not only about the product but also about the people who buy, move and use them.

Implementing Big Data analytics and automation tool makes supply chain management much easier. Automation allows clinicians to spend more time delivering high-quality care and less time to find for products availability. Technology like RFID (radio frequency identification) has been used for tracking products. The stocking products are fitted with a scannable tag which can provide information about items, manufacturing date, expiry date and shipping date, which allows providers to track the object throughout its life cycle. Predicting the number and type of patient and the supplies required allows maintaining the stock at its optimum level. For the stock, level decreases automatic stock ordering is done (Castle & Szymanski, 2008) (Uzsoy, 2005).

4.12. Drug Discovery and Development Analysis

Drug discovery requires and processing and analysing of unstructured and structured biomedical data obtained from various surveys and experiments. This includes data regarding gene sequencing, protein interaction data, drug data, electronic patient records and clinical trials, self-reporting data etc. These data collected in a huge amount from various sources over time has enriched the medical information base. The pharmaceutical company, while designing a new drug or applying clinical trial, applies analytics to these data to infer knowledge and to build a predictive model for new drug design. This usage of past data has made the drug discovery and development faster in comparison to the traditional method (Jawadekar, 2016).

4.13. Big Data for Personalised Healthcare

There is a rapid advancement in genomic technologies. With large sources of data, it is easier for healthcare professionals to understand the disease mechanisms which leads to better treatment of patients. Many diseases have preventable risk factors. A clear understanding of disease characteristics helps in personalized healthcare and thus reduces the chances of getting the disease. Healthcare professional takes patient's history, do the physical examination and laboratory testing to identify the risk of disease in future. The application of Big Data in this direction makes the process fast and easy. Analytic on patient's health and medical profile gives a personalized medical view which is specific to a patient. The personalized profile for treatment is derived not only from the particular patient's electronic medical report but also from other similar types of patients' case records. Personalized healthcare enables disease risk profiling, disease management plans and wellness plan for an individual patient.

4.14. Infection Prevention, Prediction, and Control

According to the European Centre for disease prevention & control, every year estimated 100,000 patients are infected with hospital-acquired infection (HAI). It is estimated that around 37,000 people died with direct consequences of infections per year. The World Health Organization (WHO) has strict guidelines which can minimize the risk of spreading infections. Some guidelines are easy to follow and some are hard to implement due to limited technology. In this direction, Big Data technology integrates genomics with epidemiology data in order to not just control but also to prevent as well as envisage the possibility of the spread of infections within hospitals and clinics ("TF7 Healthcare subgroup", 2016).

4.15. Health Insurance Fraud Detection

Healthcare fraud is a big problem all over the world. Over the last decade, the healthcare industry had spent billions of dollars on improper claims. More than 1.5 million people have been victimized. These statistics represent avoidable healthcare cost. Healthcare industry is applying analytical controls throughout the treatment process and also incorporating the claims review process. Review process incorporates rule-based data analytics and predictive modelling. The treatment procedure carried and the medicine administrated over the patient is analysed for similar symptom cases to find out whether the treatment and drug used are legitimate as per the context or vague one ("Seven Big Data Examples That Have Improved Healthcare Operations", 2016).

5. USE CASE EXAMPLES

5.1. Asthmapolis

Asthmapolis has launched a GPS enabled tracker called propeller that records the usage of asthma medicine by asthmatics. It helps the medical practitioner to treat asthma more effectively. Propeller[4] uses Bluetooth sensors-based inhaler, mobile application, and advanced analytics. The sensor records information that when and where the patient suffered from an asthma attack and used the inhaler. The information is transferred to a centralized database to be combined with the information at the Center for Disease Control. The combined information identifies the trends and catalyst of asthma attacks in individuals and aggregating the pattern with mass population. This leading information would help the physician to identify when the risk of an asthma attack is higher, and further help them in personalized treatment for asthma patients.

5.2. 23andMe

23andMe[5] is a privately-held personal genomics and biotechnology company. The company is named for 23 pairs of the chromosome in a normal human cell. It is saliva-based direct to consumer genetic testing business. 23andMe extract the genome information from the person saliva for delivering back to the customer. The company has built a huge genetic information bank. The aggregated customer data are available for research team employed by 23andMe and other scientific groups for inherited disorders and other diseases. 23andMe provides raw genetic data which in its original form are not meaningful in different genetic studies. Promethease a personalized online tool for health genetic information processes the raw data from 23andMe and provides personal DNA report (Ramsey, 2015).

5.3. USC Medical Monitor

Parkinson's disease is affecting millions of people today. By 2030 it will be doubled. Since this disease affects a patient's movement, it is important to monitor the patient's mobility condition. In the University of Southern California, computer scientists are teamed up with neurologists, kinesiologist & public health experts to fight against Parkinson's disease (Nambiar et al., 2013). They use different types of devices to monitor patient's movement throughout the day and gather a large amount of data about patient's abnormal movements through 3D sensors, mobile devices and from wearable sensors. The acquired patient data is fitted into algorithms which analyses the kind of changes in movements. The analysed data and reports are sent to researchers and caregivers. Depending on the motion abnormalities alert are sent to the caregiver, depending on which they prescribe appropriate medication and exercises (Nambiar et al., 2013).

5.4. GNS Healthcare and Aetna

Applying Big Data analytics, GNS Healthcare[6] in collaboration with Aetna[7], an insurance-based company aims to treat and prevent metabolic syndrome. The metabolic syndrome can increase the risk of heart disease, strokes and diabetes. GNS uses the claims and health information from Aetna, as a platform called - Reverse Engineering, Forward Simulation (REFS) to create data-driven models. GNS healthcare analyses the risk of getting metabolic syndrome depending on the five conditions i.e. increased waist size, high blood pressure, high triglyceride level, HDL cholesterol and high blood sugar. GNS analysed the data of 37000 Aetna's customers who participated voluntarily in the screening program of metabolic syndrome (Nambiar et al., 2013). The analysed data includes claims, records, pharmacy claims, demographics, laboratory test, biometric screening. GNS & Aetna team uses two analytical models:

1. Claim based model
2. Both claim and biometric data based model

Both analytical models predicted future risk of metabolic syndrome in both population and individual (Nambiar et al., 2013).

5.5. WestMed Medical Group

In the WestMed medical group, as the medical practice growing day by day, the number of physicians grows from 16 to 250. The physicians are seeing 250,000 patients with annual revenue of $255 million ("7 Big Data Use Cases for Healthcare", 2016). Using Big Data, the medical practitioner is now capable of analysing more than 2,200 procedures. The Big Data has helped in streamlining the workflow, shifted clinical work from doctors to nurses, reduced unnecessary testing, and improved patient satisfaction.

5.6. HealthCore (WellPoint)

Healthcore[8] is a clinical outcome research subsidiary of Wellpoint Inc. Healthcore has a team of highly experienced researchers including physicians, pharmacists, epidemiologists, health economists and scientists. They measure safety, efficacy, and effectiveness, compliance of drug, medical devices, and care management interventions in the real-world settings ("Epidomiology and Genomics Research Program", 2018). The Healthcore uses data from different sources like health plan providers, patient's reported information, clinical information from physicians that allows the researchers to answer complex clinical, economic and health policy questions. HealthCore interprets health data and estimates the influence of disease, their treatment and care on the outcome.

5.7. Evolent Health

Evolent Health[9] (previously Valence Health) provides value-based care solutions for health sector like hospitals, health systems and physicians to help them to effectively manage patient populations. Based on each client requirements, customized value-based care model for clinically integrated networks, population health management, health plan administration & TPA, risk adjustment, pharmacy benefit management is designed, built and managed. To handle customer's enormous and heterogeneous data, Evolent Health has adopted Big Data technology. Evolent health has been using MapR for building data repository for storing huge data. MapR offers a distributed data platform to store and analyze Big Data in a distributed fashion which is linearly scalable which can be extended just by adding more machines and/or CPUs, without changing the application code. The MapR platform delivers enterprise-grade security, reliability & real-time performance which lowers both hardware and operational costs of most applications and data. Evolent consumes 3000 inbound data feeds with 45 different types of data. This data includes lab test result, patients' health records, prescriptions, pharmacy records and claims and payment records which are used to make decisions about improving healthcare outcomes & reimbursement. Prior to the MapR, the company takes 20 hours to 22 hours to process millions of data. But MapR cuts the time to 20 minutes, which also requires less hardware.

5.8. United Healthcare

United Healthcare[10] provides health benefits and services to millions of people. Their payment team has the tough task of ensuring the claims are paid correctly and on time and not paying for the fraudulent services. They shifted to a predictive modelling environment based on Hadoop which provides a flexible (seamless integration of new tools and technologies) and cost-effective platform with enterprise-grade features (e.g. high availability and disaster recovery). Bringing the information about claims, prescriptions, plan participants, contracted care providers and associated claim review outcomes to a single framework thus people at United Healthcare are able to identify inaccurate claims in a systematic and repeatable way ("UnitedHealthcare uses Hadoop to Detect Health Care Fraud, Waste and Abuse", 2018). With the help of the data integration from different data silo, it has become easier to find out the fraudulent. United Healthcare also started using NLP to better understand customer satisfaction by converting records of customer's voice (who calls to its call enter) into text and search the indications of customer's dissatisfaction.

5.9. OptumInsight

Optum Labs[11], a collaborative research and development initiative of the Optum Inc of United Health Group and the Mayo Clinic, is pursuing a variety of Big Data analytics projects aiming to improve patient care and costs reduction. It is combining electronic medical record from Mayo & other healthcare organization with claims data from United Healthcare to understand and provide better and more effective health care and also to analyze the total cost of care for specific procedures or diseases (Cambridge & Rochester, 2013).

5.10. Liaison Technologies

Liaison Technology[12] offers a cloud-based solution which provides organizations with the ability to integrate, manage and secure data across the enterprise. They are particularly active in the healthcare industry where a patient's record may be stored in many systems in different formats. The storage is updated in real-time as per the streaming data so that the user always gets the up-to-date view of the data in a single location and in a most suitable format (McDonald, 2017).

5.11. Novartis Genomics

Next Generation Sequencing[13] (NGS), a research initiative carried out at Genomics Institute of the Novartis Research Foundation, is a Big Data application that deals with a huge volume of heterogeneous data. The data includes genome information and other medical data. NGS requires heavy interaction with diverse data from external organizations for experimental and other associated data. The Novartis Genomics suffers from two problems, one integrating heterogeneous datasets and the other in integrating public datasets. To address the problem Big Data technologies like MapReduce and Apache Spark are being used by Novartis. As a result, the combined Spark & MapReduce based workflow and integration layer allow the company's life science researchers to meaningfully take advantage of thousands of experiments that different public organization have conducted (McDonald, 2017) and thus helped in accelerating drug research.

6. CHALLENGES

The major challenges of using the Big Data in healthcare is that health data is completely distributed i.e. one cannot find a complete repository of data related to a patient at one location and in a homogeneous form (Lebied, 2017). The above statement basically points out that we'll need new infrastructure so that data can collaborate together. We have to add other new technologies to the existing older ones like predictive analysis, machine learning and graph analytics (Lebied, 2017). Some important challenges in healthcare Big Data are discussed below.

6.1. Expertise

Whenever a new technology is introduced, expertise on that technology is not achieved overnight. We must understand that most of the hospital IT staffs are not trained to used Big Data. They are familiar with SQL programming. To resolve this knowledge gap quickly and cost-effectively Big Data must allow itself to be extremely user-friendly.

The whole scenario here is that if the expertise of the user is not in the current technology he/she will lose interest in it very quickly and the investment in the technology will be dead. To avoid such mishaps, we the organisations which convert to the Big Data architecture must use various tools which help in bridging the gap between the new technology and the old. The tools must allow for the usage of the languages know previously i.e. the architecture must have backward compatibility. Creating a correct balance of backward compatibility and the new architecture must be balanced for the results.

6.2. Costly Processing and Analysis

The most common challenge in any data processing architecture is that the cost of processing the data. The medical data which comes from various pathological tests itself comes at a huge cost due to the requirement of sophisticated equipment's required to conduct the test. Add to this cost the processing charges for the additional analysis of the data to diagnose a specific disease. To understand the cost and analysis of the medical data, we must come to terms that present-day medical diagnosis and the further prognosis are completely based on the symptoms shown by the patient. These symptoms can be the same for multiple diseases thus leading to a further increase in cost for the diagnosis of the disease. We can very well say that proper handling of the data and its analysis is a very big challenge.

6.3. Security and Privacy

The collection of health data and creating EHR is the way of digitalizing the health data. The major problem with digitalization is the security of the data as well as maintaining the privacy of the patient to whom the data belongs to. The analysis of healthcare data must be done with keeping in mind that under no circumstances the privacy and the personal information of the patient are known anyone including the system i.e. a level of privacy encryption must be imposed on the data that is to be analysed (Patil & Seshadri, 2014). The security architecture of the cloud (or where ever the data is stored) must prevent data breaches and even if breaches cannot be completely avoided try to make sure that data is not traceable to any patient to whom they belong.

6.4. Ransomware Threat

Ransomware is classified as programs that infect the victim's system and prevents the victim from using the system until the ransom is paid. Ransomware basically encrypts the user's files and data and withholds the key to decryption as ransom. Hospitals are particularly vulnerable to this type of attack as the security systems employed by them are not up to the mark thus making the hospitals and medical data repositories as soft targets for such attacks. One can easily understand this as hospitals need their data on a day-to-day basis as the patients' lives depend on the data generated. To process healthcare data, we must up the security from various sources from where the data is collected so that the main systems are not compromised by these attacks.

Ransomware threats can be further reduced by utilising proper antivirus software's as well as having strict monitoring of the data. Also, regular backups of data to places which are completely secure can help from prevention as well as recovery of the valuable data.

6.5. E-Mail Vulnerability in Healthcare

E-mail vulnerability emanates from the various ways in which an email can be used to install a malicious code in the system which in turn can lead to theft of data. As more and more health data are being digitalized, health institutions are falling prey to more and more email-based attacks like phishing, where the people working in those institutions are conned into activating the attack themselves. To remove or to fight against such vulnerabilities, we must follow a three-step approach which includes proactively monitoring the threats to the continuous management of security ("Email Vulnerability in Healthcare", 2017). Also, we must bank for the worst possibility that the data is siphoned off and go for rapid incident response and recovery.

6.6. Data Governance

Data governance is the practice of managing the data assets throughout the lifecycle of the asset so that it meets the organizational needs throughout its lifetime as well as maintains its integrity (Bresnick, 2016). Data governance is required for the health data because as we are digitalizing the data if it is not properly organized, updated and maintained then that data cannot be used for anything other record keeping. We must understand that data governance is important for analytics perspective. To find more from the data we need the data to be organized rather than just being electronic. Some possible solutions to this can be that healthcare institutions hire dedicated data entry operators in their company.

6.7. Data Management

As the digitalization of the healthcare data is done, the need to manage such data also grows. We can't implement traditional methods as our analysis model is based on Big Data architecture. We must manage the data in such a way so that the maximum amount of data is always available for processing. Below are the ways via which data can be managed ("TF7 Healthcare subgroup", 2016):

- **Data Quality:** The quality of data used for processing is important as if we feed low-quality data to the system the analysis of the data will not be worth the effort. We need to focus on data quality as it is the only raw material in the system which will be used to generate valuable results. For every data that is used we must be aware of how the data was collected, conditions under which the observations were made, and how the contents were processed and transformed. This enables reproducibility of experiments as well as the reliability of the data. The quality of the data can significantly influence the conclusion of the whole analysis.
- **Data Quantity:** The quantity of data used for analytics plays a very large role in the healthcare sector. We must understand that this sector is knowledge-intensive and requires data and analytics to improve its practices. The quantity of data used in the analysis, allows us to draw greater insights into the processes. Also, if the quantity of data is less, then the whole analysis can sometimes become questionable as lack of data may not provide proper authenticity to the analysis.
- **Multi-Modal Data:** The healthcare data as mentioned earlier comes from various sources. All these data have various formats used by their respective system. This data can be further classified into structured and unstructured data. The system should accept both the data and try to find synergy among it. This type of integration of data from all sources are helpful in finding new cures for diseases or finding the genomic point of view of disease i.e. can a disease be genetically transferred to the next generation or even if transferred will it remain dormant or not. These types of analysis require data from all the kinds of sources like ancestry of a person, family history of

diseases, his/her habits as well as of their family's etc. thus we can say that multi-modal data integration and analysis plays a pivotal role in healthcare analysis.

- **Data Access:** All the analysis of the data and its inference is only possible when and only when access to data is provided. The biggest challenge of today is getting the data i.e. getting access to the data after bypassing the various privacy laws, security barriers etc. and to add hurt to the injury these laws vary from country to country. The health data is highly fragmented i.e. data is distributed among hospitals, pathologies or even specialists whom the patients contact. One of the possible solutions could be that we ask patients to willingly give their data to the analytic system so that all the red tape can be cut easily.
- **Patient-Generated Data:** The patient-generated data (PGD) refers to the data which is generated by the patient's devices and gives us an insight about the patient's habits and can also let us know about the diseases he/she is prone to or maybe suffering from. PGD also provides ways to monitor recently released patients from hospitals and continuously monitor their progress. The major challenge in PGD is that there are various types of devices, a present which is all not compatible with each other as there is no standardization about them. This causes problems and conflicts with the data that is generated.
- **Data Integration:** As it is already known that health data is heterogeneous, so before performing analytics on it we need to integrate the data from all the sources. The data integration in itself is a very big challenge as the data that is provided may be or may not be structurally compatible to each other i.e. they all may exhibit a level of structural heterogeneity if this remains the analysis can be incomplete or inconclusive. To solve this problem, we can use information extraction mechanisms in conjunction with machine learning and semantic web technologies which will help us to get homogeneously integrated data for analysis.

6.8. Fragmented Analytics

As the cost of centralized analytics systems is very high, the industries are now moving towards fragmented analytics model i.e. we analyse the heterogeneous data in fragments and then try to combine the analytics results (Bresnick, 2015). For the healthcare industry, it is assumed that it will not be successful to a very large extent as it is considered to fail at data integration and reporting of states. The Fragmented analytics model is a cheap way of implementing any data analytics system, thus a possible solution can be to maintain tables which show a correlation which previously exists among data and then use that table for data integration and reporting.

6.9. Choosing the Right Healthcare Big Data Analytics Tools

Till now we have seen the various challenges that plague the Big Data applications in healthcare. Adding further to that, we would like to elaborate on how choosing the right Big Data tool also a challenge. We must understand here that the tools must be chosen on the basis of use otherwise we'll end up increasing the cost of the whole architecture, and not even get the proper result. For example, suppose we want to use the Big Data architecture for clinical analysis and not for qualitative benchmarking (Bresnick, 2015). We must understand that the organisations must self-evaluate them and then order better tools which provide better optimisations and digestible reports (Bresnick, 2016).

7. HEALTHCARE BIG DATA IMPLEMENTATION ENVIRONMENTS

7.1. Platforms and Tools

Big Data is implemented in the healthcare domain using various tools. Below some tools and their uses are mentioned:

7.1.1. The Hadoop Distributed File System (HDFS)

The HDFS (Shvachko et al., 2010) is a cluster file system which is used to store structured and unstructured Big Data across multiple systems in a large-scale cluster (Sarkar, 2017). It allows Hadoop to process the massively-scaled volume of data in a fault-tolerant manner. HDFS is used in the healthcare system to collect and aggregate related data while maintaining the data security and privacy in an effectively better way compared to traditional storage systems (Raghupathi & Raghupathi, 2014) (Sarkar, 2017).

7.1.2. MapReduce

MapReduce[14] is a programming model for implementing, analysing and generating Big Data sets. The programming model is composed of the map and reduce methods. The map methods do filtering and data sorting whereas the reduce method summarizes the data. The MapReduce follows the divide-and-conquer approach i.e. it solves by reducing the problem into smaller sub-problems or the input data into independent chunks which are processed completely in parallel, and then the result is combined (Raghupathi & Raghupathi, 2014) (Sarkar, 2017). This algorithm provides a fault-tolerant and flexible way to analyse large data sets over distributed architecture. For large data sets like health data, the data is analysed over a distributed architecture and then the results are collected from different points of processing and combined.

7.1.3. Pig and PigLatin

Pig[15] is a data processing architecture built on top of Hadoop. Pig is designed for making Hadoop simpler to approach and use. The Pig tool can be used for easy and faster cleaning and analyses of big data sets. The pig execution has two modes the Local and Hadoop mode. The PigLatin is a script-based language to express data flow, data input and operation on data to produce the desired output (Hurwitz et al., 2013). The simple and easy to write PigLatin language is used to write programs that bring the structured, unstructured and semi-structured data to the fold which is used to convert and accommodate heterogeneous health data.

7.1.4. Hive

Apache Hive[16] is data warehouse software built over the top of Apache Hadoop. It facilitates data summarization, query writing and processing, and data analysis. Hive helps us easily write queries for getting the results. Hive is a support architecture which supports the structured query language (SQL). It allows the programmers to write queries similar to SQL thus allowing, people to use the Big Data architecture who are unfamiliar with it (Raghupathi & Raghupathi, 2014). Hive helps in maintaining the backward compatibility with the older systems, which worked on SQL, thus allowing for people trained SQL to directly work in the Big Data architecture.

7.1.5. Zookeeper

Apache Zookeeper[17] is a centralized service for distributed systems, it provides maintaining configuration information, registry naming, distributed synchronization and group services. Zookeeper allows synchronization across the resource cluster i.e. it maintains some control regarding which process should use which resource. It helps in parallel computing, by providing centralized resource management services (Raghupathi & Raghupathi, 2014).

7.1.6. HBase

HBase[18] is a Hadoop database which works on non-SQL approach and is easily able to hold all types of data. It is architecturally placed above the HDFS (Hadoop Distributed File System) (Raghupathi & Raghupathi, 2014). It helps in assimilating heterogeneous data and allows reading and writing, randomly in Big Data.

7.1.7. Cassandra

Cassandra[19] is a distributed database system which helps in handling large quantities of data spread across various utility servers (Raghupathi & Raghupathi, 2014). This database helps in health data analysis by allowing us to easily access the data stored on various servers.

7.1.8. Oozie

Oozie[20] is basically used to streamline workflow among tasks (Raghupathi & Raghupathi, 2014). It works by creating synchs among the various parties/processes involved in the system so that conflict does not occur and the workflow moves smoothly.

7.1.9. Mahout

Mahout[21] provides machine learning applications that are helpful in the predictive analysis of healthcare Big Data (Raghupathi & Raghupathi, 2014). It helps in creating applications such that they can learn from past data and able to correlate and analyse similar situations which give results faster, thus making the system more efficient.

7.1.10. Avro

Avro ("Apache Avro™ 1.8.2 Documentation", 2017) provides data serialization services (Raghupathi & Raghupathi, 2014). In healthcare industries, serialization of patients' medical history helps in diagnosing the disease he/she is suffering from or may suffer (observing some pre-symptoms).

7.1.11. Lucene

Apache Lucene[22] is one of the most widely used frameworks for information retrieval. It offers efficient text searching and analysis. It can be used to explore the EMR to satisfy patient-related queries. It can effectively be used in the diagnosis and analysing patient's reports (Raghupathi & Raghupathi, 2014). Also, Lucene can help in analysing the patient's handwriting which can determine his/her psychological state.

7.2. Architectures

7.2.1. Cloud Computing

Cloud architecture provides the most promising architecture for the health industry to switch over to the Big Data platform. Cloud allows the trouble-free and uncomplicated way to collect data in one place and then distribute it among its specialized facilities for further processing thus allowing for a secure way of processing and analysing the data (Pramanik et al., 2018). The cloud architecture provides a centralized data repository from which data is readily accessible for the Big Data analytics. The security of these structures is dependable; also, they allow the usage of the redundancy for reliability. The redundancy in the cloud architecture allows the system to have a protection against possible crashes.

7.2.2. In-Memory Computing

This is a fairly new architecture which provides real-time analysis (Mian et al., 2014). This architecture involves in-memory SQL databases. The basic advantage of in-memory computing is that it is much faster than the traditional systems as disk access time is removed from the equation. This type of architecture is suitable where real-time analysis of data is required (Pramanik & Choudhury, 2018). This architecture can be used even with non-SQL databases. The only drawback of it is that if the system crashes for any reason recovery is near impossible.

7.3. Infrastructure for Big Data in Healthcare

7.3.1. Cisco

Cisco major focus of research is IoT (Internet of Things). For such purpose, Cisco is also working on the processing architecture of IoT data called Fog (Cisco, 2015) (Pramanik et al. 2018). The major application of Fog and IoT is in the healthcare sector. The use of IoT has enabled the health industry, to create a right strategy to deliver the proper healthcare to the patients. Physicians are now able to use the clouds and all the computing powers to securely know about their patient's wellbeing as well as are able to diagnose the disease at an early stage even if the patient is at some distance away from them.

The mobility is the key here which allows the physicians, patients and the administration to be on the same page and provide the best medical care available to the patient.

7.3.2. Watson Health

Watson Health[23] is a complete package developed by IBM, which helps in all aspects of health. It has artificial intelligence as well as machine learning capabilities that help in providing effective diagnosis and medication of the diseases and reduces the job of the hospital staff and people in patient care. Watson can learn about the patient's medical history and is able to provide recommendations to the physician of all the possible new drugs or techniques available in the market, thus saving the time of the physicians to go through all the literature.

7.3.3. Philips HealthSuite

HealthSuite ("About HealthSuite", 2018) is an open cloud-based digital platform designed for the continuous health and personalized care of the user. The suite contains the power of analysing, sharing and orchestrating healthcare services. The analysis part utilizes the machine learning algorithms and various predictive analysis techniques. The sharing features are basically the interoperability of the platform form multiple devices. The orchestrating basically implement the workflow synch, communication like task etc. ("A Cloud-based Platform: Purpose-built for Healthcare", 2018).

8. CONCLUSION

Big Data has influenced almost all the industries in recent years. Healthcare is also no exception. In fact, the healthcare industry is the largest producer of the digital data. Big Data technologies have opened up new opportunities in healthcare. It not only has brought the advantages to the patients but also to the healthcare units and hospitals. To maximise the benefits, careful consideration should be given in adopting the right Big Data tools and the underlying architecture. Though Big Data technology has a significant impact on modern healthcare it needs to progress further to realise its fullest potential. The traditional healthcare system is still lacking in becoming accustomed to the 'big' change. Nevertheless, Big Data has set healthcare industry on the righteous trajectory of rapid transformation and that will surely bring startling benefits to the mankind.

REFERENCES

A Cloud-based Platform: Purpose-built for Healthcare. (2018). Retrieved July 24, 2017, from http://www.usa.philips.com/healthcare/innovation/about-health-suite

About HealthSuite. (2018). Retrieved April 29, 2018, from https://www.philips.co.in/healthcare/innovation/about-health-suite

Apache Avro™ 1.8.2 Documentation. (2017, August 2). Retrieved April 29, 2018, from https://avro.apache.org/docs/current/

Big Data Use Cases for Healthcare. (2016, October 8). Retrieved July 24, 2017, from http://www.ingrammicroadvisor.com/data-center/7-big-data-use-cases-for-healthcare

Bresnick, J. (2015, September 18). *Healthcare Big Data Analytics Suffers from "Fragmented" Approach.* Retrieved May 26, 2017, from http://healthitanalytics.com/news/healthcare-big-data-analytics-suffers-from-fragmented-approach

Bresnick, J. (2015, January 13). *How to Select a Big Data Analytics, Business Intelligence Vendor.* Retrieved July 14, 2017, from https://healthitanalytics.com/news/how-to-select-a-big-data-analytics-business-intelligence-vendor

Bresnick, J. (2016a). *How to Choose the Right Healthcare Big Data Analytics Tools.* Retrieved July 14, 2017, from https://healthitanalytics.com/features/how-to-choose-the-right-healthcare-big-data-analytics-tools

Bresnick, J. (2016b). *The Difference Between Big Data and Smart Data in Healthcare.* Retrieved July 14, 2017, from https://healthitanalytics.com/features/the-difference-between-big-data-and-smart-data-in-healthcare

Bresnick, J. (2016c). *The Role of Healthcare Data Governance in Big Data Analytics.* Retrieved July 14, 2017, from https://healthitanalytics.com/features/the-role-of-healthcare-data-governance-in-big-data-analytics

Bresnick, J. (2017, June 5). *Understanding the Many V's of Healthcare Big Data Analytics.* Retrieved July 20, 2018, from Health IT Analytics: https://healthitanalytics.com/news/understanding-the-many-vs-of-healthcare-big-data-analytics

Brown, N. (2015, September 11). *Healthcare Data Growth: An Exponential Problem.* Retrieved August 8, 2017, from http://www.nextech.com/blog/healthcare-data-growth-an-exponential-problem

Cambridge, Mass & Rochester, Minn. (2013, January 15). *Optum, Mayo Clinic Partner to Launch Optum Labs: An Open, Collaborative Research and Innovation Facility Focused on Better Care for Patients.* Retrieved April 20, 2018, from https://www.optum.com/about/news/optum-labs.html

Castle, B. L., & Szymanski, G. (2008). Supply Chain Management on Clinical Units. In eBusiness in Healthcare (pp. 197-217). London: Springe.

Cisco. (2015). *Fog Computing and the Internet of Things: Extend.* Cisco. Retrieved from https://www.cisco.com/c/dam/en_us/solutions/trends/iot/docs/computing-overview.pdf

Crapo, J. (2017). *Big Data in Healthcare: Separating The Hype From The Reality.* Retrieved July 27, 2017, from https://www.healthcatalyst.com/healthcare-big-data-realities

Disch, W. (2016, August 11). *How to Use Big Data to Improve Patient Engagement.* Retrieved 8 2017, from http://data-informed.com/how-to-use-big-data-to-improve-patient-engagement/

Eastwood, B. (2013, April 23). *6 Big Data Analytics Use Cases for Healthcare IT.* Retrieved July 24, 2017, from http://www.cio.com/article/2386531/healthcare/healthcare-6-big-data-analytics-use-cases-for-healthcare-it.html

Epidomiology and Genomics Research Program. (2018, April 5). Retrieved April 29, 2018, from https://epi.grants.cancer.gov/pharm/pharmacoepi_db/healthcore.html

Evolve, I. P. (2017). *Email Vulnerability in Healthcare.* Retrieved from http://www.evolveip.net/lp/email-vulnerability-healthcare

Flatiron. (2017). *Community Oncology.* Retrieved 8 2017, from https://flatiron.com/community-oncology/

Groves, P., Kayyali, B., Knott, D., & Kuiken, S. V. (2013). *The 'big data' revolution in healthcare.* McKinsey & Company.

HealtIT.gov. (2016, November 4). *Electronic Prescribing of Controlled Substances (EPCS).* Retrieved 8 2017, from https://www.healthit.gov/opioids/epcs

Hurwitz, J., Nugent, A., Halper, F., & Kaufman, M. (2013). *Hadoop Pig and Pig Latin for Big Data.* Wiley.

IDC. (2014). *The Digital Universe Driving Data Growth in Healthcare.* IDC. Retrieved August 7, 2017, from http://www.emc.com/analyst-report/digital-universe-healthcare-vertical-report-ar.pdf

Jawadekar, D. M. (2016, August 4). *Big Data and Pharmaceutical Drug Discovery.* Retrieved August 2017, from https://pharma.elsevier.com/pharma-rd/big-data-and-pharmaceutical-drug-discovery/

Lebied, M. (2017, May 24). *9 Examples of Big Data Analytics in Healthcare That Can Save People.* Retrieved July 26, 2017, from http://www.datapine.com/blog/big-data-examples-in-healthcare/

Leventhal, R. (2014, January 10). *Industry expert: "Big data is closer than it appears".* Retrieved August 2017, from https://www.healthcare-informatics.com/article/how-healthcare-organizations-can-turn-big-data-smart-data

Leventhal, R. (2014, December 4). *Report: Healthcare Data is Growing Exponentially, Needs Protection.* Retrieved August 7, 2017, from https://www.healthcare-informatics.com/news-item/report-healthcare-data-growing-exponentially-needs-protection

marketsandmarkets.com. (2016). *Healthcare Analytics/Medical Analytics Market.* Retrieved August 7, 2017, from http://www.marketsandmarkets.com/Market-Reports/healthcare-data-analytics-market-905.html

Marr, B. (2016, February 16). *How Big Data Is Transforming Medicine.* Retrieved August 2017, from https://www.forbes.com/sites/bernardmarr/2016/02/16/how-big-data-is-transforming-medicine/#244b70277ddc

McDonald, C. (2017, February 27). *5 Big Data Production Examples in Healthcare.* Retrieved July 24, 2017, from https://mapr.com/blog/5-big-data-production-examples-healthcare/

Mian, M., Teredesai, A., Hazel, D., Pokuri, S., & Uppala, K. (2014). In-Memory Analysis for Healthcare Big Data. *IEEE International Congress on Big Data.*

Nambiar, R., Sethi, A., Bhardwaj, R., & Vargheese, R. (2013). A Look at Challenges and Opportunities of Big Data Analytics in Healthcare. *IEEE International Conference on Big Data.* 10.1109/BigData.2013.6691753

Orcutt, M. (2016, June 29). *The Rocket Fuel for Biden's "Cancer Moonshot"? Big Data.* Retrieved April 29, 2018, from https://www.technologyreview.com/s/601784/white-house-cancer-moonshot-data/

Patil, H. K., & Seshadri, R. (2014). Big data security and privacy issues in healthcare. *IEEE International Congress on Big Data.*

Pramanik, P. K. D., & Choudhury, P. (2018). IoT Data Processing: The Different Archetypes and their Security & Privacy Assessments. In *Internet of Things (IoT) Security: Fundamentals, Techniques and Applications.* River Publishers. doi:10.4018/978-1-5225-4044-1.ch007

Pramanik, P. K. D., Pal, S., Brahmachari, A., & Choudhury, P. (2018). Processing IoT Data: From Cloud to Fog. It's Time to be Down-to-Earth. In Applications of Security, Mobile, Analytic and Cloud (SMAC) Technologies for Effective Information Processing and Management. pp. 124-148. IGI Global. doi:10.4018/978-1-5225-4044-1.ch007

Pramanik, P. K. D., Upadhyay, B., Pal, S., & Pal, T. (2018). Internet of Things, Smart Sensors, and Pervasive Systems: Enabling the Connected and Pervasive Health Care. In *Healthcare Data Analytics and Management.* Elsevier.

Raghupathi, W., & Raghupathi, V. (2014). Big data analytics in healthcare: promise and potential. *Health Information Science and Systems, 2*(3).

Ramsey, L. (2015, December 23). *I tried 23andMe's new genetics test - and now I know why the company caused such a stir.* Retrieved August 2017, from http://www.businessinsider.in/I-tried-23andMes-new-genetics-test-and-now-I-know-why-the-company-caused-such-a-stir/articleshow/50302664.cms

Revolutionizing the Healthcare Industry with Big Data, Analytics and Visualization. (2015). Retrieved August 2, 2018, from https://www.einfochips.com/whitepaper/Revolutionizing-the-Healthcare-Industry-with-Big-Data-Analytics-and-Visualization.pdf

Sarkar, B. K. (2017). Big data for secure healthcare system: A conceptual design. *Complex Intelligent Systems, 3*(2), 133–151. doi:10.100740747-017-0040-1

Seven Big Data Examples That Have Improved Healthcare Operations. (2016, April 19). Retrieved July 24, 2017, from Ingram Micro Advisor: http://www.ingrammicroadvisor.com/data-center/seven-big-data-examples-that-have-improved-healthcare-operations

Shah, S. (2016, February 18). *Why patient engagement is so challenging to achieve.* Retrieved August 2, 2018, from http://www.ibmbigdatahub.com/blog/why-patient-engagement-so-challenging-achieve

Shvachko, K., Kuang, H., Radia, S., & Chansler, R. (2010). The Hadoop Distributed File System. In *IEEE 26th Symposium on Mass Storage Systems and Technologies (MSST).* IEEE.

Srinivasan, U., & Arunasalam, B. (2013). *Leveraging Big Data Analytics to Reduce Healthcare Costs.* IEEE Computer Society.

TF7 Healthcare Subgroup. (2016, December 21). *Big Data Technologies in Healthcare: Needs, opportunities and challenges.* Retrieved July 24, 2017, from http://www.bdva.eu/sites/default/files/Big%20Data%20Technologies%20in%20Healthcare.pdf

United Healthcare uses Hadoop to Detect Health Care Fraud, Waste and Abuse. (2018). Retrieved April 20, 2018, from https://mapr.com/customers/unitedhealthcare/

Uzsoy, R. (2005). *Supply-Chain Management and Health Care Delivery: Pursuing a System-Level Understanding*. Retrieved 2017, from https://www.ncbi.nlm.nih.gov/books/NBK22867/

ENDNOTES

1. https://fluneryou.org/#/
2. https://twitter.com/search?q=%23Germtracker
3. http://www.gocap.me/
4. https://www.propellerhealth.com/
5. https://www.23andme.com/
6. http://www.gnshealthcare.com/
7. https://www.aetna.com/
8. https://www.healthcore.com/
9. https://www.evolenthealth.com/valence-health
10. https://www.uhc.com/
11. https://www.optumlabs.com/
12. https://www.liaison.com/
13. https://www.novartis.com/tags/next-generation-sequencing
14. http://hadoop.apache.org/
15. http://pig.apache.org/
16. https://hive.apache.org/
17. https://zookeeper.apache.org/
18. https://hbase.apache.org/
19. http://cassandra.apache.org/
20. http://oozie.apache.org/
21. https://mahout.apache.org/
22. https://lucene.apache.org/
23. https://www.ibm.com/watson/health/

This research was previously published in Intelligent Systems for Healthcare Management and Delivery; pages 72-100, copyright year 2019 by Medical Information Science Reference (an imprint of IGI Global).

Chapter 7
A Brief Survey on Big Data in Healthcare

Ebru Aydindag Bayrak

https://orcid.org/0000-0002-2637-9245

Istanbul University-Cerrahpaşa, Turkey

Pinar Kirci

Bursa Uludağ University, Turkey

ABSTRACT

This article presents a brief introduction to big data and big data analytics and also their roles in the healthcare system. A definite range of scientific researches about big data analytics in the healthcare system have been reviewed. The definition of big data, the components of big data, medical big data sources, used big data technologies in present, and big data analytics in healthcare have been examined under the different titles. Also, the historical development process of big data analytics has been mentioned. As a known big data analytics technology, Apache Hadoop technology and its core components with tools have been explained briefly. Moreover, a glance of some of the big data analytics tools or platforms apart from Hadoop eco-system were given. The main goal is to help researchers or specialists with giving an opinion about the rising importance of used big data analytics in healthcare systems.

1. INTRODUCTION

The technological developments helped us in producing more data that cannot be easily processed with currently available technologies. Thus, a new term 'big data' is created to describe the data that is large and not processed. Healthcare systems are generating huge amounts of data that present many positive and negative situations at the same time. For this reason, big data management and its analysis in healthcare sector are important (Dash et al., 2019).

Healthcare data increase day by day with the improvement of technology. The correct analysis of this data will increase the quality of maintenance and reduce the costs. This kind of data (big data) have some features such as high volume, variety, high speed production etc. Because of these features, analyz-

DOI: 10.4018/978-1-6684-3662-2.ch007

ing data with traditional hardware and software platforms are pretty hard. Hence, choosing appropriate platform for analyzing and managing big data is very important (Nazari et al., 2019).

Considering the studies related to big data and big data analytics in the field of health in the literature, it is seen that quite a lot of studies have presented. Especially in recent years, it has been seen that there is a great increase in the number of studies on this subject. Some of them can be expressed as follows.

Galetsi et al. (2020) have studied on big data analytics in healthcare. Theoretical frameworks, techniques and prospects about big data analytics have been explained. They have aimed to present a systematic overview of the literature in order to show how much big data analytics has managed to contribute the healthcare system. Shilo et al. (2020) characterized health data by several axes that represent different components of the data. They described the potential and hardship of using big data in healthcare resources. They aimed to contribute to the continued argument of the potential of big data resources to improve the understanding of health and disease. McCall (2020) reviewed the interest in the use of big data in healthcare. Many big data analytics examples were explained for health in Silicon Valley. Alghunaim and Al-Baity (2019) studied on the problem of breast cancer prediction in the big data context. Support Vector Machine, Random Forest and Decision Tree used for machine learning classification by applying on each dataset. Apache Spark was used as a big data framework. Also, big data framework Spark was compared with WEKA traditional data processing environment. Bayrak and Kirci (2019) studied on intelligent big data analytics and machine learning systems for early diagnosis of neurological disorders. Many researches about intelligent big data analysis were reviewed in their study. Also, most used platforms or tools for big data analytics was explained. Carnimeo et al. (2019) was aimed to study a new health care network based on big data analytics for Parkinson's disease (PD). According to healthcare network, collected data during motor examinations of PD patients were analyzed and acquired knowledge was used to create a diagnostic report for patients. Dhayne et al. (2019) searched the topic of big medical data integration solutions. Data integration technologies, tools and applications was examined in the study. They focused on finding the strength and weakness of data integration technologies. Especially, they explained data integration and it is the most important factor for healthcare sector. El Hanafi et al. (2019) studied on characterization of big data platforms for medical data. They described the big data environment with different components based on Hadoop Ecosystem. It was claimed that this system can be useful for helping the doctors to pursue their patients remotely. Nazari et al. (2019) investigated definition of the big data and the big data sources. In concern with big data, the advantages and challenges of big data, big data applications, big data analysis and big data platforms were explained. Palanisamy and Thirunavukarasu (2019) reviewed various healthcare frameworks and summarized their important ideas to learn the impact of big data in healthcare. The implications of big data tools in enhancing healthcare frameworks were considered. The big data tools were grouped data integration tools, machine learning tools, scalable searching and processing tools, visual data analytical tools and real-time and stream data processing tools. Uçar and İlkılıç (2019) worked on epistemological and ethical issues of the big data used in healthcare. Especially rather than whether big data was used in healthcare or not, they asked the question of "how" and in which conditions and in what moral lines should people use big data? Wang and Alexander (2019) explained big health data, big data in healthcare systems, applications, benefits and challenges of Big Data Analytics in healthcare system. They also presented a comparison of tools used for analyzing big data. Bahri et al. (2018) was aimed to explain big data technologies on the performance and outcomes of healthcare system. They explained big data process, technologies, and big data applications in healthcare sector. Big data application on healthcare was classified in five groups as Healthcare monitoring, healthcare prediction, recommendation systems, healthcare knowledge system and healthcare management system. Chiroma el. (2018) surveyed the progress on Artificial Neural Networks (ANN) for big data analytics. They examined the application of ANN approaches on big data analytics. They explained that their study can be used by researchers as a criterion for future. Kouanou et al. (2018) studied on big data analytics for biomedical images and showed examples that were reported in the literature and new methods used in processing. They aimed to present a workflow for the management and analysis of biomedical image data which is based on big data technology. They designed two architectures to perform the image classification step. First architecture was based on the Hadoop framework and the second one was based on the Spark. Karabay and Ulaş (2017) described different types of tools that were mostly used in analysis of big data. The usage of big data, big data analyse methods and various big data technologies were mentioned in their study. Also, big data processing tools was explained and they were compared in terms of features such as operating system support, speed, real-time analysis and scalability etc.

The presented chapter is organized as follows. In Section 2, what is big data, the components of big data, big data sources and big data technologies in present are explained. In Section 3, big data analytics in healthcare system and some of the big data analytics tools /platforms are additionally presented. Section 4 continues with discussion and the chapter ends with conclusion by proposing concluding remarks in Section 5.

2. BIG DATA

IBM explains that every day 2.5 exabytes (EB) of data are created. CISCO estimates that, by 2020, 50 billion devices will be connected to internet and networks. The costs of enterprises on Information Technology (IT) infrastructure of the digital universe and telecommunications will increase in the rate of 40% between 2012 and 2020. And, Big Data will be responsible of nearly 40%. Furthermore, International Data Corporation (IDC) reckons that the 23 percent of the information in the digital world (or 643 EB) would be beneficial for Big Data. It comprises of data originated from embedded and medical devices, surveillance footage, entertainment, social media, as well as consumer images (Akoka et al., 2017).

The term 'big data' is defined in lots of works, and a globally adopted definition of big data has not been achieved yet in the research community. Big data is a subject which is growing with great popularity and can be described as a huge dataset that is characterized based on the 'five V's' (Chiroma et al., 2018):

1. Volume means that the size of the dataset is very large;
2. Variety means that the data set is in different forms;
3. Velocity means that the content of the data adapts constantly;
4. Veracity means that the dataset has many options or interoperation variables in a mixed analysis;
5. Value means that the values in the dataset are huge and the density is very low (Figure 1).

Although the three components of the Big Data concept were met by the year it was created, today, new facts have added to these items and the number of components were increased to 5V. In fact, now it is considered as big data has 7V components rather than a 5V component (Çevik ve Özdemir, 2018):

6. Data Validity indicates that data sets may be valid for any application but not suitable for another applications;
7. Data Variability refers to the exclusion or destruction of data whose storage period has expired.

Globally, the use of big data in healthcare keep on increasing, Google's parent company, Alphabet, spent US$2.1 billion to acquire FitBit. All over the world, healthcare system is interested in the use of big data and Silicon Valley is the one important part of this fact. Fifteen studies used big data in Silicon Valley, they are summarized in the following (McCall, 2020):

1. Komodo Health, traced the journey of 320 million de-identified US patients to understand health and disease at a scale;
2. Google Verily is a subsidiary company of Google's Alphabet and it purposes to make the world's health data beneficial, thus people will be happy and have healthy lives;
3. Helix uses its genome-sequencing possibilities to map sickness progression and identify new interference for sickness;
4. Ellipsis Health improved a vital sign tool for mental health and wellness for the detection of anxiety and depression;
5. Catalia Health system has a Wellness Coach robot which is called as Mabu. It holds daily and autonomous data that is derived from artificial intelligence generated conversations from patient;
6. Human Dx is both an educational tool and an AI-based decision tool that has big data obtained from clinicians and trainees globally;
7. Flatiron Health purposes to learn from the experience of every patient with cancer in its network by obtaining data from electronic health records;
8. PryAmes is a sensor platform for continuous blood pressure monitoring;
9. LunaDNA is a community-owned and health data sharing platform for health research;
10. Evidation is a virtual research site that collects big data from people's mobile apps, wearable sensors and devices;
11. Propeller Health is a digital health platform company for searching chronic obstructive pulmonary and asthma diseases;
12. Verana Health gathers the largest clinical databases to contribute researches;
13. Tidepool is an organization that has data of diabetes;
14. Bigfoot Biomedical is another start-up in the diabetes field;
15. Freenome uses next generation blood tests based on artificial intelligence for early detection of cancer disease.

Several big data sources in healthcare are available, such as clinical data, electronic health records, biometric data, registration data, patient reports, internet data, image data, biomarker data and administrative data (Nazir et al., 2019). Also, healthcare stakeholders and big data sources are patients, medical practitioners, healthcare insurers, hospital operators, the studies about clinical and pharma (Palamisamy and Thirunavukarasu, 2019).

According to "Data Never Sleeps 7.0" project that was prepared by Domo (2019), by 2020 there will be 40x more bytes of data than stars in the observable universe. It can be find out with how much data is generated in every minute of every day with some of the most popular platforms and companies in 2019 (Figure 2). For example; YouTube users watch 4,500,000 videos, Instagram users post 55,140 photos, Twitter users send 511,200 tweets. When the global internet population growth is examined, internet population is increasing enormously year by year. As of January 2019, used percentage of internet reached 56.1% of the world's population and this rate is equal to 4.13 billion people (Domo, 2019).

Figure 1. The five components of big data (Adapted from Nazir et al. 2019)

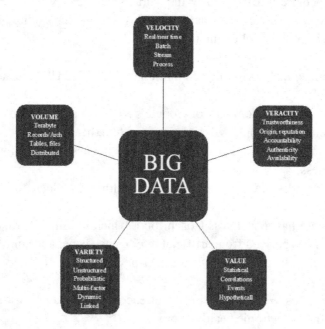

Figure 2. The spectacular picture of big data increase. 7th edition of Data Never Sleeps is related to how much data is being created in every minute in 2019 [Adapted from Domo].

According to all of these presented information, it can be said that big data was formed in the early 2000s as a concept. Surely one of the most significant factors effecting the concept was presented at the Davos Summit in 2012, and "data" was stated as an economic value. Big data is a concept used for expressing the volumetric size of the data at first, now it gained another meaning with expressing all of the processes from the storage of data to the information. The concept of "big data analytics" is also frequently used instead of the big data concept (Uçar and İlkılıç, 2019).

3. BIG DATA ANALYTICS IN HEALTHCARE

The research communities in computer science and statistics have many working fields but statistical computing and machine learning began to play a major role in data mining, because the origins of big data analytics can be traced back to the 1970s or before.

In the present day, the volume and scale of data have increased dramatically due to the risen capability of computing power and automation. The data are referred to as very large databases or massive data sets among the computer science and statistics. According to the period of appearance of several methodologies about data analysis: data mining, knowledge discovery in databases (KDD) and statistical learning, this part is the first wave of big data analytics (Figure 3). Since the year of 2000, big data analytics have been successfully adopted in many disciplines: business schools, management schools, and informatics (bioinformatics, health informatics, systems informatics etc.). This period is called as the second wave (Tsui et al., 2019).

Figure 3. The historical development process of big data analytics [Adapted from Tsui et al., 2019]

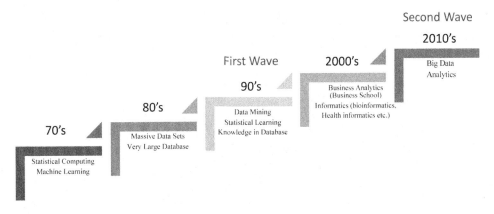

Big data analytics is the use of enhanced analytic techniques against huge, various data sets that include structured, semi-structured and unstructured data, from several sources, and between size of terabytes to zettabytes. Big data is a term applied to data sets whose size or type overcome the ability of classic relational databases to catch, run and handle the data with low latency. Analysis of big data give a chance to researchers and business users for having better and faster decisions by using data that was inaccessible or unusable data before (IBM,2020). Big data analytics refers to the use of a cutting-edge analytical tools to be able to effectively analyze and get information from big data that is high in the way of variety, volume, and velocity (Ghasemaghaei, 2020).

The analytical abilities of big data techniques and technologies that can be acquired from stored big data are useful for medical diagnosis, making predictions, resource allocations, recommendations and personal treatment plans. Big data process can be grouped as four steps: big data generation, big data acquisition, big data storage and big data analysis (Figure 4). This process is also called as big data chain value. (Bahri et al. 2018). If the data belong to healthcare industry, then the intensive and interactive dynamic big data platforms can be used, such as innovative technologies and tools to improve patient care and services in healthcare (Galetsi et al., 2020).

The most challenging parts for big data in healthcare are data privacy, data leakage, data security, effective use of big medical data, information security, wrong use of health data and misunderstanding unstructured clinical notes etc. Big data have a great opportunity to improve healthcare management and increase healthcare industry to a higher level (Bhattacharya, 2018).

Big data analytics in healthcare system have been grouped as five processes: Data Acquisition, Data Storage, Data Management, Data Analytics and Data Visualization & Report. Also, the Figure 5 shows the process of big data analytics in healthcare management (Senthilkumar et al., 2018).

The big data analytics in healthcare system is in the early stage of its evaluation. For this reason, some handicaps and problems may emerge in the application areas. Any development about big data analytics can be much better for some important issues such as; accurate classification of a disease, quick decision making for a sickness and early diagnosis of many health problems.

Figure 4. Big data process can be grouped in 4 steps that can be called as Big data chain value [Adapted from Bahri et al., 2018]

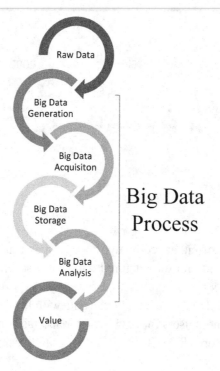

Figure 5. Big Data Analytics process in healthcare system [Adapted from Senthilkumar et al., 2018]

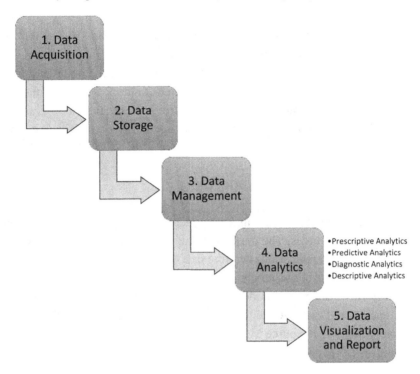

3.1. HADOOP

Apache Hadoop is a well-recognized Big Data technology that has been used by an important supporting community. It was proposed to prevent the complexity and the low performance encounter when Big Data is processed and analyzed with using traditional technologies (Oussous et al., 2018).

Among the software or platforms used in big data analytics, Hadoop software architecture, primarily uses Map-Reduce technology and HDFS (Hadoop Distributed File System). Hadoop is currently used in big data analytics for many leading IT companies, including Amazon, Yahoo, Facebook, Twitter, LinkedIn, IBM and Adobe. Hadoop architecture has two basic components, these are HDFS and Map-Reduce. The operations that will be performed in Hadoop are typically written as a job and given to the HDFS server cluster. HDFS works based on the cluster computing. In the cluster computing, it also means parallel processing architecture, servers with nodes are kept in rack cabinets (Aktan, 2018).

Hadoop is a software framework and it is developed to handle certain types of big data sets on a distributed system. It is developed with the inspiration of Google MapReduce and Google file system to process big-scale data between clustered computers. Hadoop is an open source ecosystem that combines a distributed file system called Hadoop Distributed File System (HDFS) with Hadoop MapReduce features (Karabay and Ulaş, 2017).

The core components of Hadoop HDFS, YARN and MapReduce can be explained as following.

3.1.1. HDFS (Hadoop Distributed File System)

HDFS is the file system component of Hadoop eco-system which stores file system metadata and it is known as blocks. HDFS is designed as a cost-effective and fault tolerant structure. HDFS gives file permission and authentication for all files. HDFS comprises of the name node and data nodes. HDFS works based on a master-slave architecture. A HDFS cluster contains a single name node, which is a master server that conducts the file system namespace and directories in the form of hierarchy. Data node contains two files. The first file is made up of data and the second file comprises of block's generation stamp (Hussain et al., 2019).

3.1.2. YARN (Yet Another Resource Negotiator)

YARN has been projected as the resource management framework of Hadoop. Hadoop Yarn ensures effective management of the resources. The purpose of the resource management technology is to partition system resources to various applications running in a Hadoop cluster. It is also used to schedule the conduct of tasks on different parts of clusters (El Hanafi et al., 2019). YARN is the central resource that was used by Hadoop. It traces the cluster nodes and all relevant processing operations. YARN permits Hadoop to perform operational activities without necessity of batch tasks to finish. Also, it has four fundamental components that are Resource Manager, Node Manager, Application Master and Container (Baig et al., 2019).

3.1.3. MAP REDUCE

MapReduce was suggested by Google for the first time. The map function filters the data to be processed and the Reduce function returns the analysis of the data processing as a result. When they get together, MapReduce system was appeared (Karabay and Ulaş, 2017). For processing big data, MapReduce is a well-known method to perform distributed storage and parallel computing. MapReduce is a programming model and an associated implementation for generating and processing big datasets and is convenient for semi structured or unstructured data (Dhayne et al., 2019).

The MapReduce, is used to process large data files in HDFS, it uses two functions for processing data. Map function is used to analyze and filter the data, and the Reduce function is used to get results from the data (Demirci, 2018).

4. SOME APACHE HADOOP TOOLS

4.1. Apache Spark

Apache Spark is a big data frame for the quick processes of datasets on various workloads. It can deal with interactive, batch, iterative and streaming data. Spark is accepted as 100 times faster in memory and 10 times faster on disk than Hadoop which is one of the most famous big data environments (Alghunaim et al., 2019). Apache Spark stores and processes data in memory. Spark not only processes data, but also provides Spark Machine Learning (MLlib) for machine learning, GraphX for graphic processing, Spark SQL components for SQL support and Spark Streaming for streaming data (Figure 6). It also offers the possibility for developing with using languages such as R, Scala Java, Python. Thus, they make the application provide great convenience for development (Demirci, 2018).

4.2. Apache Storm

Storm is an open source framework to analyze big data in real time and it is consisted of spouts and bolts. In a storm program, a combination of a spout and a bolt is called topology. Spout can produce data or install data from an input and Bolt processes input streams and generates output streams (Benhlima, 2018). Apache Storm is another option for using the substitute of Hadoop MapReduce when we need real-time and heavy processing. Thereby, when our analytic solution is expected to process huge data as fastly, Apache Storm is the best performer for presenting such solutions (Harerimana et al., 2018).

Figure 6. The ecosystem of Apache Spark [Adapted from Spark, n.d.]

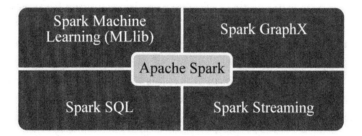

4.3. Apache Cassandra

Cassandra is an Apache project, it is built on a distributed database system. It has NoSQL system and it is developed by Facebook for inbox searching. It has two million columns in a single row. It is highly scalable, accessible, robust and reliable and has zero point of failure. Cassandra is used by several companies such as Facebook, Twitter, and Amazon. It is inapplicable, if the use of data aggregation operation, sub query, and join operations are needed (Baig et al., 2019).

4.4. Apache Flink

Flink is a framework for all components of Hadoop eco-system and it is the framework for Streaming data. It has many advantages such as processing of data without latency and solving the memory exception problem. Flink also interacts with lots of devices that have several storage systems for processing the data, and it also optimizes the program before practice (Kumar et al., 2019).

4.5. Apache Zookeeper

Zookeeper can be used by different applications to coordinate the distributed processing of Hadoop clusters. It maintains the common objects needed in large cluster environments, including configuration information and the hierarchical naming space. Zookeeper also provides the reliability of application.

If an application master dies, Zookeeper gets involved to create a new application master to be able to keep on the tasks (Kumar and Singh, 2018).

4.6. Apache Hive

Apache Hive is a data warehouse system, it is formed by Facebook in order to ease the usage of Hadoop.

It has an interactive interface with a variety of functions that are useful for data analysis and also, it is mostly used for structured data. The collected data is stored in a structured database that is easy and understandable for all users. Apache Hive database is administrated with a HQL language that has the same syntax like SQL language. HQL transforms queries into MapReduce jobs that are processed like batch tasks (Bahri et al., 2018). Hive is a data warehouse framework, it is used for querying and data analysis on Hadoop eco-system and it is developed by Apache. It uses HiveQL that is similar to SQL, to manage and query structured data. Hive's most important property is its convenience about translating the written codes. The codes are written in Hive and they are converted into Java MapReduce codes at the background. Because of this property, there is no need to learn Java program (Karabay and Ulaş, 2017).

4.7. Apache Kafka

Apache Kafka is a distributed streaming platform that has three key capabilities. These are publishing and subscribing streams of records, store streams of records by a fault-tolerant way and processing streams of records when they happen (Apache Kafka, n.d.). Apache Kafka is the storage platform for non-structured data. This platform is frequently used in real-time data processing and it can adjust how many days of data will be kept in the topic with based on the given configurations. Owing to this configuration, the data thrown into Kafka environment will not occupy a nonessential space in the system after processing (Özer, 2019).

4.8. Apache Pig

Apache Pig is a large-scale data analysis platform based on Hadoop eco-system. It ensures a language called PigLatin that has similar features as SQL language. The complier of PigLatin turns SQL-like data analysis requests into a series of optimized MapReduce transactions. Apache Pig offers easy operations and programming interfaces for massive, complex data-parallel computing. For Apache Pig's main structure and running process it can be said that it just like Hive (Yu and Zhou, 2019).

4.9. Mahout

Mahout is an open source machine learning library which is developed by Apache. Mahout can be added on top of Hadoop for performing algorithms by way of MapReduce. Also, it is designed to study on their platforms. It has the advantage of providing scalable and influent implementation of large scale machine learning applications and algorithms. Mahout library ensures to use analytical capabilities and multiple optimized algorithms. For instance, it offers libraries for classification, clustering, frequent pattern mining, collaborative filtering and text mining. Besides, additional tools involve dimensionality reduction, topic modeling, text vectorization, similarity measures, a math library and more than this (Oussous et al. 2018).

5. OTHER BIG DATA ANALYTICS TOOLS /PLATFORMS

SAP HANA was discovered by SAP company to process big data in real time. It provides a fast operation by using the in-memory database technology that contains continuously increasing big data. Owing to its in-memory technology, it has the ability to make big, instant, comparative, fast decisions and to analyze in real time. SAP HANA is not just a software that performs data control, analysis and integration processes, also with hardware it is a bundled data platform (Karabay and Ulaş, 2019).

BigML, is a scalable and programmable machine learning platform that ensures several tools to perform machine learning tasks such as classification, clustering, regression, association rules and anomaly detection. It can integrate the property of machine learning with cloud infrastructure to build cost-effective applications with high flexibility, reliability and scalability (Palanisamy and Thirunavukarasu, 2019).

KNIME is called as Konstanz Information Miner, it is an open source tool for data analytics, integration and reporting platform. It integrates different elements for data mining and machine learning through its modular data pipelining concept. Its graphical user interface allows the assembly of nodes for data pre-processing, data modelling, data visualization and data analysis. Since 2006, it has been widely used in pharmaceutical industry researches, but now it is also used in different areas like healthcare systems, customer data analysis, financial data analysis and business intelligence systems (Sampathrajan,2018).

6. DISCUSSION

In this chapter, it is aimed to present a specific information to the researchers by examining the studies on big data analysis in the field of healthcare. The application of big data analytics in health were reviewed. The most striking of these studies are tried to be summarized. It has been observed that the studies of big data analytics have been conducted on many different health problems (cancer, neurological diseases, etc.). How big data is defined in various sources is given and also big data studies in the field of health in Silicon Valley are mentioned.

The stages of big data analysis and big data analytics applied in the field of health are specified. In addition, various big data analytics platforms are mentioned. The number of presented studies, the utilized tools and platforms that can be used for big data analytics is quite high. This chapter also focuses on Hadoop architecture. Some components of the Hadoop eco-system have been studied under separate titles. It is clearly seen that big data has grown and continues growing with an incredible rate until today. Therefore, it can be said that the studies in big data and big data analytics will continue to increase.

7. CONCLUSION

This chapter presents a brief approach on big data and big data analytics and also about their roles in healthcare system. A definite range of scientific researches about big data analytics in healthcare system is mentioned.

Apache Hadoop eco-system has been tried to be explained because it is mostly used as big data analytics for lots of studies. Its core components HDFS, YARN and MapReduce are explained and also some Hadoop tools used as big data analytics such as Spark, Storm, Mahout, Pig, Hive etc. are examined.

Moreover, a glance is taken over some of the big data analytics tools or platforms apart from Hadoop eco-system.

This chapter provides an opinion of how health (medical) big data can be used as a source for big data analytics. The main aim behind this chapter is to assist the researchers or experts to provide an idea and understand about big data analytics which can be used for solving several health problems.

The big data analytics in healthcare system can be said that is in the early stage of its evaluation. For this reason, some handicaps and problems can happen in the field of application areas. Each one of the presented developments about big data analytics can provide much better ideas for some important issues such as; accurate classification of a disease, quick decision making for a sickness and early diagnosis of different health problems.

REFERENCES

Akoka, J., Comyn-Wattiau, I., & Laoufi, N. (2017). Research on Big Data–A systematic mapping study. *Computer Standards & Interfaces*, *54*, 105–115. doi:10.1016/j.csi.2017.01.004

Aktan, E. (2018). Büyük veri: Uygulama alanları, analitiği ve güvenlik boyutu. *Bilgi Yönetimi*, *1*(1), 1–22. doi:10.33721/by.403010

Alghunaim, S., & Al-Baity, H. H. (2019). On the Scalability of Machine-Learning Algorithms for Breast Cancer Prediction in Big Data Context. *IEEE Access: Practical Innovations, Open Solutions*, 7, 91535–91546. doi:10.1109/ACCESS.2019.2927080

Apache Kafka. (n.d.). https://kafka.apache.org/intro.html

Apache Spark. (n.d.). https://spark.apache.org/

Bahri, S., Zoghlami, N., Abed, M., & Tavares, J. M. R. (2018). Big data for healthcare: A survey. *IEEE Access: Practical Innovations, Open Solutions*, 7, 7397–7408. doi:10.1109/ACCESS.2018.2889180

Baig, M. I., Shuib, L., & Yadegaridehkordi, E. (2019). Big Data Tools: Advantages and Disadvantages. *Journal of Soft Computing and Decision Support Systems*, *6*(6), 14–20.

Bayrak, E. A., & Kirci, P. (2019). Intelligent Big Data Analytics in Health. In *Early Detection of Neurological Disorders Using Machine Learning Systems* (pp. 252–291). IGI Global. doi:10.4018/978-1-5225-8567-1.ch014

Benhlima, L. (2018). Big data management for healthcare systems: Architecture, requirements, and implementation. *Advances in Bioinformatics*. PMID:30034468

Bhattacharya, D. (2018). Big Data Management and Growth Enhancement. *International Research Journal of Engineering and Technology*, *5*(10), 1769–1774.

Carnimeo, L., Trotta, G. F., Brunetti, A., Cascarano, G. D., Buongiorno, D., Loconsole, C., ... Bevilacqua, V. (2019). Proposal of a health care network based on big data analytics for pds. *Journal of Engineering (Stevenage, England)*, *2019*(6), 4603–4611. doi:10.1049/joe.2018.5142

Çevik, Ö. Ü. N. K., & Özdemir, Ö. G. M. (2018, december). Büyük Veri: Tanımı ve Oluşumu. In International Congress of Management Economy and Policy 2018 Spring Proceedings Book (p. 29). Academic Press.

Chiroma, H., Abdullahi, U. A., Alarood, A. A., Gabralla, L. A., Rana, N., Shuib, L., ... Herawan, T. (2018). Progress on Artificial Neural Networks for Big Data Analytics: A Survey. *IEEE Access: Practical Innovations, Open Solutions*, *7*, 70535–70551. doi:10.1109/ACCESS.2018.2880694

Dash, S., Shakyawar, S. K., Sharma, M., & Kaushik, S. (2019). Big data in healthcare: Management, analysis and future prospects. *Journal of Big Data*, *6*(1), 54. doi:10.118640537-019-0217-0

Demirci, C. (2018). *Büyük veri platformlarından hadoop ile örnek veri analizi*. Academic Press.

Dhayne, H., Haque, R., Kilany, R., & Taher, Y. (2019). In Search of Big Medical Data Integration Solutions-A Comprehensive Survey. *IEEE Access: Practical Innovations, Open Solutions*, *7*, 91265–91290. doi:10.1109/ACCESS.2019.2927491

Domo. (n.d.). https://www.domo.com/learn/data-never-sleeps-7

El Hanafi, H. E. A., Afifi, N., & Belhadaoui, H. (2019). *Characterization of Big Data Platforms for Medical Data* (No. 1593). EasyChair.

Galetsi, P., Katsaliaki, K., & Kumar, S. (2020). Big data analytics in health sector: Theoretical framework, techniques and prospects. *International Journal of Information Management*, *50*, 206–216. doi:10.1016/j.ijinfomgt.2019.05.003

Ghasemaghaei, M. (2020). The role of positive and negative valence factors on the impact of bigness of data on big data analytics usage. *International Journal of Information Management*, *50*, 395–404. doi:10.1016/j.ijinfomgt.2018.12.011

Hussain, T., Sanga, A., & Mongia, S. (2019). *Big Data Hadoop Tools and Technologies: A Review*. Available at SSRN 3462554

IBM. (n.d.). *Big data analytics*. https://www.ibm.com/analytics/hadoop/big-data-analytics

Karabay, B., & Ulaş, M. (2017). Büyük Veri İşlemede Yaygın Kullanılan Araçların Karşılaştırılması. *8th International Advanced Technologies Symposium (IATS'17)*.

Kouanou, A. T., Tchiotsop, D., Kengne, R., Zephirin, D. T., Armele, N. M. A., & Tchinda, R. (2018). An optimal big data workflow for biomedical image analysis. *Informatics in Medicine Unlocked*, *11*, 68–74. doi:10.1016/j.imu.2018.05.001

Kumar, J. S., Raghavendra, B. K., & Raghavendra, S. (2019). Big data Processing Comparison using Pig and Hive. *International Journal on Computer Science and Engineering*, *7*, 173–178.

Kumar, S., & Singh, M. (2018). Big data analytics for healthcare industry: Impact, applications, and tools. *Big Data Mining and Analytics*, *2*(1), 48–57. doi:10.26599/BDMA.2018.9020031

McCall, B. (2020). 15 ways Silicon Valley is harnessing Big Data for health. *Nature Medicine*, *26*(1), 7–10. doi:10.103841591-019-0708-8 PMID:31932786

Nazari, E., Shahriari, M. H., & Tabesh, H. (2019). BigData Analysis in Healthcare: Apache Hadoop, Apache spark and Apache Flink. *Frontiers in Health Informatics*, *8*(1), 14. doi:10.30699/fhi.v8i1.180

Nazir, S., Nawaz, M., Adnan, A., Shahzad, S., & Asadi, S. (2019). Big Data Features, Applications, and Analytics in Cardiology—A Systematic Literature Review. *IEEE Access: Practical Innovations, Open Solutions*, *7*, 143742–143771. doi:10.1109/ACCESS.2019.2941898

Oussous, A., Benjelloun, F. Z., Lahcen, A. A., & Belfkih, S. (2018). Big Data technologies: A survey. *Journal of King Saud University-Computer and Information Sciences*, *30*(4), 431–448. doi:10.1016/j.jksuci.2017.06.001

Özer, S. (2019). *Büyük Veri Teknolojileri ve Veri Madenciliği Yöntemleri ile Medikal Veri Analizi* (Master Thesis). Marmara University, Science and Engineering Institute.

Palanisamy, V., & Thirunavukarasu, R. (2019). Implications of big data analytics in developing healthcare frameworks–A review. *Journal of King Saud University-Computer and Information Sciences*, *31*(4), 415–425. doi:10.1016/j.jksuci.2017.12.007

Sampathrajan, S. (2018). A Study of Big Data Practices in Various Open Source Tools. *International Journal of New Technologies in Science and Engineering*, *5*(7), 27–34.

Shilo, S., Rossman, H., & Segal, E. (2020). Axes of a revolution: Challenges and promises of big data in healthcare. *Nature Medicine*, *26*(1), 29–38. doi:10.103841591-019-0727-5 PMID:31932803

Tsui, K. L., Zhao, Y., & Wang, D. (2019). Big Data Opportunities: System Health Monitoring and Management. *IEEE Access: Practical Innovations, Open Solutions*, *7*, 68853–68867. doi:10.1109/ACCESS.2019.2917891

Uçar, A., & İlkılıç, İ. (2019). Büyük Verinin Sağlık Hizmetlerinde Kullanımında Epistemolojik ve Etik Sorunlar. *Sağlık Bilimlerinde İleri Araştırmalar Dergisi*, *2*(2), 80–92.

Wang, L., & Alexander, C. A. (2019). Big data analytics in healthcare systems. *International Journal of Mathematical. Engineering and Management Sciences*, *4*(1), 17–26.

Yu, J. H., & Zhou, Z. M. (2019). Components and Development in Big Data System: A Survey. *Journal of Electronic Science and Technology*, *17*(1), 51–72.

This research was previously published in the International Journal of Big Data and Analytics in Healthcare (IJBDAH), 5(1); pages 1-18, copyright year 2020 by IGI Publishing (an imprint of IGI Global).

Section 2
Development and Design Methodologies

Chapter 8
Big Data Analytics and Models

Ferdi Sönmez
ⓘ https://orcid.org/0000-0002-5761-3866
Istanbul Arel University, Turkey

Ziya Nazım Perdahçı
ⓘ https://orcid.org/0000-0002-1210-2448
Mimar Sinan Fine Arts University, Turkey

Mehmet Nafiz Aydın
Kadir Has University, Turkey

ABSTRACT

When uncertainty is regarded as a surprise and an event in the minds, it can be said that individuals can change the future view. Market, financial, operational, social, environmental, institutional and humanitarian risks and uncertainties are the inherent realities of the modern world. Life is suffused with randomness and volatility; everything momentous that occurs in the illustrious sweep of history, or in our individual lives, is an outcome of uncertainty. An important implication of such uncertainty is the financial instability engendered to the victims of different sorts of perils. This chapter is intended to explore big data analytics as a comprehensive technique for processing large amounts of data to uncover insights. Several techniques before big data analytics like financial econometrics and optimization models have been used. Therefore, initially these techniques are mentioned. Then, how big data analytics has altered the methods of analysis is mentioned. Lastly, cases promoting big data analytics are mentioned.

INTRODUCTION

Uncertainty is expressed as a situation in which many different outcomes of an option can take place in the decision-making process, but the probabilities of these different outcomes are unknown. When uncertainty is regarded as a surprise and an event in the minds, it can be said that individuals can change the future view. Market, financial, operational, social, environmental, institutional and humanitarian risks and uncertainties are the inherent realities of the modern world. Life is suffused with randomness and volatility; everything momentous that occurs in the illustrious sweep of history, or in our individual

DOI: 10.4018/978-1-6684-3662-2.ch008

lives, is an outcome of uncertainty. An important implication of such uncertainty is the financial instability engendered to the victims of different sorts of perils. This chapter is intended to explore big data analytics as a comprehensive technique for processing large amounts of data to uncover insights. Several techniques before big data analytics like financial econometrics and optimization models have been used. Therefore, initially these techniques are mentioned. Then, how big data analytics has altered the methods of analysis is mentioned. Lastly, cases promoting big data analytics are mentioned.

Financial Econometric Models

This sub-section involves a comprehensive series of techniques using financial econometrics and practical applications of these techniques. This sub-section opens up the experimental subjects and techniques meet the finance, forecasting and sampling requirements including continuous-time-period sampling and an introduction to inference. The main topics of financial econometric models are Market Efficiency, Return Predictability, ARCH, GARCH, value at risk, volatility clustering, asset returns, Single and Variable linear Models, Cointegration, Conditional Heteroskedasticity, Market Microstructure, Event Analysis, Case Study Analysis Predictability, Capital Asset Pricing Models, Multi-Factor Pricing Models, Present-Price Relations, Intertemporal Equilibrium Models, and Maturity Structure Models.

Studies that examine conditional return predictability dependent on the magnitude of the information signal can be divided into two groups (Ulusavas, 2010). The first group is the ones that examine price patterns following large one-day price changes and the second group are the ones that deals with the investment strategies designed to exploit large one-day price changes. The first group, which examined price patterns following large one-day price changes, found mixed evidence. Although most of the studies found evidence of overreaction following large positive and negative one-day price change events, only a few of them found evidence of under reaction to negative price change events. However, it was noted that in the face of transaction costs, these predictable patterns do not have economic significance. The studies in the second group dealt with whether contrarian strategies or momentum strategies make abnormal profits. A contrarian investment strategy sells past winners and buys past losers relying on price reversals but a momentum strategy sells past losers and buys winners that rely on price continuations for profitability. Most of these studies documented price continuations and price reversals for different return intervals. However, these transaction intensive strategies might not be profitable if transaction costs are taken into account. Also, the contrarian investment strategies, which rely on short-term price movements, may be a manifestation of the bid-ask bounce effect.

The concept of Market Efficiency (ME) was first introduced by Fama (1965) and has been continuously studied ever since then. ME is one of the basic concepts of financial economics. It argues that in active markets, securities are invested in the best possible way by market participants. According to the Efficient Market Hypothesis, it is stated that in the active markets it is very difficult to obtain a return on market returns only with the help of past price information, (Fama, 1970). In this context; financial econometric models and machine learning techniques have also emerged as experiments where ME is experimentally tested. It refers to the instantaneous and full incorporation of all available information and expectations by market participants into financial asset prices at any given time. Therefore, in an efficient market, investors should not be able to develop investment strategies that will consistently generate abnormal profits. Bachelier (2011) described this by saying "past, present and even discounted future events are reflected in market price, but often show no apparent relation to price changes". The concept of ME is built on the "random walk theory", which claims that financial asset price changes are independent of each other and are driven by new information that arrives at the market on a random basis. Since the term "efficiency" is ambiguous, it is worth shedding some light on what it means from a capital markets stand point. There are three types of efficiency in capital markets: operational efficiency, allocational efficiency and informational efficiency. Operational efficiency (transactional efficiency) emphasizes the way resources are employed to facilitate the operation of the market. If a market facilitates the achievement of a Pareto optimal allocation of resources, it is called allocationally efficient. Under Pareto optimality, funds should be effectively allocated to the most productive investments and stock markets should provide a mechanism to channel scarce resources among computing real investments (Saraoglu, 2017).

Financial time series analysis is based on understanding how the mechanism that controls time series data works (Lkhagva, et al.., 2006). The financial time series, which are the time series of financial systems that generate data flows by the hour, minute or even by shorter periods, have a special economic value in real time as well as being frequent frequencies (Ican, 2013). This economic value has led to storing of financial time series and transferring to related parties. The returns on investment (ROI) series obtained weekly or with a higher frequency are not really independent (Teräsvirta, 2009). In this series although the observations are irrelevant or almost unrelated, the yield series contain a high degree of dependence. One of the most popular ways to explain this dependence with parameters is the autoregressive conditional heteroskedasticity (ARCH) or generalized autoregressive conditional heteroskedasticity (GARCH) model. Time series may show great volatility under some conditions or periods. Under these conditions, the assumption of constant variance is not appropriate. There are many examples of how we might want to predict the conditional variance of a series. The holders of the assets may want to consider the rate of return or the variance over the period in which the asset is held. If an asset is planned to be bought at time t and sold at time t + 1, unconditional variance will be insignificant in this case. For this reason, the distinction between conditional and unconditional variance is shown first. The ARCH models are applied to model interest rates, exchange rates, stock prices and stock index returns (Teräsvirta, 2009). The prediction of the volatility of these series is different from the prediction of the conditional average of a process because volatility, i.e. the target to be predicted, cannot be observed. The main issue that needs to be addressed here is how to measure volatility. In the modeling of financial time series, the GARCH model, which was independently proposed by Bollerslev (1986) and Taylor (1986), is used instead of the ARCH model. In this model, the conditional variance is also a linear function of its delays and is expressed by Teräsvirta (2009) as:

$$h_t = \alpha_0 + \sum_{j=1}^{q} \alpha_j \varepsilon_{t-j}^2 + \sum_{j=1}^{p} \beta_j h_{t-j}$$

The GARCH process has a constant average. If there is variance, the process is a weak stationary process. The GARCH process can be a precise stationary process without the weak stationarity feature that requires constant, mean, variance and auto covariance to be constant and unchanged over time. Precise stationary requires that the distribution function of any set of εt be constant under time transitions. Finite moments are not required for precise stationarity (Yang, 2001).

The storage and transmission of large quantities of financial data was only possible through the advancement of database technology and information infrastructure. However, it has come a long way thank to big data analytics. In parallel with this development, practitioners have started to use machine learning techniques as a solution approach to more demanding problems. The reason for this is that models can be applied to explain the observed characteristics of real-life data, and they can provide a distributed estimate of future observational values in the time series. The features based on observations in the financial time series reflect the characteristics of the data set and are addressed under three heading given below.

- Kurtosis: This criterion is a parameter that describes the graphical representation of the probability distribution of real-valued random variables. Kurtosis is calculated as:

$$kurt(X) = \frac{E[(X - \mu)^4]}{\sigma^4}$$

Here, kurt is the kurtosis, X represents the random variable, μ represents the mean of the random variable X, and σ represents the standard deviation of X. The distribution of financial assets is generally more uniform than the normal distribution. In other words, the average is more than the normal distribution. This increases the standard deviation by having a thicker tail than the normal distribution. The increase in the size of the fluctuations experienced with the integration process in the financial markets causes the time series to move away from stationary. Normal distribution is one of the methods of financial time series distribution. It is necessary to have an auxiliary function in determining the distribution of the overall risk level. The most important indicators of this distribution are kurtosis and skewness values.

- Volatility Cluster: Mandelbrot (1963) mentioned that large changes in the prices of financial assets traded in financial markets are followed by large changes, while small changes are followed by small changes, namely, volatility clusters. This indicates that price changes are affected by each other, that is to say, they are not independent. Two different time series are shown in the following two graphs. In the first graph, there is no volatility clustering, while in the second there is volatility clustering.
- Leverage Impact: The amount of volatility of the financial asset is related to the change in the price of the financial asset, that is to say, the volatility created by the decrease in the price of the financial asset is higher than the volatile created by the increase in the price of the financial asset.

Black Sholes Model

In 1997, the Black-Scholes model, which awarded Fisher Black and Myron Scholes the Nobel Prize for economy, was introduced to calculate the prices of European-based options based on non-dividend stocks (Paul and Baschnagel, 2013). The model has been developed to calculate whether the amount paid or collected when purchasing or selling an option is reasonable.

The original Black-Scholes model was designed for stock options. However, the model can be adapted to other assets by making minor changes. Black-Scholes model is used for foreign exchange options, as in foreign exchange options by central banks. In order to be able to adapt the model to foreign exchange options, the risk-free interest rate of both currencies that are subject to the option is required. For this reason, the Garman-Kohlhagen model emerged that had been adjusted according to these requirements.

Knightian Uncertainty

F. H. Knight distinguished between risk and uncertainty in his work "Risk Uncertainty and Profit" written in 1921. Following Knight's work, the economy separated risk and uncertainty. Potential risk effects can be expressed as the known outcomes of past experiences so that future values and objective probabilities can be related to these outcomes (Langlois and Cosgel, 1993). Therefore, the values of the alternative results and occurrence probabilities are becoming known. According to Knight, although risks can be reduced by empirical and statistical estimation methods, uncertainties cannot be completely removed. Knight states that the probability factor cannot be defined empirically and that the issue of uncertainty cannot be grasped in this way. Moreover, probability calculation can be done with two different approaches: logical-mathematical approach and statistical approach. The cost of risk acceptance can be determined in advance for both approaches. Knight, pioneered a third possibility of accountability, and called estimators, in which it was not possible to predetermine size and effect. Knight claimed that past events will shed light on what will happen in the future and that predictions will come to the fore when ignorance is dominated by the decisions of the individual, suggesting a mode of behavior involving convictions based on incomplete and partial knowledge, and decisions based on intuitive reasoning. Because, according to Knight, uncertainty stems from partial knowledge.

What Knight particularly emphasized is that the theory of probability cannot help in predicting the economic consequences of decisions made in an uncertain environment. Furthermore, it is not possible to completely eliminate uncertainty, which is defined as the information disruptions of the business, while it is possible to reduce the risks by empirical and statistical estimation methods. Uncertainty can be thought of as one of the important contributions to the theory of economics, as 'a factor that cannot be replaced with information' as opposed to 'incomplete information'.

Optimization Models

Optimization is the process of selecting the best solution for a problem, subject to various constraints, from a set of available alternatives. Decision variables are the set of values that represent the decisions to be made and implemented (e.g., type of technology to invest in, number of stocks to be invested). Optimization under uncertainty has been extensively studied in stochastic programs, the optimal control theory, Markov decision processes, statistical decision theory and stochastic dynamic programming.

Deterministic mathematical programming is an important research field in modeling and analyzing the systems that involve complex decision making that cannot be handled through non-mathematical and non-computational approaches (e.g., intuition, experience based). This research field can be restrictive in its practicality, because of the assumption that the model parameters are always known with certainty. For example, in supply chain networks, the supply process is not always precise because of fluctuations or disruptions that might happen during the period of supply. These fluctuations can occur due to seasonality, quality problems, transportation problems or disruptions in supply resources. In production planning, the production capacity is not precise because of the unexpected events that can happen during production, or unexpected changes in production requirements such as specific tools, machines, etc. Deterministic mathematical programming cannot account for these uncertainties and their effect on the solution except in a few instances and only to a certain degree such as in the case of linear programming where sensitivity analysis can be employed. Furthermore, deterministic mathematical models do not consider possible future scenarios that are subject to changes in parameter values when optimizing problems (Chiralaksanakul and Mahadevan, 2007). Therefore, SP models are introduced as an extension of deterministic mathematical programs in order to deal with uncertain parameters in the system.

Although the aforementioned techniques are related to the proposed work in coping with uncertainty, the authors do not discuss these methods because the theory of these techniques are developed and improved independently from Stochastic Programming (SP) literature (Chiralaksanakul and Mahadevan, 2007; Aydin, 2012). In today's business environment, companies around the world are struggling with decision making under uncertainty related to their supply chain and production planning and often resort to myopic planning or consider very few "most likely" scenarios for their long-term planning. SP problems with recourse were first introduced by Dantzig in 1955 for mathematical programs with uncertainties (Dantzig, 2010). Since then, SP has become one of the most important methods to optimize systems that include uncertain parameters or variables in some or all aspects of the model. The most important assumption in SP is that the probability distributions of the random variables are known. A commonly used objective of the SP is to identify a feasible solution that is optimal for the expected value function over all possible realizations (Solak, 2007). Other objectives include identification of robust solutions and solutions that are optimal with respect to a pre-specified trade-off between the expected value function and its variability.

In order to determine the size of an SP problem, the dimensions of the mathematical model and the number of realizations of random vectors need to be considered. If the model's random vectors have continuous distribution or have infinitely many dimensions, then the optimization of such SP models are typically impossible. One alternative is to approximate the uncertainty through scenario aggregation or discretizing the continuous probability distributions. In the multi-stage model, the complexity continues to escalate because in this model the problem size also grows exponentially with the number of decision stages subject to uncertainty.

When the SP models are very large or the underlying mixed-integer problem is difficult, solving the SP as a single mathematical programming problem is impractical due to computational restrictions. Often, decomposition-based methods are adjusted to break the problem down to sub problems. These sub problems are then solved iteratively while enforcing those aspects of the problem relaxed for decomposition. One such decomposition method is the Progressive Hedging Algorithm (PHA) (Rockafellar & Wets, 1991). SP models are decomposed by scenarios rather than by time stages. PHA converges to the optimal solution when SP models convex programs. In cases where the decisions are integer, PHA is used as a heuristic method (Lokketangen & Woodruff, 1996; Fan & Liu 2010; Watson & Woodruff 2011).

Machine Learning

The machine learning model can be defined as a search for computational methods to test new knowledge skills and new ways to organize existing knowledge (Witten et al.., 2005). Different learning strategies are used in learning systems. The system that will do the learning and the learning algorithm used will vary depending on these strategies. In general, there are two basic strategies to learn from training data.

In the first strategy, Supervised Learning, the entire training data was labeled (Witten et al., 2005). This labeling process is usually done by an external mechanism (usually a human) and is therefore called consultative learning. The creation of a set of input-output pairs (training sample) of the training set is an example of advisory learning. Artificial neural networks, decision trees, bass learning, support vector machines are the most frequently used counseling methods. Artificial neural networks are a mixed model based on the model of human neurons. A neural network predicts one or more output with a given input set (Bramer, 2007). In decision trees that provide an advantage for decision makers in terms of easy interpretation and intelligibility, the learned model is shown as classification rules or decision tree. Independent features are separated into classes by the divide-and-conquer algorithm (Witten et al., 2005). The aim is to keep the depth of the tree at a minimum while grouping together data as similar as possible while the tree is being constructed. Thus, when the complexity (entropy) is reduced to a minimum, the gain at the maximum level (obtained information) is obtained. The Bayesian methods calculate the possible aggregation distribution. In some applications, data do not have class labels. In this case, the structure in the data has to be discovered. The second strategy, Unsupervised Learning, shows only input values in the system. And the system is expected to learn the relationships between the parameters in the examples themselves. However, no information is provided about what the correct outputs are. This type of learning tries to find rules in untagged training data, to retrieve cluster tags and sometimes to remove poultry numbers.

Support Vector Machines

Support Vector Machines (SVM), which is a machine learning method, is based on statistical learning theory and structural risk minimization principle (Bramer, 2007). Compared with other classification methods, SVM is a preferred method with high reliability, robustness to learning by heart, and levels of success in nonlinear classification, even though the training period is quite long (Celik, 2017). SVM is a consultative learning algorithm that aims to maximize the margin between support vectors that are determined dependent on the decision line. SVMs do not require assumptions of statistical estimation methods. SVMs can be used to classify entities as bankruptcy risk estimation and credit risk estimation.

Neural Networks

Artificial neurons, which have a structure similar to that of biological neurons, form artificial neural networks (NNs) by forming bonds between them, just as they are in biological neurons. The fact that many of the systems used in daily life have nonlinear structures render conventional methods ineffective in solving these problems, which increases the use of NNs in almost every field (Sönmez & Bülbül, 2015). Interest in NNs is increasing day by day in all areas of life, with features such as learning to possess, generalization, adaptability, speed, fault tolerance and non-linearity in solving complex problems. NN learns with examples. NNs will be able to generalize the problem using real events. Successful results cannot be achieved if the event cannot be shown to the network in all its aspects. It's not that the network is troubled; it's not showing well to the network. In order for NN to work safely, training and performance needs to be tested first. NNs can produce information by generalizing about unseen samples (Bramer, 2007). After being trained, NNs may produce results, even if there are missing data in the incoming new samples. NNs have a Distributed Memory that the information is spread over the network, and the values of the connections of the cells with each other show the knowledge of the network. NNs can model non-linear relationships that are difficult or impossible to model mathematically.

Genetic Algorithms

The basis of Genetic Algorithms (GA) is based on the survival and adaptation of the best. GA is a search method (Kartal, 2015) obtained by computer application that is created by simulating the conservation of nature and natural selection principle. Probability has a fundamental role for the genetic algorithm, which is a stochastic algorithm. The most important feature of GA, which is closely related to the concepts of natural selection and natural genetic mechanism, is to select new solutions to be produced in a probabilistic manner according to the fitness value of the existing solutions (the value of the objective function). The generation of the initial population uses probabilistic methods for selection of individuals for genetic operations in populations and the selection of points on the selected individual to apply genetic operators such as crossing or mutation. Parameter selection is another important step in GA because parameters have a significant effect on the performance of the genetic algorithm. Many studies have been carried out on these parameters, also called control parameters (Witten et al., 2005). The success or failure of the GA depends on the choice of these parameter values. GAs are among the methods used in bankruptcy prediction models, because the search space is large and complex, it is difficult to solve with existing information, the problem cannot be expressed by a certain mathematical model, and it is effective and useful when the desired result is not obtained from traditional optimization methods (Bramer, 2007).

Bayesian Models

Bayesian belief networks, which are a result of progress in artificial intelligence studies, provide decision makers with cognitive maps in the decision making process. Although the relationships expressed in Bayesian belief networks do not necessarily have to be causal, they are quite effective when causal. Bayesian belief networks use the advantages of not requiring strict statistical assumptions, graphically presenting a set of conditional independence constraints between a given number of variables and their corresponding conditional probability distributions in a chain-like fashion. Bayesian belief networks are casual maps that present a specialist's knowledge with some kind of graph based on probability theory. Bayesian belief networks are used to determine the importance and priority of causal factors along with the use of missing information and details. They provide practicality in analyzing variable and complex systems as the main advantage when historical data is acquired. Compared to other information maps, Bayesian belief networks use Bayes' theorem to find certainty factors for the interaction between decision variables.

By the 1980s, probability-based approaches have begun to be used and the commonly used logit and probit models have been developed. Neural networks models and genetic algorithms began to be used in 1990 when artificial intelligence became widespread in the 1990s. In the 2000s, the Hazard and Bayesian Approaches, which can be interpreted more easily with increasing environmental uncertainty and include uncertainty modeling, have begun to be used in modeling firms' failures.

Big Data

Big data is a business intelligence technique that differs from others of its kind. The term big data was first used by computer scientists in the mid 90's. The progress of technology and the rapid development of the Internet have made the power of knowledge come to the forefront (Dincerden, 2017). Many different types of data, including social media posts, continuously recorded log files, meteorological data, sensor data, GPS data, and space data are increasing constantly. Big data is a large collection of data clusters that consist of complex structures. It is not entirely possible to use conventional methods in processing big data. New techniques are being developed to store, process, analyze and visualize this type of data. The acquisition of meaningful data from big data communities and the useful information gained during the data analysis process help companies and organizations gain richer and deeper insights and a competitive edge. For this reason, big data applications should be analyzed and implemented as accurately as possible. The data are growing at a great speed, making it difficult to process large amounts of exabytes. The main difficulty in transporting such large quantities of data is the rapid increase in volumes compared to computing resources. The term big data, used today, is an inadequate term as it only indicates the size of the data and not its other existing features. Big data structures can be defined by associating with the following properties known as the 4Vs (Gandomi & Haider, 2015; Dincerden, 2017).

- Volume: Volume refers to the magnitude of data. The magnitude of data produced in recent years has increased tremendously. Due to its volume, big data cannot be analyzed by using conventional data processing methods, as these methods usually have high time complexities. While many traditional business intelligence algorithms are used to process gigabytes and terabytes, petabytes can be processed using big data analytics. However, volume definitions are relative and vary according to factors such as time and data type. What is considered to be big data today may not be so in the future, as storage capacities will increase and allow bigger data sets to be captured.
- Velocity: The increase in the collection speed of the data collected daily makes it necessary to develop technologies and methods that enable storage operations to be performed in a shorter time. Big data cannot be analyzed using traditional methods, which have high time complexities, due to its velocity. While previous data warehouses are updated weekly and evolved with daily updates, new technologies including big data are used to cope with the decision making speed and incoming data rate of new data.
- Variety: The growing variety of data sources leads to the accumulation of various information, such as structural and non-structural textures. Today, there is a wide variety of content to be analyzed, including social media comments, blogs, medical record notes, photographs, videos, textual data, as well as new types of digitizing data. The variety of data is due to continually emerging technologies. Data structure is generally evaluated as structured, semi-structured or non-structured.
- Value: The critical issue today is the development of new technologies that offer new ways of creating value by transforming raw data into information. Users can use and run stored queries and therefore extract important results from the filtered data obtained and also sort the data by size. These reports help companies discover business trends that can change their strategies. The data stored by different institutions and organizations is used for the data analyses of these institutions and organizations. The results obtained from the analyses serve as a guide for companies to achieve a higher profit rate. Above all, the analysis of the instantaneous data for the financial sector and its sub-sectors is of the utmost value, as it offers great advantages over other competitors.

Big Data Sources

Archives, sensor data, machine log data, social media, public web, business applications, data storage, various media, and various documents can be considered as big data sources. Data sets are growing rapidly due to the equipment that generates digital data getting cheaper and the data sources becoming more widespread. Traditional structured data was easier to store and analyze with the existing Relational Database Management Systems (RDBMS) even in large volumes. This structured data is now joined by semi-structured data such as XML and RSS feeds and unstructured data, which comes from diverse data sources including various different sensors and also web sources such as logs, click streams and mostly social media and comes in various data types such as texts, photos, videos and audio. Streaming data analytics is a sub-concept of big data analytics that specializes in processing streaming data. Most of the time streaming data comes from continuous data sources that analytics has to be done on flowing data which can either be structured or unstructured. This is different than the traditional store and process systems. In the traditional systems input data is first stored in a database, file system or memory which can be based on the nature of the system.

Big Data Analytics

Big data analytics (Gandomi & Haider, 2015) is a general term used for advanced data analysis techniques such as statistical analysis, data mining, machine learning, natural language processing, text analysis, and data visualization. Big data analysis is the implementation of advanced data analysis techniques to analyze large volumes of data. The concept of big data analytics involves the latest technology in data analysis and processing, in order to rapidly create valuable information from various data types (Gandomi & Haider, 2015; Dincerden, 2017). Based on the literature, the evolution of big data analytics is illustrated in Figure 1.

The following features form the basis of life cycle management of the big data analytics.

- Including structured data, semi-structured and unstructured data.
- Complex and dynamically changing data relationships.
- Achieving semantic via data and relationships.
- Increased development of the data model in the whole data cycle for a better expandability.
- Timely and error-free data development effect.

Figure 1. Evolution of big data analytics
(Arunachalam et al., 2018)

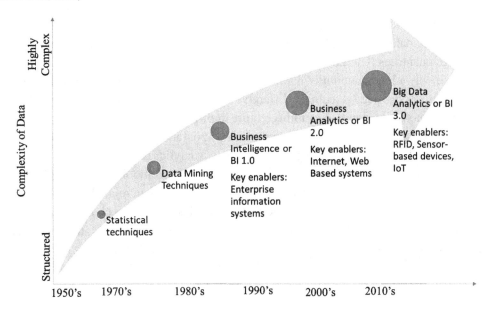

- Data distribution in different regions as multi-source and heterogeneous.

In big data analysis, a large amount of data that can affect an operation must first be analyzed. However, the complexity of the data to be analyzed and the need for specific algorithms to support such processes for various applications are difficult to analyze. Big data analytics has two main purposes: to understand the relationships between different properties and to develop effective methods of data mining that can accurately predict future observations.

Today, there are various devices that produce large amounts of data. A big data analytics platform is needed analyze such data. There are several vendors providing big data analytics platforms and software:

1.   Actian Analytics Platform
2.   Amazon Web Service
3.   Cloudera Enterprise Bigdata
4.   Google BigQuery
5.   Hortonworks Data Platform
6.   IBM Bigdata Analytics,
7.   HP Bigdata
8.   MapR
9.   Microsoft Bigdata
10.   Oracle Bigdata Analytics
11.   Pivotal Bigdata
12.   SAP Bigdata Analytics
13.   Tableau Software bigdata
14.   Teradata Bigdata Analytics

The speed of access to structured and unstructured data has also increased over time. However, there is a great need for techniques that can analyze and deliver such large amounts of data quickly. Data mining, statistical analysis and machine learning are among such analysis techniques (Cil, 2012). For example, data mining can automatically find valuable and interesting patterns in a big data set. In this respect, data mining is widely used in various fields such as basic sciences, engineering, medicine and trade. By utilizing big data analytics, highly useful hidden information regarding the business world is uncovered in large quantities (Cil, 2012).

Big Data is not only a large amount of data, but it also consists of data bits in different formats. For this reason, high processing speed is required. Effective data mining algorithms should be used to analyze big data. It should be noted that these algorithms require high-performance processors. In addition, some facilitators are developing. For example, the storage and computation requirements of big data analytics are now being effectively met by cloud computing. Big Data Analytics has five technical fields, including Big Data analysis, test analysis, web analysis, network analysis, and mobile analysis (Cil et al., 2013). There is an increase in the rise of semi-structured and unstructured data related to temporary and one-time extraction, decomposition, processing, indexing and analysis in new technological environments. Big Data Analytics allows businesses to analyze structured, semi-structured, and unstructured data. For instance, the finance department of a company makes more consistent financial decisions with the information it receives through the financial decision support system using Big Data Analytics.

Big data analysis can be applied to specific data types. However, computer science and many traditional statistical techniques are still widely used in Big Data analysis (Cil et al., 2013). There are a number of techniques that can actually be used when a project is launched. Several traditional data analysis methods used to analyze Big Data are briefly reviewed below.

- Data Mining: There are a range of different financial information systems tools. Data mining is one of these tools and is considered very important. Data mining is the process of extracting hidden information in a multitude of states and variants of data using a combination of statistical analysis techniques and artificial intelligence algorithms. Furthermore, data mining is a tool for discovering information and data mining techniques are used in financial decision-making processes (Uzar, 2013). The aim of data mining is to create decision-making models for predicting future behavior based on the analysis of past activities. Data mining is a multidisciplinary field that bridges many technical fields such as data base technology, statistics, artificial intelligence, machine learning, pattern recognition and data visualization.

- Association rule: The analysis of association rules is one of the widely used methods of data mining. It is the process of extraction of rules based on associations, relations and correlations between the data. Interesting relationships between data objects and synchronous situations are investigated. As an example of an association rule, customers who buy X and Y products can buy C product with 80% probability can be given as an example for an association rule. These kinds of association rules are meaningful if the situation related to the objects in question is frequently repeated (Birand et al.., 2012). These techniques, however, are also important in the context of the acquisition of valuable information from various events which seem not to have remarkable relations (Uzar, 2013). The discovery of some relationships that are not immediately noticeable among the various qualities in a database, where a large number of databases are stored, can help in strategic decision making. However, deriving these relationships from a large number of data, which is called cooperative mining, is not a simple process.

- Clustering Analysis: The clustering analysis provides summary information to the investigator by grouping the ungrouped data by their similarities. Grouping according to specific criteria allows creating upper groups that provide summary information by decreasing the data. In clustering analysis, there is no distinction between dependent and independent variables, unlike other highly variable techniques (Erduran, 2017). Clustering analysis is similar to Discriminant Analysis because it is often used to group data. However, the groups are pre-determined in the separation analysis and do not change during the analysis. The facts that the dependent / independent variable is not differentiated and the objects are brought together because of their characteristics are similar to factor analysis.

- Text Mining: One of the successful analysis tools developed to make meaningful aggregate of information gathered from textual data sources is text mining, a version of data mining. Text mining is defined as the automatic extraction of information from different written sources, the extraction of key items and the creation of links or hypotheses to form new facts with the information extracted. Text mining, which is different from web search, can be described as a variation of data mining. The most important feature that distinguishes text mining from data mining is the extraction of information from natural language texts rather than structured databases (Hearst, 1999). Text mining is the process of converting irregular text formatted data into digital form and extracting the qualified information in it. In the literature, it is also known as text data mining and knowledge discovery from textual databases (Oguz, 2009). Other widely used and well known methods are regression analysis and statistical analysis.

Social Media Analytics and Sentiment Analytics

According to the research of We Are Social, a global social agency, there are 4 billion internet users active around the world today; with 3 billion of these users active on Social Media (We Are Social, 2018). Social Networks are graph structures that consist of social actors/agents and relationships between these actors. Social networks are often self-organizing, complex and emergent. (Newman, 2010) Most social networks are not randomly distributed networks, where relationships between actors are distributed randomly but Scale-free networks, where relations are distributed according to a power law (Yilmaz, 2017). Social network analysis assumes that relationships among groups are important. Social network analysis evaluates, analyzes, and visually presents which nodes are communicating with each other, what facilitates the flow of information between these nodes based on the forms of relations between nodes. The social networking approach uses mathematical graph theory and statistical analysis techniques. However, it differs from the classical statistical methodology by examining its actors as a community rather than individuals. The actors that form the community and the relations, information, experiences between the actors are of fundamental interest to network theory. Each inter-node relation is represented with its own graph. In the original graphical model, the dots on the graphic represent the actors, and the lines connecting the points that represent the relationship between the actors are called the relationship.

Sentiment analysis is the measurement of people's attitude according to their writings with respect to a topic or context. The writings may include emotions, ratings, and perceptions. Sentiment analysis relies on natural language processing and machine learning to make sense of documents and classify them accordingly.

Sentiment analysis is onerous due to the high complexity of natural languages, as expressions are often hard to quantify and similar ideas can be written in many different ways which makes it hard for a computer to analyze pattern in the text. In addition to these difficulties, sentiment can be expressed with no apparent positive or negative words. With the rise of social media and the online abundance of ratings and reviews, online opinions have become an important issue for business and politics. Sentiment analysis can measure public opinions and provide intelligence using a large amount of data available online.

Use Cases

Banking and finance sector have very suitable use cases for big data projects. Fraud use cases, audit use cases, credit risk reporting, customer analytics, customer based pricing are samples of use cases. Agencies like The Securities Exchange Commission (SEC), which is maintaining fair and orderly functioning of securities markets and facilitating capital formation, is monitoring financial market activity by using network analytics and non-linear programming in big data platforms. A fraud use case and a credit risk analysis use case are mentioned below.

Fraud Use Case

Despite all the precautions taken to prevent fraud, it still continues to take place in various forms. In terms of supervisors and business management, it is important to reveal the fraud in time (Silahtaroglu,

2016; Akdemir, 2016). With the development of technology, the examination process has progressed over time, and by searching through data, proactively searching for abnormalities that may be a sign of cheating has come to the forefront. Thus, possible tricks can be detected at early stages and the operator can overcome this process with minimal harm. The banking and finance sector has suitable use cases for big data studies. Fraud crimes, credit ratings, audit use cases, credit risk analyses, customer analytics, are samples of use cases. Two of the greatest advantages brought to this sector by big data are real-time monitoring of transactions and fraud detection.

Studies carried out on national and international level to detect and prevent fraud crimes, which are almost as old as human history, are promising. However, it is known that the losses caused by fraudulent events in social and economic terms continue throughout the world (Levi & Burrows, 2008). Efforts to reduce fraud in every country and industry continue to increase. To this end, an effective system needs to be built and managed, in particular by making information sharing transparent between interested parties. At this point, governance and information systems have a vital importance.

The banking and securities sector has very suitable use cases for big data projects. Fraud use cases, audit use cases, credit risk reporting, customer analytics, customer based pricing are samples of use cases. The Securities Exchange Commission (SEC) monitors financial market activity by using network analytics and non-Linear Programming (NLP) in big data platforms. This enables to detect illegal trading activities in the financial markets.

Undoubtedly, one of the sectors that stand out both in economic terms and potential fraud issues is insurance. It is estimated that the loss due to fraud in this sector is billions of dollars (Thornton et al., 2014) and it is considered that especially accident-related fraud cases are a serious problem for the economy and institutions of a country. In connection with the detection of fraud, the effective use of information and communication technologies (ICT) offers new opportunities, but it is a daunting task to identify staged accident fraud cases.

In recent years, the role of ICT on the agenda of corporations and companies has been to contribute to business intelligence. In the insurance sector, large-scale digital transformation projects have been initiated to change the traditional way of doing business and to eliminate the clutter of legacy systems. While technology-focused solutions seem to create new opportunities to detect fraud, new fraud tactics emerge due to the weaknesses of information systems in many sectors where digital data are used. In other words, existing information systems are based on business processes, making it difficult to detect fraudulent traffic accidents and events.

International software vendors have been adding relational analysis-based software modules for fraud detection to their product ranges and are executing joint projects with the leading companies in the insurance industry. There seem to be a limited number of software products in the world that claim to be able to detect potential staged accident fraud cases. It is believed that fraudsters often exploit their interactions with humans and objects for criminal deceptions that lead to personal or financial gain.

In order to identify the complex relationships that are easily lost within information systems one needs to employ network science (that is, the science of networked relations), which enables scientists to discover new mathematical models for describing, predicting, and prescribing things and their interactions embedded in complex systems.

Stochastic based approaches to fraud detection have been adopted by using machine learning techniques. Srivastava et al. (2008) adopt stochastic approach to credit card fraud detection by using Hidden Markov Model. They present results that the model is successful for detecting fraudulent credit card purchases where the digital trace data is based on sequence of operations in credit card transactions. The model essentially reflects the normal behavior of a cardholder and in case the next transaction does not comply with the expected behavior it is considered to be fraudulent. Maes et al. (2002) applied artificial neural networks and Bayesian belief networks to credit card fraud detection and showed promising results on real-world financial data. The data used is provided by Europay International that licenses the MasterCard credit card brand in Europe. The dataset consists of credit card transactions with useful features that are anonymized. The proposed method, so-called Receiver Operating Curve (ROC), is claimed to successfully classify fraudulent transactions.

Abdallah et al. (2016) emphasized that the prevention and detection features of information systems are both needed to support protection mechanisms against fraud. Each fraud context, such as health, traffic accidents and finance, has distinguishing characteristics and is subjected to investigation in terms of various approaches and techniques. For instance, Van Vlasselaer et al.. (2016) proposed a network-based approach for detecting security fraud. Our approach as we elaborate with a use case below is similar to such approach, but we give special importance on validity issues for using digital trace data from a network science perspective (Aydin et al., 2018).

Akoglu et al. (2015) argue that earlier works on time series analysis for detecting anomalies can be associated with such statistical techniques as an auto-regressive or integrated moving average process (ARMA or ARIMA). They also provide a review on time series and data streams related fraud detection in the context of graph model. Graph-based fraud detection that uses time series data is also labeled as dynamic or temporal network analysis. Essentially dynamic time series of graph data can be considered as the aggregation of static graphs in which each snapshot may correspond to a slice of data. Regarding for fraud detection by static graphs one can use a bipartite graph for network representation. As shall be elaborated further our case is a demonstration of how to use bipartite graph model for stage accident fraud in the insurance domain.

As a case study, we consider the accident report service of Insurance Information and Monitoring Center (IIMC) of Turkey. According to the Center's official web site (www.sbm.org.tr), the Turkish government founded IIMC to collect all insurance data in a shared data base for the purpose of protecting the rights of insurance companies and the rights of the public sector. One of the missions of the Center is the prevention of fraud. The Center carries out projects to identify organized insurance fraud. The fraud initiative was first limited to "crash-for-cash" fraud detection in motor vehicle accidents (Button & Brooks, 2016), and later use cases were extended to other branches such as health, fire, life and individual accident insurance as well.

The Center provides a special online service that allows insurance companies and individuals to report accidents. We obtained information regarding what gets logged into the IIMC database as insurance companies interact with each other through the service. We learned that there are eight distinct stages in the claim evaluation process before the decision is made to pay a claim. Each accident reported to the system is assigned a unique accident identification number, which is the only piece of information that IIMC use to differentiate between accidents.

Reported vehicle collisions between drivers are rare incidents as drivers take every evasive action possible to avoid accidents, especially ones that result in loss of life and property. If we think about who we have been involved in an accident with, we might have been involved in collisions with a few drivers or around a dozen drivers at most and there are thousands of drivers in the district we live. This means that almost every driver that we could potentially be involved in an accident with, we do not collide with. Or, almost every possible collision between drivers in the World is non-collision, that is, avoidance, it is not registered in the data base; so data collected by centers like IIMC in this respect is sparse; as opposed to dense data in a world where every driver is colliding with each other Moreover, the relation between collision and evasive action was studied by Fuji and Tanaka (1971) who inferred that only one evasive action in 100,000 may fail.

Many systems can be regarded as networks, sets of things and their interactions. In a graphic representation of a network, nodes (or vertices) are the things of interest, and interacting nodes are joined in pairs by arcs (or links). A network is a mathematical object specifically designed to represent sparse data, and network science is concerned with analyzing and modeling such systems (Newman, 2010).

Let us regard the sparse data of recorded the vehicle accidents on the IIMC data base as a network. To emphasize this, from now on, we will refer to the network produced by the drivers who have been involved in accidents as the "faulty evasive action network" (FEAN). To put it simply, accident occurrence means concurrent failure of evasive action by one or several drivers. In FEAN the objects of interest are the drivers, and the drivers are joined in pairs by arcs if they fail to take evasive action, i.e., were involved in an accident.

The network science approach to sparse data turns the staged accident fraud detection problem into pattern recognition on FEAN, in which the task is to identify the structural patterns within the network associated with normative accident events, and consequently pinpoint the unusual patterns that go against the grain. What shape does the FEAN take? Mathematically, if we assume that a collision between two drivers occurs one in 100,000 encounters, the probability of multiple accidents happening between the same driver as to be next to none (i.e., around one in ten billion). Thus, we can hypothesize that the vanishingly small probability of multiple accidents between the same drivers result in a network that takes a tree like structure, in which root nodes correspond to the drivers who tend to be involved in at least three (possibly more) accidents and the leaf nodes correspond to the drivers who were involved in (at most) two accidents. The next question is what unusual patterns does the network reveal? Following the same line of reasoning we can hypothesize that the exceedingly rare loop structures that signify multiple accidents between the same drivers are strong candidates for crash-for-cash staged fraud.

The dataset that we collected from one of the insurance companies constitutes a select part of the event-based digital trace data retrieved from the IIMC. In the data set, the recorded stages relate to the trace left by the process of evaluating accident insurance claims in the automobile category of the insurance industry. By its very nature, trace data is longitudinal data, as the recorded stages occur in time. So, the network structure that we produced is an aggregation of events over a period of time, namely eight years and two months. The network we produced is an aggregation of approved insurance claims only, that is, either private insurance companies or the IIMC Commission for Automobile Accidents or both agreed to pay claim compensation for material and physical damage via the insured vehicle depending on the claims filed.

Technically speaking, we model FEAN as a special kind of tree network that is a forest. Forests are acyclic tree networks. That is, there is no pathway that starts and ends in the same driver node. By definition, all forests are two-mode (bipartite) networks having no loops or multiple edges. The model permits us to combine both the drivers who are involved in an accident and the accident identification number assigned to the reported accident event. The model is indicative of both the general forest structure of FEAN and IIMC. Unusual patterns within FEAN may indicate possible fraud cases.

A typical scenario for fraudulent reporting of automobile accidents, commonly referred to as staged accident fraud, is given as follows: Suppose that two fraudsters, who will be referred to as A and B, report two staged accidents. In order not to be caught by the authorities, A and B allegedly drive different cars and different districts are selected for the staged accidents. The districts may or may not be within the same city. IIMC logs the chassis numbers (abbreviated to C, see the Figure 2) of the cars, and the district of the accident (abbreviated to L, see the Figure 2) which is incorporated into the FEAN model.

Unusual patterns such as this loop (Figure 2) within FEAN may indicate possible fraud cases. Drivers A and B report that they were involved in two road accidents, in two distinct locations, L_1 and L_2 while driving different cars C_1, C_2, C_3, and C_4. In an FEAN of 3,974,190 nodes and 3,024,772 edges reconstructed from IIMC data of paid claims we have observed 955,625 disconnected network components. Each network component contains at least one accident event. Of these 955,625 components 5,555 of them contain loop structures such as shown in Figure 2. We have devised an algorithm that searches for fraudster networks based on location and vehicle chassis numbers. The algorithm detected 28 network components that contain accident events for which both the districts of the events and all chassis numbers differ. In other words, according to what is filed to IMMS two drivers were involved in two accident events while driving four different cars in two different districts.

Figure 2. Fraudster network

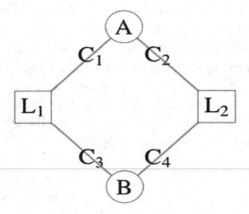

More sophisticated algorithms can be devised that can incorporate the time of the accident events as well to search for fraudster networks.

However, a graphical model alone, no matter how sophisticated it is, cannot be expected to accurately determine staged insurance fraud. Each and every fraudster network detected by the FEAN model begs verification, which is the important role of loss adjusters, who should always have the last word in fraudulent claims.

Credit Risk Analytics Use Case

Based on the needs of the organizations in the sector and the continually innovative solutions in the industry, revealing new infrastructure and applications, and shaping works with successful Research and Development activities are inevitable. Consequently, volume of credit, important and inevitable source of support for activities or financial needs of organizations and individuals, has experienced tremendous growth in recent years. The increase of the volume of the loan portfolio has brought significant gains for financial institutions, especially banks.

Improvement of the ability to manage sectoral, economic and geopolitical risks and further changes will contribute to economic recovery and development across organizations, sectors and even countries. Credit risk is one of the major risks faced by finance sector, especially commercial banks, and has an important effect on the profitability ratios. Credit rating refers to a relative opinion on the credit worthiness of an independent and aforementioned entity created by credit rating agencies or groups on the credit risk of the borrower, where the party is a state, financial institution, company or a financial asset issued (Zan et al, 2004). In other words, the rating is the activity of rating and classification of the risk status and pay ability of enterprises or capital market institutions, with capital market instruments representing the indebtedness, principal money, interest and similar liabilities in the light of certain criteria by credit rating agencies. Above-mentioned rating activity is conducted by examining, evaluating and classifying the ability of businesses or countries to meet the financial obligations of their liquidity, profitability and financial structure by taking into account the sectoral, economic, financial, political and social conditions (Zan et al, 2004; Wang et al, 2018). Credit rating is an important source of information on the risk to the parties involved (Zan et al, 2004; Kılıçaslan and Giter, 2016). This reduces the representation costs resulting from not having equal information between the parties and contributes to the more effective and effective work of the markets (Kılıçaslan and Giter, 2016). Opportunities for investors, exporters and other entrepreneurs have emerged with the increase in the credit supply and demand in the financial markets together with globalization and this has led to the opening of new national and international markets to the banks, especially banks and credit markets. The fact that credit marketing institutions do not fully recognize the region, the sector and the customer has brought various challenges which leads to high emphasis on credit rating (Shi et al, 2016).

Consequently, the credit rating or scoring systems are extremely important in the decision making process for banks and other financial institutions that lend to customers. In today's intense competition environment, in order to perform financial analysis for clients, financial institutions are forced to rely on very high costs and tend to use software packages and solutions, or to trust the methodologies of their staff, which may not be analytical or academic or even not based on present methodologies. An increase in the number of potential applicants has helped to develop the automated credit approval procedures. Financial institutions constitute various internal credit assessment models that reveal the relationships between variables affecting credit scoring. In the literature, statistics and machine learning techniques for credit ratings have been widely studied. According to the findings obtained from previously mentioned studies, while statistical methods like discriminant analysis, linear regression, and ANOVA are very effective in the selection of variables, the machine learning techniques are effective in ensuring provision. Such methods have become increasingly more important in recent years with the growth in commercial loans. Although there are a wide range of applied statistical methods in the literature, they are limited due to commercial confidentiality. Since data collection is difficult, the development of the customer credit rating model has been implemented later on compared to commercial credit rating. Banks must diminish the risk in their operations, since the financial crisis reveals the current banking risk. In recent years, many financial institutions and researchers have examined many different credit rating models, due to the publicly available data in some countries (Wang et al, 2018). In bank loans, scope of credit rating models used are not broad scope and banks mainly adopt the mortgage method. Damage becomes inevitable when the mortgaged property is depreciated. Banks should make better use of their capital and capital should include the data in the database. Banks should use customer data in better ways. The Bank relies on model and algorithm in lending business and direct marketing, not on machine learning (Wang et al, 2018). Multivariate discriminant analysis and logistic regression (LR) have been used as statistical methods to determine the credit worthiness. Many studies (Sheen, 2005; Landajo et al., 2007) showed that the decision trees or NNs, exhibit more consistent results regarding the determination of bankruptcy and the estimation of credit worthiness than discriminant analysis or logistic regression. However, some studies (Hsieh, 2004; Lee & Chen, 2005) focused on the strengths of different models, including hybrid methodologies. Studies related with credit scoring and credit rating problems have shown that machine learning techniques are superior to statistical techniques (Luo et al, 2017; Wang et al, 2018). Decision certainty on the applicant's credit score/rating or worthiness minimizes potential losses and helps to increase the lending capacity of financial institutions. Additionally, this increase has also helped the development of advanced techniques that control the financial health of the borrower and intervening great accuracy on credit scoring and rating.

As a case study we consider loan data for issuing the decision on the assessment of customers' demand for credit and acceptance of loan requests. The purpose of the credit score model is to classify the credit applicants in seven groups: starting from those who will be able to pay back liabilities (good credit rating or good performance class) and ending with those who will fail to fulfill the financial obligations and need to be deprived of credit as a consequence the high risk (bad credit rating or low performance class). Hence, the credit score represents a person's likelihood of being able to pay back the loan. Poor credit worthiness shows that there is a high risk on a loan, and thus may lead to the rejection of application or high interest rates for borrowing.

The dataset that we collected from (Kaggle Inc., 2019) involves 74 attributes and 887,000 instances. It has been seen that it is possible to use up to 34 variables, which are re-examined in the original data set, as the input variable and 1 variable as the class variable which shows the customer's discrete class. 7 discrete classes for estimation have been created for the class variable. We have removed irrelevant attributes that may affect the accuracy of classification. Variables that cannot be converted to numeric values or non-categorical variables are excluded from the data set. We have run ANOVA on the data set. The variable has been considered relevant and informative with regard to the credit rating decision on the basis of the difference (significant / low p-value). We have eliminated attributes with relatively high p-values. Also, rows and columns with many missing values have been neglected. As a consequence, we selected 34 attributes with 100,000 instances. We have used scalar normalization to scale numeric attributes between 0 and 1. MLP and SVM classifiers have been used. Levenberg-Marquardt Back Propagation Algorithm is preferred because it has an effective learning algorithm with little computational time for each iteration (Anyaeche and Ighravwe, 2013; Lavanya and Parveentaj, 2013), since we have been dealing with a big dataset in this case study.

To provide reliable estimation and to minimize the impact of data dependence on credit rating model development, k-fold cross-validation (10-fold) is used. Here, the entire credit data set is randomly separated into 10 subunits and layers of approximately equal size. After one of the 10 groups is separated as a test group, the remaining 9 (k-1) groups are trained on each fold. After training is completed, accuracy performance is calculated on the test group. This process is repeated 10 times so that the remaining groups taken as test data set at least once. Finally, the average of 10 different accuracy values is taken. Consequently, each model has been trained and tested by 10 times. It is contemplated that a prediction obtained from 10-fold cross validation will be more reliable than a prediction that is commonly applied using a single validation set.

The SVM classifier has obtained prediction accuracy comparable to that of MLP as around 85%. However, the MLP classifier was slightly slower and less accurate (81%) than the SVM classifier. Machine learning classification and feature selection methods have been applied in Python environment.

CONCLUSION

Big data analytics is used in the finance field for purposes such as estimation of stock prices, pricing of company treasuries, portfolio management, direct marketing, and credit dealing, understanding and managing financial risk, forecasting exchange rates, and credit rating. Big data analytics is also used to predict financial distress and crises. Risks and uncertainties are driving factors of financial distress and crises. Market, financial, operational, social, environmental, institutional and humanitarian risks and uncertainties are the inherent realities of the modern world. Several techniques like financial econometrics and optimization models have been used to uncover insights on risks and uncertainties. Basically, this chapter is intended to explore big data analytics as a comprehensive technique for processing large amounts of data to uncover insights. Elaborate use cases have been given for the readers to derive full understanding of the importance of the subject. Moreover, the focus is on how big data has altered the methods of conventional analysis techniques in these cases. The chapter has tried to illustrate with detailed examples of how big data models help managers to manage risk.

REFERENCES

Abdallah, A., Maarof, M. A., & Zainal, A. (2016). Fraud detection system: A survey. *Journal of Network and Computer Applications*, *68*, 90–113. doi:10.1016/j.jnca.2016.04.007

Abdou, H. A. (2009). Genetic programming for credit scoring: The case of Egyptian public sector banks. *Expert Systems with Applications*, *36*(9), 11402–11417. doi:10.1016/j.eswa.2009.01.076

Akdemir, C. (2016). *Detecting Fraud by Using Data Mining Techniques and an Application in Retail Sector* (Doctoral Dissertation). Marmara University Social Sciences Institute, Istanbul, Turkey.

Akoglu, L., Tong, H., & Koutra, D. (2015). Graph based anomaly detection and description: A survey. *Data Mining and Knowledge Discovery*, *29*(3), 626–688. doi:10.100710618-014-0365-y

Arunachalam, D., Kumar, N., & Kawalek, J. P. (2018). Understanding big data analytics capabilities in supply chain management: Unravelling the issues, challenges and implications for practice. *Transportation Research Part E, Logistics and Transportation Review*, *114*, 416–436. doi:10.1016/j.tre.2017.04.001

Aydin, M. N., Kariniauskaite, D., & Perdahci, N. Z. (2018). Validity Issues of Digital Trace Data for Platform as a Service: A Network Science Perspective. Proceedings of Trends and Advances in Information Systems and Technologies. WorldCIST'18 2018. doi:10.1007/978-3-319-77703-0_65

Bachelier, L. (2011). *Louis Bachelier's theory of speculation: the origins of modern finance*. Princeton, NJ: Princeton University Press; doi:10.1515/9781400829309

Birant, D., Kut, A., Ventura, M., Altınok, H., Altınok, B., Altınok, E., & Ihlamur, M. (2012). *A New Approach for Quality Function Deployment: An Application*. Paper presented at Akademik Bilisim 2010, Mugla, Turkey.

Bramer, M. (2007). *Principles of data mining*. London: Springer.

Button, M., & Brooks, G. (2016). From 'shallow'to 'deep'policing:'crash-for-cash'insurance fraud investigation in England and Wales and the need for greater regulation. *Policing and Society*, *26*(2), 210–229. doi:10.1080/10439463.2014.942847

Celik, S. (2017). Applying Web Usage Mining for the Analysis of Web Log Files. *Istanbul Business Research*, *46*(1), 62–75.

Chiralaksanakul, A., & Mahadevan, S. (2007). Decoupled approach to multidisciplinary design optimization under uncertainty. *Optimization and Engineering*, *8*(1), 21–42. doi:10.100711081-007-9014-2

Cil, I. (2012). Consumption universes based supermarket layout through association rule mining and multidimensional scaling. *Expert Systems with Applications*, *39*(10), 8611–8625. doi:10.1016/j.eswa.2012.01.192

Cil, I., & Turkan, Y. S. (2013). An ANP-based assessment model for lean enterprise transformation. *International Journal of Advanced Manufacturing Technology*, *64*(5-8), 1113–1130. doi:10.100700170-012-4047-x

Dantzig, G. B. (2010). Linear programming under uncertainty. In *Stochastic programming* (pp. 1–11). New York, NY: Springer. doi:10.1007/978-1-4419-1642-6_1

Dincerden, E. (2017). *Is Zekasi ve Stratejik Yonetim*. Istanbul: Beta Basım Dagitim Co.

Fama, E. F. (1965). The behavior of stock-market prices. *The Journal of Business*, *38*(1), 34–105. doi:10.1086/294743

Fama, E. F. (1970). Efficient capital markets: A review of theory and empirical work. *The Journal of Finance*, *25*(2), 383–417. doi:10.2307/2325486

Fan, Y., & Liu, C. (2010). Solving stochastic transportation network protection problems using the progressive hedging-based method. *Networks and Spatial Economics*, *10*(2), 193–208. doi:10.100711067-008-9062-y

Fujii, Y., & Tanaka, K. (1971). Traffic capacity. *Journal of Navigation*, *24*(4), 543–552. doi:10.1017/S0373463300022384

Gandomi, A., & Haider, M. (2015). Beyond the hype: Big data concepts, methods, and analytics. *International Journal of Information Management*, *35*(2), 137–144. doi:10.1016/j.ijinfomgt.2014.10.007

Hearst, M. A. (1999). Untangling Text Data Mining. In *Proceedings of the 37th Annual Meeting of the Association for Computational Linguistics on Computational Linguistics*. Association for Computational Linguistics. 10.3115/1034678.1034679

Hsieh, N.-C. (2005). Hybrid mining approach in the design of credit scoring models. *Expert Systems with Applications*, *28*(4), 655–665. doi:10.1016/j.eswa.2004.12.022

Ican, O. (2013). *Determining the Functional Structure of Financial Time Series by Means of Genetic Learning*. Anadolu University, Graduate School of Social Sciences.

Kaggle Inc. (2019). *Loan data set*. [Data file]. Retrieved from https://www.kaggle.com/prateikmahendra/loan-data

Kartal, B. (2015). *Financial Portfolio Optimization with Artifical Bee Colony Algorithm*. Istanbul University, Social Sciences Institute.

Kılıçaslan, H., & Giter, M. S. (2016). Kredi Derecelendirme ve Ortaya Çıkan Sorunlar [Credit Rating and Emerging Issues]. *Maliye Araştırmaları Dergisi, 2*(1), 61–81.

Landajo, M., Andres, J. D., & Lorca, P. (2007). Robust neural modeling for the cross-sectional analysis of accounting information. *European Journal of Operational Research, 177*(2), 1232–1252. doi:10.1016/j.ejor.2005.10.064

Langlois, R. N., & Cosgel, M. M. (1993). Frank Knight on risk, uncertainty, and the firm: A new interpretation. *Economic Inquiry, 31*(3), 456–465. doi:10.1111/j.1465-7295.1993.tb01305.x

Lee, T.-S., & Chen, I.-F. (2005). A two-stage hybrid credit scoring model using artificial neural networks and multivariate adaptive regression splines. *Expert Systems with Applications, 28*(4), 743–752. doi:10.1016/j.eswa.2004.12.031

Levi, M., & Burrows, J. (2008). Measuring the impact of fraud in the UK: A conceptual and empirical journey. *British Journal of Criminology, 48*(3), 293–318. doi:10.1093/bjc/azn001

Lkhagva, B., Suzuki, Y., & Kawagoe, K. (2006, April). New time series data representation ESAX for financial applications. In *22nd International Conference on Data Engineering Workshops (ICDEW'06)* (pp. x115-x115). IEEE. 10.1109/ICDEW.2006.99

Løkketangen, A., & Woodruff, D. L. (1996). Progressive hedging and tabu search applied to mixed integer (0, 1) multistage stochastic programming. *Journal of Heuristics, 2*(2), 111–128. doi:10.1007/BF00247208

Luo, C., Wu, D., & Wu, D. (2017). A deep learning approach for credit scoring using credit default swaps. *Engineering Applications of Artificial Intelligence, 65*, 465–470. doi:10.1016/j.engappai.2016.12.002

Maes, S., Tuyls, K., Vanschoenwinkel, B., & Manderick, B. (2002). *Credit card fraud detection using Bayesian and neural networks*. Paper presented at 1st International Naiso Congress on Neuro Fuzzy Technologies, Havana, Cuba.

Mandelbrot, B. B. (1963). The variation of certain speculative prices. *The Journal of Business, 24*, 392–417.

Newman, M. (2010). *Networks: an introduction*. Oxford, UK: Oxford University Press. doi:10.1093/acprof:oso/9780199206650.001.0001

Paul, W., & Baschnagel, J. (2013). *Stochastic processes*. Heidelberg, Germany: Springer. doi:10.1007/978-3-319-00327-6

Rockafellar, R. T., & Wets, R. J. B. (1991). Scenarios and policy aggregation in optimization under uncertainty. *Mathematics of Operations Research, 16*(1), 119–147. doi:10.1287/moor.16.1.119

Saraoglu, A. C. (2017). *Stock Price Reactions to Dividend Changes: a Comparative Test of Signalling Theory and Market Efficiency in The Emerging Emea Stock Markets* (Doctoral Dissertation). Kadir Has University, Istanbul, Turkey.

Sheen, J. N. (2005). Fuzzy financial profitability analyses of demand side management alternatives from participant perspective. *Information Sciences, 169*(3-4), 329–364. doi:10.1016/j.ins.2004.05.007

Shi, B., Chen, N., & Wang, J. (2016). A credit rating model of microfinance based on fuzzy cluster analysis and fuzzy pattern recognition: Empirical evidence from Chinese 2,157 small private businesses. *Journal of Intelligent & Fuzzy Systems, 31*(6), 3095–3102. doi:10.3233/JIFS-169195

Silahtaroglu, G. (2016). *Veri madenciliği*. Istanbul: Papatya Press.

Solak, S. (2007). *Efficient solution procedures for multistage stochastic formulations of two problem classes*. Georgia Institute of Technology.

Sönmez, F., & Bülbül, S. (2015). An intelligent software model design for estimating deposit banks profitability with soft computing techniques. *Neural Network World, 25*(3), 319–345. doi:10.14311/NNW.2015.25.017

Srivastava, A., Kundu, A., Sural, S., & Majumdar, A. (2008). Credit card fraud detection using hidden Markov model. *IEEE Transactions on Dependable and Secure Computing, 5*(1), 37–48. doi:10.1109/TDSC.2007.70228

Teräsvirta, T. (2009). An Introduction to Univariate GARCH Models. In T. Mikosch, J. P. Kreiß, R. Davis, & T. Andersen (Eds.), *Handbook of Financial Time Series*. Heidelberg, Germany: Springer. doi:10.1007/978-3-540-71297-8_1

Thornton, D., van Capelleveen, G., Poel, M., van Hillegersberg, J., & Mueller, R. (2014, April). *Outlier-based health insurance fraud detection for us medicaid data*. Paper presented at 16th International Conference on Enterprise Information Systems, ICEIS 2014, Lisbon, Portugal.

Ulusavas, O. (2010). *Short Term Predictable Patterns Following Price Shocks Conditional On Characteristics of Information Signals, Foreign Investment and Investor Confidence: Evidence from Istanbul Stock Exchange* (Doctoral Dissertation). Yeditepe University, Istanbul, Turkey.

Uzar, C. (2013). *The Usage of Data Mining Technology in Financial Information System: an Application on Borsa Istanbul* (Doctoral Dissertation). Dokuz Eylül University Social Sciences Institute, Izmir, Turkey.

Van Vlasselaer, V., Eliassi-Rad, T., Akoglu, L., Snoeck, M., & Baesens, B. (2016). Gotcha! Network-based fraud detection for social security fraud. *Management Science, 63*(9), 3090–3110. doi:10.1287/mnsc.2016.2489

Wang, D., Zhang, Z., Bai, R., & Mao, Y. (2018). A hybrid system with filter approach and multiple population genetic algorithm for feature selection in credit scoring. *Journal of Computational and Applied Mathematics, 329*, 307–321. doi:10.1016/j.cam.2017.04.036

Watson, J. P., & Woodruff, D. L. (2011). Progressive hedging innovations for a class of stochastic mixed-integer resource allocation problems. *Computational Management Science, 8*(4), 355–370. doi:10.100710287-010-0125-4

Witten, I. H., Paynter, G. W., Frank, E., Gutwin, C., & Nevill-Manning, C. G. (2005). KEA: Practical Automated Keyphrase Extraction. In Design and Usability of Digital Libraries: Case Studies in the Asia Pacific (pp. 129-152). IGI Global.

Yildiz, E. G. (2017). *Analysis of Online Customer Complaints by Data Mining* (Doctoral Dissertation). Trakya University Social Sciences Institute, Edirne, Turkey.

Yilmaz, S. E. (2017). *Evaluation of the Ability of the Social Network Analysis Method about Establishment of the Relations and Contradictions in Prescribing Characteristics, with the Real World Data* (Doctoral Dissertation). Istanbul University, Institute of Health Science, Istanbul, Turkey.

Zan, H., Hsinchun, C., Chia-Jung, H., Wun-Hwa, C., & Soushan, W. (2004). Credit rating analysis with support vector machines and neural networks: A market comparative study. *Decision Support Systems*, *37*(4), 543–558. doi:10.1016/S0167-9236(03)00086-1

Chapter 9
Developing a Method to Valuate the Collection of Big Data

Colleen Carraher Wolverton

University of Louisiana at Lafayette, Department of Management, Lafayette, USA

Brandi N. Guidry Hollier

University of Louisiana at Lafayette, Department of Management, Lafayette, USA

Michael W. Totaro

University of Louisiana at Lafayette, School of Computing and Informatics, Lafayette, USA

Lise Anne D. Slatten

University of Louisiana at Lafayette, Department of Management, Lafayette, USA

ABSTRACT

Although organizations recognize the potential of "big data," implementation of data analytics processes can consume a considerable amount of resources. The authors propose that when organizations are considering this costly and often risky investment, they need a systematic method to evaluate the costs of data collection associated with the implementation of a new data and analytics (D & A) strategy or an expansion of an existing effort. Therefore, in this article, a new dimension of big data is proposed which is incorporated into a theoretically justified and systematic method for quantifying the costs and benefits of the data collection process. By estimating the worth of data, organizations can more efficiently focus on streamlining the collection of the most beneficial data and jettisoning less valuable data collection efforts.

INTRODUCTION

Interest in data and analytics (D & A) by business, healthcare, government, and numerous other entities continues to increase exponentially. By definition, analytics involves quantitative and/or qualitative analysis of data in an effort to categorize and identify patterns to unveil meaningful trends. It also encompasses various business intelligence initiatives (Gartner, 2017). Data and analytics support decision-making

DOI: 10.4018/978-1-6684-3662-2.ch009

through a better understanding of an organization's customers and its products, as well as identification of possible risks to the firm (Yaqoob et al., 2016). The interest in this area is due in no small measure to the recent availability of computational and analytical tools necessary to store, access, organize, and analyze such massive text and imagery data. In fact, there is a growing interdependence between computational modeling and data analytics, which is not without unique technical challenges, particularly in the areas of science and engineering (Reed & Dongarra, 2015). The prominence of "big data" was made evident in August 2010 when it, along with healthcare and national security, was positioned by the White House, Office of Management and Budget (OMB), and the Office of Science & Technology Policy (OSTP) as a national priority (Kaisler, Armour, Espinosa, & Money, 2013). According to Gartner (2017), big data is "high-volume, high-velocity and/or high-variety information assets that demand cost-effective, innovative forms of information processing that enable enhanced insight, decision making, and process automation."

Investment in big data and analytics continues to increase rapidly. A recent Forbes article declared that worldwide revenues for business analytics and big data will increase from $130.1 billion in 2016 to more than $203 billion in 2020 (Press, 2017). Such investment growth appears to reflect a considerable interest by organizations of all types and sizes in big data and data analytics.

With such significant investment in and continuing growth of big data and analytics, it is not unreasonable to conclude that organizations believe that big data and analytics can improve business performance. In fact, the MIT Center for Digital Business sought to test the hypothesis that data-driven organizations would generally be better performers (McAfee, Brynjolfsson, & Davenport, 2012) than other organizations. Their results indicate that companies in the top third of those organizations that use data-driven decision making were approximately 5% more productive and 6% more profitable than their competitors. Such findings demonstrate the importance of the use of big data and data analytics by corporations.

Although organizations recognize the potential of "big data," implementation of data analytics processes can consume a considerable amount of resources (Raghupathi & Raghupathi, 2014). Indeed, the amount of financial investment and time resources necessary to effectively implement a new data analytics initiative in an organization is significantly more than traditional analytics approaches (Raghupathi & Raghupathi, 2014). Furthermore, D & A projects can be risky, as Gartner estimates that they falter 60% of the time (Carande, Lipinski, & Gusher, 2017).

We propose that when organizations are considering this costly and risky investment, they need a systematic method to evaluate the costs of data collection associated with the implementation of a new D & A strategy or an expansion of an existing effort. While any new process will involve the use of organizational resources, this is not always easily quantified. Ward, Daniel, and Peppard (2008) offer ways of overcoming the difficulties of this quantification, several of which are pertinent and adaptable to the valuation model presented herein: estimations of detailed internal evidence, modeling or simulation, and benchmarking of existing cutting-edge processes of first-mover corporations or comparable processes in other industries. In this paper, we propose a new dimension of big data which we incorporate into a theoretically justified and systematic method for quantifying the costs and benefits of the data collection process. Such an approach will bring economic and effective solutions to improve business decision making.

The remainder of the paper is organized as follows: first, we propose a new dimension of big data: valuation. We then present the systematic method for organizations to evaluate the value of a particular D & A initiative. Finally, practical implications of the method are offered.

VALUATION

Information is power. The three dimensions of big data have often been defined as volume, variety, and velocity (Kaisler et al., 2013). We will now describe each of the extant dimensions.

Volume

The amount of data available has grown exponentially with 90% of data in the world produced in less than the last five years (Wu, Zhu, Wu, & Ding, 2014). Organizations are developing ways to obtain useful information from the volume of available data today. At the most basic level, organizations must understand how to work with the size and variety of data and how to use this information in a forward-thinking manner (Wu et al., 2014). Other important considerations include ownership of the information, access, collection and storage of the data. The ability to apply a valuation dimension to the management of the volume of data and sheer number of records available will allow for strategic decision making.

Variety

Structured (numbers, dates, and strings) and unstructured data (surveillance video, product evaluations, weather data, mobile data, audio recordings, and social media data) provide the basis for the many types of data available today from customers, vendors, and nearly all aspects of human activity. A variety of data types yields information that can be dissected and stratified along a wide variety of dimensions resulting in diverse data representations. Such richness can also increase the inefficiency in how information is shared across the organization (Seddon & Currie, 2017). The variety and differences bring challenges to organizations, although we posit that an understanding of the collection methods and storing of the most valued data can yield sustainable competitive advantage.

Velocity

Data coming from different sources flowing at different speeds can challenge traditional database storage systems. Data management and processing issues also add to the challenges. The rapid collection of large-scale information and timely analysis of data in real-time (or nearly real-time) impacts access to information that can influence all aspects of business operations. Pressure to collect and process data as fast as possible can also create bottlenecks in an organization. These performance bottlenecks create the need for continuous investment of large-scale budget resources in order to craft effective infrastructure solutions (Seddon & Currie, 2017). The ability to quickly conduct a value assessment on the management and processing of incoming data provides managers with the ability to make decisions regarding access to the information and its uses. Nearly all business transactions today depend on the speed of data creation.

Valuation

In addition to these extant dimensions, we propose a new dimension: valuation. Although researchers have declared the notion of value and value creation as imperative in D & A (McAfee et al., 2012), discussion around the topic has remained mainly superficial (McAfee et al., 2012). Therefore, we seek to fill this gap in the literature through the development of a systematic method for organizations to evaluate the value of a particular D & A initiative.

For decades, corporations have sought to amass large amounts of data to provide them with better decision-making power (Chen, Chiang, & Storey, 2012). However, over time, we postulate that organizations have accumulated a nimiety of data, much of which may never be utilized or provide any benefit to the organization. This study describes a sustainable method for quantifying the costs and benefits of the data collection process. Specifically, we present a tool that can be used to systematically valuate the collection of new data. By estimating the worth of data, organizations can more efficiently focus on streamlining the collection of the most beneficial data and jettisoning less valuable data collection efforts.

In order to collect, distribute, and analyze new information within an organization and to ultimately position the organization to realize performance improvements, as a result, business processes must be changed (Sharma, Mithas, & Kankanhalli, 2014). Sharma et al. (2014) argue that the transformation of business processes, particularly decision-making processes and those related to resource allocation, is a necessary step. According to Côrte-Real, Oliveira, and Ruivo (2017), big data analytics creates value for business. It results in a more agile organization through knowledge management and its effect on process change (Côrte-Real et al., 2017). It is important to note, however, that it takes valuable time and financial resources to implement such changes. As these resources are scarce commodities, organizations must focus on thoroughly evaluating the numerous costs associated with the implementation of new data collection processes. By valuating the collection of new data, we can determine whether there is a reasonable business case for the collection of new data. Thus, in order to valuate new data collection for organizations, we have adapted the classification framework for building a business case for IT investments from Ward et al. (2008) to develop a customized cost–benefit analysis (CBA) metric. This will provide organizations with a tool to compare the costs of obtaining new data with the benefits of having the new information.

THE VALUATION PROCESS

The technological, financial, and organizational cost factors expended to change business processes can be high, and thus must be justified (Mutschler & Reichert, 2012). Through a review of the literature, we have developed a process to valuate the costs and benefits of each relevant data set. We began by adapting Ward et al.'s (2008) framework to analyze the costs and risks associated with the existing data collection process in addition to the new data collection process. The framework should be evaluated to assess both the current data collection process in addition to augmenting new data sets into the data collection process.

First, the organization should create a baseline evaluation of the current process involved in collecting the data. Although organizations traditionally focus on only financial costs to collecting data, additional costs and risks such as time investments and data security risks to collecting the data should also be calculated. Many small and medium-sized firms had difficulties with data security prior to the onset of big data. With the increase in the amount, complexity, and layers of data, organizations are faced with the potential for more security risks and breaches than ever before (Marr, 2017). According to the 2017 Poneman Institute Cost of Data Breach Study of 419 organizations in 11 counties, the average cost per breach was approximately $3.6 million. Organizations should analyze the financial cost, time investment, level of difficulty to collect data, level of complexity to collect data, and conduct a data security risk analysis associated with the collection, processing, analyzing, distribution, and retention of that data. Generally, a cross-functional team should be assembled to properly develop this calculation. Table 1 provides the framework for this analysis.

Table 1. Evaluation of costs of data collection

		Process				
		Collecting	Processing	Analyzing	Distributing	Retaining
Costs and Risks	Financial cost					
	Time investment					
	Data security risks					
	Level of difficulty to collect data					
	Level of complexity of collect data					

The costs and risks should be described both qualitatively in addition to being scored quantitatively. Figure 1 specifies examples of quantitative measures to be utilized to evaluate each cost and risk in the data collection process. This mixed-methods approach is often referred to as superior to the mono-method approach (Johnson and Onwuegbuzie 2004).

After having calculated the costs associated with collecting the data, we will now discuss the customized data valuation measures. By analyzing the value of the current data collection processes, we can determine whether the collection of this data should be continued. Furthermore, by analyzing the value of collecting new data sources, we can determine whether their inclusion can be justified.

MEASURING VALUE OF DATA

In order to quantify the value of certain qualitative variables, we have developed scales to measure these constructs. Specifically, in order to quantify the benefits from the analysis of this data, we have developed a measure which analyzes the extent to which collection of specific data would provide certain benefits. An organization would utilize this survey (refer to Table 2) to collect the data to estimate the values of these constructs. We have included examples of benefits, although the specific benefits could be customized to reflect the origination's desired benefits. Therefore, a benefit total can be calculated from this measure, which can be utilized to compare benefits from each data collection effort.

Finally, the organization should compare the results from the two data valuation steps and provide recommendations for the most valuable data from the findings, including data that is currently being collected and new data collection opportunities. By evaluating the benefits associated with the current data collection process in addition to the benefits that could be achieved by collecting new data, the organization can systematically analyze whether the collection, processing, analysis, distribution, and retention of certain data sets will result in financial or operational benefits to the firm. Other, more subjective benefits, such as increased value for customers, risk reduction, or enhanced decision-making abilities are equally important to consider. Organizations should begin with a global measure of the perceived overall value of each data set, and then determine the perceived value of the anticipated benefits.

Figure 1. Quantitative measure of data collection costs

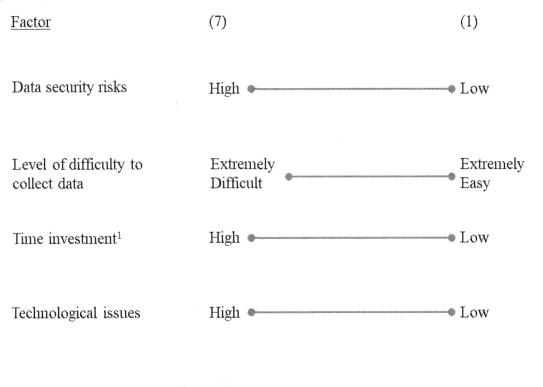

[1]Organizations should collect an actual time investment amount for data sets that are currently being used. Then, an estimated measure of the time investment for the collection of new data sets should be developed. In addition, organizations should collect time investment estimates from related industries that are utilizing similar data sets.

Table 2. Evaluation of benefits of data collection

| | | To What Extent Would Collection of [xxx] Data Provide the Following Benefits....* | | |
		To a Great Extent (7)	To Some Extent (4)	Not at All (1)
Benefits	Identify new customers			
	Increase customer service ratings			
	Decrease injuries on the job			
	Identify best job candidates			

*For existing data sets, it should read "To what extent does collection of [xxx] data provide the following benefits…"

We have adapted the Polonetsky, Tene, and Jerome (2014) data benefit-risk analysis tool to incorporate cost and valuation. By graphing each data collection effort based upon its calculated benefits and costs, an organization can categorize the data collection into one of the four categories (Figure 2).

Figure 2. D & A valuation categorization

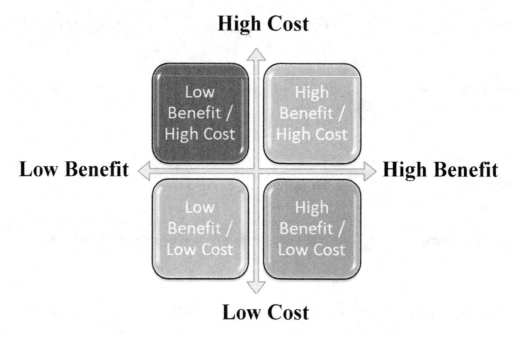

Data collection efforts that fall into low benefit/high cost should be discontinued or never started; so, we have indicated that with red (upper left quadrant). Data collection efforts that fall into high benefit/ low cost should be continued or started; so, we have indicated that with green (lower right quadrant). The other two categories, namely high benefit/high cost and low benefit/low cost (upper right and lower left quadrants) are indicated with yellow, as each organization should determine whether the data collection efforts provide enough value in their specific industry or to their specific organization. For example, at an organization characterized by a profusion of monetary reserves, we would recommend that high benefit/ high-cost data would be more valuable for the organization than low benefit/ low-cost data.

IMPLICATIONS

As with most assets and resources, organizations today must consider cost-benefit trade-offs when determining whether the collection, processing, analysis, distribution, and retention of certain data sets are worthwhile to the firm. As Sharma et al. (2014) concluded, managers must realize the importance of transforming the process of decision making in their organizations in order to better realize the benefits of big data analytics. We posit that this change in business processes requires the use of valuable resources and, therefore, the decision to move forward requires careful evaluation. The systematic data valuation process we have presented in this paper can be utilized by organizational leaders to methodically compare the costs and benefits of the data collection process. Therefore, our approach should accommodate economic and effective solutions to improve business decision making. Valuation as a fourth dimension of big data provides organizations with a more comprehensive view of both internal and external data sources. It is important to bear in mind that the various dimensions of big data—volume, variety, velocity, and our proposed valuation—are interdependent, which suggests that, as one dimension changes, one or more other dimensions are more likely to change as well (Gandomi & Haider, 2015).

CONCLUSION

The implications of big data are more than just technological and have "the potential to unleash enormous value creating new winners and losers" (Mayer-Schönberger & Cukier, 2013, p. 192). Indeed, big data is becoming an integral component of business strategy for all types of businesses, government entities, and nonprofit organizations. Some are farther along than others in understanding how to effectively use and re-use information and data collected from groups like customers, competitors, vendors and other data sources to impact the bottom line. We have presented a valuation tool to estimate the costs and benefits of data collection processes that can assist organizations in better understanding the ways data can be valuable as a resource, a means of sparking innovation, and a tool for decision making now and into the future.

REFERENCES

Carande, C., Lipinski, P., & Gusher, T. (2017). How to integrate data and analytics into every part of your organization. [online]. *Harvard Business Review*.

Chen, H., Chiang, R. H., & Storey, V. C. (2012). Business intelligence and analytics: From big data to big impact. *Management Information Systems Quarterly*, *36*(4), 1165–1188. doi:10.2307/41703503

Côrte-Real, N., Oliveira, T., & Ruivo, P. (2017). Assessing business value of Big Data Analytics in European firms. *Journal of Business Research*, *70*, 379–390. doi:10.1016/j.jbusres.2016.08.011

Gandomi, A., & Haider, M. (2015). Beyond the hype: Big data concepts, methods, and analytics. *International Journal of Information Management*, *35*(2), 137–144. doi:10.1016/j.ijinfomgt.2014.10.007

Gartner. (2017). Gartner IT Glossary. Retrieved from https://www.gartner.com/it-glossary/big-data

Kaisler, S., Armour, F., Espinosa, J. A., & Money, W. (2013). Big data: Issues and challenges moving forward. *Paper presented at the 2013 46th Hawaii International Conference on System Sciences (HICSS)* (pp. 995-1004).

Marr, B. (2017, June). 3 Massive Big Data Problems everyone should know about. Forbes.

Mayer-Schönberger, V., & Cukier, K. (2013). Big data: A revolution that will transform how we live, work, and think. Houghton Mifflin Harcourt.

McAfee, A., Brynjolfsson, E., & Davenport, T. H. (2012). Big data: The management revolution. *Harvard Business Review*, (October), 59–68. PMID:23074865

Mutschler, B., & Reichert, M. (2012). Understanding the costs of business process management technology. In M. Glykas (Ed.), *Business Process Management* (pp. 157–194). Berlin, Germany: Springer; http://dbis.eprints.uni-ulm.de/742/1/BPM_MuRe11.pdf

Polonetsky, J., Tene, O., & Jerome, J. (2014, September 14). Benefit-risk analysis for big data projects: Future of Privacy Forum. Retrieved from https://pdfs.semanticscholar.org/62b4/1973f204c6fc78d2283 3133e17ac09ea9022.pdf

Ponemon, L. (2017, July 26). 2017 Ponemon Institute cost of a data breach study. *SecurityIntelligence*. Retrieve from https://securityintelligence.com/media/2017-ponemon-institute-cost-of-a-data-breach-study/

Press, G. (2017, January 20). 6 predictions for the $203 billion big data analytics market. *Forbes*.

Raghupathi, W., & Raghupathi, V. (2014). Big data analytics in healthcare: promise and potential. *Health information science and systems*, 2(1), 3.

Reed, D. A., & Dongarra, J. (2015). Exascale computing and big data. *Communications of the ACM*, 58(7), 56–68. doi:10.1145/2699414

Seddon, J. J., & Currie, W. L. (2017). A model for unpacking big data analytics in high-frequency trading. *Journal of Business Research*, 70, 300–307. doi:10.1016/j.jbusres.2016.08.003

Sharma, R., Mithas, S., & Kankanhalli, A. (2014). Transforming decision-making processes: A research agenda for understanding the impact of business analytics on organisations. *European Journal of Information Systems*, 23(4), 433–441. doi:10.1057/ejis.2014.17

Ward, J., Daniel, E., & Peppard, J. (2008). Building better business cases for IT investments. *MIS Quarterly Executive*, 7(1), 1–15.

Wu, X., Zhu, X., Wu, G.-Q., & Ding, W. (2014). Data mining with big data. *IEEE Transactions on Knowledge and Data Engineering*, 26(1), 97–107. doi:10.1109/TKDE.2013.109

Yaqoob, I., Hashem, I. A. T., Gani, A., Mokhtar, S., Ahmed, E., Anuar, N. B., & Vasilakos, A. V. (2016). Big data: From beginning to future. *International Journal of Information Management*, 36(6), 1231–1247. doi:10.1016/j.ijinfomgt.2016.07.009

This research was previously published in the International Journal of Strategic Decision Sciences (IJSDS), 10(1); pages 1-9, copyright year 2019 by IGI Publishing (an imprint of IGI Global).

Chapter 10

Big–Data–Based Architectures and Techniques:
Big Data Reference Architecture

Gopala Krishna Behara
Wipro Technologies, India

ABSTRACT

This chapter covers the essentials of big data analytics ecosystems primarily from the business and technology context. It delivers insight into key concepts and terminology that define the essence of big data and the promise it holds to deliver sophisticated business insights. The various characteristics that distinguish big data datasets are articulated. It also describes the conceptual and logical reference architecture to manage a huge volume of data generated by various data sources of an enterprise. It also covers drivers, opportunities, and benefits of big data analytics implementation applicable to the real world.

INTRODUCTION

In Information Age, we are overwhelmed with data, ways to store, process, analyze, interpret, consume and act upon the data. The term Big Data is quite vague and ill defined. The word "Big" is too generic and the question is how "Big" is considered as "Big" and how "Small" is small (Smith, 2013) is relative to time, space and circumstance. The size of "Big Data" is always evolving and the meaning of Big Data Volume would lie between Terabyte (TB) and Zettabyte (ZB) range. The concept of big data is the explosion of data from the Internet, cloud, data center, mobile, Internet of things, sensors and domains that possess and process huge datasets. Cisco claimed that humans have entered the ZB era in 2015 (Cisco, 2017).

Based on social media statistics 2018, the face book claimed that, there are over 300 million photos uploaded to Facebook every day (Nowak & Spiller, 2017). On an average 300 hours of videos are uploaded every minute on You Tube (YouTube, 2017). Approximately, 42 billion texts are sent and 1.6

DOI: 10.4018/978-1-6684-3662-2.ch010

billion photos shared through Whatsapp daily (Stout, 2018). Since 2005, business investment in hardware, software, talent, and services has increased as much as 50 percent, to $4 trillion (Rijmenam, 2018).

In 2005, Roger Mougalas from O'Reilly Media coined the term Big Data for the first time. It refers to a large set of data that is almost impossible to manage and process using traditional business intelligence tools. During the same year, Yahoo created Hadoop. This was built on top of Google's MapReduce. Its goal was to index the entire World Wide Web (Rijmenam, 2018).

In 2009, the Indian government decides to take an iris scan, fingerprint and photograph of all of its 1.2 billion inhabitants. All this data is stored in the largest biometric database in the world (Chandra, 2018).

In 2010, at Technomy conference, Eric Schmidt stated, "There were 5 Exabyte's of information created by the entire world between the dawn of civilization and 2003. Now that same amount is created every two days." (Schmidt, 2010).

In 2011, McKinsey released a report on Big Data which claimed that, the next frontier for innovation, competition, and productivity, states that in 2018 the USA alone will face a shortage of 140.000 – 190.000 data scientist as well as 1.5 million data managers (Manyika, 2011).

Another detailed review was contributed by Visualizing.org (Hewlett Packard Enterprise, 2017) in Big Data. It is focused on the time line of how to implement Big Data Analytics. Its historical description is mainly determined by events related to the Big Data push by many internet and IT companies such as Google, YouTube, Yahoo, Facebook, Twitter and Apple. It emphasized the significant impact of Hadoop in the history of Big Data Analytics.

In the past few years, there has been a massive increase in Big Data startups, trying to deal with Big Data and helping organizations to understand Big Data and more and more companies are slowly adopting and moving towards Big Data.

Figure 1 shows the history of Big Data and its eco system.

Figure 1. History of Big Data

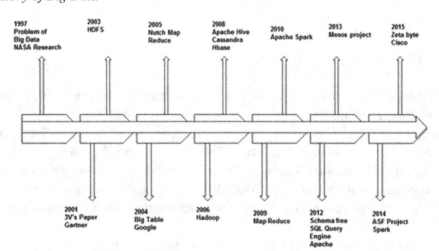

The data sources and their formats are continuous to grow in variety and complexity. Few list of sources includes the public web, social media, mobile applications, federal, state and local records and databases, commercial databases that aggregate individual data from a spectrum of commercial transactions and public records, geospatial data, surveys and traditional offline documents scanned by optical character recognition into electronic form. The advent of the more Internet enabled devices and sensors expands the capacity to collect data from physical entities, including sensors and radio-frequency identification (RFID) chips. Personal location data can come from GPS chips, cell-tower triangulation of mobile devices, mapping of wireless networks, and in-person payments (Manyika, 2011). The big challenge is, how do we consume those data sources and transform them into actionable information Big Data describes a data management strategy that integrates many new types of data and data management alongside traditional data.

There exist many sources, which predict exponential data growth toward 2020 and beyond. Human- and machine-generated data is experiencing an overall 10x faster growth rate than traditional business data, and machine data is increasing even more rapidly at 50x the growth rate.

IDC predicts that by 2020, 50% of all business analytics software will incorporate prescriptive analytics built on cognitive computing technology, and the amount of high-value data will double, making 60% of information delivered to decision makers actionable (Hewlett Packard Enterprise, 2017). 75% of Big Data is helping government departments to improve the quality of citizen's life style (Mullich, 2013; Wedutenko & Keeing, 2014).

The objective of this chapter is to describe the aspects of big data, definition, drivers, principles, scenarios, best practices and architectures.

BACKGROUND

Today, the data that we deal with is diverse. Users create content like blog posts, tweets, social network interactions, etc. To tackle the challenges of managing this data, a new breed of technologies has emerged.

Data architecture earlier designed primarily for batch processing of mostly structured data and created to address specific Business Units, Enterprise needs. It lacks in the ability to support data democratization, ad-hoc analytics, machine learning/artificial intelligence (ML/AI), complex data governance and security needs - all of which are critical to building a true data driven enterprise.

These new technologies are more complex than traditional databases. These systems can scale to vastly larger sets of data, but using these technologies effectively requires a fundamentally new set of techniques.

Enterprises that do not actively transform themselves to become data driven are left behind, their basic existence questioned. CXOs recognize the threat and the opportunity, and are eager to deploy a modern data architecture that can not only help them store a wide variety of large amounts volume of data but also provides an enterprise-wide analytic platform. This can empower every single employee in the organization to take data driven decisions in real-time, with little or no support from IT.

Big data addresses large, diverse, complex, longitudinal, and/or distributed datasets generated from instruments, sensors, Internet transactions, email, video, click streams, and/or all other digital sources available today and in the future (National Science Foundation, 2012). It describes a holistic information management strategy that includes and integrates many new types of data and data management alongside traditional data. The boundaries of what constitutes a Big Data problem are also changing due to the ever shifting and advancing landscape of software and hardware technology.

Thirty years ago, one gigabyte of data could amount to a Big Data problem and require special purpose computing resources. Now, gigabytes of data are commonplace and can be easily transmitted, processed and stored on consumer-oriented devices. Data within Big Data environments generally accumulates from enterprise applications, sensors and external sources. Enterprise applications consume this processed data directly or can fed into a data warehouse to enrich existing data there.

The results obtained through the processing of Big Data can lead to a wide range of insights and benefits, such as,

- Operational optimization
- Actionable intelligence
- Identification of new markets
- Accurate predictions
- Fault and fraud detection
- Improved decision-making

Concepts and Terminology

The following are the fundamental concepts and terms used in Big Data Architectures and Techniques.

Datasets: Collections or groups of related data. Each group or dataset member shares the same set of attributes or properties as others in the same dataset. Some examples of datasets are:

- Tweets stored in a flat file
- A collection of image files in a directory
- An extract of rows from a database table stored in a CSV formatted file
- Historical weather observations that are stored as XML files

Data Analysis: Process of analyzing data to find facts, relationships, patterns, insights and trends. The overall goal of data analysis is to support better decision making.

Big Data: A massive volume of both structured and unstructured data that is so large that it's difficult to process with traditional database and software techniques

Data Analytics: A discipline that includes the management of the complete data lifecycle, which covers collecting, cleansing, organizing, storing, analyzing and governing data. Data analytics enable data-driven decision-making with scientific backing so that the decisions based on factual data and not just on experience.

Highlighted below are the four categories of analytics,

1. **Descriptive Analytics**: It addresses to answer questions about events that have already occurred. This form of analytics contextualizes data to generate information.
2. **Diagnostic Analytics**: It aim to determine the cause of a phenomenon that occurred in the past using questions that focus on the reason behind the event. The goal is to determine the information related to the phenomenon in order to enable answering questions that seek to determine why something has occurred.
3. **Predictive Analytics**: It helps to determine the outcome of an event that might occur in the future. Enriched information with meaning to generate knowledge that conveys how that information is related. The strength and magnitude of the associations form the basis of models to generate future predictions based on past events.

4.   **Prescriptive Analytics**: Built upon the results of predictive analytics by prescribing actions be taken. This type of analytics used to gain an advantage or mitigate a risk.

Types of Data: The data processed by Big Data solutions can be human-generated or machine-generated. Human-generated data is the result of human interaction with systems, such as online services and digital devices. Software programs and hardware devices in response to real-world events generate machine-generated data. The primary types of data are:

- Structured data
- Unstructured data
- Semi-structured data

Structured Data: Conforms to a data model or schema and is often stored in tabular form. Used to capture relationship between different entities. The data is often stored in a relational database. Generally, generation of structured data is by enterprise applications and information systems like ERP and CRM systems.

Unstructured Data: Data that does not conform to a data model or data schema. Unstructured data has a faster growth rate than structured data. This form of data is either textual or binary and often conveyed via files that are self-contained and non-relational. A text file may contain the contents of various tweets or blog postings. Binary files are often media files that contain image, audio or video data.

Semi Structured Data: This type of data has a defined level of structure and consistency, but is not relational in nature. Instead, semi-structured data is hierarchical or graph-based. This kind of data is commonly stored in files that contain text. XML and JSON files are common forms of semi-structured data.

Metadata: It provides information about a dataset's characteristics and structure. This type of data is mostly machine-generated data. The tracking of metadata is crucial to Big Data processing, storage and analysis because it provides information about the pedigree of the data and its provenance during processing. Examples of metadata include:

- XML tags providing the author and creation date of a document
- Attributes providing the file size and resolution of a digital photograph governments

CHARACTERISTICS OF BIG DATA

Big Data Analytics is an integrated Business Intelligence and Data Analytics, which includes conventional and Big Data. Comparing to the traditional data, big data has five major characteristics: Volume, Velocity, Variety, Veracity and Value (Normandeau, 2013; Hilbert, 2016; Hilbert, 2015).

- **Volume:** It indicates more data. The volume of data that processed by Big Data solutions is substantial and ever growing. High data volumes impose distinct data storage and processing demands, as well as additional data preparation, curation and management processes. Big Data requires processing high volumes of data, that is, data of unknown value. For example, twitter data feeds, clicks on a web page, network traffic, sensor-enabled equipment capturing data and many more. Typical data sources that are responsible for generating high data volumes are:

- Online transactions
- Scientific and research experiments
- Sensors, such as GPS sensors, RFIDs, smart meters and telematics
- Social media, such as Facebook and Twitter
- **Velocity**: In Big Data environments, data can arrive at fast speeds, and enormous datasets can accumulate within very short periods. From an enterprise's point of view, the velocity of data translates into the amount of time it takes for the data processing, once it enters the enterprise's perimeter. Coping with the fast inflow of data requires the enterprise to design highly elastic and available data processing solutions and corresponding data storage capabilities. Some Internet of Things (IoT) applications have health and safety ramifications that require real-time evaluation and action. Other internet-enabled smart products operate in real-time or near real-time. As an example, consumer e-commerce applications seek to combine mobile device location and personal preferences to make time sensitive offers.
- **Variety**: New unstructured data types. Unstructured and semi-structured data types, such as text, audio, and video require additional processing to both derive meaning and the supporting metadata. Unstructured data has many of the same requirements as structured data, such as summarization, lineage, auditability, and privacy. Further complexity arises when data from a known source changes without notice.
- **Veracity**: Quality or fidelity of data. Assessment of Data that enters Big Data environments for quality, which can lead to data processing activities to resolve invalid data and remove noise. Data with a high signal-to-noise ratio has more veracity than data with a lower ratio. Data that is acquired in a controlled manner, for example via online customer registrations, usually contains less noise than data acquired via uncontrolled sources, such as blog postings
- **Value**: There is a range of quantitative and investigative techniques to derive value from data. The cost of data storage and compute has exponentially decreased, thus providing an abundance of data from which statistical sampling and other techniques become relevant, and meaningful.

Figure 2. Big Data Characteristics

Volume	Velocity	Variety	Veracity	Volume
Data at Scale	Data In Motion	Data In Many Forms	Data Uncertainty	Data Usage
Terabytes to petabytes of data	Batch to Streaming Analysis of streaming data to enable decisions within fractions of a second	Structured, unstructured, text, multimedia	Managing the reliability and predictability of inherently imprecise data types	Managing the Cost, Storage and Time for data processing

DRIVERS OF BIG DATA

Easy and timely retrieval and analysis of related and unrelated information is crucial for enterprise to meet and improve mission requirements that vary across business units. Enterprises are collecting, procuring, storing and processing increasing quantities of data. This is occurring in an effort to find new insights that can drive more efficient and effective operations, provide management the ability to steer the business proactively and allow the C-suite to better formulate and assess their strategic initiatives. Ultimately, enterprises are looking for new ways to gain a competitive edge. Thus, the need for techniques and technologies that can extract meaningful information and insights has increased. Computational approaches, statistical techniques and data warehousing have advanced to the point where they have merged, each bringing their specific techniques and tools that allow the performance of Big Data analysis. The maturity of these fields of practice inspired and enabled much of the core functionality expected from contemporary Big Data solutions, environments and platforms.

Data continues to be generated and digitally archived at increasing rates driven by customer initiatives, sensors, customer interactions and program transactions. For example, Government organizations are beginning to deploy Big Data technologies to analyze massive data sets as well as mine data to prevent bad actors from committing acts of terror and/or to prevent waste, fraud, and abuse (Kalil, 2012; Department of Defense, 2012).

Figure 3 depicts the drivers of Big Data. Big Data drivers are explained below.

Figure 3. Drivers of Big Data and Analytics

Business

Enterprises today are looking for improvement in marketing, enhance customer experience, improve operational efficiencies, identify fraud and waste, prevent compliance failures and achieve other outcomes that directly affect top- and bottom-line business performance. Big Data analytics helps in discovering new business initiatives. This is the opportunity to enable innovative new business models.

Digitization

Today for all businesses, digital mediums have replaced physical mediums as the de facto communications and delivery mechanism. The use of digital artifacts saves both time and cost as distribution is supported by the vast pre-existing infrastructure of the Internet. As consumers connect to a business through their interaction with these digital substitutes, it leads to an opportunity to collect detailed data by leveraging Big Data Analytics. Collecting detailed data can be important for businesses because mining this data allows customized marketing, automated recommendations and the development of optimized product features.

Explosion of Mobile Devices

The increased use of smart phones Users expect to be able to access their information anywhere and anytime. To the extent that visualizations, analytics, or operationalized big data/analytics are part of the mobile experience.

Real-Time Sensor Data

The coverage of Internet and Wi-Fi networks has enabled more people and their devices to be continuously active in virtual communities. Usage of Internet based connected sensors, Internet of Things and Smart Internet connected devices has resulted in massive increase in the number of available data streams demanding the need for Big Data Analytics. These data streams are public and channeled directly to corporations for analysis.

Growth of Social Media

Customers today are providing feedback on product/item to enterprise, in near real time through various channels. This leads the businesses to consider customer feedback on their service and product offerings in their strategic planning. As a result, businesses are storing increasing amounts of data on customer interactions within their customer relationship management systems (CRM) and from harvesting customer reviews, complaints and praise from social media sites. This information feeds Big Data analysis algorithms that surface the voice of the customer in an attempt to provide better levels of service, increase sales, enable targeted marketing and even create new products and services. Businesses have realized that branding activity no longer managed by internal marketing activities. In addition, enterprises and its customers are co-creating the product brands and corporate reputation. For this reason, businesses are increasingly interested in incorporating publicly available datasets from social media and other external data sources.

Cloud Computing

Cloud computing plays an essential role in data analytics. In many scenarios, it act as a data source, providing real-time streams, analytical services, and as a device transaction hub. Businesses have the opportunity to leverage highly scalable, on-demand IT resources for storage and processing capabilities provided by cloud environments in order to build-out scalable Big Data solutions that can carry out large-scale processing tasks. The ability of a cloud to dynamically scale based upon load allows for the creation of resilient analytic environments that maximize efficient utilization of ICT resources. Cloud computing can provide three essential ingredients required for a Big Data solution: external datasets, scalable processing capabilities and vast amounts of storage.

Cyber Security

Big Data security strategy should be align with the enterprise practices and policies already established, avoid duplicate implementations, and manage centrally across the environments.

Enterprise security management seeks to centralize access, authorize resources, and govern through comprehensive audit practices. Adding a diversity of Big Data technologies, data sources, and uses adds requirements to these practices.

Advanced Analytical Capability

Technological advancement in data collection, storage, analytics and visualization allows the enterprises to increase the amount of data they generate and produce actionable intelligence to support real time decision making. It helps the capability to foresee key events and take appropriate and timely actions. Better utilization of data, not merely for producing statistical reports on the past but intelligent reports that throw light on the future.

PRINCIPLES OF BIG DATA

Architecture principles provide a basis for decision making when developing Big Data solutions and design. These principles will be extended with Organization specific architecture principles and requirements (Blockow, 2018; Forrest, 2016). They form a structured set of ideas that collectively define and guide development of a solution architecture, from values through to design and implementation, harmonizing decision making across an organization.

The following are the principles to guide enterprises in their approach to big data.

- **Data is an Asset**: Data is an asset that has a specific and measurable value to the Enterprise and managed
- **Data is Shared**: Users have access to the data necessary to perform their duties; therefore, data is shared across enterprise functions and organizations
- **Data Trustee**: Each data element has a trustee accountable for data quality.
- **Common Vocabulary and Data Definitions**: Data definition is consistent throughout Enterprise, and the definitions are understandable and available to all users.
- **Data Security**: Data is protected from unauthorized use and disclosure.
- **Data Privacy**: that privacy and data protection is considered throughout the entire life cycle of a big data project. All data sharing will conform to relevant regulatory and business requirements
- **Data Integrity and the Transparency of Processes**: Each party to a big data analytics project must be aware of, and abide by their responsibilities regarding: the provision of source data and the obligation to establish and maintain adequate controls over the use of personal or other sensitive data
- **Data Skills and Capabilities**: Skills and expertise in data analytics were shared amongst enterprises and industry, where appropriate. Resources such as data sets and the analytical models used to interrogate them, as well as the infrastructure necessary to perform these computations and shared amongst business units where appropriate and possible to do so.

- **Collaboration with Industry and Academia**: The industry, research and academic sectors have been working on big data analytics projects for some time and continue to invest heavily in the skills, technologies and techniques involved with big data analysis.

BIG DATA ARCHITECTURE FRAMEWORK

The diagram below depicts the high-level architecture framework of traditional data, structured in nature. It has two data sources that use integration (ELT/ETL/Change Data Capture) techniques to transfer data into a DBMS data warehouse or operational data store, and then offer a wide variety of analytical capabilities to reveal the data. Some of these analytic capabilities include dashboards, reporting, EPM/BI applications, summary and statistical query, semantic interpretations for textual data, and visualization tools for high-density data.

Figure 4. Traditional Architecture Components

A big data architecture, designed to handle the ingestion, processing, and analysis of data that is too large or complex for traditional database systems. Conceptual Architecture of the Big Data Analytics shown in Figure below. It illustrates key components and flows and highlights the emergence of the Data repository and various forms of new and traditional data collection.

Figure 5. Conceptual Reference Architecture

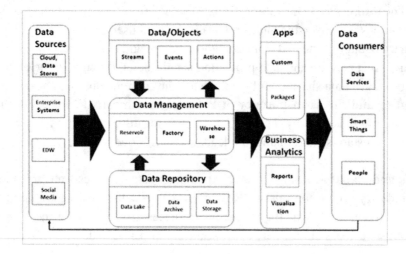

Big data solutions typically involve one or more of the following types of workload:

- Batch processing of big data sources at rest.
- Real-time processing of big data in motion.
- Interactive exploration of big data.
- Predictive analytics and machine learning.

Description of these primary components:

- **Stream Data:** Components that process data in-flight (streams) to identify actionable events and then determine next best action based on decision context and event profile data and persist in a durable storage system. The decision context relies on data in the data reservoir or other enterprise information stores.
- **Reservoir:** Economical, scale-out storage and parallel processing for data that does not have stringent requirements for data formalization or modelling. Typically manifested as a Hadoop cluster or staging area in a relational database.
- **Factory:** Management and orchestration of data into and between the Data Reservoir and Enterprise Information Store as well as the rapid provisioning of data.
- **Warehouse**: Large scale formalized and modelled business critical data store, typically manifested by a Data Warehouse or Data Marts.
- **Data Repository:** A set of data stores, processing engines, and analysis tools separate from the data management activities to facilitate the discovery of new knowledge. Key requirements include rapid data provisioning and sub setting, data security/governance, and rapid statistical processing for large data sets.
- **Business Analytics:** A range of end user and analytic tools for business Intelligence, faceted navigation, and data mining analytic tools including dashboards, reports, and mobile access for timely and accurate reporting.
- **Applications:** A collection of prebuilt adapters and application programming interfaces that enable all data sources and processing directly integrated into custom or packaged business applications.

BIG DATA LOGICAL ARCHITECTURE

The following diagram shows logical application architecture of Big Data Analytics System with key components and layers. A detailed description of these components and layers are provided in this section. While there exist many standard logical architectures for the Big Data Analytics (Wu, 2014; Angelov, 2012; Chen, 2014; Ahmed & Karypis, 2012; Klein, 2017), the author tried to arrive a detailed and concise Big Data Logical Reference Architecture based on practical experience across various domains and technologies.

Figure 6. Logical Application Architecture View

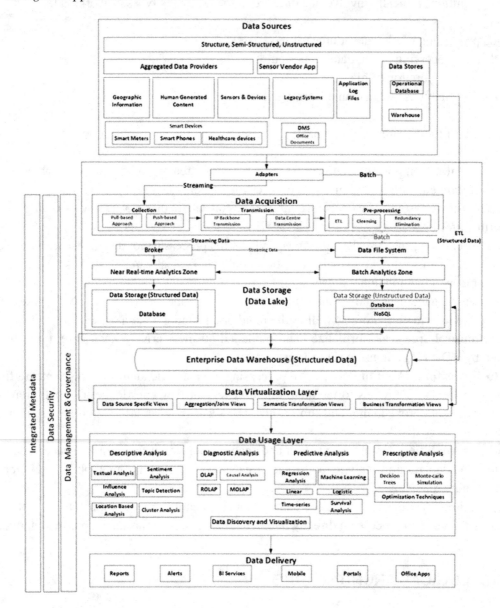

Below is the brief description of each of the logical application architecture layers,

Data Sources and Types

The data sources provide the insight required to solve the business problem. The data sources are structured, semi-structured, and unstructured, and it comes from many sources. Big Data Analytics solution shall support processing of all types of data from a variety of sources. Given below is an indicative list of data sources, and categories. All big data solutions start with one or more data sources. Examples include,

- Application data stores, such as relational databases.
- Static files produced by applications, such as web server log files.
- Real-time data sources, such as IoT device.

Table 1. Structured and Unstructured data for Internal and External systems

Category	Internal
Structured	Departmental Database, Data Hubs, Data Warehouse, Data Marts
Semi/Unstructured	e-Mails, Documents, XML documents
Category	**External**
Structured	Sensor Data, Log Stream Data, Web sites, Satellite Data, Social media, Bioinformatics, Blogs/Articles
Semi/Unstructured	Documents, E-mails, Audio-visuals, Stream data and Web Analytics data

Data Acquisition and Enrich

Relevant push or pull-based mechanisms are used for collecting data from various data sources. Data acquisition provide the capability to hold and transmit raw data collected from various sources to data. The acquisition layer provides the mechanism to cleanse different types of data like traditional, sensor based, log data and data from internet.

- **Streaming Data**: Streaming data comprises of unstructured data coming in from various sources. The data shall be held in a buffer area and when a set limit is reached, it shall be transmitted to Data Analytics system (Hold-Transmit). After capturing real-time messages, the solution must process them by filtering, aggregating, and otherwise preparing the data for analysis. The processed stream data is written to an output sink.
- **Batch Data**: Batch data is normally extracted from enterprise systems using ETL or ELT processes. Structured data may be loaded directly to Data Warehouse, and unstructured/semi structured data to Hadoop or equivalent(or better) unstructured data processing platform. Both ETL and ELT support complex transformations such as cleansing, reformatting, aggregating, and converting large volumes of data from many sources. Because the data sets are so large, often a big data solution must process data files using long-running batch jobs to filter, aggregate, and otherwise prepare the data for analysis.
- **Near Real-Time Data Analytics Zone**: It process incoming stream data in real time to provide quick insights into the data. This data may then be persisted on Hadoop system. Near real-time analytics shall provide capabilities like log stream analysis, sensor data analysis etc. The real-time analytics system must be able to quickly identify useful data and that is not useful. Near real-time data shall augment insights obtained from batch analysis.
- **Batch Data Analytics Zone**: Batch data zone ingest large amount of data in batch mode, and also insights obtained in Real-time analytical zone.

Data Storage

Data for batch processing operations is typically stored in a distributed file store that can hold high volumes of large files in various formats. This type of data store is called Data Lake.

- **Data Lake**: A data lake is a storage repository that holds a vast amount of raw data in its native format, including structured, semi-structured, and unstructured data. The data structure and requirements are not defined until the data is needed. It stores all data while making it faster to get up and running with batch, streaming and interactive analytics. The lake can serve as a staging area for the data warehouse, the location of more carefully treated data for reporting and anlaysis in batch mode. The data lake accepts input from various sources and can preserve both the original data fidelity and the lineage of data transformations.

The features of the Data lake are:

- **Collect Everything:** A Data Lake contains all data, both raw sources over extended periods of time as well as any processed data.
- **Dive in Anywhere:** A Data Lake enables users across multiple business units to refine, explore and enrich data on their terms.
- **Flexible Access:** A Data Lake enables multiple data access patterns across a shared infrastructure: batch, interactive, online, search, in-memory and other processing engines.

Enterprise Data Warehouse

A Data warehouse stores whole of enterprise data, comprising of structured data from enterprise database and data hubs. The data warehouse supports massively Parallel processing and share-nothing architecture and provide optimal performance considering structured and unstructured data. It designed in such a way; it has no single point of failure.

Data Virtualization Layer

Data Virtualization acts as the intermediary and abstraction layer between the information consumers and all sources of data that may contribute to the interaction. It hides cryptic names of tables and columns from users and provide business friendly definitions of data that be used to create reports even by non-technical people. In addition, the data abstraction layer has the capability to access structured, unstructured, or both data in a single query. The query language is standard RDBMS, and query initiated at any level should have ability to process data from all data stores (structured and unstructured). The layer supports a strong optimizer to tune query execution, for response time as well as throughput.

Data Consumers and Delivery

It describes how enterprise users and applications consume output from Big Data Analytics system. This may be in the form of Big Data Analytics Services, alerts on emails and phones, actions, integration with office applications like word, excel etc., collaboration(discussion threads etc.), mobile and so on. The Delivery layer supports delivery through the following mechanisms:

1. **Big Data Analytics Services**: It offers ability to embed actions, alerts, and reports in other application, tool or UI. They shall have ability to refresh automatically based on predefined schedule.
2. **Alerts**: This is to notify stakeholders if a certain event has occurred. Alerts may be delivered in the form of email, reports, or messages.
3. **Actions**: Enable users take some action based on alerts or reports. For example: removing a duplicate record or fixing a corrupted data.
4. **Portal**: Portals provide mechanism to catalogue and index, classify, and search for Big Data Analytics objects such as reports or dashboards. All Big Data Analytics reports to be made available to department users on the portals, based on the roles and responsibilities.
5. **Mobile:** Reports, dashboards, and portals shall be accessible on Mobile devices too.
6. **Office Applications**: The system should integrate with Standard Office products at the minimum. The data and reports should be importable and exportable from/to Office products.

Integrated Meta Data Management

Metadata repository needs to be created for both Structured and Unstructured data. Whether it is for structured data or unstructured, metadata contain enough information to understand, track, explore, clean, and Transform data. Big Data Analytics has the capability to apply metadata on incoming data without any manual intervention.

- **Metadata for Structured Data (DWH)**: It includes Technical, Business, and Process metadata. Besides these, rules of precedence such as which source tables can update which data elements in which order of precedence must be defined and stored.
- **Metadata for Unstructured Data**: Contains rules, definitions, and datasets that help filter out valuable data from incoming data streams or batch load, and persist only such data that are useful. Metadata should enable lineage tracking of data that is loaded into Big Data Analytics system
- **Reusing Data Objects**: Standard queries, models, and metadata can be moved into one layer and virtualise it so that these objects may be reused

Data Security

Data security considerations specific to big data include:

- Increased value of the information asset as enterprises enrich their data, its aggregation and the insights derived from it.
- The increasing range of data acquisition channels and their potential vulnerability.
- The unknowability of the content of unstructured data sources upon acquisition.
- Increased distribution of physical and virtual locations of data storage.

More details about the Big Data Security is explained in the Secuirty Architecture Section of this chapter.

Data Usage Layer

Different users may want different types of outputs based on their role, responsibilities, and functions. The goal of most big data solutions is to provide insights into the data through analysis and reporting. To empower users to analyze the data, the architecture may include a data modeling layer, such as a multidimensional OLAP cube or tabular data model in Azure Analysis Services. It might also support self-service BI, using the modeling and visualization technologies in Microsoft Power BI or Microsoft Excel. Analysis and reporting can also take the form of interactive data exploration by data scientists or data analysts. Big Data Analytics shall provide the following usage capabilities:

- **Reports and Ad-hoc Queries**: Analytical reporting (based on data warehouse/Datamart). The system shall provide scripting language, ability to handle complex headers, footers, nested subtotals, and multiple report bands on a single page.
- The system shall support simple, medium, and complex queries against both structured and unstructured data.
- **Online Analytical Processing (OLAP)**: Slicing and dicing, measuring dependent variables against multiple independent variables. It enables users regroup, re-aggregate, and re-sort by dimensions.
- **Advanced Analytics**: This includes predictive, prescriptive, descriptive, causal, statistical, spatial, and mathematical analysis, using structured and unstructured data
- **Dashboards**: Displays variety of information in one page/screen. Typically they display Key Performance Indicators visually.
- **Textual Analytics**: Textual analytics refers to the process of deriving high-quality information from text in documents, emails, Government orders, web, etc. This is useful in sentiment analysis, understand hot topics of discussion in public, and maintaining government image.
- **Performance Management**: Analytical data can be used by departments to understand their performance, and reasons for current levels of performance measured in terms of KPIs.
- **Data Mining, Discovery, and Visualisation**: It is about searching for patterns and values within data streams such as sensor based data, social media, satellite images etc. Data exploration is primarily used by Data scientists or statisticians to create new Analytical models and test them so that they can be used for Analytics.

Data Management and Governance

Data Governance is a process of managing data assets of an enterprise. It includes the rules, policies, procedures, roles and responsibilities that guide overall management of an enterprise's data. It provides the guidance to ensure that data is accurate and consistent, complete, available and secure. Governance is not a onetime event - it is a continual process of maintaining, monitoring and improving the enterprise important asset.

Enterprises have the governance responsibility to align disparate data types and certify data quality. Governance provides the structure to enable:

- The decision making processes that an enterprise uses to ensure the integrity of its key data items.
- Fast and effective decision making in times of ambiguity.

- Adherence to policies, standards and alignment to overall data management approach.

Improved Governance

- Data-analysis-based insights improving quality of governance.
- Data-analysis-driven decisions leading to right planning and right targeting.
- Insights leading to effective regulation and better governance.
- Recommendations and interventions to improve performances.

Principles of Data Governance are:

- **Enterprise Asset**: Data is recognized as a key business asset and will be organized, stored, distributed and managed to allow sharing across the Enterprise.
- **Conformance**: The logical structure of data will be independent of Applications and will conform to defined Logical Data Models and common data formats.
- **Stewards and Owership**: Each data element has a corporate steward accountable for data ownership and data quality.
- **Shared**: Users have access to the data necessary to perform their duties; therefore, data is shared across Enterprise functions and Business Units.
- **Accessible**: Data is accessible for users to perform their functions from any location and by any approved mechanisms.
- **Secure**: Data is protected from unauthorized use and disclosure.
- **Timely:** The Systems, Applications and Databases will be designed to make data available anytime and anyplace.
- **Available:** All shared data will have the capability to be continuously available based on agreed business need.
- **Interoperable Information**: Data must be managed in such a way as to achieve information interoperability.
- **Common Vacabulary**: Data is defined consistently throughout the Enterprise, and the definitions are understandable and available to all users.
- **Meta Data Repository**: An integrated, centralized Metadata Repository.
- **Data Capture**: All primary data will be captured once at the point of creation and stored and managed to enable appropriate levels of sharing across the Enterprise.

BIG DATA SECURITY ARCHITECTURE

Security today involves far more than just password protection, anti-malware solutions, and network encryption. It requires a continuous application of security measures to manage and control access to valuable electronic assets of an enterprise. Big Data security approach shall ensure that the right people, internal or external, get access to the appropriate data and information at right time and place, within the right channel (National Security Agency, Central Security Services, 2011; Smith & Hallman, 2013). The security prevents and safeguards against malicious attacks and protects enterprise data assets by securing and encrypting data while it is in-motion or at-rest. It also enables organizations to separate roles and responsibilities and protect sensitive data without compromising privileged user access.

Based on the author experience in Big Data Architectures, the core components of the Big Data Security Framework are classified as:

- **Data Management**: Secure data storage and transaction logs
- **Identity and Access Management:** Role based access control for data components
- **Data Protection and Privacy:** Scalable privacy preserving data mining and analytics
- **Network Security:** Network access control allows traffic to approved levels
- **Infrastructure Security and Integrity:** Secure computations in distributed programming

Figure 7 is the logical architecture for the big data security approach:

Figure 7. Big Data Security Architecture View

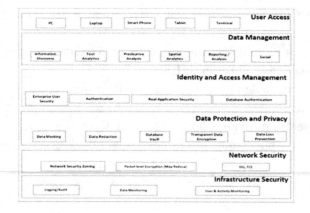

The various data security capabilities are:

- Authentication and authorization of users, applications and databases
- Privileged user access and administration
- Data encryption and redaction, application level cryptographic protection
- Data masking and sub setting, performed in batch or real time
- Separation of roles and responsibilities, role based access control
- Transport security
- Network security, data protection in transit and network zoning and authorization components
- Database activity monitoring, alerting, blocking, auditing and compliance reporting

IOT ANALYTICS ARCHITECTURE

Imagine a world where billions of objects can sense, communicate and share information and are inter connected over public or private Internet Protocol (IP) networks. These interconnected objects have data regularly collected, analyzed and used to initiate action, providing a wealth of intelligence for planning, management and decision-making. This is called Internet of Things (IOT) (Morris, 2014; Wang, 2017; Greenough, 2014; Rohling, 2014).

These devices are producing Zetabytes of data every month. The transmissions typically consist of high velocity semi-structured data streams that must land in highly scalable data management systems. The following diagram depicts the IoT logical reference architecture as three tiers: 1.) Edge; 2.) Platform, and; 3.) Enterprise. These tiers process the data flows and control flows based on usage activities across the enterprise systems.

Figure 8. IoT Analytics Architecture View

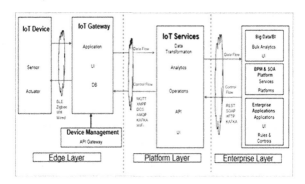

1. **Edge**: Consists of IoT devices and the IoT gateway. The architectural characteristics of this tier, including its breadth of distribution and location, depend on the specific use cases of the enterprise.

It is common for IoT devices to communicate using a relatively short range and specialized proximity network, due to power and processing limitations.

The IoT gateway contains a data store for IoT device data, one or more services to analyze data streaming from the IoT devices or from the data store, and control applications.

The IoT gateway provides endpoints for device connectivity, facilitating bidirectional communication with the enterprise systems. It also implements edge intelligence with different levels of processing capabilities.

2. **Platform**: Receives, processes and forwards control commands from the Enterprise tier to the Edge tier. The Platform tier consolidates, processes and analyses data flows from the Edge tier, and provides management functions for devices and assets. It also offers non-domain-specific services such as data operations and analytics.
3. **Enterprise**: Receives data flows from the Edge and Platform tiers, and issues control commands to these tiers. The Enterprise tier implements enterprise domain-specific applications and decision support systems, and provides interfaces to end users, including operations.

The different networks used to connect these three tiers are:

1. The ***proximity network*** connects the sensors, actuators, devices, control systems and assets, collectively called edge nodes. It typically connects these edge nodes in one or more clusters to a gateway that bridges to other networks.

2. The ***access network*** enables data and control flows between the Edge and the Platform tiers. It may be a corporate network, or a private network overlaid over the public Internet or a 4G/5G network.

3. The ***service network*** enables connectivity between the services in the platform tier and the enterprise tier, and the services within each tier. It may be an overlay private network over the public Internet, or the Internet itself, allowing enterprise-grade security between end-users and various services.

Users of the IoT system include both humans and digital users. Humans typically interact with the IoT system using one or more kinds of user devices – smartphones, personal computers, tablets or specialized devices. In all cases, the IoT system provides some form of application that connects the human user with the rest of the IoT system.

In some scenarios, immediate action must be taken when data is first transmitted (as when a sensor reports a critical problem that could damage equipment or cause injury) or where it would be possible alleviate some other preventable situation (such as relieving a highway traffic jam). Event processing engines designed to take certain pre-programmed actions quickly by analyzing the data streams while data is still in motion or when data has landed in NoSQL database front-ends or Hadoop. The rules applied usually based on analysis of previous similar data streams and known outcomes.

BIG DATA ANALYSIS TECHNIQUES

Big Data analysis blends traditional statistical data analysis approaches with computational ones. In any fast moving field like Big Data, there are always opportunities for innovation. An example of this is the question of how to blend statistical and computational approaches for a given analytical problem. Statistical techniques are commonly preferred for exploratory data analysis, after which computational techniques that advantage the insight gleaned from the statistical study of a dataset can be apply (Buhler, 2016; We, 2014; Oracle Corporation, 2015; Lopes & Ribeiro, 2015; NIST, 2015; Labrinidis & Jagadish, 2012).

The shift from batch to real-time presents other challenges, as real-time techniques need to leverage computationally efficient algorithms. The following are the basic types of data analysis:

- Quantitative analysis
- Qualitative analysis
- Data mining
- Statistical analysis
- Machine learning
- Semantic analysis
- Visual analysis
- **Quantitative Analysis**: Quantitative analysis is a data analysis technique that focuses on quantifying the patterns and correlations found in the data. Based on statistical practices, this technique involves analysing a large number of observations from a dataset. Since the sample size is large,

the results can be applied in a generalized manner to the entire dataset. Quantitative analysis results are absolute in nature and used for numerical comparisons.

- **Qualitative Analysis**: Qualitative analysis is a data analysis technique that focuses on describing various data qualities using words. It involves analysing a smaller sample in greater depth compared to quantitative data analysis. Extending these results to entire dataset is not possible due to the small sample size. The analysis results state only that the figures were "not as high as," and do not provide a numerical difference.
- **Data Mining**: Data mining, also known as data discovery, is a specialized form of data analysis that targets large datasets. In relation to Big Data analysis, data mining generally refers to automated, software-based techniques that sift through massive datasets to identify patterns and trends. Specifically, it involves extracting hidden or unknown patterns in the data with the intention of identifying previously unknown patterns. Data mining forms the basis for predictive analytics and business intelligence (BI).
- **Statistical Analysis**: Statistical analysis uses statistical methods based on mathematical formulas as a means for analysing data. Statistical analysis is most often quantitative, but can also be qualitative. This type of analysis commonly used to describe datasets via summarization, such as providing the mean, median, or mode of statistics associated with the dataset. In addition, it is used to infer patterns and relationships within the dataset, such as regression and correlation.
- **Machine Learning**: Humans are good at spotting patterns and relationships within data. Unfortunately, we cannot process large amounts of data very quickly. Machines, on the other hand, are very adept at processing large amounts of data quickly, but only if they know how. If human knowledge combined with the processing speed of machines, machines will be able to process large amounts of data without requiring much human intervention. This is the basic concept of machine learning.
- **Semantic Analysis**: A fragment of text or speech data can carry different meanings in different contexts, whereas a complete sentence may retain its meaning, even if structured in different ways. In order for the machines to extract valuable information, text and speech data needs to understand by the machines in the same way as humans do. Semantic analysis represents practices for extracting meaningful information from textual and speech data.
- **Visual Analysis**: Visual analysis is a form of data analysis that involves the graphic representation of data to enable or enhance its visual perception. Based on the premise that humans can understand and draw conclusions from graphics more quickly than from text, visual analysis acts as a discovery tool in the field of Big Data. The objective is to use graphic representations to develop a deeper understanding of the data being analysed. Specifically, it helps identify and highlight hidden patterns, correlations and anomalies. Visual analysis, directly related to exploratory data analysis as it encourages the formulation of questions from different angles.

INDICATIVE BUSINESS SCENARIOS OF BIG DATA IN GOVERNMENT

The following lists summarizes representative categories where Big Data Analytics system will be used to improve Government and department processes.

Integrated Services

- Analyzing the content in electronic and social media and other sources to understand public sentiment on the programs of the Government, conducting a root-cause analysis and suggesting appropriate interventions and mid-course corrections to improve the delivery of the programs.
- Predicting a disaster and identifying the areas likely to be affected, and suggesting advance interventions required to mitigate the adverse impact on the population.
- Analyzing the Text inputs (unstructured data) in the Grievance system and the popular print media, identifying of key problem areas (Region / Type of Problem / Frequency/Severity) and suggesting suitable remedial action.
- Designing a Happiness Index, appropriate to the socio-economic profile of the Government agency, supporting the Government in conducting approriate sample surveys, Analyzing the results and making suitable recommendations for enhancement of the Index.

Service Delivery

- Analyzing the medium-term impact of development and welfare schemes, identifying the gaps and realigning the schemes for enhanced effectiveness.
- Analyzing the geographical spread of various schemes and making corrections for even distribution.
- Conduct sentiment analysis based on social media and electronic media, and provide appropriate inputs for action by the municipality.
- Qualitative and Quantitative analysis of potable drinking water supplied to the rural people in the habitations as per defined norms through implementation of various water supply schemes under different programs in the government.

Statistics

- Analyzing the patterns of public expenditure on top 10 sectors of the economy, identifying the correlations with the progress in achieving the relevant Sustainable Development Goals and suggesting the desired areas and sectors for intervention.
- Analyzing the trends of growth of GSDP, geographically and sector-wise, identifying causal factors for high and low growth rates and suggesting the right mix of interventions required to optimize the growth rate of the economy of the Government.
- Analysis of trends of cropped areas and economics of various crops area wise over the last 5 years, and the demand-supply position for different agricultural produce across the country and to arrive at the optimised crop area planning for various crops in different agro-climatic regions of the Government and giving decision support to agricultural planners.
- Analysis of soil health records of the last 5 years, along with the crops grown during the period, rainfall, irrigation, yield and other parameters, to arrive at a plan for maximising micro-nutrient corrections, through focused interventions.

Productivity Gain

- To monitor the condition of the roads and provide advance recommendations on optimal resource utilisation for producing best impact on taxpayers.
- Identify leakages of taxes and other major revenues, conduct causal analysis and provide decision support.
- Monitor the sanitary conditions, analyse w.r.t climatic and othe rconditions and predict the outbreak of communicable diseases to enable the department to take corrective action.
- Analysis of global commodity prices and provision of advisories to farmers on the export markets to be preferred for exporting grain and horticultural products.
- Integrating climatic, economic, and social data along with quality of healthcare provided, identify geographic regions that are vulnerable to Viral diseases and providing decision support to the department (realtime).
- Usage of IOT for Smart City to improve the quality of the life of the Citizen.

BIG DATA BEST PRACTICES

The following are the best practices for the Big Data Architectures:

Business

- **Align Big Data with Business Goals**: Advice business of an enterprise on how to apply big data techniques to accomplish their goals. For example, understand e-commerce behaviour, derive sentiment from social media and customer support interactions and understand statistical correlation methods and their relevance for customer, product, manufacturing, or engineering data. Even though Big Data is a newer IT frontier and there is an obvious excitement to master something new, it is important to base new investments in skills, organization, or infrastructure with a strong business-driven context to guarantee ongoing project investments and funding. Determine how Big Data support and enable enterprise business architecture and top IT priorities.
- **Consolidate Enterprise Data**: Today enterprises have an overwhelming amount of data available in the form of structured and unstructured application data (documents, files, logs, click streams, events, social media, images, videos and more). All this data is either poorly captured or not easily accessible by employees due to the siloed nature of old data architectures. Big Data Analytics helps in establishing an enterprise-wide common data platform that makes data available from a central location.
- **Align with the Cloud Operating Model**: Big Data processes and users require access to broad array of resources for both iterative experimentation and running production jobs. Data across the data realms (transactions, master data, reference, and summarized) is part of a Big Data solution. Private and Public cloud provisioning and security strategy plays an integral role in supporting these changing requirements.

- **Manage Operations**: Operationalizing insights requires a repeatable and scalable process for developing numerous analytic models and a reliable architecture for deploying these models into production applications. Ease of operationalization is an important characteristic of a successful modern data architecture.

Technical

- **Unstructured and Structured Data**: It is certainly valuable to analyse Big Data on its own. However, by connecting and integrating low density Big Data with the structured data you are already using today, you can bring even greater business clarity. For example, there is a difference in distinguishing all sentiment from that of only your best customers. Whether you are capturing customer, product, equipment, or environmental Big Data, an appropriate goal is to add more relevant data points to your core master and analytical summaries, which can lead to better conclusions. For these reasons, many see Big Data as an integral extension of enterprise existing business intelligence and data warehousing platform and information architecture.

- **Partition Data**: Partition data files and data structures such as tables, based on temporal periods that match the processing schedule. That simplifies data ingestion and job scheduling, and makes it easier to troubleshoot failures.

- **Schema-on-Read Semantics**: Use *schema-on-read* semantics, which project a schema onto the data when the data is processing, not when the data is stored. This builds flexibility into the solution, and prevents bottlenecks during data ingestion caused by data validation and type checking.

- **Cloud**: Incorporate on premise and cloud Organizations have different criteria for determining which workloads run on premise vs cloud. The criteria could involve internal or external policies regarding location of data stored; availability of an application/system in the cloud; availability of capacity for running a specific workload, etc. It is important for a modern architecture to support a hybrid environment as it is fast becoming the new operating reality for enterprises.

- **Process Data In-Place**: Traditional BI solutions often use an extract, transform, and load (ETL) process to move data into a data warehouse. With larger volumes data, and a greater variety of formats, big data solutions generally use variations of ETL, such as transform, extract, and load (TEL). With this approach, the data processed within the distributed data store, transforming it to the required structure, before moving the transformed data into an analytical data store.

- **Orchestrate Data Ingestion**: In some cases, existing business applications may write data files for batch processing directly into data storage, where Data Lake Analytics consume it. To orchestrate the ingestion of data from on-premises or external data sources into the data lake. Use an orchestration workflow or pipeline, to achieve a predictable and centrally manageable fashion.

- **Automate Processes:** At a time when data volume, variety and number of sources are ever-increasing, automation plays a key role in keeping the data driven culture alive. Data pipeline automation, automation of data cataloging (using ML/AI) and such, help in near real-time availability of consumable data.

Governance

- **Support from Management**: Get C-suite support Building a data driven enterprise needs deep collaboration between various functions across the organization. Many challenges pertaining to people, policies, data ownership and sharing will arise. For the initiative to succeed, a top-down mandate with a clear mission and approval framework to resolve logjams is required.

- **Culture Cultivation**: Develop a data driven culture Building a data driven enterprise is more about people and culture than technology. To ensure employees replace their gut-based decision making with a more thoughtful, data driven approach, it is important to sensitize employees to the need for, and advantages of, being data driven. Orientation and training sessions on how to use data and analytics as part of their daily operations will play a key role in the successful implementation and adoption of a modern data architecture.

- **Data Governance**: Data is a shared asset for any enterprise. Data governance assumes an important role and needs a well thought out enterprise wide strategy coupled with strong execution. It needs a framework that transcends enterprise silos to establish how data assets managed, accessed by employees. Data quality, lineage, security, discovery, self-serve access, compliance, legal hold and information lifecycle management need to be given due importance as part of the data governance strategy. To achieve a comprehensive governance strategy, put together a strategy team representing the legal and compliance departments, IT operations, line of business stakeholders, and application/ information owners. Further, enterprises need to implement a comprehensive communication program to sensitize employees about the need for the governance policy and their adherence to it.

- **Data Community**: Build a data community Data democratization needs trusted guardians who can help data consumers use the right data in its relevant form. Building a data community comprising IT managers, data engineers, data scientists and functional experts is crucial for enabling a trusted data environment for business users. This community is responsible for the availability of centralized data dictionaries, MDM, data enrichment, data preparation, pre-prepared data models, business formulae, algorithms and such to the business users. This greatly helps business users to quickly extract insights without having to worry about the data quality or the trustworthiness of the data available.

- **Skills and Governance**: Organizations implementing Big Data solutions and strategies should assess skills requirement early and often and should proactively identify any potential skills gaps. Skills gaps can be addressed by training / cross-training existing resources, hiring new resources, or leveraging consulting firms.

- **No Big Bang**: Do not try to do everything at once. Deploying a modern data architecture is a big initiative and is heavily influenced by technology, policies and people. Though it is important to approach this in a holistic manner, it is not necessary to do it all at once. Enterprises can realize benefits by implementing modern data architecture even for a single function and use the lessons learned for the next phase.

FUTURE RESEARCH DIRECTIONS

Big data analytics is gaining so much attention these days and there were number of research problems that need to be addressed going forward. Few research directions for the future are highlighted below.

Many different models like fuzzy sets, rough sets, soft sets, neural networks, their generalizations and hybrid models are used in analyzing the data. The challenges in analyzing the data may affect performance, efficiency and scalability of the data intensive computing systems. Fast processing while achieving high performance and high throughput, and storing it efficiently for future use is another issue. Expressing data access requirements of applications and designing programming language abstractions to exploit parallelism are an immediate need.

- **Data Life Cycle of Big Data Analytics:** Most of the customer requirements today demanding real-time performance of the big data analytics. This leads for the definition of data life cycle, the value it can provide and the computing process to make the analytics process real time. This increases the value of the analysis (Boyd & Crawford, 2012). A proper data filtering techniques need to be developed to ensure correctness of the data (Nielsen & Chuang, 2000) in Big Data Analysis. The availability of data that is complete and reliable is a big challenge. In most of the cases, data is very limited and do not show clear distribution, resulting to misleading conclusions. A method to overcome these problems needs proper attention and sometimes handling of unbalanced data sets leads to biased conclusion.

- **Storage and Retrieval Data:** Multidimensional data should be integrated with analytics over big data. With the explosion of smart phones, the Images, Audios and Videos are being generated at an unremarkable pace. However, storage, retrieval and processing of these unstructured data require immense research in each dimension.

- **Big Data Computations:** Apart from current big data paradigms like Map-Reduce, other paradigms such as YarcData (Big Data Graph Analytics) and High-Performance Computing cluster (HPCC explores Hadoop alternatives), are being explored.

- **Algorithms for Real Time Processing:** The pace at which data is being generated and the expectations from these algorithms may not be met, if the desired time delay is not met.

- **Smart Storage Devices:** The demand for storing digital information is increasing continuously. Purchasing and using available storage devices cannot meet this demand. Research towards developing efficient storage device that can replace the need for HDFS systems that is fault tolerant can improve the data processing activity and replace the need for software management layer.

- **Quantum Computing for Big Data Analytics:** A quantum computer has memory that is exponentially larger than its physical size and can manipulate an exponential set of inputs simultaneously (Hashem, 2015). Quantum computing provides a way to merge the quantum mechanics to process the information. In traditional computer, information is presented by long strings of bits which encode either a zero or a one. On the other hand a quantum computer uses quantum bits or qubits. The difference between qubit and bit is that, a qubit is a quantum system that encodes the zero and the one into two distinguishable quantum states. Therefore, it can be capitalized on the phenomena of superposition and entanglement. It is because qubits behave quantumly. For example, 100 qubits in quantum systems require 2100 complex values to be stored in a classic computer system. It means that many big data problems can be solved much faster by larger scale quantum computers compared with classical computers. Hence it is a challenge for this generation to built a quantum computer and facilitate quantum computing to solve big data problems.

- **Cloud Computing for Big Data Analytics:** Big data application using cloud computing should support data analytic and development. The cloud environment should provide tools that allow data scientists and business analysts to interactively and collaboratively explore knowledge acquisition data for further processing and extracting results. This can help to solve large applications that may arise in various domains (Chen, 2012). In addition, cloud computing should also enable scaling of tools from virtual technologies into new technologies like spark, R, and other types of big data processing techniques. The major issues are privacy concerns relating to the hosting of data on public servers, and the storage of data from human studies. All these issues will take big data and cloud computing to a high level of development.
- **IoT for Big Data Analytics:** An IoT device generates continuous streams of data and the researchers can develop tools to extract meaningful information from these data using machine learning techniques. Understanding these streams of data generated from IoT devices and analyzing them to get meaningful information is a challenging issue and it leads to big data analytics. Machine learning algorithms and computational intelligence techniques is the only solution to handle big data from IoT prospective. Key technologies that are associated with IoT are also discussed in many research papers.
- **Machine Learning for Big Data Analytics:** Research in the area of machine learning for big data has focused on data processing, algorithm implementation, and optimization. Many of the machine learning tools for big data are started recently needs drastic change to adopt it. Author, argue that while each of the tools has their advantages and limitations, more efficient tools can be developed for dealing with problems inherent to big data. These efficient tools to be developed must have provision to handle noisy and imbalance data, uncertainty and inconsistency, and missing values.

CONCLUSION

Modern businesses are evolving and are constantly demanding more from their Information Management systems. No longer satisfied with standardized reporting by a limited set of users, modern businesses manage by fact, demanding faster and more pervasive access to information on which to base critical business decisions. This change to the volume, velocity and reach of the information is in turn forcing changes to the solution architecture and technology that underpins the solutions.

Big Data employs the tenet of "bringing the analytical capabilities to the data" versus the traditional processes of "bringing the data to the analytical capabilities through staging, extracting, transforming and loading," thus eliminating the high cost of moving data.

In Big Data world, data storage platforms are not restricted to a predefined rigid data model and data systems are capable of handling all kinds of structured and unstructured data. Big data offers capabilities such as deploying data storage/processing from new sources such as external social media data, market data, communications, interaction with customers via digital channels, etc. with unconstrained scalability and flexibility to adapt to constantly changing data landscape.

The following are the Outcome and recommendations on the usage of Big Data Analytics:

- To provide insights into how current business scenario's are performing, and Why(Descriptive and Causal Analyses).
- Design of Better Projects by being more customer centric and effective.
- To determine likely future scenarios and recommend best courses of action (Predictive and Prescriptive Analyses).
- To gauge sentiments of customers, and understand their perceptions of and attitudes towards enterprise products, policies.
- To provide a system of dashboards that enable administrators monitor and implement enterprise programs effectively.
- To improve collaboration among various stakeholders.
- To provide a tool for research in Data Sciences and statistical analysis.
- Enhanced customer Satisfaction through participation in decision-making.
- Formulation of the Right Policies that factor the needs of the people.
- Enhanced transparency of public institutions through feedback & social audit.
- Increased Trust between enterprise & customer allows the free flow of the information.
- Real-time fraud monitoring can be done by integrating large amounts of diverse, structured and unstructured high-velocity data.
- Real-time location information to provide more accurate traffic and drive-time information by analyzing the commute patterns, drive times to and from work.

Big Data also opens up a range of new design and implementation patterns that can make Information Management solutions less brittle, speed development reduce costs and generally improve business delivery. When designed appropriately, they can combine these benefits without giving up the things the business has come to expect and value such as good governance, data quality and robustness.

Finally, Big Data Analytics is not about adopting a technology solution. It is about leveraging tools that enable enterprise to operate more effectively through making informed decisions and where needed, in real time.

ACKNOWLEDGMENT

The author would like to thank Hari Kishan Burle, Raju Alluri of Architecture Group of Wipro Technologies for giving us the required time and support in many ways in bringing this chapter as part of Global Enterprise Architecture Practice efforts. This research received no specific grant from any funding agency in the public, commercial, or not-for-profit sectors.

REFERENCES

Ahmed, R., & Karypis, G. (2012). Algorithms for Mining the Evolution of Conserved Relational States in Dynamic Networks. *Knowledge and Information Systems*, *33*(3), 603–630. doi:10.100710115-012-0537-2

Angelov, S., Grefen, P., & Greefhorst, D. (2012). A framework for analysis and design of software reference architectures. *Journal of Information and Software Technology*, *54*(4), 417–431. doi:10.1016/j.infsof.2011.11.009

Blockow, D. (2018). *Big Data Architecture Principles*. Data to Decision CRC. Retrieved from https://www.d2dcrc.com.au/blog/big-data-architecture-principles/

Boyd & Crawford. (2012). *Six Provocations for Big Data. Proceeding of A Decade in Internet Time: Symposium on the Dynamics of the Internet and Society*. Retrieved from: https://papers.ssrn.com/sol3/papers.cfm?abstract_id=1926431

Buhler, P. (2016). *Big Data Fundamentals: Concepts, Drivers & Techniques*. Prentice Hall.

Chandra, S. (2018). *India's Biometric Identity Program Is Rooting Out Corruption*. Retrieved from: https://slate.com/technology/2018/08/aadhaar-indias-biometric-identity-program-is-working-but-privacy-concerns-remain.html

Chen, M., Mao, S., & Liu, Y. (2014). Big data: A survey. *Mobile Networks and Applications*, *19*(2), 171–209. doi:10.100711036-013-0489-0

Chen, X. (2012). Article. *Research on Key Technology and Applications for Internet of Things*, *33*, 561–566.

Cisco. (2017). *The Zettabyte Era: Trends and Analysis*. Retrieved from: http://www.cisco.com/c/en/us/solutions/collateral/service-provider/visual-networking-index-vni/VNI_Hyperconnectivity_WP.html

Department of Defence. (2012). *Big Data Across the Federal Government*. Executive Office of the President. Retrieved from: https://www.hsdl.org/?view&did=742609

Enterprise, H. P. (2017). *The Exponential Growth of Data*. Retrieved from: https://insidebigdata.com/2017/02/16/the-exponential-growth-of-data/

Forrest, C. (2016). 5 architectural principles for building big data systems on AWS. *TechRepublic*. Retrieved from: https://www.techrepublic.com/article/5-architectural-principles-for-building-big-data-systems-on-aws/

Greenough, J. (2014). *The 'Internet of Things' Will Be The World's Most Massive Device Market And Save Companies Billions Of Dollars. BI Intelligence reports*. Retrieved form: https://www.businessinsider.in/The-Internet-of-Things-Will-Be-The-Worlds-Most-Massive-Device-Market-And-Save-Companies-Billions-Of-Dollars/articleshow/44766662.cms

Hashem, I., Yaqoob, I., Anuar, N. B., Mokhtar, S., Gani, A., & Ullah Khan, S. (2015). The rise of "big data" on cloud computing: Review and open research issues. *Information Systems*, *47*, 98–115. doi:10.1016/j.is.2014.07.006

Hilbert, M. (2015). What is Big Data. *YouTube*. Retrieved from: https://www.youtube.com/watch?v=XRVIh1h47sA

Hilbert, M. (2016). Big Data for Development: A Review of Promises and Challenges. *Development Policy Review*, *34*(1), 135–174. doi:10.1111/dpr.12142

Kalil, T. (2012). *Big Data is a Big Deal*. The White House. Retrieved from: https://obamawhitehouse.archives.gov/blog/2012/03/29/big-data-big-deal

Klein, J. (2017). *Reference Architectures for Big Data Systems*. Carnegie Mellon University Software Engineering Institute. Retrieved from: https://insights.sei.cmu.edu/sei_blog/2017/05/reference-architectures-for-big-data-systems.html

Labrinidis, A., & Jagadish, H. V. (2012). Challenges and opportunities with big data. *Proceeding of VLDB Endowment, 5*(12), 2032–2033.

Lopes & Ribeiro. (2015). GPUMLib: An Efficient Open-source GPU Machine Learning Library. *Machine Learning for Adaptive Many-Core Machines - A Practical Approach, 7*, 15–36.

Manyika. (2011). *Big data: The next frontier for innovation, competition, and productivity*. McKinsey Global Institute. Retrieved from: http://www.mckinsey.com/insights/business_technology/big_data_the_next_frontier_for_innovation

Morris, H. (2014). *A Software Platform for Operational Technology Innovation*. International Data Corporation. Retrieved from: https://www.predix.com/sites/default/files/IDC_OT_Final_whitepaper_249120.pdf

Mullich, J. (2013). *Closing the Big Data Gap in Public Sector*. SAP, Bloomberg Inc.

National Science Foundation. (2012). *Core Techniques and Technologies for Advancing Big Data Science & Engineering (BIGDATA)* (Publication Number: 12-499). Retrieved from: http://www.nsf.gov/pubs/2012/nsf12499/nsf12499.pdf

National Security Agency, Central Security Services. (2011). *Groundbreaking Ceremony Held for $1.2 Billion Utah Data Center*. NSA Press. Retrieved from: https://www.nsa.gov/news-features/press-room/press-releases/2011/utah-groundbreaking-ceremony.shtml

Nielsen & Chuang. (2000). Quantum Computation and Quantum Information. Cambridge University Press.

NIST. (2015). *NIST Big Data Interoperability Framework: Use Cases and General Requirements*. NIST Big Data Public Working Group (Publication number 1500-3). Retrieved from: https://bigdatawg.nist.gov/_uploadfiles/NIST.SP.1500-3.pdf

Normandeau. (2013). *Beyond Volume, Variety and Velocity is the Issue of Big Data Veracity*. Big Data Innovation Summit. Retrieved from: https://insidebigdata.com/2013/09/12/beyond-volume-variety-velocity-issue-big-data-veracity/

Nowak & Spiller. (2017). *Two Billion People Coming Together on Facebook*. Facebook News.

Oracle Corporation. (2015). *An Enterprise Architect's Guide to Big Data*. Oracle Corporation. Retrieved from: https://www.oracle.com/technetwork/topics/entarch/articles/oea-big-data-guide-1522052.pdf

Rijmenam, M. (2018). *A Short History Of Big Data*. Retrieved from: https://datafloq.com/read/big-data-history/239

Rohling, G. (2014). *Facts and Forecasts: Billions of Things, Trillions of Dollars*. Siemens - Internet of Things: Facts and Forecasts. Retrieved from: https://www.siemens.com/innovation/en/home/pictures-of-the-future/digitalization-and-software/internet-of-things-facts-and-forecasts.html

Schmidt, E. (2010). *Techonomy*. Retrieved from: https://www.youtube.com/watch?utm_source=datafloq&utm_medium=ref&utm_campaign=datafloq&v=UAcCIsrAq70

Smith, T. P. (2013). *How big is big and how small is small, the size of everything and why.* Oxford University Press.

Smith & Hallman. (2013). NSA Spying Controversy Highlights Embrace Of Big Data. *The Huffington Post.* Retrieved from: https://www.huffingtonpost.in/entry/nsa-big-data_n_3423482

Stout. (2018). *Social Media Statistics 2018: What You Need to Know.* Retrieved from: https://dustn.tv/social-media-statistics/

Wang, J. (2017). Big Data Driven Smart Transportation: the Underlying Story of IoT Transformed Mobility. *The WIOMAX SmartIoT Blog.* Retrieved from: http://www.wiomax.com/big-data-driven-smart-transportation-the-underlying-big-story-of-smart-iot-transformed-mobility/

We, H. (2014). *SAP and Hortonworks Reference Architecture.* SAP AG.

Wedutenko & Keeing. (2014). *Big data and the public sector: strategy and guidance.* Clayton Utz Insights.

Wu, X. (2014). Data Mining with Big Data. *IEEE Transactions on Knowledge and Data Engineering,* 26(1), 97–107. doi:10.1109/TKDE.2013.109

YouTube. (2017). *YouTube by the Numbers.* Retrieved from: https://www.youtube.com/yt/about/press/

KEY TERMS AND DEFINITIONS

Cloud Computing: Cloud computing is an ICT sourcing and delivery model for enabling convenient, on-demand network access to a shared pool of configurable computing resources (e.g., networks, servers, storage, applications, and services) that can be rapidly provisioned and released with minimal management effort or service provider interaction.

Data Exhaust: Data exhaust (or digital exhaust) refers to the by-products of human usage of the internet, including structured and unstructured data, especially in relation to past interactions.

ETL: Extract, transform, load.

OLAP: Online analytical processing.

OLTP: Online transaction processing.

Open Data: Data which meets the following criteria: accessible (ideally via the internet) at no more than the cost of reproduction, without limitations based on user identity or intent. In a digital, machine readable format for interoperation with other data; and free of restriction on use or redistribution in its licensing conditions.

Structured Data: The term-structured data refers to data that is identifiable and organized in a structured way. The most common form of structured data is a database where specific information is stored based on a methodology of columns and rows. Structured data is machine readable and efficiently organized for human readers.

Unstructured Data: The term unstructured data refers to any data, that has little identifiable structure. Images, videos, email, documents, and text fall into the category of unstructured data.

Chapter 11
Big Data Analytics in Cloud Computing:
Effective Deployment of Data Analytics Tools

Rajganesh Nagarajan
A. V. C. College of Engineering, India

Ramkumar Thirunavukarasu
VIT University, India

ABSTRACT

In this chapter, the authors consider different categories of data, which are processed by the big data analytics tools. The challenges with respect to the big data processing are identified and a solution with the help of cloud computing is highlighted. Since the emergence of cloud computing is highly advocated because of its pay-per-use concept, the data processing tools can be effectively deployed within cloud computing and certainly reduce the investment cost. In addition, this chapter talks about the big data platforms, tools, and applications with data visualization concept. Finally, the applications of data analytics are discussed for future research.

INTRODUCTION

Big data is an evolving term that describes huge amount of structured, semi-structured and unstructured data. In addition, big data (Kolomvatsos et al., 2015) refers to the use of predictive analytics, behavior analytics, or advanced data analytics for extracting the real inside values from different kind of data (Boyd et al., 2012). The basic characteristics of big data includes volume, variety and velocity (Hilbert & Martin, 2016). Volume represents the quantity of generated and stored data. The size of the data is the key factor to determine the value and its potential insight for considering the whether it is big data or not. Variety includes the data type and its nature such as structured, semi-structured and unstructured

DOI: 10.4018/978-1-6684-3662-2.ch011

data. Velocity represents the speed of the data in which generated and processed to meet the demands and challenges.

Big data environments require clusters of computing servers to support the tools that process the structured, semi-structured and unstructured data. Though big data offers various kinds of analysis such as descriptive modeling, predictive modeling, and prescriptive modeling, it is crucial to analyze and synthesize interesting pattern from diversified data sources. This makes cloud based data analytics, a viable research field and open new research avenues in modeling and analyzing complex data. Furthermore, cloud services enable infrastructures to be scaled up and down rapidly, adapting the system to the actual demand. Hence, this chapter addresses the importance of cloud computing in order to support the big data analytics. In such circumstances, the primary features of cloud computing such as on-demand provisioning, pay-per-usage provides significant improvement in the process of data analytics. The important challenges of big data are discussed and further research directions with the aid of cloud computing is presented.

CATEGORIES OF BIGDATA AND CHALLENGES ASSOCIATED

With the advent of internet and smart devices, the manipulation of data increases rapidly. In addition, there is no such common mechanism followed for the representation of data. In such scenario, it is important to process different kinds of data (Agresti & Kateri, 2011) before formulating the information. With respect to the existing data processing mechanisms, it is essential to invent a new data processing methodology with less capital investment. Accordingly, cloud computing has been highly recommended to incorporate the data processing activities by running the new data analytics tools. Hence, this section highlights the various categories of big data and its processing tool. Finally, the incorporation of cloud computing enhances the data analytics process in an effective manner.

Categories of Data

1. **Structured Data**: Refers to any kind of data that has a proper format and resides in a record or file. Structured data (Chang et al., 2008) are easy to input, query, store, and analyse. Examples of structured data include numbers, words, and dates.
2. **Semi-Structured Data:** The data that are not following the conventional or relational data base system are called as semi-structured data (Sagiroglu & Sinanc, 2013). The data are not organized in table format. In order to analyse the semi-structured data, the complex rules must be used.
3. **Unstructured Data:** The text messages, location information, videos, and social media information (Feldman & Sanger, 2007) are data that do not follow any prescribed format. Always the size of this data is increasing because of the use of new technological devices such as smartphones. Therefore, the understanding of such data become a more challenging one.

Challenges in Big Data

The challenges in big data require more attention to avoid the failure of technology with some unpleasant results. Some of the identified challenges (Labrinidis et al., 2012; Chen et al., 2014) are given here to understand the common issues.

Data Storage

The volume, velocity and variety of big data leads to storage challenges. Storage of data on traditional device such as Hard Disk Drives (HDD) is very tedious and the data protection mechanisms are inefficient (Robinson, 2012). In addition, the traditional storage systems failed to scale up for the effective handling of big data. However, cloud computing provides the facility such as Amazon S3, Elastic Block Store to address big data storage challenges.

Processing of Reliable Data

Because of diversified nature, the processing of data becomes inefficient and affects the quality of data. Hence, the feature selection methods has to be considered for processing the data.

Accessing of Data

The inadequate platform and the programming language complicates the data access among the various resources. As a result, the effectiveness of data access have not achieved.

Processing of Complex Data

The analysis of data such as image, video, and the representation of the physical as well as the living world is very complex. It is necessary to reinvent the big data tools with programming architectures to capture, store and analyze the data in an effective manner.

Data Visualization

Data visualization discovers unknown correlations to improve decision-making (Nasser & Tariq, 2015) process. Though the big data is heterogeneous in structure and semantics, the visualization is critical to make sense of big data (Chen et al., 2014). Similarly, the real time visualization and interaction is always difficult (Sun et al., 2012; Nasser & Tariq, 2015).

Privacy and Security

A more sensitive issue of the big data is the privacy and security. The inner details of the data are shared and used by many user. Therefore, it is important to ensure the security of the personal's information while processing the data for any commercial purpose.

Data Quality

The complex and heterogeneity (Lohr, 2012) nature of big data makes data accuracy and completeness is a difficult one. The quality of the data includes the features such as, accuracy, completeness, redundancy and consistency (Chen et al., 2014). With respect to the case of social media, the data are highly skewed in space with different time and demographic details. Therefore, controlling of data redundancy in the collection point is needed. Similarly, data consistency and integrity becomes a challenging one (Khan et al., 2014).

EMERGENCE OF CLOUD COMPUTING

According to National Institute of Standards and Technology (NIST), the cloud computing is defined as, 'a model for enabling convenient, on-demand network access to a shared pool of configurable computing resources that can be rapidly provisioned and released with minimal management effort or service provider interaction'. In short, cloud computing involves deploying groups of remote servers and software networks that allow centralized data storage and online access to computer services or resources. The implementation of cloud computing has been realized with 3 service models, 4 deployment models, and 5 characteristics (Zhang et al., 2010; Rajganesh & Ramkumar, 2016) is shown in Figure 1.

Figure 1. Cloud computing architecture

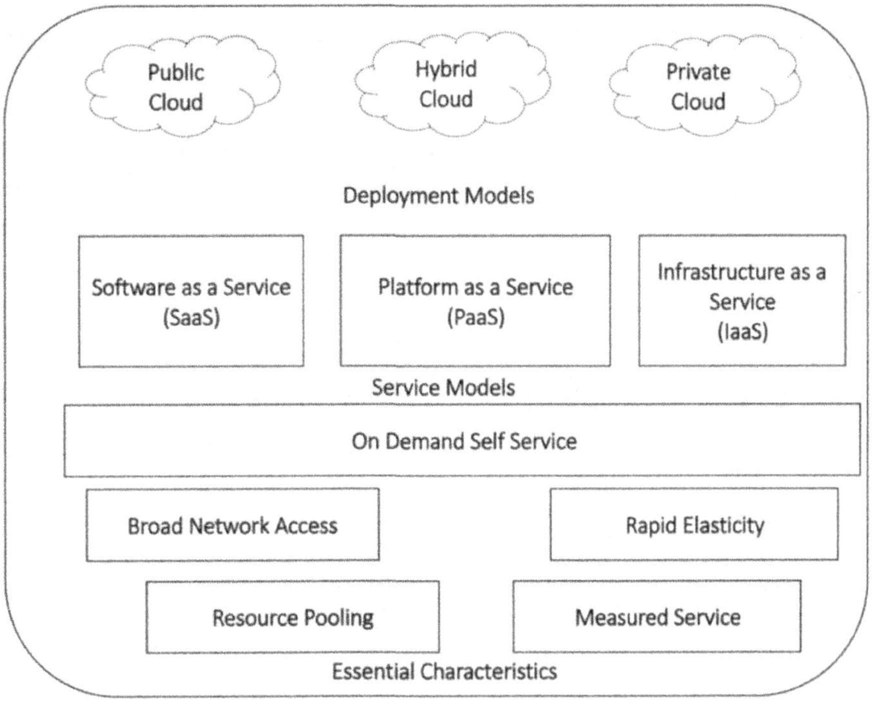

Deployment Model

As per the nature of consumption, the type of cloud are labelled as public, private and hybrid (Hu et al., 2011). In public cloud, the services are offered as open access for all the public. In private cloud, the services are offered for the exclusive use of single person or an organization which comprising many business units. Hybrid cloud contains a combination of both public and private type clouds (Sabahi, 2011).

Public Cloud

Theoretically, there may be no difference between public and private clouds. However, the security consideration may be significantly different for services like storage, applications, and networks. Some of the public cloud service providers are Amazon Web Services (AWS), Oracle, Microsoft and Google. Generally, these providers own and operate the infrastructure at their data centre and provide access to cloud user via the Internet.

Private Cloud

A cloud infrastructure resources provided to a single organization and solely utilized by the authorized team in order to ensure the resource security is called private cloud. With this cloud type, the organization is expected to re-evaluate the decisions about existing resources. It can improve business, but every step in the project raises security issues that must be addressed to prevent serious vulnerabilities.

Hybrid Cloud

A composition of two or more clouds for offering the benefits of multiple deployment models is achieved with the hybrid type of cloud. Hybrid cloud is composed of public, private, and community cloud services from various service providers. Hence, it allows the cloud user to extend either the capacity or the capability of a cloud service, by aggregation, integration or customization with another cloud service. Hybrid cloud depend upon the factors such as data security and control, amenability requirements, and the applications an organization uses.

Service Models

The service models provides Software, Platform, and Infrastructure services to the cloud user and the layered architecture is shown in Figure 2.

Figure 2. Layered architecture of service models

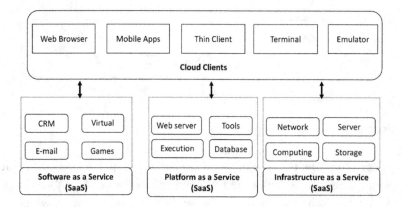

The *Software as a Service (SaaS)* model allows the consumers to avail the predefined compound functionalities from the cloud service provider. The objective is to deliver the application services as per user requirements. Hence, the end users need not worry about the issues such as installation and future maintenance overheads.

The second service called *Platform as a Service (PaaS)* is an implausible model for offering the computing platform that includes operating systems, program-developing environment, web servers and database systems to the cloud user. From this model, the user can share the platform resources.

The third service namely, *Infrastructure as a Service (IaaS)* meant for delivering the cloud computing infrastructure such as physical computers, storage, network and related resources for the deployment of user operating system, application software. Through this, the users can own the peripherals and configure as per their wish. In short, the major offering (Rimal et al., 2009) of the cloud is classified as computational services, storage and other services such as scheduling and management of tasks, provision of user access interface, web APIs, framework for programming.

Characteristics of Cloud Computing

Cloud computing exhibits five important characteristics namely, on demand self-service, broad network access, resource pooling, rapid elasticity, and measured service.

On-demand self-service. A cloud user are provisioned the computing capabilities (server, network storage) as per their need without requiring human interaction.

Broad network access. The utilization of resources over the network through the standard mechanisms that helps the user to avail the services from their terminal.

Resource pooling. The effective allocation of resources among the requested service user can be obtained with this characteristic. Hence, the provider's computing resources are pooled to serve multiple consumers with different physical and virtual resources. These resources can be dynamically assigned and reassigned according to user's need.

Rapid elasticity. The resource capabilities can be elastically provisioned to meet out the dynamic need of cloud user.

Measured service. Every cloud systems control and optimize the resource through the metering capability. Resource usage can be monitored, controlled, and reported immediately for assisting the cloud provider and user.

The cloud computing has been greatly differing from the concept of big data based on following reasons: (i) In cloud computing (Mell, 2011), resources have been utilized from the third-party vendors and the data ownership will be on the hand of service provider, whereas the resources have been utilized in an in-house model at big data. (ii) In big data, the computational part must be moved towards the data, whereas in cloud computing, data have been moved towards the location of the computing processors. However, several research issues such as data variety, volume, storage, integration, and visualization of data are to be addressed and their risks need to be mitigated before using the big data with cloud computing. Cloud computing plays a critical role in Big Data Analytics (BDA) process as it offers on-demand access for computing infrastructure, data, and application services (Armbrust et al., 2010). Due to the massive dataset, the improved computational capacity with less cost becomes more attention for implementing the BDA.

BIG DATA ANALYTICS IN CLOUD ENVIRONMENT

The 3 V's of big data represents the semantic meaning of data. Whereas, big data analytics represents pragmatic meaning of big data (Wu et al., 2016), is shown in Figure 3.

Figure 3. Pragmatic meaning of big data

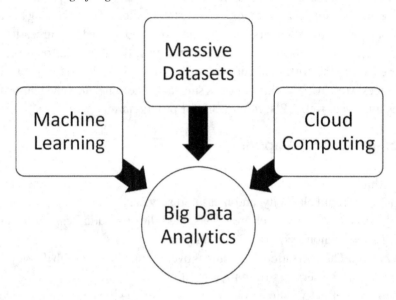

Big Data Analytics

The process of examining different data to uncover hidden patterns, unknown correlations, market trends, customer preferences, and other useful information is termed as big data analytics. Most of the companies implement Big Data Analytics to make more informed business decisions. Big data analytics gives analytics professionals, such as data scientists and predictive modelers, the ability to analyze big data from multiple and varied sources, including transactional data and other structured data.

The processing requirements of Big data may also make traditional data warehousing a poor fit. As a result, newer, bigger data analytics environments and technologies have emerged, including Hadoop, MapReduce and NoSQL databases. These technologies can use the cloud computing platforms to serve better for the user needs and reduces the installation cost of these tools from the customer point.

Data Analytics in Cloud Computing

The effectiveness of data analytics through the cloud computing is mostly preferred by the data owners. The nature of cloud computing will always simplify the work with respect to the cost and time. Also, the demand for the analytics tools have been fulfilled in cloud computing with its service categories such as Infrastructure as a Service (IaaS), Platform as a Service (PaaS) and Software as a Service (SaaS). Processing the big data with cloud computing improves the performance with less investment. Figure 4 shows the integration of the big data with the cloud computing architecture. The various big data sources have been processed with in the cloud computing and reduces the computation and storage cost. Normally, the existing data processing methodologies are having the limitation in order to process the big data sources. By using the various services of cloud computing, it is better to improve the effectiveness of the data with respect to the customer's need.

Figure 4. Data analytics in cloud computing

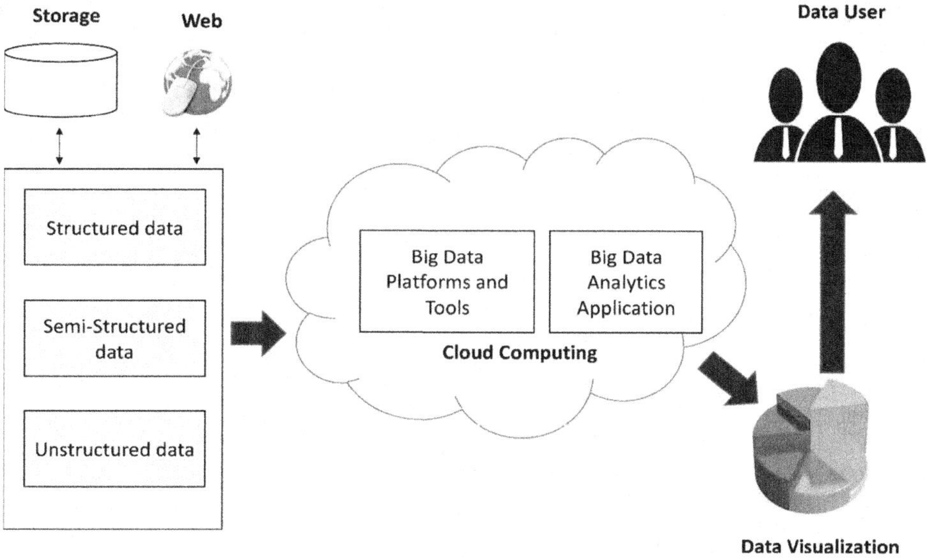

BIG DATA PLATFORMS: TOOLS AND APPLICATIONS

Nowadays, there are thousands of big data tools available to process the data. All of them promising to save the time, money and help the user to understand the data in a simple way (Dhar, 2013).

Cloud Based Big Data Analytics Tools

Data analytics tools (Witten et al., 2016; Vukotic & Gardner, 2016) automatically collect, clean, and analyze data for making decision. Table 1 elaborates the usage of tools with its pros and cons. In addition, the most important open source tools, which are commonly used to process the data is given.

Hadoop

The Apache distributed data processing software is so pervasive that often the terms 'Hadoop' and 'big data' are used synonymously (Strang & Sun, 2017). The Apache foundation extend the capabilities of Hadoop by adding additional projects. In addition, many vendors offer supported versions of Hadoop and related technologies in Windows and Linux platforms. The Hadoop project provides the basic services for building a cloud computing environment with hardware and software to support the user tasks. The two fundamental pieces of Hadoop are the MapReduce framework and the Hadoop Distributed File System (HDFS).

MapReduce

MapReduce is a programming model (Wang et al., 2017) developed by Google for writing applications that rapidly process huge amounts of data. The independent nature MapReduce allows other computing platforms to work together. The following Figure 5 shows the MapReduce architecture with mapper and reducer classes.

Figure 5. MapReduce framework

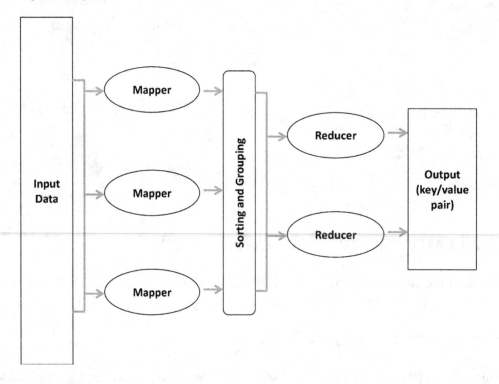

MapReduce includes two major functions, called 'Map' and 'Reduce'. The Map function is applied in parallel to every input (*key*, *value*) pair, and produces new set of intermediate (key, value) pairs. With the help of MapReduce library, all the produced intermediate (*key*, *value*) pairs are sorted and grouped based on the '*key*' part. Finally, the Reduce function is applied in parallel to each group producing the collection of values as output.

Hadoop Distributed File System (HDFS)

HDFS is a file system that is designed for use with MapReduce jobs that read large chunks of input, process it, and write potentially large chunks of output. In HDFS the file data is simply mirrored to multiple storage nodes. With this replication of data nodes, the availability of data is achieved.

HDFS contains two nodes called Name node and Data node. Name node handles management of the file system metadata, and provides management and control services. Data node provides block storage and retrieval services. HDFS is designed for specific type of applications. Hence, it is not a general-purpose file system; it does not need all the requirements of a general distributed file system.

GridGain

GridGrain is supported in Windows, Linux and OS X platforms. It is an alternative to Hadoop's MapReduce (Belcastro, 2017) and is compatible with the Hadoop Distributed File System (HDFS). GridGain includes an in-memory data grid, database, streaming analytics in a single platform. Through this, user can create modern, scalable, real-time applications for digital transformation. In addition, GridGain can scale horizontally by adding the cluster node for automatic rebalancing of workload.

GridGain can integrates with the with the existing database technologies such as RDBMS, NoSQL and Hadoop. The presence of API's in GridGain allows it to work with other programming paradigms also. GridGain integrates with many common management and data processing operations and can run on premises of public cloud such as, AWS, Mirosoft Azure, Google Cloud Platform.

Key Benefits

- In-memory computing platform
- Scalable to petabytes of in-memory data
- Easy integration with other databases
- Less complexity
- Low cost - built on open source software

Key Features

- In-memory Data Grid and Database
- Streaming Analytics
- Continuous Learning Framework
- ACID transactions
- Unified API
- Optional native persistence
- Native support for Spark, Cassandra, MongoDB, YARN, Docker and Kubernetes

High Performance Computing Cluster Systems

High Performance Computing Cluster (HPCC) (Zong, 2017) is developed by LexisNexis Risk Solutions to offer superior performance to Hadoop. Linux supports it and a paid version is available. The HPCC system includes two processing environments namely, Data refinery and Roxie.

Data refinery is used for processing the huge volumes of raw data of any type. Also, performs the operations such as data extraction, cleansing, transformation, record linking and entity resolution, large-scale ad-hoc complex analytics, and creation of keyed data and indexes to support high-performance structured queries and data warehouse applications. The data refinery is also referred to as *Thor*.

The second part, *Roxie* is designed as an online high-performance structured query and analysis platform and functions as a rapid data delivery engine. Roxie utilizes a distributed indexed file system to provide parallel processing of queries using an optimized execution environment. The functionalities of a Roxie cluster is similar to Hadoop and provides real time predictable query latencies. Both Thor and Roxie clusters utilize the ECL programming language for implementing applications, increasing continuity and programmer productivity.

Application Areas

- *Computer aided engineering (CAE)*. Automotive design and testing, transportation, structural, mechanical design.
- *Chemical engineering*. Process and molecular design.
- *Digital content creation (DCC) and distribution*. Computer aided graphics in film and Media.
- *Economics/financial*. Portfolio management and automated trading.
- *Electronic design and automation (EDA)*. Electronic component design and verification.
- *Geosciences and geo-engineering*. Oil and gas exploration and reservoir modelling.
- *Mechanical design and drafting*. 2D and 3D design and verification, mechanical Modelling.
- *Defense and energy*. Nuclear stewardship, basic and applied research.
- *Government labs/University/academic*. Basic and applied research.
- *Weather forecasting*. Near term and climate/earth modelling.

Storm

Storm offers distributed real-time computation capabilities and often described as the 'Hadoop of Real-time'. Storm is simple, highly scalable, robust, fault tolerant and works with nearly all programming languages. Storm has the use cases such as real time analytics, online machine learning, continuous computation, and distributed RPC. It is owned by Twitter and its platform is Linux.

The Apache Storm cluster comprises following critical components:

- **Nodes:** There are two types of nodes, i.e., Master Node and Worker Node. The Master Node executes a daemon Nimbus that assigns tasks to machines and monitors their performances. On the other hand, the Worker Node runs the daemon called Supervisor, which assigns the tasks to other worker node and operates them as per the need.

- **Components:** Storm has three critical components namely Topology, Stream, and Spout. Topology is a network made of Stream and Spout. Stream is an unbounded pipeline of tuples and Spout is the source of the data streams, which converts the data into the tuple of streams and sends to the bolts to be processed.

Table 1. Data analytics tools: An overview

S. No	Name of the Tool	Definition	Uses	Limitations
1	Tableau Public	Communicates insights through data visualization	Publish interactive data visualizations in to the web. No programming skills required. Shared through email or social media.	Data is public. Limited data size. Cannot connect with R.
2	OpenRefine (Google Refine)	A data cleaning software that helps to get everything ready for analysis. It is based on relational database tables.	Messy data cleaning. Transformation of data. Parsing of data from websites.	Not suitable for large datasets. It does not work very well with big data.
3	Knime	A tool to manipulate, analyze, and modeling data in an intuitive way via visual programming.	Drop and Drag based method. Supports programming languages.	Poor data visualization.
4	RapidMiner	Provides machine learning procedures and data mining including data visualization, processing, statistical modeling, deployment, evaluation, and predictive analytics.	Performs business analytics, predictive analysis, text mining, data mining, and machine learning. Used for application development, rapid prototyping, training, education, and research.	Size constraints problem with respect to the increase of rows. More hardware resources are needed.
5	Google Fusion Tables	A free and incredible tool for data analysis, mapping, and large dataset visualization.	Easy filtering and summarizing of row data. Allows table merging for better visualization.	Limitation in rows processing. The size is limited to 1MB only.
6	NodeXL	A free open source visualization and analysis software for providing the exact calculations.	Data Import. Graph visualization and Graph Analysis. Data Representation. Elements of a graph structure like nodes and edges.	Multiple seeding terms. Data extractions in different time interval.
7	Wolfram Alpha	It is a computational knowledge engine allows getting answers for factual queries directly.	Provides detailed responses to technical searches. Providing information charts and graphs.	It can only deal with number and facts, not with viewpoints. Limited Computation Time for Each query.
8	Google Search Operators	Instantly filters Google results to get most relevant and useful information.	Fast in filtering of data. Help to discover new information or market research.	-
9	DataIKU DSS	A collaborative data science software platform that helps team build, prototype, explore, and deliver their own data products more efficiently.	Provides an interactive visual interface. Faster in data preparation.	Limited visualization capabilities. Difficult to compile entire code into a single document. Need to integrate with SPARK.

Data Visualization

An important step in data analytics is the data visualization process. The goal is to communicate the information very clearly and effectively to the users. According to Friedman (1998), the goal of data visualization is "to communicate information clearly and effectively through graphical means". It doesn't mean that data visualization (Langseth et al., 2017) needs to look boring to be functional or extremely sophisticated to look beautiful.

Terminology in Data Visualization

Data visualization (Nolan & Perrett, 2016) involves specific terminology such as;

- **Categorical:** Text labels describing the nature of the data, such as 'Name' or 'Age'. This term also covers qualitative (non-numerical) data.
- **Quantitative:** Numerical measures, such as '25' to represent the age in years.

Two primary types of information displays are tables and graphs.

- A *table* contains quantitative data organized into rows and columns with categorical labels.
- A *graph* is used to show relationship among data and portrays values as *visual objects* (e.g., lines, bars, or points). Numerical values are displayed within an area delineated by one or more *axes*. These axes provide *scales* (quantitative and categorical) used to label and assign values to the visual objects. The following Figure 6 shows the decision tree generated with the help of R Studio for the input values of cloud infrastructure services (Nagarajan & Thirunavukarasu, 2018). The input values are given in the form of *.csv* file. The selection of services are considering either the storage capacity or the computational speed with a small change in the price value.

Figure 6. Data visualization through R studio

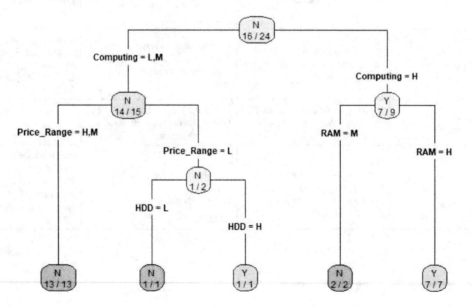

APPLICATIONS OF DATA ANALYTICS

Big data management strategies and best practices (Gunasekaran et al., 2016) are still evolving, but joining the big data, movement has become an imperative for companies across a wide variety of industries. Here, some of the application area is highlighted which are mostly benefited from the big data.

Internet Search

All the search engines are make use of data science algorithms to deliver the best result for the user query. By considering the popular search engine such as Google, it processes more than 20 petabytes of data every day. It is possible because of the data analytics only.

Recommender Systems

Based on the user needs, right prediction of services or products is a challenging one. Internet giants like Amazon, Twitter, Google Play, Netflix, Linkedin uses this system to improve user experience. The recommendation have been made based on the previous search results of a user.

Speech Recognition

Some of the best example of speech recognition products are Google Voice, Siri, Cortana etc. The usage of speech recognition feature really uses the data analytics for the easy understanding and its action sequences.

Price Comparison in Websites

Products comparison based on price and feature is a challenging in the existing data processing applications. Now, the data analytics tools are emerged to enhance the data processing. PriceGrabber, PriceRunner, Junglee, Shopzilla, DealTime are some examples of price comparison websites. Nowadays, price comparison can be found in almost every domain such as technology, hospitality, automobiles, durables, apparels etc.

Fraud and Risk Detection

In a marketing environment, the bad debts causes a loss for the companies every year. However, they had many data, collected during the initial paper work while sanctioning loans. They decided to bring in data science practices in order to rescue them out of losses. Over the years, banking companies learned to divide and conquer data via customer profiling, past expenditures, and other essential variables to analyze the probabilities of risk and default. Moreover, it also helped to push their banking products based on customer's purchasing power.

CONCLUSION

At present, the big data analytics through cloud computing has been established as one of the hot topics. The different categories of data and their processing with the data analytics tools are briefly explained in this overview. Besides, the overall challenges in the processing of big data is addressed. The effectiveness of data analytics through the cloud computing is mostly preferred by the data owners, since the nature of cloud computing simplifies the work with respect to the cost and time. The chapter outlines the cloud-based open source tools, which are commonly used to process the data towards to communicate the information very clearly and effectively to the users. Followed that, the need for the data visualization is justified with few terminologies. Finally, the important applications of the data analytics are pointed out for further work.

REFERENCES

Agresti, A., & Kateri, M. (2011). *Categorical data analysis*. Springer Berlin Heidelberg.

Armbrust, M., Fox, A., Griffith, R., Joseph, A. D., Katz, R., Konwinski, A., & Zaharia, M. (2010). A view of cloud computing. *Communications of the ACM*, *53*(4), 50–58. doi:10.1145/1721654.1721672

Belcastro, L., Marozzo, F., Talia, D., & Trunfio, P. (2017). Big Data Analysis on Clouds. In *Handbook of Big Data Technologies* (pp. 101–142). Springer International Publishing. doi:10.1007/978-3-319-49340-4_4

Boyd, D., & Crawford, K. (2012). Critical questions for big data: Provocations for a cultural, technological, and scholarly phenomenon. *Information Communication and Society*, *15*(5), 662–679.

Chang, F., Dean, J., Ghemawat, S., Hsieh, W. C., Wallach, D. A., Burrows, M., & Gruber, R. E. (2008). Bigtable: A distributed storage system for structured data. *ACM Transactions on Computer Systems*, *26*(2), 4.

Chen & Zhang. (2014). Data-intensive applications, challenges, techniques and technologies: A survey on Big Data. *Information Sciences*, *275*, 314–347.

Chen, Z. K., Yang, S. Q., Tan, S., Zhao, H., He, L., Zhang, G., & Yang, H. Y. (2014). The Data Allocation Strategy Based on Load in NoSQL Database. *Applied Mechanics and Materials*, *513–517*, 1464–1469.

Dhar, V. (2013). Data science and prediction. *Communications of the ACM*, *56*(12), 64–73.

Feldman, R., & Sanger, J. (2007). *The text mining handbook: advanced approaches in analyzing unstructured data*. Cambridge University Press.

Friedman, J. H. (1998). Data mining and statistics: What's the connection? *Computing Science and Statistics*, *29*(1), 3–9.

Gunasekaran, A., Kumar Tiwari, M., Dubey, R., & Fosso Wamba, S. (2016). Big data and predictive analytics applications in supply chain management. *Computers & Industrial Engineering*, *101*(C), 525–527.

Hilbert & Martin. (2016). Big data for development: A review of promises and challenges. *Development Policy Review*, *34*(1), 135–174.

Hu, F., Qiu, M., Li, J., Grant, T., Taylor, D., McCaleb, S., & Hamner, R. (2011). A review on cloud computing: Design challenges in architecture and security. *CIT. Journal of Computing and Information Technology*, *19*(1), 25–55. doi:10.2498/cit.1001864

Khan, N., Yaqoob, I., Hashem, I. A. T., Inayat, Z., Mahmoud Ali, W. K., Alam, M., ... Gani, A. (2014). Big Data: Survey, Technologies, Opportunities, and Challenges. *The Scientific World Journal*, 1–18. PMID:25136682

Kolomvatsos, K., Anagnostopoulos, C., & Hadjiefthymiades, S. (2015). An efficient time optimized scheme for progressive analytics in big data. *Big Data Research*, *2*(4), 155–165. doi:10.1016/j.bdr.2015.02.001

Labrinidis, A., & Jagadish, H. V. (2012). Challenges and opportunities with big data. *Proceedings of the VLDB Endowment International Conference on Very Large Data Bases*, *5*(12), 2032–2033. doi:10.14778/2367502.2367572

Langseth, J., Aref, F., Alarcon, J., & Lindner, W., III. (2017). *U.S. Patent No. 9,612,742*. Washington, DC: U.S. Patent and Trademark Office.

Lohr, S. (2012). The age of big data. *New York Times*, p. 11.

Mell, P., & Grance, T. (2011). *The NIST definition of cloud computing*. Gaithersburg, MD: Computer Security Division, Information Technology Laboratory, National Institute of Standards and Technology, United States Department of Commerce. doi:10.6028/NIST.SP.800-145

Nagarajan, R., & Thirunavukarasu, R. (2018). A fuzzy-based decision-making broker for effective identification and selection of cloud infrastructure services. *Soft Computing*. doi:10.100700500-018-3534-x

Nasser, T., & Tariq, R. S. (2015). Big Data Challenges. *Journal of Computer Engineering & Information Technology*, *4*(3), 1–10.

Nolan, D., & Perrett, J. (2016). Teaching and learning data visualization: Ideas and assignments. *The American Statistician*, *70*(3), 260–269. doi:10.1080/00031305.2015.1123651

Rajganesh, N., & Ramkumar, T. (2016). A review on broker based cloud service model. *CIT. Journal of Computing and Information Technology*, *24*(3), 283–292. doi:10.20532/cit.2016.1002778

Rimal, B. P., Choi, E., & Lumb, I. (2009). *A taxonomy and survey of cloud computing systems*. INC, IMS and IDC. doi:10.1109/NCM.2009.218

Robinson, S. (2012). *The Storage and Transfer Challenges of Big Data*. Retrieved from http://sloanreview.mit.edu/article/the-storage-and-transfer-challenges-of-big-data/

Sabahi, F. (2011). Cloud computing security threats and responses. *IEEE 3rd International Conference on Communication Software and Networks (ICCSN)*, 245-249. 10.1109/ICCSN.2011.6014715

Sagiroglu, S., & Sinanc, D. (2013). Big data: A review. *IEEE International Conference on Collaboration Technologies and Systems (CTS)*, 42-47. 10.1109/CTS.2013.6567202

Strang, K. D., & Sun, Z. (2017). Analyzing relationships in terrorism big data using Hadoop and statistics. *Journal of Computer Information Systems*, *57*(1), 67–75. doi:10.1080/08874417.2016.1181497

Sun, M., Li, J., Yang, C., Schmidt, G. A., Bambacus, M., Cahalan, R., ... Li, Z. (2012). A Web-Based Geovisual Analytical System for Climate Studies. *Future Internet*, *4*(4), 1069–1085. doi:10.3390/fi4041069

Vukotic, I., & Gardner, R. (2016). *Big Data Analytics Tools as Applied to ATLAS Event Data* (No. ATL-SOFT-SLIDE-2016-649). ATL-COM-SOFT-2016-079.

Wang, C. S., Lin, S. L., & Chang, J. Y. (2017). MapReduce-Based Frequent Pattern Mining Framework with Multiple Item Support. In *Asian Conference on Intelligent Information and Database Systems*. Springer. 10.1007/978-3-319-54430-4_7

Witten, I. H., Frank, E., Hall, M. A., & Pal, C. J. (2016). *Data Mining: Practical machine learning tools and techniques*. Morgan Kaufmann.

Wu, C., Buyya, R., & Ramamohanarao, K. (2016). *Big Data Analytics= Machine Learning+ Cloud Computing*. arXiv preprint arXiv:1601.03115

Zhang, Q., Cheng, L., & Boutaba, R. (2010). Cloud computing: State-of-the-art and research challenges. *Journal of Internet Services and Applications*, *1*(1), 7–18. doi:10.100713174-010-0007-6

Zong, Z., Ge, R., & Gu, Q. (2017). *Marcher: A Heterogeneous System Supporting Energy-Aware High-Performance Computing and Big Data Analytics*. Big Data Research.

This research was previously published in Novel Practices and Trends in Grid and Cloud Computing; pages 325-341, copyright year 2019 by Engineering Science Reference (an imprint of IGI Global).

Chapter 12
Decision Framework for Engaging Cloud–Based Big Data Analytics Vendors

Emmanuel Wusuhon Yanibo Ayaburi
University of Texas Rio Grande Valley, USA

Michele Maasberg
iD https://orcid.org/0000-0003-4306-0559
Louisiana Tech University, USA

Jaeung Lee
iD https://orcid.org/0000-0002-9869-050X
Louisiana Tech University, USA

ABSTRACT

Organizations face both opportunities and risks with big data analytics vendors, and the risks are now profound, as data has been likened to the oil of the digital era. The growing body of research at the nexus of big data analytics and cloud computing is examined from the economic perspective, based on agency theory (AT). A conceptual framework is developed for analyzing these opportunities and challenges regarding the use of big data analytics and cloud computing in e-business environments. This framework allows organizations to engage in contracts that target competitive parity with their service-oriented decision support system (SODSS) to achieve a competitive advantage related to their core business model. A unique contribution of this paper is its perspective on how to engage a vendor contractually to achieve this competitive advantage. The framework provides insights for a manager in selecting a vendor for cloud-based big data services.

INTRODUCTION

The proliferation of mobile devices and the ability of almost any electronic device to connect to the

DOI: 10.4018/978-1-6684-3662-2.ch012

Internet have significantly increased the amount of data generated by businesses daily. This increase in the magnitude of data is called *big data* (Hashem et al., 2015); it is difficult to store, process, and analyze using traditional tools, such as relational databases. Big data is distinguished from traditional data by volume, velocity, variety, veracity, and value (Marr, 2015). These characteristics help business managers to make important decisions in real time (Höchtl, Parycek, & Schöllhammer, 2016). The nature and origin of these characteristics can be explained by the data life cycle where a business collects, stores, processes, and makes meaning out of the data at their disposal from generation to insight. Figure 1 illustrates a typical data life cycle where a business uses the insights obtained from the processed data to gather more data. The data life cycle process leads to challenges that typical businesses do not face in their daily operations in dealing with big data, often prohibiting insights if the business is unprepared to handle them.

Many organizations are unable to manage their existing smaller data, and big data adds a layer of complexity, as capabilities are necessary with analytics and storage (Troester, 2012). Thus, despite the pervasiveness of big data technologies, many e-business firms are unable to achieve the elusive status of success (Gupta & George, 2016).

Figure 1. Data life cycle

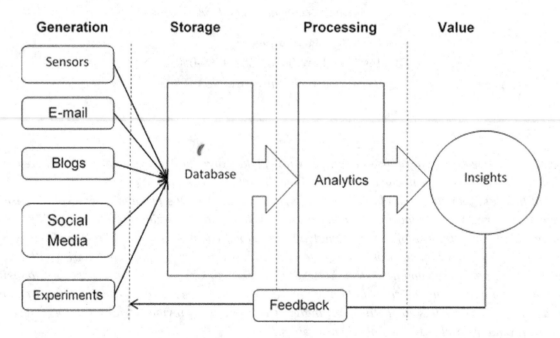

This study posits that one explanation for organizations missing out on the success of big data relates to the nature and effect of the contract between vendors providing cloud-based data analytic services and clients receiving those services. Among the opportunities for big data and analytics in the cloud is an ecosystem conceptually referred to as a *Service-Oriented Decision Support System (SODSS)*. Demirkan and Delen (2013) suggest that value can be created through the implementation of accrued knowledge from the interactions of service systems that involve people, technology, organizations, and shared information. There are challenges as vendors, usually third parties, are required to manage these processes unless the core competency of the organization is technology, particularly related to big data, analytics, and the cloud. This study complements prior studies such as Pakath (2015) and Yu (2016) that provide insights for businesses to create value from big data analytics. This study seeks to enhance understanding of economic benefits of analytics literature by investigating the following research questions:

Question 1: What challenges do e-business organizations face in using cloud-based big data analytics?
Question 2: What decision factors should e-business organizations consider in their contracts with agents regarding cloud-based big data analytics to achieve competitive parity?
Question 3: How should e-business organizations manage their contracts with cloud-based big data analytics vendors?

In response to these questions, this study develops a theoretical framework to understand the opportunities and challenges of big data analytics in cloud computing for e-businesses (Amit & Zott, 2001) from an economic perspective to maximize competitive parity (Mata, Fuerst, & Barney, 1995). The findings provide insights to e-business firms into how they can make the most from the potential data available to them and understand the challenges in the process, particularly their decision-making regarding the type of vendor for big data. The rate of adoption of data analytics tools suggests that most firms would continue to use the services of third-party vendors. An examination of client decisions and issues in contracting vendors reduces uncertainties in adopting analytics.

BACKGROUND: CLOUD-BASED DATA ANALYTICS CHALLENGES

Data Scalability and Availability

The rise of big data, from the proliferation of sensors and the ability to measure things at minute levels, has led to the production of petabytes of data in almost all kinds of electronic business. Much of this data is of little interest and should be filtered. Cloud providers still lack round-the-clock service as they experience outages, notable among these is the famous Amazon Web Services (AWS) 2012 outage (Williams, 2012). This places extra responsibility on e-business firms to monitor their services. Some businesses use internal or third-party tools to supervise usage, Service Level Agreements (SLAs), performance, robustness, and business dependency.

Data Integrity

The data gathered in electronic transactions do not always come in a form that can be effectively analyzed. However, collecting data at the original sources and aggregating them can be a technical challenge for most e-business firms. Therefore, generated big data might not always be giving accurate information. For example, reviewers sometimes misinform other reviewers, and customer service personnel may not process customer complaints they deem detrimental to their jobs. This presents challenges regarding the validity of gathered data.

Data Quality

Big data can be highly noisy, dynamic, untrustworthy, inter-related, and heterogeneous (Xindong Wu, Xingquan Zhu, Gong-Qing Wu, & Wei Ding, 2014). Nonetheless, big data is still valuable because information obtained from the analysis of data or web mining usually empowers individuals, leading to the discovery of hidden patterns and knowledge. Information redundancy can help compensate for missing data and enhance the efficiency of these analyses. The value of big data analysis in e-business is enhanced if analysis can be done robustly under difficult conditions such as limited data. The quality of the needed information depends on the ability to coordinate disparate database systems. Despite advances in cloud-based analytics, gathering high-quality data from e-business sites is still a challenge (Xindong Wu et al., 2014).

Loss of Control

Some concerns of e-business firms' transitioning to cloud-based big data analytics include security and privacy of customer data (Chen, Chiang, & Storey, 2012). This is because data that resides outside the corporate firewall presents data owners' challenges in the exercise of control and oversight in data protection. Cloud infrastructure hacking can affect multiple clients. E-business firms would have to incur extra cost to purchase additional security applications and encrypt files across several servers (Chen et al., 2012).

Lock-In

SLA of some cloud-based big data analytics providers may be inadequate to guarantee availability, scalability, and ease of data mobility (Subashini & Kavitha, 2011). Thus, some e-business firms may have justified concerns when things that are not under their control go wrong. The loss of control over data to the cloud provider is a valid concern when the accountability for the safety, security, and proper use of its business data are poorly negotiated in cloud-based big data analytics contracts (Subashini & Kavitha, 2011). One key recommendation for selecting the service provider is for an e-business firm to have an alternative for cloud disaster recovery, in case the disaster is a bankrupt service provider (Behrend et al., 2011). This reduces their exposure to being locked into one provider.

THEORY AND DECISION FRAMEWORK FOR ECONOMIC ANALYSIS

Agency Theory in Cloud-Based Big Data Analytics for E-Business

Agency Theory (AT) deals with issues that arise when two or more parties are engaged in a transaction in which a decision made by one party affects the other parties in the transactions. Actions and decisions by vendors of big data analytics affect the relationship with e-business firms. AT highlights issues of goal incongruence between an *agent* (cloud big data analytics vendors and brokers) and a *principal* (e-business user firms). Some have applied it in other areas, such as understanding outsourcing relationships (Tiwana & Bush, 2007). AT suggests that information asymmetry is the underlying key to understanding principal-agent problems, as the agent is assumed to possess private information about the type and nature of cloud-based big data analytics services that the principal is not privy to, or can only be able to acquire with added cost and effort. Instituting behavioral and outcome controls in contracts as suggested by AT to protect e-business clients will only be successful if the principal (client firm) can confidently specify current and future requirements for the privacy and security of its data generation and analytic activities. Extra demands from principals will not always be in the agent's (service providers) interests as it requires charging the client extra for anything that is not in the contract. That will ultimately affect the provider's profitability (Gottschalk & Solli-Sæther, 2005). With the inability to negotiate a contract that covers every possible situation (Bakos & Brynjolfsson, 1993), some cloud-based analytics providers could hide behind their inefficiencies to fully deliver their substandard services, such as insecure virtualization. Providers may blame any non-favorable outcomes to outside forces.

Agents

Cloud Vendors

Client firms using cloud-based services such as Infrastructure as a Service (IaaS) can pay for exactly the amount of service used, similar to electricity, water, and storage services. This ability to pay as needed enables firms to store more data generated during their operation without having to worry about limitations to their physical devices. As a result, data can be generated in large volumes and at a faster rate than before. Thus, the big data phenomenon is largely driven by the ability of firms to generate and store data with little or no constraints. Some examples of IaaS providers include AWS, which offers computation and storage services, Windows Azure, which is believed to be a natural fit for clients working on Microsoft platforms, Google Cloud Storage, Google BigQeury, and Google Cloud SQL. Additionally, Google Compute Engine is also touted to be best suited for big data, data warehousing, high-performance computing, and other analytics-focused applications such as Rackspace Open Cloud, IBM SmartCloud Enterprise, and HP Enterprise Converged Infrastructure.

Cloud Brokers/Integrators

Cloud Service Brokerage (CSB) functions as intermediaries between client firms and cloud service providers. The intermediary services provided by these brokerages include aggregating multiple cloud services and integrating cloud services with in-house apps. In some instances, these brokerages provide customizable cloud services to meet the needs of clients. The three roles for CSBs are aggregation, integration, and customization. A CSB-as-aggregator pulls together multiple cloud services and provides them to the end customer, essentially acting as a reseller. The integration role, meanwhile, calls for the broker to link cloud services and on-premises systems while customization involves the tweaking of cloud services to meet the customer's needs or the creation of applications to run in the cloud setting. Some examples of brokers include AWS Marketplace, Dell Boomi, Rackspace Cloud Tools Marketplace, SoftChoice Cloud, and SaaSMax. Annual IT spending on these CSB services is forecasted to reach approximately $160 billion by 2018 (Gartner, 2015).

Cloud-Based Big Data Analytics Contract Challenges

Agent Underperformance

E-business firms expect the continuous provision of cloud services year-round to deliver flawless services to their clients. These goals will be hampered severely if their IT infrastructure is unavailable since their entire operation is online. Contracts in the form of SLAs of most cloud providers such as AWS promise 99% availability and with a promise to pay for any downtime (Amazon Web Services, 2013). However, these come with caveats such as establishing the cause of downtime to be reasonably within the service provider's control, prompting some industry experts such as Gartner researchers to describe such cloud SLAs as having little usefulness. It is, therefore, very possible for service providers to blame underperformance, from service outages to the caveats in their SLAs, to minimize their losses. A case in point is the famous outage of AWS for 23 hours affecting service to Netflix and other online businesses around Christmas Eve in 2012 when media service providers such as Netflix are in peak demand. AWS attributed this challenge to failures in its load balancers and offered its standard apologies to make up for it (Mann, 2013). Therefore, it is challenging for e-business firms to graciously hand over their mission-critical services to third-party cloud-based big data analytics vendors for fear it might go down for almost a whole day with immeasurable negative consequences and no compensation. Firms' inability to assess vendors' capabilities and SLA caveats properly creates asymmetries in information, which leads to heightened chances of moral hazards (Pallas, 2014). E-business firms bear more risk than service providers in these transactions. Prior studies, such as Mao, Lee, & Deng, (2008) suggest that client firms' trust in or control over the vendor could improve the performance of the vendor.

Agent Shirking

Cloud-based big data analytics operate under the premise that integrated resources are better used than disparate ones because users have varying demands for computing resources at different times. Aggregating these computing and analytic demands, service providers can meet the needs of many e-business firms with limited resources compared to each firm having their own computing resources. This is no minor task for service providers, as they need to accurately predict user requirements and invest in analytic, server, spare, and backup capacities in an optimal manner. Excess investments in these areas means increased costs for vendors, which ultimately get transferred to the e-business firms requiring their services. Thus, cloud vendors are in a constant dilemma about their investments in capacity, since their goal is to maximize the benefits for their shareholders and not their clients. This creates information asymmetries about how to guarantee services from adequate server capacity/backups and maximizing vendor profits. Clients unaware of these capacities could encourage vendors to shirking their responsibility to provide backups for clients, as stated in most SLAs. Vendors expect clients to attribute poor services to a spike in demand for services from multiple clients. For instance, Nirvanix, a cloud storage service headquartered in San Diego, in pursuit of their singular goal of maximizing value for its creditors, shirked their responsibility to provide continuous storage services to their clients as stated in their SLA and decided to close their services by filing chapter 11 bankruptcy protections (Lowe, 2013). Although alternative plans were made to transfer its customers to IBM, most of their clients were unaware of prior actions of their providers until they received their two weeks' notice. Little thought was given to how the change of service providers would impact their clients' business.

Data Poaching and IP Theft

As these e-business firms share the same resources, vendors must provide another layer of security such that rival firms do not have access to data of a competitor. Increased data federation and protection of firm data increase the operational cost of vendors as there is the need to monitor data centers constantly for breaches. However, user firms, such as e-business firms located in Europe, are required by the European Union (EU) regulations to store their data within the EU. For instance, as of October 2015, it is illegal for storage providers to transfer data outcomes from the EU to the US, even if that is an economically viable option leading giant cloud vendors such as AWS and Facebook to start building full-scale data centers in Europe (Drozdiak & Schechner, 2015). For example, Box.com, an online file sharing and personal cloud content management service for businesses handed a user's entire account over to a stranger, who removed the client's account (Tynan, 2013). Although Box.com was able to find the cause and implement new procedures to prevent future occurrence, this human error heightens the concern of moral hazards for e-business firms wanting to adopt cloud-based big data analytic tools. For example, rival firms in Europe could end up having their data stored next to each other in the same data center, and if the data center suffers from "Box.com syndrome," the consequence could be far more disastrous. Thus, the fear of IP theft is real for e-business firms. Vendors' motivation to provide this additional layer of protection in addition to building data centers contained within a geographical location remains an open question. Considering the challenges discussed here, this study proposes that:

Proposition 1: E-business firms will be more likely to use cloud-based big data analytics services when brokers and vendors show competence in handling contractual challenges.

Transaction Challenges

Transaction Costs

Transaction costs arise because it is impossible to write a comprehensive contract to cover all possible situations, giving rise to subsequent renegotiations when the balance of power between the transacting parties shifts (Williamson, 1979). If transaction costs offset production cost advantages of the external supplier, the firm subsumes the activity. Using Transaction Cost Economics (TCE) as their theoretical basis for argument, Ang & Straub (1998) concluded that the sourcing decision is often seen as a rational decision made by firms that have considered transaction-related factors such as asset specificity, environmental uncertainty, and other types of transaction costs. Whenever an activity is conducted under conditions of high uncertainty, or whenever an activity requires specific assets, transaction costs, the costs of writing, monitoring, and enforcing contracts are likely to be high. When transaction costs are high, outsourcing is deemed to be relatively inefficient compared with internal, hierarchical administration (Gottschalk & Solli-Sæther, 2005). Increased legislation about the storage location of cloud data has been a global issue. Therefore, the direct and indirect expenses (TCE) of negotiating, monitoring, and enforcing explicit and implicit contracts between a client firm and cloud big data analytic vendors will guide the initial decision to use cloud-based data analytic services (Tiwana & Bush, 2007).

Network Externalities

An externality, or spillover effect, is a cost or benefit that is incurred by someone who is not involved in the trade. Positive network externalities are a form of benefit arising from a network when the value of adding an extra node or edge is felt by every other part of the network (Liu, Gal-Or, Kemerer, & Smith, 2011). Technological changes that allow us to connect and share data more easily are disrupting established business models. Network externalities occur in the case of data because data is only informative when it is interpreted. The value of each datum increases with the volume of other data that it may be connected with as the context and range of analysis that is possible increases (Gower, 2012). This has prompted some to advocate for open data. This is because data is typically non-excludable, implying that prohibiting the sharing of data in many cases is practically unenforceable.

Switching Costs

Gottschalk & Solli-Sæther, (2005) concluded in their study of critical success factors of IT outsourcing that organizations can minimize transaction costs by relying less on specific IT assets, increasing transaction frequency, and reducing complexity and uncertainty in IT tasks. However, software stacks in cloud computing have improved interoperability among platforms, but with little standardization, most of the storage APIs for cloud computing are still proprietary or at least have not been the subject of active standardization (Armbrust et al., 2010). Thus, client firms who use cloud-based big data analytics cannot easily extract their data and programs from one site to run on another or easily switch between service providers. Concern about data-lock-in is preventing some organizations from adopting cloud computing. Although lock-in is desirable to service providers, client firms are susceptible to price increases and reliability problems because of increased switching costs. For instance, on August 8, 2008, online storage service provider, The Linkup, formerly known as MediaMax, could not account for 45% of customer data after it shut down due to failure in their attempt to move files of over 20,000 customers to a different platform (Brodkin, 2008).

Adverse Selection and Incomplete Contracts

Adverse selection, a related agency problem, could occur when the analytics service provider has relevant private information unknown to its clients. The asymmetry of information may lead an e-business firm to make bad decisions, such as doing more business with less profitable or riskier cloud providers. Usually, the shorter the time frame of the service arrangement, the less time each party will invest in writing a contract. For the uncertainty of the future, if a third party service arrangement is for a long time, parties will invest more time designing contracts that will protect their future bargaining powers (Holdup) subsequently resulting in the writing of an extensive contract (Susarla, Subramanyam, & Karhade, 2010). Thus, the SLA between client firms and service providers might not cover aspects of the usage of cloud-based big data analytics leading to an incomplete contract (Bakos & Brynjolfsson, 1993). The potential adverse selection on the part of e-business firms or issues arising from the incomplete nature of the contract (SLA) could lead to higher switching costs or transaction costs for client firms (Tuttle, Harrell, & Harrison, 1997). This suggests that:

Proposition 2: The higher the level of network effects generated using cloud-based analytics, the less likely the e-business organization will be concerned about transaction uncertainty such as possible switching cost or adverse vendor selection.

Countermeasures

Monitoring

AT generally focuses on problems of providing incentives in a variety of settings (McAfee & McMillan, 1986, 1987). To mitigate the moral hazard problems caused by agents, principals implement incentive-based contracts that compensate agents based on observable outcomes. Incentive mechanisms and monitoring of any contract result in the reduction of uncertainty, especially when information is constantly updated over the course of the contract. Benchmark, as a form of monitoring agent actions, can help reduce uncertainty about the capabilities of vendors and the consequences of their actions. Although cloud vendors have information about the quality of their cloud-based data analytic tools in data generation, integration, security controls, and status of the standards of their technologies, user client firms might lack the appropriate capability to assess these capabilities. Industry experts such as Gartner, IDC, Forrester, and TalkinCloud are better positioned to evaluate the capabilities and behaviors of vendors than user firms. These industry experts annually evaluate vendors and rank vendors in reports such as the Gartner magic quadrant and the Talkin' Cloud 100 Report (e.g., Gartner magic quadrant 2014 and 2015 and Talkin' Cloud 100 Report 2014 and 2015). As the audiences of these reports include big client firms, vendors will implement systems that produce quality information to user firms, rather than peruse opportunistic behavior to the detriment of their user client firms. Vendors will try to maintain good ratings in these reports to attract business, gain the trust of potential clients, and avoid the negative effect low ranking will have on their stocks. Also, the vendor firm leadership gets extra compensation for achieving or maintaining good rankings.

Screening and Signaling

Third party cloud-based data analytics is a form of outsourcing. Like firms engaged in outsourcing contracts, e-business firms using cloud-based analytics are also confronted with the issue of incomplete contracts in guiding the behavior of parties involved in the transaction. Vendors aiming at maximizing their revenue might oversell their capabilities, or clients might not be able to fully document their analytics needs as these may change over time. Information asymmetry or incomplete contracts could give rise to agency problems. AT suggests that a principal could reduce its chances of suffering opportunistic behavior problems by having an appropriate contract that reduces the information asymmetry between them and their vendors (Eisenhardt, 1989). It is in the crafting of these contracts and the actual implementation of these contracts that the expertise of Brokers and Integrators of cloud-based big data analytics are necessary.

Based on the information and services provided by brokers and integrators, user firms can pick up signals about the potential of vendors and screen out vendors that will likely deliver unsatisfactory results. Effective signals allow brokers and vendors who deliver quality service to differentiate from those who deliver substandard service (Pavlou, Liang, & Xue, 2007). Therefore:

Proposition 3: The more efficient the countermeasures (i.e., monitoring, signaling, and screening) are in the industry, the less likely e-business firm will be concerned about contracts with vendors and the analytics services sourced in the cloud.

Figure 2 displays a proposed theoretical framework to assist firms in making the best decision in the use of cloud-based data analytics complemented by propositions 1–3 that results in increased efficiency in operation, better relationship with customers, and increased revenue in the decision-making process.

Figure 2. Proposed framework for analysis of e-business management in the era of big data and cloud computing

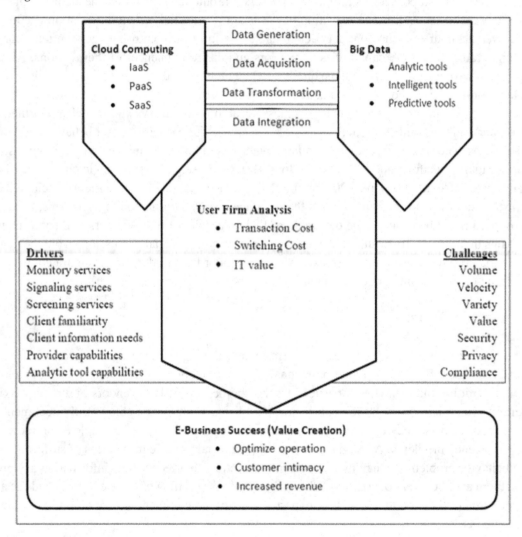

FRAMEWORK EVALUATION

Vendor Denologix and Clients MANULIFE, AVIVA, and BMO Bank Group

Although there are many different big data analytics vendors, the vendors that successfully manage contractual relationships with their clients will dominate the market. For example, Denologix clients have enjoyed success with their big data and business intelligence services. Denologix is a Canadian IT firm that offers information management planning, development, integration, and support services for transactional and business intelligence systems to its clients. Contracts between Denologix and most of its clients are not public. The following analyzes the propositions advanced in this study based upon publicly available information about Denologix and its clients.

Contractual Challenges (Proposition 1)

A firm's uncertainty is reduced when involved in the design of the services delivered or when given control over vendor performance. This alleviates concerns about underperformance and increases trust in the big data vendor. Denologix, in its relationship with Manulife Financial Corporation, a Canadian based insurance and financial services provider company, has earned the trust of the insurance company to manage its most prized asset - customer data. A testimony of Denologix's reputation of trustworthiness is from a director of MANULIFE: "I have worked with Denologix for over a decade now. . . This vendor is amazing. I'm happy I chose Denologix and would do it again" (Denologix Information Management, 2019). When a vendor places the interest of clients at the behest of the shareholder, the vendor treats the trust of the e-business firm with care. Such a vendor will not shirk its responsibility to a business firm (Pavlou et al., 2007). Denologis has attempted to reduce concerns about potential shirking of its responsibility to its client. This is confirmed by a senior manager at AVIVA, another client:

Their team is very honest. Their leaders are very transparent and open. Partnerships like this, you don't find anywhere. I met very few vendors that I could say that I trusted. This vendor is amazing. I am happy I chose Denologix and would do it again. (Denologix Information Management, 2019)

Transaction Challenges (Proposition 2)

E-businesses sometimes experience storage needs or analytical capability demand bursts due to external events, but they waste capacity if they overestimate the spike (Armbrust et al., 2010). This creates transaction challenges, including transaction costs, switching costs, and network externalities between big data vendors and their clients. These challenges will play a big role in creating value for clients. The more clients that are using a vendor's big data analytics, the more other consumers will be willing to use the vendors. This can only happen, however, if the vendor consistently adheres to standards. Many clients expect service level agreement uptimes and data accuracy of 99.99% or higher (Marston, Li, Bandyopadhyay, Zhang, & Ghalsasi, 2011). This is a huge task for most vendors. Denologix has developed the Data Accuracy Index (dxINDEX) a benchmark to help companies understand if the data they are working with is performing at optimum levels. Denologix has worked with some of its clients to improve the quality and integration of their data. For instance, the director of the Canadian Imperial Bank of Commerce (CIBC) had this to say about their relationship with Denologix:

Their ability to understand customer needs is quite special. Denologix was very good at listening to us and coming up with solutions, which they were able to sell to our own internal clients easily. They know how to maintain the highest standard of professionalism and accountability. (Denologix Information Management, 2019)

Countermeasures (Proposition 3)

The provision of information that aids user firms to screen services of vendors is critical to realizing the value of cloud-based big data analytics. Clutch, a global market insight provider, makes information available to guide user firms in their decisions to select a good cloud-based big data analytics vendor. On its leader board, Clutch recognized Denologix as a Clutch Global Leader. This leader board includes over 475 companies from around the world. Clutch has ranked Denologix as one of the top 10 Big Data Analytics Companies in 2018 (Patrick, 2018). This has the potential to reduce uncertainty from any client of Denologix, including CIBC, may have. The Vice President of SAS had this to say about Denologix: "I have nothing but good things to say about them" (Denologix Information Management, 2019). This is an important monitoring and signaling service provided by Clutch. This leader board reports on the services of over 200 analytics vendors around the world. Clutch uses the services of expertise, as well as verified cases for its ranking of vendors. According to Clutch, some of the top big data brokers include Altoros, CBIG Consulting, KPI Partners, LatentView Analytics, Beyond the Arc, Anthem Marketing Solutions, VISUAL BI SOLUTIONS, InData Labs, cBEYONData (Formerly DCS Consulting), Denologix, Pinnacle Solutions, DataRoot Labs, Pragmatic Works, SoftwareMill, and Altar.io. Denologix's ranking demonstrates the value it has created for its clients. For example, Bank of Montreal, operating as BMO Financial Group, invested in an advanced IFRS 9 solution with the aid of Denologix, allowing BMO to exceed its credit risk monitoring and analysis target. Thus, the screening and signaling services provided by Clutch is a big step towards minimizing the chances of transaction failure.

IMPLICATIONS

This study, in addition to discussing cloud-based big data analytics technologies, presents a model that enables firms to create competitive parity by focusing on issues that threaten their contracts with vendors. The proposed framework systematically achieves competitive parity with data analytics by designing contracts that protect the objectives of e-business firms. Cloud-based big data clients can reduce uncertainty in their contracts with vendors and thus improve the probability of success using data analytics. The proposed theoretical framework is a decision-making tool for e-businesses and suggests that addressing transaction challenges such as shirking, underperformance, moral hazards, and data theft are fundamental to value creation instead of being merely implicit premises. Clients' efforts to maintain flexible and adaptable contracts with vendors will have to avoid some of these challenges and provide guarantees that help the process of value creation needed for competitive parity. This study enriches value creation research from an agency perspective. From a theoretical standpoint, AT and transaction cost theory provide insights into the governance of the provision of cloud-based data analytics services best suited for third parties vendors, the risks associated with providing services, and how to mitigate the risk effectively. The study reveals the essential elements, links, and path-to-value chains for an understanding of cloud-based big data analytic enabled value creation. As indicated by Gupta and George

(2016), creating value with big data analytics is a complex process requiring human skills and intangible resources. The discussion in this study enriches the theoretical perspective and complements prior studies such as Xie, Wu, Xiao, and Hu (2016) on how big data resources could become cooperative assets.

MANAGERIAL INSIGHTS

Most IT managers must make the decision to use cloud-based analytic tools. However, managers are overloaded with different promises and capabilities by different vendors. This study highlights key factors to be considered when choosing and contracting as many managers are still in the early phase of technology adoption. The framework developed in this study provides a guide in the decision-making process to use cloud-based big data analytics. The study details how the interest of vendors and clients' firms might be misaligned and provides a new way of thinking for understanding the value of big data analytics. Organizations should carefully consider, understand, and reduce the risk of engaging the services of cloud-based data analytics and create competitive parity to enjoy the benefits of cloud computing as a strategic asset (Pakath, 2015). Additionally, an organization should analyze their preparedness by evaluating their organizations' management support and the complexity of integrating the cloud-based analytics with their local technology (Oliveira et al., 2014; Low et al., 2011). When selecting a vendor, IT managers should eliminate any vendor who poses contractual challenges to minimize risks.

Furthermore, IT managers will have to justify the selection of a vendor by evaluating both the direct and indirect way cloud-based analytics enhances their innovativeness (Oliveira et al., 2014). When the level of network effects generated using cloud-based analytics is high, IT managers will have to be concerned about transaction uncertainty, such as possible switching costs or adverse vendor selection. The level of competitive pressure in the industry influences the adoption and selection of cloud-based analytics tools, but their use should yield network benefits (Alshamaila et al., 2013).

Additionally, IT managers must consider security, privacy, and ethicality in selecting a cloud-based analytics vendor to optimize their returns (Sun et al., 2018). Even when IT managers make the best vendor selection, the institute practical measures such as monitoring, signaling, and screening to mitigate any unforeseen challenges. The more efficient the countermeasures are in the industry, the less concerned IT managers will be about contracts with vendors. In addition to the preceding, IT capability or competence in maintaining data (Hsu et al., 2014; Kwon et al., 2014) and carefully analyzing uncertainties about the involved costs in prioritizing the vendors should be considered (Raguseo, 2018). Figure 3 summarizes the key factors that influence IT managers' cloud-based analytics vendor selection.

CONCLUSION

The framework proposed here opens new areas of research for examining the role of enablers and situations that would lead to delivering economic value to big data clients and vendors. This is because there is little information on SLA contracts and risk transfer designs that provide an optimal set of guidelines for clients considering the adoption of cloud-based big data analytics. The framework suggests that unique moral hazards, agent shirking, data theft, and switching cost issues should be included intimately in SLA design considerations.

Figure 3. Vendor contracting decision factors

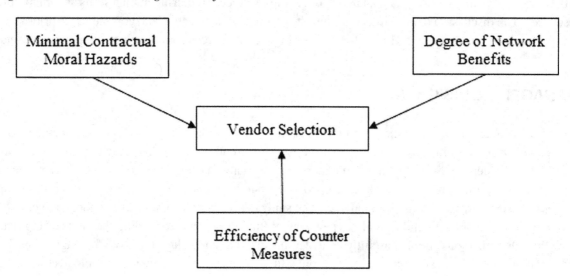

REFERENCES

Alshamaila, Y., Savvas, P., & Feng, L. (2013). Cloud computing adoption by SMEs in the north east of England. *Journal of Enterprise Information Management, 26*(3), 250–275. doi:10.1108/17410391311325225

Amazon Web Services. (2013, June 1). *Amazon Compute Service Level Agreement.* https://aws.amazon.com/ec2/sla/

Amit, R., & Zott, C. (2001). Value creation in e-business. *Strategic Management Journal, 22*(6–7), 493–520. doi:10.1002mj.187

Ang, S., & Straub, D. W. (1998). Production and transaction economies and IS outsourcing: A study of the US banking industry. *Management Information Systems Quarterly, 22*(4), 535–552. doi:10.2307/249554

Armbrust, M., Fox, A., Griffith, R., Joseph, A. D., Katz, R., Konwinski, A., Lee, G., Patterson, D., Rabkin, A., Stoica, I., & Zaharia, M. (2010). A view of cloud computing. *Communications of the ACM, 53*(4), 50–58. doi:10.1145/1721654.1721672

Bakos, J. Y., & Brynjolfsson, E. (1993). Information technology, incentives, and the optimal number of suppliers. *Journal of Management Information Systems, 10*(2), 37–53. doi:10.1080/07421222.1993.11517999

Behrend, T. S., Weibe, E. N., London, J. E., & Johnson, E. C. (2011). Cloud computing adoption and usage in community colleges. *Behaviour & Information Technology, 30*(2), 231–240. doi:10.1080/0144929X.2010.489118

Brodkin, J. (2008, August 11). Loss of customer data spurs closure of online storage service "The Linkup." *Network World.* https://www.networkworld.com/article/2274737/data-center/loss-of-customer-data-spurs-closure-of-online-storage-service--the-linkup-.html

Chen, H., Chiang, R. H., & Storey, V. C. (2012). Business intelligence and analytics: From big data to big impact. *Management Information Systems Quarterly*, *36*(4), 1165–1188. doi:10.2307/41703503

Demirkan, H., & Delen, D. (2013). Leveraging the capabilities of service-oriented decision support systems: Putting analytics and big data in cloud. *Decision Support Systems*, *55*(1), 412–421. doi:10.1016/j.dss.2012.05.048

Denologix Information Management. (2019). *Testimonials: Reviewed & Approved*. https://www.denologix.com/company/

Drozdiak, N., & Schechner, S. (2015, October 6). EU court says data-transfer pact with U.S. violates privacy. *The Wall Street Journal*. https://www.wsj.com/articles/eu-court-strikes-down-trans-atlantic-safe-harbor-data-transfer-pact-1444121361

Eisenhardt, K. M. (1989). Agency theory: An assessment and review. *Academy of Management Review*, *14*(1), 57–74. doi:10.5465/amr.1989.4279003

Gartner. (2015, February 13). *Forecast: Public cloud service brokerage, 4Q14*. https://www.gartner.com/doc/2985118/forecast-public-cloud-service-brokerage

Gottschalk, P., & Solli-Sæther, H. (2005). Critical success factors from IT outsourcing theories: An empirical study. *Industrial Management & Data Systems*, *105*(6), 685–702. doi:10.1108/02635570510606941

Gower, R. (2012). The economics of open data. *Infonomics Limited*. http://www.infonomics.ltd.uk/blog/2012/10/25/the-economics-of-open-data/

Gupta, M., & George, J. F. (2016). Toward the development of a big data analytics capability. *Information & Management*, *53*(8), 1049–1064. doi:10.1016/j.im.2016.07.004

Hashem, I. A. T., Yaqoob, I., Anuar, N. B., Mokhtar, S., Gani, A., & Ullah Khan, S. (2015). The rise of "big data" on cloud computing: Review and open research issues. *Information Systems*, *47*, 98–115. doi:10.1016/j.is.2014.07.006

Höchtl, J., Parycek, P., & Schöllhammer, R. (2016). Big data in the policy cycle: Policy decision making in the digital era. *Journal of Organizational Computing and Electronic Commerce*, *26*(1–2), 147–169. doi:10.1080/10919392.2015.1125187

Hsu, P., Soumya, R., & Yu-Yu, L. (2014). Examining cloud computing adoption intention, pricing mechanism, and deployment model. *International Journal of Information Management*, *34*(4), 474–488. doi:10.1016/j.ijinfomgt.2014.04.006

Kwon, O., Namyeon, L., & Bongsik, S. (2014). Data quality management, data usage experience and acquisition intention of big data analytics. *International Journal of Information Management*, *34*(3), 387–394. doi:10.1016/j.ijinfomgt.2014.02.002

Liu, C. Z., Gal-Or, E., Kemerer, C. F., & Smith, M. D. (2011). Compatibility and proprietary standards: The impact of conversion technologies in IT markets with network effects. *Information Systems Research*, *22*(1), 188–207. doi:10.1287/isre.1090.0255

Low, C., Yahsueh, C., & Mingchang, W. (2011). Understanding the determinants of cloud computing adoption. *Industrial Management & Data Systems*, *111*(7), 1006–1023. doi:10.1108/02635571111161262

Lowe, S. (2013, October 28). *The cloud does not protect you from mistakes and failures*. http://wikibon. org/wiki/v/The_Cloud_Does_Not_Protect_You_From_Mistakes_and_Failures

Mann, A. (2013, January 7). Time to stop forgiving cloud providers for repeated failures. *Andi Mann– Ubergeek*. http://pleasediscuss.com/andimann/20130107/time-to-stop-forgiving-cloud-providers-for-repeated-failures/

Mao, J.-Y., Lee, J.-N., & Deng, C.-P. (2008). Vendors' perspectives on trust and control in offshore information systems outsourcing. *Information & Management*, *45*(7), 482–492. doi:10.1016/j.im.2008.07.003

Marr, B. (2015). *Big data: Using SMART big data, analytics and metrics to make better decisions and improve performance*. Wiley.

Marston, S., Li, Z., Bandyopadhyay, S., Zhang, J., & Ghalsasi, A. (2011). Cloud computing—The business perspective. *Decision Support Systems*, *51*(1), 176–189. doi:10.1016/j.dss.2010.12.006

Mata, F. J., Fuerst, W. L., & Barney, J. B. (1995). Information technology and sustained competitive advantage: A resource-based analysis. *Management Information Systems Quarterly*, *19*(4), 487–505. doi:10.2307/249630

McAfee, R. P., & McMillan, J. (1986). Bidding for contracts: A principal-agent analysis. *The RAND Journal of Economics*, *17*(3), 326. doi:10.2307/2555714

McAfee, R. P., & McMillan, J. (1987). Competition for Agency Contracts. *The RAND Journal of Economics*, *18*(2), 296. doi:10.2307/2555554

Oliveira, T., Manoj, T., & Mariana, E. (2014). Assessing the determinants of cloud computing adoption: An analysis of the manufacturing and services sectors. *Information & Management*, *51*(5), 497–510. doi:10.1016/j.im.2014.03.006

Pakath, R. (2015). Competing on the cloud: A review and synthesis of potential benefits and possible pitfalls. *Journal of Organizational Computing and Electronic Commerce*, *25*(1), 1–27. doi:10.1080/10 919392.2015.990771

Pallas, F. (2014). An agency perspective to cloud computing. In *International Conference on Grid Economics and Business Models* (pp. 36–51). Springer. https://link.springer.com/chapter/10.1007/978-3-319-14609-6_3

Patrick, S. (2018). Best big data analytics companies. *Clutch*. https://clutch.co/it-services/analytics

Pavlou, P. A., Liang, H., & Xue, Y. (2007). Understanding and mitigating uncertainty in online exchange relationships: A principal-agent perspective. *Management Information Systems Quarterly*, *31*(1), 105–136. doi:10.2307/25148783

Raguseo, E. (2018). Big data technologies: An empirical investigation on their adoption, benefits and risks for companies. *International Journal of Information Management*, *38*(1), 187–195. doi:10.1016/j. ijinfomgt.2017.07.008

Subashini, S., & Kavitha, V. (2011). A survey on security issues in service delivery models of cloud computing. *Journal of Network and Computer Applications, 34*(1), 1–11. doi:10.1016/j.jnca.2010.07.006

Susarla, A., Subramanyam, R., & Karhade, P. (2010). Contractual provisions to mitigate holdup: Evidence from information technology outsourcing. *Information Systems Research, 21*(1), 37–55. doi:10.1287/isre.1080.0204

Tiwana, A., & Bush, A. (2007). A comparison of transaction cost, agency, and knowledge-based predictors of IT outsourcing decisions: A U.S.–Japan cross-cultural field study. *Journal of Management Information Systems, 24*(1), 259–300. doi:10.2753/MIS0742-1222240108

Troester, M. (2012). *Big data meets big data analytics: Three key technologies for extracting real-time business value from the big data, that threatens to overwhelm traditional computing architectures* [White Paper]. SAS Institute Inc.

Tuttle, B., Harrell, A., & Harrison, P. (1997). Moral hazard, ethical considerations, and the decision to implement an information system. *Journal of Management Information Systems, 13*(4), 7–27. doi:10.1080/07421222.1997.11518140

Tynan, D. (2013, October 23). How Box.com allowed a complete stranger to delete all my files. *ITworld*. https://www.itworld.com/article/2833267/how-box-com-allowed-a-complete-stranger-to-delete-all-my-files.html

Williams, A. (2012, October 27). Amazon Web Services outage caused by memory leak and failure in monitoring alarm. *TechCrunch*. https://techcrunch.com/2012/10/27/amazon-web-services-outage-caused-by-memory-leak-and-failure-in-monitoring-alarm/

Williamson, O. E. (1979). Transaction-cost economics: The governance of contractual relations. *The Journal of Law & Economics, 22*(2), 233–261. doi:10.1086/466942

Wu, X., Zhu, X., Wu, G. Q., & Ding, W. (2014). Data mining with big data. *IEEE Transactions on Knowledge and Data Engineering, 26*(1), 97–107. doi:10.1109/TKDE.2013.109

Xie, K., Wu, Y., Xiao, J., & Hu, Q. (2016). Value co-creation between firms and customers: The role of big data-based cooperative assets. *Information & Management, 53*(8), 1034–1048. doi:10.1016/j.im.2016.06.003

Yu, C.-C. (2016). A value-centric business model framework for managing open data applications. *Journal of Organizational Computing and Electronic Commerce, 26*(1–2), 80–115. doi:10.1080/10919392.2015.1125175

This research was previously published in the Journal of Cases on Information Technology (JCIT), 22(4); pages 60-74, copyright year 2020 by IGI Publishing (an imprint of IGI Global).

Chapter 13
Big Data and High–Performance Analyses and Processes

Ramgopal Kashyap

ⓘ https://orcid.org/0000-0002-5352-1286

Amity University, Raipur, India

ABSTRACT

The period of vast information and examination has arrived and is changing the world significantly. The field of information frameworks ought to be at the bleeding edge of comprehension and decipher-ing the effect of the two innovations and administration to lead the endeavors of business to inquire about in the information period. In this chapter, the author investigates administrative issues of business change coming about because of the original appropriation and inventive uses of information sciences in business. The author ends by giving an analysis of big data that covers all the analytical processes and future research headings.

INTRODUCTION

The world has transformed into data society that hugely depends on information. Since data frameworks create colossal measures of records each day, consistently, it appears the world is achieving the level of information over burden. It is evident that keeping in mind the end goal to process such volumes of information a huge limit is required regarding stockpiling and figuring assets. Though the development of limit is restricted by the advancement of equipment and advances, the development of the information volume is in reality boundless. Getting more particular, these days numerous associations has embraced and extensively utilize data frameworks running on mechanical stages, numerous their motivation has progressed toward becoming dependent on information. In the developed association's information specifically influence the rationale of business forms; data has turned into a center of their business or business end. Thus business requests the information, besides accessibility of particular information in particular time. More unpredictable also, hazardous basic leadership process depends on rightness and straightforwardness of information.

DOI: 10.4018/978-1-6684-3662-2.ch013

Motivation

The intriguing driver identified with this subject says that the development of information is boundless. What is the general public going to do about the information overburden? The most effective method to deal with and additionally to process all the information? It appears as though we are having the big data issue. Another driver for this subject is recovering the data not to assemble all information for further examination. Among every one of the information, how to recover the applicable data and inside a required time? Which examination ought to be connected to information? What is the harmony between the cost of recovery and estimation of that data? What are the expenses of the ability to recover wanted data? It appears as though it is about the benefit, exchange off between estimation of data, the cost to get it. Furthermore to the two drivers the test is to picture the data such that its esteem is far reaching and justifiable. The primary issue is the data over burden. Examination in the conventional mode, as far as the big data, is securing information that may or may not be required for examination. This all requires a creative perspective, an alternate approach, design or framework, assuming any. A superior investigation is one of them. Embracing innovation requires to process, find and break down these gigantic informational indexes that can't be managed utilizing conventional databases and models because of the absence of limit assets as far as calculation and capacity. Elite investigation speaks to one of the creative methodologies that can be connected on the expanding volumes, speed and assortment of information.

Goals

Enormous data phenomenon, which is described by the quick development of volume, assortment and speed of information data resources, flourishes the change in perspective in explanatory information preparing. High Performance Analytics (HPA) can be considered as one of the methodologies. The point of the postulation is an exploration outline, order, and talks on issues and difficulties on the spearheading condition of specialty of cutting edge examination using different strategies HPA techniques that could raise and improve the calculation execution of examination. Considering the way that they chose a region of research is as of now being refined and formalized and at the same time is rising quickly in restrictive definitions and arrangements from various sellers, the objective of the theory is to arrange and give outline and review with finish and reliable picture about the region of high performance analytics. In addition, usage of these strategies might be exhibited in down to earth task including handling of immense dataset.

Outcome

The extent of the theory is committed to research and methodologies of big data and high performance Analytics. A hypothetical piece of the theory is a result of complete investigate that abridges a condition of craftsmanship diagram for this issue, characterizes the drivers and results of big data phenomenon, and presents approaches for dealing with big data, in specific approach given High Performance Analytics. Particularly the result of the examination is situated on a review of HPA, order, qualities and focal points of particular strategy for HPA using the different mix of framework assets. A functional piece of the proposal is a result of exploratory task that incorporates explanatory preparing of expansive dataset utilizing investigative stage from SAS Institute. The analysis exhibits scientific handling for chosen HPA strategies that are talked about in hypothetical part. One a player in the analysis incorporates forming diverse scientific situations on which the preferences and accommodation of HPA stage are illustrated.

PROBLEM IDENTIFICATION AND SUMMARY

As said in the presentation a main issue of this postulation is information, information preparing, extricating data and stuff around it. Let us first begin with hypothetical approach of issue.

Theoretical Problem

The information volume speaks to a test all things considered, not simply like that, ought to be put inside a set. The accessible information like client information in their business setting that develops in all measurements are point by point in segments later, and they connected information with expository and execution limit (Kuner, Cate, Millard & Svantesson, 2012), delineated in Figure 1.

Thinking about the genuine patterns, when all of lines are developing, the accessibility of information has overburdened a capacity to break down information examination, and in addition an ability to utilize the investigation either to run investigation or store examination registering and capacity limit. An information hole communicates the powerlessness to break down information because of the restricted expository procedures may incorporate information mining calculations, characteristic dialect handling, and so on, e.g. propelled feeling investigation of printed remarks of web based life (Hassani-Mahmooei, Berecki-Gisolf & Collie, 2017). An execution hole communicates failure to use investigation because of the restricted accessibility of assets may incorporate handling units, information stockpiles, and so forth for asked for a timeframe, e.g. undertaking to process the all day by day exchange at bank in asked for configuration of the clearing house more than one night.

Figure 1. The information volume challenge

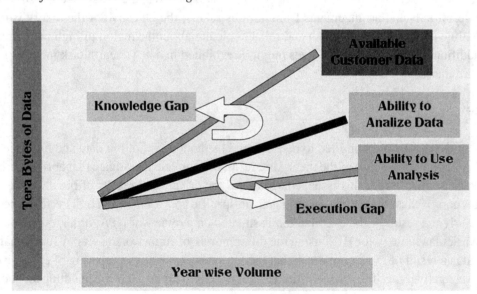

WHERE IS THE ISSUE?

While an execution limit as far as equipment is developing a pretty much stable rate, information volumes are developing exponentially. In this way the learning hole is getting more extensive, and the territory of the lost data openings in set of accessible information containing the data significant regarding the data needs. The point is to boost the arrangement of important information that conceivably contains the profitable data. Hence, the volume and accessibility of information are not an issue instead of the preparing and association of information.

Enormous Information and Examination

Enormous information postures the two openings and difficulties for organizations to extricate esteem from enormous information, it must be prepared and examined in an opportune way, and the outcomes require being accessible so to have the capacity to impact positive change or impact business choices. The adequacy additionally depends on an association having the correct mix of individuals, process and innovation by unadulterated definition. Investigation is the disclosure and correspondence of important examples in information. However for business, investigation ought to be seen as the broad utilization of information, factual also, quantitative examination, utilizing informative and prescient models to drive reality based business administration choices and activities.

Examination streamlines key procedures, capacities and parts it can be utilized to total both interior and outer information analytics process is shown in figure 2. It empowers associations to meet partner announcing requests, oversee gigantic information volumes, advertising preferences, oversee hazard, enhance controls and, eventually, improve hierarchical execution by turning data into knowledge (Ahmadvand & Goudarzi, 2017). An investigation can distinguish creative open doors in key procedures, capacities and parts. It makes an impetus for advancement and change and by testing the norm; it can help to make new conceivable outcomes for the business and its clients. Advanced methods can enable organizations to find underlying drivers, examine micro segments of their business sectors, change procedures and make exact expectations about future occasions or clients' inclination to purchase, agitate or lock in.

It is never again enough for organizations to just comprehend current process or tasks with a view on enhancing what as of now exists when there is presently the ability to address if a process is applicable to the business, or whether there is another method for tackling a specific issue. The key driver for development inside associations is to continually challenge existing practices instead of reliably acknowledging the same. Most associations have intricate and divided design scenes that make the strong resemblance and scattering of information troublesome. The major goal of picture division is to segment the information picture into important non-covering locales sections for assist examination or perception. There is an assortment of methodologies tending to this undertaking, misusing different picture properties to accomplish the given objective (Kashyap and Gautam, 2017a). They traverse from low-level methods utilizing power limits, edge following or district developing, over chart based and measurable methodologies, to show based calculations also, other more elevated amount techniques. As of late, the mix based arrangement has been presented, where the last parcel is shaped utilizing a blend of aftereffects of a few division techniques and subsequently repressing their inadequacies (Kashyap, Gautam and Tiwari, 2018). In spite of the long-lasting push to grow fantastic division calculations, there has not been any all inclusive division technique discussed. Under these conditions, there is a predicament which strategy to decide for given specific informational collection and whether the mix of

Figure 2. Analytics process

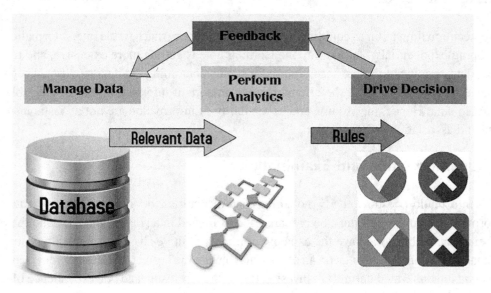

division results would be valuable (Kashyap, Gautam, 2017b). This endeavors to answer these inquiries for characterized classification of picture handling information set of pictures of minuscule images the execution of a few division techniques on pictures of minute examples in three unique modalities was broke down. The arrangement of ten quality lists was utilized to accomplish assessment as goal as could be expected under the circumstances. We appeared that there was no single division technique which altogether beat the others in the concentrated set. The normal execution of the techniques was at that point assessed with the conclusion that Mean Shift calculation played out the best and can be viewed as the best division technique by and large(Kashyap, Anderson, 2018). New logical arrangements are playing an essential part in empowering a viable Intelligent Enterprise (IE) is given in figure 2. An IE makes a single view over your association by using a mix of standard detailing and information perception (Rho & Vasilakos, 2017):

- Data from numerous source frameworks is rinsed, standardized and ordered
- External feeds can be assembled from the most recent research, best practice rules, benchmarks and other online vaults (Kashyap, R., & Piersson, A. D., 2018)
- Use of upgraded perception procedures, benchmarking files and dashboards can illuminate administration and shoppers by means of cell phones, PCs, tablets, and so on. In house or then again remotely

All organizations need to begin pondering gathering and utilizing significant huge information. Information driven choices can lessen wastefulness between the business, legitimate and IT, advance existing data resources and address separates between various elements of an association. In any case, it is important that the best information and the most progressive scientific devices and systems amount to nothing in the event that they are not being utilized by individuals who are asking the right inquiries. Enormous information, rising stockpiling innovation stages and the most recent diagnostic calculations are empowering influences to business achievement not a certification of it.

HUGE INFORMATION DRIVERS

The advantages and dangers of enormous information while there is almost certainly that the huge information upset has made generous advantages to organizations and customers alike, there are proportionate dangers that accompany utilizing huge information big data drivers is given in the figure 3.

Figure 3. Big data drivers

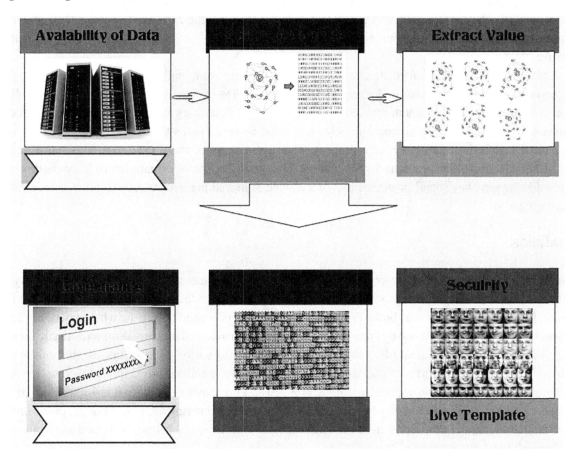

The need to anchor delicate information, to ensure private data and to oversee information quality, exists whether informational collections are huge or little (Rey-del-Castillo & Cardeñosa, 2016). Be that as it may, the particular properties of huge information volume, assortment, speed, and veracity make new sorts of dangers that requires an extensive procedure to empower an organization to use huge information while staying away from the traps. This ought to be done in an organized manner with the goal that organizations can begin to understand the advantages of enormous information in venture with dealing with the dangers. The accompanying pages take a gander at the conceivable outcomes and dangers related with huge information and give cases of how enormous information is being utilized to understand a portion of the unpredictable issues organizations confront today. We distinguish conventional and new dangers and contemplations for the seven key advances to progress: administration,

administration, engineering, utilization, quality, security and protection (Waterman & Hendler, 2013). The nature of informational collections and the deduction drawn from such informational collections are progressively winding up more basic what's more; associations need to fabricate quality and checking capacities and parameters for huge information. For instance, adjusting an information mistake can be considerably more exorbitant than getting the information right the first time and getting the information wrong can be calamitous what's more, significantly more expensive to the association if not remedied. For a long time the human services environment has grasped huge information. With the capacity to catch each patient touch point, the measure of information inside the social insurance biological system has detonated. The development of new information sources and the capacity to squash that information with existing information sources is advancing huge information is making the likelihood of new positive patient results.

A portion of these new information sources incorporate the combination of infection registries, tissue registries and genomic data, and afterward adjusting them to important utilizes clinical models. It is characterizing key care treatment approaches in light of new hereditary bits of knowledge and clinical convention coordinating calculations, and characterizing centered patient care treatment bits of knowledge prior inside the care conveyance process. The incentive from these new enormous information bits of knowledge will be precious for the patient. The quality of the information will likewise directly affect driving new key social insurance bits of knowledge in making superb results while successfully overseeing costs.

Analytics

Investigation is another popular expression in the innovation business and it "alludes to our capacity to gather and utilize information to produce bits of knowledge that educate certainty based basic leadership" before, the information that was broke down was for the most part used to foresee what may occur later on and was completely held onto by enterprises, for example, banks and protection organizations, yet not by associations, for example, retailers. Enormous data and investigation go as an inseparable unit in the current innovative age. Enormous data examination utilizes prescient and prescriptive examination and is changing the investigation scene (Hussain & Roy, 2016). Prescient examination utilizes information from the past to anticipate what may happen, and its probability occurring later on. Though, prescriptive examination is taking information from the past, utilizing it to choose what ought to be done alongside accomplish ideal outcomes.

Methodologies

The issue has diverse settling approaches theoretically; the information hole can be shut by constraining or diminishing development of information. Clearly, this is not going to happen. Explanatory limit is resolved and subject to look into cutting edge examination. All things considered, having developed level of examination may be a decent approach except if the investigation is physically conceivable to keep running on transfer innovations and equipment. The execution hole can be conceivably shut by expanding use limit, for example, disseminated or parallel preparing restricted by level of division of undertaking going with extra units for preparing CPU, RAM and putting away information. This approach has drawback in overall restricted assets and won't tackle the issue because of high proportion supply: demand of information. Aside from limit another point of view of improving might be input itself. Is all information required? Important to break down or store? In view of the prerequisites the repetitive or insignificant information that holds little, assuming any, data can be sifted through, with danger of lost data opportunity in missing information yet we don't realize what we don't have the foggiest idea. By applying "brute force" calculation on entire dataset the issue is starting over from the beginning.

Insights to Foresights

Progressed Analytics can be appropriate for different business investigation with respect to investigate client patterns conduct, rivalry, misrepresentation recognition, wastefulness in business process Capacity Maturity Model (CMMI), showcase crate examination conditions, causalities, relations in items' deals, and so on (Weber, Königsberger, Kassner & Mitschang, 2017). All that really matters is various examination utilizations can be arranged by the speed of information with time conditions continuous, group preparing, or to the assortment of information organized, semi structured, unstructured. Review of utilization cases for examination is delineated in Figure 4.

Figure 4. Big data and high performance analysis

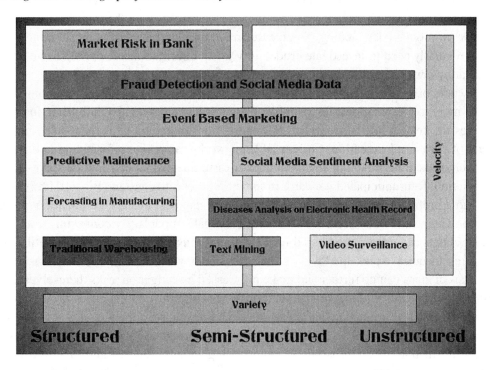

It is vital to specify that examination can recover helpful data from information that may speaks to bits of knowledge. With facilitate examination can be possibly move into premonitions. New developing region of investigation is spoken to by unstructured information content with expansive utilization of online life (Lomotey & Deters, 2015). Content examination distinguishes and separates the important data and translates mines and structures it to uncover examples, conclusions and connections inside and among records.

- Automated content order makes data looks far quicker and then some successful than manual or review labeling strategies.
- Ontology administration joins content storehouses together, authorizing information quality with predictable and deliberately characterized connections.
- Sentiment investigation naturally finds and recognizes assumption communicated in online materials, for example, person to person communication destinations, remarks and websites on the Web, and from inside electronic archives.
- Text mining gives intense approaches to investigate unstructured information accumulations and find already obscure ideas and examples.

Business Intelligence

BI and OLAP normally spend significant time in questioning, announcing, and breaking down chronicled information to comprehend and contrast comes about with date or for particular eras previously. Associations can utilize BI and OLAP counts to extend a perspective of what the numbers say is probably going to happen later on (Kekwaletswe & Lesole, 2016). In any case, progressed investigation can give a considerably more profound comprehension of why what more, a deductively based, prescient perspective is without bounds. Progressed examination gives clients with the capacity to investigate numerous factors to refine understanding. To give this more profound level of understanding, progressed examination regularly need to investigate crude, nitty gritty information as opposed to littler examples and accumulations, which are usually utilized for BI and OLAP.

BI frameworks offers client connections through dashboard interfaces that incorporate information get to what's more, representations, for example, diagrams and charts with cautions, pointers, and different changes trackers. While conventional BI reports now and again gives just static and restricted perspectives of chronicled execution. Current BI frameworks can revive information in dashboards all the more much of the time, enabling clients to track measurements that can caution spikes, plunges, or different deviations from anticipated standards in something closer to constant. What BI frameworks need is both the more profound, more exploratory point of view that best in class examination can give, and the bits of knowledge driven by prescient and other systematic models. By connecting with dashboard gateways, BI clients can devour progressed investigation through representations, and utilize information disclosure capacities to pick up a "why" comprehension of what the BI execution measurements are appearing. Associations can go further and make progressed investigation tasks themselves the drivers, and execute BI dashboards and measurements to give sees into the consequences of the logical tasks. Illustrations incorporate examination that gives understanding into consumer loyalty, accomplishment in extortion anticipation (Arbel, 2015). A vital piece of huge information investigation capacities is access to enormous information. Business associations are ending up increasingly mindful of the estimation of information. The development in business information usage rate is specifically identified with the huge information development rate. Five information composes are distinguished: open information, private information, information debilitate, network information, and self evaluation information. The meanings of these information writes are source particular information e.g., non individual information when they characterize the accompanying information composes (Tromp, Pechenizkiy & Gaber, 2017). • Public information are regularly free information given by legislative establishments, private associations or people. • Private information is association claimed information. • Data deplete speaks to information with no or little incentive in its own unique situation yet may give profitable intel when associated with other information. ● Community information is, for example, Facebook, Twitter and other web based social networking created information. ● Self measurement information is information produced from wearable advancements like savvy watches, wellness groups and so forth (N. Smith, 2015). Information can be additionally isolated into outside and inner information: ● Internal information is hierarchical information made by the authoritative procedures. Illustrations are stock updates, deals, exchanges or other inside procedures. ● External information are information from outside sources, either open, private yet achievable through purchasing or exchanging, network information among others.

Huge Data Analytics

Enormous Data Analytics can be portrayed with the accompanying chain of activities with information to reveal groupings or connections and uncover useful perceptions: (Figure 5)

Figure 5. The handling ventures of big data analytics

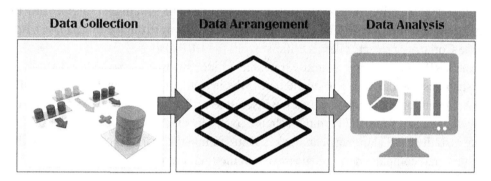

Huge data analytics offers an organization an understanding perspective inside its structure and acquires radiant data for present and future business arrangements. The objective for big data researchers is to pick up learning, got from the information preparing. Ongoing information alludes to floods of information that are conveyed specifically after information accumulation. So, there exists no deferral in the change from crude information accumulation to the data gave from continuous information (Kashyap, 2019a). Beside continuous information, organizations additionally confer assets to extricate an incentive from present and verifiable information. Over the top accentuation on constant information can lead bring about difficulties and disappointment of information driven basic leadership (Diesner, 2015). The accessibility of present and verifiable information is important to position constant information into setting of examples and patterns. Further, "right time information" and noteworthy information should be given to help basic leadership. Henceforth, applicable information should be assembled and incorporated for particular necessities or situations, types and source of data is given in table1.

The Principle of Work

As indicated by the plan, the interchange between big data and the organization is portrayed by the accompanying advances:

Table 1. Sort of data and data sources

S.N.	Types of Data	
1.	Organized Data	Table and Records
2.	Unstructured Data	Human Language, Audio and Video
3.	Semi Structured Data	XML and Similar Standards
4.	Occasion Data	Messages (typically in Real Time)
5.	Complex Data	Hierarchical or Legacy Sources
6.	Spatial Data	Long/Lat Coordinates and GPS Output
7.	Online networking Data	Blogs, Tweets and Social Networks
8.	Logical Data	Astronomy, Genomes and Physics
9.	Machine Generated Data	Sensors, RFID and Devices
10.	Metadata	Data that depicts the substance of other information

1. The creation information, produced amid the assembling of the Intelligent Engineering Products, is sent to the organization's ERP where the information is put away in the social databases. Additionally, the Case Company protects client's criticism into the ERP also.

2. Next, the ERP programming naturally transmits crude information to the big data Analytics Tool that distributes it in the SQL Server and makes the investigation to show the working effectiveness of the seller in different zones: apparatus use, time utilization, execution rate, false coefficient, quality degree, and so forth (Tromp, Pechenizkiy & Gaber, 2017).

3. At long last, the Case Company can track and streamline the work process, deal with the business procedures and complete new enhancements in the foundation procedure.

Figure 6. The working guideline of the big data analytics tool

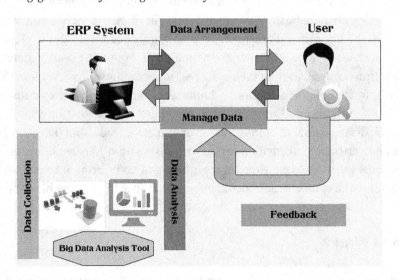

The investigation result can be hard to get with one preliminary extra information investigation works can be rehashed for a few times by confirming the outcome and deciding the estimation of examination result. The procedure of enormous information investigation may concede in every examination procedure so that the powerful result can be obtained just by rehashed exhibitions of different strategies as shown in figure 7.

Figure 7. Big data analytics process

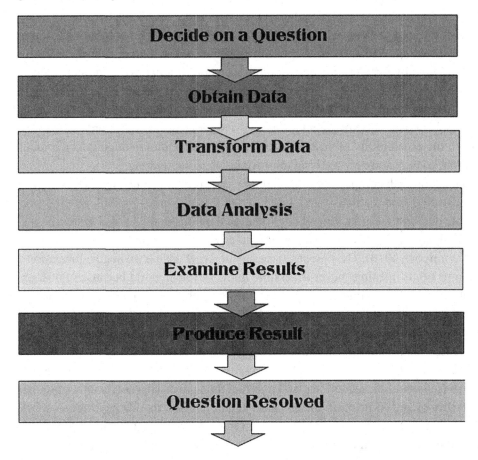

Methodological paradigms and difficulties of big data methodologically, enormous information enables us to use both expectation and causal investigation. Best in class enormous information research and practice draws on an assortment of systems from machine learning, established measurements, and econometrics, to plan of tests industry calls this A/B or multivariate testing to test existing speculations and theories, creating new speculations, and making vast scale business esteem (Yu, Yurovsky & Xu, 2011). From the point of view of logical request, the whole comprehensively associated organized economy currently can be conceived as a large scale true lab where scientists can outline and lead analyses and gather the information expected to acquire answers to an assortment of inquiries including (1) impacts of companion impact, (2) effects of the impact of dynamic ties, (3) effects of namelessness on online connections, (4) comes about from elective estimating methodologies for advanced media, (5)

the influence of painstakingly composed cutting edge recommender frameworks, and (6) the changing inclination structures of Generation Y and Z shoppers. Breaking down these issues absolutely present methodological difficulties, however we see the difficulties as open doors for capable analysts.

The enormous information techniques specified above have likewise raised contentions. Late disclosures from two well known sites, Facebook and OkCupid, both of which explored different avenues regarding their clients, have started enthusiasm for the subject of what, if any, fitting applications exist for utilization of the online social space as a research center for promoting our comprehension of human conduct (Davalos & Merchant, 2015). The key question is whether such experimentation by organizations or potentially by scholastics as a team with organizations gives advantages to society everywhere, and, assuming this is the case, what moral examination is proper and implementable? We contend that there is a solid case for such experimentation, not simply to maintain a strategic distance from expensive awful choices, yet additionally for quest for better comprehension of what drives human social communications. Awful choices hurt all that really matters of organizations as well as they cost society since terrible choices result in a misallocation of basic assets. As far back as that phlebotomy was a useful medicinal practice, precisely composed experimentation has driven logical investigation and learning disclosure. Presently, with the accessibility of vast scale experimentation yielding huge information, the potential for examination, testing, and new learning improvement are captivating.

While connecting with companions and scanning for sentimental accomplices go back to the posterity of Adam and Eve. The reality is that a huge part of this movement is direct on the web an ongoing PNAS examine demonstrates that 33% of later relational unions in the United States, begin from a web-based dating webpage in vigorously designed computerized stages with highlights that can be controlled (Soltani & Navimipour, 2016). The immense measure of small scale level huge information about human communications offers openings never accessible in the physical world because of cost or infeasibility of equivalent information accumulation. We currently have chances to produce new causal experiences, to test the viability of age old dependable guidelines and standards that represent social cooperation's. We can thoroughly test existing hypotheses and assemble and test new hypotheses. In short, we can go where social researchers could just dream of going before.

This conveys us to the need to precisely address the issue of regardless of whether such extensive scale field analyses would cause more societal mischief than great. This net thought of societal advantage is unquestionably of key enthusiasm for our individual colleges' morals and human subjects advisory groups otherwise called institutional audit sheets. Organizations need to take a leaf out of, or maybe team up with, the scholarly community and set up comparative morals advisory groups managing human subjects (Kashyap, 2019b). On the off chance that, as a general public, we put stock in interest about us as an animal varieties, at that point we have to gain from what probing the on the web social chart lets us know. As usual, we require our foundations to make up for lost time to innovation. Utilizing enormous information and investigation accompanies a large group of difficulties, a large number of which are ripe ground for future research. Huge information is more minds boggling to oversee than standard corporate information. Previously, organizations for the most part oversaw well structured information. In any case, organizations presently need to oversee a lot of inner and outer information that oftentimes will be unstructured or approximately organized. Including suitable what's more, entrepreneurial review information from any of the nearly omnipresent overview choices, firms currently can confront an enormous exhibit of inside, outer, and overview information.

Pervasive Informing

Today, people and organizations record what they find fascinating, store this data for themselves or others, what's more, share the information for individual and additionally business purposes. For effortlessness, we allude to this marvel as omnipresent illuminating since a definitive objective is to educate somebody about something extending from a brilliant dish, somebody's heartbeat, video catches, social cooperation's, vehicle tasks, and road reconnaissance for all intents and purposes any piece of data. Universal illuminating is conceivable in light of mechanical propels in versatile registering, video gushing, social organizing, savvy vehicles, and the Internet of things. Data snatching and trading are undoubtedly simple; the challenge is to discover an incentive in setting aside the opportunity to finish such assignments (Ding, Erickson, Kellogg & Patterson, 2011). The issue is whether one can utilize huge information and information investigation to get genuine esteem. Can an organization become more acquainted with its clients better? Can the organization distinguish its generally important customers and improve benefits through giving these clients with more customized client connections or better client administrations? Can the organization use data to increase more grounded advertise position? The difficulties from omnipresent advising incorporate growing far better enormous information building and examination to oversee and use enormous information to convey business esteem.

Usage Environments

From an unadulterated stockpiling point of view, stack situations, for example, Hadoop have been acquainted with oversee huge information 3D shapes. As with any new innovation, such creating situations ought to be drawn closer with clear vision and sound feedback. As noted (Nurika, Hassan & Zakaria, 2017), anyway delightful the methodology, one ought to at times take a gander at the outcomes. In many cases, stack situations remain vigorously underutilized with the danger of presenting yet another expensive heritage trouble and imperiling future huge information driven developments. More moderate inmemory setups could exhibit an intriguing option in the travel towards the develop enormous information association.

COORDINATION ISSUES

A key enormous information challenge for any firm is to distinguish and unravel the interrelationships of the huge information shape and draw out the esteem suggestions by connecting the different information streams utilizing properly characterized one of a kind identifiers, it might end up conceivable to get a more total picture of client conduct (Mynarz, 2014). In a protection setting, a system of connected elements for example, claims, petitioners, policyholders, autos, locally available diagnostics gadgets, auto repair shops, charge cards, and portable numbers may be built to disclose an extraordinary point of view on complex intrigue practices or extortion designs.

Esteem Assessment

The troublesome effect and imaginative utilizations of enormous information cause genuine difficulties for the expository systems and models that will be manufactured. These models fundamentally begin from traditional measurements, econometrics, machine learning, or manmade reasoning. A key normal for these explanatory strategies is that they center on improving a particular precision paradigm or insights based target work e.g., limiting a mean squared blunder or augmenting probability. Ordinarily, execution is abridged utilizing comparing factual measures that can be troublesome to comprehend for end clients or no experts (Thompson, Varvel, Sasinowski & Burke, 2016). As diagnostic models acquire and more impact in the key choices of a firm, it is vital to connect this correspondence hole to create the important trust. In particular, to pick up trust in an investigative model, the two information researchers and chiefs ought to receive a most widely used language in which the idea of significant worth assumes a key part. This achieves an entirely new point of view on the development, execution, and assessment of a diagnostic model. As such, other as unadulterated factual execution e.g., estimated utilizing misclassification rates, mean squared mistakes, Gini bends, top decile, genuine esteem based criteria turn into the prevailing components. The suitable criteria are exceptionally needy upon the particular business setting.

Expository Models Ought to Be Justifiable to Chiefs

Clearly, this has a subjective component to it and relies upon both the portrayal and formal multifaceted nature of the systematic model and additionally the instruction or foundation of the end client. Black box investigative models in light of exceptionally complex scientific recipes are probably not going to be trusted to bolster key business procedures, for example, credit hazard estimation, misrepresentation identification, or even therapeutic finding. However, in the event that a discovery strategy conveys precise restorative analyze over and over, would the patient driven specialist select for less precise yet effortlessly reasonable choices? Esteem based execution basis concerns operational productivity including model assessment, show checking, and demonstrate refreshing (Kashyap & Tiwari, 2018). The first of these allude to the assets that are expected to assemble the fundamental information inputs, preprocess them, run them through the model, and follow up on the acquired yield. Continuously basic leadership settings, quick model assessment are a key prerequisite. Consider the case of charge card misrepresentation location, where regularly a choice should be made in less than five seconds after the exchange is started. Recommender frameworks are another case where any client activity or occasion for instance, recorded utilizing area based administrations (Angelis & Kanavos, 2013). Notwithstanding model assessment endeavors, operational proficiency likewise involves the assets expected to screen, back test, and, where pertinent, stretch test the scientific models. At long last, the model must be invigorated or refreshed as new information develops or business conditions change. The organization that can recognize changing conditions and rapidly adjust its models is the organization that will succeed.

Overseeing Analytic Decisions

Drawing out choice prepared derivations from huge information investigation impacts and improves the association's basic leadership. With examination, we will see more choices being mechanized, in this manner affecting the choice procedures and obligations all through the association. With choices being mechanized possibly in light of enormous information examination, overseeing and demonstrating business choices is a rising test. Associations are intensely engaged with improving their business forms and empowering fast and compelling response to new difficulties, openings, or controls. By expressly demonstrating choices and the rationale behind them, choices can be overseen independently from the procedures, drastically expanding business spryness. This requires understandable choice examination methods for business (Ploskas, Stiakakis & Fouliras, 2014) and in addition strategies and measures to depict, show, what's more, oversee business basic leadership. The choice model what's more, documentation is such a standard for choice displaying, received by the Object Management Group, to conquer any hindrance between business process outline and business choices.

Quantifiable Profit and Trust

At long last, a diagnostic model should include monetary incentive by either producing benefits or cutting expenses or both. A profit driven assessment of a diagnostic model is vital to create trust crosswise over different levels and specialty units in any association. Administrative choices are ordinarily in view of monetary return, as opposed to a factually critical explanatory model, furthermore, that is the place examination can produce question and hence fall short. It is our firm conviction this ought to be catalyzed by more research in no less than two territories. To start with, inventive methodologies ought to be created to precisely measure the arrival on venture of an investigative model considering the add up to cost of model proprietorship, including aberrant and opportunity expenses, and covering an adequately long and fitting time skyline. As a next subject on the exploration plan, the subsequent monetary bits of knowledge and measures ought to be specifically installed into a systematic model building process, as opposed to simply utilized as ex post assessment measures (Batarseh, Yang & Deng, 2017). In particular, logical models should never again indiscriminately center around improving a probability work or limiting a misclassification rate, however go for including business esteem where it is important, considering all the previously mentioned criteria. At exactly that point will the vital trust be acquired over all choice levels and specialty units in a firm?

STRATEGIES FOR ANALYZING BIG DATA: A NEW APPROACH

When you utilize SQL inquiries to look into money related numbers or OLAP devices to create deals estimates, you for the most part comprehend what sort of information you have and what it can let you know. Income, topography and time all identify with each other in unsurprising ways. You don't really comprehend what the appropriate responses are nevertheless you do know how the different components of the informational collection identify with each other. BI clients regularly run standard reports from organized databases that have been deliberately displayed to use these connections. Enormous information investigation includes making "sense" out of huge volumes of shifted information that in its crude frame does not have an information model to characterize what every component implies with regards to the others. There are a few new issues you ought to consider as you set out on this new sort of investigation: Discovery in numerous cases you don't generally comprehend what you have and how unique informational indexes identify with each other (Kashyap, 2019). You should make sense of it through a procedure of investigation and disclosure. Iteration because the genuine connections are not generally known ahead of time, revealing understanding is frequently an iterative process as you discover the appropriate responses that you look for. The idea of emphasis is that it here and there drives you down a way that ends up being a deadlock. That is alright experimentation is a piece of the procedure. Numerous investigators and industry specialists recommend that you begin with little, very much characterized ventures, gain from each cycle, and continuously proceed onward to the following thought or field of request (Yang & Yecies, 2016). Flexible Capacity because of the iterative idea of huge information examination is set up to invest more energy and use more assets to take care of issues.

Mining and predicting big information investigation isn't highly contrasting. You don't generally know how the different information components identify with each other (Kashyap, 2019c). As you mine the information to find examples and connections, prescient investigation can yield the experiences that you look for. Decision Management considers the exchange volume and speed. On the off chance that you are utilizing huge information investigation to drive numerous operational choices, for example, customizing a site or provoking call focus specialists about the propensities and exercises of buyers at that point you have to think about how to mechanize and improve the execution of every one of those activities.

For instance you may have no clue regardless of whether social information reveals insight into deals patterns. The test comes with making sense of which information components identify with which other information components, and in what limit. The procedure of disclosure not just includes investigating the information to see how you can utilize it yet in addition deciding how it identifies with your conventional endeavor information. New kinds of request involve what happened, as well as why. For instance, a key metric for some, and organizations is client agitate. It's genuinely simple to evaluate stir. Yet, for what reason does it happen? Examining call information records, client bolster request, internet based life analysis, and other client input would all be able to help clarify why clients imperfection (Pan, Wang & Han, 2016). Comparative methodologies can be utilized with different sorts of information and in different circumstances. For what reason did deals fall in a given store? For what reason do certain patients survive longer than others? Try to locate the correct information, find the shrouded connections, and examine it accurately.

Huge Data Analysis Requirements

In the past segment, Techniques for analyzing big data, we talked about some of strategies you can use to discover which means and find shrouded connections in enormous information. Here are three huge necessities for directing this request in a practical way:

1. Limit information development
2. Utilize existing aptitudes
3. Take care of information security

Limiting information development is tied in with moderating figuring assets. In customary investigation situations, information is conveyed to the PC, handled, and after that sent to the following goal. For instance, creation information may be separated from e business frameworks, changed into social information write, and stacked into an operational information store organized for detailing. Yet, the volume of information develops, this kind of ETL engineering moves toward becoming progressively less effective. There's simply an excessive amount of information to move around. It bodes well to store and process the information in a similar place. With new information and new information sources comes the need to obtain new abilities. The current range of abilities will figure out where investigation should and ought to be possible (Horton & Tambe, 2015). At the point when the imperative abilities are deficient with regards to, a mix of preparing, procuring and new instruments will address the issue. Since most associations have more individuals who can dissect information utilizing SQL than utilizing MapReduce, it is critical to have the capacity to help the two kinds of handling. Information security is basic for some corporate applications. Information distribution center clients are acclimated not exclusively to deliberately characterized measurements and measurements and properties, additionally to a dependable arrangement of organization strategies and security controls. These thorough procedures are regularly missing with unstructured information sources and open source investigation instruments. Focus on the security and information administration necessities of every investigation venture and make beyond any doubt that the devices you are utilizing can oblige those prerequisites.

Database Processing With Oracle Advanced Analytics

Most Oracle clients are exceptionally acquainted with SQL as a dialect for question, announcing, and examination of organized information. It is the accepted standard for investigation and the innovation that underlies most BI apparatuses. R is a prevalent open source programming dialect for factual examination. Investigators, information researchers, scientists, and scholastics generally utilize R, prompting a developing pool of R software engineers. When information has been stacked into Oracle Database, clients can profit themselves of Oracle Advanced Analytics (OAA) to reveal shrouded connections in the information. Prophet Advanced Analytics, an alternative of Oracle Database Enterprise Release, offers a mix of intense in database calculations and open source R calculations, available through SQL and R dialects. It joins elite information mining capacities with the open source R dialect to empower prescient investigation, information mining, content mining, measurable examination, progressed numerical calculations and intuitive design all inside the database (Jin, Liu & Qi, 2012). Prophet Advanced Analytics gives all center scientific capacities and dialects on great in database engineering. These explanatory capacities incorporate information mining calculations actualized in the database, local SQL capacities for fundamental factual procedures, and incorporation with open source R for measurable programming and access to a more extensive arrangement of measurable methods.

This intense diagnostic condition offers an enormous scope of capacities to Oracle Database clients handling enormous information extends by limiting information development and guaranteeing intrinsic security, versatility, and execution (Waoo, Kashyap, & Jaiswal, 2010). It incorporates information mining apparatuses that let you make complex models and convey them on expansive informational collections. You can use the consequences of these prescient models inside BI applications. For instance, you can utilize relapse models to foresee client age in view of obtaining conduct and statistic information. You can likewise assemble and apply prescient models that assistance you focus on your best clients, create nitty gritty client profiles, find and counteract misrepresentation, and understand numerous other scientific difficulties.

Productive Data Mining

The information mining instruments in OAA empower information investigators to work specifically with information inside the database, investigate the information graphically, manufacture and assess numerous information mining models, and send forecasts and bits of knowledge all through the undertaking. It incorporates information digging calculations for characterization, bunching, advertises container investigation, misrepresentation identification, and content mining that can be connected to settle an extensive variety of information driven issues. It additionally incorporates a dozen calculations that you can use to fabricate and send prescient applications that consequently mine star diagram information to convey constant outcomes and expectations. Since the information, models and results stay in the Prophet Database, information development is wiped out, data dormancy is limited and security is kept up. Utilizing standard SQL charges you can get to elite calculations in the database to mine tables, sees, star constructions, and value based and unstructured information (Bacardit & Llorà, 2013). Any individual who can get to information put away in an Oracle Database can get to OAA comes about, expectations, suggestions, and revelations utilizing standard reports and BI instruments.

Factual Analysis With R

Prophet Advanced Analytics has been intended to empower analysts to utilize R on vast informational indexes. Investigative models can be composed in R. The related tables and perspectives in Oracle Database show up as R objects. Therefore there is no compelling reason to compose SQL proclamations. Examiners can compose R code to control the information in the database. By running R programs right in the database, there is no compelling reason to move information around. This coordinated engineering guarantees extraordinary security and execution, since you can apply enormous, versatile equipment assets to complex issues. OAA underpins existing R contents and outsider bundles too. All current R improvement abilities, devices, and contents can run straightforwardly with OAA, and scale against information put away in Oracle Database 11g. The tight mix between R, Oracle Database, and Hadoop empowers examiners to keep in touch with R content that can keep running in three distinct conditions: a workstation running open source R, Hadoop running with Oracle big data connectors, and Oracle Database (Duque Barrachina & O'Driscoll, 2014). It is anything but difficult to connect the consequences of the investigation to business examination devices, for example, Prophet Business Intelligence and Oracle Analytics, as portrayed in the accompanying area.

Connecting Hadoop and Oracle Database

There are two distinct alternatives for connecting information and interval brings about Hadoop with your Oracle information distribution center. Contingent upon your utilization case, you might need to stack Hadoop information into the information stockroom, or abandon it set up and simply inquiry it utilizing SQL. Prophet Loader for Hadoop gives a simple method to stack HDFS information into an Oracle information stockroom. MapReduce to make advanced informational collections that can be proficiently stacked into Oracle Database. Not at all like other Hadoop loaders, has it created Oracle inward configurations, allowing it to stack information speedier with less framework assets. Once stacked, the information can be gotten to with conventional SQL based Business Intelligence devices (Hossen, Moniruzzaman & Hossain, 2015). Prophet SQL Connector for HDFS is a fast connector for getting to HDFS information straightforwardly from Oracle Database, conquering any hindrance amongst HDFS and information distribution center conditions. The information put away in HDFS can at that point be questioned by means of SQL, joined with information put away in Oracle Database, or stacked into Oracle Database.

Prophet's Big Data Platform

Prophet has three built frameworks that illuminate distinctive parts of the huge information issue. Every stage incorporates all the essential equipment and programming important for extraordinary information handling. All parts are pre coordinated what's more, prepared to send and work. Prophet has done the diligent work of integrating these built frameworks so that you can extricate an incentive from your information by means of a progressed huge information stage with coordinated investigation (Kashyap and Tiwari, 2017). This finish arrangement incorporates different frameworks dealing with information procurement, stacking, capacity, administration, investigation, combination and introduction so you can rapidly remove an incentive from enormous information with coordinated examination. Prophet big data Appliance incorporates a mix of open source programming and concentrated programming created by Oracle to address huge information prerequisites. Dwelling at the front end of the enormous information lifecycle, it is intended to secure and arrange enormous information proficiently, and to be the savviest stage to run Hadoop (AlMahmoud, Damiani, Otrok & Al-Hammadi, 2017). For additional data on the adequacy of this approach, see the white paper "Getting real about big data: Build Versus Buy" from the Enterprise Strategy Group. Prophet Exadata Database Machine conveys extraordinary execution and versatility for a wide range of database applications. It is the speediest stage accessible for running Oracle Database and the related investigation talked about in this chapter.

Prophet analytics is a built framework that incorporates an endeavor BI stage, in memory investigation programming, what's more, equipment upgraded for expansive scale examination. With apparatuses for cutting edge information perception and investigation, it empowers clients to acquire significant understanding from a lot of information. At the point when Oracle Analytics is utilized with Prophet Advanced Analytics, clients have a far reaching stage that conveys understanding into key business subjects, for example, beat forecast, item suggestions, conclusion examination, and misrepresentation alarming.

Analytics for the Enterprise

Associations in each industry are endeavoring to comprehend the monstrous deluge of huge information, and additionally to create diagnostic stages that can orchestrate conventional organized information with semi organized and unstructured sources of data. At the point when appropriately caught and investigated, enormous information can give interesting bits of knowledge into advertise patterns, gear disappointments, purchasing behaviors, support cycles and numerous different business issues, bringing down expenses, and empowering more focused on business choices. To get an incentive from enormous information, you require a strong arrangement of answers for catching, handling, and breaking down the information, from obtaining the information and finding new bits of knowledge to settling on repeatable choices and scaling the related data frameworks. Prophet advanced analytics is perfect for revealing shrouded connections in enormous information sources. Regardless of whether you have to foresee client conduct, envision cross/up offer openings, enhance showcasing effort reaction rates, counteract agitate, dissect "advertise containers" to find affiliations, examples and connections, use influencers in interpersonal organizations, decrease misrepresentation, or foresee future request, Oracle Advanced Analytics can help (Ravada, 2015). At the point when utilized as a part of conjunction with open source instruments, for example, Hadoop and MapReduce, this intense systematic arrangement conveys all that you have to procure, sort out, break down and expand the estimation of huge information inside the undertaking while satisfying crucial prerequisites for limiting information development, utilizing existing ranges of abilities, and guaranteeing elevated amounts of security.

- A major information investigation arrangement comprises of administrations or calculations that adventure both machine ability information driven administrations and human knowledge collaboration centric administrations.
- To encourage and guarantee the reconciliation of machine capacity and human knowledge, joining driven administrations are expected to help clients connect with the two information driven

administrations and joint effort driven administrations and give instruments to incorporate the aftereffect of two sorts of administrations.

- All administrations or calculations together help the enormous information change from crude organization to learning item (bottom up) or from theory to assets (top down) (Kuiler, 2014).
- Human knowledge ought to be associated with the entire procedure of information change, including designing information driven administrations, deciphering the aftereffect of information driven administrations, working together with different specialists on translating and sharing the outcomes.

Figure 8. Conceptual architecture of big data analytics

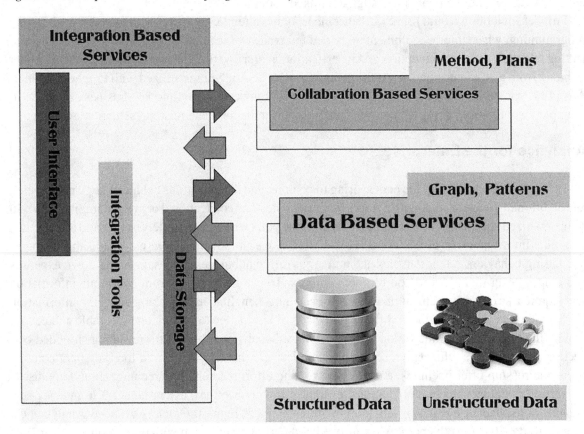

As appeared in the design graph (Figure 8), there are three sorts of segments.

- Data driven administrations, which abuse substantial information handling innovation to genuinely look, break down and total information from heterogeneous information sources. The contribution of the information driven administrations is organized or potentially unstructured information from heterogeneous information sources. The yield of information driven administrations is looked or separated data, found examples or records and so forth. The information driven administrations expect to enhance the procedures of individual sense making (Luo, Zhang, Zukerman & Qiao, 2014).

- Collaboration driven administrations, which bolster individuals and their communication by catching and sharing assets, sentiments, contentions and remarks among members, so to encourage the aggregate comprehension of the issues identified with information investigation. The contribution of the joint effort driven administrations could be the yield of information driven administrations and in addition the cooperation's remarks, contentions and talks and so on (Luo, Zhang, Zukerman & Qiao, 2014) figure 9 shown this concept for social media. The learning item theory, techniques and so on ought to be the result of their association. The joint effort driven administrations intend to help synergistic sense making.

- Integration driven administrations, which bolster information driven administrations and coordinated effort driven administrations. Coordination driven administrations are to guarantee and encourage the consistent coordination of the autonomous administrations created. Related capacities incorporate UI, information stockpiling and coordination components and so on. The mix driven administrations actualized in Dicode venture are the Dicode Workbench, the Dicode ONtology and the Storage Service (Dafferianto Trinugroho, 2014).

Figure 9. Conceptual architecture for big dataanalytics in social media monitoring

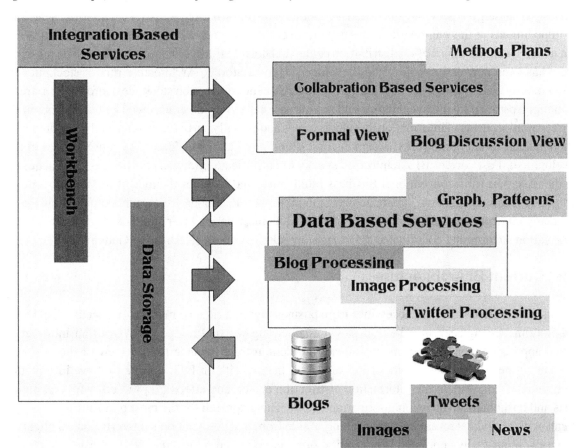

This approach opens up an additional channel to necessities displaying and examination, which depends on changing and breaking down hypothetical models from sociology and subjective science to a plan curio. The exploration work announced in this section gives a delineation of how hypothetical models were chosen and connected to the examination and outline of the design as shown in figure 9. We trust this unobtrusive endeavor at bringing sociology or psychological science models into prerequisite designing will supplement the conventional necessity displaying process. Considerably more work is expected to refine to meet the down to earth necessities of prerequisites expert and architects.

Approaches to Deal With Big Data

Huge data can be viewed as issue, then again as happenstance this area contains methodologies of taking care of the relative huge information from point of view of design, procedures, foundation, and advancements.

Approaches

The conventional BI engineering can be considered as a beginning stage for structures with its process counting arranging territory, information distribution center, information stores, ETL, and so on. Searching for impediments of this engineering, one may discover that it is probably not going to store all information in focal, venture information distribution center and not all information are important to be put away. There has been new design approaches developed: Hybrid Storage Architecture mix of stockpiles for different information composes and organizes, impermanent information stockpiles, information stream handling, Upstream Intelligence logical and measurable capacities are connected right off the bat in the process amid securing of information that incorporates additionally particular Stream and event preparing based manage based frameworks, design distinguishing proof (Askitas, 2016). As consequences of this development, Post current BI Architecture speaks to an intricate arrangement that has been acquired, for the most part from conventional Business Intelligence and includes the idea of mixture stockpiling design, upstream insight, and stream an occasion preparing. Postmodern BI Architecture comprises of circulated information distribution center, merged Meta information layer, composed administration of information streams and coordinated effort learning administration (Kashyap & Gautam, 2017).

Post Current BI Architecture

Because of assorted variety of necessities from business symmetrical BI models advanced: a Top Down and Bottom Up engineering. The Top Down engineering worried a report driven or an information driven approach where an information stockroom demonstrate is made first in view of the business/ announcing necessities. Procedure of this approach begins with an ETL routine to move information from source framework to the information distribution center, and afterward proceeds with making reports and dashboards to question information in DW. This approach for the most part fulfills easygoing clients with periodical revealing and checking. Aside from that, association's interests control clients to chip away at specially appointed investigation or undertakings in innovative work division. With past approach control clients are left aside to utilize specially appointed spreadsheets, independent/neighborhood database occasions, SQL and information mining workbenches with Top Down approach control

Figure 10. Top down Vs. bottom up approach architecture

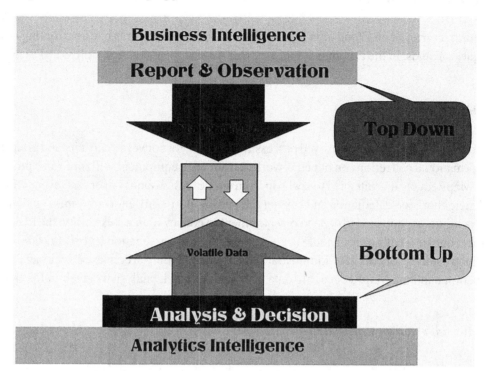

clients discover BI instruments unyielding and a data warehousing structure excessively constrained for their worries (Kekwaletswe & Lesole, 2016). Open door for Bottom Up design approach has shown up.

The Bottom Up approach suits better for business examiners and information researchers who require the impromptu investigation of any information source, both inside and outside corporate limits, working intimately with business directors to improve existing procedures. Post present day BI design is an aftereffect of development of information warehousing structures, information administration programs and adding progressed investigation to adjust the dynamic between top down and base up necessities. This compositional idea is otherwise called half and half engineering portrayed in the Figure 10. Huge Data and HPA don't change information warehousing or BI structures. They basically supplement them with new advancements and get to techniques better custom made to meet the data prerequisites. Cross breed design can alternatively contain following correlative innovations like: •Hadoop bunches to help stockpiling for semi organized information, utilized as a part of arranging region or then again expository sandboxes •Streaming and Complex Event Processing Engines to help consistent insight, utilized as smart sensors that can be connected to streams with extensive volume of information and screen blend of occasions •Analytical Sandbox to support examination handling, specially appointed questions, to fulfill short-term investigation needs, utilized as a passages for other BI frameworks •Non social database framework to store unstructured or crude information, utilized as a part of expository sandbox, or arranging region •Data center point to encourage different frameworks and applications instead of to have revealing or investigation applications specifically, information stockroom utilized as a center (Shmueli, 2017).

Big Data Analytics Tools

BDA structures, conveyed on Cloud or in house data center, have end up basic to confronting the computational request errands. In the accompanying, we exhibit a review of the most utilized BDA apparatuses in writing.

Apache Hadoop

Apache Hadoop is an open source conveyed processing structure for conveyed capacity and group handling of huge informational collections on bunches worked from ware equipment utilizing basic programming models i.e. MapReduce. It is intended to scale up from single to thousands of servers, every one of which offers both neighborhood calculation and capacity. It permits preparing enormous information by utilizing bunch handling. As opposed to depend on equipment to convey high accessibility, the library itself is intended to recognize what's more, handle disappointments at the application layer (Mavridis & Karatza, 2017). Hadoop center segments give administrations to work planning, a conveyed document framework and information handling MapReduce, big data analytics for batch analysis is given in the figure 11.

Figure 11. Big data analytics structure batch analysis

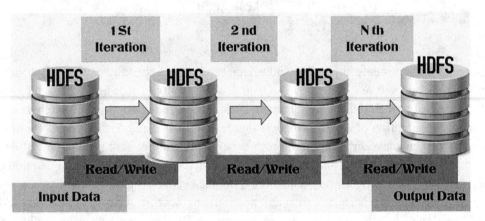

Apache Kafka

Apache Kafka is a quick, versatile, strong, and blame tolerant publish subscribe informing framework. Kafka is regularly utilized as a part of place of conventional message merchants like JMS and AMQP due to its higher throughput, unwavering quality and replication [Kafka] figure 12 is demonstrating the structure streaming analysis. Apache Kafka can work in blend with various frameworks for constant investigation and the rendering of gushing information, for example, Apache Storm, Apache HBase or Apache Spark. More often than not, it is utilized for two kind of utilization, growing constant information work processes, trading messages between frameworks or applications in a dependable way, and ongoing spilling applications that change or respond to the information stream (Shaheen, 2017). Kafka is a message representative on a level plane adaptable, and blame tolerant. Despite the utilization case,

Figure 12. Big data analytics structure streaming analysis

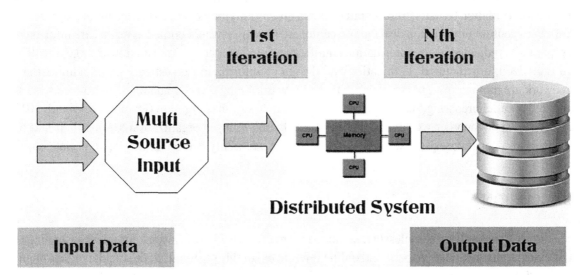

Kafka agent's huge streams of messages for low inactivity investigation in the Apache Hadoop biological system.

DISCUSSION

Enormous data phenomenon has been depicted in this segment with its causalities, definitions, impacts and effects. Mention that the change in perspective from information driven approach towards data driven approach might be seen dangerously on the conventional thought of focal information stockroom and physically authorized information respectability and consistency. Instead of that, it makes integral arrangements that fulfill necessities for adaptability and flexibility supporting information investigation. Data Driven Approach is a beginning stage for Upstream Insight. Enormous data rearranges engineering in that way that Post Modern BI Architecture created in mélange of Hybrid Storage Architecture Analytical Sandboxes, Hadoop, NoSQL, RDBMS, Upstream Intelligence especially bolstered by Complex Event Processing and customary information warehousing (Omidi & Alipour, 2016). Another wonderful thought, following the Hybrid Storage Architecture, is Information Federation that urges to find information on different apparatuses in different structures what's more, designs. Anyway it underpins examination and guarantees giving of constant access to information by means of essentially brought together information get to having the BI design thoroughly expanded post modern BI Architecture, there are however advances that flourish for creative ways to deal with handle Big Data. Region of high execution examination isn't extensively characterized and mapped. The advancement of HPA is for the most part determined by business interest for having data after effects of information handling instantly and by accessibility of assets framework figuring, substantial memory with coordinate.

Diagnostic stages of HPA shift among the merchants and as a rule are actualized as restrictive arrangements. Specialization of stages depends on business prerequisites and business applications. Additionally different specialized drivers influence the usage of stage, which can be for example number of customers/supporters regarding applications and clients, information volumes, kind of information, fit in the worldwide design of BI arrangement e.g. arranging territory, data warehouse, subordinate/autonomous information bazaars, impromptu research and prototyping office. Talking about patterns, data storehouses venture information distribution center are moving towards pooled assets where information are separate as indicated by the information significance need preparing, information arrange organized, semi organized, unstructured. Foundation and design of information investigation and administration framework are moving from being execution tuned towards being directly adaptable in linkage with disseminated parallel preparing, network figuring, and in memory investigation (Hamoud & Obaid, 2013). Adaptability spurs another worldview that movements on premises organization towards half and half customary and apparatuses situated arrangement, where versatility can be flexible with private cloud.

CONCLUSION

Since the big data has been ceaselessly recognized for many years there is a considerable measure inquire about done in writing, white papers, and online references. In this postulation, the big data Phenomenon is outlined in a review including its causalities, definition, impact and effects. It speaks to a beginning stage and driver for High Performance Analytics regarding crude material that contains shrouded data, examples and esteem. Closing from look into, big data, with its dynamic measurements, ought not to be considered as an issue, as opposed to circumstance to transform it into advantage. Elite Analytics is broadly inquired about in this postulation as an approach towards taking care of big data because of this region it is as yet rising, being refined and formalized among sellers, explore on HPA is trying keeping in mind the end goal to bring diagram, characterization of HPA strategies and methods database analytics and parallel registering, their attributes, and fitting utilization. HPA is driven by business world with wide necessities to figure comes about as quick as conceivable on the biggest dataset. The development HPA winds up conceivable with innovative advancement very large memory, 64bit address, Grid Computing and moderateness of equipment costs, price: performance marker. For the time being, HPA can be viewed as an answer corresponding to the Business Intelligence, yet exceedingly on premises the advancement will proceed further. The research could be stretched out to jump into HPA arrangements from other merchants contrasting different restrictive methodologies in subtle elements. Test assignments as it has been outlined, exhibit the execution of HPA approach on vast datasets. Distinctive logical activities and their mixes have been chosen to exhibit the advantages of logical stage in light of In Memory Analytics approach. In Memory Analytics engineering has found as helpful for the calculation extraordinary activities connection, slant lines, gauging, percentile, since all information are stacked in memory and can be specifically tended to. There are a few constraints of trial assignments. For the future work, the investigative activities can be tried on explanatory stages that actualize other HPA approaches, moreover against conventional approach in Business Intelligence e.g. OLAP. Once in a while, sellers offer the explanatory stage that would actualize all talked about HPA approaches and on the off chance that, it is testing to perform them on a similar framework foundation. Defeating the restrictions, the examinations are adequate for looking at the execution of investigative activity among each other, to recognize focal points and advantages of chose systematic stage.

REFERENCES

Ahmadvand, H., & Goudarzi, M. (2017). Using Data Variety for Efficient Progressive Big Data Processing in Warehouse-Scale Computers. *IEEE Computer Architecture Letters*, *16*(2), 166–169. doi:10.1109/LCA.2016.2636293

AlMahmoud, A., Damiani, E., Otrok, H., & Al-Hammadi, Y. (2017). Spamdoop: A privacy-preserving Big Data platform for collaborative spam detection. *IEEE Transactions on Big Data*, 1-1. doi:10.1109/tbdata.2017.2716409

Angelis, A., & Kanavos, P. (2013). A Multiple Criteria Decision Analysis Framework For Value Based Assessment Of New Medical Technologies. *Value in Health*, *16*(3), A53. doi:10.1016/j.jval.2013.03.302

Arbel, L. (2015). Data loss prevention: The business case. *Computer Fraud & Security*, *2015*(5), 13–16. doi:10.1016/S1361-3723(15)30037-3

Askitas, N. (2016). Big Data is a big deal but how much data do we need? *Asta Wirtschafts- Und Sozialstatistisches Archiv*, *10*(2-3), 113-125. doi:10.1007/s11943-016-0191-3

Bacardit, J., & Llorà, X. (2013). Large-scale data mining using genetics-based machine learning. *Wiley Interdisciplinary Reviews. Data Mining and Knowledge Discovery*, *3*(1), 37–61. doi:10.1002/widm.1078

Batarseh, F., Yang, R., & Deng, L. (2017). A comprehensive model for management and validation of federal big data analytical systems. *Big Data Analytics*, *2*(1), 2. doi:10.118641044-016-0017-x

Dafferianto Trinugroho, Y. (2014). Information Integration Platform for Patient-Centric Healthcare Services: Design, Prototype and Dependability Aspects. *Future Internet*, *6*(1), 126–154. doi:10.3390/fi6010126

Davalos, S., & Merchant, A. (2015). Using Big Data to Study Psychological Constructs: Nostalgia on Facebook. *Journal of Psychology & Psychotherapy*, *05*(06). doi:10.4172/2161-0487.1000221

Diesner, J. (2015). Small decisions with big impact on data analytics. *Big Data & Society*, *2*(2), 205395171561718. doi:10.1177/2053951715617185

Ding, X., Erickson, T., Kellogg, W., & Patterson, D. (2011). Informing and performing: Investigating how mediated sociality becomes visible. *Personal and Ubiquitous Computing*, *16*(8), 1095–1117. doi:10.100700779-011-0443-8

Duque Barrachina, A., & O'Driscoll, A. (2014). A big data methodology for categorising technical support requests using Hadoop and Mahout. *Journal Of Big Data*, *1*(1), 1. doi:10.1186/2196-1115-1-1

Hamoud, A., & Obaid, T. (2013). *Building Data Warehouse for Diseases Registry: First Step for Clinical Data Warehouse*. SSRN Electronic Journal. doi:10.2139srn.3061599

Hassani-Mahmooei, B., Berecki-Gisolf, J., & Collie, A. (2017). Using Bayesian Model Averaging to Analyse Hierarchical Health Data: Model implementation and application to linked health service use data. *International Journal For Population Data Science*, *1*(1). doi:10.23889/ijpds.v1i1.89

Horton, J., & Tambe, P. (2015). Labor Economists Get Their Microscope: Big Data and Labor Market Analysis. *Big Data*, 3(3), 130–137. doi:10.1089/big.2015.0017 PMID:27442956

Hossen, A., Moniruzzaman, A., & Hossain, S. (2015). Performance Evaluation of Hadoop and Oracle Platform for Distributed Parallel Processing in Big Data Environments. *International Journal Of Database Theory And Application*, 8(5), 15–26. doi:10.14257/ijdta.2015.8.5.02

Hussain, A., & Roy, A. (2016). The emerging era of Big Data Analytics. *Big Data Analytics*, 1(1), 4. doi:10.118641044-016-0004-2

Jin, C., Liu, N., & Qi, L. (2012). Research and Application of Data Archiving based on Oracle Dual Database Structure. *Journal of Software*, 7(4). doi:10.4304/jsw.7.4.844-848

Kashyap, R. (2019a). Security, Reliability, and Performance Assessment for Healthcare Biometrics. In D. Kisku, P. Gupta, & J. Sing (Eds.), Design and Implementation of Healthcare Biometric Systems (pp. 29-54). Hershey, PA: IGI Global. doi:10.4018/978-1-5225-7525-2.ch002

Kashyap, R. (2019b). Security, Reliability, and Performance Assessment for Healthcare Biometrics. In D. Kisku, P. Gupta, & J. Sing (Eds.), Design and Implementation of Healthcare Biometric Systems (pp. 29-54). Hershey, PA: IGI Global. doi:10.4018/978-1-5225-7525-2.ch002

Kashyap, R. (2019c). Biometric Authentication Techniques and E-Learning. In A. Kumar (Ed.), *Biometric Authentication in Online Learning Environments* (pp. 236–265). Hershey, PA: IGI Global; doi:10.4018/978-1-5225-7724-9.ch010

Kashyap, R., & Gautam, P. (2017). Fast medical image segmentation using energy-based method. Biometrics. *Concepts, Methodologies, Tools, and Applications*, 3(1), 1017–1042.

Kashyap, R., & Piersson, A. D. (2018). Big Data Challenges and Solutions in the Medical Industries. In V. Tiwari, R. Thakur, B. Tiwari, & S. Gupta (Eds.), *Handbook of Research on Pattern Engineering System Development for Big Data Analytics* (pp. 1–24). Hershey, PA: IGI Global; doi:10.4018/978-1-5225-3870-7.ch001

Kashyap, R., & Tiwari, V. (2017). Energy-based active contour method for image segmentation. *International Journal of Electronic Healthcare*, 9(2–3), 210–225.

Kashyap, R., & Tiwari, V. (2018). Active contours using global models for medical image segmentation. *International Journal of Computational Systems Engineering*, 4(2/3), 195. doi:10.1504/ijcsyse.2018.091404

Kekwaletswe, R., & Lesole, T. (2016). A Framework for Improving Business Intelligence through Master Data Management. *Journal of South African Business Research*, 1-12. doi:10.5171/2016.473749

Kekwaletswe, R., & Lesole, T. (2016). A Framework for Improving Business Intelligence through Master Data Management. Journal of South African Business Research, 1-12. doi:10.5171/2016.473749

Kuiler, E. (2014). From Big Data to Knowledge: An Ontological Approach to Big Data Analytics. *The Review of Policy Research*, 31(4), 311–318. doi:10.1111/ropr.12077

Kuner, C., Cate, F., Millard, C., & Svantesson, D. (2012). The challenge of 'big data' for data protection. *International Data Privacy Law*, 2(2), 47–49. doi:10.1093/idpl/ips003

Lomotey, R., & Deters, R. (2015). Unstructured data mining: Use case for CouchDB. *International Journal Of Big Data Intelligence*, *2*(3), 168. doi:10.1504/IJBDI.2015.070597

Luo, H., Zhang, H., Zukerman, M., & Qiao, C. (2014). An incrementally deployable network architecture to support both data-centric and host-centric services. *IEEE Network*, *28*(4), 58–65. doi:10.1109/MNET.2014.6863133

Luo, H., Zhang, H., Zukerman, M., & Qiao, C. (2014). An incrementally deployable network architecture to support both data-centric and host-centric services. *IEEE Network*, *28*(4), 58–65. doi:10.1109/MNET.2014.6863133

Mavridis, I., & Karatza, H. (2017). Performance evaluation of cloud-based log file analysis with Apache Hadoop and Apache Spark. *Journal of Systems and Software*, *125*, 133–151. doi:10.1016/j.jss.2016.11.037

Mynarz, J. (2014). Integration of public procurement data using linked data. *Journal of Systems Integration*, 19-31. doi:10.20470/jsi.v5i4.213

Nurika, O., Hassan, M., & Zakaria, N. (2017). Implementation of Network Cards Optimizations in Hadoop Cluster Data Transmissions. *ICST Transactions On Ubiquitous Environments*, *4*(12), 153506. doi:10.4108/eai.21-12-2017.153506

Omidi, M., & Alipour, M. (2016). Why NOSQL And The Necessity of Movement Toward The NOSQL Data Base. *IOSR Journal Of Computer Engineering*, *18*(05), 116–118. doi:10.9790/0661-180502116118

Pan, E., Wang, D., & Han, Z. (2016). Analyzing Big Smart Metering Data Towards Differentiated User Services: A Sublinear Approach. *IEEE Transactions On Big Data*, *2*(3), 249–261. doi:10.1109/TBDATA.2016.2599924

Ploskas, N., Stiakakis, E., & Fouliras, P. (2014). Assessing Computer Network Efficiency Using Data Envelopment Analysis and Multicriteria Decision Analysis Techniques. *Journal Of Multi-Criteria Decision Analysis*, *22*(5-6), 260–278. doi:10.1002/mcda.1533

Ravada, S. (2015). Big data spatial analytics for enterprise applications. *SIGSPATIAL Special*, *6*(2), 34–41. doi:10.1145/2744700.2744705

Rey-del-Castillo, P., & Cardeñosa, J. (2016). An Exercise in Exploring Big Data for Producing Reliable Statistical Information. *Big Data*, *4*(2), 120–128. doi:10.1089/big.2015.0045 PMID:27441716

Rho, S., & Vasilakos, A. (2017). Intelligent collaborative system and service in value network for enterprise computing. *Enterprise Information Systems*, *12*(1), 1–3. doi:10.1080/17517575.2016.1238962

Shaheen, J. (2017). Apache Kafka: Real Time Implementation with Kafka Architecture Review. *International Journal Of Advanced Science And Technology*, *109*, 35–42. doi:10.14257/ijast.2017.109.04

Shmueli, G. (2017). Research Dilemmas with Behavioral Big Data. *Big Data*, *5*(2), 98–119. doi:10.1089/big.2016.0043 PMID:28632441

Smith, N. (2015). Wearable Tech: Smart Watches. *Engineering & Technology*, *10*(4), 20–21. doi:10.1049/et.2015.0451

Soltani, Z., & Navimipour, N. (2016). Customer relationship management mechanisms: A systematic review of the state of the art literature and recommendations for future research. *Computers in Human Behavior*, *61*, 667–688. doi:10.1016/j.chb.2016.03.008

Thompson, S., Varvel, S., Sasinowski, M., & Burke, J. (2016). From Value Assessment to Value Co-creation: Informing Clinical Decision-Making with Medical Claims Data. *Big Data*, *4*(3), 141–147. doi:10.1089/big.2015.0030 PMID:27642718

Tromp, E., Pechenizkiy, M., & Gaber, M. (2017). Expressive modeling for trusted big data analytics: Techniques and applications in sentiment analysis. *Big Data Analytics*, *2*(1), 5. doi:10.118641044-016-0018-9

Tromp, E., Pechenizkiy, M., & Gaber, M. (2017). Expressive modeling for trusted big data analytics: Techniques and applications in sentiment analysis. *Big Data Analytics*, *2*(1), 5. doi:10.118641044-016-0018-9

Waterman, K., & Hendler, J. (2013). Getting the Dirt on Big Data. *Big Data*, *1*(3), 137–140. doi:10.1089/big.2013.0026 PMID:27442195

Weber, C., Königsberger, J., Kassner, L., & Mitschang, B. (2017). M2DDM – A Maturity Model for Data-Driven Manufacturing. *Procedia CIRP*, *63*, 173–178. doi:10.1016/j.procir.2017.03.309

Yang, J., & Yecies, B. (2016). Mining Chinese social media UGC: A big-data framework for analyzing Douban movie reviews. *Journal Of Big Data*, *3*(1), 3. doi:10.118640537-015-0037-9

Yu, C., Yurovsky, D., & Xu, T. (2011). Visual Data Mining: An Exploratory Approach to Analyzing Temporal Patterns of Eye Movements. *Infancy*, *17*(1), 33–60. doi:10.1111/j.1532-7078.2011.00095.x

KEY TERMS AND DEFINITIONS

DM: Data mining Information mining is the way toward finding designs in expansive informational indexes including strategies at the convergence of machine learning, measurements, and database systems. An interdisciplinary subfield of computer science, it is a fundamental procedure where in insightful strategies are connected to extricate information patterns the general objective of which is to separate data from an informational index and change it into a justifiable structure for facilitate use. Aside from the crude examination step, it includes database and information administration angles, information pre-handling, model and surmising contemplations, intriguing quality measurements, multifaceted nature contemplations, post-preparing of found structures, perception, and online updating. Data mining is the investigation venture of the "learning revelation in databases" process, or KDD. The term is a misnomer, in light of the fact that the objective is the extraction of examples and learning from a lot of information, not the extraction (mining) of information itself.

HPDA: High performance data analytics with information investigation the procedure use HPC's utilization of parallel handling to run ground-breaking scientific programming at speeds higher than a teraflop or (a trillion gliding point tasks for each second). Through this approach, it is conceivable to rapidly inspect expansive informational indexes, making determinations about the data they contain. Some examination workloads improve the situation with HPC instead of standard figure framework. While some "huge information" errands are proposed to be executed on item equipment in"scale out" engineering, there are sure circumstances where ultra-quick, high-limit HPC "scale up" approaches are favored. This is the space of HPDA. Drivers incorporate a touchy time allotment for examination, e.g. ongoing, high-recurrence stock exchanging or exceedingly complex investigation issues found in logical research.

Chapter 14
A Conceptual Model for Describing the Integration of Decision Aspect into Big Data

Fatma Chiheb
LRDSI Laboratory, Saad Dahlab University, Blida, Algeria

Fatima Boumahdi
LRDSI Laboratory, Saad Dahlab University, Blida, Algeria

Hafida Bouarfa
LRDSI Laboratory, Saad Dahlab University, Blida, Algeria

ABSTRACT

Big Data is an important topic for discussion and research. It has gained this importance due to the meaningful value that could be extracted from these data. The application of Big Data in the modern business allows enterprises to take faster and smarter decisions, achieving a real competitive advantage. However, a lot of Big Data projects provide disappointing results that don't address the decision-makers' needs due to many reasons. The main reason for this failure can be summarized in neglecting the study of the decision-making aspect of these projects. In light of this challenge, this study proposes the integration of decision aspect into Big Data as a solution. Therefore, this article presents three main contributions: 1) Clarify the definition of Big Data; 2) Presents BD-Da model, a conceptual model describes the levels that should be considered to develop a Big Data project aiming to solve a problem that calls a decision; 3) Describes a particular, logical, requirements-like approach that explains how a company develops a Big Data analytics project to support decision-making.

DOI: 10.4018/978-1-6684-3662-2.ch014

INTRODUCTION

We are living in an era where we are witnessing massive and continuous production of data with different formats (videos, images, text, etc.) by users on social media, IoT devices, smart devices, and other sources. We can say that we have entered the era of Big Data, where Big Data has increasingly become an important area for discussion and research. A large number of scientists and researchers of many disciplines have written on this important subject. Big Data has acquired this importance because of the significant value that can be derived from the processing and analysis of this data (Panneerselvam, Liu, & Hill, An Introduction to Big Data, 2015).

Big Data can play a leading role in today's organization's decision-making. Nowadays, there is a popular idea, that Big Data enables businesses to create a powerful foundation for making better, faster, evidence supported, and more reliable decisions (Janeiro & Eduardsen, 2018). Probst et al. (2013) stated that the application of Big Data in modern business provides insights and business intelligence in real-time, such as trends and characteristics of their customers, enabling companies to react quickly and optimize their decision-making processes, which in turn can lead to improved business performance and a competitive advantage (Probst, et al., 2013). Similarly, Kościelniak and Puto (2015) stated that if organizations succeed to incorporate Big Data tools and methods into their businesses to extract the correct and beneficial information from the data, they can support their decision-making to make faster and more adequate decisions leading to cost reduction, development of new products and creation of optimized tenders and emergence of market trends, thus they can create sustainable competitive advantage (Kościelniak & Puto, 2015). For instance, Brynjolfsson, Hitt, and Kim (2011) found that companies that make data-based decisions can lead to a 5-6% productivity increase.

Data is a strategic asset but is worthless if it is not used constructively and appropriately to provide valuable results (Marr, 2015). All today's organizations aim to adopt big data, while little is known about the effective operation of Big Data analytics in business problem solving or decision-making (Akter, Bandara, Hani, Wamba, Foropon, & Papadopoulos, 2019). As a result, a lot of Big Data projects developed by organizations failed or fall short of their objectives. For instance, a survey conducted by Infochimps (2012) indicated that 55% of Big Data projects provide disappointing results, while Gartner warned that 60% of big data projects would fail and be abandoned through 2017 (as cited in (Grover, Chiang, Liang, & Zhang, 2018)).

The literature has shown that the reason these projects fail to produce the desired results lies in the way these projects have been developed since organizations generally focus on data itself and Data Analytics without a focus on decision-making which is the actual use of Big Data. In this context, Taylor (2017) explained that the focus on identifying the required data, the analytical technology to be used, and the workflow without focusing on decision-making per se prevents projects of data mining and predictive analyzes of obtaining the desired value. In another study, Infochimps (2012) explained that the main reason for the failure of Big Data projects was the lack of communication between managers who presented a global vision of the project – a global vision of the decision to be made and the desired information from data analysis – and Big Data analytical team responsible for actually implementing. Besides, the lack of business context around the data and the lack of expertise on business hinder the overall understanding of business, business objectives, and its use in decision support (Infochimps, 2012).

This paper contributes to the current essential need to understand how to develop an effective big data project to support decision-making within organizations. Despite recognizing the vital role of big data in supporting decision-making on the organization, most studies are focusing on technological aspects of big data, neglecting the study of decision aspect which is the actual use of big data. Motivated by this challenge, the main research question the authors address in this paper is the following one: what are the aspects that should be considered in the development of a big data project aiming to solve a decision-making problem in the organization?

In order to answer the research question of this paper, we first need to answer this secondary question: what are the concepts related to Big Data in the literature? And to answer the secondary question, a bibliographic search had to be performed to find the papers that define these concepts, providing theoretical support for the construction of the integrated model proposed in this study. Therefore, the authors thought that a Systematic Literature Review (SLR) methodology is an appropriate and useful approach to make the review process more precise and less biased since the SLR is a means of evaluating and interpreting all available research relevant to a particular research question, topic area, or phenomenon of interest using a trustworthy, rigorous, and auditable methodology (Kitchenham, 2004). Accordingly, the present paper conducted a SLR approach to provide a comprehensive understanding of the concept of big data. As a result, it is found that Big Data cannot be viewed only in terms of data but there are other concepts that should be considered in defining, they are: datasets with new characteristics, data analytics lifecycle, technology, analytical techniques, insight, and decision-making.

Then, this study proposes Big Data with Decision aspect (BD-Da) model. On the basis of the six concepts associated with big data and the results of related studies about the integration of big data and decision-making process, the authors developed the model BD-Da. The model BD-Da divides these concepts to three levels that have to be taken on consideration in the development of a big data project aiming to solve a decision-making problem in the organization. These levels are Data level, Data analytics level, and decision level.

The rest of this paper is organized as follows: Section 2 introduces related works and background information on key concepts related to the study including Big Data, the decision-making process in the organization, and decision modeling. Section 3 illustrates the research methodology followed in order to clarify the concept of Big Data. Section 4 analyzes and interprets the results obtained from the SLR process. Section 5 presents the model BD-Da, while section 6 discusses our proposed model. Finally, in Section 7 we conclude this paper.

BACKGROUND AND RELATED WORKS

Big Data Concept

There is an ongoing increase in the number of publications that address Big Data. For instance, a search performed on Google Scholar for the keyword "Big Data" generated 50 million scholarly works of research in many disciplines within 0.04s. The repeated use of the term Big Data in different contexts has been accompanied by an increase in the number of existent Big Data definitions. As a result, there is no common definition to the term Big Data in the literature, but there are diverse and even often contradictory definitions that describe this term (De Mauro, Greco, & Grimaldi, 2015). This contradiction led to ambiguity and confusion among researchers and practitioners which, in turn, could hinder the effective development of this subject (De Mauro, Greco, & Grimaldi, 2015). For instance, the study Emmanuel and Stanier (2016) explained that the absence of a comprehensive definition of Big Data presents a challenge to their research in developing big data quality dimensions due to the ambiguity about the concept of Big Data, as well as the confusion of Big Data characteristics and data quality characteristics; some Big Data definitions identify characteristics of data quality as the characteristics that distinguish Big Data which make the process of identifying Big Data quality concepts and tools more difficult.

In the literature, there are many studies have attempted to analyze the different definition of big data to provide a clear and concise common definition for this concept that would eliminate ambiguity and reduce confusion related to its usage. Among them:

- Ward and Barker (2013) found that the different definitions of Big Data in the literature cover at least one of the following aspects: size (massive volume of data), complexity of data, and technologies used to handle sizable or complex dataset (tools and techniques).
- Hu, Wen, Chua, and Li (2014) specified three categories of definition that are important to define the different aspects of big data. They are attributive definitions, comparative definitions, and architectural definitions.
- Li, Wang, and Ma (2014) found that the existing definitions of Big Data can be arranged into six categories. The first category focus on the characteristics of the data, the second focus on data analysis technology, the third focuses on the commercial value of data, the fourth focuses on the structure of big data, the fifth focuses on magnitude and source of the data, and some definitions refer to big data as a phenomenon – this latter category of definitions is not prevailing.
- On the basis of a review of the literature on Big Data and the analysis of its previous definitions, De Mauro, Greco, and Grimaldi (2015) stated that there are four main themes associated with Big Data definitions in current literature. They are (1) information: the information created is characterized by 'Volume', 'Velocity' and 'Variety'. (2) Specific technology & (3) Methods are required for Big Data analysis. (4): Impact: extract valuable information from Big Data that impact companies and societies.
- Emmanuel & Stanier (2016) reviewed and discussed the different definitions of big data to provide an alternative definition. As a result, they determined three complementary elements that define the term big data: the data characteristics, Architectures and processing, and Applications of Big Data.

Decision-Making Process in the Organization

Forman and Selly (2001) defined decision-making that it is a process of choosing among alternative courses of action in order to attain goals and objectives. Simon (1960) claimed that the whole process of managerial decision-making is synonymous with managing.

The role of managers in an organization is to make decisions; managers decide whether employees will be assigned or dismissed, sales managers decide discount rates or special pricing plans, and so on. Simon (1960) has classified the different decisions made by managers into two main types of managerial decisions regarding the structure of these problems, namely, programmed and Non-programmed decisions. In addition to those two categories, Gorry and Scott Morton (1971) later defined another class of decisions that comes between programmed and non-programmed decisions, namely semi-structured decision.

- **Programmed Decisions:** this kind of decisions is made to solve routine problems which that are highly structured, well understood, and typically repetitive. These kinds of problem have standard solution methods. The first time the organization encounters this problem, it may need a great effort to make a decision and solve the problem. To resolve the problem for the first time, it requires a systems approach, but as a result of this approach, the problem will have an algorithmic solution that can be applied to find an acceptable solution each time the same problem occurs (Montana & Charnov, 2000).

- **Non-Programmed Decisions:** will be made to solve those problems that are fuzzy, complex, not highly structured, happen infrequently, there are no to routine or systematic procedures to solve them. These decisions could be supported by advanced decision support tools, including Big Data, but could not be automated since the abilities of managers and human intuition is often a basis in decision-making (Montana & Charnov, 2000).

- **Semi-Structured Decision:** the semi-structured problems have some structured elements and some other unstructured elements. Solving a semi-structured problem involves the combination of both standard solution procedures and human judgment (Efraim, 2011).

There is another classification of the managerial decisions based on the organizational levels that make these decisions proposed by Anthony (1965) (as cited in (Efraim, 2011)). Anthony has defined three categories of decisions, namely, strategic, tactical and operational decisions.

- **Strategic Decisions:** are those decisions made at the highest level of management. They are complex, infrequent, and very influential decisions that determine the goals, the purpose, and direction of business organization, and its relation to external environments. These decisions need large numbers of people, time and money. They are usually non-programmed in nature (Montana & Charnov, 2000).

- **Tactical or Administrative Decisions:** these decisions concern the implementation of strategic decisions. They are made by the midlevel managers such as divisional or departmental managers. They are less impactful, more specific and concrete, and more action-oriented than strategic decisions because strategic decisions are applied to all departments within the organization, tactical decisions articulate the objectives of enterprise in a specific departmental manner (Montana & Charnov, 2000).

- **Operational Decisions:** those decisions related to the course of daily operations of the enterprise made on the lowest of management level. These decisions are administrative in nature, taken repetitively, and less risky. They are designed to finalize the tactical decisions. (Montana & Charnov, 2000)

Decision-making is the heart of all managerial functions, and that a rich decision-making process is the basis for the success of enterprise because decision-making is absolutely necessary to gain and maintain a competitive advantage (Forman & Selly, 2001). Literature offers a series of decision-making process models that clearly defined phases of a decision-making process to follow in order to reach a good decision. For instance, Simon (1960) defined a decision-making process involved three phases, they are intelligence, design, and choice phase (the model IDC): (I) intelligence phase refers to searching the environment for conditions, problem or opportunity, calling for decision; (D) Design phase refers to the development and analysis of alternative solutions to the problem or opportunity; (C) Choice phase refers to the selection of one or more of alternatives available. Simon later added a fourth phase, implementation and Monitoring can be considered a fifth phase-a form of feedback (as cited in (Efraim, 2011)).

Having analyzing many models of the decision-making process, the authors have observed that these models are divided into three basic phases: defining the decision, generating and evaluating alternatives, and choosing an alternative or more. Some models include implementation and assessing the choices. These phases correspond to Simon's decision-making process phases, namely, intelligence, design, choice, implementation, and review. The relationship of these models with Simon's model is presented in *Table 1*.

Table 1. The relationship between the model IDC and previous models

Simon (1960)	Intelligence	Design	Choice	Implementation	Review
(Mintzberg, Raisinghani, & Theoret, 1976)	Identification phase	Development phase	Selection phase		
(Courtney, 2001)	• Problem Recognition • Problem Definition	• Alternative Generation • Model development	Choice	implementation	
(Parker & Moseley, 2008)	• State the Decision • Develop Objectives • Classify Objectives into Musts and Wants. • Weigh the Wants most important Wants	• Generate Alternatives • Screen Alternatives through the Musts • Compare Alternatives against the Wants • Identify Adverse Consequences	Make the Best Balanced Choice		Review the Data
(Lunenburg, 2010)	Identifying the problem	• Generating alternatives • Evaluating alternatives	Choosing an alternative	Implementing the decision	Evaluating decision effectiveness
(Negulescu, 2014)	• Defining the problem. • Gathering information	Identifying the alternatives.	• Finding consensus and selecting the alternative. • Foreseeing consequences of the decision.	Implementing the alternative	
(Martin, 2016)	• Change-Needing Situational Analysis (identify situation that require decision) • Challenge Framing and Causal Analysis	Generating Solution Ideas	Choosing a Solution Set	Implementation and Aftermath Planning	
(Litherland, 2017)	• Defining the problem • Identifying and limiting the factors	• Development of potential solutions • Analysis of the alternatives	Selecting the best alternative	Implementing the decision	Establishing a control and evaluation system
(Arndt, 2018)	Identification of problem	• Development of alternatives • Analyze of alternatives	Selection of an alternatives	Implementation of the alternative	Evaluation of decision effectiveness

Decision Model and Notation (DMN) Standard

Big Data provides an unparalleled opportunity for organizations to make faster and smarter knowledge-driven decision. To leverage this opportunity, organization need a deep understanding of these decisions and their requirements to be able to connect the knowledge extracted from big data to their decisions (Decker & Debevoise, 2015). The decision modeling is a powerful technique to represent decisions and their requirements in a clear, concise, and understandable format (Taylor, 2016b). In this context, a new standard has been developed by the OMG, the Decision Model and Notation (DMN) standard for modeling business decisions. Version 1.0 of DMN was released by OMG (Object Management Group) on Dec 2014 (Decker & Debevoise, 2015). The main objective of DMN is to provide an easily understandable common notation for all business users (OMG, 2016).

The decision modeling using DMN standard includes two levels, decision requirements diagrams (DRD) and decision logic, which could be used independently or in conjunction in a decision model (OMG, 2016). DRD comprises a set of elements, and the interrelationship between them. These elements define the decision that will be made, and how it depends on other decisions, policies or regulation (knowledge source), business knowledge (knowledge model) and input data (OMG, 2016). While decision logic specifies the logic used to make individual decisions such as business rules, decision tables, or executable analytic models to allow validation and/or automation of the decision-making processes (OMG, 2016).

Three main uses of DMN can be discerned. It can be used to model human decision and its requirements within an organization using a DRD, model the requirements for automated decision-making, or implementing automated decision-making (OMG, 2016).

Decision Requirements modeling can be used to model any decision whether it is a strategic, tactical or operational decision, as long as this decision worth modeling. If a decision is dynamic, the way of making this decision change often, there is a wide set of alternatives solution to choose from, many policies or regulations to apply, or if it bases upon a lot of data then this decision worth modeling (Taylor, 2016b).

Big Data-Driven Decision-Making Models

While the use of big data tends to improve the decision-making which helps organizations to make better decisions, the integration of big data analytics into the decision-making process within organizations remains a challenge (Akter, Bandara, Hani, Wamba, Foropon, & Papadopoulos, 2019). In the literature, the authors found that there are relatively few studies that have tried to meet this challenge and integrate big data into the decision-making process.

Poleto, de Carvalho, and Costa (2015, 2017) proposed an integrated model combines the elements necessary to apply the Big Data concept during the phases of the decision-making process. Their model is based on the integration of Big Data, Business Intelligence (BI) and the Decision Support System (DSS) with the model IDC. They explained that the model IDC could be supported by analyzing Big Data using BI tools to provide business information that support decision-makers to make better decisions. While a DSS may be implemented to predict the most adequate solutions among the alternatives proposed to solve the problem.

In another study, Elgendy and Elragal (2016) proposed a framework called "B-DAD Framework". The B-DAD framework integrates Big Data tools, architecture, and analysis into the model IDC. To evaluate and demonstrate their framework, they performed a study in the area of retail. Their goal was to identify promotional products, when they should be offered, and to study the influence of social media using rational data (collected from the POS and ERP system) and social media data (collected from Facebook).

Turet and Costa (2018) also proposed a decision-making model based on the analysis of large amounts of data to support public security decision-making to reduce the number of crimes in the region. Their paper is based on studying a real scenario in a police department in the northeast of Brazil- where there is a continuing need to take action to reduce the number of crimes in the region - and proposes a model for decision-making based on analyzing large amounts of data. Their proposed model includes three main steps: data acquisition, data management, and decision-making process. This model proposes the collection and analysis of large amount of data to identify the areas with the highest number of crimes, identify types of crimes, propose alternative courses of action to reduce crime in the area, set criteria to evaluate the alternatives, use multi-criteria methods to evaluate the alternatives and chose the most appropriate one to implement.

Based on a SLR and qualitative studies, Akter, Bandara, Hani, Wamba, Foropon, and Papadopoulos (2019) have identified six interrelated and iterative key steps that provide a clear and helpful guide to employ BDA in decision-making: define the problem or the decision that is expected to be addressed by big data analytics, review relevant past findings and context to avoid replication and pitfalls, select the variables and develop the model that represent the problem, collect all relevant data from different sources to measure and test the model, analyze the data to gain insights, take actions on the problem based on the insights gained from big data.

Another study proposed a new decision-making process model (Chiheb, Boumahdi, & Bouarfa, 2019) that integrates big data into the phase of the model IDC.

Our study is another attempt to propose a solution that assists managers to take advantage of the power of Big Data to create opportunities to resolve a specific organizational problem. This study proposes a model defines three aspects namely: data aspects, data analytics aspect, and decision aspects. Our study focuses on defining these aspects, including decision aspect which was excluded in big data projects. To define the decision aspect in our model, the authors resorted to two key elements, namely: the decision-making process and decision-modeling using the extended model and notation oDMN+. Some studies provide cogent illustrations of the contribution of decision modeling to correctly framing the problem and identifying the right data analysis models that will be built in data analytics level.

For instance, Taylor (Taylor, 2016a, 2017) have harnessed decision modeling using DMN standard with CRISP-DM methodology to strengthen their data analytics projects. They have proposed developing a decision requirements model in the first phase of CRISP-DM methodology, which is Business Understanding phase, to frame their analytic requirements. Thus, they ensure a clear understanding of the business and an effective start-up of the project. The new DMN-based approach has helped the analytical team revitalize previously unsolvable projects due to the erroneous beginnings of these projects that led to a misunderstanding of their objectives. The use of DMN provided a common language between the business client and the analytics team. It allows teams to understand the context around a decision such as the objectives or metrics that are affected by the decision, input data, knowledge sources, and other decisions are needed to make the decision.

Another study (Horita, Albuquerque, Marchezini, & Mendiondo, 2017) argued that decision modeling using DMN standard is not enough to model decision in a Big Bata context. Horita, Albuquerque, Marchezini, and Mendiondo explained that DMN succeeded to represent the connection between decisions and the information required, however it failed to represent the connection between the information and the data sources that provide this information. They stated that the data created nowadays is provided from different sources and at any time new data sources could appear, therefore the organization relies on Big Data to make their decisions need to identify the various possible sources of data that can provide the information required for these decisions. To addressee this need, they developed the extended model and notation oDMN+ based on DMN standard. Their extended model and notation oDMN+ allows describing the connection between decision-making, the information required and the different data sources that could provide the information needed to support these decisions. They argued that the use of oDMN+ in a case study showed that their contribution has allowed decision-makers to find the most useful data sources that provide more accurate information for particular decisions and thus speed up these decisions. It also helped them to find alternatives data sources that can be adopted to meet the requirements of the decision-makers.

The main difference between this study and the previous studies is that this study is the only one between these studies that aimed to define the concept of Big Data from a decision-making perspective. In this context, this study defines and organizes the different aspects of Big Data that should be considered in order to develop a Big Data project aiming to solve a problem that calls a decision. This study proposed a model that describes Big Data aspects, the whole concepts that constitute each aspect, as well as the relationship between them. Besides the concepts associated with Big Data in the literature, new concepts are proposed about Big Data with a Decision Aspect (BD-DA), in particular, the concept of decision aspect: decision, decision model, alternative, and the choice. Defining decision aspect allows framing correctly the decision that will be made and the business information desired from data analytics.

Furthermore, this study describes a particular, logical, requirements-like approach to develop a big data analytics project to support decision-making. Unlike the previous studies that only emphasized the importance of recognizing the problem and properly framing the problem to make smart and sufficient decisions, our study proposed decision modeling using oDMN + as a technique to provide strong support for this step as it will support collaboration and communication between decision-makers and big data experts.

RESEARCH METHODOLOGY

To provide an overview of existing definitions associated to the term "Big Data" in the literature, this study followed a SLR approach following the process proposed by (Kitchenham, 2004) and applied by many studies such as (Akter, Bandara, Hani, Wamba, Foropon, & Papadopoulos, 2019). As part of the process, we developed a protocol that specified the research questions, search strategy, inclusion and exclusion criteria, data extraction, and synthesis of studies.

In order to discuss and clarify the definition of Big Data in the literature and provide a clear definition of the different aspects of big data. This work investigates the following research question: what are the concepts related to Big Data in the literature?

Our search started on March 26, 2019 and ended on April 24, 2019. The first step in the search strategy is the definition of the literature sources. Scopus is considered as a good starting point since Scopus is the largest abstract and citation database of peer-reviewed research literature. It covers more than 24,600 active titles from more than 5,000 international publishers (Elsevier, 2017). Thus, it provided a comprehensive overview of the world's scientific research output across all disciplines.

Having defined literature sources, the authors applied a search process that consists of search criteria construction and manual selection process.

This process sought to identify the literature that includes the different definitions of big data in the literature and the existing studies that attempted to studies these definitions. At first, the authors identified relevant publications by forming a search string that returns the articles including the keywords "big data definition (s), definition(s) of big data, define(s/ing) big data" in (title, keywords, or abstract) of the article. This search string returned 126 results. We limited the results to the articles and conferences papers that are written in English, a total of 93 papers were identified. After that, in the Manual selection process, we read the abstracts, to choose the relevant papers, if it is not clear from the abstract; we read a part of the text or the full text of each of the resulting papers. The inclusion/exclusion criteria used to select each paper is: If the paper is a peer-reviewed paper that contains an explicit definition of big data, include it, otherwise exclude it. At this stage, 10 papers not found were excluded while 83 papers were downloaded and reviewed: among them, 17 papers did not meet the eligibility criteria were excluded, and 66 papers were included. After that, 08 additional articles have been added through going backward by reviewing the interesting references cited in the included papers. These additional papers have been included since they meet the eligibility criteria: peer-reviewed journal or conferences papers that are written in English, the paper provides at least one explicit definition to the term big data. At the end of the search process phase, we had a final list of 74 papers and 86 different definitions.

While this review focuses on the definitions of big data in the literature, the 65 articles, which were defined throughout the papers selection process, have been read in whole or in part. All the explicit definitions of Big Data mentioned in these articles have been extracted and organized into a three-column table (reference of definition, definition, the concepts included in the definition). All these definitions are studied one by one to define the concepts included in them. As a result, we found that the definition of big data related to six concepts. Each definition includes at least one of them, namely: datasets with new characteristics, data analytic lifecycle, technology, analytical techniques, insight (Value), and impact (decision-making).

ANALYSIS AND INTERPRETATION

In this section, the authors analyze and interpret the results obtained from the SLR process to clarify big data definition and determine the different aspects of big data.

Drawing on analyzing a non-exhaustive list of existing Big Data definitions that were found and the results of previous works that attempted to explain the definition for the term Big Data, the authors noticed that the term Big Data was defined from different perspectives. Some definitions were proposed by academic researchers and others were proposed by relevant companies such as IBM, Microsoft, Oracle, Hadoop, etc. With different points of view, there was a variance between these definitions that were similar in some elements and differ in others. Sometimes, the same paper had to give different definitions to the term Big Data to provide a clear and comprehensive definition. In this context, Hu, Wen, Chua, and Li (2014) stated that it was almost impossible to reach a consensus on the definition of Big Data, therefore, the use of many definitions to define the term "Big Data" was a logical choice where each definition focuses on a specific aspect.

The result of our study shows that the term Big Data is frequently associated with six concepts where each definition includes at least one of them. They are: datasets with new characteristics, data analytic lifecycle, technology, analytical techniques, insight (value), and impact (decision-making).

- **Datasets with new characteristics:** a category of definitions emphasized the new characteristics of data compared to traditional data. The year 2001 is considered as a major milestone in the definition of Big Data when Laney described three essential dimensions of Big Data: volume, velocity, and variety (as cited in (Ylijoki & Porras, 2016)). The model 3Vs extended to the model 4Vs, 5Vs, 6Vs, and 7Vs. IBM proposed model 4Vs by adding veracity as the fourth V of Big Data; the model 3V was extended to the 5Vs model by adding value and veracity; another study has extended the model 3Vs by adding Veracity, Variability, and Visualization to define 6Vs model; while there are two alternatives of the 7Vs model: 3Vs with Veracity, Validity, Volatility, and

Value; and the second 7Vs model includes 3Vs with Value, Veracity, Variability, and Complexity (Emmanuel & Stanier, 2016). Emmanuel and Stanier (2016) discussed these extended models where they explained that the model 3V was widely accepted as a definition of Big Data, whereas the extended models were contentious because they cause confusion between the attributes of Big Data, and other elements of data that are associated with data quality and data management and they are not elements uniquely descriptive of Big Data. The 5 Vs, which includes veracity and value with Volume, Variety, and Velocity, is the most extension used in literature (Emmanuel & Stanier, 2016). In this study, this study adopts the 4 Vs approach proposed by IBM that includes: Volume, Variety, Velocity, and Veracity, while Value is not considered as a character of Big Data. We give a definition of these elements below.

- **Volume:** the characteristic the most associated with Big Data that distinguishes Big Data from traditional data, it considers the high size of data generated every day by machine and human sources (Schroeck, Shockley, Smart, Romero-Morales, & Tufano, 2012).IBM reported that 2.5 quintillion of data are created each day (IBM, n.d).

- **Velocity:** considers the speediness of data production, processing and analyzing (Schroeck, Shockley, Smart, Romero-Morales, & Tufano, 2012). For instance, IBM reported that every 60 seconds, there are 72 hours of footage uploaded in YouTube, 216,000 Instagram posts, and 204 million of email sent (IBM, n.d). As well as, Data processing and analysis of data demand real-time results generation.

- **Variety:** focuses on the diversity of data sources and the diversity of data type created (Schroeck, Shockley, Smart, Romero-Morales, & Tufano, 2012).Organizations need to handle different types of data, including structured data such as traditional database systems; semi-structured such as XML data; and unstructured data such as text, images, web data, sensor data, audio, video, and so on. In this context, IBM reported that 90% of generated data was unstructured data and that 80% of data came in the format of videos, images, and documents (IBM, n.d.).

- **Veracity:** focuses on the quality of data associated with certain types of sources. The quality of data is related to the degree of reliability of this data. Organizations make their decisions based on analysis results of some uncertain and inaccurate data such as sentiment and truthfulness in humans, weather conditions, and economic factors (Schroeck, Shockley, Smart, Romero-Morales, & Tufano, 2012). For instance, IBM reported that 1 in 3 of business leaders don't trust the information which they use to make decisions (IBM, n.d.). Despite the uncertainty in the data, it can't be ignored because it stills contains valuable information.

- **Data analytic lifecycle:** some definitions linked Big Data to the process of collection, storage, processing, and analyzing data to gain value from this data. In this sense, the study (Ward & Barker, 2013) stated that Big Data is mainly associated with two ideas: data storage and data analysis.

- **Technology:** another category of definitions emphasized the need for new technological tools that enable the collection, storage, processing, and analyzing of these amounts of data since the traditional data management technologies are unable to deal with the characteristics of Big Data.

- **Analytical techniques:** there is a category of definitions which focused on that the analyzing of these datasets requires the application of powerful analytical techniques in order to extract information from structured and unstructured data.

- **Insight (Value):** some definitions focused on the hidden value in these large amounts of a wide variety of data, which is considered in some studies as the fifth V of Big Data. Value indicates that there is so much potential and highly useful hidden insight in such a huge volume of data. Ylijoki and Porras (2016) stated that this value is associated with the use of data and is not one of the features that characterize this data since this value has to be extracted from this data by applying analytics. Therefore, it suggested separating data and its usage to remove the ambiguous and incoherency of the definition. It also suggested using the term Big Data insights to describe the value of Big Data. Our study adopts the idea which claimed that the value is not a characteristic of data. While Value is the fundamental feature that gives Big Data this increasing importance (Panneerselvam, Liu, & Hill, 2015). Thus, Value or insight is an integral part of the concepts that define the term Big Data.
- **Impact (decision-making):** Wang, Xu, Fujita, and Liu (2016) stated that the objective of Big Data processing is to exploit knowledge from data for scientific purposes such as: investigating natural phenomena, acquiring new knowledge or correcting existing knowledge by analyzing the data generated from different sources. Or in order to support making intelligent decisions in real-time in Big Data environment (Wang, Xu, Fujita, & Liu, 2016). In this study, the authors define Big Data from a decision-making perspective, thus we focus only on the impact of Big Data on improving the decision-making.

THE MODEL BD-DA: BIG DATA WITH DECISION ASPECT MODEL

BD-Da Model Levels

Our Model BD-Da represents a conceptual model that illustrates the integration of decision aspect into Big Data. Drawing on the six concepts associated with Big Data definitions, the model BD-Da distinguishes three levels of Big Data that have to be considered in order to develop a Big Data project aiming to support a decision-making in organizations. They are: Data level, Data analytics level, and decision level as they are depicted in Figure 1.

- **Data Level:** focuses on defining the datasets that will be used, i.e., the features that characterize Big Data namely 4V, as well as, the different internal and external sources that provide this data.
- **Data Analytic Level:** Big Data hides significant valuable insights that enable decision-makers to make faster and smarter decisions. This level focuses on achieving this insight by collecting, storing, processing, and analyzing these huge amounts of data through the application of powerful analytical techniques and the use of new tools capable of handling Big Data characteristics. Having obtained the desired information, it must be visualized and presented to decision-makers in a structured and understandable format to be exploited at Decision Level.
- **Decision Level:** it acts the decision aspect of Big Data that was excluded in Big Data projects. It focuses on linking the value of Big Data to its actual use which is supporting decision-making. This sight bases on two elements: the model IDC that includes intelligence, design and choice phase; and decision modeling using the extended model oDMN+ standard.

Figure 1. The levels of the model BD-Da

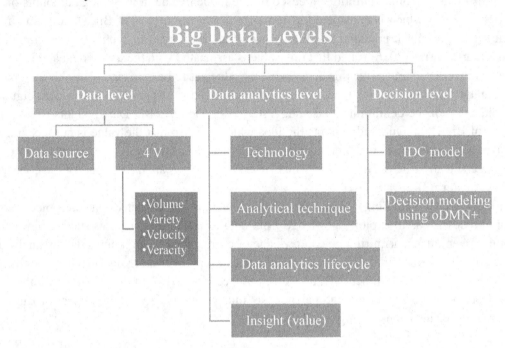

The Model BD-Da: Presentation

Figure 2 represents BD-Da Model. BD-Da Model represents the concept of Big Data based on six concepts, namely: datasets with new characteristics, data analytics lifecycle, technology, analytical techniques, insight, and decision-making. BD-Da categorizes these concepts into three levels that should be considered in order to develop a successful Big Data projects, namely: data level, data analytics level, and decision level. In the following, each component of our proposed model is explained.

Decision Problem

Dietrich, Heller, and Yang (2015) pointed out that starting a Big Data analytics project by collecting and analyzing data without taking sufficient time to understand the objectives and requirements of the project, and framing the correct business problem is a common mistake that is committed in the projects of Big Data analytics. This mistake leads to generate value without impact and fall short of its objectives due to the mismatch between the objective and the available data or misunderstanding of the project's objectives. They also explained that a successful Big Data project starts with understanding the business domain and framing the business problem (correspondent to the Discovery phase of their lifecycle proposed). Framing the business problem of the project means defining the main goals, the needs that have to be achieved in business terms, and the requirements to meet these needs (Dietrich, Heller, & Yang, 2015).

For a Big Data analytics project, which aims to support decision-making within the organization, we can associate the project's problem framing with defining decisions that will be made and their requirements (correspondent to intelligence phase of the model IDC). Consequently, we link the desired insights from Big Data projects to their actual use which is the support of decision-making. Defining decision requirements includes defining the data and the knowledge necessary for this decision, thus defining the data that will be used and the models that will be built in Data analytics level. In this context, the authors propose the modeling of these decisions to better understand these decisions and their requirements from data and data analysis.

Decision Model

In order to clearly define the decision will be made and specify its requirements, we can use DMN standard to model decisions and their requirements. The goal of using DMN in this step is to represent decisions in a clear, simple and unambiguous way and to facilitate communication and collaboration between decision-makers and analytics team.

Figure 2. The model BD-Da

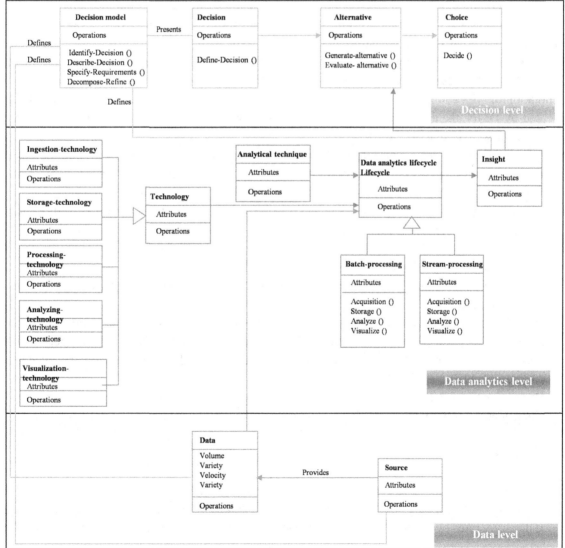

Let's remind that decision requirements modeling can be used to model strategic, tactical, and operational decision in order to describe human decision-making, semi-automate, or automate decisions. In this context, for programmed decision or semi-programmed decision where the goal is to semi-automate or automate this decision, we can use decision logic to describe DRD. For non-programmed decisions, such as strategic decisions that are usually non-programmed in nature, we can develop a DRD and describe it using a natural language or the Semantics of Business Vocabulary and Rules (SBVR) rather than decision logic.

SVBR is a standard published by OMG. Its aim is to formulate a business vocabulary to overcome the ambiguity of the business term, which can then be applied in business rules to be unambiguously and clearly formulated. The formulation of rules in SBVR follows a natural language pattern and is intended more for business than it is for IT which facilitate business transformation independently of IS design. (Hall & Odd, 2018)

The modeling of decision-making process using DMN allows supporting collaboration between decision makers and the analytical team of Big Data and due to the understandable common notation that facilities communication and collaboration between decision-makers and analytics team and allows the good understanding of data and the knowledge desired from Big Data analytics. However, it failed in presenting the connection between the information and the data sources that provided them. While the addition provided by oDMN+ allows filling this gap. The extended model oDMN+ based on DMN standard allows Data sources' modeling. In this context, the authors suggest the use of the extended model and notation oDMN+ to model the decision rather than DMN model because, besides the advantages presented by DMN, the addition provided by oDMN+ allows defining and representing the potential alternatives of sources that provide data.

To develop the decision model using oDMN+, we define four steps. These steps are similar to steps proposed by the reference (Taylor, 2016b) to build decision model using DMN standard. The use of oDMN+ requires adding some necessary modifications to be adapted to oDMN + changes.

The paper (Taylor, 2016b) explained four iterative steps to develop an effective Decision Requirements Model using DMN standard. These steps are:

- Identify the decisions that are the center of interest of this project.
- **Describe Decisions**: name, short description for each decision, and how improving these decisions will influence business.
- **Specify Decision Requirements**: Specify the requirements of decision (information and knowledge) and combine them into a Decision Requirements Diagram. In this step, we need also to identify the different data sources that could provide the input information required because these data source will be modeled using oDMN+.
- **Decompose and Refine the Model:** If a decision needs information coming from other decisions, identify additional decisions needed and describe them and specify their requirements.

Data Sources

We are currently living in an era where data flows intensively and continuously into all areas of our activities. These data can be generated by humans such as emails, researches, documents, log files, and diverse data generated by social media websites; machines such as computer networks, sensors, satellite, mobile phone applications, and prediction of security breaches; or business processes such as transactional data, corporate data, and government agencies data (Aggi & Jain, 2018).

Therefore, in addition to the internal sources of data, today's organizations have numerous and countless external sources, which have the potential to provide new kind of information. The developer model using oDMN + identifies the different source that can provide the data needed for our project.

Data with New Characteristics

Data is the key element associated with Big Data concept. It is the raw material used in producing the business information. This data is created continuously by multiple sources. It differs from traditional data in their characteristics known as 4Vs: volume, variety, velocity, and veracity. Decision model developed using oDMN+ defines the data required that have to be collected and analyzed in our project.

Data Analytics Lifecycle

Organizations need to use information extracted from Big Data to improve their decision-making process. To transform raw data defined by decision model at Decision level into insight exploitable by decision-makers, these data residing in multiples sources have to pass through a sequence of phases known as Big Data lifecycle. These data have to be collected, stored, processed, and analyzed to turn the data into useful and valuable information. Then this information has to be presented in a structured view and displayed to decision-makers to be exploited in making better decisions. In general, there are two processing models for Big Data, namely, batch processing and stream processing (Kolomvatsos & Hadjiefthymiades, 2015). The choice between them depends on the latency that is demanded.

- **The batch processing:** is designed to address the volume of Big Data. It works with data that have already been stored in a storage system over a period of time, ignoring the new data produced once a batch processing has started. It depends on parallel distributed processing system. It provides stability and reliability however it has high latency, so it is not suitable for real-time applications. (Rubén & Muhammad, 2014)
- **Streaming Processing or real-time processing:** is oriented to handle stream data with high velocity using the diskless approach to achieve low latency; stream processing allows acquisition and analyzing the data as they are generated, it allows the processing of data in real time by analyzing sequence of small sets of data that are stored in memory. It works well with the applications that require real-time processing of data streams from heterogeneous sources. (Rubén & Muhammad, 2014)

Generally, the overall Big Data analytics lifecycle can be divided into four main phases (Google Cloud, 2018; Rubén & Muhammad, 2014):

- **Data acquisition (ingestion):** is the process of collecting data from various sources, filtering, and cleaning it before placing it in a data storage system.
- **Data storage:** after the data has been acquired, they need to be stored in order to be processed and analyzed in subsequent phases. Batch processing employs a storage system such as HDFS to store data while stream processing uses in-memory approach.

- **Data analysis:** once the data has been cleaned and stored, in this phase the data is processed and analyzed by applying various models, techniques and algorithms to transform the raw data into actionable information.
- **Data exploitation and visualization:** this phase concerns presenting the information resulting from the analysis in a structured view to decision makers, which facilitates the extraction of knowledge and participation among decision-makers to generate alternatives in decision level.

Technology

The characteristics of Big Data outweigh the ability of classic hardware environments and software tools to handle such high-volume, high-velocity, and high-variety data. Indeed, Traditional data technologies and platforms lack the storage capacity, scalability, flexibility, and performance required to handle Big Data (Oussous, Benjelloun, Lahcen, & Belfkih, 2017). To cope with the complexity of the new data, much work has been carried out to develop new tools that can handle data in an effective way during the different phases of data analytics lifecycle. As a result, a countless number of tools and technologies that offer more flexibility, scalability, and performance have been developed to store, process and analyze such volume of structured and unstructured data (Oussous, Benjelloun, Lahcen, & Belfkih, 2017). Below are examples of Big Data technologies available. They are categorized into five categories: data storage tools, data processing tools, data ingestion tools, data analytics tools, and data visualization tools.

- **Data Storage Tools:** file system such as Hadoop, wide column NoSQL databases systems such as Hbase and Cassandra, document store NoSQL systems such as CouchDB and MongoDB, key-value store NoSQL systems such as Redis, and Graph DBMS NoSQL systems such as Neo4j.
- **Data Processing Tools:** batching processing tools such as: Hadoop MapReduce, Spark, Pig, Hive, etc. Stream processing tools such as: Flink, Spark streaming, Strom, Samza, etc.
- **Data Ingestion Tools:** Batch processing tools such as Sqoop and Chukwa. And stream processing tools such as Flume, Nifi, and Kafka.
- **Data Analytics Tools:** batch processing tools such as Mahout, H2O, and Spark MLlib. And stream processing tools such as SAMOA.
- **Data Visualization Tools:** batch processing tools such as Tableau and Pentaho. And stream processing tools such as Zoomdata.

Analytical Techniques

Big Data value can't be captured by applying the traditional analytical techniques used with small relational datasets. To overcome the limits of traditional techniques and analyze Big Data efficiently, new analytical techniques need to be developed to analyze the new types of data, and traditional once have to be adapted with the volume, velocity and variety of data.

These data analytical techniques include many disciplines that usually interfere with each other (Wang, Xu, Fujita, & Liu, 2016). According to (Aggi & Jain, 2018), the main data techniques of Big Data analytics are: (1) advanced machine learning techniques including classification, clustering, regression, association analyze, graph analyze and decision tree; (2) Advanced statistics analytics techniques; and (3) Advanced data mining techniques. These techniques are applied to analyze the data with new characteristics. They are applicable to text analytics, audio analytics, video analytics, social media analytics, and so on (Aggi & Jain, 2018).

Insight (Value)

Organizations are struggling to process the high-volume, high-velocity, and high-variety nature of Big Data in order to obtain the hidden meaningful value of Big Data (Panneerselvam, Liu, & Hill, An Introduction to Big Data, 2015). This value lies in the insight extracted from Big Data by processing and analyzing the raw data. This insight has the potential to strengthen decision-making in the organization in order to make faster and smarter decision. The insight desired from Big Data project is defined at Decision level by decision model while Data analytics level is responsible for capturing this insight from raw data at Data level.

For instance, the study (Ram, Zhang, Williams, & Pengetnze, 2015) extracted the potential number of asthmatics who will visit the emergency department in a particular area by analyzing emergency department data, Twitter data, Google search data, and environmental sensor data. Another study (Zhang, Zhang, Cheng, & Chen, 2016) succeeded in identifying the high potentials luxury car buyers using car owners and telecom users' data. While the study (Nayak, Pai, & Pai, 2016) was able to predict trends in the Indian stock market daily and monthly through processing news, social media data, and historical price. In another study (Shirdastian, Laroche, & Richard, 2017) used social media data collected from Twitter to derive out the authenticity and sentiments polarity towards the brand "Starbucks". The study (Colleoni, Rozza, & Arvidsson, 2014) also used Twitter data in order to classify users according to their political orientation (Democrats or as Republicans) based on the political content in tweets.

Alternatives and Choices

The creation, development, and analysis of alternative courses of action to solve the decision problem are a significant step in solving decision problem (correspondent to Design phase of Simon's model). The insights resulted from Big Data analytics level support strongly this task. Decision makers rely on new information, their knowledge, and their experiences to propose alternatives courses of action. In addition, the criteria to be used in judging and evaluating each alternative are identified.

After defining alternatives and criteria for evaluation, these alternatives are evaluated to know the impact that will have each one of them on business. To evaluate the alternatives, the reference (Poleto, de Carvalho, & Costa, 2015) proposed the implementation of a DSS to predict the most adequate solutions among the alternatives proposed. While study (Elgendy & Elragal, 2016) stated that Visualization, reporting, information boards, what-if scenarios, and exploratory techniques can be used to evaluate these alternatives. And the study (Turet & Costa, 2018) proposed the use of multi-criteria methods to evaluate the alternatives and chose the most appropriate one.

The choice is to make the actual decision; based on the findings of the evaluation, decision makers choose an alternative or a set of alternatives that will solve the problem to be implemented.

DISCUSSION AND IMPLICATIONS

This research paper derives its significance from the importance of the impact of Big Data on decision-making within organizations. Making adequate and smart decisions is a vital part of the success of any organization. As Big Data has the potential to improve the quality of decision-making within the organization, it is necessary to recognize the concept of Big Data and to apply correctly Big Data within an organization to improve the quality of their decisions. Therefore, this study has important implications practice and research on Big Data-based decision-making within organizations.

In the first place, our study examined a set of definitions of "Big Data" and proposed a set of concepts that define the concept Big Data from a decision-making perspective, that we believe will contribute to clarifying the ambiguity and confusion among researchers and practitioners about the definition of Big Data from a decision-making perspective.

Second, our study suggested that in order to reap the most benefits from Big Data, practitioners and researchers should not only focus on data aspect and data analytics aspect when studying and developing a Big Data project to support decision-making but also go beyond this and study the decision aspect of this project. This is particularly important because the decision aspect allows relating the value extracted from Big Data with its actual use which is decision-making. Therefore, a clear understanding of these decisions, how these decisions will be made, and their requirements of data and knowledge allows framing the correct business problem, thus it gives a strong start to a Big Data project to provide the result desired from decision-makers.

Moreover, this study describes a particular, logical, requirements-like approach that explains how a company develops a Big Data analytics project to support decision-making. Our proposed approach begins with finding, identifying, and formulating the problem that needs to take a decision, then identifies the various requirements from data and knowledge that able to support those decisions and model them using oDMN+. After that, all the required data are then gathered from internal and external sources, stored and managed in an appropriate Big Data storage system (such as HDFS or NoSQL systems), processed, and analyzed to gain new insights. Next, alternative solutions to the problem are developed and evaluated based on the insight extracted. This approach has important practical implications:

First, the collaboration between decision-makers and analysts within organizational decision processes need to be addressed in order to prevent misunderstanding and support the efficacious use of Big Data in decision-making. Our proposed model, basing on decision modeling, is a feasible solution in this regard. The application of our approach to develop a Big Data project aiming to support the decision making can bridge the gap of misunderstanding between domain experts (managers) and analysts. Decision-modeling supports collaboration between decision-makers and the team of analysts due to the understandable common notation that facilities communication and collaboration between them.

In addition, another radically different approach from our proposed approach has recently emerged. It was based on simply collecting a lot of data, then looking for patterns that might provide useful insights that may support decisions—these insights are previously unknown. For example, the proposed framework "B-DAD" depends on this approach (Elgendy & Elragal, 2016). B-DAD framework bases on gathering all sorts of data available, processing, organizing and analyzing to extract whichever information can be brought out of it. Then the decision-makers see how this information can support their decisions that could be unknown beforehand (Elgendy & Elragal, 2016). On the one hand, this approach is considered the big promise and innovation of Big Data Analytics by some people. On the other hand, the collection of a lot of data from multiple data sources available, which tend to know everything without focusing on identifying the useful data that is actually needed to provide necessary business insights for their objectives, is highly inadvisable since this strategy is likely to fail (Marr, 2015). Marr (2015) has argued that it is important to begin a Big Data project with finding, identifying, and formulating the right problem question that a Big Data project was trying to answer. In this context, our requirements-like approach, based on oDMN+ allows companies to better exploit Big Data for providing business real-time insights to help make adequate decisions with optimizing time and price of applying a Big Data project. The model developed explicitly defines the data and data sources to be used, the questions that should be answered, the policies and regulations that will be applied, and data analytics that will be developed to answer these questions. As a result, companies can identify much easier the data needed and unanswered questions in their business to tackle them with Big Data instead of focusing on all data. Collecting, managing, and processing a lot of data has become an increasingly difficult problem in the era of Big Data and can generate lots of answers to things that don't really matter (Marr, 2015).

All the previous studies that were interested in integrating Big Data and decision-making, including our proposed model, begin with identifying the problem and formulating the problem that calls decision-making. In this phase, it is important to differentiate between the problem symptoms and the problem itself. Sometimes, what is considered as a problem (such as lower sales last month) may not be a problem, but symptoms of the problem which is not always easy to differentiate between them and the real problem (Efraim, 2011). The definition of the problem can be determined by monitoring and analyzing internal and external data. In this scope, it is favorable to follow the approach that bases on collecting all the relevant data to bring out whichever information that could define the real problem to identify the problem that calls a decision. Then, we start the application of our requirements-like approach that includes decision-modeling using oDMN+.

Furthermore, we want to point out that we should not ignore the virtues of small data in the era of Big Data. Small data will continue to be a vital part of the research landscape. It has a long history of development across private and public organizations and businesses, with established methodologies and modes of analysis, and a record of producing meaningful answers (Kitchin & Lauriault, 2015). In this context, although that our study focuses on Big Data, our approach described above is also applicable for small data since it provides ingredients that are very useful for a generic approach that defines data as a basis for decision making including small data that could also benefit from the technological evolution resulting from the emergence of Big data.

Ultimately, we present some threats to the validity of our SLR review based on the threats to validity and their influences presented defined by (Zhou, Jin, Zhang, Li, & Huang, 2016). First, one of the main limitations of the review is that we may not have identified all relevant publications for many reasons; the search string used in the automatic search is incomplete, thus, we couldn't identify all relevant publications in the database source used. Besides, library resources used to search for primary studies do not include some important resources databases; it was restricted to Scopus only. However, we combined the method of automatic search and manual search. As a result, new papers were included. These papers were identified by searching the references of included studies. Some of these studies were indexed by Scopus but were not found with the search terms used in the review. A further search-related limitation of the review is that there are some inaccessible or unfound papers that we couldn't download. It is therefore probable that a number of definitions included in these studies were excluded. Although we contacted the authors of inaccessible papers, we couldn't obtain all of these papers. Bias in study selection may be another threat to validity. In this SLR, we developed a protocol that specified the research questions, search strategy, inclusion and exclusion criteria, data extraction, and synthesis of studies. We completely use the inclusion and exclusion criteria for selecting the paper included in this study. The paper selected to be included are only the papers that contain all the inclusion criteria and do not include any of the exclusion criteria predefined.

CONCLUSION

Big Data has become a hot topic that is increasingly attracting researchers' attention in many disciplines due to the valuable knowledge and actionable insight that could be generated. This value has the potential to improve the decision-making process in the organization to make faster and smarter decisions. Therefore, organizations today believe that they have to adopt Big Data to maintain their competitive advantage.

Despite the importance of Big Data in these organizations, according to many surveys, there are a great number of Big Data projects that have fallen short of the objectives desired. There are many reasons for the failure of these projects. We can summarize the main reasons behind the failure of these projects in the way these projects have been developed since they ignored the decision aspect. The main objective of this work is to develop a conceptual model that integrates the decision aspect into Big Data that allows associating the value extracted and its actual use. For the development of this model:

- First of all, the authors worked on understanding the Big Data concept. In this context, we conducted a SLR approach. As a result, we defined six basic concepts associated with Big Data definitions, which are: datasets with new characteristics, data analytics lifecycle, technology, analytical techniques, insight, and decision-making.
- Then, drawing on the concepts associated with Big Data definitions, the authors identified three levels of Big Data that have to be taken into consideration in order to develop a Big Data project aiming to solve a decision problem. They are data level, data analytics level, and decision level. To define decision aspect, the authors resorted to Decision modeling and the model IDC.
- Finally, we developed a conceptual model that is called the model BD-Da. It describes the three levels of Big Data, the constituents of each level and the relationships between them.

Our study provides two main contributions: the first one clarifies and defines the Big Data concept and the second one is to investigate the possibility of integrating Big Data and the decision-making to support decision-makers for making better and faster data-driven decisions.

Ultimately, the limitations of this work should be noted. Our model stills a theoretical model that bases on a theoretical study without applying the proposed model to solve a real decision problem in a Big Data environment. However, this study highlights the three points of view that should be analyzed in order to develop a Big Data project.

REFERENCES

Aggi, M. K., & Jain, S. (2018). survey towards an integration of big data analytics to big insights for value-creation. *Information Processing & Management, 54*(5), 758–790. doi:10.1016/j.ipm.2018.01.010

Akter, S., Bandara, R., Hani, U., Wamba, S. F., Foropon, C., & Papadopoulos, T. (2019). Analytics-based decision-making for service systems: A qualitative study and agenda for future research. *International Journal of Information Management*, *48*, 85–95. doi:10.1016/j.ijinfomgt.2019.01.020

Arndt, H. (2018). *Knowledge discovery and anomalies—towards a dynamic decision-making model for medical informatics* [Doctoral dissertation]. Stellenbosch University.

Brynjolfsson, E., Hitt, L. M., & Kim, H. H. (2011). Strength in numbers: How does data-driven decisionmaking affect firm performance?

Casado, R., & Younas, M. (2015). Emerging trends and technologies in big data processing. *Concurrency and Computation*, *27*(8), 2078–2091.

Chiheb, F., Boumahdi, F., & Bouarfa, H. (2019). A New Model for Integrating Big Data into Phases of Decision-Making Process. *Procedia Computer Science*, *151*, 636–642. doi:10.1016/j.procs.2019.04.085

Colleoni, E., Rozza, A., & Arvidsson, A. (2014). Echo chamber or public sphere? Predicting political orientation and measuring political homophily in Twitter using big data. *Journal of Communication*, *64*(2), 317–332. doi:10.1111/jcom.12084

Courtney, J. F. (2001). Decision making and knowledge management in inquiring organizations: Toward a new decision-making paradigm for DSS. *Decision Support Systems*, *31*(1), 17–38. doi:10.1016/S0167-9236(00)00117-2

De Mauro, A., Greco, M., & Grimaldi, M. (2015). What is big data? A consensual definition and a review of key research topics. In A. I. P. Dans (Ed.), AIP conference proceedings (pp. 97–104). Academic Press. doi:10.1063/1.4907823

Decker, G., & Debevoise, T. (2015, April). Quick Guide to Decision Modeling using DMN 1.0. Signavio, Inc.

Dietrich, D., Heller, B., & Yang, B. (2015). *Data Science & Big Data Analytics: Discovering, Analyzing, Visualizing and Presenting Data*. John Wiley & Sons, Inc.

Efraim, T. (2011). Decision decision-making systems, modeling, and support. Pearson Education India.

Elgendy, N., & Elragal, A. (2016). Big data analytics in support of the decision making process. *Procedia Computer Science*, *100*, 1071–1084. doi:10.1016/j.procs.2016.09.251

Elsevier. (2017). *Scopus Content Coverage Guide*.

Emmanuel, I., & Stanier, C. (2016). Defining big data. *Proceedings of the International Conference on Big Data and Advanced Wireless Technologies*. Academic Press. 10.1145/3010089.3010090

Forest, H., Foo, E., Rose, D., & Berenzon, D. (2014). Big Data, how it can become a differentiator. Deutsche Bank.

Forman, E. H., & Selly, M. A. (2001). Introduction: Management Decision-Making Today. In Decision by objectives: how to convince others that you are right (p. 1). Scientific, World.

Google Cloud. (2018, October 17). *Data Lifecycle*. Retrieved from https://cloud.google.com/solutions/data-lifecycle-cloud-platform

Gorry, G. A., & Scott Morton, M. S. (1971). A framework for management information systems.

Grover, V., Chiang, R. H., Liang, T.-P., & Zhang, D. (2018). Creating Strategic Business Value from Big Data Analytics: A Research Framework. *Journal of Management Information Systems*, *35*(2), 388–423. doi:10.1080/07421222.2018.1451951

Hall, O., & Odd, S. (2018). *Business Decisions or Rules – Why not Both? The Views of Three Decision Modelling Experts*.

Horita, F. E., Albuquerque, J. P., Marchezini, V., & Mendiondo, E. M. (2017). Bridging the gap between decision-making and emerging big data sources: An application of a model-based framework to disaster management in Brazil. *Decision Support Systems*, 97.

Hu, H., Wen, Y., Chua, T.-S., & Li, X. (2014). Toward scalable systems for big data analytics: A technology tutorial. *IEEE Access : Practical Innovations, Open Solutions*.

IBM. (n.d.). *Extracting business value from the 4 V's of big data*. Retrieved from https://www.ibmbig-datahub.com/infographic/extracting-business-value-4-vs-big-data

Infochimps. (2012). CIOs & Big Data: What Your IT Team Wants You to Know. *Infochimps*. Retrieved from http://www.infochimps.com/resources/report-cios-big-data-what-your-it-team-wants-you-to-know-6/

Janeiro, J., & Eduardsen, J. S. (2018). *How can big data affect uncertainty in strategic decision-making?* Aalborg University.

Kitchenham, B. (2004). *Procedures for performing systematic reviews*. Keele, UK: Keele University.

Kitchin, R., & Lauriault, T. P. (2015). Small data in the era of big data. *GeoJournal*, *80*(4), 463–475. doi:10.100710708-014-9601-7

Kolomvatsos, K., & Hadjiefthymiades, S. (2015). An efficient time optimized scheme for progressive analytics in big data. *Big Data Research*, *2*(4), 155–165. doi:10.1016/j.bdr.2015.02.001

Kościelniak, H., & Puto, A. (2015). BIG DATA in decision making processes of enterprises. *Procedia Computer Science*, *65*, 1052–1058. doi:10.1016/j.procs.2015.09.053

Li, T. Z., Wang, S. H., & Ma, J. (2014). Study on Fair Definitions and Application Modes of Big Data. *Applied Mechanics and Materials*.

Litherland, N. (2017, September 26). *Decision-Making Process of Managers*. Récupéré sur bizfluent: https://bizfluent.com/how-does-5280248-decisionmaking-process-managers.html

Lunenburg, F. C. (2010). The decision making process. *National Forum of Educational Administration and Supervision Journal, 27*(4), 12.

Marr, B. (2015). *Big Data: Too Many Answers, Not Enough Questions*. Forbes.

Martin, T. N. (2016). *Smart Decisions: The Art of Strategic Thinking for the Decision Making Process*. Springer. doi:10.1057/9781137537003

Mintzberg, H., Raisinghani, D., & Theoret, A. (1976). The structure of" unstructured" decision processes. *Administrative Science Quarterly, 21*(2), 246–275. doi:10.2307/2392045

Montana, P. J., & Charnov, B. H. (2000). Management Decision-Making: Types and Styles. In P. J. Montana, & B. H. Charnov (Eds.), Business Review Books Management Third Edition (pp. 86-105).

Nayak, A., Pai, M. M., & Pai, R. M. (2016). Prediction models for Indian stock market. *Procedia Computer Science, 89*, 441–449. doi:10.1016/j.procs.2016.06.096

Negulescu, O. (2014). Using a decision-making process model in strategic management. *Review of General Management.*

OMG. (2016, May). Decision Model and Notation (DMN) V1.1 with change bars.

Oussous, A., Benjelloun, F.-Z., Lahcen, A. A., & Belfkih, S. (2017). Big Data technologies: A survey. *Journal of King Saud University-Computer and Information Sciences, 30*(4), 431-448.

Panneerselvam, J., Liu, L., & Hill, R. (2015). An Introduction to Big Data. In B. Akhgar, G. B. Saathoff, H. R. Arabnia et al. (Eds.), Application of Big Data for National Security (pp. 3-13). Elsevier. doi:10.1016/B978-0-12-801967-2.00001-X

Panneerselvam, J., Liu, L., & Hill, R. (2015). *An Introduction to Big Data. In Application of Big Data for National Security* (pp. 3–13). Elsevier. doi:10.1016/B978-0-12-801967-2.00001-X

Parker, J. S., & Moseley, J. D. (2008). Kepner-Tregoe decision analysis as a tool to aid route selection Part 1. *Organic Process Research \& Development, 12*(6), 1041-1043.

Poleto, T., de Carvalho, V. D., & Costa, A. P. (2017). The Full Knowledge of Big Data in the Integration of Inter- Organizational Information: An Approach Focused on Decision Making. *International Journal of Decision Support System Technology, 9*(1), 16–31. doi:10.4018/IJDSST.2017010102

Poleto, T., de Carvalho, V. D. H., & Costa, A. P. C. S. (2015, May). The roles of big data in the decision-support process: an empirical investigation. *Proceedings of the International conference on decision support system technology* (pp. 10-21). Cham: Springer.

Provost, F., & Fawcett, T. (2013). Data science and its relationship to big data and data-driven decision making. *Big Data, 1*(1), 51–59. doi:10.1089/big.2013.1508 PMID:27447038

Ram, S., Zhang, W., Williams, M., & Pengetnze, Y. (2015). Predicting asthma-related emergency department visits using big data. *IEEE Journal of Biomedical and Health Informatics, 19*(4), 1216–1223. doi:10.1109/JBHI.2015.2404829 PMID:25706935

Schroeck, M., Shockley, R., Smart, J., Romero-Morales, D., & Tufano, P. (2012). Analytics: The real-world use of big data. *IBM Global Business Services, 12*, 1–20.

Shirdastian, H., Laroche, M., & Richard, M.-O. (2017). Using big data analytics to study brand authenticity sentiments: The case of Starbucks on Twitter. *International Journal of Information Management.*

Simon, H. A. (1960). The executive as decision maker. *The new science of management decision*, 1-7.

Taylor, J. (2016a). *Bringing Clarity to Data Science Projects with Decision Modeling: A Case Study.* International Institute for Analytics.

Taylor, J. (2016b). *Decision Modeling with DMN.* Decision Management Solutions.

Taylor, J. (2017). *Framing Analytic Requirements.* Decision Management Solutions.

Turet, J. G., & Costa, A. P. (2018). Big Data Analytics to Improve the Decision-Making Process in Public Safety: A Case Study in Northeast Brazil. *Proceedings of the International Conference on Decision Support System Technology.* Academic Press. 10.1007/978-3-319-90315-6_7

Wang, H., Xu, Z., Fujita, H., & Liu, S. (2016). Towards felicitous decision making: An overview on challenges and trends of Big Data. *Information Sciences*, *367*, 747–765. doi:10.1016/j.ins.2016.07.007

Ward, J. S. (2013). Undefined by data: a survey of big data definitions.

Ward, J. S., & Barker, A. (2013). Undefined by data: a survey of big data definitions.

Ylijoki, O., & Porras, J. (2016). Perspectives to definition of big data: A mapping study and discussion. *Journal of Innovation Management*, *4*(1), 69–91. doi:10.24840/2183-0606_004.001_0006

Zhang, H., Zhang, L., Cheng, X., & Chen, W. (2016). A novel precision marketing model based on telecom big data analysis for luxury cars. *Proceedings of the 2016 16th International Symposium on Communications and Information Technologies (ISCIT)* (pp. 307-311). IEEE.

Zhou, X., Jin, Y., Zhang, H., Li, S., & Huang, X. (2016). A map of threats to validity of systematic literature reviews in software engineering. *Proceedings of the 2016 23rd Asia-Pacific Software Engineering Conference (APSEC)* (pp. 153-160). Academic Press.

This research was previously published in the International Journal of Information System Modeling and Design (IJISMD), 10(4); pages 1-23, copyright year 2019 by IGI Publishing (an imprint of IGI Global).

Chapter 15
Toward a Conceptualization of Big Data Value Chain:
From Business Problems to Value Creation

Rim Louati

https://orcid.org/0000-0003-1905-153X

University of Sfax Higher Institute of Business Administration, Tunisia

Sonia Mekadmi

University of Carthage Institute of Higher Commercial Studies, Tunisia

ABSTRACT

The generation of digital devices such as web 2.0, smartphones, social media and sensors has led to a growing rate of data creation. The volume of data available today for organizations is big. Data are produced extensively every day in many forms and from many different sources. Accordingly, firms in several industries are increasingly interested in how to leverage on these "big data" to draw valuable insights from the various kinds of data and to create business value. The aim of this chapter is to provide an integrated view of big data management. A conceptualization of big data value chain is proposed as a research model to help firms understand how to cope with challenges, risks and benefits of big data. The suggested big data value chain recognizes the interdependence between processes, from business problem identification and data capture to generation of valuable insights and decision making. This framework could provide some guidance to business executives and IT practitioners who are going to conduct big data projects in the near future.

INTRODUCTION

The increasing digitalization of organizations, coupled with the advances in the capabilities of technology, has led to the explosion of data in different formats from various digital sources. The volumes of data amassed by organizations are "big" (McDonald and Léveillé, 2014). According to estimates, the volume of business data, across almost all companies worldwide, doubles every 1.2 years (McKinsey

DOI: 10.4018/978-1-6684-3662-2.ch015

Global Institute, 2012; Chen and Zang, 2014). The volume of data available today is measured in zetta-bytes (ZB) – a measure equal to one trillion gigabytes (GB) and equivalent to the data storage capacity of about 250 billion DVDs (Alharthi *et al.*, 2017). As a consequence, companies in many industries are increasingly interested in how to leverage on these "big data" to draw insights from the various kinds of data available to them and gain an in-depth understanding of the hidden values in order to exploit new opportunities (Tan et al., 2015; Raguseo, 2018). The International Data Corporation (IDC, 2017) fore-casted that "Big data and business analytics worldwide revenues, which reached $49.1 billion worldwide in 2016, are expected to maintain a compound annual growth rate (CAGR) of 11.9% through 2020 when revenues will be more than $210 billion".

Big data is a nascent concept introduced to describe the tremendous quantity of data that requires to be managed in organizations. The proliferation of digital devices such as web 2.0, smartphones, social media and sensors has led to a growing rate of data creation and is driving an increasing need for real-time analytics and evidence-based decisions. Notwithstanding the emerging nature of big Data, the origin of the concept is not new. It was introduced by the Gartner analyst Doug Laney in a research note from 2001 in which he noted: *"While enterprises struggle to consolidate systems and collapse redundant da-tabases to enable greater operational, analytical, and collaborative consistencies, changing economic conditions have made this job more difficult. E-commerce, in particular, has exploded data management challenges along three dimensions: volume, velocity and variety"* (p. 1).

Big data is a new concern for organizations. The objectives of big data initiatives are generally focused on data value (McDonald and Lévéillé, 2014). With big data, firms can extract new insights about their markets, customers and products which are important to innovation. However, as noted by McAfee et al. (2012), businesses are collecting more data than they know what to do with. In this way, managers should define a clear strategy for how to use big data to respond to business problems and support firms' innovation capabilities. The main challenges for ensuring this strategy are both related to the development of skills and a new decision-making culture to turn all this data into a competitive advantage (Raguseo, 2018), and to the establishment of a robust IT architecture that enables acquisition, storage and analysis of very huge data sets (Barton and Court, 2012; Kumar et al., 2013; Wamba et al., 2015).

The purpose of this chapter is to provide an integrated view of big data management. A conceptu-alization of big data value chain is proposed as a research model to help firms understand how to cope with challenges, risks and benefits of big data. Value chain, a concept introduced by Porter (1985), sees an organization as a series of processes and each process adds value to the product or service for their customers (Chou, 2014). Value delivered by actions is therefore a foundation of decision-making. Value chain architecture helps to analyze the sources of value creation by identifying the main activities and processes a firm should perform and how they interact. Miller and Mork (2013) applied Porter's value chain theory into a reference model for big data value creation. However, the model is limited to the big data management process and neglected other processes like big data architecture and business process reengineering.

The purpose of defining an integrated big data value chain is to provide a holistic approach to big data management that begins with the identification of business problems explaining the need to carry out big data projects, and ends with the value creation by generating and leveraging deep customer insights. From the beginning to the end of the value chain, three interrelated processes are positioned which are related to big data management process, big data architecture and business process reengineering. The suggested value chain focuses on the interrelations between strategic, organizational and technological elements in order to extract value from big data. Such a definition is needed for strategic planning and alignment of the elements, and thus should not only be of academic interest, but also have important managerial implications.

Based on a literature review, this paper first describes the big data concept and its dimensions and characteristics, and then proposes a research model conceptualizing the main issues that need to be considered when managing big data. After this discussion, the different components of the big data value chain are described in detail. Finally, the conclusion section and directions for future research are given.

BIG DATA CONCEPT AND DIMENSIONS

The term big data is used to characterize the massive volume of data generated by digital machines and computing devices, cloud-based solutions, business management processes, etc. This volume of data is very difficult to manage using traditional data analysis tools. The importance of big data can be explained by the fact that data are produced extensively every day in many forms and from many different sources. Organizations have now more data to use than ever before. This data may be internal or external, structured or unstructured (Raguseo, 2018). Companies are searching for new technological solutions in order to harness this 'big' quantity of data and therefore to understand patterns of consumer activity and to deliver new business insights.

Laney (2001) suggested that Volume, Variety, and Velocity (or the three V's) are the three dimensions of challenges in data management. The Three V's have emerged as the main characteristics to describe big data (Gandomi and Haider, 2015; Gartner, 2017). *Volume* refers to the size of data. The huge quantity of data currently gathered by organizations is reported in multiple terabytes and petabytes. But the concept of big data goes beyond volume. *Variety* which is the multidimensionality and heterogeneity of data formats and sources, including various types of structured, semi-structured, and unstructured data. *Velocity* is related to the frequency or the speed of data generation and/or analysis and delivery. Drawing on the ubiquity of the Vs definition, others include two additional Vs (5 Vs) namely value and veracity. *Value* highlights the need of creating economic benefits or business value from the available big data. *Veracity* emphasizes the importance of data quality and the level of trust in various data sources (White, 2012; Lee, 2017).

There are also other definitions that stress the role of advanced technologies to enable the capture, storage, management and analysis of big data (Wamba et al., 2015). The term big data designates not only data, but also the tools and techniques used for capturing, analyzing, processing, and managing these massive, complex, and rapidly evolving data sets (Alharthi *et al.*, 2017).

In this way, big data can be defined as a holistic strategy and a set of cost-effective and innovative techniques and technologies to manage the volume, variety, velocity, value and veracity of data in order to get enhanced insights for decision-making and business value creation. Big data requires taking into account the main characteristics of data (the 5 Vs), the desired outcomes from its analysis and the means to achieve those benefits. Big data must bring a chain value for an organization.

CONCEPTUALIZING BIG DATA VALUE CHAIN

Value creation is a challenge for every firm seeking a sustainable competitive advantage. The value added to their product or service plays an important role while business executives are deciding to invest in a vital project. It is therefore necessary to target high value-adding processes within an organization for enhancing the final value delivered to its customers. In that sense, Porter (1985) proposed the value-chain concept, describing an organization as a series of activities and processes that culminate in value creation. Whereas applying value analysis into IT context, Smith and McKeen (2003) identified three stages of generating an IT value in business processes, including identification of potential opportunities for adding value, conversion of those opportunities into effective applications of technology for the process, and realization of that applications for developing IT value (Chou, 2014).

Big data value creation may also be examined through a value chain model. Miller and Mork (2013) adapted Porter's value chain theory for big data management. The aim of this framework was to examine how to bring disparate data together and manage them in an organized process from data capture to valuable information creation that can inform decision making at the enterprise level. Although interesting, the suggested value chain is restricted to the big data management process without taking into account other processes like big data architecture and business process reengineering. Then, we propose an integrated big data value chain, which aims to manage big data across a continuum from business problem identification to value creation. As illustrated in Figure 1, big data value creation model consists of five components: business problem identification, big data management process, big data architecture, business process reengineering, and big data value creation. The suggested big data value chain gets closer to the Smith and McKeen (2003) logic's. The only difference is that the conversion phase has been divided into three processes linked to the management and application of big data technologies. The framework targets simultaneously strategic, organizational and technological aspects related to effective management of big data projects. The individual components of the research model are discussed below.

Figure 1. Big data value chain

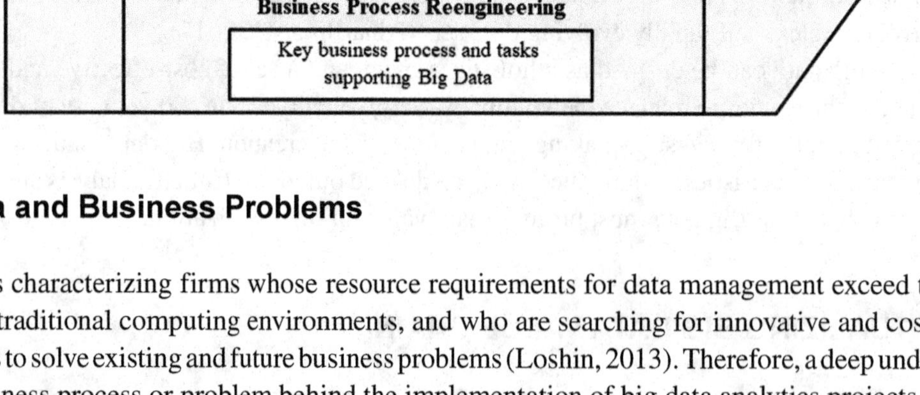

Big Data and Business Problems

Big data is characterizing firms whose resource requirements for data management exceed their capabilities of traditional computing environments, and who are searching for innovative and cost-effective techniques to solve existing and future business problems (Loshin, 2013). Therefore, a deep understanding of the business process or problem behind the implementation of big data analytics projects is the first critical step. Senior management and business stakeholders of the project must set the right expectations about what the management of big data can achieve for their organization, and the possible insights that can be generated from it (Dutta and Bose, 2015).

There are many examples of business problems explaining the need to carry out big data projects in multiple companies belonging to different industries. Besides the giants of the web, like Amazon, Google and Facebook, who are multiplying initiatives to exploit their big data, a significant number of firms, both in traditional sectors and e-commerce, are trying to understand their business needs in order to set targets for achievement in a big data project. The most noteworthy case is the retail sector which is searching to build a culture of customer data-driven decision making. Confronted with the competition of e-commerce, retailers must innovate in stores and rely on big data to cope with online business competitors. All the signs are now leading a strategy of digitalization of the retail outlet and try to mix the digital, the mobile and the store to collect as much information as possible. For a big retailer, the objective is naturally to convert the occasional visitors into customers. Analysis of the behavior is thus crucial to react at best to the abandonments of shopping cart, to bring back the visitor on the site and urge him to convert its visit in act of purchase with a multi-channel approach, whether it is on mobile, in shop, on the Web or via the call center. Hence, big data offer possibilities to track customers during their customer journey, and optimize advertising campaigns and budgets. Technical analysis of customer journeys has become an important feature for retailers, who follow the customer when he or she seeks information, compares products, and ultimately takes the decision to purchase a product and buy it. For example, the number one Retailer in UK "Tesco" has created a powerful data collection engine through the combination of data obtained from loyalty cards, scanners, Web sites, and market research, in order to systematically turn big data into customer insights and insights into business decisions (Leeflang et al., 2014).

Other business problems can be encountered in the financial sector, telecommunications, transport, etc. For instance, credit card companies need to analyze fraudulent behavior with stolen credit cards. Based on this analysis, they can automatically block credit cards that show payment patterns frequently displayed with stolen credit cards, in order to reduce the financial risk for both the customer and the credit card company. Yet another example is Telecommunications companies who are submerged by big data from their call center records. The results of data analysis can help them determine what segments of their market are experiencing particular technical issues, and develop enhanced technical support services targeted to specific demographic segments (McDonald and Lévéillé, 2014). Railway companies can use their own travel data and data provided by navigation systems to provide information to customers on their expected travel time by train and by car. This helps customers make more grounded decisions on their choice of travel mode.

In another instance, the tremendous growth of social media and consumer-generated content on the Internet had impacted hospitality industry. Websites including TripAdvisor.com, and online travel agencies (OTAs) such as Expedia and Travelocity, had allowed consumers to post their ratings and reviews regarding their experiences with hotel properties they have stayed at in the past. Customer reviews reflect the way consumers describe, relive, reconstruct, and share their experiences. Because other consumers are tapping into this information for travel planning purposes, customer reviews can generate a huge impact on travel planning and subsequently attitudes and behavioral intentions. Hotels can indeed apply big data analytic techniques, like text mining approach, to a large quantity of consumer reviews extracted from social websites to deconstruct hotel guest experience and examine its association with satisfaction ratings (Xiang et al., 2015).

One last example is related to airline companies. In airports, every minute counts, including schedules of arrival of the flights: if a plane lands before the ground staff is ready to accommodate it, the passengers and the crew find themselves blocked. If the plane is presented later that envisaged, staff remains seated doing nothing and the costs rise. Also, airline companies have commonly the issue of waiting times for landing with a variation between the estimated hour and the effective hour of landing. In search of a better customer service, those companies must offer the right estimated hour of landing (ETA). They need to collect instantaneously a large set of information by combining the weather conditions data, the schedules of flights, and diverse other factors with data coming from the airplane pilot and radar tracking stations. Big data analytics can allow an airline company to know when its planes are going to land and organizing itself accordingly, saving as a result several costs in every airport (McAfee and Brynjolfsson, 2013).

Note that all examples assume that data-driven customer insights are gaining the most challenge in different businesses such as retail, financial, high-tech, and telecom companies. The same challenge is ubiquitous in every Internet company. Big data allows better planning, and thus to better decision making.

Big Data Management Process

Considering the complexity of big data management, due to its high-volume, high velocity and high variety, initiatives taken by organizations must involve the development of processes and systems designed to capture, examine, store, analyze, visualize and otherwise exploit data from existing systems and databases.

Typically, as shown in Fig. 1, valuable insights and knowledge extracted from big data require the management of a series of stages or sub-processes, beginning with the acquisition of data from one or several sources, and proceeding through steps that include the examination and storage of data, data analysis and modeling, data visualization and the eventual production of statistics, reports and other forms of information (McDonald and Léveillé, 2014; Chen and Zang, 2014). Different challenges are facing firms in each sub-process:

- **Data Acquisition:** Data requirements are different due to different organizations' needs and problems. First, it is essential for a company to understand what information it needs in order to create as much value as possible (Tan et al., 2015). This helps identify data sources and capture the right data. A better management of big data depends on the integration of multiple sources of data, including structured data such as historical business transactions, Internet traffic (e.g., clickstreams), mobile transactions, customer surveys, etc. and unstructured data obtained from social media sources, sensor networks, customer interaction emails, user-generated content, etc. Often, these unstructured data give additional insights that can augment insights generated from structured data. Thus, the accessibility of Big Data sources is on the top priority of the knowledge creation process. Big Data should be accessed easily and rapidly for further analysis (Chen and Zang, 2014).
- **Data Storage and Curation:** It is important for organizations to meet their bulk storage requirements in big data management process for experimental databases, array storage for statistical computations, and large output files (Tan et al., 2015). However, challenges in Big Data storage include data inconsistence and incompleteness, scalability, timeliness, redundancy and data security. The pre-processing of the data is necessary before it is stored to improve its quality and

simplify its authentication, retrieval, reuse and preservation over time. Thus, a number of data pre-processing techniques, including data cleaning, data integration, data transformation and data reduction, can be used to remove noise and correct inconsistencies from datasets (Chen and Zang, 2014). The unstructured data may require going through text tagging and annotation for creation of metadata, using new variables like product, customer, location, etc. This metadata in turn could serve as a dimension of analysis for the structured data (Dutta and Bose, 2015). Hence, a well-constructed data is the prior step to data analysis.

- **Data Analysis and Visualization:** The main characteristic of Big Data is its volume. So, the biggest and most important challenge is analysis of the large amount of data. Data analytics can be used to help managers generate lots of useful information. Analytics is the practice of using and interpreting data to extract insights that can help firms make better fact-based decisions with the ultimate aim of driving strategy and improving performance (Tan et al., 2015). Various data mining techniques can be used on the collected data in order to generate lots of useful information, identify trends in the data and discover underlying reasons explaining the trend. The choice of quantitative modeling technique depends on the type of business problem which is solved as well as the nature of data. For structured data analysis, statistical approaches such as factor analysis, regression, structural equation modeling, etc. as well as machine learning approaches such as decision trees, neural networks, clustering, among others, can be used. For unstructured data analysis, text mining can be used for identification of important concepts and their interrelationships as well as extraction of important reviews and terms related to concepts and analysis of sentiments expressed about these concepts (Dutta and Bose, 2015). Furthermore, data visualization techniques can be used to represent knowledge more intuitively and effectively. Different graphs with both aesthetic form and functionality are necessary to transmit information easily by providing knowledge hidden in the complex and big data sets (Chen and Zang, 2014).

Big Data Architecture

With big data, firms can extract new insights about their markets, customers and products which are important to innovation. However, managers must define a clear strategy for how to use big data to support firms' innovation capabilities. The main challenge for ensuring this strategy is the establishment of a robust IT architecture that enables acquisition, storage and analysis of very huge data sets (Barton and Court, 2012; Kumar et al., 2013; Wamba et al., 2015). Organizations need to use and develop new techniques and technologies to manage volume, variety and velocity of big data that often remain beyond traditional IT capabilities. IT infrastructure is especially required to support the two main sub-processes of managing big data: data storage and data analytics. As shown in figure 2, data storage involves technologies to capture and store data and to prepare and retrieve it for analysis. Data analytics, on the other hand, refer to techniques and technologies used to analyze and make sense from big data (Gandomi and Haider, 2015).

Architecture for Big Data Storage

An efficient accessible architecture is required to the storage and management of large data sets and for achieving availability and reliability of big data. However, the rapid growth of data has restricted the capability of existing storage technologies to manage big data. Even though traditional database systems

Figure 2. Big data architecture

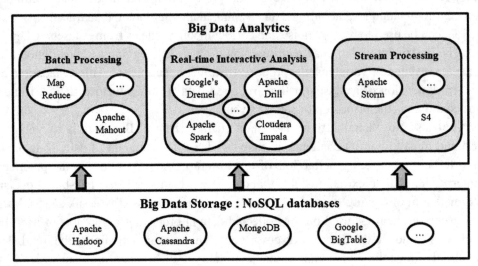

are able to handle the Volume associated with Big Data, they are inadequate when dealing with the Variety and Velocity of Big Data (Madden 2012, Dutta and Bose, 2015).

Generally, traditional storage systems are utilized to store data through structured Relational Database Management Systems (RDBMS) (Hashem et al., 2015). For example, a data warehouse is a popular relational database system that is used to store and manage large-scale datasets. The data warehouse is Standard Query Language (SQL) based database system which is mainly responsible to store structured data that is sourced from the operational systems. Although some Big Data analytic platforms, like SQL stream and Cloudera Impala, still use SQL in their database systems, because SQL is more reliable and simpler query language with high performance in stream Big Data real-time analytics, the most popular big data architectures use NoSQL database, also called "Not Only SQL", to store and manage unstructured data or non-relational data for large and distributed data management and database design (Chen and Zang, 2014; Self and Voorhis, 2015).

The most famous used NoSQL database is Apache Hadoop which is an open-source Software framework written in Java that allows the distributed processing of large datasets across clusters of commodity. Hadoop provides high reliability and a high fault tolerance to applications by maintaining multiple working copies of data and redistributing the failed node (Tian and Zhao, 2015). Its scalability is enhanced by the parallel and fast processing of petabytes of data (Lam, 2010; Tan et al., 2015). The most significant feature of Hadoop is that the storage system is not physically separated from the processing system. Other NoSQL implementations include Apache Cassandra, MongoDB, Google BigTable, etc.

It should be noted that big data utilizes distributed storage technology based on cloud computing rather than local storage attached to a computer or electronic device. Big data analysis is driven by using virtualized technologies like Hadoop clusters. Virtualization is a process of resource sharing and isolation of underlying hardware to increase computer resource utilization, efficiency, security and scalability. Therefore, cloud computing not only provides facilities for the computation and processing of big data but also serves as a service model for minimizing infrastructure maintenance cost (Hashem et al., 2015).

Architecture for Big Data Analytics

Big data analytics is a new research paradigm that can help organizations to analyze a mix of structured, semi-structured and unstructured data in search of new business insights. A diverse set of analytical tools can be used to transform large data sets containing a variety of data types into valuable information and then action. The analytical findings enable companies to understand business environment, customer needs, competitors, strategic stakeholders, market characteristics, products and more generally to predict future trends from the data and make more informed business decisions (Aiden and Michel, 2014; Xiang et al., 2015).

There are an increasing number of tools and platforms developed to optimize the time of processing on distributed databases and make sense of Big Data. Current technologies for big data computing can be divided into three categories, namely, batch processing technologies, real-time interactive analysis technologies and stream processing technologies (Chen and Zang, 2014; Tian and Zhao, 2015):

- **Batch Processing Technologies:** Batch processing is the execution of frequently used programs ("jobs") with minimum human interaction. Jobs can run to completion without any manual intervention. Batch process jobs are designed so that all input data are pre-defined through scripts or command-line parameters. A job takes a set of data files as input, processes the data, and produces a set of output data files. The input data are collected into *batches* or sets of records and each batch is processed as a unit. The output is another *batch* that can be restated for computation. Batch processes are used when a real-time response is not critical in data transmission. The files to be transmitted are gathered over a period and then sent together as a batch. The major benefit of batch processing is the ability to share computer resources between users and programs and shift job processing time to other resources that are less busy. Most batch processing technologies are based on the Apache Hadoop framework which provides infrastructures and platforms for other analytical Big Data applications, such as MapReduce and Apache Mahout. These systems are built on Hadoop, and have specific usages in different domains like data mining and machine learning;
- **Real-Time Interactive Analysis Technologies:** Nowadays, many organizations need the continuous access and processing of events and data in real time to gain constant awareness and take immediate action. The most important requirement of real-time analysis is the response to user needs in real time. The interactive analysis processes the data in an interactive environment, allowing users to undertake their own analysis of information. The user is directly connected to the computer and so can interact with it in real time. The data can be reviewed, compared and analyzed in tabular or graphic format or both at the same time (Chen and Zang, 2014; Tian and Zhao, 2015). Hadoop does well in processing large amount of data in parallel. However, Hadoop is designed for batch processing, but is not a real-time and high performance tool. In recent years, Open source Big Data systems have emerged to address the need not only for scalable batch processing, but also real-time interactive processing. Google's Dremel, Apache Drill, Apache Spark and Cloudera Impala are the most prominent technologies based on real-time and interactive analysis;
- **Stream Processing Technologies:** When the data volume is large, the requirement for real-time response is high, and the data sources are continuous, the data is considered as a data stream. A data stream is an accumulation of data records that are unbounded in number and time distribution. Data streams are now very common. Log streams, click streams, message streams, and event streams are some examples. Stream processing technologies are designed to process large

real-time streams of data. They enable applications such as real-time trading in financial services, fraud detection, process monitoring, location-based services in telecommunications, ad delivery, real-time searches and analysis of social networks. Actually, there are a few stream processing frameworks. Storm from Twitter and S4 (Simple Scalable Streaming System) from Yahoo! Inc. are two notable ones that are designed for big data streams (Tian and Zhao, 2015). Both frameworks are written in Java but their programming model is different.

To capture Big Data value and benefit their specified purposes, firms need to develop high-level computer architecture for data storage management and data analysis. Big data techniques and technologies are still emerging and will certainly grow much more in the future so that businesses need to wade in or risk being left behind.

Business Process Reengineering

In the last few years, a lot has been written about Big Data either in academic literature or in professional magazines (Gandomi and Haider, 2015; Wamba et al., 2015; Wamba and Mishra, 2017) and also about BPR (Business Process Reengineering), BPM (Business Process Management), and BPI (Business process Improvement) (Anand et al., 2013). However, few research efforts have been done to review and explain the relationship between both concepts. How can they co-exist and how can they be mutually supportive? How could an organization combine them to deliver real business benefits? Big data is expected to help organizations improve substantially their business processes and redefine their business model (Mishra et al., 2016) through BPR (Business Process Reengineering) and BPM (Business Process Management).

Originally pioneered in the early 1990's by Hammer and Champy, BPR is an approach to redesign management by radically transforming core processes, often using Information technology, to enable sustainable improvements and thus successfully create long lasting costumer value (Jha et al., 2016). BPR has been criticized as too risky and too radical. More flexible and less risky than BPR, BPM (Business Process Management) is a business practice that covers techniques and methods aiming at studying, identifying, changing and monitoring business processes to ensure they run smoothly and can be improved over time. It is about to manage performance of existing processes in a smooth and continuous manner rather than removing and replacing them by "perfect processes" at one time.

Companies willing to successfully integrate a Big Data technology will face issues related not only to their information and data architecture but also to how to make their business processes more intelligent. First of all, companies should identify business processes which are using unstructured and semi structured data. They should then determine the critical processes that need to be radically changed in order to release quick wins in the area of business performance improvement and cost reduction undertakings. The way decisions are made has known a fundamental change, by relying on multi-source and semantically enriched data. Traditionally, business processes generate structured data. This kind of data is indeed helpful in solving numerous business issues but when isolated from other data sources, it may improve existing processes that are on the way to become obsolete and unprofitable. Besides, decisions based on these processes overlook unstructured and often external data that, undoubtedly, contain valuable business information which can be analyzed to improve overall performance. The real concern is not to rely on a sole data source overlooking the other ones, but to understand what variety of data is required for analysis and what additional variables will enhance or refine the analytical result. Only in this way, can the organization reach BPR outcomes.

Big data databases are supported by systems which are themselves supported by business processes. Consequently, "Any effort to understand the organizational context from the perspective of big data on the one hand and records retention and disposition on the other should be based on the business process that generated the data in the first place" (McDonald and Lévéillé, 2014, p. 107). There is an obvious relation between big data and business processes. Big data analytics need to be combined with business processes to improve operations and offer innovative services to customers. Business processes need to be reengineered for big data analytics.

Big Data strategy could be utilized as a mean to support reengineering and thus to transform business processes into more intelligent. Based on the Six Sigma tool (Tennant, 2001) for process improvement, Jha et al. (2016) proposed a methodology to develop a Big Data strategy for reengineering. They identified six steps for applying this strategy: data from different sources (internal, external, social media…); key business process supporting the key tasks; key tasks that need to be accomplished to be successful; desired outcome and critical success factors; business initiatives that support the business strategy; and finally, big data strategy.

Reengineering is in turn an imperative step to make Big Data strategy feasible (figure 3). Park et al. (2017) proposed a modeling framework for BPR using big data analytics and goal orientation, called IRIS. This model consists of two parts, business modeling part and big data part. The authors defined a modeling language which helps diagnose as-is processes according to business goals and transform them into to-be processes with insights supported by big data. The model shows why, what and how concretely big data analytics may serve BPR and BPM initiatives.

Figure 3. Relationship between big data and business process reengineering

Big Data Value

"You can't manage what you can't measure!" and *"If you can't measure it you can't improve it!"* These famous and very old management philosophies frequently attributed to both Perter Drucker and Edwards Deming (McAfee and Brynjolfsson, 2013), are more accurate and recent than ever. They represent the key driving force behind the emergence of Big Data solutions.

Not very long ago, companies have been making business decisions based on transactional data stored on relational databases. With the advent of big data, they are using less structured data (weblogs, social media, email, sensors, and photographs) which have more volume, velocity and variety than any data used so far. Even though very useful, they are still characterized by relatively " low value density " especially due to their volume (Gandomi and Haider, 2015). Volume is not Value. Having more data does not mean delivering more customer value. Customer value results from new insights into customers and from building deeper relationships with them. Also, velocity is not value because companies must take action on these insights in order to identify new opportunities which might increase customer engagement and then value creation. The velocity of big data is pushing companies to make real-time decisions. The real value of big data depends heavily on the speed of the company's execution ability.

One of the key factors to survive in today's competitive business context is the ability of firms to extract value from big data so that they can understand their customer behavior trends, customize more their products and accordingly gain meaningful customer insights (Wong, 2012; Tan et al., 2015). If well filtered, deeply mined, analyzed and operationalized on time, big data may reveal a real treasure trove. The main challenge for companies is to have the maturity and the readiness to turn big data into insights, into smart decisions and finally into business value.

To extract value from Big Data, one fundamental step consists of taking a consumer-centric focus. Sophisticated and powerful quantitative tools may be used to switch from big data to customer value. To build long lasting advantage, companies must use big data to answer questions like "what will be the customer's lifetime value?" or "what will prevent a customer from switching out when a competitor offers a better price?" rather than " what price is he willing to pay?" or "what will trigger his next purchase?" Put simply, firms must shift from asking what big data can do for them, to what it can do for customers. Advanced analytic techniques such as Business Intelligence tools, data mining and predictive analytics can help answering these new questions. These tools can turn very large volumes of data derived from many different types and formats, into predictive insights for optimal marketing decision making.

Data is only as useful as it can inform metrics which might be later combined to provide the "ardently desired" insights to managers seeking to understand their customer behavior. For example, Kumar and Reinartz (2006) list marketing metrics in three categories: (1) traditional marketing metrics; (2) primary-customer based metrics; and (3) strategic customer-based value metrics. Notwithstanding their aid in determining the total value that a single buyer could provide a firm, the above-mentioned metrics do not provide much deeper insights about future customer purchasing behavior because they assume that a customer's past buying behavior and future buying behavior will be similar. A complementary metric more accurate to predict the future profitability of a customer is the CLV "customer Lifetime Value" metric (Kumar and Reinartz, 2006; Kumar and Rajan, 2012; Kumar et al., 2013). It is probably the most powerful metric for measuring the true value of a company's customer and for giving weight to customer relationship. This forward-looking metric does not prioritize loyalty over profitability, it rather makes certain whether a consumer is going to be profitable and for how long. It allows firms to learn about the consumer's personal behavior and then to develop personalized initiatives that improve profit and retention. Calculating customer's lifetime value is not a trivial task. It involves an incredible amount of data which need to be thoroughly tracked and analyzed. Big data sets can help calculate CLV and other significant metrics by creating extremely precise pictures that take into account a variety of environmental variables such as demographics.

All key metrics are then brought into a single display called "dashboard", thereby avoiding potential problems such as data overload, disseminated data, managerial biases and lack of transparency and accountability (Pauwels et al., 2009). In big data analytics, reporting the insights gathered from the analysis of large and disparate data sources is the ultimate step of the process. Before big data, dashboard and data visualization offered limited benefits because organizations were unable to access large data sets without applying batch processing which may take sometimes several days. Big data applications make data more accessible for all company's levels and actors including consumers.

CONCLUSION

Today, big data has been recognized by the IT industry and business executives as an opportunity for any organization that knows how to capitalize on it. More and more managers view data as a significant driver of innovation and an important source of value creation and competitive advantage. Firms can use likes, tweets, click streams, videos and other unstructured sources to extract new insights about their products, customers, and markets. The challenge here is to develop new ideas and products or improve customer service processes using several data sources.

Various types of benefits can be gained from the use of big data. Its practice can bring substantial value in such areas as product and market development, market demand predictions, customer experience and loyalty, and operational efficiency (Yin and Kaynak, 2015; Raguseo, 2018). In other words, this new concept adds new value chain to companies by offering them the possibility to get strategic data which are relevant to decision making and action. However, this value may not be easy to be discovered. To get the most out of the big data, firms must identify its value realization processes to manage data holistically from business problem identification and data capture to decision making.

Data volume, variety, velocity and veracity are significant impediments to value creation. So, the paper's primary focus has been on the conceptualization of a big data value chain for helping managers in their quest to take advantage and gain valuable insights from huge sets of data. The paper first defines what is meant by big data by describing its various dimensions. Then, a big data value chain model is proposed by identifying five components: (1) business problem, (2) big data management process, (3) big data architecture, (4) business process reengineering, and (5) big data value creation.

After giving some examples of business problems underlying the need to implement big data projects, this paper lays down a number of challenges that big data management comes across, including the choice of support technologies for big data acquisition, storage, analysis and visualization; the management and improvement of business processes that generate this data; and the setting of appropriate metrics and KPIs to control value creation. The suggested big data value chain recognizes the interdependence between processes, from business problem identification and data capture to generation of valuable insights and decision making. This framework could provide some guidance to business executives and IT practitioners who are going to conduct big data projects in the near future.

To illustrate the usefulness of our research model for business and to better explain the relationships between its components, we can take fund distribution industry as a practical example. Financial Companies operating in fund management industry are facing a fragmented and complex market burdened by the weight of many intermediaries. This causes slow transactions and too many relationships. Moreover, clients or fund buyers, in order to select the most appropriate investment product, they require reliable financial information about products offered by fund promoters. Therefore, there is a need for a global solution to digitalize and enhance the efficiency of the entire fund distribution chain. The main driver here is clients' needs for relevant, accurate and up-to-date information about products. In order to achieve this goal, financial institutions need to ensure the management of a series of big data levels, starting with capture and storage of a wide range of data (static, transactional & historical fund data, fund marketing documentation, etc.) from internal and external data sources like market data vendors and web scraping, and ending with processing and analysis of large amount of data to perform custom analytics from reporting to predictive. For architecture, fund managers can leverage Big Data technologies to make the fund distribution process easier and more efficient. They can first create a central distributed platform for big data storage and dissemination enabling an easy access to fund data for both distributors and investors. They can then use big data analytics tools to help investors, distributors, and fund manufacturers explore fund data to compare and select funds according to multiple criteria. The digital platform could transform fund liability management and support functions like commercial, marketing, legal and risk functions. It could also simplify processes for order execution and support new and optimized straight through processing (STP) transaction placement and management functions in a controlled and streamlined process across the fund distribution chain, addressing thus the transparency challenge raised by new regulations. This initiative will significantly improve customer knowledge and the new investor on-boarding experience, for both the investor and the promoter, in terms of speed, simplicity, and transparency. It will also enable to transform the revenue model by optimizing costs structure and providing added-value distribution services through online monitoring with dashboard and big data analytics technologies.

Looking beyond this research, there is a need for more practical research analyzing challenges to big data within business, as well as a need for organizational culture changes to encourage data-based decision making. Companies need to cultivate a data-driven culture. A culture in which the business is empowered to make better use of data, in which business teams are more autonomous in the ways they use data, and people are aware of how data can be beneficial and how it can lead to new opportunities.

Future studies should be carried out to validate the structure of this conceptual model by testing it among companies belonging to different industries such as financial institutions, retailers, hotels, etc. Conducting case studies in companies who are adopting or willing to adopt big data technologies is necessary in order to understand the dynamics of their adoption and confirm or not the different components of the proposed big data value chain and their eventual interrelationships.

REFERENCES

Aiden, E., & Michel, J. B. (2014). The Predictive Power of Big Data. *Newsweek*. Retrieved from http://www.newsweek.com/predictive-power-big-data-225125

Alharthi, A., Krotov, V., & Bowman, M. (2017). *Addressing barriers to big data*. Business Horizons.

Anand, A., Wamba, S. F., & Gnanzou, D. (2013). A Literature Review on Business Process Management, Business Process Reengineering, and Business Process Innovation. In *Workshop on Enterprise and Organizational Modeling and Simulation* (pp. 1-23). Springer.

Barton, D., & Court, D. (2012). Making advanced analytics work for you. *Harvard Business Review*, *90*(10), 78. PMID:23074867

Chen, Ph., & Zhang, Ch.-Y. (2014). Data-intensive applications, challenges, techniques and technologies: A survey on Big Data. Information Sciences, 275(10), 314-347.

Chou, D. C. (2014). Cloud Computing: A Value Creation Model. *Computer Standards & Interfaces*. doi:10.1016/j.csi.2014.10.001

Dutta, D. & Bose, I. (2015). Managing a Big Data Project: The Case of Ramco Cements Limited. *International Journal of Production Economics: Manufacturing Systems, Strategy & Design*, 1-51.

Gandomi, A., & Haider, M. (2015). Beyond the hype: Big data concepts, methods, and analytics. *International Journal of Information Management*, *35*(2), 137–144. doi:10.1016/j.ijinfomgt.2014.10.007

Gartner. (2017). Big data. Retrieved from http://www.gartner.com/it-glossary/big-data

Hashem, I. A. T., Yaqoob, I., Anuar, N. B., Mokhtar, S., Gani, A., & Khan, S. U. (2015). The rise of "big data" on cloud computing: Review and open research issues. *Information Systems*, *47*, 98–115. doi:10.1016/j.is.2014.07.006

IDC. (2017). Worldwide Semiannual Big Data and Analytics Spending Guide. Retrieved from https://www.idc.com/getdoc.jsp?containerId=prUS42371417

Jha, M., Jha, S., & O'Brien, L. (2016). Combining Big Data Analytics with Business Process using Reengineering.

Kumar, V., Chattaraman, V., Neghina, C., Skiera, B., Aksoy, L., Buoye, A., & Henseler, J. (2013). Data-driven services marketing in a connected world. *Journal of Service Management*, *24*(3), 330–352. doi:10.1108/09564231311327021

Kumar, V., & Rajan, B. (2012). Customer lifetime value management: strategies to measure and maximize customer profitability. In V. Shankar & G.S. Carpenter (Eds.), Handbook of Marketing Strategy (pp. 107-134). Edward Elgar Publishing.

Kumar, V., & Reinartz, W. J. (2006). *Customer Relationship Management: A Databased Approach*. Hoboken, NJ: Wiley.

Lam, C. (2010). *Hadoop in Action*. Greenwich, CT, USA: Manning Publications Co.

Laney, D. (2001). *3D Data Management: Controlling Data Volume, Velocity and Variety, Application Delivery Strategy. Gartner*. Retrieved from http://blogs.gartner.com/doug-laney/files/2012/01/ad949-3D-Data-Management-Controlling-Data-Volume-Velocity-and-Variety.pdf

Lee, I. (2017). Big data: Dimensions, evolution, impacts, and challenges. *Business Horizons*. doi:10.1016/j.bushor.2017.01.004

Leeflang, P. S. H., Verhoef, P. C., Dahlström, P., & Freundt, T. (2014). Challenges and solutions for marketing in a digital era. *European Management Journal*, *32*(1), 1–12. doi:10.1016/j.emj.2013.12.001

Loshin, D. (2013). *Market and Business Drivers for Big Data Analytics*.

Madden, S. (2012). From databases to Big Data. *IEEE Internet Computing*, *16*(3), 4–6. doi:10.1109/MIC.2012.50

McAfee, A., & Brynjolfsson, E. (2013). Le Big Data, une revolution du management. *Harvard Business Review*, (Avril-Mai), 1–9.

McAfee, A., Brynjolfsson, E., Davenport, T. H., Patil, D. J., & Barton, D. (2012). Big data: The management revolution. *Harvard Business Review*, *90*(10), 61–67. PMID:23074865

McDonald, J., & Léveillé, V. (2014). Whither the retention schedule in the era of big data and open data? *Records Management Journal*, *24*(2), 99–121. doi:10.1108/RMJ-01-2014-0010

McKinsey Global Institute. (2012). *Big data: The Next Frontier for Innovation*, Competition, and Productivity.

Miller, H. G., & Mork, P. (2013). *From data to decisions: a value chain for big data. In IT Pro* (pp. 57–59). IEEE.

Mishra, D., Gunasekaran, A., Papadopoulos, T., & Childe, S. (2016). Big Data and Supply Chain Management: A Review and Bibliometric Analysis. *Annals of Operations Research*. doi:10.100710479-016-2236-y

Park, G., Chung, L., & Khan, L. (2017). A Modeling Framework for Business Process Reengineering Using Big Data Analytics and A Goal-Orientation.

Pauwels, K., Ambler, T., Clark, B. H., LaPointe, P., Reibstein, D., Skiera, B., ... Wiesel, T. (2009). Dashboards as a service: Why, how, and what research is needed? *Journal of Service Research, 12*(2), 175–189. doi:10.1177/1094670509344213

Porter, M. E. (1985). *Competitive Advantage: Creating and Sustaining Superior Performance*. New York: The Free Press.

Raguseo, E. (2018). Big data technologies: An empirical investigation on their adoption, benefits and risks for companies. *International Journal of Information Management, 38*(1), 187–195. doi:10.1016/j.ijinfomgt.2017.07.008

Self, R. J., & Voorhis, D. (2015). Tools and technologies for the implementation of big data, In Application of Big Data for National Security (pp. 140-154).

Smith, H. A., & McKeen, J. D. (2003). Developments in practice VII: Developing and delivering the IT value proposition. *Communications of the Association for Information Systems, 11*, 25.

Tan, K.H., Zhan, Y.Z., & Ji, G. Ye F. and Chang, Ch. (2015). Harvesting big data to enhance supply chain innovation capabilities: An analytic infrastructure based on deduction graph. *International Journal of Production Economics*, 1–11.

Tennant, G. (2001). *Six Sigma: SPC and TQM in Manufacturing and Services*. Gower Publishing, Ltd.

Tian, W., & Zhao, Y. (2015). *Big Data Technologies and Cloud Computing*. In *Optimized Cloud Resource Management and Scheduling* (pp. 17–49). doi:10.1016/B978-0-12-801476-9.00002-1

Wamba, F. S., Akter, S., Edwards, A., Chopin, G., & Gnanzou, D. (2015). How 'big data' can make big impact: Findings from a systematic review and a longitudinal case study. *International Journal of Production Economics*, 1–33. doi:10.1016/j.ijpe.2014.12.031

Wamba, F. S., & Mishra, D. (2017). Big data integration with business processes: A literature review. *Business Process Management Journal, 23*(3). doi:10.1108/BPMJ-02-2017-0047

White, M. (2012). Digital workplaces: Vision and reality. *Business Information Review, 29*(4), 205–214. doi:10.1177/0266382112470412

Wong, D. (2012). *Data is the Next Frontier, Analytics the New Tool: Five Trends in Big Data and Analytics, and Their Implications for Innovation and Organisations*. London: Big Innovation Centre.

Xiang, Z., Schwartz, Z., Gerdes, J. H. Jr, & Uysal, M. (2015). What can big data and text analytics tell us about hotel guest experience and satisfaction? *International Journal of Hospitality Management, 44*(January), 120–130. doi:10.1016/j.ijhm.2014.10.013

Yin, S., & Kaynak, O. (2015). Big Data for Modern Industry: Challenges and Trends. *Proceedings of the IEEE, 103*(2), 143–146. doi:10.1109/JPROC.2015.2388958

Chapter 16
Role of Big Data in Internet of Things Networks

Vijayalakshmi Saravanan
University of Waterloo, Canada

Fatima Hussain
Ryerson University, Canada

Naik Kshirasagar
University of Waterloo, Canada

ABSTRACT

With recent advancement in cyber-physical systems and technological revolutions, internet of things is the focus of research in industry as well as in academia. IoT is not only a research and technological revolution but in fact a revolution in our daily life. It is considered a new era of smart lifestyle and has a deep impact on everyday errands. Its applications include but are not limited to smart home, smart transportation, smart health, smart security, and smart surveillance. A large number of devices connected in all these application networks generates an enormous amount of data. This leads to problems in data storage, efficient data processing, and intelligent data analytics. In this chapter, the authors discuss the role of big data and related challenges in IoT networks and various data analytics platforms, used for the IoT domain. In addition to this, they present and discuss the architectural model of big data in IoT along with various future research challenges. Afterward, they discuss smart health and smart transportation as a case study to supplement the presented architectural model.

1. INTRODUCTION

The Internet-of-Things (IoT) concept traces its origins the back to late 90s and it referred to the interoperability of devices using RFID technology. With the explosion of cheap mobile devices with a wide array of sensors, IoT has transformed into a large-scale network of heterogeneous devices that are connected via wired or wireless internet. Today, a widely accepted definition of the modern IoT is "a network

DOI: 10.4018/978-1-6684-3662-2.ch016

infrastructure comprised of interconnected "smart things" having self-healing and self-configuring characteristics. These smart things refer to physical and virtual entities capable of sensing and gathering information, having smart interfaces with interoperability capability using standard communication technologies." (Xu, He and Li, 2014) & (van Kranenburg, 2007)).

This new revolution in terms of IoT has led to a generation of huge volumes of data contributed by billions of devices connected to the internet (Bloem et al., 2013; Tannahill & Jamshidi, 2014; Zikopoulos, Eaton, Deroos, Deutsch, & Lapis, 2012). Recent estimates suggest that several zettabytes (ZB) of data have been created and processed today, a quantity that vastly exceeds the data created and stored since the dawn of human civilization until 2003 (Chen, Mao and Liu, 2014). Naturally, such an explosion in generated data has mandated that Big Data storage, processing, and analytics technologies go hand-n-hand with the IoT, with Big Data tools today being an indispensable backbone for the operation of the IoT.

The creation of the new IoT has opened up new vistas in exploiting the power of information in ways never seen before. Efficient utilization of the massive volume of data generated by industrial sensors can help increase the efficiency of industrial manufacturing processes, while data from smart devices can enhance a wide variety of human experiences ranging from home environmental control to tailored social media content. Further, big data analytics can help governments and businesses make critical decisions and improve policy-making towards economic growth (Cebr, 2016).

The objective of this chapter is to present an overview of big data, its storage and processing which serve as key enablers for IoT applications. We discuss the concept of Big Data along with its importance in IoT, in section 2, followed by the architectural framework of the IoT in section 3. Section 4 covers state of the art techniques used in IoT applications. Afterward, we present two applications of IoT in intelligent transportation networks and healthcare services, as a case study in section 5. These case studies are used to illustrate the power of Big Data technologies coupled with the IoT framework. In section 6, we highlight challenges in the adaptation of Big Data in IoT, along with some future directions. We conclude the chapter in section 7.

2. IMPORTANCE OF BIG DATA INTERNET OF THINGS

This section provides a general overview of Big Data and its usability in the IoT domain. The notion of Big Data trails back to the realization of engines such as; Yahoo and Google and large-scale experiments performed by European Organization for Nuclear Research (CERN) supercollider (Arkady, Perera and Georgakopoulos, 2013). Today, with Cloud technologies, smartphones and massive social media networks, Big Data is a ubiquitous industry worth nearly 125 billion USD.

2.1. Big Data: The Definition

Big Data is usually characterized by five properties, referred to as the 5V's in Figure 1.

2.1.1 Volume

Typically, Big Data means massive volumes of data, usually in terabytes (TB), petabytes (PB), zettabytes (ZB) or more.

Figure 1. Characteristics of Big Data
(Dr. Asif Q. Gill 2012)

2.1.2. Variety

The data consists of a mixture of structured, unstructured and quasi-structured information, drawn from such vastly heterogeneous sources as RFID, web searches, social media, mobile sensors like GPS and accelerometers, high fidelity industrial sensors, video streaming etc.

2.1.3 Velocity

Big Data arrives at varying speeds ranging from milliseconds to days to years and has differing requirements on the speed with which it is to be processed.

2.1.5 Value

Some researchers consider value as a key characteristic of Big Data, with data being considered valuable if useful information (from a business or engineering perspective) can be extracted from large data sets where individual data points may not carry any value by themselves.

2.1.6 Veracity

It means accuracy and credibility of data. This becomes increasingly relevant when large numbers of users in the IoT may be reluctant to report truthful data due to privacy and security concerns.

2.2. IoT Landscape and Scope of Big Data

The explosive growth of the IoT landscape and the subsequent creation of large-scale cyber-physical-human networks has made Big Data tools critical to every IoT application. Data generated from devices were already big even before the arrival of IoT. Now, this data is projected to double every two years to reach an estimated 35 ZB (zettabytes) with more than 50 billion estimated devices by the year 2020. Figure 2 shows the exponential increase in the data generated from the IoT with the number of connected devices according to data from the McKinsey Global Institute. The factors driving more devices to join the IoT is clear: larger computing power (cloud computing) with lower cost, extensive wireless connectivity, and ease of low-power sensing.

Figure 3 shows the Gartner Hype Cycle for emerging technologies in 2014, revealing IoT to be among the most disruptive technologies in this decade and predicting the subsequent emergence of Big Data motivated by the extensive integration of IoT into everyday life. Today, big data is a disruptive technology and have the potential to create a potential for personal analytics and human-machine interaction that has never been encountered before. However, Big Data technologies must surmount several key barriers including standards, security and privacy, efficient storage and analysis and network infrastructure. In the following lines, we discuss the current state-of-the-art and associated challenges in processing, storage, and Big Data analytics, in the context of its role as a key enabler of IoT.

Figure 2. Availability of Data on Internet of Things
(Source: McKinsey Global Institute Analysis)

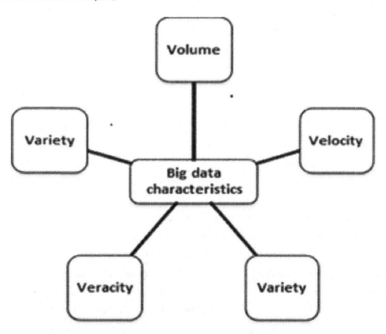

Big data architecture for IoT applications is important in the sense that it provides a reliable data-handling scheme, capable of being scaled and adapted by any type of infrastructure. Figure 4 depicts the three main high-level tasks that must be accomplished by the Big Data architecture.

Figure 3.

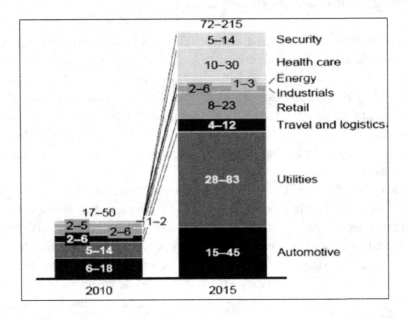

- Data Collection

In the IoT paradigm, data is acquired from various resources such as the internet, social media, mobile sensors, RFID etc. as well as conventional database management systems like RDBMS. The volume of data acquired in this manner is in accordance with Moore's law (Forsth, 2012; Kurzweil & Grossman, 2005).

- Data Management

Several powerful Big Data technologies like MapReduce and NoSQL used to retrieve data effectively from heterogeneous sources and process it according to application needs

- Data Utilization

The processed data is mined using various learning techniques and is used to infer applicable information, which can be visualized and applied for prediction and analysis.

Figure 5 shows a sample of Big Data architecture for IoT (Figueiredo, 2015). In such typical architecture, data is collected from heterogeneous sources that may be unstructured is sent through streaming processed where it is processed, eventually becoming structured as it moves through the architecture. At this stage, the data is extracted for analytics, queries or visualization. Its complexity is characterized by various factors such as; available input and outputs and correlation among them, and the timescales involved (Suh, 2005; Xu, Wang, Bi, & Yu, 2014; Bi & Lang, 2007; Bi, Lang, Shen, & Wang, 2008; Bi & Zhang, 2011). Any Big Data architecture for IoT applications must possess the following characteristics (Figueiredo, 2015; Cecchinel et al., 2014).

3.1. Characteristics of Big Data in IoT Applications

3.1.1. Flexibility and Scalability

The architecture must be able to handle heterogeneous data from a variety of sources, as well as different data scales ranging from TB to ZB in terms of data volumes.

3.1.2. Reconfigurability

The architecture must, preferably, be remotely reconfigurable when deployed in on-site locations.

3.1.3. Interfacing

The architecture must support easy interfacing of devices both to retrieve data for analytics and visualization as well as for data collection. Heterogeneous devices such as smartphones, medical imagining devices, and implants, automotive sensors etc. must be an interface for IoT applications.

3.1.4. Storage

Efficient storage of data is critical for fast feature extraction and correlation studies to identify interrelated data. In the context of IoT, this is crucial to extract user preferences to provide value-added services such as product suggestions.

3.1.5. Batch Processing

This is essential to analyze large quantities of data quickly and efficiently.

3.1.6. Visualization

For some IoT applications, such as industrial process control, effective data visualization will provide operators with the ability to make better decisions in critical time-frames.

3.1.7. Reliability

A good architecture must be tolerant of human error, hardware failure, and data inaccuracies.

3.2. Task Models

The efficient implementation of Big Data architectures that can handle the rapidly growing volume of data also requires new task models that address the following challenges.

Figure 4. Big Data and IoT: High-Level Architecture
(Designed by the authors)

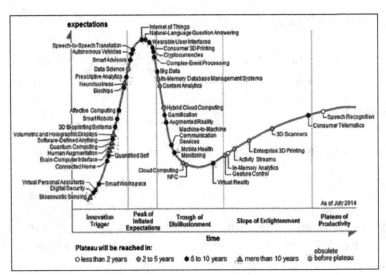

3.2.1. Task Parallelism

This refers to the breaking down of the non-sequential program segments into multiple tasks that are simultaneously executed on multiple cores. Due to the overheads associated with parallel programming languages, the complexity of parallel processing code increases. This calls for new architectural models and programming languages for task parallelism that reduce these overheads.

3.2.2. Data Parallelism

This refers to the simultaneous execution of a function on all elements of a dataset using multiple cores. With large and highly distributed datasets, the computational time for this operation increases due to the overhead associated with the need to distribute the code across many nodes for parallelized implementation. This calls for new ways to process data in parallel. The introduction of the Hadoop MapReduce programming model is one step in this direction.

To enable real-time IoT applications meeting the above architectural requirements, new big data techniques must be developed (Taylor, 2013). In the following sections, we will describe these techniques in more details

3.3. Architectural Challenges for Big Data in IoT

Though Big Data and associated tools/ technologies have been used for predictive analysis for many years (Earley, 2014), now it is facing many challenges because of new requirements of data storage and analytics of heterogeneous and massive volume of data generated from IoT devices. Advanced Big Data tools and techniques are being developed to sense and store data after being gathered from various IoT applications, adapting effectively to the dynamic nature of IoT enterprises. Many researchers have discussed the technical and architectural challenges associated with Big Data tools (Assuncao, Calheiros,

Figure 5. Typical Big Data Architecture for IoT Applications
(Source: Figueiredo, 2015)

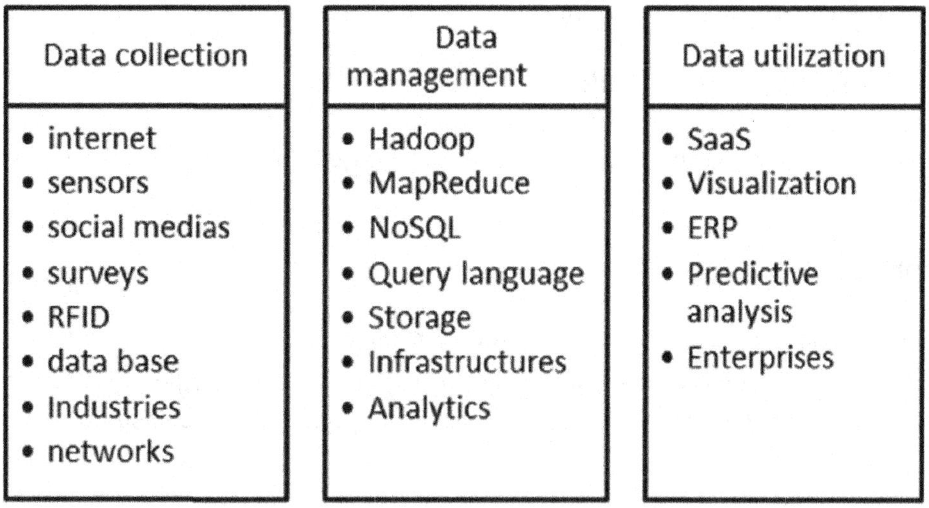

Data collection	Data management	Data utilization
• internet • sensors • social medias • surveys • RFID • data base • Industries • networks	• Hadoop • MapReduce • NoSQL • Query language • Storage • Infrastructures • Analytics	• SaaS • Visualization • ERP • Predictive analysis • Enterprises

Bianchi, Netto, and Buyya, 2014); most common challenges for various IoT applications are discussed in Hegeman et al. (2013). Bloem et al. (2013) discuss three main technical challenges - data scalability, data integration and ten core technologies to process data -. Besides the technical challenges presented by these authors, the integration of Big Data tools into IoT applications requires expertise in this domain. Currently, the lack of organization support is also a key challenge in this regard. In addition, lack of skill set and talent required for data analytics. (Forfas, 2014).

According to Moore's law, CPU performance gain doubles every 18 months. Nevertheless, the pace of growth of Big Data volumes has outpaced the processing speed, with the consequences that several architectures challenges lie ahead on the road to using Big Data effectively. The issue of systems being CPU intensive while being poor I/O intensive is a common challenge for both traditional and Big Data architectures. This motivates the need for massively and embarrassingly parallel paradigms. Due to the large volume of data, a variety of formats, representations, and models, I/O parallelism has become the key architecture challenge for Big Data. In recent years, distributed systems like the Hadoop and MapReduce have been widely adopted to address this challenge (Dean & Ghemawat, 2008). However, the use of Hadoop works with an assumption, that data does not share memory on a single machine. To overcome such challenges along with the rapidly growing volume of data, new task models that address both task and data parallelism must be developed.

4. TECHNIQUES AND TOOLS USED IN BIG DATA

A huge amount of data generated by IoT applications poses a critical challenge for high-performance computing industries to develop scalable and, parallelized solutions to process this data. The use of a wide array of techniques like machine learning, graph analysis, statistical analysis, and signal processing in conjunction with classical Big Data programming tools in present-day IoT applications has made it critical for programmers and software engineers to be well versed in a wide array of topics including domain-specific issues and scalable system programming. Scalable programming, distributed storage, parallelized programming, and multi-core execution have become especially relevant due to the need to analyze large volumes of heterogeneous data that go beyond available technologies.

4.1. Big Data Management Tools

In recent years, the following tools have been extensively used for big data processing, storage, and analytics.

4.1.1 MapReduce

Typical tools for MapReduce include Pig, Caffeine, Hadoop, Hive, S4, Kafka, MapR, Acunu, and Flume. Hadoop is the popular tool used nowadays. It supports Java and Python; the most widely used languages. PIG and PigLatin; being dataflow languages are specifically developed and used to simplify this MapReduce process.

4.1.2 Database Management

- **NoSQL:** MongoDB, CouchDB, Cassandra, Redis, BigTable, HBase, Hypertable, Voldemort, Riak, ZooKeeper
  - **HBase:** HBase is a column-oriented database built on HDFS and MapReduce jobs.
  - **BigTable:** It is a distributed, high performance, proprietary data storage system built on the Google file system (Chang et al., 2008).
- **Hive and HiveQL:** Is used to process ad-hoc queries for data in Hadoop. It supports HiveQL, which is like SQL but has comparatively less support than SQL.

4.1.3 Data Storage

HDFS (Hadoop distributed file system), S3 (Simple storage services)
Servers: EC2, Google App Engine, Elastic, Beanstalk, Heroku

4.1.4 Data Processing

R, Yahoo! Pipes, Mechanical Turk, Solr/Lucene, ElasticSearch, Datameer, BigSheets, Tinkerpop

We now examine two of the most popular Big Data processing frameworks, MapReduce and Hadoop, in detail.

4.2. MapReduce

It is a data processing computational framework applied to large datasets by employing distributed algorithms on clusters. This framework comprises user-defined Map and Reduce functions as well as a MapReduce library. Data is processed in parallel using map functions, whose output is sorted and processed by reducing functions. The MapReduce library parallelizes the data processing by breaking it down into smaller chunks that are processed using a master/slave implementation. Typically, the MapReduce framework is implemented in six steps as follows.

Step 1: Read data value from the Hadoop Distributed File Systems (HDFS).
Step 2: Split the task into small tasks.
Step 3: Input key/value pairs to Map function to generate intermediate key/value pairs.
Step 4: From the output of the Map function, identify and send all pairs with the same key to the Reduce function.
Step 5: Sort the input to the reduce function by key.
Step 6: Write the reduced output into the HDFS.

The slave tasks in this setup are processed parallel without communicating with one another. This framework, while allowing for efficient data parallelization, also handles load balancing, data distribution, and fault tolerance. Alternative MapReduce implementations have also been proposed by (Jiang et al. (2010); Chen et al. (2010); Mao et al. (2010b); Ranger et al. (2007b); Talbot et al. (2011) and Yoo et al. (2009)).

Several authors have explored optimization techniques for processing large numbers of datasets using multi-core processors. For example, two such optimization techniques on the Hadoop framework are proposed in Kumar et al. (2013). Several investigations regarding performance of multi-core processors has been done (Gough, Siddha, & Chen (2007); Saha et al. (2007); Boyd-Wickizer et.al. (2008); Zhu, Sreedhar, Hu, & Gao (2007)) and the performance bottlenecks that arise in systems using MapReduce libraries have also been explored (Mao, Morris, & Kaashoek, 2010a). A recent study showed that the Phoenix library results in a better performance than the PThreads used in multi-core processors (Ranger, Raghuraman, Penmetsa, Bradski, & Kozyrakis, 2007a). While some studies have pointed out the limitations of Hadoop implementations in dealing with data that has a high variety (J Dean et al. (2008) and D. Jiang (2014), hybrid architectures have been proposed (A. Abouzeid (2009); D. J. DeWitt (2013)) to overcome these drawbacks. The implementation of these architectures requires efficient processing techniques for structured and graph data.

4.3. Hadoop Model

The Hadoop model was developed to facilitate the parallel processing of large datasets on clusters. The Hadoop model can simultaneously run multiple tasks at a single node, allowing for an efficient multi-core implementation (Haggarty, Knottenbelt, & Bradley, 2009). Typically, a Hadoop model architecture comprises of a Hadoop Distributed File System (HDFS) for data storage coupled with a MapReduce framework for a large-scale data processing. Recently, a new Hadoop model as shown in Figure 6, known as the Hadoop NextGen-MapReduce model, comprising of the following components has been proposed.

4.3.1 Cluster

The cluster is the hardware component of this model, comprising of connected nodes (computers) that are partitioned into racks.

4.3.2 YARN

The YARN comprises three main components as shown in Figure 8, and provides the computational resources (such as processors and memory) that are required for the implementation of the Hadoop NextGen-MapReduce model.

- **Resource Manager:** Every cluster has one Resource Manager which allocates resources to all applications in the system. In other words, the Resource Manager acts as a Master node.
- **Node Manager:** Node Managers are slave nodes used as containers to run client application programs. There are several Node Managers in every cluster and can allocate various resources to the clusters. This allocation is performed on the available cores and the cluster's memory.
- **Client:** The client submits the application program to the Resource Manager to be processed.

4.3.3 HDFS

The HDFS is a distributed file storage system. The development of the HDFS was motivated by the issue of data locality. Locality refers to the scenario where the data to be processed is not located at the same node that processes it, leading to a decrease in parallel processing performance. The HDFS addressed this issue by allowing data to be processed at the same node in which it is stored, leading to increased processing speeds (White, 2009).

4.3.4 Storage

These are alternative storage options like the Simple Storage Service (S3) that may be used by certain applications.

4.3.5 MapReduce

The MapReduce implementation lies in this layer.

One drawback of the Hadoop model is that the Master Node may sometimes become unresponsive to file requests from the client nodes due to the increased number of Meta files in slave nodes, pertaining to additional tasks (Dong et al., 2012).

5. BIG DATA ANALYTICS: IoT APPLICATION CASE STUDIES

Due to advancements in the IoT and sensor technologies, Big Data analytics has become critical to process different data and make effective decisions based on the available information (Lee, Lapira, Bagheri, & Kao, 2013; King, Lyu, & Yang, 201; SAS, 2014). Big data analytics encompasses many analysis tools such as regression analysis, neural networks, cluster analysis and decision trees (Davis, 2014) and refers to analytical techniques and technologies that can handle extreme data models (Bloem et al., 2013). Typically, these techniques differ from classical data analytics techniques in that they combine tools like pattern recognition and machine learning with standard statistical tools. Rapid developments in big date analytics has made it currently possible to efficiently process large volumes of data (Barlow, 2013).

This section discusses Big Data analytics in two IoT application domains - transportation networks and healthcare. Our aim is to illustrate how Big Data can help transform these specific domains. We also provide an overview of related problems and challenges. We do not attempt to compare different approaches. Rather, we seek to highlight the challenges of Big Data analytics in IoT using various sources from literature.

Figure 6. Hadoop Architecture
(http://ercoppa.github.io/HadoopInternals/HadoopArchitectureOverview.html)

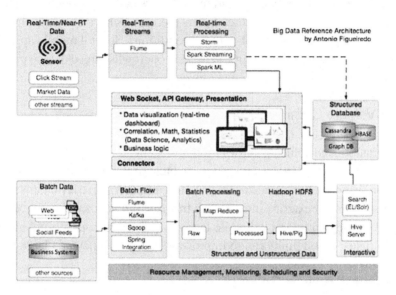

Figure 7. Hadoop NextGen-MapReduce Model
(YARN)(http://ercoppa.github.io/HadoopInternals/HadoopArchitectureOverview.html)

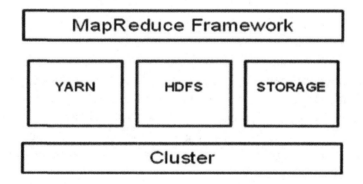

5.1. Smart Transportation System

Every year, traffic jams in the United States alone result in 7 billion wasted man hours and 3 billion gallons of wasted fuel, with an economic cost of over 160 billion USD (Lomax et al., 2015). Further, road crashes cause nearly 1.3 million fatalities and cost 518 billion USD annually (ASIRT, 2016). Increased information about road conditions like hazards and congestion provided to drivers real-time can lead to a more efficient use of the transportation network, minimizing traffic jams and crashes. Today, three main technological advances have contributed to the collection and dissemination of this information to drivers on the road. These technologies will form the cornerstone of future research in IoT-enabled Intelligent Transportation Systems (ITS).

5.1.1 Vehicles as Data Sources

Most vehicles are enabled with GPS systems and most drivers have smartphones, enabled with an array of sensors, connected to the internet. Therefore, drivers themselves have become sources of data that can be processed to extract useful information about road conditions. Several mobile applications like Waze have already successfully used this community-generated or crowdsourced data to provide vehicles with preferred routes and accurate estimates of travel time.

5.1.2 Vehicle-to-Vehicle Communication

The introduction of automated vehicles allows for direct Vehicle-to-Vehicle (V2V) communication of traffic conditions and vehicle data such as engine parameters over wireless networks. With this information, vehicles can jointly prevent or eliminate small-scale (microscopic) traffic jams and avoid collisions at a local level without need for external intervention from the traffic management centers. This frees up the resources of the traffic controllers to handle large-scale (macroscopic) problems like dynamically coordinating traffic lights, speed limits etc. to improve system efficiency at a large-scale level.

5.1.3 Vehicle-to-Infrastructure Communication

Traffic lights and other sensors on the road generate data regularly and communicate this data to traffic management centers. With Vehicle-to-Infrastructure (V2I) communication technology, this data can now be used to directly provide vehicles with useful information about their environment and provide early warning of accidents or other hazardous conditions. This information can then be exchanged among vehicles using V2V communication infrastructure to manage traffic at a microscopic level. Data communicated to a central traffic management center and combined with historical data and weather conditions to predict traffic jams and change traffic light sequences and road signs to reduce system-wide congestion.

The US Department of Transportation (Burt et al., 2014) predicts that volume of connected vehicle data in the United States will be of the order of 10 to 27 petabytes per second, if only Basic Safety Messages (BSM) are transmitted. This highlights the challenge for Big Data analytics in future transportation networks. The following are examples of the types of data will be collected and transmitted over IoT in future ITS.

- **Vehicle-Level:** GPS location, speed, acceleration, braking.
- **Infrastructure-Level:** Traffic light times, number of cars passing through in a time interval (traffic flow), dynamic speed limit settings, traffic density.
- **Ancillary Data:** Weather reports, road conditions, demographics, driver route choices, historical data.

Clearly, this data has high variety as well as volume. Therefore, efficient Big Data architectures must be developed to clean up bad data, eliminate redundant information and store the processed data efficiently for analytics. Several researchers have worked towards addressing this problem. For example, the TransDec (Transportation Decision-making) system was developed by the Integrated Media Systems Center (IMSC) at University of Southern California to efficiently store, analyze and visualize data from the Los Angeles Metropolitan Authority. Figure 8 shows the architecture of the TransDec system. In this architecture, data pertaining to road traffic (e.g., traffic density, traffic flow, road occupancy), public transportation (e.g., GPS locations, delay information), ramp meters and other events (e.g., collisions, casualties, ambulance arrival times) are acquired, aggregated and stored in the Microsoft Azure Cloud Platform (Jagadish et al., 2014). This data is then analyzed using several machine learning techniques to accurately predict traffic evolution patterns in various segments of the network.

5.2. Smart Transportation and Associated Challenges

With the introduction of new sources of data like automated vehicles and ancillary sensors, novel learning techniques that combine local vehicle-level data with system-level data like traffic density maps and road conditions to make accurate predictions about traffic patterns, travel times, likelihood of traffic jams etc. must be developed. The following are specific research directions for Big Data analytics in ITS.

5.2.1 Human-Level Applications and Tailored Services

With data like location and user behavioral patterns gathered from personal mobile devices, it is possible to match users with tailored services that foresee the user's needs at particular times of the day. New service providers can mine user data from social networks, smart home sensors and mobile devices to match users with carpooling or ride-sharing services. From the Big Data analytics perspective, this will require the development of learning algorithms that can derive useful information from multi-modal heterogeneous data that may not necessarily be linked to the user's transportation preferences, like weather data and home sensor data (Burt et al., 2014).

5.2.2 Network-Level Applications and Performance Optimization

While users will derive benefits like targeted transportation services from Big Data enabled ITS, traffic management centers can use this user generated data to improve network performance. In this domain, a key Big Data analytics challenge is in the development of accurate traffic prediction models from dynamic user data, road data and weather conditions. These models can then be used to design traffic light schedules, dynamic speed limits and other network-level controls to optimize network throughput. User route preference data also used to predict congested routes at a particular time and incentivize users to stay off the road at particular times or take routes other than their preferred one to minimize overall network travel time.

5.2.3 Security and Privacy

Some data like user GPS locations may be used by attackers to determine a user's identity (Jagadish et al., 2014). Therefore, data storage mechanisms that protect user privacy will be particularly relevant in

ITS that are powered by crowdsourced data. The collection of large amounts of crowdsourced data also brings the challenge of identifying the veracity of this data, since users may report false data, especially on social networks, to protect their privacy. In this case, the large volume and redundancy of Big Data must be intelligently exploited to develop analytics algorithms that extract useful information by correcting for the errors associated with possibly inaccurate data.

The integration of Big Data analytics will transform ITS as it will contribute to billions of dollars being saved at the network-level and provide a more personalized and improved travel experience at the individual user-level.

5.3. Smart Health Care

In this section, we explore how Big Data and IoT-enabled technologies have drastically transformed healthcare applications to become more efficient. The availability of cheap and portable mobile sensors provides an opportunity for continuous monitoring of vital signs and other functions of the human body. With the next generation IoT technologies, information about a patient's health status will be available 24/7, opening up the potential for timely preventive as well as reactive care. Further, collection of patient data over longer periods of time can enhance diagnosis by providing the ability to study various trends that emerge in the data over time. In this section, we present an overview of IoT-enabled healthcare systems, personalized medicine and disease risk prediction.

Current health care systems use standalone desktops and laptops to capture, store and transfer patient data through an integrated healthcare infrastructure to primary care doctors, specialists and emergency responders. This data, usually referred to as an electronic health record, electronic medical record or personal health record/history (Häyrinen, K., et.al, 2008), usually comprises the medical history of the patient including test results, past ailments, medication provided etc. Today, with the ubiquity of smartphones and other IoT devices combined with easy-to-use mobile applications, this data can further be expanded to reflect daily records of a patient's heart rate, stress levels, blood sugar, sleep activity, blood pressure and other vital signs. Further, a patient's dietary habits (intake of calories), exercise routine and other day-to-day activities can be incorporated to get a more complete picture of the patient's health (Swan, M., 2012).

In Feldman et al. (2012), it is predicted that data generated from healthcare applications will reach 25K petabytes in 2020. This large volume of data collected from various health care systems drives the big data challenges in this domain. Data generated from healthcare applications is typically very heterogeneous ranging from radiology records to daily heart rate trends and vastly differing arrival and processing time scales. While lab test result data is typically available every few months, data from personal patient monitors may arrive every hour or even every minute. Heterogeneity also arises in data storage, where data can be stored in spread sheet applications like Excel, databases and the Hadoop data storage system. Further, while traditional patient electronic health records are structure with tagged name, age and other fields, the vast majority of data available from personal monitoring devices is unstructured or semi-structured. Therefore, this data will first need to be converted to a structured form by a combination of machine learning and data mining techniques. The structured data can then be processed through healthcare software to analyze trends and allow doctors to take preventive action that reduce readmissions to hospitals (Figure 9).

Figure 8. TransDec Architecture
Source: http://imsc.usc.edu/intelligent-transportation.html

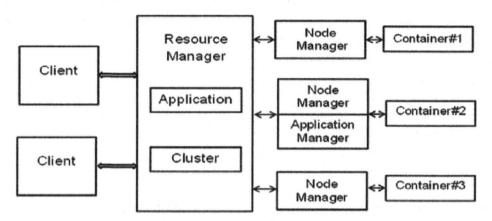

In Islam et al. (2015), the analysis of this data is divided into single-condition and clustered condition analysis. In this framework, single-condition pertains to an individual disease or condition or parameter that is monitored. Examples of single-condition analysis include blood sugar or body temperature monitoring to ensure that these parameters are within desired limits. Clustered-condition deals with predicting trends across several diseases or conditions that are tied together. Preventive healthcare for conditions like heart attacks fall under this category. While single-condition analysis can be carried out locally, clustered-condition analysis requires the analysis of patterns in data collected over a considerable period. A variety of machine learning techniques need to be developed along with efficient parallelized implementations to accomplish this.

5.4 Smart Health and Associated Challenges

We posit that future research in IoT-enabled healthcare will involve the following key directions (Raghupathi et al., 2014).

5.4.1 Evidence-Based Patient-Oriented Personalized Medicine

Patient electronic health records, personal monitoring device data and clinical data will be used to provide personalized healthcare solutions, predict risk of certain health conditions and reduce readmission rates.

5.4.2 Large-Scale Analytics

Analysis of trends across data collected from many patients will be used to identify those at risk of particular conditions or in need of preventive care. These predictive analytics tools can be used for the prevention of chronic disease like diabetics.

5.4.3 Public Health

Rapid analysis of the spread of epidemics will enable faster response and prevent crises by driving accelerated drug discovery and vaccine development.

5.4.4 Genome Analysis

The advent of cost-effective genetic analysis tools will allow genetic data to augment patient profiles in making healthcare decisions.

5.4.5 Security and Privacy

While the benefits of Big Data in the healthcare domain are evident, attention must be paid to the information security and privacy issues that arise with storing and processing patient data. Further, regulatory issues like obtaining permission to use or share certain datasets require careful examination.

With the above-mentioned objectives, big data can revolutionize the healthcare system by supporting more genomics research, changing data into information, support healthcare providers and self-care, increasing general awareness of using integrated communication technologies and expanding the ecosystem to provide efficient healthcare services.

Figure 9. Big data & IoT in healthcare

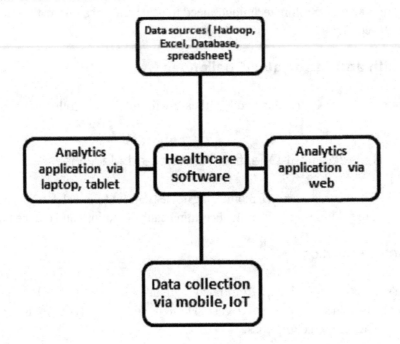

6. CHALLENGES AND FUTURE DIRECTIONS

One area where further research is needed is analysis of a variety of social media platforms that could provide useful insight. Future research can also consider benchmarking social media data to other existing sources of information such as (server logs of web pages). Future researchers can also analyze how traffic statistics change on individual pages. This analysis can serve as a useful further measure of what the public is currently thinking. It can then be benchmarked against the results from social media data analysis.

7. CONCLUSION

IoT has revolutionized the future of infrastructure networks with the proliferation of many internet-enabled devices capable of being interconnected. However, the massive amount of heterogeneous data generated by the IoT has made the storage, processing and analysis of this data very challenging. Naturally, this calls for the inclusion of all those tools and techniques specific for Big Data analysis. This chapter presents a detailed overview of the architectural challenges for Big Data in IoT along with current tools for Big Data analytics, processing and storage. Big Data challenges in IoT are also illustrated via two emerging applications – smart transportation systems and smart healthcare. Although lots of research has been done in this domain but lots of more research and development is required in various categories such as; Big Data computer architecture, advanced storage techniques, I/O and data-driven techniques. Cloud computing, bio-inspired and quantum computing are few to mention.

ACKNOWLEDGMENT

First and foremost, the authors would like to thank "God Almighty". I, Vijayalakshmi Saravanan would like to express my special thanks to the "Schlumberger Foundation Faculty for the Future" (FFTF) who awarded me a Postdoctoral fellowship opportunity, which helped me in doing a lot of research, in the field of Computer Science and Engineering. During this chapter writing, I came to know many new things and innovative ideas in my research field. I am thankful to them. Last but not the least, my sincere thanks to my dear husband, Mohan Radhakrishnan and my beloved parents, G. Saravanan & S. Selvi who supported me a lot throughout the writing process that helped in the successful completion of this chapter. I also thank Sivaranjani S, University of Notre dame, US for the consistent support.

REFERENCES

Abouzeid, A., Bajda-Pawlikowski, K., Abadi, D., Silberschatz, A., & Rasin, A. (2009). HadoopDB: an architectural hybrid of MapReduce and DBMS technologies for analytical workloads. *Proceedings of the VLDB Endowment, 2*(1), 922-933. Retrieved on April 19, 2016 from http://www.vldb.org/pvldb/2/vldb09-861.pdf

Anuganti, V. (2012). Typical "big" data architecture. *Venu Anuganti Blog.* Retrieved on April 4, 2016 from http://venublog.com/2012/11/30/typical-big-data-architecture/

ASIRT. (n.d.). Retrieved from https://asirt.org/initiatives/informing-road-users/road-safety-facts/road-crash-statistics

Assuncao, M. D., Calheiros, R. N., Bianchi, S., Netto, M. A. S., & Buyya, R. (2014). Big Data and clouds: Trends and future directions. *Journal of Parallel and Distributed Computing.* doi:10.1016/j.jpdc.2014.08.003

Atzori, L., Iera, A., & Morabito, G. (2010). The internet of things: A survey. *Computer Networks, 54*(15), 2787–2805. doi:10.1016/j.comnet.2010.05.010

Barlow, M. (2013). *Real-time big data analytics: emerging architecture.* Sebastopol, CA: O'Reilly Media.

Bi, Z. M., & Lang, S. Y. T. (2007). A framework for CAD- and sensor-based robotic coating automation. *IEEE Transactions on Industrial Informatics, 3*(1), 84–91. doi:10.1109/TII.2007.891309

Bi, Z. M., Lang, S. Y. T., Shen, W. M., & Wang, L. (2008). Reconfigurable manufacturing systems: The state of the art. *International Journal of Production Research, 46*(4), 967–992. doi:10.1080/00207540600905646

Bi, Z. M., & Zhang, W. J. (2011). Modularity technology in manufacturing: Taxonomy and issues. *International Journal of Advanced Manufacturing Technology, 18*(5), 381–390. doi:10.1007001700170062

Bloem, J., van Doorn, M., Duivestein, S., van Manen, T., van Ommeren, E., & Sackdeva, S. (2013). *No more secrets with big data analytics.* Retrieved from http://vint.sogeti.com/wp-content/uploads/ 2013/11/ Sogeti_NoMoreSecrets.pdf

Bloem, J., van Doorn, M., Duivestein, S., van Manen, T., van Ommeren, E., & Sackdeva, S. (2013). *No more secrets with big data analytics.* Retrieved from http://vint.sogeti.com/wp-content/uploads/ 2013/11/ Sogeti_NoMoreSecrets.pdf

Burt, M., Cuddy, M., & Razo, M. (2014). *Big Data's Implications for Transportation Operations: An Exploration.* US Department of Transportation White Paper. Retrieved from http://ntl.bts.gov/ lib/55000/55000/55002/Big_Data_Implications_FHWA-JPO-14-157.pdf

Cebr. (2016). *The Value of Big Data and the Internet of Things to the UK Economy.* Cebr Report for SAS.

Cecchinel, C. (2014). An architecture to support the collection of big data in the internet of things. In *2014 IEEE World Congress on Services.* IEEE. 10.1109/SERVICES.2014.83

Chang, F., Dean, J., Ghemawat, S., Hsieh, W. C., Wallach, D. A., Burrows, M., & Gruber, R. E. (2008). BigTable: A distributed storage system for structured data. *ACM Trans. Comput. Syst., 26*(2), 4:1–4:26. Retrieved on April 4, 2016 from http://static.googleusercontent.com/media/research.google.com/en// archive/bigtable-osdi06.pdf

Chen, M., Mao, S., & Liu, Y. (2014). Big data: A survey. *Mobile Networks and Applications, 19*(2), 171–209. doi:10.100711036-013-0489-0

Chen, R., Chen, H., & Zang, B. (2010). Tiled-MapReduce: optimizing resource usages of data-parallel applications on multicore with tiling. In *Proceedings of the 19th International Conference on Parallel architectures and compilation techniques* (pp. 523-534). ACM. Retrieved on April 4, 2016 from http://www.csee.ogi.edu/~zak/cs506-pslc/tiledmr.pdf

Da Xu, L., He, W., & Li, S. (2014). Internet of things in industries: A survey. *IEEE Transactions on Industrial Informatics*, *10*(4), 2233–2243. doi:10.1109/TII.2014.2300753

Davenport, T. H., Barth, P., & Bean, R. (2012). How 'Big Data' is different. *MIT Sloan Management Review*, *54*(1), 22–24. Retrieved from http://www.hbs.edu/faculty/Pages/item.aspx?num=43026

Davis, C. K. (2014). Beyond data and analytics. *Communications of the ACM*, *57*(6), 39–41. doi:10.1145/2602326

Dean, J., & Ghemawat, S. (2008). MapReduce: simplified data processing on large clusters. *Communications of the ACM, 51*(1), 107-113. Retrieved on April 4, 2016 from http://static.googleusercontent.com/media/research.google.com/en//archive/mapreduce-osdi04.pdf

DeWitt, D. J., Halverson, A., Nehme, R., Shankar, S., Aguilar-Saborit, J., Avanes, A., & Gramling, J. (2013). Split query processing in polybase. In *Proceedings of the 2013 ACM SIGMOD International Conference on Management of Data* (pp. 1255-1266). ACM. Retrieved on April 4, 2016 from https://pdfs.semanticscholar.org/3fd5/fdfd1a672a613de8a2b266676f577de9bcf1.pdf

Dong, B., Qiu, J., Zheng, Q., Zhong, X., Li, J., & Li, Y. (2010). A novel approach to improving the efficiency of storing and accessing small files on Hadoop: a case study by PowerPoint files. In *2010 IEEE International Conference on Services Computing* (pp. 65-72). IEEE. Retrieved on April 4, 2016 from http://ieeexplore.ieee.org/xpl/login.jsp?tp=&arnumber=5557216&url=http%3A%2F%2Fieeexplore.ieee.org%2Fxpls%2Fabs_all.jsp%3Farnumber%3D5557216

Dong, B., Zheng, Q., Tian, F., Chao, K.-M., Ma, R., & Anane, R. (2012). An optimized approach for storing and accessing small files on cloud storage. *Journal of Network and Computer Applications*, *35*(6), 1847–1862. doi:10.1016/j.jnca.2012.07.009

Earley, S. (2014). *Big data and predictive analytics: What is new? IT Pro*. IEEE Computer Society.

Feldman, B., Martin, E. M., & Skotnes, T. (2012). Big Data in Healthcare Hype and Hope. *Dr. Bonnie, 360*.

Figueiredo. (n.d.). *Keeping up with Big data*. Retrieved from https://www.linkedin.com/pulse/keeping-up-big-data-antonio-figueiredo

Forfas. (2014). *Assessing the demand for big data and analytics skills 2013–2020*. Retrieved from http://www.forfas.ie/media/07052014- Assessing_the_Demand_for_Big_Data_and_Analytics_Skills- Publication.pdf

Forsyth Communications. (2012). *For big data analytics there's no such thing as too big the compelling economics and technology of big data computing*. Retrieved from http://www.cisco.com/c/dam/ en/us/solutions/data-center-virtualization/big_data_wp.pdf

Franks, B. (2012). *Taming the Big Data tidal wave: Finding opportunities in huge data streams with advanced analytics* (1st ed.). Wiley Publishing. doi:10.1002/9781119204275

Ghemawat, S., Gobioff, H., & Leung, S. T. (2003). The Google file system. *ACM SIGOPS Operating Systems Review, 37*(5), 29-43. Retrieved on April 4, 2016 from http://static.googleusercontent.com/media/research.google.com/en//archive/gfs-sosp2003.pdf

Gough, C., Siddha, S., & Chen, K. (2007). Kernel scalability—expanding the horizon beyond fine grain locks. *Proceedings of the Linux Symposium,* 153-165. Retrieved on April 4, 2016 from https://www.kernel.org/doc/ols/2007/ols2007v1-pages-153-166.pdf

Haggarty, O. J., Knottenbelt, W. J., & Bradley, J. T. (2009). Distributed response time analysis of GSPN models with MapReduce. *Simulation, 85*(8), 497–509. doi:10.1177/0037549709340785

Häyrinen, K., Saranto, K., & Nykänen, P. (2008). Definition, structure, content, use and impacts of electronic health records: A review of the research literature. *International Journal of Medical Informatics, 77*(5), 291–304. doi:10.1016/j.ijmedinf.2007.09.001 PMID:17951106

Hegeman, T., Ghit, B., Capota, M., HIdders, J., Epema, D., & Iosup, A. (2013). *The BTWorld use case for big data analytics: Description, MapReduce logical workflow, and empirical evaluation.* Retrieved from http://www.pds.ewi.tudelft.nl/~iosup/btworld-mapreduce-workflow13ieeebigdata.pdf

Islam, S. M. (2015). The internet of things for health care: A comprehensive survey. *IEEE Access: Practical Innovations, Open Solutions, 3,* 678–708. doi:10.1109/ACCESS.2015.2437951

Jagadish, H. V., Gehrke, J., Labrinidis, A., Papakonstantinou, Y., Patel, J. M., Ramakrishnan, R., & Shahabi, C. (2014). Big data and its technical challenges. *Communications of the ACM, 57*(7), 86–94. doi:10.1145/2611567

Jiang, D., Chen, G., Ooi, B. C., Tan, K. L., & Wu, S. (2014). epiC: an extensible and scalable system for processing big data. *Proceedings of the VLDB Endowment, 7*(7), 541-552. Retrieved on April 4, 2016 from http://www.nus.edu.sg/dpr/files/research_highlights/2015_01Jan_epiC.pdf

Jiang, W., Ravi, V. T., & Agrawal, G. (2010). A map-reduce system with an alternate API for multi-core environments. In *Proceedings of the 2010 10th IEEE/ACM International Conference on Cluster, Cloud and Grid Computing* (pp. 84-93). IEEE Computer Society. Retrieved on April 4, 2016 from http://web.cse.ohio-state.edu/~agrawal/allpapers/ccgrid10.pdf

King, I., Lyu, M. R., & Yang, H. (2013). *Online learning for big data analytics.* Retrieved from http://cci.drexel.edu/bigdata/bigdata2013/ieee.bigdata.tutorial.1.slides.pdf

Kumar, K. A., Gluck, J., Deshpande, A., & Lin, J. (2013). Hone: "scaling down" Hadoop on shared-memory systems. *Proc. VLDB Endow., 6*(12), 1354–1357. Retrieved on April 4, 2016 from http://www.vldb.org/pvldb/vol6/p1354-kumar.pdf

Kurzweil, R., & Grossman, T. (2005). *Fantastic voyage: Live long enough to live forever. Plume.* New York: Rodale Inc.

Lee, J., Lapira, E., Bagheri, B., & Kao, H. (2013). Recent advances and trends in predictive manufacturing systems in big data environment. *Manufacturing Letters, 1*(1), 38–41. doi:10.1016/j.mfglet.2013.09.005

Liu, X., Han, J., Zhong, Y., Han, C., & He, X. (2009). Implementing WebGIS on Hadoop: A case study of improving small file I/O performance on HDFS. In *IEEE International Conference on Cluster Computing and Workshops* (pp. 1-8). IEEE. Retrieved on April 4, 2016 from http://ieeexplore.ieee.org/stamp/stamp.jsp?tp=&arnumber=5289196

Lomax, T., Schrank, D., & Eisele, B. (2015). *Annual Urban Mobility Scorecard.* Retrieved from http://mobility.tamu.edu/ums/

Manyika, J., Chui, M., Brown, B., Bughin, J., Dobbs, R., Roxburgh, C., & Byers, A. H. (2011). *Big Data: The Next Frontier for Innovation, Competition and Productivity.* McKinsey Global Institute. Retrieved on April 4, 2016 from http://www.fujitsu.com/us/Images/03_Michael_Chui.pdf

Mao, Y., Morris, R., & Kaashoek, M. F. (2010). Optimizing MapReduce for multicore architectures. In *Computer Science and Artificial Intelligence Laboratory.* Massachusetts Institute of Technology, Tech. Rep. Retrieved on April 4, 2016 from http://citeseerx.ist.psu.edu/viewdoc/download;jsessionid=F539 BF63A34B2D6D8F9B472F9A007144?doi=10.1.1.186.5309&rep=rep1&type=pdf

Raden, N. (2012). *Big data analytics architecture: Putting all your eggs in three baskets.* Hired Brains, Inc. Retrieved on April 4, 2016 from https://site.teradata.com/Microsite/raden-research-paper/landing/.ashx

Ranger, C., Raghuraman, R., Penmetsa, A., Bradski, G., & Kozyrakis, C. (2007). Evaluating MapReduce for multi-core and multiprocessor systems. In *IEEE 13th International Symposium on High Performance Computer Architecture HPCA 2007* (pp. 13-24). IEEE. Retrieved on April 4, 2016 from http://csl.stanford.edu/~christos/publications/2007.cmp_mapreduce.hpca.pdf

Saha, B., Adl-Tabatabai, A. R., Ghuloum, A., Rajagopalan, M., Hudson, R. L., Petersen, L., & Rohillah, A. (2007). Enabling scalability and performance in a large scale CMP environment. *ACM SIGOPS Operating Systems Review, 41*(3), 73-86. Retrieved on April 4, 2016 from http://leafpetersen.com/leaf/publications/eurosys2007/mcrt-eurosys.pdf

SAS. (2014). *Big data meets big data analytics: Three key technologies for extracting real-time business value from the big data that threatens to overwhelm traditional computing architectures.* Retrieved from http://www.sas.com/content/dam/SAS/en_us/doc/whitepaper1/big-data-meetsbig-data-analytics-105777.pdf

Schaller, R. R. (1997). Moore's law: Past, present, and future. *IEEE Spectrum, 34*(6), 52–59. doi:10.1109/6.591665

Schonlau, M. (2002). The clustergram: A graph for visualizing hierarchical and nonhierarchical cluster analyses. *Stata Journal, 2*(4), 391-402. Retrieved on April 4, 2016 from http://schonlau.net/publication/02stata_clustergram.pdf

Schultz, T. (2013). Turning healthcare challenges into big data opportunities: A use-case review across the pharmaceutical development lifecycle. *Bulletin of the American Society for Information Science and Technology, 39*(5), 34–40. doi:10.1002/bult.2013.1720390508

Suh, N. P. (2005). *Complexity: theory and applications.* Oxford, UK: Oxford University Press.

Swan, M. (2012). Sensor mania! the internet of things, wearable computing, objective metrics, and the quantified self-2.0. *Journal of Sensor and Actuator Networks*, *1*(3), 217–253. doi:10.3390/jsan1030217

Talbot, J., Yoo, R. M., & Kozyrakis, C. (2011). Phoenix++: modular MapReduce for shared-memory systems. In *Proceedings of the Second International Workshop on MapReduce and its Applications* (pp. 9-16). ACM. Retrieved on April 4, 2016 from http://csl.stanford.edu/~christos/publications/2011.phoenixplus.mapreduce.pdf

Tannahill, B. K., & Jamshidi, M. (2014). Systems of systems and big data analytics – bridging the gap. *Computers & Electrical Engineering*, *40*(1), 2–15. doi:10.1016/j.compeleceng.2013.11.016

Taylor, J. (2013). *Delivering customer value faster with big data analytics*. Retrieved from http://www.fico.com/en/wp- content/secure_upload/DeliveringCustomerValueFasterWithBigDataAnalytics.pdf

Think Big Analytics. (2013). *Big data reference architecture*. Retrieved on April 4, 2016 from http://thinkbiganalytics.com/leading_big_data_technologies/big-data-reference-architecture/

van Kranenburg, R. (2007). *The Internet of Things: A Critique of Ambient Technology and the All-Seeing Network of RFID*. Amsterdam: Institute of Network Cultures.

Viégas, F. B., Wattenberg, M., & Dave, K. (2004). Studying cooperation and conflict between authors with history flow visualizations. In *Proceedings of the SIGCHI Conference on Human Factors in Computing Systems* (pp. 575-582). ACM. Retrieved on April 4, 2016 from http://alumni.media.mit.edu/~fviegas/papers/history_flow.pdf

Vijayalakshmi, S., Anpalagan, A., Kothari, D. P., Woungang, I., & Obaidat, M. S. (2014). An analytical study of resource division and its impact on power and performance of multi-core processors. *The Journal of Supercomputing*, *68*(3), 1265–1279. doi:10.100711227-014-1086-0

White, T. (2009). *Hadoop: The definitive guide* (1st ed.). O'Reilly Media, Inc. Retrieved on April 4, 2016 from http://ce.sysu.edu.cn/hope/UploadFiles/Education/2011/10/201110221516245419.pdf

Whitepaper. (2012). *Challenges and opportunities with BigData* (Tech. Rep.). Retrieved on April 4, 2016 from https://www.purdue.edu/discoverypark/cyber/assets/pdfs/BigDataWhitePaper.pdf

Xu, L. D., Wang, C., Bi, Z. M., & Yu, J. (2014). Object-oriented templates for automated assembly planning of complex products. *IEEE Transactions on Automation Science and Engineering*, *11*(2), 492–503. doi:10.1109/TASE.2012.2232652

Yoo, R. M., Romano, A., & Kozyrakis, C. (2009). Phoenix rebirth: Scalable MapReduce on a large-scale shared-memory system. In *Workload Characterization, 2009. IISWC 2009. IEEE International Symposium on* (pp. 198-207). IEEE. Retrieved on April 4, 2016 from http://csl.stanford.edu/~christos/publications/2009.scalable_phoenix.iiswc.pdf

Zaslavsky, A., Perera, C., & Georgakopoulos, D. (2013). *Sensing as a service and big data*. arXiv preprint arXiv:1301.0159

Zhu, W., Sreedhar, V. C., Hu, Z., & Gao, G. R. (2007). Synchronization state buffer: supporting efficient fine-grain synchronization on many-core architectures. *ACM SIGARCH Computer Architecture News*, *35*(2), 35-45. Retrieved on April 4, 2016 from http://www.capsl.udel.edu/pub/doc/papers/ISCA2007.pdf

Zikopoulos, P., Eaton, C., Deroos, D., Deutsch, T., & Lapis, G. (2012). *Understanding big data: Analytics for enterprise class Hadoop and streaming data.* New York: McGraw-Hill.

ADDITIONAL READING

Adamov, A. (2012). Distributed file system as a basis of data-intensive computing. *In Application of Information and Communication Technologies (AICT), 2012 6th International Conference on Application of Information and Communication Technologies (pp. 1-3).* IEEE. Retrieved on April 4, 2016 from http://ieeexplore.ieee.org/stamp/stamp.jsp?tp=&arnumber=6398484

Assuncao, M. D., Calheiros, R. N., Bianchi, S., Netto, M. A., & Buyya, R. (2013). Big Data computing and clouds: challenges, solutions, and future directions. *arXiv preprint arXiv:1312.4722.* Retrieved on April 4, 2016 from http://arxiv.org/pdf/1312.4722.pdf

Assunção, M. D., Calheiros, R. N., Bianchi, S., Netto, M. A., & Buyya, R. (2015). Big Data computing and clouds: Trends and future directions. *Journal of Parallel and Distributed Computing, 79,* 3–15. doi:10.1016/j.jpdc.2014.08.003

Bahga, A., & Madisetti, V. K. (2012). Analyzing massive machine maintenance data in a computing cloud. *IEEE Transactions on Parallel and Distributed Systems, 23*(10), 1831–1843. doi:10.1109/TPDS.2011.306

Bahga, A., & Madisetti, V. K. (2013). Performance evaluation approach for multi-tier cloud applications. *Journal of Software Engineering and Applications, 6*(02), 74–83. doi:10.4236/jsea.2013.62012

Barbarossa, S., & Scutari, G. (2007). Bio-inspired sensor network design. *IEEE Signal Processing Magazine, 24*(3), 26–35. doi:10.1109/MSP.2007.361599

Bekkerman, R., Bilenko, M., & Langford, J. (Eds.). (2011). *Scaling up machine learning: Parallel and distributed approaches.* Missing city, state: Cambridge University Press. Retrieved on April 4, 2016 from http://hunch.net/~large_scale_survey/SUML.pdf

Bertone, P., & Gerstein, M. (2001). Integrative data mining: the new direction in bioinformatics. *Engineering in Medicine and Biology Magazine, IEEE,20(4), 33-40.* Retrieved on April 4, 2016 from http://ieeexplore.ieee.org/stamp/stamp.jsp?arnumber=940042

Bryant, R. E. (2007). *Data-intensive supercomputing: The case for DISC.* Retrieved on April 4, 2016 from https://www.cs.cmu.edu/~bryant/pubdir/cmu-cs-07-128.pdf

Bryant, R. E. (2011). Data-intensive scalable computing for scientific applications. *Computing in Science & Engineering, 13*(6), 25–33. doi:10.1109/MCSE.2011.73

Byungik Ahn, J. (2012). Neuron machine: Parallel and pipelined digital neurocomputing architecture. *In Computational Intelligence and Cybernetics (CyberneticsCom), 2012 IEEE International Conference on Computational Intelligence and Cybernetics (pp. 143-147).* IEEE. Retrieved on April 4, 2016 from http://ieeexplore.ieee.org/stamp/stamp.jsp?arnumber=6381635

Chang, F., Dean, J., Ghemawat, S., Hsieh, W. C., Wallach, D. A., Burrows, M., & Gruber, R. E. (2008). BigTable: A distributed storage system for structured data. *ACM Transactions on Computer Systems*, *26*(2), 4. doi:10.1145/1365815.1365816

Chen, C. P., & Zhang, C. Y. (2014). Data-intensive applications, challenges, techniques and technologies: A survey on Big Data. *Information Sciences*, *275*, 314–347. doi:10.1016/j.ins.2014.01.015

Chen, M., Mao, S., & Liu, Y. (2014). Big data: A survey. *Mobile Networks and Applications*, *19*(2), 171–209. doi:10.100711036-013-0489-0

Dean, J., & Ghemawat, S. (2008). MapReduce: Simplified data processing on large clusters. *Communications of the ACM*, *51*(1), 107–113. doi:10.1145/1327452.1327492

Del Río, S., López, V., Benítez, J. M., & Herrera, F. (2014). On the use of MapReduce for imbalanced big data using random forest. *Information Sciences*, *285*, 112–137. doi:10.1016/j.ins.2014.03.043

Di Ciaccio, A., Coli, M., & Ibanez, J. M. A. (Eds.). (2012). *Advanced statistical methods for the analysis of large data-sets*. Missing city, state: Springer Science & Business Media Retrieved on April 4, 2016 from http://www.springer.com/us/book/9783642210365

Forbes, N. (2000). Biologically inspired computing. *Computing in Science & Engineering*, *2*(6), 83–87. doi:10.1109/5992.881711

Fujimoto, Y., Fukuda, N., & Akabane, T. (1992). Massively parallel architectures for large scale neural network simulations. *IEEE Transactions on Neural Networks*, *3*(6), 876–888. doi:10.1109/72.165590 PMID:18276485

Garber, L. (2012). Using in-memory analytics to quickly crunch big data. *Computer*, *45*(10), 16–18. doi:10.1109/MC.2012.358

García, A. O., Bourov, S., Hammad, A., Hartmann, V., Jejkal, T., Otte, J. C., . . . Stotzka, R. (2011). Data-intensive analysis for scientific experiments at the large scale data facility. *In Large Data Analysis and Visualization (LDAV), 2011 IEEE Symposium on Large Data Analysis and Visualization (pp. 125-126)*. IEEE. Retrieved on April 4, 2016 from http://ieeexplore.ieee.org/xpl/login.jsp?tp=&arnumber=6092331&url=http%3A%2F%2Fieeexplore.ieee.org%2Fxpls%2Fabs_all.jsp%3Farnumber%3D6092331

Ghemawat, S., Gobioff, H., & Leung, S. T. (2003). The Google file system. *In ACM SIGOPS operating systems review (Vol. 37, No. 5, pp. 29-43)*. ACM. Retrieved on April 4, 2016 from http://static.google-usercontent.com/media/research.google.com/en//archive/gfs-sosp2003.pdf

Gillick, D., Faria, A., & DeNero, J. (2006). *MapReduce: Distributed computing for machine learning*. Berkley, Volume 18. Retrieved on April 4, 2016 from https://www.researchgate.net/profile/Dan_Gillick/publication/237563704_MapReduce_Distributed_Computing_for_Machine_Learning/links/551c00630cf20d5fbde24350.pdf

Gokhale, M., Cohen, J., Yoo, A., Miller, W. M., Jacob, A., Ulmer, C., & Pearce, R. (2008). Hardware technologies for high-performance data-intensive computing. *Computer*, *41*(4), 60–68. doi:10.1109/MC.2008.125

Gorton, I., Greenfield, P., Szalay, A., & Williams, R. (2008). Data-intensive computing in the 21st century. *Computer*, *41*(4), 30–32. doi:10.1109/MC.2008.122

Hashem, I. A. T., Yaqoob, I., Anuar, N. B., Mokhtar, S., Gani, A., & Khan, S. U. (2015). The rise of "big data" on cloud computing: Review and open research issues. *Information Systems, 47, 98-115*. Elsevier. Retrieved on April 4, 2016 from http://www.sciencedirect.com/science/article/pii/S0306437914001288

Jacobs, A. (2009). The pathologies of big data. *Communications of the ACM*, *52*(8), 36–44. doi:10.1145/1536616.1536632

Jagadish, H. V., Gehrke, J., Labrinidis, A., Papakonstantinou, Y., Patel, J. M., Ramakrishnan, R., & Shahabi, C. (2014). Big data and its technical challenges. *Communications of the ACM*, *57*(7), 86–94. doi:10.1145/2611567

Jagadish, H. V., Gehrke, J., Labrinidis, A., Papakonstantinou, Y., Patel, J. M., Ramakrishnan, R., & Shahabi, C. (2014). Big data and its technical challenges. *Communications of the ACM*, *57*(7), 86–94. doi:10.1145/2611567

Jiang, D., Ooi, B. C., Shi, L., & Wu, S. (2010). The performance of MapReduce: An in-depth study. *Proceedings of the VLDB Endowment, 3(1-2), 472-483*. VLDB Endowment. Retrieved on April 4, 2016 from http://www.vldb.org/pvldb/vldb2010/papers/E03.pdf

Jiang, D., Tung, A. K., & Chen, G. (2011). Map-join-reduce: Towards scalable and efficient data analysis on large clusters. *IEEE Transactions on Knowledge and Data Engineering*, *23*(9), 1299–1311. doi:10.1109/TKDE.2010.248

Jordan, J. M., & Lin, D. K. (2014). Statistics for big data: Are statisticians ready for big data? *Journal of the Chinese Statistical Association*, *52*(1), 133–149.

Kambatla, K., Kollias, G., Kumar, V., & Grama, A. (2014). Trends in big data analytics. *Journal of Parallel and Distributed Computing*, *74*(7), 2561–2573. doi:10.1016/j.jpdc.2014.01.003

Kasavajhala, V. (2011). Solid state drive vs. hard disk drive price and performance study. Proc. Dell Tech. White Paper, 8-9. Retrieved on April 4, 2016 from http://www.dell.com/downloads/global/products/pvaul/en/ssd_vs_hdd_price_and_performance_study.pdf

Kim, W. (2009). Parallel clustering algorithms: survey. CSC 8530 Parallel Algorithms, Spring 2009, Georgia State University, Atlanta, GA. Retrieved on April 4, 2016 from http://grid.cs.gsu.edu/~wkim/index_files/SurveyParallelClustering.html

Klemens, B. (Ed.). (2008). *Modeling with data: tools and techniques for scientific computing*. Missing city, state: Princeton University Press. Retrieved on April 4, 2016 from http://press.princeton.edu/titles/8706.html

Konwinski, A. (2009). Improving mapreduce performance in heterogeneous environments. Technical Report of EECS Department, University of California, Berkeley, no. UCB/EECS-2009-183. Retrieved on April 4, 2016 from http://digitalassets.lib.berkeley.edu/techreports/ucb/text/EECS-2009-183.pdf

Kouzes, R. T., Anderson, G. A., Elbert, S. T., Gorton, I., & Gracio, D. K. (2009). The changing paradigm of data-intensive computing. *Computer*, *42*(1), 26–34. doi:10.1109/MC.2009.26

Kraft, S., Casale, G., Jula, A., Kilpatrick, P., & Greer, D. (2012). Wiq: work-intensive query scheduling for in-memory database systems. *In 2012 IEEE 5th International Conference on Cloud Computing (CLOUD) (pp. 33-40). IEEE*. Retrieved on April 4, 2016 from http://ieeexplore.ieee.org/xpl/login.jsp?tp=&arnumber=6253486&url=http%3A%2F%2Fieeexplore.ieee.org%2Fxpls%2Fabs_all.jsp%3Farnumber%3D6253486

Landset, S., Khoshgoftaar, T. M., Richter, A. N., & Hasanin, T. (2015). A survey of open source tools for machine learning with big data in the Hadoop ecosystem. *Journal of Big Data*, 2(1), 1–36. doi:10.118640537-015-0032-1

LaValle, S., Lesser, E., Shockley, R., Hopkins, M. S., & Kruschwitz, N. (2011). Big data, analytics and the path from insights to value. *MIT Sloan Management Review*, 52(2), 21.

Liu, C., Yang, C., Zhang, X., & Chen, J. (2015). External integrity verification for outsourced big data in cloud and IoT: A big picture. *Future Generation Computer Systems*, 49, 58–67. doi:10.1016/j.future.2014.08.007

Loughran, S., Calero, J. M. A., Farrell, A., Kirschnick, J., & Guijarro, J. (2012). Dynamic cloud deployment of a MapReduce architecture. *IEEE Internet Computing*, 16(6), 40–50. doi:10.1109/MIC.2011.163

Lynch, C. (2008). Big data: How do your data grow? *Nature*, 455(7209), 28–29. doi:10.1038/455028a PMID:18769419

Mackey, G., Sehrish, S., Bent, J., Lopez, J., Habib, S., & Wang, J. (2008). Introducing map-reduce to high end computing. *In Petascale Data Storage Workshop, 2008. PDSW'08. 3Rd (pp. 1-6)*. IEEE. Retrieved on April 4, 2016 from http://ieeexplore.ieee.org/xpl/login.jsp?tp=&arnumber=4811889&url=http%3A%2F%2Fieeexplore.ieee.org%2Fxpls%2Fabs_all.jsp%3Farnumber%3D4811889

McAfee, A., Brynjolfsson, E., Davenport, T. H., Patil, D. J., & Barton, D. (2012). Big data. The management revolution. *Harvard Business Review*, 90(10), 61–67. PMID:23074865

Nielsen, M. (2009). The Fourth Paradigm: Data-Intensive Scientific Discovery edited by Tony Hey, Stewart Tansley & Kristin Tolle. *Nature-London, 462(7274), 722-722*. Retrieved on April 4, 2016 from http://research.microsoft.com/en-us/collaboration/fourthparadigm/4th_paradigm_book_complete_lr.pdf

Pébay, P., Thompson, D., Bennett, J., & Mascarenhas, A. (2011). Design and performance of a scalable, parallel statistics toolkit. *In Parallel and Distributed Processing Workshops and Ph.D. Forum (IPDPSW), 2011 IEEE International Symposium on (pp. 1475-1484)*. IEEE. Retrieved on April 4, 2016 from http://ieeexplore.ieee.org/xpl/login.jsp?tp=&arnumber=6009003&url=http%3A%2F%2Fieeexplore.ieee.org%2Fxpls%2Fabs_all.jsp%3Farnumber%3D6009003

Savitz, E. (2012). Gartner: 10 Critical Tech Trends for the Next Five Years. Retrieved on April 4, 2016 from http://www.forbes.com/sites/ericsavitz/2012/10/22/gartner-10-critical-tech-trends-for-the-next-five-years/#39e9ca1f4c6f

Shah, A. H. S., & Capellá, J. (2012). Good Data Won't Guarantee Good Decisions. *Harvard Business Review, The Magazine*. Retrieved on April 4, 2016 from http://hbr.org/2012/04/good-data-wont-guarantee-good-decisions/ar/1

Shvachko, K., Kuang, H., Radia, S., & Chansler, R. (2010). The Hadoop distributed file system. *In 2010 IEEE 26th Symposium on Mass Storage Systems and Technologies (MSST) (pp. 1-10)* Incline Village, NV. IEEE. Retrieved on April 4, 2016 from http://pages.cs.wisc.edu/~akella/CS838/F15/838-CloudPapers/hdfs.pdf

Szalay, A. (2011). Extreme data-intensive scientific computing. *Computing in Science & Engineering, 13*(6), 34–41. doi:10.1109/MCSE.2011.74

Thusoo, A., Sarma, J. S., Jain, N., Shao, Z., Chakka, P., Anthony, S., & Murthy, R. (2009). Hive: A warehousing solution over a map-reduce framework. *Proceedings of the VLDB Endowment International Conference on Very Large Data Bases, 2*(2), 1626–1629. doi:10.14778/1687553.1687609

Wu, X., Zhu, X., Wu, G. Q., & Ding, W. (2014). Data mining with big data. *IEEE Transactions on Knowledge and Data Engineering, 26*(1), 97–107. doi:10.1109/TKDE.2013.109

Chapter 17
Big Data Analytics and IoT in Smart City Applications

Mamata Rath
ⓘ https://orcid.org/0000-0002-2277-1012
Birla School of Management, Birla Global University, India

ABSTRACT

Big data analytics is a sophisticated approach for fusion of large data sets that include a collection of data elements to expose hidden prototype, undetected associations, showcase business logic, client inclinations, and other helpful business information. Big data analytics involves challenging techniques to mine and extract relevant data that includes the actions of penetrating a database, effectively mining the data, querying and inspecting data committed to enhance the technical execution of various task segments. The capacity to synthesize a lot of data can enable an association to manage impressive data that can influence the business.

INTRODUCTION

There are many Real Time Applications of Big Data Analytics in Smart City based systems, that incorporates Smart City idea, big data innovations, ongoing big data analytics, urban improvement, data and correspondence innovation, Internet of Things. Technological insurgency in the ongoing past has empowered the idea of Smart City for urban advancement. Smart City idea is imagined with the destinations of giving better administrations to the residents and improves the personal satisfaction. Data and Communication Technology (ICT) and Internet of Things (IoT) made smart city applications as a lot less difficult and compelling. Big data advances assume a significant job in smart city applications. This examination work gives an outline of the job of big data in structure smart city applications and proposes a system for continuous big data analytics. Constant big data analytics help in settling on better choices and progressively precise forecasts at opportune time to offer better administrations to the residents. Here, we focus on t some of significant arrangements and administrations for the smart city where the continuous big data analytics and IoT helps in improving the nature of administrations in smart city applications.

DOI: 10.4018/978-1-6684-3662-2.ch017

There are learning models developed quality education in smart urban communities, that incorporates long transient memory systems, IoT smart city data examination, data and correspondence advancements, sustainable urban life, IoT based administrations, IoT data forecast, Internet of Things idea, profound learning strategies, profound learning methods, IoT based smart city applications, city partners, air quality expectation, profound learning model, smart city forecast problems.In ongoing years, Internet of Things (IoT) idea has turned into a promising exploration point in numerous zones including industry, trade and training. Smart urban areas utilize IoT based administrations and applications to make a sustainable urban life. By utilizing data and correspondence advances, IoT empowers smart urban communities to make city partners progressively mindful, intuitive and productive. With the expansion in number of IoT based smart city applications, the measure of data created by these applications is expanded enormously. Governments and city partners play it safe to process these data and anticipate future impacts to guarantee sustainable advancement. In expectation setting, profound learning procedures have been utilized for a few guaging issues in big data. This motivates us to utilize profound learning techniques for forecast of IoT data. Thus, in exploration work by many eminent researchers, novel profound learning models are proposed for breaking down IoT smart city data. The analysts present novel model dependent on Long Short Term Memory (LSTM) systems to foresee future estimations of air quality in a smart city. The assessment consequences of the proposed model are seen as promising and they demonstrate that the model can be utilized in other smart city forecast issues also.

Different Computing Platforms for Big Data Analytics in Electric Vehicle Infrastructures have been developed that incorporate data-concentrated investigation, carbon impression, SG mix, figuring stages, dispersed distributed computing, EV joining, smart vehicular applications, omnipresent arrangement, IoT gadgets, smart matrix mix, wise transportation framework, transport situated smart urban areas, Big Data analytics stages, EV rollout, BDA exercises, structural layers, electric vehicle foundations, ITS, TOSC, appropriated edge-haze computing.With the development of consistently developing smart vehicular applications and pervasive sending of IoT gadgets crosswise over various engineering layers of Intelligent Transportation System (ITS), data-escalated examination rises to be a significant test. Without incredible correspondence and computational help, different vehicular applications and administrations will at present remain in the idea stage and can't be tried in the daily life. In this examination work, the specialists think about the instance of Electric Vehicle (EV) to Smart Grid (SG) combination. The EVs are key players for Transport Oriented Smart Cities (TOSC) as they help urban areas to end up greener by lessening discharges and carbon impression. The analysts break down various use-cases in EV to SG combination to demonstrate how Big Data Analytics (BDA) stages can assume an essential job towards effective EV rollout. The analysts at that point present two figuring stages in particular, dispersed distributed computing and edge/haze registering. The scientists featured the distinctive highlights of each towards supporting BDA exercises in EV reconciliation. At long last, the specialists give a detailed outline of chances, patterns, and difficulties of both these processing strategies.

Big data analytics require advances and technical mechanism that can change a lot of organized, unstructured, and semi-organized data into a more reasonable data and metadata design for explanatory procedures. The calculations utilized as a part of these explanatory instruments must find examples, patterns, and relationships over an assortment of time skylines in the data . In the wake of breaking down the data, these instruments envision the discoveries in tables, diagrams, and spatial outlines for proficient decision making. Along these lines, big data investigation is a genuine test for some applications due to data unpredictability and the adaptability of basic calculations that help such procedures. acquiring supportive data from big data investigation is a basic issue that requires adaptable logical calculations and strategies to return all around planned outcomes, though current methods and calculations are wasteful to deal with big data analytics. In this manner, huge framework and extra applications are important to help data parallelism. In addition, data sources, for example, rapid data stream got from various data sources, have diverse configurations, which makes coordinating different hotspots for analytics arrangements basic . Subsequently, the assessment is centered around the execution of current calculations utilized as a part of big data investigation, which isn't rising directly with the fast increment in computational assets .

By and large, when the expression "big data," is coined, people quickly think about enormous data volumes. In case these were the main reason behind medicinal services administrations to get the better approach for taking care of data, they could regulate without, in light of the way that most of them could contain what they have in a solid social database. In 2001, Doug Laney depicted the "3 Vs" of enormous and complex data as "Volume, Velocity and Variety.". While restorative administrations CIOs could benefit by all of the three, the highlight should be on combination. This is an example experienced by human administrations, just as by all endeavors. Figure 1 demonstrates Big data applications in different fields. Beside customary patient data contained in substance, there are various pictures and sounds recorded, from x-shafts and ultrasounds, to Doppler and MRI imaging. A couple of experts particularly need that their talks with patients be recorded for the patient's bit of leeway. This get-together of dissimilar data is generally unstructured and can't be mentioned in the immaculate tables and sections of a social database. This is the spot big databases, as Hadoop, score. In any case, it is one thing to store big data and extremely another to recoup it truly. Data analysts who can design procedures to remove significant data from the non-successive and evidently unpredictable big databases are presently popular.

These techniques are challenging and hard to solve, however the IT business is beginning to convey activities that make significant data extraction less demanding. There is additionally a move to a half breed database structure, where data is put away in both a social and a "NoSQL" database. Where social insurance elements have handled this obstacle, the outcome is an all encompassing perspective of the patient, which expels a portion of the unpredictability of finding for the medicinal professional and makes life less difficult for the patient. It likewise opens the path for the move to machine-to-machine (M2M) correspondence and the utilization of computerized reasoning to filter through and investigate data transmitted from the sensors gathering it. The future guarantee is examination that will screen well-being more than ever however there are likewise further issues that should be tended to, for example, data protection and security. Figure 2 represents various smart applications in smart city using Internet of Things.

Figure 1. Applications of Big data Analytics in various fields

Security and Banking	Manufacturing and Production
Communications and Media	Education & Training
Health Care Applications	Energy Sectors and Utilities
Transportations	Home Appliances

Figure 2. Applications of IoT in Smart City

Applications of IoT in Smart City	
Smart Traffic Management	Smart Industry
Smart Energy and Smart Grid	Smart healthcare
Smart Transportations	Smart Home Appliances

For analysis of major type of business process, Big Data helps in transforming major selling practice by improved techniques and accurate analysis of presented data. As shown in fig.1 some of such process are Banking and Security, Media and communication, Health Care Sector, Manufacturing, Training and Education, Insurance, Transportation, Energy and utilities. Using big data analytics in all these fields improves the quality of the process and results improved output. The Organisation of the paper has been done as follows. The Second section describes the Literature Review. Section 3 presents applications of big data analytics and IoT in smart city and at last Section 4 concludes the chapter.

2. BACKGROUND

This section presents background of the topic with literature study. Manjunatha, B. Annappa (2018) present Real Time Big Data Analytics in Smart City Applications, that incorporates Smart City idea, big data innovations, ongoing big data analytics, urban improvement, data and correspondence innovation, Internet of Things.Technological insurgency in the ongoing past has empowered the idea of Smart City for urban advancement. Smart City idea is imagined with the destinations of giving better administrations to the residents and improves the personal satisfaction. Data and Communication Technology (ICT) and Internet of Things (IoT) made smart city applications as a lot less difficult and compelling. Big data advances assume a significant job in smart city applications. This examination work gives an outline of the job of big data in structure smart city applications and proposes a system for continuous big data analytics. Constant big data analytics help in settling on better choices and progressively precise forecasts at opportune time to offer better administrations to the residents. Here, the analysts talked about some of significant arrangements and administrations for the smart city where the continuous big data analytics helps in improving the nature of administrations in smart city applications.

M. U. Azimayek (2017) present A profound learning model for air quality expectation in smart urban communities, that incorporates LSTM, long transient memory systems, IoT smart city data examination, data and correspondence advancements, sustainable urban life, IoT based administrations, IoT data forecast, Internet of Things idea, profound learning strategies, profound learning methods, IoT based smart city applications, city partners, air quality expectation, profound learning model, smart city forecast problems.In ongoing years, Internet of Things (IoT) idea has turned into a promising exploration point in numerous zones including industry, trade and training. Smart urban areas utilize IoT based administrations and applications to make a sustainable urban life. By utilizing data and correspondence advances, IoT empowers smart urban communities to make city partners progressively mindful, intuitive and productive. With the expansion in number of IoT based smart city applications, the measure of data created by these applications is expanded enormously. Governments and city partners play it safe to process these data and anticipate future impacts to guarantee sustainable advancement. In expectation setting, profound learning procedures have been utilized for a few guaging issues in big data. This motivates us to utilize profound learning techniques for forecast of IoT data. Thus, in this exploration work, a novel profound learning model is proposed for breaking down IoT smart city data. The analysts propose a novel model dependent on Long Short Term Memory (LSTM) systems to foresee future estimations of air quality in a smart city. The assessment consequences of the proposed model are seen as promising and they demonstrate that the model can be utilized in other smart city forecast issues also. Table 1. Illustrates details of literature survey carried out in this research work.

Table 1. Details of literature survey carried out in this research work

Literature Study Reference	year	Research Topic	Associated Concepts related to Respective Research
Manjunatha, B. Annappa	2018	Real Time Big Data Analytics in Smart City Applications	Smart City concept, big data technologies, real-time big data analytics, urban development, information and communication technology, Internet of Things
M. U. Azimayek	2017	A deep learning model for air quality prediction in smart cities	LSTM, long short term memory networks, IoT smart city data analysis, information and communication technologies, sustainable urban life, IoT based services, IoT data prediction, Internet of Things concept, deep learning methods, deep learning techniques, IoT based smart city applications, city stakeholders, air quality prediction, deep learning model, smart city prediction problems
B. Cheng, S. Longo, F. Cirillo, M. Bauer, E. Kovacs	2015	Building a Big Data Platform for Smart Cities: Experience and Lessons from Santander	Big Data platform, Internet of Things, IoT, human activities, context-awareness, system architecture, live city data and analytics platform, CiDAP, SmartSantander, smart city data platforms
M. M. Hussain, M. M. S. Beg, M. S. Alam, M. Krishnamurthy, Q. M. Ali	2018	Computing Platforms for Big Data Analytics in Electric Vehicle Infrastructures	data-intensive analysis, carbon footprint, SG integration, computing platforms, distributed cloud computing, EV integration, smart vehicular applications, ubiquitous deployment, IoT devices, smart grid integration, intelligent transportation system, transport oriented smart cities, Big Data analytics platforms, EV rollout, BDA activities, architectural layers, electric vehicle infrastructures, ITS, TOSC, distributed edge-fog computing
S. A. Shah, D. Z. Seker, M. M. Rathore, S. Hameed, S. Ben Yahia, D. Draheim	2019	Towards Disaster Resilient Smart Cities: Can Internet of Things and Big Data Analytics Be the Game Changers?	IoT, big data analytics technologies, BDA technologies, disaster management activities, smart city incentives, data harvesting, data aggregation, data pre-processing, smart buildings, city pollution, natural disasters, disaster resilient smart cities, Internet of Things, DRSC environment, Hadoop Ecosystem, Spark, traffic simulator, Twitter, emergency evacuation path
M. R. Bashir, A. Q. Gill	2016	Towards an IoT Big Data Analytics Framework: Smart Buildings Systems	IoT Big Data analytics, IBDA framework, smart building system, data storage, data analysis

continues on following page

Table 1. Continued

Literature Study Reference	year	Research Topic	Associated Concepts related to Respective Research
P. Bellini, P. Nesi, M. Paolucci, I. Zaza	2018	Smart City Architecture for Data Ingestion and Analytics: Processes and Solutions	provide support, decision support systems, interoperability, data ingestion, Sii-Mobility national smart city project, Km4City ontology, smart city data aggregation, service production, smart City architecture, smart city architectures, data analytics processes, Internet of everything, sensors, IOT
A. Sharif, J. Li, M. Khalil, R. Kumar, M. I. Sharif, A. Sharif	2017	IoT based smart traffic management system for smart cities using big data analytics	STS, smart city, smart traffic management system, Internet of Things, IoT, Smart Traffic System, smart cities, predictive analytics, traffic density, analytical scriptures, big data analytics, data processing, public traffic data, low cost vehicle, traffic update, public traffic management
B. Ahlgren, M. Hidell, E. C. -. Ngai	2016	Internet of Things for Smart Cities: Interoperability and Open Data	Internet of Things, smart cities, interoperability, Big Data analytics, open data accessibility, cloud services, GreenIoT platform, Uppsala, Sweden
J. Chin, V. Callaghan, I. Lam	2017	Understanding and personalising smart city services using machine learning, The Internet-of-Things and Big Data	personalising smart city services, machine learning, Internet-of-Things, Big Data, artificial intelligence, IoT, ML classification algorithms, Bayes Network, NaÃ¯ve Bayesian, NB, nearest neighbour, NN, weather data, UK MetOffice, Transport for London, decision tree J48 algorithm
J. Zenkert, M. Dornhofer, C. Weber, C. Ngoukam, M. Fathi	2018	Big data analytics in smart mobility: Modeling and analysis of the Aarhus smart city dataset	intelligent services, smart urban services, intelligent networking, sensing technologies, Open Data Aarhus datasets, sensor data, city Aarhus, smart mobility, Aarhus smart city dataset, information and communication technologies, Big Data analytics, Internet of Things, IoT, R Shiny application, road traffic data analysis, pollution data analysis, MapReduce framework, Hadoop cluster
P. Manjunath, M. Prakruthi, P. Gajkumar Shah	2018	IoT Driven with Big Data Analytics and Block Chain Application Scenarios	Internet of Things, big data analytics, block chain application scenarios
S. Shukla, Balachandran K, Sumitha V S	2016	A framework for smart transportation using Big Data	Big Data, information technology, data driven decision, India, smart city project, smart transportation systems, smart traffic signals
P. Rizwan, K. Suresh, M. R. Babu	2016	Real-time smart traffic management system for smart cities by using Internet of Things and big data	real-time smart traffic management system, smart cities, Internet of Things, Big Data, STMS, traffic indicators, traffic details, low-cost vehicle detecting sensors, IoT, traffic data, real time streaming data, traffic density analysis, predictive analytics, mobile application, user interface
Y. Sun, H. Song, A. J. Jara, R. Bie	2016	Internet of Things and Big Data Analytics for Smart and Connected Communities	Italy, Trento, cultural heritage, smart tourism, TreSight, mobile crowdsensing, cyber-physical cloud computing, smart sensors, ubiquitous network, IoT, SCC, big data analytics, Internet of Things
V. Dattana, K. Gupta, A. Kush	2019	A Probability based Model for Big Data Security in Smart City	big data security, smart technologies, economic data, smart city data, smart applications, smart city critical data, data objects, transport data, data analytics, smart traffic management system, sensitive data sharing, data leakage detection, highly sensitive data, probability based model, personal data, organisational data, environment data, energy data, crisis response, emergency management, disaster resilience, bigraph, critical data security
S. N. Shukla, T. A. Champaneria	2017	Survey of various data collection ways for smart transportation domain of smart city	smart city, IoT, M2M interaction, Information and Communicaiton Technology, quality of life, smart transportation, smart transportation domain, data collection ways

continues on following page

Table 1. Continued

Literature Study Reference	year	Research Topic	Associated Concepts related to Respective Research
J. Lieberman, A. Leidner, G. Percivall, C. RÃ¶nsdorf	2017	Using big data analytics and IoT principles to keep an eye on underground infrastructure	Concept Development Study, Open Geospatial Consortium, high-quality feature data, underground urban infrastructure, nonvisual methods, UGI geodata, hidden features, diverse velocity sensing streams, high-velocity sensing streams, realistic predictive models, lower construction costs, efficient infrastructure operation, sound disaster preparedness, smart city services, IoT principles, Sensor Web observation standards, functional digital twins, hidden infrastructure, underground built environment, eye, underground infrastructure, Big Data analytics, OGC geodata
S. Nguyen, Z. Salcic, X. Zhang	2018	Big Data Processing in Fog - Smart Parking Case Study	Hadoop MapReduce, fog - smart parking, fog computing, Big Data processing, sensor-based system, data analytics tasks, data analytics system, monitoring carpark occupancy, IoT-based platform, vehicle parking, traffic congestion, traffic efficiency
C. Costa, M. Y. Santos	2016	BASIS: A big data architecture for smart cities	Big data architecture, smart cities, Internet of Things, IoT, BASIS, multiple abstraction layers, public data availability
S. V. Nandury, B. A. Begum	2017	Big data for smart grid operation in smart cities	smart grid operation, conventional power grids, smart city environment, smart grid applications, Big data analytics, smart grid management, smart grid maintenance, power generation, power consumption, power distribution, SWIFT, ICT backbone architecture
P. Nesi, G. Pantaleo, M. Paolucci, I. Zaza	2018	Auditing and Assessment of Data Traffic Flows in an IoT Architecture	data traffic flows, Internet of Things, Smart City environments, flexible smart living lab, Smart City data, automated decision-making processes, data flows, connected IoT devices, data-driven applications, data shadow, IoT Smart City Architecture, Snap4City framework, DevDash tools, AMMA tools
M. E. ARASS, I. Tikito, N. Souissi	2018	An Audit Framework for Data Lifecycles in a Big Data context	Internet of Things, Big data lifecycles, data usage context, data collection, data management, Big data context, audit framework
M. M. Rathore, A. Ahmad, A. Paul	2016	IoT-based smart city development using big data analytical approach	IoT-based smart city development, Big Data analytical approach, urban public development, city development, Internet, smart city system, smart home sensors, vehicular networking, weather sensors, water sensors, smart parking sensors, surveillance objects, Hadoop ecosystem, data generation, data collection, data aggregation, data classification, data filtration, data preprocessing, spark
P. J. Navarathna, V. P. Malagi	2018	Artificial Intelligence in Smart City Analysis	AI, fully functional smart city, artificial intelligence, sustainable development, growing fields, conventional cities, smart cities

B. Cheng, S. Longo, F. Cirillo, M. Bauer, E. Kovacs (2015) present Building a Big Data Platform for Smart Cities: Experience and Lessons from Santander, that incorporates Big Data stage, Internet of Things, IoT, human exercises, setting mindfulness, framework design, live city data and analytics stage, CiDAP, SmartSantander, smart city data platforms.The Internet of Things (IoT) is currently forming exploration work ' s urban areas to make them increasingly associated, helpful, and keen. In any case, this change will profoundly depend on extricated qualities and bits of knowledge from the big data created by research work ' s urban areas by means of sensors, gadgets, and human exercises. Many existing examinations and tasks have been done to make research work ' s urban communities smart, concentrating more on the most proficient method to send different sensors and gadgets and after that gather data from them. Be that as it may, this is only the initial move towards smart urban areas and following stage will be to utilize the gathered data and empower setting mindfulness and insight into a wide range of uses and administrations by means of an adaptable big data stage. In this examination work, the scientists present the framework engineering and the significant structure issues of a live City Data and Analytics Platform, in particular CiDAP. All the more critically, the scientists offer research work ' s experience and exercises gained from structure this reasonable framework for an enormous scale running smart city proving ground, SmartSantander. Research work ' s work gives a significant guide to future Smart City stage planners with the goal that they can anticipate some training issues and allude to research work ' s arrangement when building their very own smart city data stages.

M. M. Hussain, M. M. S. Ask, M. S. Alam, M. Krishnamurthy, Q. M. Ali (2018) present Computing Platforms for Big Data Analytics in Electric Vehicle Infrastructures, that incorporates data-concentrated investigation, carbon impression, SG mix, figuring stages, dispersed distributed computing, EV joining, smart vehicular applications, omnipresent arrangement, IoT gadgets, smart matrix mix, wise transportation framework, transport situated smart urban areas, Big Data analytics stages, EV rollout, BDA exercises, structural layers, electric vehicle foundations, ITS, TOSC, appropriated edge-haze computing. With the development of consistently developing smart vehicular applications and pervasive sending of IoT gadgets crosswise over various engineering layers of Intelligent Transportation System (ITS), data-escalated examination rises to be a significant test. Without incredible correspondence and computational help, different vehicular applications and administrations will at present remain in the idea stage and can't be tried in the daily life. In this examination work, the specialists think about the instance of Electric Vehicle (EV) to Smart Grid (SG) combination. The EVs are key players for Transport Oriented Smart Cities (TOSC) as they help urban areas to end up greener by lessening discharges and carbon impression. The analysts break down various use-cases in EV to SG combination to demonstrate how Big Data Analytics (BDA) stages can assume an essential job towards effective EV rollout. The analysts at that point present two figuring stages in particular, dispersed distributed computing and edge/haze registering. The scientists featured the distinctive highlights of each towards supporting BDA exercises in EV reconciliation. At long last, the specialists give a detailed outline of chances, patterns, and difficulties of both these processing strategies.

S. A. Shah, D. Z. Seker, M. M. Rathore, S. Hameed, S. Ben Yahia, D. Draheim (2019) present Towards Disaster Resilient Smart Cities: Can Internet of Things and Big Data Analytics Be the Game Changers?, that incorporates IoT, big data analytics advancements, BDA innovations, catastrophe the board exercises, smart city motivations, data reaping, data collection, data pre-handling, smart structures, city contamination, cataclysmic events, fiasco strong smart urban areas, Internet of Things, DRSC condition, Hadoop Ecosystem, Spark, traffic test system, Twitter, crisis clearing path. Disasters (characteristic or man-made) can be deadly to human life, nature, and framework. The ongoing headways in the Internet of Things (IoT) and the advancement in big data analytics (BDA) advances have given an open chance to grow exceptionally required debacle versatile smart city conditions. In this exploration work, the specialists propose and talk about the novel reference design and theory of a debacle versatile smart city (DRSC) through the mix of the IoT and BDA advances. The proposed engineering offers a nonexclusive answer for debacle the board exercises in smart city motivations. A mix of the Hadoop Ecosystem and Spark are checked on to build up a productive DRSC condition that supports both ongoing and disconnected investigation. The execution model of nature comprises of data collecting, data total, data pre-handling, and big data analytics and administration stage. An assortment of datasets (i.e., smart structures, city contamination, traffic test system, and twitter) are used for the approval and assessment of the framework to recognize and create alarms for a fire in a structure, contamination level in the city, crisis departure way, and the gathering of data about catastrophic events (i.e., seismic tremors and tidal waves). The assessment of the framework effectiveness is estimated as far as handling time and throughput that shows the exhibition predominance of the proposed engineering. In addition, the key difficulties confronted are distinguished and quickly talked about.

M. R. Bashir, A. Q. Gill (2016) present Towards an IoT Big Data Analytics Framework: Smart Buildings Systems, that incorporates IoT Big Data analytics, IBDA structure, smart structure framework, data stockpiling, data analysis.There is a developing enthusiasm for IoT-empowered smart structures. In any case, the capacity and examination of enormous measure of fast continuous smart structure data is a difficult undertaking. There are various contemporary Big Data the board innovations and progressed analytics procedures that can be utilized to manage this test. There is a requirement for a coordinated IoT Big Data Analytics (IBDA) system to fill the examination hole in the Big Data Analytics domain. This exploration work presents one such IBDA structure for the capacity and investigation of constant data produced from IoT sensors conveyed inside the smart structure. The underlying form of the IBDA structure has been created by utilizing Python and the Big Data Cloudera stage. The materialness of the structure is exhibited with the assistance of a situation including the investigation of continuous smart structure data for naturally dealing with the oxygen level, iridescence and smoke/dangerous gases in various pieces of the smart structure. The underlying outcomes demonstrate that the proposed structure is fit for the reason and appears to be valuable for IoT-empowered Big Data Analytics for smart city. Table 1 displays details of literature survey carried out in this research work.

The present expansion and development in the field of Internet of Things (IoT) are giving surprising potential in the course of the novel era of healthcare. The visualization of the healthcare is expansively supported, as it progresses the perfection of life and health of people, including a few health controls. The perpetual increment of the multifaceted IoT devices in health is comprehensively tried by difficulties, for example, controlling the IoT terminal hubs utilized for health observing, continuous information handling and shrewd choice and occasion administration. Healthcare plan has been proposed by few researchers which are based with examination of vitality collecting for health observing sensors and the acknowledgment of Big Data investigation in healthcare.

In the choice of the most modern decade, there has been an expanding passion for huge information look into, particularly for health administrations applications. The requisition of the distributed computing and the Internet of Things (IoT) worldview in the healthcare field can convey a few chances to therapeutic IT, and specialists trust that it can essentially enhance healthcare administrations and add to its ceaseless and orderly advancement in a major information condition, for example, Industry 4.0 applications. In any case, the expected assets to oversee such information in a cloud-IoT condition are as yet a major test. In like manner, another model is also planned to streamline virtual machines choice (VMs) in cloud-IoT health administrations applications to productively deal with a major measure of information in incorporated industry 4.0. Industry 4.0 applications require to process and examine huge information, which originate from various sources, for example, sensor information, without human mediation. The proposed demonstrate plans to improve the execution of the healthcare frameworks by lessening the partners' demand execution time, streamlining the required stockpiling of patients' huge information and giving an ongoing information recovery component for those applications.

The inclination of universal frameworks is supported by the improvement and dynamic selection of the Internet of Things (IoT) devices and their empowering advancements. IoT has been appeared to have critical potential in high-chance Environment, Health, and Safety (EHS) enterprises. In these businesses, human lives are in question and IoT-based applications are prepared to offer protected, dependable, and effective arrangements because of their capacity to work at a fine granular level and give rich low-level data. Another research audits existing distributed research on IoT-based applications in high-hazard EHS businesses with particular prominence on healthcare industry, nourishment inventory network (FSC), mining and vitality enterprises (oil and gas and atomic), insightful transportation (e.g., associated vehicles), and building and foundation administration for crisis reaction tasks until 2016.Web of Things (WoT) offers a consistent stage to interface individuals and items to each other for improving and making our lives simpler. This vision conveys us from form based unified plans to a more circulated condition offering a tremendous measure of utilizations, for example, intelligent wearable devices, smart home, perceptive versatility, and savvy urban areas. Few research talks regarding immaterialness of IoT in healthcare and prescription by displaying an all encompassing design of IoT eHealth biological community. Healthcare is ending up progressively hard to oversee because of inadequate and less compelling healthcare administrations to meet the expanding requests of rising maturing populace with constant ailments. We suggest this requires a progress from the center driven treatment to understanding driven healthcare where every operator, for example, clinic, patient, and administrations are flawlessly associated with each other. This patient-driven IoT eHealth biological community needs a multi-layer design: (1) device, (2) mist figuring and (3) cloud to engage treatment of complex information regarding its assortment, speed, and inertness. This mist driven IoT design is trailed by different case cases of administrations and applications that are actualized on those layers. Those illustrations run from versatile health, helped living, e-drug, inserts, early cautioning frameworks, to populace checking in keen urban communities.

Over the most recent couple of years, the m-healthcare applications in light of Internet of Things (IoT) have given multi-dimensional highlights and ongoing administrations. These applications give a stage to a huge number of individuals to get health refreshes routinely for a healthier way of life. Enlistment of IoT devices in the healthcare condition have renewed numerous highlights of these applications. The huge information created by IoT devices in healthcare space is broke down on the cloud rather than exclusively depending on restricted capacity and calculation assets of handheld devices. In respect to this unique situation, a cloud-driven IoT based M-healthcare checking illness diagnosing system is proposed which predicts the potential ailment with its level of seriousness. Key wordings are characterized to produce client situated health estimations by investigating the idea of computational sciences. The structural model for brilliant understudy healthcare is intended for application situation. The outcomes are registered subsequent to preparing the health estimations in a particular setting. In few research, deliberate understudy point of view health information is created utilizing UCI dataset and medicinal sensors to anticipate the understudy with various illness seriousness. Finding plans are connected utilizing different best in class order calculations and the outcomes are registered in light of precision, affectability, specificity, and F-measure. Exploratory outcomes demonstrate that the proposed technique beats the benchmark strategies for illness forecast.

3. BIG DATA ANALYTICS AND IOT IN SMART CITY APPLICATIONS

One of the biggest obstacles obstructing to utilize big data in social insurance is the manner by which restorative data is spread crosswise over numerous sources represented by various states, clinics, and authoritative offices . Combination of these data sources would require building up another foundation where all data suppliers team up with each other. Similarly critical is actualizing new data examination instruments and procedures. Social insurance needs to get up to speed with different ventures that have effectively moved from standard relapse based techniques to more future-arranged like prescient investigation, machine learning, and chart examination. Table 2 displays details of major contributions performed on applications of big data analytics and IoT in smart city applications.

Table 2. Contributions of big data analytics and IoT in smart city

· Real Time Big Data Analytics in Smart City Applications
· A deep learning model for air quality prediction in smart cities
· Building a Big Data Platform for Smart Cities: Experience and Lessons from Santander
· Computing Platforms for Big Data Analytics in Electric Vehicle Infrastructures
· Towards Disaster Resilient Smart Cities with Focus on Internet of Things and Big Data Analytics Be the Game Changer
· Towards an IoT Big Data Analytics Framework: Smart Buildings Systems
· Smart City Architecture for Data Ingestion and Analytics: Processes and Solutions
· IoT based smart traffic management system for smart cities using big data analytics
· Internet of Things for Smart Cities and Interoperability and Open Data
· Understanding and personalising smart city services using machine learning, The Internet-of-Things and Big Data
· Big data analytics in smart mobility: Modeling and analysis of the Aarhus smart city dataset
· IoT Driven with Big Data Analytics and Block Chain Application Scenarios
· A framework for smart transportation using Big Data
· Real-time smart traffic management system for smart cities by using Internet of Things and big data
· Internet of Things and Big Data Analytics for Smart and Connected Communities
· A Probability based Model for Big Data Security in Smart City
· Survey of various data collection ways for smart transportation domain of smart city
· Using big data analytics and IoT principles to keep an eye on underground infrastructure
· Big Data Processing in Fog - Smart Parking Case Study
· BASIS: A big data architecture for smart cities
· Big data for smart grid operation in smart cities
· Auditing and Assessment of Data Traffic Flows in an IoT Architecture
· An Audit Framework for Data Lifecycles in a Big Data context
· IoT-based smart city development using big data analytical approach
· Artificial Intelligence in Smart City Analysis

Big data analytics considers the progression of a wide variety of uses. Things can be looked for, directed, analyzed, and even consolidated into aggregate beguilements. Ventures, human services, and urban regions are abusing IoT data driven frameworks to make these affiliations increasingly beneficial, along these lines, upgrading the lives of occupants. For making IoT a reality, data made by sensors, propelled cell phones, watches, and various wearables ought to be facilitated; furthermore, the significance of IoT data should be explicitly addressed. In any case, the Big Data nature of IoT data powers difficulties that ought to be tended to keeping in consideration the ultimate objective to give flexible and profitable IoT data driven establishments. These issues have been dealt with and focussed on the issues of depicting the centrality of IoT spilling data using reasoning and fusing this data in a learning outline.

The Internet-of-Things (IoT) has supposed control over the business range, and its applications fluctuate broadly from farming and social insurance to transportation. A hospital condition can be extremely upsetting, particularly for senior people and youngsters. With the consistently expanding total populace, the regular patient-physical check up has lost its viability. Thus, keen medicinal services turns out to be critical. Savvy social insurance can be actualized at all levels, beginning from temperature checking for children to following essential signs in the elderly .Data technology has progressed amid the most recent five decades to the phase where its effect is being felt by the general public in each administration that it gets from media, business, health care, shopper devices, vitality and power, and transportation domains. Amid this course of human-technology collaboration tremendous measure of data and learning exchange happens straightforwardly between specialist co-ops and their customers, and in addition by implication between customers. Since human propensity is to "investigate" its past with a specific end goal to foresee the "future", monitoring this powerfully gushing voluminous heterogeneous data, called Big Data (BD), and examining it for significantrevelation of learning that prompts esteem included business turns into a critical research action. It is in this setting research in Big Data (BD) figuring has developed. Important choices can be construct just with respect to huge information disclosure, which thus requires a decent comprehension of the attributes of the aggregated data, a fitting grouping of this enormous gathering, and a proficient investigation of it. Health care part is a basic framework since its administrations influence the lives of humans and the absence of administration coherence might be unfortunate to the economy and human lives. The huge measure of data gathered by this part from its customers is organized into sections based on importance and relevance and further processed through intelligent utilities.

4. FUTURE RESEARCH DIRECTIONS

Big data analytics and IoT are becoming the research focal point in industries and academia. Data science aims at researching big data and knowledge extraction from data. Applications of big data and data science include information science, uncertainty modeling, uncertain data analysis, machine learning, statistical learning, pattern recognition, data warehousing, and signal processing. Effective integration of technologies and analysis will result in predicting the future drift of events. Main focus of this section is to discuss open research issues in big data analytics. The research issues pertaining to big data analysis are classified into three broad categories namely internet of things (IoT), cloud computing, bio inspired computing, and quantum computing. However it is not limited to these issues.

Big Data and IoT in Mobile Communication

Internet has restructured global interrelations, the art of businesses, cultural revolutions and an unbelievable number of personal characteristics. Currently, machines are getting in on the act to control innumerable autonomous gadgets via internet and create Internet of Things (IoT). Thus, appliances are becoming the user of the internet, just like humans with the web browsers. Internet of Things is attracting the attention of recent researchers for its most promising opportunities and challenges. It has an imperative economic and societal impact for the future construction of information, network and communication technology. The new regulation of future will be eventually, everything will be connected and intelligently controlled. The concept of IoT is becoming more pertinent to the realistic world due to the development of mobile de- vices, embedded and ubiquitous communication technologies, cloud computing, and data analytics. Moreover, IoT presents challenges in combinations of volume, velocity and variety. In a broader sense, just like the internet, Internet of Things enables the devices to exist in a myriad of places and facilitates applications ranging from trivial to the crucial. Conversely, it is still mystifying to understand IoT well, including definitions, content and differences from other similar concepts. Several diversified technologies such as computational intelligence, and big-data can be incorporated together to improve the data management and knowledge discovery of large scale automation applications. Much research in this direction has been carried out by eminent researchers.

Big Data and IoT in Cloud Computing

The development of virtualization technologies have made super computing more accessible and affordable. Computing infrastructures that are hidden in virtualization software make systems to behave like a true computer, but with the flexibility of specification details such as number of processors, disk space, memory, and operating system. The use of these virtual computers is known as cloud computing which has been one of the most robust big data technique. Big Data and cloud computing technologies are developed with the importance of developing a salable and on demand availability of resources and data. Cloud computing harmonize massive data by on- demand access to configurable computing resources through virtualization techniques. The benefits of utilizing the Cloud computing include offering resources when there is a demand and pay only for the resources which is needed to develop the product. Simultaneously, it improves availability and cost reduction. Open challenges and research issues of big data and cloud computing are discussed in detail by many re- searchers which highlights the challenges in data management, data variety and velocity, data storage, data processing, and resource management. So Cloud computing helps in developing a business model for all varieties of applications with infrastructure and tools.

Evolutionary Computing and Big Data Analytics

Bio-inspired computing is a technique inspired ny nature to address complex real world problems. Biological systems are self organized without a central control. A bio-inspired cost minimization mechanism search and find the optimal data service solution on considering cost of data management and service maintenance. These techniques are developed by biological molecules such as DNA and proteins to conduct computational calculations involving storing, retrieving, and processing of data. A significant feature of such computing is that it integrates biologically derived materials to perform computational functions and receive intelligent performance. These systems are more suitable for big data applications.

Big Data Analysis in IoT and Quantum Computing Research

A quantum computer has memory that is exponentially larger than its physical size and can manipulate an exponential set of inputs simultaneously [33]. This exponential improve- ment in computer systems might be possible. If a real quantum computer is available now, it could have solved problems that are exceptionally difficult on recent computers, of course today's big data problems. The main technical difficulty in building quantum computer could soon be possible. Quantum computing provides a way to merge the quantum mechanics to process the information. In traditional computer, information is presented by long strings of bits which encode either a zero or a one. On the other hand a quantum computer uses quantum bits or qubits. The difference between qubit and bit is that, a qubit is a quantum system that encodes the zero and the one into two distinguishable quantum states. Therefore, it can be capitalized on the phenomena of superposition and entanglement. It is because qubits behave in quantum way. For example, 100 qubits in quantum systems require 2100 complex values to be stored in a classic computer system. It means that many big data problems can be solved much faster by larger scale quantum computers compared with classical computers. Hence it is a challenge for this generation to built a quantum computer and facilitate quantum computing to solve big data problems.

5. CONCLUSION

Big data analytics empowers data diggers and researchers to examine an extensive volume of data that may not be outfit utilizing customary apparatuses. Big data analytics require advances and statistical instruments that can change a lot of organized, unstructured, and semi-organized data into a more reasonable data and metadata design for explanatory procedures. There is tremendous positive potential concerning application of big data in smart city applications. The above chapter focuses on many versatile applications related to smart city and the contribution of big data analytics in IoT based systems to enhance the functionality of intelligent IoT systems.

REFERENCES

Ahlgren, B., Hidell, M., & Ngai, E. C. (2016). Internet of Things for Smart Cities: Interoperability and Open Data. *IEEE Internet Computing*, *20*(6), 52–56. doi:10.1109/MIC.2016.124

Arass, M. E., Tikito, I., & Souissi, N.(2018). An Audit Framework for Data Lifecycles in a Big Data context. *International Conference on Selected Topics in Mobile and Wireless Networking (MoWNeT)*, 1-5. doi: 10.1109/MoWNet.2018.8428883

Bashir, M. R., & Gill, A. Q. (2016). Towards an IoT Big Data Analytics Framework: Smart Buildings Systems. *IEEE 18th International Conference on High Performance Computing and Communications; IEEE 14th International Conference on Smart City; IEEE 2nd International Conference on Data Science and Systems (HPCC/SmartCity/DSS)*, 1325-1332. 10.1109/HPCC-SmartCity-DSS.2016.0188

Bellini, P., Nesi, P., Paolucci, M., & Zaza, I. (2018). Smart City Architecture for Data Ingestion and Analytics: Processes and Solutions. *2018 IEEE Fourth International Conference on Big Data Computing Service and Applications (BigDataService)*, 137-144. 10.1109/BigDataService.2018.00028

Cheng, B., Longo, S., Cirillo, F., Bauer, M., & Kovacs, E. (2015). Building a Big Data Platform for Smart Cities: Experience and Lessons from Santander. *IEEE International Congress on Big Data*, 592-599. 10.1109/BigDataCongress.2015.91

Chin, J., Callaghan, V., & Lam, I. (2017). Understanding and personalising smart city services using machine learning, The Internet-of-Things and Big Data. *IEEE 26th International Symposium on Industrial Electronics (ISIE)*, 2050-2055. 10.1109/ISIE.2017.8001570

Costa, C., & Santos, M. Y. (2016). BASIS: A big data architecture for smart cities. *SAI Computing Conference (SAI)*, 1247-1256. 10.1109/SAI.2016.7556139

Dattana, V., Gupta, K., & Kush, A. (2019). A Probability based Model for Big Data Security in Smart City. *2019 4th MEC International Conference on Big Data and Smart City (ICBDSC)*, 1-6. 10.1109/ICBDSC.2019.8645607

Hussain, M. M., Beg, M. M. S., Alam, M. S., Krishnamurthy, M., & Ali, Q. M. (2018). Computing Platforms for Big Data Analytics in Electric Vehicle Infrastructures. *4th International Conference on Big Data Computing and Communications (BIGCOM)*, 138-143. 10.1109/BIGCOM.2018.00029

Kök, I., Şimşek, M. U., & Özdemir, S. (2017). A deep learning model for air quality prediction in smart cities. *2017 IEEE International Conference on Big Data (Big Data)*, 1983-1990. 10.1109/BigData.2017.8258144

Lieberman, J., Leidner, A., Percivall, G., & Rönsdorf, C. (2017). Using big data analytics and IoT principles to keep an eye on underground infrastructure. *IEEE International Conference on Big Data (Big Data)*, 4592-4601. 10.1109/BigData.2017.8258503

Manjunath, P., Prakruthi, M., & Gajkumar Shah, P. (2018). IoT Driven with Big Data Analytics and Block Chain Application Scenarios. *Second International Conference on Green Computing and Internet of Things (ICGCIoT)*, 569-572. 10.1109/ICGCIoT.2018.8752973

Manjunatha & Annappa B. (2018). Real Time Big Data Analytics in Smart City Applications. *2018 International Conference on Communication, Computing and Internet of Things (IC3IoT)*, 279-284.doi: 10.1109/IC3IoT.2018.8668106

Nandury, S. V., & Begum, B. A. (2017). Big data for smart grid operation in smart cities. *International Conference on Wireless Communications, Signal Processing and Networking (WiSPNET)*, 1507-1511. 10.1109/WiSPNET.2017.8300013

Navarathna, P. J., & Malagi, V. P. (2018). Artificial Intelligence in Smart City Analysis. *International Conference on Smart Systems and Inventive Technology (ICSSIT)*, 44-47. 10.1109/ICSSIT.2018.8748476

Nesi, P., Pantaleo, G., Paolucci, M., & Zaza, I. (2018). Auditing and Assessment of Data Traffic Flows in an IoT Architecture. *IEEE 4th International Conference on Collaboration and Internet Computing (CIC)*, 388-391. 10.1109/CIC.2018.00058

Nguyen, S., Salcic, Z., & Zhang, X. (2018). Big Data Processing in Fog - Smart Parking Case Study. *IEEE Intl Conf on Parallel & Distributed Processing with Applications, Ubiquitous Computing & Communications, Big Data & Cloud Computing, Social Computing & Networking, Sustainable Computing & Communications (ISPA/IUCC/BDCloud/SocialCom/SustainCom)*, 127-134. doi:10.1109/BDCloud.2018.00031

Rathore, M. M., Ahmad, A., & Paul, A. (2016). IoT-based smart city development using big data analytical approach. *IEEE International Conference on Automatica (ICA-ACCA)*, 1-8. 10.1109/ICA-ACCA.2016.7778510

Rizwan, P., Suresh, K., & Babu, M. R. (2016). Real-time smart traffic management system for smart cities by using Internet of Things and big data. *International Conference on Emerging Technological Trends (ICETT)*, 1-7. . 2016.787366010.1109/ICETT.2016.7873660

Shah, S. A., Seker, D. Z., Rathore, M. M., Hameed, S., & Yahia, S. (2019). Towards Disaster Resilient Smart Cities: Can Internet of Things and Big Data Analytics Be the Game Changers? IEEE Access, 7, 91885-91903. doi:10.1109/ACCESS.2019.2928233

Sharif, A., Li, J., Khalil, M., Kumar, R., Sharif, M. I., & Sharif, A. (2017). Internet of things — smart traffic management system for smart cities using big data analytics. *2017 14th International Computer Conference on Wavelet Active Media Technology and Information Processing (ICCWAMTIP)*, 281-284. doi: 10.1109/ICCWAMTIP.2017.8301496

Shukla, S., Balachandran, K., & Sumitha, V. S. (2016). A framework for smart transportation using Big Data. *International Conference on ICT in Business Industry & Government (ICTBIG)*, 1-3. 10.1109/ICTBIG.2016.7892720

Shukla, S. N., & Champaneria, T. A. (2017). Survey of various data collection ways for smart transportation domain of smart city. *2017 International Conference on I-SMAC (IoT in Social, Mobile, Analytics and Cloud) (I-SMAC)*, 681-685. 10.1109/I-SMAC.2017.8058265

Sun, Y., Song, H., Jara, H. J., & Bie, R. (2016). Internet of Things and Big Data Analytics for Smart and Connected Communities. *IEEE Access: Practical Innovations, Open Solutions*, 4, 766–773. doi:10.1109/ACCESS.2016.2529723

Zenkert, J., Dornhofer, M., Weber, C., Ngoukam, & Fathi, M. (2018). Big data analytics in smart mobility: Modeling and analysis of the Aarhus smart city dataset. *IEEE Industrial Cyber-Physical Systems (ICPS)*, 363-368. doi:10.1109/ICPHYS.2018.8387685

KEY TERMS AND DEFINITIONS

Big Data: Big data frequently refers to data sets with sizes away from the ability of frequently used software tools to confine, curate, administer, and process data contained by a supportable elapsed instance. Big data philosophy encompasses shapeless, semi-structured and prepared data, however the main focal point is on unstructured data.

Big Data Analytics: Big data analytics is the often composite process of examining large and wide-ranging data sets, or big data, to come across information—such as concealed patterns, indefinite correlations, market development and client preferences—that can help organizations create informed business decisions.

Cloud Computing: Cloud computing is the on-demand ease of use of computer system resources, particularly data storage and computing influence, without direct active organization by the user. The expression is generally used to explain data centers obtainable to many users over the Internet.

Evolutionary Computing: In computer science, evolutionary computation is a ancestors of algorithms for comprehensive optimization inspired by biological evolution, and a coordinated section of artificial intelligence and soft computing using these algorithms.

Internet of Things: The Internet of Things (IoT) is a arrangement of organized computing devices such as mechanical equipment or digital machines, they can be objects or community that are provided with exclusive identifiers and the facility to transfer data over a set-up without requiring human-to-human or human-to-computer communication.

Mobile Communication: Mobile communication allows broadcast of voice and multimedia data via a workstation or a mobile device exclusive of having connected to any physical or fixed connection. Mobile communication is growing day by day and has become a must have for every person. Mobile communication is the exchange of voice and data using a communication facility at the same time without any physical link.

Quantum Computing: All computing systems rely on an elementary ability to store and control information. Existing computers manipulate individual bits, which accumulate information as binary 0 and 1 states. Quantum computers focus more power on quantum mechanical phenomena to direct required information.

This research was previously published in the Encyclopedia of Information Science and Technology, Fifth Edition; pages 586-601, copyright year 2021 by Engineering Science Reference (an imprint of IGI Global).

Chapter 18
Integrating Blockchain Platforms With Big Data Solutions for Regional Innovation Development

Leyla Ayvarovna Gamidullaeva
https://orcid.org/0000-0003-3042-7550
Penza State University, Russia

Vardan Mkrttchian
https://orcid.org/0000-0003-4871-5956
HHH University, Australia

Alexey Finogeev
https://orcid.org/0000-0002-4777-3364
Penza State University, Russia

ABSTRACT

The chapter discusses the creation of a mechanism for ensuring reliable and secure interaction among participants in regional innovation systems based on the establishment of smart contracts in the block-chain. The technology allows to reduce the possibility of fraud by dishonest participants, as well as to exclude the need for a third party by transferring its functions to a smart contract. This is important for ensuring confidential and transparent relations between participants in innovative projects, as well as with interested subjects of social and economic activities in the regions. The Ethereum blockchain plat-form was chosen to create smart contracts. On its basis, there were developed components to perform transactions in contracting, creating, and implementing innovations, transferring intellectual property rights, using rights and licenses for innovation, etc. The main component of the system is a distributed transaction register with digital copies of innovation objects.

DOI: 10.4018/978-1-6684-3662-2.ch018

INTRODUCTION

Today we can observe the strengthening of global communication accessibility that promotes the emergence of new economic relations on the principles of collaborative behavior.

The authors in previous research identified that the main barrier impeding efficient interaction of innovation actors in Russian Federation (RF) is high level of transaction costs. As a rule, there are growing instability and uncertainty of existing links and relationships at innovation activity stages, which, in particular, stimulate the growth of transaction costs. This determines high costs of development and implementation of innovations. Such costs are not of transformational nature associated with transformations and changes of initial resources, but of transactional one that is determined by a necessity of collaborations and mutually beneficial contacts.

The strengthening of interactions between interested participants in a regional system appears to be an important mechanism of innovation activity development from the emergence of an idea to the commercialization of innovation.

It is reasonable to use digital technologies to organize and support an innovation system that simplify and promote interactions between innovation activity participants by performing a situational analysis of large volumes of structured and unstructured data on innovation activity subjects in the regions.

The cyber-social innovation system may be considered as an intelligent information system focused on lowering the barriers to implementation of innovations by engaging a larger amount of participants in the innovation process and ensuring their intensive interaction. Its synthesis requires a mechanism that will enable different agents of innovation interaction having common development goals to create new knowledge and exchange it in a safe intelligent network.

The Internet of Things (IoT), Big Data and blockchain are three main trends that could combine to create an entirely new methods and tools for managing regional innovation system and provide their economic development. Blockchain technology provides the ability to redistribute costs across all of the participants of the peer-to-peer network, and give each peer an economic motivation to provide their (small) part of the infrastructure needed to enable the greater good. This reduces the burden on any individual peer, while allowing them to leverage the resources of all (Sun, et al., 2015).

The aim of the present chapter is to substantiate the essence, peculiarities and features of integrating blockchain platforms with Big Data intelligent analytics for regional innovation development. The study was carried out based on materials describing the development of this concept both in the whole world and its spread in the Russian economy.

BACKGROUND

The world experience in transition to the digital economy is disclosed in the works by Tapscott D. (1996), Brynjolfsson E. & Kahin B. (Eds.) (2003), Wetherbe J.C., Turban E., Leidner D.E. & McLean E.R. (2008).

Digital economy operates at three levels - markets and industries, platforms and technologies, environment (Bershadsky, et al, 2017). At the first level, suppliers and consumers interact, at the second level; competencies are formed for the development of markets and sectors of the economy. The third level is the environment that creates conditions for the development of platforms and technologies. Technological tools and management models are necessary for its successful operation and development. They will participate in all three levels, create "cross-cutting" technologies to operate in the global market and develop infrastructure for the digital economy (Mkrttchian, et al, 2016).

Many researches today are devoted to the investigation of the technologies and processes concerned with Industry 4.0 and its impact on economic development. Industry 4.0 supposes the use of network approach that is based on the ability of creating smart products and components (Kohlberg & Zühlke, 2015). According to the authors (Kohlberg & Zühlke, 2015) Industry 4.0 enables new implementation areas through the potential of Industry 4.0 technologies such as powerful, flexible and affordable Cyber Physical Systems' applications with various production types.

The Internet of Things (IoT), Big Data and blockchain are three main trends that could combine to create an entirely new methods and tools for managing regional innovation system and provide their economic development. This development looks at the 'art of the possible' and this new way of thinking could provide powerful ways for a business to run autonomously (Sun, et al., 2015).

Blockchain technology provides an alternative that allows any single participant to essentially "outsource" the management, communications and scalable infrastructure problems to the peer-to-peer network that maintains the blockchain. Instead of using a central server, a distributed public ledger will be maintained to store the transaction records of "things" and every node will possess a copy of this immutable public ledger. The "scalability" feature of blockchain can be utilized to accommodate 'things' in the IoT world (Sun, et al., 2015).

Blockchain is a specifically structured uninterrupted sequential chain of blocks (chained list, distributed register) containing information on participants and existing innovations (Swan, 2015). Copies of blockchains are stored and processed independently from each other in multiple network nodes (Franco, 2014; Antonopoulos, 2014). Originally the term referred to the completely replicated distributed data base (register) designed for the "Bitcoin" system, as the technology was initially intended for cryptocurrency transactions. Although blockchain can be applied to any interconnected information objects. Blockchain is actually a chain of blocks connected sequentially. In blockchains, the chronologically ordered data points are grouped into individual storage units called blocks. These blocks are then ordered sequentially and stored in a decentralized manner across all the participating nodes to form the blockchain (Asharaf and Adarsh, 2017).

Bughin and Manyika (2015) assumed that the crucial impact factor in competition is related with the Internet of Things (IoT) which means that senior managers and company's members must act at the system level in order to be able to solve the challenges coming from the technological disruption.

Big data and big data analytics have become the important frontier for innovation, research and development (Chen and Zhang, 2014; Laney and Jain, 2017). Big data and its emerging technologies including big data analytics have been not only making big changes in the way the business operate but also making traditional data analytics and business analytics bring forth new big opportunities for academia and enterprises (Sun, et al., 2016, Sun, et al., 2014; McAfee and Brynjolfsson, 2012).

An intelligent big data analytics becomes the disruptive technology for the age of trinity in terms of healthcare, web services, service computing, cloud computing and social networking computing (Laney and Jain, 2017).

MAIN FOCUS OF THE CHAPTER

The ubiquitous development and implementation of blockchain technology will fundamentally change the way the economy functions today and how economic transactions are carried out.

The blockchain technology was developed in order to create a decentralized model for data exchange and storage, which is controlled using a decentralized operating system. Decentralized systems cannot be controlled by a minority of participants or a single body exercising centralized management, and they are transparent to all participants, as well as self-governing.

Blockchain has strong advantages for systems where it is necessary:

The Trust: Any process where the intermediary provides a trusting relationship between the producer and the consumer (information, product or something else).

Reliability: Blockchain was created as an impenetrable fortress to protect value, especially digital assets (Figure 1).

Figure 1. Main features of blockchain

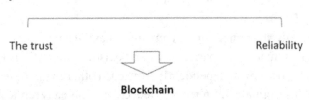

The Use of Big Data Analytics in Regional Economic Development

Big data analysis and analytics help user organizations get value in the form of more numerous and accurate business insights. Similarly, universities can get value with Big Data analytics, - one gets a host of new possibilities ranging from new ways of providing students with basic support to new ways of getting students to learn what the faculty needs them to learn. Furthermore, the rapid advancement of big data analytics make it necessary for any university to coincide it with their management and measurement.

Big data analytics can be defined as the process of collecting, organizing and analyzing big data to discover, visualize and display patterns, knowledge, and intelligence within the big data (Sun, et al., 2015). Similarly, big data analytics can be defined as techniques used to analyze, acquire and visualize knowledge and intelligence from big data (Gandomi and Haider, 2015). The main components of big data analytics include big data descriptive analytics, big data predictive analytics and big data prescriptive analytics (Sun, Zou, & Strang, 2015; Gandomi & Haider, 2015).

Big data analytics can facilitate business decisions and business goals by analyzing existing data and future trends, creating predictive models for predicting future threats and opportunities, and streamlining business processes to improve the performance of an organization using the methods mentioned (Delena and Demirkanb, 2013; Chen, et al., 2012).

The Big Data is usually characterized by five properties:

1.   **Volume:** Typically, Big Data refers to massive volumes of data, usually in zettabytes (ZB) or more.

2. **Variety:** The data consists of a mixture of structured, unstructured and semistructured information, drawn from such vastly heterogeneous sources as RFID (radio frequency identification), web searches, social media, mobile sensors like GPS and accelerometers, high fidelity industrial sensors, video streaming etc.

3. **Velocity:** Big Data arrives at varying speeds ranging from milliseconds to days to years, and has differing requirements on the speed with which it is to be processed.

4. **Value:** Some researchers consider value as a key characteristic of Big Data, with data being considered valuable if useful information (from a business or engineering perspective) can be extracted from large data sets where individual data points may not carry any value by themselves.

5. **Veracity:** This refers to the accuracy and trustworthiness of the data. This becomes increasingly relevant when large numbers of users in the IoT may be reluctant to report truthful data due to privacy and security concerns (Saravanan, et al., 2019).

The rapid growth of the IoT technologies and the creation of large-scale cyber-physical systems human networks has made Big Data tools crucial to every IoT application. Data generated from devices was already big even before the arrival of IoT. Now, this data is projected to double every two years to reach an estimated 35 ZB (zettabytes) with more than 50 billion estimated devices by the year 2020.

However, Big Data technologies must surmount several key barriers including standards, security and privacy, efficient storage and analysis and network infrastructure.

Basic requirements for implementation of Big Data:

1. **Requirements for Modern Platforms for Collection and Processing of Data:** In the IoT paradigm, data is acquired from various resources such as internet, social media, mobile sensors, RFID etc. The platform for Big Data have the technology to work with data alone (structured and unstructured), and with data in motion (powerful data streams from any type of source). Stream processing needed: overcoming the curse of dimension in data storage.

2. **Platform Must be Trained by Real Time System: the Goal of Training IT systems is Undoubtedly the Improvement of their Characteristics on two Basic Factors Influencing the Quality of the Solution:** IT awareness and intelligence. Any ideas for teaching people or systems are based on applying knowledge accumulated in the past to make decisions in the present or predict the future, on the idea of feedback from the past to the present. The processed data is mined using learning techniques to extract useful information, which can then be visualized and used for predictive analysis.

3. **Data Management:** Several powerful Big Data technologies like MapReduce and NoSQL used to retrieve data effectively from heterogeneous sources and process it according to application needs.

4. Free adaptive search and production of information: the legitimate ways of extracting information are technologically implemented through the toolkit of search platforms that provide teams of analysts (IT and business) with the possibility of free creative search in all cyberspace. Modern platforms implement the concept of free search across cyberspace under the control of a creative team, with feedback on this team.

Blockchain and Smart Contracts for Interaction Of Economic Actors

It should be noted that elements of any cyber-social system depend on the provided safe and reliable interaction within transaction processes aimed at elaboration and implementation of development mechanisms, including the innovation ones. The trending transition to digital economy means that the most processes of informational interaction should be carried out with minimal human involvement. At the same time an important role in digital economy is assigned to safety and transparency of transactions between interacting agents that should be provided by blockchain and smart contracts.

As we know, purchasing, selling and renting various products and services on the Internet and by online commerce is a complicated task. The main problem is trust relationships or a lack thereof between unacquainted transaction participants. To solve this problem it is required to address the third party for guarantees of transaction settlement. But even in this case the problem of safety is not resolved by high reliability. In risk management the technology of the distributed register (blockchain) is being applied more actively, as it reduces the probability of fraud from dishonest participants and excludes the need for the third party by transferring its functions to the intelligent system.

All data are stored in network nodes of users of the distributed register system. Each node stores a part of information in the form of data blocks or copies of such blocks. This principle makes the system virtually invincible to information threats and attacks, all the more these blocks are protected by cryptographic keys and calculated using the algorithm of hash-functions.

An example of blockchain application in intellectual property rights management in Russia is the implementation of IPChain on HyperLedger Fabric allowing to work with different information channels within a single register and determining the transaction approval policy for each of them. Hyperledger Fabric is a project of the consortium led by IBM embracing top IT companies, such as Intel, Oracle, Cisco, Digital Assets, etc. The main advantage is an adaptive algorithm designed to achieve concord between trusted nodes by means of a mechanism that performs decentralized registration of transactions in a set number of equal nodes and, in case the authenticity of results is proved, confirms a transaction. The infrastructure of IPChain includes a bound register of intellectual property objects and a transaction register with the said objects, transaction registry nodes, transaction fixing nodes, network administration nodes and trust certificate issuing nodes.

In 1994 N. Szabo (Szabo, 1997) proposed the concept of smart contracts, which became possible to realize only in 2008, when blockchain occurred. A smart contract is a special protocol intended to contribute, verify or implement the negotiation or performance of the contract by means of blockchain. This type of contracts fits any transactions. It guarantees money transfer or execution of other actions as soon as all parties have completed contract obligations. When parties conclude a smart contract, it is similar to transferring of cryptocurrency blockchain funds. After that the contract comes into effect. In order to have contract's obligations automatically complied with there is required a special environment enabling automatic execution of all contract's clauses. Thus, a smart contract can exist only within such environment, where the program code executing the contract's algorithm has access to its objects. Therefore, all relationships between parties within the contract should be mathematically formalized and feature a clean execution logic. According to transaction conditions, the smart contract's algorithm tracks accomplishments or breaches of its clauses and makes a corresponding decision automatically to ensure authenticity of contract obligations.

The objects of smart contracts may be the following:

- Interacting parties accepting or declining contract's conditions via digital signatures,
- Contract's subjects including objects in the field of contract's existence,
- Conditions that display a logic of contract clause execution in the form of a formalized mathematical description, which can be programmed in the field of contract's existence.

In turn, the existence of smart contracts requires as follows:

- Application of digital signatures on the basis of public and private keys through asymmetric encryption.
- Presence of open distributed data bases for storing of data on executable transactions with access for contracting parties.
- Availability of a distributed network to execute Ethereum, Codius, Counterparty contracts, etc.
- Digital data source validation, for example, by means of SSL certification centers.

Today modern blockchain platforms are used to develop decentralized applications (DApps). Although decentralized applications are similar to smart contracts, they have no direct connection with funds and enable to utilize blockchain for any means. DApps have no limitations in the number of participants and they are independent from market segments.

SOLUTIONS AND RECOMMENDATIONS

To create a blockchain system of interactions between regional innovation system subjects it is necessary to choose a platform and to develop a series of components on its basis that execute various transactions. The system must provide safe and reliable conclusion of contracts and accomplishment of contract obligations when developing and implementing innovations, as well as transfer of intellectual property rights, carrying out the stipulations of license agreements, transparency, protection and conservation of data on innovations and innovation companies, opportunities for rights and licenses usage monitoring in the course of innovation activities, etc.

CONCLUSION

The chapter considers questions of creation of a new mechanism providing reliable and safe interaction of regional innovation system's participants on the basis of smart contracts created in blockchain.

ACKNOWLEDGMENT

The reported study was funded by RFBR according to the projects: N° 18-010-00204, 16–07-00031, 17–307-50010, 18–07-00975.

REFERENCES

Aeternity blockchain. Retrieved from https://aeternity.com/

Antonopoulos, A. (2014). *The Blockchain. Mastering Bitcoin.* Sebastopol, CA: O'Reilly Media.

Asharaf, S., & Adarsh, S. (2017). Introduction to Blockchain Technology. In *Decentralized Computing Using Blockchain Technologies and Smart Contracts: Emerging Research and Opportunities* (pp. 10–27). Hershey, PA: IGI Global. doi:10.4018/978-1-5225-2193-8.ch002

Bershadsky, A., Bozhday, A., Evseeva, Y., Gudkov, A., & Mkrtchian, V. (2017). Techniques for adaptive graphics applications synthesis based on variability modeling technology and graph theory. *Communications in Computer and Information Science, 754,* 455–466. doi:10.1007/978-3-319-65551-2_33

Blockchain app platform. (n.d.). Retrieved from https://www.ethereum.org/

Blockchain in Russia. (2018). Retrieved from http://www.tadviser.ru/index.php/Статья:Блокчейн_в_России#cite_note-7

Blockchain platforms. (n.d.). Retrieved from http://smart-contracts.ru/platforms.html

Brynjolfsson, E., & Kahin, B. (2003). Understanding the digital economy: Data, tools, and research. *The Journal of Documentation, 59*(4), 487–490. doi:10.1108/00220410310485785

Cardano is a decentralised public blockchain and cryptocurrency project and is fully open source. Retrieved from https://www.cardano.org/en/home/

Chen, C. P., & Zhang, C.-Y. (2014). Data-intensive applications, challenges, techniques and technologies: A survey on Big Data. *Information Sciences, 275,* 314–347. doi:10.1016/j.ins.2014.01.015

Chen, H., Chiang, R., & Storey, V. (2012). Business intelligence and analytics: From big data to big impact. Decentralized platforms for smart contracts: challenges and solutions. *Management Information Systems Quarterly, 36*(4), 1165–1188. doi:10.2307/41703503

Delena, D., & Demirkanb, H. (2013). Data, information and analytics as services. *Decision Support Systems, 55*(1), 359–363. doi:10.1016/j.dss.2012.05.044

Sun, Z., Zou, H., & Strang, K. (2015, October). Big data analytics as a service for business intelligence. In *14th Conference on e-Business, e-Services and e-Society,* Delft, The Netherlands. (pp. 200-211). Cham, Switzerland: Springer. doi:. ffhal-014480310.1007/978-3-319-25013-7_16ff

Finogeev, A. G. (2004). *Simulation of systems-synergistic processes in information environments.* Penza, Russia: Penza State University.

Franco, P. (2014). *The Blockchain. Understanding Bitcoin: Cryptography, Engineering and Economics.* Hoboken, NJ: John Wiley & Sons.

Gamidullaeva, L. A. (2016). About formation of innovation management system in Russia. *Economic Revival of Russia, 4,* 50, 74-84.

Gamidullaeva, L. A. & Tolstykh, T. O. (2017, November). Transaction Costs, Institutions and Regional Innovation Development: the Case of Russia. *Proceedings of the 30th International Business Information Management Association Conference (IBIMA)*, Madrid, Spain. Vision 2020: Sustainable Economic Development, Innovation Management, and Global Growth. 2121-2135.

Gandomi, A. & Haider, M. (2015). Beyond the hype: Big data concepts, methods, and analytics. *International Journal of Information Management, 35*, 137–144.

Hyperledger Fabric is a platform for distributed ledger solutions. Retrieved from http://hyperledger-fabric.readthedocs.io/en/release-1.1/

In Russia may appear a blocking analogue of eBay in the field of intellectual property management. Retrieved from https://forklog.com/v-rossii-mozhet-poyavitsya-blokchejn-analog-ebay-v-sfere-upravleniya-intellektualnymi-pravami/

Laney, D. & Jain, A. (2017, June 20). 100 Data and Analytics Predictions Through. Retrieved from https://www.gartner.com/events-na/data-analytics/wp-content/uploads/sites/5/2017/10/Data-and-Analytics-Predictions.pdf

McAfee, A., & Brynjolfsson, E. (2012). Big data: The management revolution. *Harvard Business Review*, (October), 61–68. PMID:23074865

Minelli, M., Chambers, M., & Dhiraj, A. (2013). *Big Data, Big Analytics: Emerging Business Intelligence and Analytic Trends for Today's Businesses* (Chinese Edition 2014). Hoboken, NJ: Wiley & Sons. doi:10.1002/9781118562260

Mkrttchian, V., Kataev, M., Hwang, W., Bedi, S., & Fedotova, A. (2016). Using Plug-Avatars "hhh" Technology Education as Service-Oriented Virtual Learning Environment in Sliding Mode. Leadership and Personnel Management: Concepts, Methodologies, Tools, and Applications (4 Volumes), IRMA, (pp. 890-902). Hershey, PA: IGI Global. doi:10.4018/978-1-4666-9624-2.ch039

Official site of Ascribe company. Retrieved from https://www.ascribe.io/

Poon, J., & Dryja, T. (2016). The Bitcoin Lightning Network: scalable off-chain instant payments. Retrieved from http://lightning.network/lightning-network-paper.pdf

Smart Contracts. Explained. Partnership Material. Retrieved from https://cointelegraph.com/explained/smart-contracts-explained

Solidity is a contract-oriented, high-level language for implementing smart contracts. Retrieved from http://solidity.readthedocs.io/en/v0.4.24/

Sun, Z., Strang, K., & Yearwood, J. (2014). *Analytics service oriented architecture for enterprise information systems. Proceedings of iiWAS2014, CONFENIS,* (pp. 506–518). Hanoi, Vietnam: ACM. doi:10.1145/2684200.2684358

Sun, Z., Sun, L., & Strang, K. (2018). Big Data Analytics Services for Enhancing Business Intelligence. *Journal of Computer Information Systems, 58*(2), 162–169. doi:10.1080/08874417.2016.1220239

Swan, M. (2015). *Blockchain: Blueprint for a New Economy*. O'Reilly Media

Szabo, N. (1997). Smart Contracts: Formalizing and Securing Relationships on Public Networks. *First Monday*, 2(9), 9. doi:10.5210/fm.v2i9.548

Tapscott, D. (1996). *The digital economy: Promise and peril in the age of networked intelligence* (Vol. 1). New York, NY: McGraw-Hill. doi:10.10160099- 1333(96)90098-1

Vasin, S. M., & Gamidullaeva, L. A. (2017). Development of Russian innovation system management concept. *Innovations*, 5(223), 34–40.

Wetherbe, J. (2008). *Information technology for management: Transforming organizations in the digital economy*. Hoboken, NJ: John Wiley & Sons.

This research was previously published in Avatar-Based Models, Tools, and Innovation in the Digital Economy; pages 175-186, copyright year 2020 by Business Science Reference (an imprint of IGI Global).

Chapter 19
Big Data in Railway O&M:
A Dependability Approach

Diego Galar

Lulea University of Technology, Sweden & TECNALIA, Spain

Dammika Seneviratne

Lulea University of Technology, Sweden & TECNALIA, Spain

Uday Kumar

Lulea University of Technology, Sweden

ABSTRACT

Railway systems are complex with respect to technology and operations with the involvement of a wide range of human actors, organizations and technical solutions. For the operations and control of such complexity, a viable solution is to apply intelligent computerized systems, for instance, computerized traffic control systems for coordinating airline transportation, or advanced monitoring and diagnostic systems in vehicles. Moreover, transportation assets cannot compromise the safety of the passengers by only applying operation and maintenance activities. Indeed, safety is a more difficult goal to achieve using traditional maintenance strategies and computerized solutions come into the picture as the only option to deal with complex systems interacting among them and trying to balance the growth in technical complexity together with stable and acceptable dependability indexes. Big data analytics are expected to improve the overall performance of the railways supported by smart systems and Internet-based solutions. Operation and Maintenance will be application areas, where benefits will be visible as a consequence of big data policies due to diagnosis and prognosis capabilities provided to the whole network of processes. This chapter shows the possibilities of applying the big data concept in the railway transportation industry and the positive effects on technology and operations from a systems perspective.

DOI: 10.4018/978-1-6684-3662-2.ch019

INTRODUCTION

Industry 4.0 symbolizes a fourth generation of industrial activity as a result of the fourth industrial revolution characterized by smart systems and Internet-based solutions, Landscheidt et al. (2016). The first revolution took place in the 19th century, when production was mechanized. This meant that production was moved from the home or small workshops to large factory units and a new social class was born; the working class. The second revolution occurred in the last century when the production was electrified and parts and processes were standardized. The archetype of this revolution is Ford's assembly line. The digitization of production is usually called the third revolution marked by introduction of programmable logic controllers (PLC) in late 1960s.

The fourth industrial revolution relies on ICT evolution and data driven decision making processes by the means of big data. Two of the characteristic features of Industry 4.0 are computerization with the help of cyber-physical systems and intelligent factories that are based on the concept of "internet of things" (Amadi, 2010). Cyber-physical systems are integrated computer-based or digital components that monitor and control physical devices, also called embedded systems (Le, 2016). These systems communicate over a network usually based on internet technology, creating an "internet of things" (as opposed to social media that could be described as "internet of persons"). Combining these two concepts, we get a distributed network of embedded systems communicating with each other in an ad hoc and dynamic way. In today's competitive environment, there are unmistakable signs that human beings, organizations, cities, systems and so on are increasingly becoming interconnected, instrumented and intelligent.

The transportation sector and especially the railway have not ignored industry 4.0 and adapted most of the positive inputs, as has the aircraft industry (traditional driver of advanced O&M methodologies by the means of massive data capturing).

This is leading to improved quality of services, new savings, enhanced resource utilization and efficiency. This has also facilitated the development of the new services and business models based on the capability of industrial internet and the analytics capabilities provided by big data. Indeed, big data provides a foundation for the next generation of transportation technologies based on the use of advanced information logistics analytics to transform the current state of the art railway platforms into a network of collaborative communities seamlessly moving freight and passengers and delivering services in a planned way. It symbolizes the current trend of automation and data exchange in the transportation sector striving to adopt and adapt the new and emerging technologies to achieve new levels of effectiveness and efficiency.

Big data in railways include necessary stakeholders who instrument, interconnect and finally provide intelligence to the railway system. It means that the complete big data architecture will be comprised of cyber-physical systems, the Internet of things and cloud computing in order to have a real big data environment providing "smart railways". In fact, one of the application areas which created more expectations is a better operation and maintenance in the form of self-learning and smart systems that predict failure, make diagnoses, and trigger maintenance actions. These systems are already having high demands on data access and data quality and use multiple data sources to extract relevant information with further analytics, Lee et al. (2014). Several research projects have focused on the cyber-physical approach for developing intelligent O&M management systems for failure detection, diagnostics and prognostics, Kroll et al. (2014), Sankavaram et al. (2013) and Syed et al. (2012). So far, the main application area has been process and manufacturing industries, but it is pretty obvious that these services have a huge potential in other areas like the railway sector due to the complexity and huge amount of data generated and captured with high quality standards.

Big data analytics in railway O&M are expected to utilize the advanced technologies for predictive analytics and provides decisions based on feasibility. Therefore, big data for O&M services involves data collection, analysis, visualization and decision making for assets. Big data in O&M also addresses a common Achilles heel in asset management: a better assets status forecasting, commonly called prognosis. The estimation of the remaining useful life constitutes the basis for any operation or maintenance service in order to check the probability of mission accomplishment by the asset (Galar et al., 2012).

The 'Big data' approach can be applied to diverse sources of information and create new services based on the ontologies exploited and knowledge discovery performed (Baglee et al., 2014). This adoption of Big data may pave the ground for better Operation and Maintenance policies bridging the gap between them considering that O&M have been historically optimized in independent silos. In summary, the foundation of big data in railway O&M is built around the concepts of interconnectivity, instrumentation and intelligence for the assets by the means of successful proven technologies such industrial internet, cloud computing or industrial Internet of Things (IoT).

INSTRUMENTATION AND INTERCONNECTION

Internet of Things

The Internet of Things (IoT) is a collective term for the developments whereby machinery, vehicles, goods, appliances, clothes and other things and creatures (including humans), is equipped with tiny sensors and computers. IoT could be defined as a dynamic network infrastructure with self-configuring capabilities based on standard interoperable communication protocols where physical and virtual things have identities, physical attributes, and virtual personalities and use intelligent interfaces, and are seamlessly integrated into the information network. In short, the Internet of Things (IoT) is the network of everything—devices, vehicles, buildings and other items embedded with electronics, software, sensors, and network connectivity that enables these objects to collect and exchange data.

Industrial Internet

Industrial internet can be defined as the new and emerging technologies for managing interconnected machines and systems between its physical assets and computational capabilities (Lee et al., 2014).

The Industrial Internet of Things (IIoT) is the use of Internet of Things (IoT) technologies in manufacturing incorporating machine-to-machine communication, big data analytics, harnessing of the sensor data and robotics and automation technologies that have existed in industrial settings for years.

There are three main elements of Industrial Internet:

- **Intelligent Machines:** New ways of connecting myriad of machines, facilities, fleets and networks with advanced sensors, controls and software applications.
- **Advanced Analytics:** Harnessing the power of physics-based analytics, predictive algorithms, automation and deep domain expertise in material science, electrical engineering and other key disciplines required to understand how machines and larger systems operate.

- **People:** Connecting people, whether they work in industrial facilities, offices, hospitals or on the move, at any time to support more intelligent design, operations, maintenance as well as higher quality service and safety. Connecting and combining these elements offers new opportunities across firms and economies.

The Industrial Internet starts with embedding sensors and other advanced instrumentation in an array of machines from the simple to the highly complex. This allows the collection and analysis of an enormous amount of data, which can be used to improve machine performance, and inevitably the efficiency of the systems and networks that link them. Even the data itself can become "intelligent," instantly knowing which users it needs to reach.

The three main components of this concept are intelligent devices, intelligent systems, and digital instrumentation to industrial machines. These represent the first step in the Industrial Internet Revolution.

Several forces at work to make machines and collections of machines more intelligent are costs of deployment (instrumentation, Internet of Things), computing power (nanotechnology) and advanced analytics (Big Data Analytics).

The specific domain of railways with pervasive computer and connection via the train bus where most of the subsystems and their respective sensors are accessible is one of the most promising domains in this regard. Indeed, the interconnection by data buses inside the vehicle of different subsystems with different OEMs open the doors and create new insights for global optimization in a system of system approach replacing the old approach of local optima with reduced scope for O&M of the whole asset and its desired function.

Cyber-Physical Architecture

Cyber-Physical Systems (CPS) is defined as transformative technologies for managing interconnected systems between its physical assets and computational capabilities (Kans and Gill, 2016). The 5-level CPS structure, namely the 5C architecture, provides a step-by-step guideline for developing and deploying a CPS for manufacturing application (Liggins et al., 2015).

- **Smart Connection:** Acquiring accurate and reliable data from machines and their components is the first step in developing a Cyber-Physical System application. The data might be directly measured by sensors or obtained from controller or vehicle/track side systems such as ERP, MES, SCM and CMMS.
- **Data-to-Information Conversion:** Meaningful information to be inferred from the data. In recent years, extensive focus has been applied to develop these algorithms specifically for prognostics and health management applications. By calculating health value, estimated remaining useful life etc., the second level of CPS architecture brings context-awareness to machines.
- **Cyber:** The cyber level acts as central information hub in this architecture. Information is being pushed to it from every connected machine to form the machines network.
- **Cognition:** Implementing CPS on this level generates thorough knowledge of the monitored system. Presentation of the acquired knowledge to expert users supports the correct decision.
- **Configuration:** The configuration level is the feedback from cyber space to physical space and acts as supervisory control to make machines self-configure and self-adaptive. This stage acts as

resilience control system (RCS) to apply the corrective and preventive decisions, which have been made in cognition level, to the monitored system.

Figure 1. Architecture of CPS
Source: Liggins et al., 2015

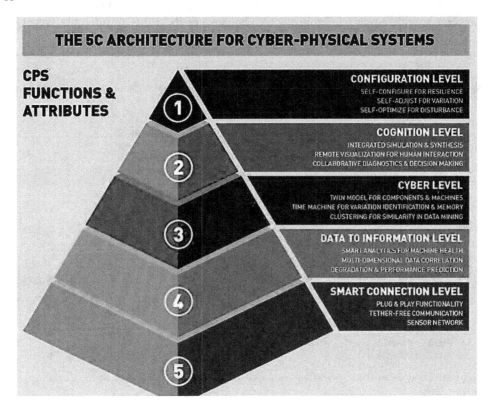

Cloud Computing

According to National Institute of Standards and Technology definition of cloud computing V15, dated 10-7-2009 (NIST, 2009), cloud computing is a model for enabling convenient, on-demand network access to a shared pool of configurable computing resources (for example, networks, servers, storage, applications, and services) that can be rapidly provisioned and released with minimal management effort or service provider interaction. Talking in terms of a cloud for industrial services cloud computing can be seen as a broad array of web-based services aimed at allowing users to obtain a wide range of functional capabilities on a 'pay-as-you-go' basis that previously required tremendous hardware and software investments and professional skills to acquire. Cloud computing is the realization of the earlier ideals of utility computing without the technical complexities or complicated deployment worries.

Therefore, the cloud is just a set of hardware, networks, storage, services, and interfaces that enables the delivery of computing as a service. For maintenance, the cloud seems to be the solution, given the large amounts of dispersed data in different repositories. The end user (maintenance or operators for infrastructure or rolling stock) do not really have to know anything about the underlying technology. The data collection and distribution applications may be dispersed throughout the network and data may be collected at a number of locations.

Figure 2 illustrates a simplified functional block diagram of data flow and communication associated with or used by the asset cloud. In particular, the diagram includes the data collection and distribution system which receive data from numerous data sources.

The cloud can maintain and store these data in the central working data store. At the same time, a user interface can provide a powerful analysis tool because of its ability to integrate layout, inventory, conditions, maintenance input, weather etc.

Figure 2. Services provided by the asset cloud

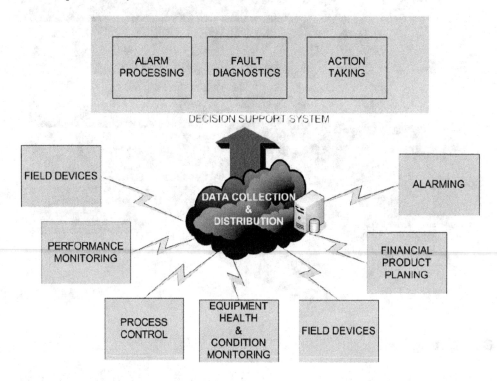

BIG DATA STATE OF THE ART

This section is divided into six parts to fully explain the state of the art in Big Data techniques relevant to the railway sector. Thus, the characteristics of current available commercial tools and the most recent outcomes from the scientific community in predictive algorithms, scalable data structures, data acquisition and communication and visualization and research outcomes in big data techniques applied to the railway operation and maintenance will be described.

Characteristics of Current Available Commercial and Open Source Tools

Big Data software tools: EU VisMaster and Zikopoulos (2011) have performed a deep survey in the visual analytics (VA) and Big Data tools currently available. The summary is described in the following points:

- **Open Source Toolkits:** A number of open-source VA toolkits exist; each covers a specific set of functionalities for visualization, analysis and interaction. For example, InfoVis Toolkit, Prefuse, Improvise and JUNG. Using existing toolkits for required functionality instead of implementing from scratch provides much efficiency while developing new VA solutions, although the level of O&M, development and user community support of open source toolkits can vary drastically. Besides, a relatively high amount of programming expertise and effort is often required to integrate these components into a new system.
- **Commercial VA Systems:** Tableau, Spotfire, QlikView, JMP, Visual Analytics, Centrifuge Jaspersoft, Board and ADVIZOR are the most relevant Big Data commercial software. They consist of long-standing software suites, which have developed out of core database or statistical data analysis suites. Common tasks of BD systems include reporting of historic and current data, performing analysis (intelligence) of data, and publishing prediction capabilities including what-if analysis.

The summary provided by Zikopoulos 2011 allows to easily draw the following conclusions:

1. There is already an important ecosystem (at least 10 very complete commercial SW tools and a similar number of open source tools) for Big Data processing. Most of them share similar features.
2. There is an important limitation in the predictive algorithms. Most of the commercial SW tools do not provide these algorithms, and those which provide them are based on simple linear predictive models such as ARIMA, Holt-Winter or Multi Variable Linear Regression.
3. Hardly all the "input information formats" are excel files, CVS and GIS.
4. The visualization techniques are limited to "control centre" standard statistical charts, georelated data and network description through tree maps. However, real time information is not displayed and neither data to maintenance personnel on-field.

The leading programming paradigm for Big Data is MapReduce. Although its fundamentals have roots in the LISP functional paradigm, the term was coined much more recently, in 2004, by Google MapReduce. While some papers were published, Google's software remained private. Then some researchers interested in the idea began to develop an open-source version. This effort, led by Dog Cutting, ended with a framework written in Java and called Hadoop.

Hadoop has become a framework for distributed storage and distributed processing of very large datasets on computer clusters built from commodity hardware. Two key ideas behind Hadoop are robustness and ease of use. A fundamental assumption is that hardware will probably fail and the system should face that. On the other hand, the functional decomposition of the problems in terms of map, shuffle and reduce modules to provide a general framework within with a linear scalability is possible with almost zero effort from the programmer.

The core of Apache Hadoop consists of a storage component, Hadoop Distributed File System (HDFS), and a processing module. Out of the core functionality a rich ecosystem of applications and tools have been or are currently being developed. Commercial support and added services are provided by a number of private corporations, e.g. Cloudera, HortonNetworks, MapR, However, the leading development is hosted within the Apache Software Foundation ApacheSF, who has boosted its development, and application. It also hosts a number of related projects: Ambari, Avro, Cassandra, Hbase, Hive, Mahout, Pig, and ZooKeeper, to name a few.

In addition, many other vendors that traditionally offer software for data processing and analysis are developing specific adaptations of Hadoop to their respective platforms, e.g. IBM, SAS or SAP.

While very effective when properly applied, the MapReduce paradigm is not universal and suffers from several limitations. For example, some of the best-known Data Mining techniques cannot easily be implemented within its framework, such as the Support Vector Machines. It does not work well for algorithms like Iterative Graph, Gradient Descent or Expectation Maximization. Some efforts have arisen to overcome these limitations. For example, extensions for particular cases, like Pregel (Google proposal for iterative graph algorithms) or Stanford's Graph Processing System.

The most effective of those newcomers is Spark. Spark was initially developed at UC Berkeley, and afterwards become a new project under the ApacheSF. Spark can access and manage a variety of data source, with a focus on HDFS, but can also connect too many other relational and non-relational database systems and data formats. So, it does not provide a new storage component. However, in contrast to Hadoop disk-based processing, Spark provides in-memory computation primitives which can boost the performance up to 100 times faster for suitable applications. In particular, it is well suited to deploy machine learning and data mining algorithms. This so clear that the previous effort to develop a Machine Learning Library on pure Hadoop, called Mahout, has been frozen in favor of native component of Spark, the MLlib, and Machine Learning Library.

Spark has become the current state-of-the-art in Big Data Processing. Anyway, this is a field in constant change and a host of open-source proposals are being developed exploring different aspects.

Big Data Techniques Applied to Railway Maintenance

This section describes first the already available SW tools to aid maintenance of the railway system and then the most important contributions from the research community in this field. Currently, SW tools to aid maintenance of the railway system can be divided in two families; on one hand, the SW tools from the rolling stock manufacturers, which to some degree are usually responsible for the operation and maintenance of the vehicles, and on the other hand, the SW tools for the infrastructure managers.

In the first family, we could include tools provided by ALSTOM, CAF or SIEMENS. They all provide similar features, for example, ALSTOM publishes the following features:

- Information management (e.g. documentation, staff, spare, task scheduling for corrective and predictive maintenance).
- Condition-based monitoring (CBM) based on vehicle parameters which are radio transmitted to a ground-based server. Unfortunately, the information to monitor is very limited to a set of parameters with very limited prediction capabilities. In general, the parameters are more alarms than performance indicators.
- Predictive data analytics for maintenance (HealthHub): algorithms to predict the future state of a given component. Monitors asset health and uses advanced data analytics to predict their remaining useful life and replace assets on a truly as-needed basis. Unfortunately, the algorithms are very limited by the amount of data available and only simple statistical regressions are provided.
- Optimization algorithms to reduce the cost of the component lifecycles. Optimization is very limited because they rely on predictive algorithms which are not accurate enough.

In the second family, different IT service providers have general purpose solutions which are typically customized for the infrastructure operator. Apart from the Integral Asset Management (IAM) service concept released by SIEMENS and probed successfully in several large infrastructures (e.g. Madrid Barajas Airport), ILOG® from IBM, RAMSYS from MERMEC group, it is worth highlighting the Maintenance Management System of THALES (6618NetTrac). This SW application provides a wide range of features such as:

- Information management (e.g. documentation, staff, spare, task scheduling for corrective and predictive maintenance)
- Condition monitoring (on-line and off-line). Unfortunately, the information to monitor is very limited to a set of parameters with very limited prediction capabilities. In general, the parameters are more alarms than performance indicators.
- Visualization (web technologies and mobile devices environment). The visualization is very limited to standard charts and reports. Advanced visualization systems to aid field work is not provided.

THALES also publishes prediction capabilities but it is limited by the reduced amount of information available and the underlying algorithm is basically a statistical correlation.

In conclusion, currently available SW tools to aid maintenance of railway systems cannot be considered Big Data technology since the sources of information actually analysed are very limited (some hundreds of MB) to either the infrastructure or the fleet. Therefore, the predictive algorithms are not accurate enough nor scalable and consequently the optimization capabilities could be significantly enhanced. Moreover, the visualization techniques are limited to different types of standard charts which give little information when dealing with Big Data in a control centre, and they do not provide "context dependent" advanced visual information to field workers.

In summary, during the last fifteen years the research community, led by Europe, has developed several projects aiming to reduce the operation and maintenance expenses of assets. Regarding the use of Big Data for predicting component failures, it is worth mentioning the following research projects:

- **Learning to Predict Train Wheel Failures:** In Kroll (2014) the goal was to optimize maintenance and operation of trains employing decision trees and Naïve Bayes. Through indirect measurement and a prediction algorithm the project achieved a predicting accuracy of 97% of wheel failures while maintaining a reasonable false alert rate (8%). Like in previous cases, the sources of information were limited since no information from the type of material, the operational information of the vehicle or the conditions of the rail was used.
- **Railway Track Geometry Defect Modelling:** Deterioration, Derailment Risk and Optimal Repair (Qing, 2012) where the goal is to predict railway track geometry defect by means of a method based on three steps:
  - Track deterioration model to study the degradation of Class II geo-defects;
  - A survival model to assess the derailment risk as a function of the track condition;
  - An optimization model under uncertainty for track repair decisions. This research project states that this methodology based on Big Data technology can reduce 20% of the total composite cost on average.
- **Predictive Maintenance Sensor Rich but Uncertain Information Quality Environment Case Study in Railroad (IBM, 2013):** The objectives are to increase network velocity by either reduc-

ing the number of derailments (attributed to mechanical -car and locomotive- faults as primary cause) and reducing intermediate maintenance calls due to false positives/alarm (by 5% from current level). The methodology employed is based on SVM (Support Vector Machine a machine learning algorithms). The presented results reveal a saving of 5% in O&M associated costs.

- **Facilitating Maintenance Decisions on the Dutch Railways Using Big Data:** The ABA Case Study Niekamp (2015) developed by the TU Delft and published recently in 2014 IEEE international conference on Big Data. This research project employs up to 1TB of data for identifying and predicting rail degradation.

The analysis of the state of the art of the research community reveals huge potential savings and this is encouraging the work in this research line. However, there is a huge distance from research to the commercial solutions in terms of technology. The research projects have not coped with the problem from a holistic point of view. The sources of information do not combine all possibilities such as track-side sensing, vehicle sensing, maintenance site information, weather conditions or fleet operational conditions. Moreover, most of the information is analyzed off-line and there are no specific tools for big data visualization (not in control centers or in field work).

SYSTEMS COMPLEXITIES IN RAILWAY TRANSPORTATION

Systems thinking is a way to understand a complex phenomenon by defining the system characteristics, its boundaries and components, and by describing the interactions between the components in the system. The systems thinking has its origins in the general systems theory developed in the 1940s as a reaction to the emerging need for new approaches to problem solving in the modern world, Sandra (2005). Instead of focusing on separate items or occurrences, these are seen as parts of a bigger whole; the system. Today, the systems approach is applied in virtually every category of science. Natural science such as biology studies ecosystems, social science studies human interactions, engineering science studies mechanical systems and computer science studies human-computer systems. Systems science and its applications can roughly be divided into two categories: hard systems and soft systems. Hard systems apply mathematical methods and simulations for quantifying the system and the interactions between components in the system. Operational research and management research are examples of hard systems approaches. The soft systems approach is applied for problems that are hard to quantify, such as those involving human interactions and conflicting viewpoints.

Railway in general is a system with a high level of complexity especially with respect to technology and operations. From the technological point of view the rail-way consists of a number of physical objects, both rolling equipment and fixed, that interact with each other. Operational conditions, usage and weather conditions are examples of variables that affect the technical systems and their performance. The performance of the technical systems in turn affects the operations. The technical objects interact with human beings, both employees with specific roles and passengers, in the creation of the main service; transportation. In addition, the objects have to be coordinated in time and space with capacity as a delimiting variable. The operations must reach the goals of punctuality, reliability, safety, and health and environment. The planning, coordination and control take place on the organizational level, where different actors and organizations interact. It is thus obvious that the railway is an excellent object for systems studies.

The railway sector has undergone big changes since the 1980's when the national railway organizations comprising infrastructure and rolling stock were deregulated and split into two parts, operators and infrastructure managers. Operators, both passengers and freight became responsible for the traffic and the infrastructure manager became responsible for the fixed assets. These companies all over the world were privatized and the traffic was fully deregulated. In this situation, the number of train-kilometers has increased steadily, mainly for passenger trains. Meanwhile, the number of actors in the railway transport industry has increased. More advanced technology in trains as well as in infrastructure and increased speed have changed the railway transportation industry. The railway transportation is a highly complex activity with respect to organization, operations and technology.

Organizational Complexity

The organizational complexity of the railway has previously been studied mainly using qualitative, or soft, approaches. Busby (2006), Amadi et al. (2010) and Gustafson et al. (2013) use a qualitative approach for understanding risk behavior and to increase safety in railway, while Kyriakidis et al. (2015) use a quantitative approach for understanding risk behavior of operators. In Nishikawa (2014), the organisational change process in Japanese railway is described from an organization cultural perspective.

Figure 3. Main functions of the railway system

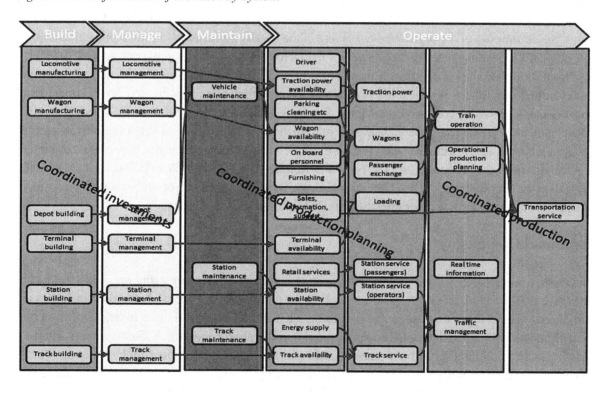

For each of the four main processes identified in Figure 3 (build, manage, maintain and operate) a number of functions are found. These functions support the main activity labelled "Transportation service" on the far right. The functions are planned and coordinated horizontally to reach this, but a vertical coordination is also required. Coordinated investments are often found on the strategic level, i.e. on the long-term planning scale, while the coordinated production planning is in the annual to weekly horizon, i.e. on the tactical level. Coordinated production is a daily operational matter. Coordinating all actors and functions within the main processes is a complex problem, with respect to both information flow and decision making. Because of the high number of actors involved in the timetabling process, there are long lead times in the planning. The timetable process for instance is a yearlong process, from the first application of capacity utilisation in February to April, to the detailed time plan in October, which is translated into the operational timetable that takes effect in December, Taneia (2012).

Operational Complexity

For addressing the operational complexity in the railway, the hard systems approach has been applied in various research, such as Moore (1993), Michalos (2016) and Kans et al. (2016). These researchers propose models for capacity, cost and schedule optimisation based on different operational research methods. The operational complexity occurs during the "operate" phase of the value chain, and especially the early stage of this phase, when assets are made available for the production. The ability to have assets available when needed is directly affected by the efficiency of maintenance, see Figure 1. The ability to provide assets when needed is a scheduling problem. Many actors have to be coordinated, for instance train owners, operators, infrastructure managers, and regulatory bodies. When put into an extraordinary situation, such as the winter season 2009 / 2010 with heavy snowfall causing delays and cancellation of trains, the complexity of the organization was one of the factors that created additional negative impact, SIS (2014). The seasonal changes are an additional factor of operational complexity, as well.

From 2000 there was a significant increase in railway transport. Especially the major routes and routes in major cities are experiencing very high capacity utilisation. This created several operational problems. The most direct is the timetabling of major bottlenecks. The speed is also reduced and this affects punctuality. Moreover, the higher capacity utilization affects the possibility of performing maintenance, which in turn affects the safety. As an example, postponed maintenance caused the derailment of a freight train south of Stockholm the 12th of November 2013, Amadi (2014). This incident affected the traffic for over one week. Therefore, maintenance windows should be considered as key factors in this complex system for smoother operation and higher customer satisfaction.

Technical Complexity

The technical complexity of the railway system has been addressed mainly using the hard systems approach. Lutchman et al. (2006) propose a model for the prediction of wheel and rail wear. In Johansson and Hassel (2010) static and functional properties of interdependent technical railway infrastructure systems are modelled, and the results could be used for vulnerability analysis. A tool for energy and wear simulation and optimisation of train traction and braking systems is proposed by Perko et al. (2016). Olsson et al. (2015) address one of the complexities in railway, i.e. the interaction between rolling elements and railway infrastructure. This complexity makes it hard to create reliable wear models. Lack of reliable models for deterioration and for assessing the condition of Swedish railway infrastructure is one of the deficiencies reported in Rong et al. (2015). The railway is a large networked system where different fixed and rolling elements interact. This diversity of technological solutions and age of the infrastructure add to the complexity. Today, the infrastructure managers simply do not know the true condition of the full railroad network. In addition, due to the interactions of technical systems and components, it is hard to assess the true cause of failure, Penna (2014), which in turn affects the detection of the true cause of train delays.

BIG DATA FOR O&M: A NEW DOMAIN FOR KNOWLEDGE DISCOVERY

The use of big Data Analytics is a standard (e.g. bank sector or pharmaceutical sector). For these sectors, there are also a great number of software tools and IT services that cover most of the end user needs. Some successful implementations of Big Data have been summarized in Whyte et al. (2016). Most businesses or industrial processes (parts of the supply chain) have not yet incorporated the Big Data concept, either for the lack of specific tools (real time communication, scalable data structures, complex predictive algorithms or visualizations tools) or the excessive cost to involve all the required stakeholders.

Whyte et al. (2016) define big data as: datasets that could not be perceived, acquired, managed, and processed by traditional Information Technology and software/hardware tools within a tolerable time. IBM researchers (Zikopoulos and Eaton, 2011) have modeled big data in terms of 3V properties: Volume, amount of data; Variety, unstructured data coming from multiple sources; and Velocity, high rate of data generation. In Lomotey and Deters (2014) this model has been extended into 5V, by adding: Value, understanding the cost and value of the data; and Veracity, the need to check accuracy of the data and data cleaning. Data Mining is one of the processes for Knowledge Discovery that aims in creation of new knowledge. Lomotey and Deters (2014) propose an Analytics-as-a-Service tool for Knowledge Discovery in Big Data. It has been indicated that existing data mining techniques have been designed for structured and schema oriented data storages. The proposed approach aims to perform topic and terms mining from unstructured data silos. In a McKinsey & Company report (Meier et al., 2010) the value that creative and effective utilization of big data could create are summarized: in U.S. medical industry it may surpass 300 billion USD; retailers may improve their profit by more than 60%. Meanwhile, the EU could save over 100 billion EUR by utilizing big data to improve the efficiency of government operations.

Big Data in Asset Management

Data produced in asset management can be described in terms of the 5Vs described by Zikopoulos and Eaton (2011) and Lomotey and Deters (2014). Data from sensors like accelerometers or acoustic sensors can be acquired at a velocity of tens of thousands of samples per second per each measuring point. Having hundreds or thousands of those points, a big volume of data is being produced. Some maintenance related data are structured while some are not, such as free text comments for performed maintenance actions or failure reports. Moreover, data from different systems are in different formats. This is the source of variety of data in asset management. This data has potential value when properly employed in asset management, but in order to achieve this, there is a need to assess and manage the veracity of the data, i.e. the data uncertainty. Finally, it is important to understand the value of data, i.e. how data can enable efficiency and effectiveness in maintenance management, for instance for improved decision making, and to choose the most cost-effective means to process the data is important.

Data mining in big asset data can discover knowledge in terms of new patterns and relations not visible at a glance. The big data approach enables incorporation of contextual information in Maintenance

Decision Support Systems (Galar et al., 2015). One example of useful knowledge that could be discovered is root cause of failure. This can provide an input for design improvement, as well as for more accurate maintenance planning.

Supporting an effective maintenance decision making process needs a trusted DSS based on knowledge discovery. The process of knowledge discovery will essentially consist of; data acquisition, to obtain relevant data and manage its content; data transition, to communicate the collected data; data fusion, to compile data and information from different sources; data mining, to analyze data to extract information and knowledge; and information extraction and visualization, to support maintenance decision; as shown in Figure 4. Figure 4 illustrates a maintenance decision based on real time data using data fusion and big data analytics and context sensing to get real time decisions and solutions for maintenance problems.

Figure 4. A generic maintenance information process

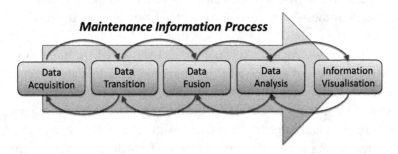

The integration of data, recorded from a multiple-sensor system, together with information from other sources to achieve inferences is known as data fusion (Liggins & Hall, 2017). Data fusion is a prerequisite when handling data from heterogeneous sources or from multiple sensors. Knowledge discovery when applied for maintenance decision support uses eMaintenance concept for integrating the data mining and knowledge discovery. To get the right decision for the context sensing is a must as illustrated in Figure 5. However, development of eMaintenance for industrial application faces a number of challenges which can be categorised into: 1. Organisational; 2. Architectural; 3. Infrastructural; 4. Content and Contextual; and 5. Integration (Karim, et al, 2016). Indeed, big data in O&M domain utilize the advanced technologies for the predictive analytics and provides decisions based on feasibility.

eMaintenance Solutions and Big Data

The on-going industrial digitalization provides enormous capabilities for railway industry to collect vast amount of data and information, from various processes and data sources such as operation, maintenance, and business processes. However, having accurate data and information available is one the prerequisites in maintenance knowledge discovery. Beside the collecting data and information, another challenge is to understand the patterns and relationships of these data useful and relevant for maintenance decisions. To deal with the challenges arising out of high volume of data generated by railway sector both infra and rolling stock, big data, advanced tools are developed and implemented so that data can be systematically processed into information and facilitate decision making with more information in real time.

The concept is captured within the framework of eMaintenance solutions and maintenance analytics as a crucial part of a wider and ambitious concept called the asset management.

Since there is no standard definition we define eMaintenance as a concept that connects all the stake holders, integrates their requirements and facilitates optimal decision making on demand or in real time to deliver the planned and expected function and services from the assets and minimizes the total business risks.

Figure 5. eMaintenance solution

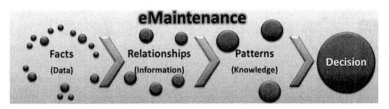

eMaintenance Challenges

e-Maintenance is the facilitator of the O&M processes by the means of ICT solutions and especially big data analytics. Indeed eMaintenance is the adaptation of big data analytics for O&M due to the special characteristics of this process, vey uncommon and entirely different from health, banking, etc.

It represents services that are aimed for managing maintenance-related information. The e-Maintenance services can be utilized during all system lifecycle phases for different purposes, such as maintenance preparation, execution, assessment and also knowledge management. Hence, it is believed that a proper eMaintenance solution should be approached from a holistic perspective. Its design should be based on appropriate strategies, methodologies and technologies (e.g., service-orientation). To identify them, however, is a very challenging task. Some of the challenges to be met are the following: Organizational challenges mainly focus on aspects related enterprise resource management. Examples of these challenges are: 1. restructuring of the organizations involved in maintenance; 2. planning of resources (e.g. material, spare-part); 3. information management; 4. knowledge management; and 5. management of heterogeneous organizations.

Architectural challenges deal with issues related to the overall architecture of eMaintenance solutions. Some of these challenges are: 1. development of a framework for development of eMaintenance; 2. development of models for decentralized data processing and analysis; 3. development of service model for decentralized data analysis; 4. development of model based prognostic tools; 5. development of model aimed for data and information visualization to support Human-Machine Interaction; and 6. development of model aimed for distributed data storage capability.

Infrastructural challenges address with issues related to provision of necessary technologies and tools that are required to meet needs and requirements when services, according to SOA, are developed, implemented and managed in an enterprise. Example of these are: 1. network infra-structure (e.g. wired and wireless); 2. authentication of services and users; 3. authorization of services and users; 4) safety and security mechanism; 5. maintainability of eMaintenance services; 6. availability performance manage-

Figure 6. O&M decision process incorporating knowledge discovery by the means of big data

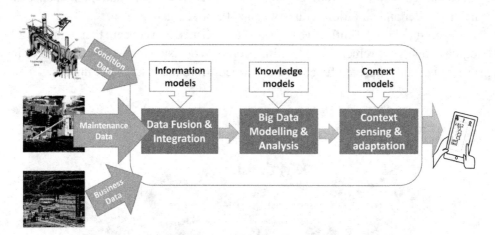

ment; and tracing and tracking mechanism.; and 7. provision of mechanism aimed for documentation and archiving

Content and contextual challenges are mainly related to data and information provided through the eMaintenance services. Some of these challenges are: 1. provision of appropriate ontology through which data from data sources (e.g. process data, product data, condition monitoring data, and business data) can smoothly and seamlessly be integrated; 2. provision of quality assurance mechanism that ensures that required data quality is fulfilled and visualized, in order to increase the quality of decision making; 3. mechanism for sensing user's current situation in order to adapt information to user's context; 4. provision of mechanism for describing various context; 5. mechanism to manage uncertainty in data sets; and 6. provision of mechanism for pattern recognition.

Integration challenges address issues related to coordination, orchestration, and integration of services and data managed by the eMaintenance solution. Some of these challenges are related to: 1. management, interaction and interactivity of services; 2. configuration management of eMaintenance services; 3. enablement of integration capability across a multi-platform and technologies.

Big Data Analytics and Knowledge Discovery in O&M

Within O&M, the process of automating the decision support and through knowledge discovery forms important parts of the decision support system looking for failure free operations. The process of knowledge discovery will essentially consist of: data acquisition from intelligent devices, to obtain relevant data and manage its content; data transition, to communicate the collected data; data fusion, to compile data and information from different sources; data mining, to analyses data to extract information and knowledge; and information extraction and visualization, to support maintenance decision in real time.

Data mining in big asset data can discover knowledge in terms of new patterns and relations not visible at a glance. The big data approach enables incorporation of contextual information in Maintenance Decision Support Systems (Galar et al., 2015). Conceptually, KDD refers to a multiple step process that can be highly interactive and iterative in the following (Fayyad & Uthurusamy, 1995; Wang, 1997).

Artificial intelligent techniques have advanced knowledge management, including knowledge acquisition, knowledge repositories, knowledge discovery, and knowledge distribution. Knowledge acquisition captures tacit and explicit knowledge from domain experts, while knowledge repositories formalize the outcomes of knowledge acquisition and integrate knowledge in distributed corporate environments. Knowledge discovery and mining approaches explore relationships and trends in the knowledge repositories to create new knowledge (Le et al., 2016).

In data integration, multiple sources or multiple data types can be integrated. By integrating multiple sources of the same data type, it is possible to compare parameters and by that retrieve an indication on the quality of the data, integrating multiple data types enables a more thorough analysis utilizing the relation between the data types and their behavior. The last step, Data visualization, is the interface between the user and the cloud by the means of web service (Figure 7).

This includes any interaction from the user. As previously mentioned, this turns into quite a complex task due to the varying character of the customers and their users. The information to visualize and the relevancy in the information will differ a lot depending on customer characteristics

Figure 7. Interface between the user and the cloud

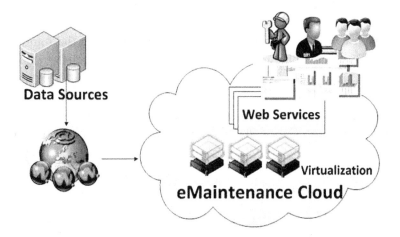

Expectations From Big Data Analytics in O&M Domain Analytics

The on-going industrial digitalization provides enormous capabilities for industry to collect vast amount of data and information i.e. railway Big Data, from various processes and data sources such as operation, maintenance, and business processes. However, having accurate data and information available is one the prerequisites in maintenance knowledge discovery. Beside the collecting data and information, another puzzle is to understand the patterns and relationships of these data useful and relevant for maintenance decisions.

Hence, the purpose of big data in O&M for railways is provide analytics which aim to facilitate operation and maintenance actions through enhanced understanding of data and information. These analytics focus in new knowledge discovery addressing the process of discovery, understanding, and communication of maintenance data from four time-related perspectives. These time related perspective match with the determination of the past, present and future state, summarized by Gartner (2012) in four questions, as it can be seen in Figure 8. What happened, why it happened, what will happen and how can we make it happen are the issues involving the determination of the state of an asset. The questions are ordered by the value of the information given by each of them, in such a way that the former has the less value and the latter the higher value. Nevertheless, obtaining this valuable information requires more and more resources as the difficulty to achieve the goals proposed by the questions is higher. The last question will be in the spotlight in the coming future in order to decide how to take advantage of a future opportunity or mitigate a future risk, getting information about the implications of each decision option. The selection of the best option, based on some given parameters, will provide a meaningful tool for improving maintenance planning and production scheduling.

- **Descriptive Analytics (Monitoring):** It focuses to discover and describe what happened in the past; and why something happened; In this phase access to data related to system operation, system condition, and expected condition is highly important. Another important aspect in order understand the relationship of events and states during the descriptive analytics is time and time frame associated with each specific log.
- **Diagnostic Analytics:** It explains the possible reasons for faults or failures, i.e., the why question and the where since diagnosis is defined by EN13306 as the fault detection, identification and localization.
- **Predictive Analytics:** It focuses to estimate what will happen in the future; The Maintenance Predictive Analytics phase of MA aims to answer: "What will happen in the future?" but also why will it happen? In this phase, the outcome from 'Descriptive Analytics' is used. Additionally, in this phase, availability of reliability data and maintainability data is necessary beside the data used in descriptive phase. In addition, in order to predict upcoming failure and fault there is a need to provide business data such as planned operation and planned maintenance to this phase.

Figure 8. The way to prescriptive analysis
Source: Gartner, 2012.

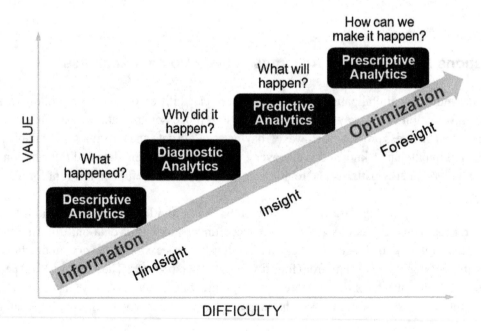

- **Prescriptive Analytics:** Which addresses what need to be done next. The Prescriptive Analytics phase aims to answer: "What needs to be done?" When dealing with Maintenance Analytics (MA) provision of appropriate information logistics is essential. The main aim of information logistics is to provide just-in-time information to targeted users and optimization of the information supply process, i.e. making the right information available at the right time and at the right point of location (Heuwinkel et al., 2003; Haseloff, 2005). Solutions for in-formation logistics need to deal with: I) time management, which addresses 'when to deliver'; II) content management, which refers to 'what to deliver'; III) communication management, which refers to 'how to deliver'; IV) con-text management, which addresses 'where and why to deliver' (Heuwinkel et al., 2003; Haseloff, 2005).

Expectations and Challenges of Big Data for Railway O&M

The objective of big data in railways are mostly foreseen as enablers of Big Data technologies in the fields of predictive algorithms from heterogeneous data sources, scalable data structures, real-time communications and visualizations techniques. This fundamental research is challenging in a sector such as the infrastructure assets maintenance and specifically to the railway environment in three different areas: railway system component degradation prediction modelling, railway infrastructure and vehicle maintenance cost prediction modelling, and infrastructure and vehicle condition monitoring.

Specifically, the objectives of the Big Data in railways follow these points:

- Real time predictive algorithms from heterogeneous data sources that will cope with privacy preserved processing, feature and instance selection, discretization, data compression, ensemble classifiers and regression models, and spatial and temporal alignment of data.
- Scalable data structures based on cross-domain data sources acquisition by means of a virtualization layer between data acquisition process and data analytics. This also includes new solutions that combine new databases capabilities to integrate heterogeneous data sources on a high-performance accessing system based on Cloud.
- Enabling Big Data Communications by means of open interface gateways with monitoring systems providing timestamp and position synchronization, heterogeneous communication support, including mobility and aggregation, and priority protocols for real-time transmission of information.
- Application of visualization techniques of info graphics and virtual/augmented reality (see Figure 9).

THE POSITIVE EFFECTS OF BIG DATA ANALYTICS ON THE RAIL-WAY TRANSPORTATION SYSTEM

This section discusses on how big data analytics can overcome organizational, operational and technical complexities in railway industries. The economic and human being effects are organizational effects, but it would be good to highlight effects on the information handling too.

Figure 9. Application of visualization techniques of info graphics and virtual/augmented reality

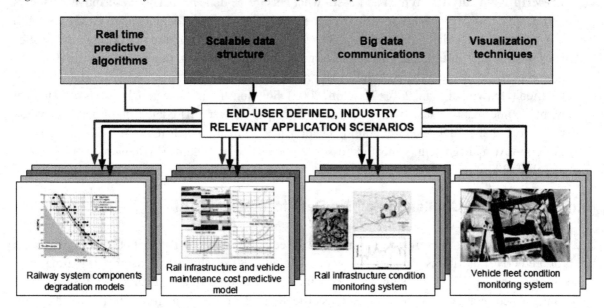

Effects on Technology

Currently deployed Traffic Management Systems (TMS) are combinations of various sub-systems with limited integration and non-standardised interfaces and display rules. In this scenario, the dramatic change will come in the way of a seamless, fully-automated TMS enabling integration with railway related services and other modes of transport.

However, the disparate number and nature of current transportation assets with distributed non-integrated and non-standardised asset registers makes the integration of data sources extremely difficult and therefore the network asset status information cannot be widely understood or exploited to inform TMS decision making (Galar, et al. 2012). Even more challenging is the integration with other information domains like maintenance related services, energy resources etc., which must be done manually. In summary operation and maintenance are completely disconnected in terms of incoming data sources and further decision making (Parida, et al. 2011).

For this purpose, new 'Business Intelligence' (BI) approaches from other sectors where success is already proven may provide Big data analytics as a technology trigger in order to harmonize and create single sources of data with accepted, adopted and exportable taxonomies and ontologies cross over infrastructure managers, contractors and service providers (Thaduri, et al, 2014). It is relevant to mention the need of 'Big data' approach to diverse sources of information and create new services based on the ontologies exploited and therefore knowledge discovery performed (Baglee, et al. 2014). This adoption of BI and Big data may pave the ground for a real Operation and Maintenance policy in transportation bridging the gap between them.

In fact, all these new O&M services lead to a common Achiles heel in asset management and specifically in transportation: a better assets status forecasting, commonly called prognosis. The estimation of the remaining useful life constitutes the basis for any operation or maintenance service in order to check the probability of mission accomplishment by the asset (Galar et al., 2012). The figure 10 below shows a common scenario where a vehicle merges its status with the infrastructure condition in order to forecast the asset condition and verify the user scenario selected in the onboard computer. The analytics are expected to provide relevant info regarding the probability of getting the desired destination according to the current condition of the car and other information sources like road condition weather etc. Relevant information regarding maintenance planning, spare parts and inspection may be provided as well and sent to the closest workshops.

Effects on Operations

Big data will enable a more automated, interoperable, interconnected and advanced traffic management systems; scalable and upgradable systems, utilising standardised products and interfaces, enabling easy migration from legacy systems; the wealth of data and information on assets and traffic status; information management systems adding the capability of nowcasting and forecasting of critical asset statuses. Indeed, the positive effects of forecasting asset status don´t provide benefits just for maintenance planning but also for traffic management.

Figure 10. Big data applied in railway transportation as a fusion of vehicles and infrastructure sources

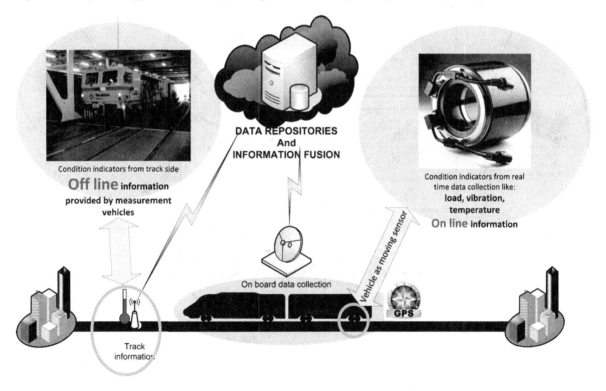

Therefore, one of the main advantages of Big data in railways will be the improvement of the traffic operation and management by the means of side benefits also gotten with the deployment big data analytics such as:

- A standardised approach to information management and dispatching system enabling an integrated Traffic Management System (TMS).
- An Information and Communication Technology (ICT) environment supporting all transport operational systems with standardised interfaces and with a plug and play framework for TMS applications.
- An advanced asset information system with the ability to 'nowcast' and forecast network asset statuses with the associated uncertainties from heterogeneous data sources.

For these reasons, a transportation system with big data analytics capabilities should be able to provide advanced automated, interoperable and interconnected; scalable and upgradable traffic management systems. All these goals will be achieved utilizing standardized products and interfaces enables easy migration from legacy systems since big data is expected to have a smooth transition from earlier attempts, failed initiatives and proprietary systems. The new traffic service that is based on the prognosis is shown in Figure 11.

Figure 11. New O&M services provided by prognosis in railway big data context

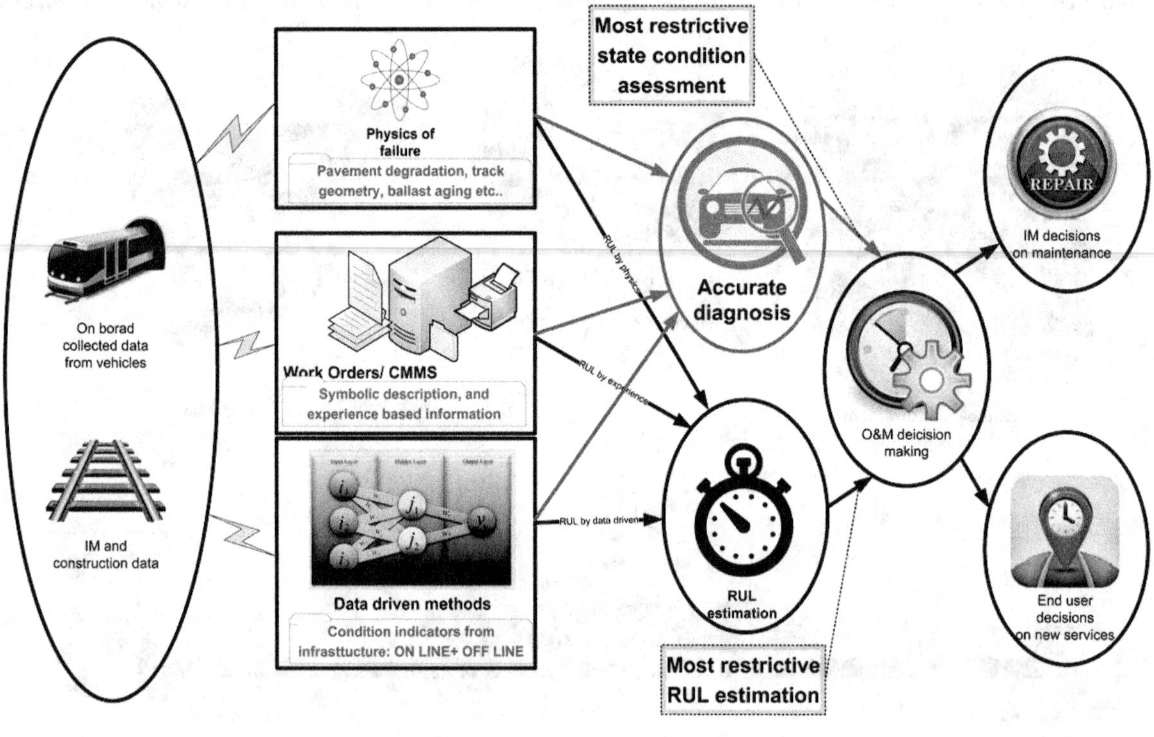

Organizational Effects (Effects on Economy and Human Beings)

Big data in railway will contribute to achieve the objectives of the Transport White Paper. In this document EU members state that "Transport is fundamental to our economy and society. Mobility is vital for the internal market and for the quality of life of citizens as they enjoy their freedom to travel. Transport enables economic growth and job creation: it must be sustainable in the light of the new challenges we face. Transport is global, so effective action requires strong international cooperation".

Considering that many European companies are world leaders in infrastructure, logistics, and traffic management systems and manufacturing of transport equipment – but as other world regions are launching huge, ambitious transport modernization and infrastructure investment programs, it is crucial that European transport continues to develop and invest to maintain its competitive position. For this purpose, a sustainable maintenance of the infrastructure and the vehicles is a "must" as a crucial tool in the European agenda.

Therefore, big data analytics in railway will provide specific benefits as follows:

- **Long-Term Needs and Socio-Economic Growth:** Big data will develop common methodology for improving infrastructure capacity, safety and environmental impacts.
- **Smarter Railway Processes:** SMARTness in transportation is closely related to operation and maintenance methodologies aiming for self-configuration, self-maintenance and self-repair systems in order to maximize capacity and utilization of the assets minimizing shutdowns. Therefore instrumented, interconnected and intelligent assets will be maintained in a very different way from traditional policies.
- **System Integration, Safety, and Interoperability:** New O&M policies by the means of big data outcomes will provide open cross borders with higher interoperability by the means of harmonization in RAMS analysis and calculations, increased safety as a consequence of increased reliability, and finally a common way to integrate systems creating complex assets as system of systems but in such a way that reliability is not affected by the complexity along the international corridors.

Last but not least, the potential benefits of Big data analytics in Energy and sustainability for the railway domain are not disregard. It is already proven that better O&M reduces energy consumption and therefor improves the carbon fingerprint of the assets both rolling stock and infrastructure, thus big data in railway will optimize operation and maintenance methodologies in a holistic approach, considering the entire life cycle of the asset in a cradle to grave approach and contributing to the sustainability of the transportation system in a significant way.

REFERENCES

Amadi-Echendu, J. E., Brown, K., Willett, R., & Mathew, J. (Eds.). (2010). Definitions, concepts and scope of engineering asset management. In Engineering Asset Management Review (Vol. 1). Springer. doi:10.1007/978-1-84996-178-3

Baglee, D., & Marttonen, S. (2014, January). The need for Big Data collection and analyses to support the development of an advanced maintenance strategy. In *Proceedings of the International Conference on Data Mining (DMIN)* (p. 3). The Steering Committee of The World Congress in Computer Science, Computer Engineering and Applied Computing (WorldComp).

Galar, D., Kans, M., & Schmidt, B. (2016). Big Data in Asset Management: Knowledge Discovery in Asset Data by the Means of Data Mining. In *Proceedings of the 10th World Congress on Engineering Asset Management (WCEAM '15)* (pp. 161-171). Springer International Publishing. 10.1007/978-3-319-27064-7_16

Galar, D., Palo, M., Van Horenbeek, A., & Pintelon, L. (2012). Integration of disparate data sources to perform maintenance prognosis and optimal decision making. Insight-non-destructive testing and condition monitoring, 54(8), 440-445.

Galar, D., Thaduri, A., Catelani, M., & Ciani, L. (2015). Context awareness for maintenance decision making: A diagnosis and prognosis approach. *Measurement*, *67*, 137–150. doi:10.1016/j.measurement.2015.01.015

Gartner. (n. d.). Gartner IT Glossary. Retrieved from http://www.gartner.com/it-glossary/big-data/

Haseloff, S. (2005). Context awareness in information logistics.

Heuwinkel, K., Deiters, W., Konigsmann, T., & Loffeler, T. (2003, May). Information logistics and wearable computing. In *Proceedings of the 23rd International Conference on Distributed Computing Systems Workshops* (pp. 283-288). IEEE. 10.1109/ICDCSW.2003.1203568

Hipkin, I. (2001). Knowledge and IS implementation: Case studies in physical asset management. *International Journal of Operations & Production Management*, *21*(10), 1358–1380. doi:10.1108/01443570110404763

Hirsch, M., Opresnik, D., Zanetti, C., & Taisch, M. (2013, September). Leveraging Assets as a Service for Business Intelligence in Manufacturing Service Ecosystems. In *Proceedings of the 2013 IEEE 10th International Conference on e-Business Engineering (ICEBE)* (pp. 162-167). IEEE. 10.1109/ICEBE.2013.25

Ingwald, A., & Kans, M. (2016). Service management models for railway infrastructure, an ecosystem perspective. In *Proceedings of the 10th World Congress on Engineering Asset Management (WCEAM '15)* (pp. 289-303). Springer International Publishing. 10.1007/978-3-319-27064-7_28

Kans, M., & Ingwald, A. (2016). Business Model Development Towards Service Management 4.0. Procedia CIRP, 47, 489-494.

Karim, R., Westerberg, J., Galar, D., & Kumar, U. (2016). Maintenance Analytics–The New Know in Maintenance. *IFAC-PapersOnLine*, *49*(28), 214–219. doi:10.1016/j.ifacol.2016.11.037

Khosrowshahi, F., Ghodous, P., & Sarshar, M. (2014). Visualization of the modeled degradation of building flooring systems in building maintenance. *Computer-Aided Civil and Infrastructure Engineering*, *29*(1), 18–30. doi:10.1111/mice.12029

Kroll, B., Schaffranek, D., Schriegel, S., & Niggemann, O. (2014, September). System modeling based on machine learning for anomaly detection and predictive maintenance in industrial plants. In Proceedings of 2014 IEEE Emerging Technology and Factory Automation (ETFA) (pp. 1-7). IEEE doi:10.1109/ETFA.2014.7005202

Landscheidt, S., & Kans, M. (2016). Method for Assessing the Total Cost of Ownership of Industrial Robots. *Procedia CIRP*, *57*, 746–751. doi:10.1016/j.procir.2016.11.129

Le, T., & Jeong, H. D. (2016). Interlinking life-cycle data spaces to support decision making in highway asset management. *Automation in Construction, 64*, 54–64. doi:10.1016/j.autcon.2015.12.016

Lee, J., Kao, H. A., & Yang, S. (2014). Service innovation and smart analytics for industry 4.0 and big data environment. Procedia CIRP, 16, 3-8.

Liggins, M. II, Hall, D., & Llinas, J. (Eds.). (2017). *Handbook of multisensor data fusion: theory and practice*. CRC press.

Lomotey, R. K., & Deters, R. (2014, April). Towards knowledge discovery in big data. In *Proceedings of the 2014 IEEE 8th International Symposium on Service Oriented System Engineering (SOSE)* (pp. 181-191). IEEE. 10.1109/SOSE.2014.25

Lutchman, R. (2006). Sustainable asset management: linking assets, people, and processes for results. DEStech Publications, Inc.

Meier, H., Roy, R., & Seliger, G. (2010). Industrial product-service systems—IPS 2. *CIRP Annals-Manufacturing Technology, 59*(2), 607–627. doi:10.1016/j.cirp.2010.05.004

Michalos, G., Sipsas, P., Makris, S., & Chryssolouris, G. (2016). Decision making logic for flexible assembly lines reconfiguration. *Robotics and Computer-integrated Manufacturing, 37*, 233–250. doi:10.1016/j.rcim.2015.04.006

Moore, J. F. (1993). Predators and prey: A new ecology of competition. *Harvard Business Review, 71*(3), 75–83. PMID:10126156

Niekamp, S., Bharadwaj, U. R., Sadhukhan, J., & Chryssanthopoulos, M. K. (2015). A multi-criteria decision support framework for sustainable asset management and challenges in its application. *Journal of Industrial and Production Engineering, 32*(1), 23–36. doi:10.1080/21681015.2014.1000401

Olsson, N. O., & Bull-Berg, H. (2015). Use of big data in project evaluations. *International Journal of Managing Projects in Business, 8*(3), 491–512. doi:10.1108/IJMPB-09-2014-0063

Park, S., Park, S. I., & Lee, S. H. (2016). Strategy on sustainable infrastructure asset management: Focus on Korea' s future policy directivity. *Renewable & Sustainable Energy Reviews, 62*, 710–722. doi:10.1016/j.rser.2016.04.073

Penna, R., Amaral, M., Espíndola, D., Botelho, S., Duarte, N., Pereira, C. E., . . . Frazzon, E. M. (2014, July). Visualization tool for cyber-physical maintenance systems. In *Proceedings of the 2014 12th IEEE International Conference on Industrial Informatics (INDIN)* (pp. 566-571). IEEE. 10.1109/IN-DIN.2014.6945575

Perko, I., & Ototsky, P. (2016). Big Data for Business Ecosystem Players. *Naše gospodarstvo [Our economy], 62*(2), 12-24.

Rong, K., Hu, G., Lin, Y., Shi, Y., & Guo, L. (2015). Understanding business ecosystem using a 6C framework in Internet-of-Things-based sectors. *International Journal of Production Economics, 159*, 41–55. doi:10.1016/j.ijpe.2014.09.003

Sankavaram, C., Kodali, A., & Pattipati, K. (2013, January). An integrated health management process for automotive cyber-physical systems. In *Proceedings of the 2013 International Conference on Computing, Networking and Communications (ICNC)* (pp. 82-86). IEEE. 10.1109/ICCNC.2013.6504058

SIS, SS-ISO 55000:2014, Asset management – Overview, principles and terminology. (2014).

Syed, B., Pal, A., Srinivasarengan, K., & Balamuralidhar, P. (2012, December). A smart transport application of cyber-physical systems: Road surface monitoring with mobile devices. In *Proceedings of the 2012 Sixth International Conference on Sensing Technology (ICST)* (pp. 8-12). IEEE.

Taneja, J., Katz, R., & Culler, D. (2012, April). Defining cps challenges in a sustainable electricity grid. In *Proceedings of the 2012 IEEE/ACM Third International Conference on Cyber-Physical Systems (ICCPS)* (pp. 119-128). IEEE. 10.1109/ICCPS.2012.20

Thaduri, A., Galar, D., & Kans, M. (2016). Maintenance 4.0 in Railway Transportation Industry. In *Proceedings of the 10th World Congress on Engineering Asset Management (WCEAM '15)* (pp. 317-331). Springer International Publishing.

Tiddens, W. W., Braaksma, A. J. J., & Tinga, T. (2015). The adoption of prognostic technologies in maintenance decision making: A multiple case study. *Procedia CIRP*, *38*, 171–176. doi:10.1016/j.procir.2015.08.028

Wang, G., Gunasekaran, A., Ngai, E. W., & Papadopoulos, T. (2016). Big data analytics in logistics and supply chain management: Certain investigations for research and applications. *International Journal of Production Economics*, *176*, 98–110. doi:10.1016/j.ijpe.2016.03.014

Whyte, J., Stasis, A., & Lindkvist, C. (2016). Managing change in the delivery of complex projects: Configuration management, asset information and big data. *International Journal of Project Management*, *34*(2), 339–351. doi:10.1016/j.ijproman.2015.02.006

Zikopoulos, P., & Eaton, C. (2011). *Understanding big data: Analytics for enterprise class hadoop and streaming data*. McGraw-Hill Osborne Media.

This research was previously published in Innovative Applications of Big Data in the Railway Industry; pages 1-26, copyright year 2018 by Engineering Science Reference (an imprint of IGI Global).

Chapter 20
Usage and Analysis of Big Data in E-Health Domain

Sushruta Mishra
C. V. Raman College of Engineering, India

Hrudaya Kumar Tripathy
KIIT University, India

Brojo Kishore Mishra
iD https://orcid.org/0000-0002-7836-052X
C. V. Raman College of Engineering, India

Soumya Sahoo
C. V. Raman College of Engineering, India

ABSTRACT

Big data analytics is a growth area with the potential to provide useful insight in healthcare. Big Data can unify all patient related data to get a 360-degree view of the patient to analyze and predict outcomes. It can improve clinical practices, new drug development and health care financing process. It offers a lot of benefits such as early disease detection, fraud detection and better healthcare quality and efficiency. This chapter introduces the Big Data concept and characteristics, health care data and some major issues of Big Data. These issues include Big Data benefits, its applications and opportunities in medical areas and health care. Methods and technology progress about Big Data are presented in this study. Big Data challenges in medical applications and health care are also discussed. While many dimensions of big data still present issues in its use and adoption, such as managing the volume, variety, velocity, veracity, and value, the accuracy, integrity, and semantic interpretation are of greater concern in clinical application.

DOI: 10.4018/978-1-6684-3662-2.ch020

INTRODUCTION

Over the past 20 years, data has increased in a large scale in various fields. According to a report from International Data Corporation (IDC), in 2011, the overall created and copied data volume in the world was 1.8ZB ($\approx$ 1021B), which increased by nearly nine times within five years (Gantz, J. & Reinsel, D. 2011). This figure will double at least every two years in the near future. Under the explosive increase of global data, the term of big data is mainly used to describe enormous datasets. Compared with traditional datasets, big data typically includes masses of unstructured data that need more real-time analysis. Recently, industries become interested in the high potential of big data, and many government agencies announced major plans to accelerate big data research and applications (Fact sheet 2012). In addition, issues on big data are often covered in public media, such as The Economist (Cukier, K. 2010, Drowning in numbers 2011), New York Times (Lohr, S. 2012) and National Public Radio (Yuki, N. 2011). Two premier scientific journals, Nature and Science, also opened special columns to discuss the challenges and impacts of big data (Big data 2008,Special online collection 2011). The era of big data has come beyond all doubt (Manyika, J. et al. 2011)The current international population exceeds 7.2 billion (Worldometers 2014), and over 2 billion of these people are connected to the Internet. Furthermore, 5 billion individuals are using various mobile devices, according to McKinsey (2013). As a result of this technological revolution, these millions of people are generating tremendous amounts of data through the increased use of such devices. In particular, remote sensors continuously produce much heterogeneous data that are either structured or unstructured. This data is known as Big Data (Che, D.,et al. 2013). Figure 1. groups the critical issues in Big Data into three categories based on the commonality of the challenge.

Figure 1. Challenges in Big Data

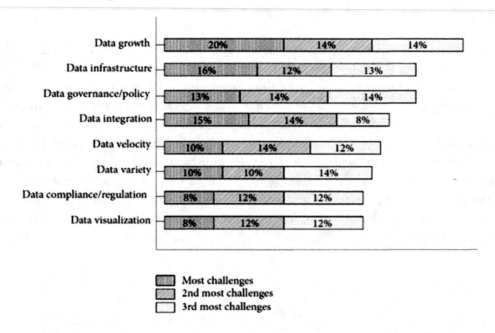

Big data is a largest buzz phrases in domain of IT, new technologies of personal communication driving the big data new trend and internet population grew day by day but it never reach by 100%. The need of big data generated from the large companies like face book, yahoo, Google, YouTube etc for the purpose of analysis of enormous amount of data which is in unstructured form or even in structured form. Google contains the large amount of information. So; there is the need of Big Data Analytics that is the processing of the complex and massive datasets this data is different from structured data in terms of five parameters –variety, volume, value, veracity and velocity (5V's). The five V's (volume, variety, velocity, value, veracity) are the challenges of big data management shown in Figure 2 which are:

- **Volume:** Data is ever-growing day by day of alltypes ever MB, PB, YB, ZB, KB, TB of information. The data results into large files. Excessive volume of data is main issue of storage. This main issue is resolved by reducing storage cost. Data volumes are expected to grow 50 times by 2020.
- **Variety:** Data sources are extremely heterogeneous. The files comes in various formats and of any type, it may be structured or unstructured such as text, audio, videos, log files and more. The varieties are endless, and the data enters the network without having been quantified or qualified in any way.
- **Velocity:** The data comes at high speed.Sometimes 1 minute is too late so big data is time sensitive. Some organisations data velocity is main challenge. The social media messages and credit card transactions done in millisecond and data generated by this putting in to databases.
- **Value:** It is a most important v in big data. Value is main buzz for big data because it is important for businesses, IT infrastructure system to store large amount of values in database.
- **Veracity:** The increase in the range of values typical of a large data set. When we dealing with high volume, velocity and variety of data, the all of data are not going 100% correct, there will be dirty data. Big data and analytics technologies work with these types of data.

Figure 2. The five dimensions of big data

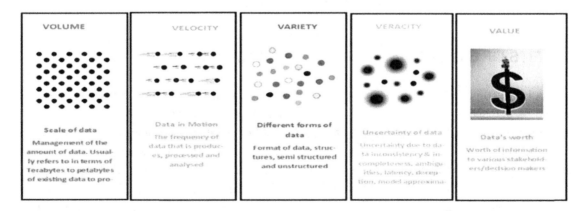

HEALTH CARE DATA

Big data in healthcare refers to electronic health data sets so large and complex that it is difficult to manage with traditional or common data management methods and traditional software and/or hardware Data in healthcare can be categorized as follows:

- **Genomic Data:** It refers to genotyping, gene expression and DNA sequence.
- **Clinical Data:** About 80% of this type data are unstructured documents, images and clinical or transcribed notes.
- Structured data (e.g., laboratory data, structured EMR/HER).
- Unstructured data (e.g., post-op notes, diagnostic testing reports, patient discharge summaries, unstructured EMR/HER and medical images such as radiological images and X-ray images).
- Semi-structured data (e.g., copy-paste from other structure source).
- **Behaviour Data and Patient Sentiment Data:** Web and social media data (Search engines, Internet consumer use and networking sites (Facebook, Twitter, Linkedin, blog, health plan websites and smartphone, etc.).
- Mobility sensor data or streamed data (data in motion, e.g., electroencephalography data). They are from regular medical monitoring and home monitoring, tele-health, sensor-based wireless and smart devices.
- **Health Publication and Clinical Reference Data:** Text-based publications (journals articles, clinical research and medical reference material) and clinical text-based reference practice guidelines and health product (e.g., drug information) data.
- **Administrative, Business and External Data:** Insurance claims and related financial data, billing and scheduling.
- **Biometric Data:** Fingerprints, handwriting and iris scans, etc.
- **Other Miscellaneous Data:** Device data, adverse events and patient feedback, etc.
- The content from portal or Personal Health Records (PHR) messaging (such as e-mails) between the patient and the provider team; the data generated in the PHR.

BENEFITS OF BIG DATA IN MEDICAL APPLICATIONS

Big data is recognized as a multidisciplinary information processing system. Areas of business, government, media, and in particular healthcare, are increasingly incorporating big data into information processing systems. To make effective use of the potential of big data in healthcare, an understanding of what the 2.5 quintillion bytes of data consists of, where they reside, are they raw, processed or derived artifacts, and what the delineation between public and private access is required. Effective large-scale analysis often requires the collection of heterogeneous data from multiple sources. For example, obtaining the 360-degrees health view of a patient(or a population) benefits from integrating and analyzing the medical health record along with Internet available environmental data and then even with readings from multiple types of meters (for example, glucose meters, heart meters, accelerometers, among others).Applying advanced analytics to patient profiles, characteristics and the cost and outcomes of care can help identify the most clinically and cost effective treatments, proactively identify individuals who would benefit from preventative care or lifestyle changes. Big Data could help reduce waste and inefficiency in the following three areas:

1. **Clinical Operations:** Determine more clinically relevant and cost-effective ways to diagnose and treat patients.
2. **Research & Development:** (1) lower attrition and produce a leaner, faster, moretargeted R&D pipeline in drugs and devices with the help of predictive modeling; (2) improve clinicaltrial design, thus reducing trial failures and speeding new treatments to market; and (3) identify follow-on indications and discover adverse effects before products reach the market.
3. **Public Health:** (1) analyze disease patterns and track disease outbreaks and transmission to improve public health surveillance and speed response; (2) faster develop more accurately targeted vaccines and (3) turn large amounts of data into actionable information.

Big Data benefits in medical applications and health care can be summarized as follows:

1. Improvement of health outcomes through more accurate and precise diagnoses; identification of patients who are at risk of adverse outcomes; and customization of care at the level of the individual patient (personalized medicine).
2. Reduction of costs through earlier detection of disease; elimination of unnecessary and duplicate care; reduction in variations in care; and elimination of erroneous and improper claims submissions.
3. Predicting and managing obesity and health risks; detecting health care fraud more quickly and efficiently (Certain developments or outcomes may be predicted and/or estimated based on vast amounts of historical data).
4. Decreasing inappropriate Emergency Department (ED) utilization by using statistical models to identify the best ED services or care alternatives that are more appropriate, more convenient and lower in cost according to health conditions, prior use of health care.

OPPORTUNITIES OF BIG DATA IN HEALTH CARE

Big Data can provide support across all aspects of health care. Big Data analytics has gained traction in genomics; epidemic spread prediction, clinical outcome, fraud detection, pharmaceutical development and personalized patient care, etc. There are potential applications in these areas. The specific applications of Big Data in the areas are as follows.

*   **Genomics Analytics:** Genomic data is becoming critical to the complete patient record. Combining patient genomic data with clinical data helps cancer treatment.
*   **Flu Outbreak Prediction and Control:** In public and population health, continuously aggregating and analyzing public health data helps detect and manage potential disease out breaks. Big Data analytics can mine web-based and social media data topredict flu outbreaks based on consumer search, social content and query activity.
*   **Clinical Outcome Analytics:** Clinical analytics can be performed through unifying clinical, financial and operation data for efficient clinical decisions. Blue Cross and Blue Shield of North

Carolina, USA has provided several promising examples of how Big Data can be used to reduce the cost of care, predict and manage health risks and improve clinical outcomes.

- **Fraud Detection and Prevention:** Identifying, predicting and minimizing fraud can be implemented by using advanced analytic systems for fraud detection and checking the accuracy and consistency of claims. Big Data predictive modeling can be used by health care payers for fraud prevention. Fraud waste and abuse analytics can be performed in analyzing claims and benefits of Veterans benefits and education fraud.

- **Medical Device Design and Manufacturing:** Big Data tools enable a broader set of anatomical configurations, device materials, delivery methods and tissue interactions to be evaluated. Computational methods and Big Data can play an important role in medical device design and manufacturing.

- **Personalized Patient Care:** Healthcare is moving from a disease-centered model towards a patient-centered model. In a disease-centered model, physicians' decision making is centered on the clinical expertise and data from medical evidence and various tests. In a patient-centered model, patients actively participate in their own care and receive services focused on individual needs and preferences. The patient-centric model creates a personalized disease risk profile, as well as a disease management plan and wellness plan for an individual. Personalized healthcare is a data-driven approach. With the increase in the use of electronic medical records, Big Data will facilitate to bring proactive and personalized patient care. In the near future, new big data-derived linkages will prompt timely updates of patient triage, diagnostic assistance and clinical guidelines to allow more precise and personalized treatment to improve clinical outcome for patients.

- **E-Consultation and Tele-Diagnosis:** In the future, the aggregated ECG and images from hospitals worldwide will become big data, which should be used to develop an e-consultation program helping on-site practitioners deliver appropriate treatment. Real-time tele-consultation and tele-diagnosis of ECG and images can be practiced via an e-platform for clinical, research and educational purposes. Big Data analytics can predict over 50% deaths with fewer false positives as compared with the traditional ECG analysis, conducted based on a smaller segment of ECG signals.

- **Pharmaceuticals and Medicine:** The ability of pharmaceutical companies to continue bringing new life-saving/life enhancing medicines to patients in a timely, yet cost-effective manner will dependent on their ability to manage big data generated during all phases of pharmaceutical development. Integration of clinical, healthcare, patents, safety and public research data will provide key insights into decision making for target selection and lead optimization through Big Data analytics for drug discovery.

- **Medical Education:** Visual analytics was explored as a tool for finding ways of representing big data from the medical curriculum of an undergraduate medical program. A possible use of Big Data in the medical education context is to: (1) identify data connections and the relations between them; (2) determine data's roles in the lowest level of a course and in the overall picture of the medical program; (3) perceive and analyze the curriculum in terms of identifying whether knowledge, skills and attitude are constructed through the alignment of teaching methods and assessment towards learning outcomes and (4) perform gap analysis by comparing different states in which data can be found to identify possible discrepancies.

- **Smart Health and Wellbeing:** Business Intelligence and Analytics (BI&A) and the related field of Big Data analytics have become increasingly important in the business communities. Big Data has brought great opportunities in medical applications and health care. Big Data applications will expand to more areas (such as telemedicine and digital hospitals), further improve medical service and deliver extensive value-based care. Big Data applications and opportunities need technology support.

APPLICATION OF BIG DATA IN RURAL HEALTHCARE

Problem Statement

Health care is one of the greatest concerns in India. While, those living in cities and big towns have access to high end health services, the millions of people living in rural India, particularly in the remote parts of the country face problems of inadequate facilities and poor access to healthcare. Many experts, including researchers, policy makers and practitioners identified that, there is a big gap in the knowledge about innovations in public and private health financing and delivery. The inefficiencies and inequities in the public health care access in India have pushed forward the need for creative thinking and innovative solutions to strengthen the same. The problems existing in the health care scenario provides apparent calls for the need to change the existing structure of the present health care services by applying big data analytics. This section identifies the massive shortage of proper health care facilities and addresses how to provide greater access to primary health care services in rural India. The objective is to present the reforms in the health care sector and boosts the discussions on how government can harness innovations in the big data analytics to improve the rural health care system. Now, the digital health care solutions has transformed the health care system to become much more efficient, less expensive and achieve better quality than before with the introduction of Big data analytics in health care. To offer better services to the people, the health care system needs to evolve and innovate continuously. The following are the key points that make the performance of health center better and people live healthier.

- Measure, store and analyze the data to improve treatment quality.
- Manage revenue costs by reducing un-necessary tests.
- Improve preventive care and increase patient & physician's satisfaction.

Adoption of big data in healthcare (Liu,W. & Park, E.K. 2014)significantly increases security and patients primary concerns and recommends the patient information to be stored in data center's with varying levels of security. As per the health insurance acts, EHR security must be taken as a high priority to ensure patient safety. As per the above discussions, the e-Health service data can be considered as a Big Data because of its variety of data with huge volumes flowing with high velocity. Some of the solutions to the e-Health service big data include the predominant current technologies (Harsh,K.P. &Ravi Seshadri.R) like HDFS, Map Reduce, Hadoop, STORM etc. At present, with the increase in number of hospitals and rural health care centers, the health care system seems to have improved. Also, it is observed that e- Health care doctors, technicians, nurses and other administration staff are not in good pace with the kind of growth that the health care is exhibiting, the report says that, US spends 18% of its GDP on health care, where as India spends only 4% of GDP. D. Peter Augustine (Peter A.D.,Leveraging 2014) has noticed the need for big data analytics in India's health care system and concludes how to overcome the realistic challenges involving the government and its policies. The doctors, medical professionals and others using this technology suggest how to achieve better outcomes at lower costs.This section describes the existing health care in India while focusing on the problems in the existing healthcare system. It provides the big ideas to provide better health care to the rural population of India, presenting the big data analytics in health care system

Existing Healthcare in Rural India

Rural India contains over 68% of India's total population, and half of all residents of rural areas live below the poverty line, struggling for better and easy access to health care and services. Accessing primary health care to the population residing in rural India is still a challenge. Health issues being experienced by rural people are many and diverse – from severe malaria to uncontrolled diabetes, from a badly infected wound to cancer.

Figure 3. Structural Outline of Rural Public Health Care System in India

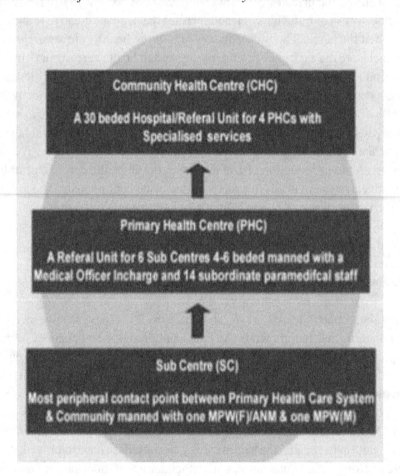

Mr. Arnab Mukherji (Mukherji, A) has pointed out that, the main issue in the Indian health care system is inequity in Healthcare. To overcome the inequity in healthcare system, the Government of India has launched the National Rural Health Mission (NHRM) in 2005. The aim of this mission is to

provide effective healthcare to India's rural population. The thrust of this mission is on establishing a fully functional, community owned, decentralized health delivery system with inter-sectoral convergence at all levels, to ensure simultaneous action on a wide range of determinants of health such as water, sanitation, education, nutrition, social and gender equality. Institutional integration within the fragmented health sector was expected to provide a focus on outcomes, measured against Indian Public Health Standards for all health facilities. Though it is hard to believe, the fact is, compared to government health sector the private health sector has highly skilled doctors and the facilities are world-class using the latest laboratory equipment's and innovative technology. Though, the aim of National Rural Health Mission (NRHM) is to provide effective health care to rural population, the hospitals located in remote villages are not equipped with well qualified doctors and sophisticated equipment due to several unknown reasons like the doctors may not be interested to reside in village to serve the rural population, lack of funds to procure and supply required infrastructure to all the remote hospitals. To access the high-end private sector facilities, people are spending large amounts of money on treatment which in-turn affects their livelihoods and slowly poor people are becoming poorer. In such cases, the concept of Telemedicine along with big data analytics is the better alternative to treat the patients in rural areas.

The Rural public health care system in India as depicted in Figure 3 has three different levels of health care access. At the lowest level, we have Sub Centre (SC) and on top of that there will be a Primary Health Centre (PHC). This PHC is the referral unit for 6 sub centers and PHC contains 4 to 6 beds and Medical officer in-charge along with 14 subordinate paramedical staff. After the Primary health center, a 30 bedded hospital called Community Health Centre (CHC) which will be a referral unit for 4 PHC's. To access primary health care services, the rural patient's visits the Sub center. The Health workers at the sub center first take note of the vitals and symptoms of the patient, record them using the proposed system and if possible, they will try to resolve the issues themselves. If the case is too complex to handle, they send the corresponding criticality level and escalate it to the next level i.e. primary health center, this level consists of a pool of medical officers connected to the network via our proposed method. Any medical officer available online at this level will try to resolve this issue by requesting for more information or by providing suitable recommendations. But, if a medical officer feels that the case cannot be resolved at this level, He / She suggests an immediate short time remedy, modifies criticality level if necessary and escalates it to the next level. i.e., the community health center. At this level, a similar pool of specialist doctors available online will try to resolve the case with their medical expertise. If, however the case is too critical for them as well, they provide their immediate suggestions and escalate the case to the city hospital level. Who, being the final point of contact will resolve the issue of the patient. At any point in this process, if a doctor feels that a physical consultation is necessary, he/she can suggest the same through our system to the patients and diagnose the patient physically. Electronic Health Records (EHR's) in the proposed system are sorted first by criticality and then by timestamp and also the proposed system should not allow two doctors at the same level to handle the case simultaneously.

Big Ideas to Fix Rural Healthcare in India

Seven big ideas are presented here to fix rural health care in India and bridge the gap between quality and affordability in government hospitals. These ideas will enable us to access the services on par with the private super specialty hospitals. Further, the implementation of these ideas will provide cheaper, better and easier health care facilities to the citizens of India.

- **E-Health File:** The creation of a e-Health care file for each patient, where all health care providers and patients themselves were able to submit information (with the consent of the patient). Both subjective data, symptom diaries, lab data, image diagnostics, pathology reports etc., could be filed. To overcome the information overload from the massive amounts of data, Big Data Analytics could be employed for the processing of the data and obtain the desired results with great accuracy in reasonable time.

- **Creating Awareness With Chronic Diseases:** The system must identify and create awareness among the people with the common chronic diseases at particular areas, through which we can prevent diseases. These chronic diseases are responsible for the 75% of health care spending due to lack of awareness and prior care.

- **Prescribe:** Paper based prescriptions are archaic and lead to several miseries each year due to errors in prescription. But if every doctor is provided with an electronic prescription system, it would improve safety by making prescriptions easier to read and providing instant checks on drug interactions, dosages, and a patient's medication history.

- **Electronic Medical Records:** Medical Experts agree that electronic medical records (EMRs) are a must for the better health care in India. But, at present only few hospital are maintaining EMR's, mainly because of cost, privacy issues, and the lack of one compatible, easy-to-use infrastructure.

- **Stop Unnecessary Treatments:** Doctors should avoid trial and error type of medication. The problem must be examined thoroughly by performing the required diagnostic tests during the preliminary days of disease. The right treatment should be suggested at the first visit only which avoids the disease to become more critical. Most of the issues are arising with the misdiagnosis and wrong treatment during the early stages.

- **Reduce Infant Mortality:** The Infant Mortality rate in our country is substantially large compared to other countries. Though, the government has several schemes for the pregnant women, those were not yielding better results due to the lack of proper medical care. If the proper care is taken towards the pregnant women, definitely the new-born baby will be healthy in all aspects to make India healthy.

- **Tele Medicine:** Doctors can often diagnose or prescribe without seeing the patient. The patient has to physically appear before the nearby health centre, where the nurses or health workers will diagnose at first level, note the symptoms and informs the high level specialist doctors about the case. After examining the reports, the specialist doctor suggests the treatment through health worker which reduces costs and creates satisfaction by virtual communication of patients and doctors to discuss medication changes and test results through an online system.

Applying Big Data Analytics in Health Care

We live in the age of big data. The amount of data created in the world up to and including 2005 is now created every two days. Big data is a platform for importing, storing and analyzing data to uncover information not previously known. This explosion of the data changing the way people think about everything. From the cutting edge scientific research to the monetization of social media and exchanging the way people think about healthcare analytics too. However, the health care has not kept pace with big data. Big Data Healthcare is the drive to capitalize on growing patient and health system data availability to generate healthcare innovation. By making smart use of the ever-increasing amount of data available, we find new insights by re-examining the data or combining it with other information. In healthcare this means not just mining patient records, medical images, diagnostic reports etc., for insights, diagnoses and decision support device, but also continuous analysis of the data streams produced for and by every patient in a hospital, at home and even while on the move via mobile devices (Mohanty, S . et al. 2013)Even today the majority of health care analytics is performed by doing monthly data refreshes in relational databases that produce pre-processed reports. A fair gap is often missing lab test is often 45 days old, as the data flow move from batched data fields to real time fields from transactional systems and streaming data from analytical modeling devices. This old model of analytics will fail. Analysis will need to be done on that spot moment not in the pre-processed form. Data refreshes need to be done in real-time not once in a month. The data analysis tools of today are likely yellow pages phone book in the era of Internet Search Engine. They are becoming more obsolete with each passing day. The traditional health care analytic tools are built on tools developed by IBM in 1970, more than 40 years ago.If all the three parties (payer, provider, pharmaceutical company) (Edwin M.F) work collaboratively and share data/insight, disease management programs will become cost-effective and deliver improved patient outcomes at a scale that will further optimize overall health-care cost structure.The term "E-health" (Zwicker,M. et al.2012)defined by WHO: "a new term used to describe the combined use of electronic communication and information technology in the health sector". E-health is the main driver for three significant changes within the health care environment(Zwicker,M. et al.2012)

- Patients to become better informed.
- Patients to become more active and empowered in their health care.
- Healthcare to become more efficient.

It is referred in the Cognizant 20-20 insights by Cognizant, (. Hamilton,B 2012)Big data solutions attempt to cost-effectively solve the challenges of large and fast-growing data volumes realize its potential analytical value. For instance, trend analytics allow you to figure out what happened, while root cause and predictive analytics enable understanding of why it happened and what it is likely to happen in future. All healthcare constituents – patients, payers, providers, groups, researchers, governments etc. – will be impacted by big data, which can predict how these players are likely to behave, encourage desirable behavior. These applications of big data can be tested, refined and optimized quickly and inexpensively and will radically change healthcare delivery and research. The healthcare domain has been an easy target for people who seek easy money by using fraud methods (Konasan,V. et al. 2012) Healthcare fraud is expected to continue to rise as people live longer. The white paper by trend analytics (Konasan,V. et al. 2012) reveals that healthcare fraud prevention has resulted savings of nearly $4.1 billion in 2011. A big data platform has ability to sift through a huge amount of historical data in relatively shorter amount of time, so that the business transactions can use fraud detection on real time. Though, the big data analytics in healthcare plays a crucial role to provide better health care services, provide analysis on the historical data to uncover hidden information, the big data analytics has the challenges like Heterogeneity and Incompleteness of data, scale, timeliness, privacy and Human Collaboration(Konasan, V. et al. 2012) The future research is all about to overcome the challenges and use big data analytics in healthcare to uncover the knowledge from the raw unstructured data.

Concluding Remarks

Big data analytics in healthcare is evolving into a promising field for providing insight from very large data sets and improving outcomes while reducing costs. In this section, an overview of the issues faced by the rural population residing in remote parts of the country in accessing the primary health care is addressed in detail. Also, discussed how the big data analytics are beneficial to transform rural healthcare by gaining insight from their clinical and other data repositories and make informed decisions. It discusses about the big data and its characteristics, methods and challenges and suggests how to overcome the underlying problems being faced by the health care industry. Also presents the big ideas to fix the healthcare system in India. Achieving better outcomes at lower costs has become very important for health care which can be achieved through the implementation of this section using Hadoop HDFS and MapReduce to uncover the information lying in big health data sets.

CONCLUSION

Big Data is going to continue growing during the next years, and each data scientist will have to manage much more amount of data every year. This data is going to be more diverse, larger, and faster. Big Data is becoming the new Final Frontier for scientific data research and for business applications. Big Data is based on data obtained from the whole process of diagnosis and treatment of each case. Big Data analytics can perform predictive modeling to determine which patients are most likely to benefit from a care management plan. It is moving forward quickly in population health and quality measurement. Big Data offers a lot of benefits such as disease prevention, reduced medical errors and the right care at the right time and better medical outcomes. In addition, Big Data can improve the Research and Development (R&D) and translation of new therapies. Big data has great potential to improve medicine, guide clinicians in delivering value-based care. Big Data has challenges in medical applications and healthcare. These challenges include consolidating and processing segmented data, aggregating and analyzing unstructured data, indexing and processing continuously streaming data, privacy, data leakage, information security and lack of infrastructure and unified standards, etc. Our study discusses about the big data and its characteristics, methods and challenges and suggests how to overcome the underlying problems being faced by the health care industry. It also presents the big ideas to fix the healthcare system in India. The implementation part can be done using HDFS (Hadoop File System) for the huge data storage and Hadoop Map Reduce with Amazon Web Services. The use of big data analytics across the healthcare organization and healthcare industry will mine the doctor's lab transcript's using text mining and co-relation to patient outcomes and location aware application analytics for enhancing customer experience. Achieving better outcomes at lower costs has become very important for health care which can be achieved through the implementation of this chapter using Hadoop HDFS and Map Reduce to uncover the information lying in big health data sets.

REFERENCES

Big data. (2008). Retrieved from http://www.nature.com/news/specials/bigdata/ index.html

Che, D., Safran, M., & Peng, Z. (2013). From Big Data to Big Data Mining: challenges, issues, and opportunities. In *Database Systems for Advanced Applications* (pp. 1–15). Berlin, Germany: Springer. doi:10.1007/978-3-642-40270-8_1

Cukier, K. (2010). *Data, data everywhere: a special report on managing information. Economist Newspaper*.

Drowning in numbers - digital data will flood the planet - and help us understand it better. (n.d.). Retrieved from http://www.economist.com/blogs/daily chart/2011/11/bigdata-0

Edwin, M. F. (n.d.). *Big Data Healthcare, An overview of the challenges in data intensive health care*. Discussion Paper. Academic Press.

Fact sheet. (2012). *Big data across the federal government*. Retrieved from http:// www.whitehouse.gov/ sites/default/files/microsites/ostp/big data fact sheet 3 29 2012.pdf

Gantz, J., & Reinsel, D. (2011). Extracting value from chaos. *IDC iView*, 1–12.

Hamilton, B. (2012). *Big Data is the Future of Healthcare*. Cognizant 20-20 Insights.

Harsh, K.P., & Seshadri, R. (n.d.). *Big data security and privacy issues in healthcare*. Academic Press.

Konasani, V., Biswas, M., & Koleth, P.K. (2012). *Healthcare Fraud Management using Big Data Analytics*. A Whitepaper by Trendwise Analytics.

Liu, W., & Park, E. K. (2014). Big Data as an e-Health Service. *International Conference on Computing, Networking and Communications*, 982-988.

Lohr, S. (2012). The age of big data. *New York Times*, p. 11.

Manyika, J., Chui, M., Brown, B., Bughin, J., Dobbs, R., Roxburgh, C., & Byers, A.H. (2011). *Big data: The next frontier for innovation, competition, and productivity*. Report McKinsey Global Institute.

Mohanty, S., Jagadeesh, M., & Srivatsa, H. (2013). *Big Data Imperatives*. Apress Publications. doi:10.1007/978-1-4302-4873-6

Mukherji, A. (n.d.). *Indian Healthcare system: Challenges and Opportunities*. Retrieved from http:// tejas.iimb.ac.in/interviews/41.php

National Rural Health Mission (NRHM). (n.d.). Retrieved from http://nrhm.gov.in/

Peter, A. D. (2014). Big Data Analytics and Hadoop in Developing Indias Healthcare Services. *International Journal of Computers and Applications*, 89(16), 44–50. doi:10.5120/15719-4622

Special online collection: dealing with big data. (2011). Retrieved from http:// www.sciencemag.org/ site/special/data/

Worldometers. (2014). *Real time world statistics*. Retrieved from http://www.worldometers.info/world-population/

Yuki, N. (2011). *Following digital breadcrumbs to big data gold*. Retrieved from http://www.npr. org/2011/11/29/142521910/thedigitalbreadcrumbsthat-lead-to-big-data

Yuki, N. (2011). *The search for analysts to make sense of big data.* Retrieved from http://www.npr. org/2011/11/30/142893065/the-searchforanalyststo-make-sense-of-big-data

Zwicker, M., Seitz, J., & Wickramasinghe, N. (2012). Identifying Critical Issues for Developing Successful E-Health Solutions. *Proceedings of the Pacific Asia Conference on Information Systems (PACIS).* Retrieved from http://aisel.aisnet.org/pacis2012/33

This research was previously published in Big Data Management and the Internet of Things for Improved Health Systems; pages 230-242, copyright year 2018 by Medical Information Science Reference (an imprint of IGI Global).

Chapter 21
Intelligent Techniques for Analysis of Big Data About Healthcare and Medical Records

Pinar Kirci
Istanbul University, Turkey

ABSTRACT

To define huge datasets, the term of big data is used. The considered "4 V" datasets imply volume, variety, velocity and value for many areas especially in medical images, electronic medical records (EMR) and biometrics data. To process and manage such datasets at storage, analysis and visualization states are challenging processes. Recent improvements in communication and transmission technologies provide efficient solutions. Big data solutions should be multithreaded and data access approaches should be tailored to big amounts of semi-structured/unstructured data. Software programming frameworks with a distributed file system (DFS) that owns more units compared with the disk blocks in an operating system to multithread computing task are utilized to cope with these difficulties. Huge datasets in data storage and analysis of healthcare industry need new solutions because old fashioned and traditional analytic tools become useless.

INTRODUCTION

In the work of Mayer-Schönberger and Cukier (2013), people have collected vast amounts of data for centuries in libraries since ancient times, thus collecting and accumulating data is not new for human race. Today, they want to keep whole of the considered data. Companies want to gather the data of their suppliers, customers and staff. Also, the data of business transactions, of purchases and sales, of expenses and profits for many years. Nearly twenty years ago, this kind of data were kept in books and files. But today it is impossible to keep this kind of valuable data in files because it is not safe and there is not enough space. Today, electronic storage on databases is utilized to keep data. Thus, people save time, space, money and effort with keeping the past and present data of the companies with larger databases, faster processing computers and greater storage capacities. Larger databases are provided by

DOI: 10.4018/978-1-6684-3662-2.ch021

ever improving computer technology. Databases are a kind of two-dimensional table of data and thus they grow in two ways as in the number of rows and the number of columns. These rows and columns keep various types of data including names, expiration dates, addresses, salaries of customers, goods, purchase and staffs. In time, the data entries increase but there is no need to remove older entries because today storage is not a problem, thus gathering and keeping data is easier. Besides, with one barcode scanner, much of the vital data can be easily gathered about a product such as transaction's time and date, payment type and customer's data. Also, internet presents large amounts of data, easy access, gathering and storing only with a click.

According to Mayer-Schönberger and Cukier (2013), in addition to the ever growing databases, many databases come together and form data warehouses. Nowadays, even small companies need data warehouses instead of using a database because of the variety of data needed. By connecting databases, it is easier to reach large amounts of data such as several petabytes, thus relationships are emerged among many variables and vast amounts of data can be received from data warehouses so that this will rise to data mining. But it is obvious that in a few years data warehouses will be insufficient because of the ascending data. Therefore, Cloud Computing is offered together with online storage of data with vast networks of servers. The data that cannot be handled by traditional database technology because of its unstructured nature or large amounts is called as big data. It is composed of three V's which are volume, velocity and variability. Velocity is the speed of the processes which are data collection, storage and analysis. It is easy to handle numerical data but video clips, music and text recognition including unstructured data is more complex and difficult for processing. Thus, sometimes veracity *named* fourth V emerges because truth is an important factor. In a day, Google handles nearly 24 petabytes of data, 3 billion comments are left in Facebook and 400 million messages are left on Twitter. This means that at every minute nearly five exabytes of data circulates over the world.

Obaidat et al. (2011) discuss that the security, efficiency, patient based, seasonableness, impartialness and efficiency over different nations are basic goals that should be ensured for the development of healthcare. These goals were mentioned by The American Institute of Medicine. A mobile data infrastructure that includes telemedicine systems and information processing techniques for patients' needs will be able to ensure these aims. Lately, wearable and pervasive sensors, working with personal mobile devices addresses new e-health systems which are pervasive healthcare systems. The system combines patient based and hospital based systems with ensuring medical workflow inside the facility with collecting more data.

The authors of Kenny (2014) and Obaidat et al. (2011) discuss in their research that with the technological developments, keeping, processing and storing data will be less expensive because of less space requirement. Sensor usage will provide more data collection and transmission to wherever the data is required. Monitoring of engines, people, environment and machinery will also make life easier with collecting more data. Besides, with the help of collecting private and health data by remote health monitoring improves the life quality of patients in their own homes. Personal Health Systems with wearable sensors gather, process, store and send medical data ensuring the life standards of patients by monitoring and communicating with external devices. All of these advancements will be provided with smaller devices for big data storage and processing. In the last ten years, for keeping a definite amount of data, smaller volume of space was needed. With the recent developments in nanotechnology, storage units are produced in the atomic level. Furthermore, increasing the data processing speed is another vital topic. Today, parallel arrangement of computers is used to improve the data processing speed.

Kenny (2014) discuss in the work that data is stored since ancient times in libraries. Today, every kind of data is collected and stored by libraries, companies and governments. Formerly, customer and staff informations, business transactions' records, purchases' records, and expenses' records were kept in files. And data were used only for having data about the past and present days of the company. Data were not utilized for future predictions. Then, electronic storage on databases was emerged and widely used because of its space saving structure. And as databases became bigger and computers presented faster processing and more storage space, data are started to be used for forecasting and making decisions about the future. The growth of databases is emerged in two ways: in the number of rows and the number of columns. Every one of a row is an entry for a new data: a new staff, a new supplier and sale for instance. And every one of a column includes the variables such as staff names, birthdates, addresses, product types. But the amount of stored data was growing with time and storing of collected data became a big problem that needed urgent solution. In our daily routine during twenty four hours when we purchase a product, barcodes are scanned over the product to record the sale and transaction together with all of the containing data: the date and payment type, etc. Personal details of the customers are collected according to the payment type: store credit card, loyalty card for instance. A user's every click provides new data for companies because of the high usage rates of internet but all of the collected data are not needed or useful, they are gathered because it is easy to gather and store them.

According to Kenny (2014) databases are grown and come together to present data warehouses. By bringing together some databases, huge amounts of data such as several petabytes can be processed. Data warehouses provide us to be able to use relationships between many different variables in addition to large amounts of data. These presented relationships improve data mining and forecasting about future decisions and opportunities. Every year the rise in the amount of data accelerates and data warehouses become inadequate in time. Lately, Cloud computing is presented to provide storage with an external provider. And big networks of servers are used to propose online storage together with data analysis.

Raghupathi&Raghupathi (2014) showed in their work that in healthcare and medical industry, large quantities of data are produced because of record keeping requirement. Until today, most of the data is kept as hard copies but this method is getting inadequate and clumsy. Thus, digitization of the huge amounts of data is presented and attracted great attention. By this means, the quality of healthcare delivery is improved. The improvement in healthcare improves clinical decision support, disease surveillance and decrease the healthcare and medical treatment costs. Contemporarily, in healthcare, big data is composed of huge and complicated electronic health data sets. It is very troublesome to conduct these datasets by traditional data management tools and methods. Health data sets have huge volume and a variety of data types. Also, it must be conducted as fast as possible to answer needs of medical industry. Big data in the healthcare industry is composed of clinical data and clinical decision support systems which are physician's written notes and prescriptions, medical imaging, pharmacy and laboratory. And also patient data in electronic patient records (EPRs); machine generated and sensor data with monitoring vital signs are known as health data. With understanding and managing the relations and patterns within the big data, health care can be improved and many lives can be saved. Thus, researches about big data are increased in every area to be able to provide best decisions.

BACKGROUND

The author of Dean (2014) showed in the work that big data is emerged in the late 1990s. The big data is composed of quickly growing data volumes far beyond what people imagined would ever occur. Today, in addition to the volume of data, the usage of it is more important for companies and goverments. It is vital for a company to be able to use all of the gathered data without wasting it. And they want to gather all of the possible data because the data will be utilized for definite aims and purposes today or in the future to gain improvements. Organizations and companies need data to make decisions and improvements to produce better products or to make better decisions. Thus, organizations try to collect as much as data they could possibly gather.

According to Dean (2014) most important type of data is personal data which is any type of data that can define a person directly or indirectly. The produced amount of data in the year of 2012 was 2.8 zettabytes. International Data Corporation (IDC) announced that this estimated amount of data would be doubled every year. It is very challenging to decide how much of that data is utilizable and functional in such a big amount of data because some part of the data consist of downloaded movies, streamed audio, emails, Excel spreadsheets and so on. In addition to this, there is information type of data which is nondirect data such as traffic camera footage, GPS coordinates from our phones travelling over the internet. There is too much data to collect, process and store thus it is more important to collect right data instead of collecting all of the data. To be able to gather right data, computers help people to improve their domain knowledge so we will not struggle to store and process the useless type of data.

Dean (2014) showed in the work that the main reason of ever growing amounts of data is recently proposed technologies like Internet, Internet Protocol version 6 (IPv6), social media, improved telecommunications, technologies such as RFID, sensors and the reduced per unit cost of manufacturing electronics. From the beginning, big data got many developments. There are many milestones in the timeline of big data. Most important of them in big data usage and the future of analytics are presented according to the years.

The authors of Dean (2014), Davies (2012), CMS.gov. (2016), Chaouchi & Laurent-Maknavicius (2009) and Obaidat et al. (2011) discuss in their research that information processing technology has provided essential improvements since the 1970s. With the emergence of personal computers, every person could work on one machine in the 1980s.

In the year of 1981, robust and easily implemented Internet Protocol version 4 (Ipv4) was presented. Later, Internet Protocol version 6 (Ipv6) was published (Dean, 2014; Davies, 2012; CMS.gov., 2016; Chaouchi, Laurent-Maknavicius, 2009; Obaidat, Denko, Woungang, 2011).

Dean (2014) showed in the work that in the year of 1991, Internet (World Wide Web) was proposed together with Hypertext Transfer Protocol (HTTP) which is presented as the standard for sharing data.

Dean (2014) showed in the work that in the year of 1995, Sun presented Java and the Java platform. Java became the second best known language after C programming language. Java was used for the web applications and as the main standard for middle-tier applications. These applications were utilized at recording and storing web traffic. Also, during the year of 1995, Global Positioning System (GPS) which was presented in the year of 1970s by Defense Advanced Research Projects Agency (DARPA) for military applications became more popular. But in time GPS usage areas were widen including navigation in everyday applications.

In the year of 1998, an open source relational database NoSQL was used for large data sets. And Google was proposed.

In the year of 1999, the Internet of Things was introduced (Dean, 2014).

Personal computers developed and became mobile devices for instance the Laptop and SmartPhone in the 1990s.

In the year of 2001, Wikipedia was presented as an encyclopedia.

The authors of Dean (2014), Davies (2012), CMS.gov. (2016), Chaouchi & Laurent-Maknavicius (2009) and Obaidat et al. (2011) discuss in their research that in the year of 2001, IEEE 802.16-2001 (IEE 01) was approved. The second version of IEEE 802.16-2004 (IEE 04) was presented in 2004. IEEE-802.16e-2006 (IEE 06b) was published in 2006.

According to Dean (2014) in the year of 2002, a short distance data transfer standard whose name is The Bluetooth Version 1.1 was improved in wireless technology .

According to Dean (2014) in the year of 2003, LinkedIn was introduced as a social networking website

According to Dean (2014) in the year of 2004, Facebook was introduced as the social networking service.

According to Dean (2014) in the year of 2005, the Apache Hadoop project was launched.

According to Dean (2014) in the year of 2007, the iPhone was presented by Apple.

According to Dean (2014) in the year of 2011, for NoSQL databases, UnQL was introduced as a query language. And the address spaces were assigned to IPv4 pools.

Dean (2014) discusses in the research that in the healthcare industry, data is getting more valuable because for the twenty years it was understood that the data can be utilized to evolve customer satisfaction, evolve patient care and provide bigger values to shareholders. In the healthcare industry today, data can be gathered from many sources but in the past claim forms and prescription drugs can be used as the only information source for healthcare providers. Many different types of data are now potentially available: physician notes, radiology reports, etc. But it is very difficult to use this data in decision making because it is unstructured. And approximately 80% of all data is unstructured. Also, medical records are most complex and the hardest data to work with because of its shorthand and abbreviations. Thus, medical records require more attention and caution while organizing the including data. With using the data at businesses' disposal and convert that data to useful information, they provide better healthcare, better products for the patients and also businesses will diminish costs and improve revenue.

Dean (2014) showed in the research that in the United States, Medicare Advantage service have nearly 41 millions of patients. Medicare Advantage is a health insurance plan that presents better service when compared to standard Medicare plan which is for older adults and those with disabilities. In Medicare Advantage, there is a star rating between one to five stars. There are five different rating systems. CAHPS (Consumer Assessment of Healthcare Providers and Systems), HEDIS (Healthcare Effectiveness Data and Information Set), HOS (Health Outcomes Survey), IRE (Independent Review Entity), (CMS) Centers for Medicare & Medicaid Services. The Centers for Medicare & Medicaid Services (CMS) implement many patient experience surveys and ask patients about ratings of their health care providers.

According to Dean (2014) the main aim of Consumer Assessment of Healthcare Providers and Systems (CAHPS) program is providing data for healthcare purchasers, consumers, health plans and policy makers with many CAHPS surveys. The program evolves patient surveys which are needed to compare results by asking patients to report on and score their experiences about healthcare. And the program produces tools for sponsors to provide useful data for patients and healthcare providers.

According to Dean (2014) healthcare Effectiveness Data and Information Set (HEDIS) considers many health issues: high blood pressure control, diabetes care, asthma medication, screening of breast cancer, antidepressant medication and also immunization status and weight/body mass index assessment at childhood and adolescence. Then the program presents data for customers.

According to Dean (2014) the Medicare Health Outcomes Survey (HOS) program collects health situation data from Medicare managed care. The collected data is utilized for mainly improving health, public reporting and plan accountability.

According to Dean (2014) independent Review Entity (IRE) is presented for people who think that they have been unfairly treated under their plan benefits. The Medicare health plans are rated with five categories for managing chronic conditions, member experience about the health plan, health plan customer service, member problems considering services and also staying healthy with screenings and tests.

Dean (2014) discussed in the research that it is obvious that members' thoughts and feelings about their health plans are vital for providing the continuity of star rating. And the star rating is very important for reimbursement of the plan for services it presents. Patient satisfaction is predicted by the predictive modeling for healthcare providers to help them consider extra care requiring patients. Thus, better medical care and better medical outcomes are provided for patients. By this means, the healthcare provider uses patient's capital for essential and fundamental topics for the patient.

ARCHITECTURE OF BIG DATA ANALYTICS

According to Raghupathi and Raghupathi (2014) big data analytics in healthcare is similar to that of a traditional health analytics. The main difference between them is the execution of processing. In healthcare, the application of big data analytics is supported and become widespread with Hadoop and MapReduce platforms.

5 Healthcare applications of Hadoop and Big data (2015) showed that in healthcare, to be able to store data in its native form, the basic technology is Hadoop. Without considering the speed of ingest and data format, everything can be brought into Hadoop. It is estimated that the amount of health records will reach tens of billions in the year of 2016. Hence cost efficient implementations are needed for storage of huge unstructured data sets and parallel data processing. Hadoop technology is a good solution for these problems processing large amounts of data by MapReduce engine and HDFS. The human DNA is composed of nearly 3 billion base pairs and to be able to fight cancer, the considered data have to be organized. The Hadoop technology helps in solving the mapping of DNA problem. Also, to work with big data, many hospitals utilize Hadoop to compete with unstructured data. Furthermore, healthcare insurance companies use Big Data Analytics for fraud detection. Various data types are used to find fraudsters such as call center notes, data of medical claims, wages, etc.

According to Raghupathi and Raghupathi (2014) big data in healthcare has internal sources, external sources, multiple formats, multiple locations and multiple applications as presented in Figure 1. The internal sources are composed of CPOE (Computer based Physician Order Entry), electronic health records and clinical decision support systems. External sources include government sources, laboratories and pharmacies. Multiple formats have flat files, .csv and relational tables. Multiple locations are geographic as well as in various healthcare providers' sites. Multiple applications are composed of transaction processing applications and databases.

According to Raghupathi & Raghupathi (2014) sources and data types are composed of Web and social media data (Clickstream data from Facebook, health plan websites and Twitter), Machine to machine data (data from remote sensors and other vital sign devices), Big transaction data (health care claims and other billing records), Biometric data (blood pressure, finger prints, pulse, genetics and retinal scans types of data) and human generated data (EMRs, physicians notes and email).

According to Raghupathi & Raghupathi (2014) in big data analytics, the data is pooled. The data is in a raw state in the second component. Thus raw state data is processed/transformed. Middleware, extract, transform and load (ETL), data warehousing and traditional format CSV are the options. Middleware is a service oriented architectural option. In data warehousing, data is aggregated and become ready to process. With extract, transform and load (ETL), data is cleansed. According to the structured or unstructured data, many formats can be used. The data input approach, analytics models, distributed design and tool selection are decided in the next component. For big data analytics, Hadoop (Apache platform) is a notable platform and it is presented in Figure 2 with other used platforms. It is improved as the open source distributed data processing platform. Queries, reports, Online Analytical Analysis (OLAP) and data mining applications of big data analytics in healthcare are presented in the last component. With mathematics, economics, computer science and various fields, many methods are improved and adapted to aggregate, manage, examine and visualize big data in healthcare.

Figure 1. Main components of big data
Raghupathi, Raghupathi, 2014.

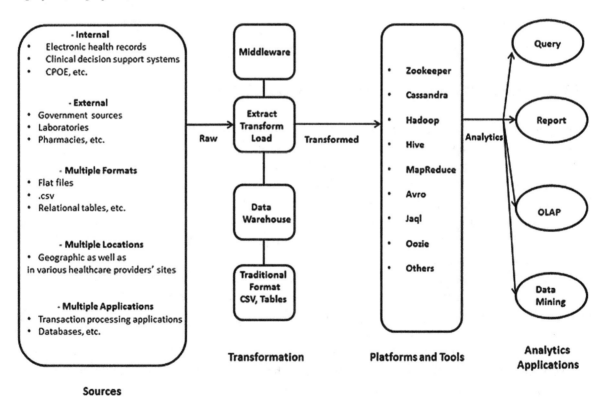

Figure 2. Basic Hadoop components
Mohanty, Jagadeesh, Srivatsa, 2013; Raghupathi, Raghupathi, 2014.

Tools and Platforms in Healthcare	Definition
The Hadoop Distributed File System (HDFS)	HDFS partitions the data into smaller parts and dispense it over different servers or nodes.
MapReduce	MapReduce is a software framework. It ensures the interface for the dispensation of sub-tasks. Also,it provides the collection of outputs.
Hive	Hive is a Hadoop-based data warehouse. It uses Structure Query Language (SQL) with the Hadoop platform.
HBase	HBase is a non-relational database that provides for low-latency. It is placed on top of HDFS

HEALTHCARE AND MEDICAL RECORDS ANALYSIS

According to Mohanty et al. (2013) in data storage and analysis, the increase in datasets of clinical areas present advantages but also cause many drawbacks. Because of the insuppressible rise in big data, many problems emerge, thus new solutions are required. With the developments in communication technology, multithreaded solutions were emerged for big data analysis. Big data and analytics opportunities are different from data warehousing. The opportunities are business hypothesis driven and frequently revolve about exploratory activities. To take advantage of big data analytics, a business use case is needed to be improved. In Figure 3, the industry wide use cases are presented with the big data characteristics of velocity, volume and variety.

According to Mohanty et al. (2013) the big data has a ubiquitous structure. It is utilized to convey real-time data, huge quantities of data, next generation data management capabilities, social media analytics like concepts. Contemporarily, the main aim of the organizations is to process and analyze big amounts of information with novel methods.

The authors of Mohammed et al. (2014), Kwiatkowska et al. (2007), Zhou et al. (2008), Hu et al. (2012), Sammon et al. (2009), Støa et al. (2008) and Mohanty et al. (2013) discuss in their research that for thousands of years, the data have been produced by human beings. The data generation have been accelerated for the last twenty years with digital structures. But most of the data have not been collected and also most of the collected part is thought as useless. The people have not known how to collect and process data properly. Then it is realized that the most important part of an enterprise is data. After discovering the real value of data for an enterprise, data silos for enterprises were established. Initially, the data was a structured type, standardized and a few terabytes big. Basically, big data is composed of

Figure 3. 3Vs in healthcare
Mohanty, Jagadeesh, Srivatsa, 2013.

Industry	Use Case	Volume	Velocity	Variety
Health and Life Sciences	- Revealing of counterfeiting	yes	yes	yes
	- Standards of ill people's maintenance	yes		yes
	- Collected information search of diagnosis	yes	yes	yes
	- Discovery of drug and improvement analysis	yes		yes
	- Explorations and improvements	yes		yes
Public Sector	-Smart city and e-governance	yes	yes	yes
	-Consumption of energy and carbon footprint administration	yes	yes	yes
Resources	- Smart grid and smart meters	yes	yes	yes
	- Seismic data search	yes	yes	yes

interactive data and transactional data. Emerged technologies mastered the art of managing volumes of transaction data. By the way, variety and velocity characteristics are inserted to the permanently and steadily expanding data by the interactive data. Vital and huge business values can be achieved from data. The raw data can be transformed to action guiding wisdom step by step. At first, the raw data is transformed to information then to the knowledge and finally to the actionable insight by collecting, organizing, summarizing, analyzing, synthesizing and decision making respectively.

According to Mohammed et al. (2014), Kwiatkowska et al. (2007), Zhou et al. (2008), Hu et al. (2012), Sammon et al. (2009), Støa et al. (2008) and Mohanty et al. (2013) enterprises' raw data collections were transformed to actionable wisdom by Enterprise Data Warehouse (EDW), Business Intelligence (BI) and analytics during the first years of 2000s. Thus, enterprises' business applications' most complimental and important sections are composed of mainly healthcare analytics, customer analytics, product analytics and financial analytics using structured data. Enterprises function type has been effected by the pervasive structure of the internet because most of the businesses have been changed into "digital" business structures. So, the amount of data have risen and new dimensions have been contributed to the definition of data by the effect of new applications: cloud computing, social media applications and software-as-a-service applications, for instance. These novel data sources are used for presenting and marketing of products to end users by Twitter, LinkedIn and Facebook. For enterprises, data have became a vital business factor. And it is defined as two types: internal data and external data. Internal data is composed of enterprise application data and external data is consisted of web data. Then, the term big data is proposed. But it has been very challenging to manage such a huge amount of data with using the traditional and old data management principles because of its heterogeneous structure over many platforms and business functions. In addition to this, there is a big amount of unused data which is found in the enterprise firewalls. This data is old and raw, thus processing it will be complicated and expensive for standard information systems.

The authors of Mohammed et al. (2014), Kwiatkowska et al. (2007), Zhou et al. (2008), Hu et al. (2012), Sammon et al. (2009), Støa et al. (2008) and Mohanty et al. (2013) discuss in their research that today, data involves the events which are gathered and stored as sound, text, graphics, numbers, images, video and signals. Some industries have been interested in big data for ages. Most remarkable of them are genomics and biomedical research of life sciences, meteorology and physics of physical sciences and also defense, and treasury of government. Gathering and processing is a big problem for these industries. They utilize mash-up of custom developed technologies and complex programs. Big data is comprised of a polystructured nature, thus it causes the concerns to increase about how an industry will use the poly-structure nature owning data. Because, database content is structured data, log files or XML files are semi-structured data and also, text documents or web pages or graphics are unstructured data.

According to Mohammed et al. (2014), Kwiatkowska et al. (2007), Zhou et al. (2008), Hu et al. (2012), Sammon et al. (2009), Støa et al. (2008) and Mohanty et al. (2013) by the help of big data age, all sizes of enterprises could use novel technologies and processes. And companies had the most out of big data analytics. In supply chain and manufacturing, with using on-board GPS and RFID (Radio Frequency Identification) sensors, logistics and manufacturing is performed and during these operations big amounts of data emerges. The gained data is used for cost optimization and operational optimization. In healthcare and life sciences, to improve patient care and public health management, electronical medical records systems are examined. In Financial services, to provide fraud detection and increasing successful trades, banking transaction and stock market data which are produced by capital markets are used. In media and telecommunications, text messages, streaming media and smartphones are used to examine the user interests and needs.

The authors of Mohammed et al. (2014), Kwiatkowska et al. (2007), Zhou et al. (2008), Hu et al. (2012), Sammon et al. (2009), Støa et al. (2008) and Mohanty et al. (2013) discuss in their research that the big data value across industries in McKinsey's analysis's most important ones are about health care, banking, communications and media services and also government. The volume of data in healthcare providers is medium. Velocity of data is high. Variety of data is medium. And, the volume of data in banking and securities is high. Velocity of data is high. Variety of data is low. In communications and media services, the volume of data is high. Velocity of data is high. Variety of data is high. In government, the volume of data is high. Velocity of data is medium. Variety of data is high. In manufacturing, the volume of data is high. Velocity of data is high. Variety of data is high. In addition to this, all of the industries' potential big data value is high.

According to the authors of Mohammed et al. (2014), Kwiatkowska et al. (2007), Zhou et al. (2008), Hu et al. (2012), Sammon et al. (2009), Støa et al. (2008) and Mohanty et al. (2013) basic difficulties occur in visualizing, analyzing and storing the data. And as a solution, computing clusters owning software programming frameworks are used to overcome corresponding difficulties together with collections of commodity hardware with conventional processors. Distributed file system (DFS) and software programming frameworks are used together. The file system includes more units than disk blocks in an operating system. In case of data losses during data transmission over a network, for preventing data losses, data replication is ensured by DFS. Analytics is used in dataset processing

According to the authors of Mohammed et al. (2014), Kwiatkowska et al. (2007), Zhou et al. (2008), Hu et al. (2012), Sammon et al. (2009), Støa et al. (2008) and Mohanty et al. (2013) Three types of analytics are proposed:

1. Descriptive analytics is a process of summarizing the dataset which is under an examination. It is utilized to produce standard reports for addressing some questions such as What is the problem? and What happened? but it does not explain about the future.
2. Predictive analytics is used for predicting the future. The historical datasets' statistical models are used in it. Questions like "Why is this happening? and What will happen next?" are considered.
3. Prescriptive analytics helps in using various scenarios of the data model mostly in the optimization problems. Questions like "What will happen if this scenario of resource utilization is used? What is the best scenario?" are considered.

According to Mohanty et al. (2013) lately, patients ask questions to gain more information about their healthcare options. Thus, they put forward ideas for their care. In healthcare systems, the main data sources are patient demographics and medical history, diagnostic, clinical trials data and drug effectiveness index. The increasing expenses in healthcare forces governments to work on financial incentives about health outcomes where the patient's care is the main factor. There are many main factors for providers; the costs are lowered by payers and pharmaceutical companies and ordered outcomes are also obtained by them because treatments, visits and tests are important for providers. Also, pharmaceutical companies deal with managing costs. The cost of healthcare can be decreased by utilizing data together with providers, payers and pharmaceutical companies. Thus, patient outcomes will be improved. Providers, payers and pharmaceutical companies have variable data type in healthcare. To examine disease progression broadly, patients' past and today is considered by providers. Payers consider patients' medical data from labs and their health history. But, pharmaceutical companies consider patients' clinical trial data instead of personal patient data. The healthcare systems are not combined with variable data origins. The required connections are given over a big data analytics platform in Figure 4.

Figure 4. Basic healthcare system
Mohanty, Jagadeesh, Srivatsa, 2013.

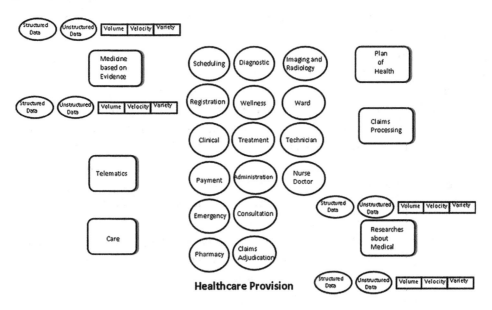

Mohanty et al. (2013) showed in the work that in a healthcare management program, patients who have a chronic condition are given potential inclusion. In a healthcare management program, many questions about patient's medical history may be utilized by healthcare professionals. The collected answers are evaluated by analytic models. And, the produced results are used to propose suggestions to the considered healthcare professional, thus healthcare professional decides if the program level is convenient for the patient about the disease treatment program. Next, the patient is followed by in home visits, phone calls, text messages and with many other ways on a continuing schedule after leaving the outpatient office corresponding with the patient's program. And if the patient does not participate appointments or lab tests then to be able to determine the in-home visits, the data gained from provider and payer is used.

Electronic Medical Records

According to Bhargava (2011) in the last twenty years, payers and patients consider Health information technologies (HIT) and electronic medical records (EMRs) in the United States. EMR is composed of records of a patient's health data which is gathered by licensed clinicians. EMRs are composed of vital data thus they can be used to improve the quality of patient's healthcare and prevent medical errors. And EMRs will prevent medical errors, decrease healthcare costs and develop patient's satisfaction. Also, physicians use EMR while making decisions about patients and storing patient data.

Clinical Big Data Analysis

Mohammed et al. (2014) discuss in the work that lately, the used, collected, stored data amounts increased and this enormous data amount is named with Big Data. The big data about clinical datasets include biomedical data, laboratory information management system (LIMS) data, electronic medical records (EMR), gene expression data, biometrics data, medical images and test utilization data. To store, visualize, process and analyze these datasets is very challenging and complicated. Thus, novel software programming frameworks to multithread computing tasks have been improved and presented to overcome these problems.Considered programming frameworks are used to gain their parallelism from computing clusters that are composed of many processors and hardware. At the begining, a distributed file system (DFS) that features more units when compared to disk blocks in a conventional operating system is used by software programming frameworks. In addition to this, data replication is gained with DFS. It provides redundant data in case of frequent media failures during data transmission over the network.

According to Mohammed et al. (2014) the increase in usage of huge datasets in a clinical setting produces challenges and opportunities in data storage and analysis. This is known as "big data" that challenges usual analytic tools. It will need new solutions adapted from various areas. Lately, information and communication technology had many improvements and thus proposed many valuable solutions for big data analysis in terms of efficiency and scalability. It is crucial that those big data solutions are multithreaded. Also, these data access methods are tailored to big amounts of semi-structured/unstructured data. The MapReduce programming framework utilizes two tasks. These tasks are well known in functional programming which are Map and Reduce. MapReduce is proposed as a new parallel processing framework. Hadoop is presented as its open source implementation on a computing node or on clusters. It is very challenging and complex to gather and process these huge datasets by old and conventional mechanisms. The MapReduce framework is used to process big amounts of data which is on top of the Hadoop distributed file system. By utilizing a MapReduce algorithm the query is investigated easily and the gathered data that include biomedical, clinical and biometric data is analyzed. Bioinformatics datasets include biological data: protein structure and DNA sequence of patients. Biomedical signal datasets include electrocardiography (ECG), electroencephalography (EEG) which are the vital signs of patients.

Kwiatkowska et al. (2007) showed in the work that Clinical prediction rules (CPR) are used for providing diagnosis, prognosis and treatment. Clinical prediction rules (CPR) are utilized in expediting the diagnosis and treatment to be able to gather some values by the help of laboratory tests, medical history and physical examination. In some situations, many patients may require faster diagnosis and treatment because of their vital situation. To utilize CPRs, they need to be formed, then validated and at last they need to be considered in clinical systems.

According to Kwiatkowska et al. (2007) with older methods, it takes time to form CPRs but with latest improvements this process is more easier than before. Today, machine learning methods are used to form rules with the help of automated or semiautomated rule induction from data. Diagnosed patients' data in clinical records are reused by this type of data driven approach. Thus, the cost of data gain is minimized with reusing of medical data. Also, it helps to reach the exceptional medical data. By the way, re-analysis of heterogeneous sources' data includes many difficulties.

According to Kwiatkowska et al. (2007) in Sampling, various gathering methods and criteria of inclusion is utilized in clinical studies together with sampling methods.

According to Kwiatkowska et al. (2007) in Referral, primary-care practitioners refer a patient to a specialist. The considered data includes a preselected group's widespread disease.

According to Kwiatkowska et al. (2007) in Selection, clinical data sets are constructed according to the patients having distinct properties like gender, ethnicity and other properties.

According to Kwiatkowska et al. (2007) in Method, different types of measurements of outcome is utilized in clinical studies.

According to Kwiatkowska et al. (2007) in Clinical spectrum, seriousness of a disease and sequence of medical problems are involved and presented in records of patients.

According to Kwiatkowska et al. (2007) in the knowledge discovery (KD) process, smart data analysis is needed for secondary usage of medical data.

In the work of Zhou et al. (2008) conventional chinese medicine (TCM) theories are found in the clinical data of the daily clinical processes which is utilized as main data resource. The considered data warehouse system is composed of electronic medical record system and daily clinical data. The system is proposed for TCM clinical researches and includes extraction and transformation loading tool, clinical data schema, online analytical analysis (OLAP) and data mining functionalities. The proposed system owns various types of data about diseases from nearly 20,000 inpatient and 20,000 outpatient. The considered diseases are coronary heart disease, diabetes and stroke. Traditional Chinese medicine (TCM) is an old, entrenched and notable medical structure which is distinct from today's medical and clinical systems having no experimental practice in laboratory. Today, Chinese medical formulas are from daily clinical practice. TCM clinical study is based on clinical practices by synthesized treatment based on syndrome differentiation (STSD) with enormous clinical data storage. To provide storage and management for huge amounts of data, data warehouse is proposed as a solution. The presented technical solution is used for many applications in various areas such as in clinical decision processes, laboratory test data analysis, adverse drug events and also in financial analysis. Clinical data warehouse task is composed of entityattribute- value (EAV) data structure, bitemporal data and many-to-many relationships.

Patient Data

In the work of Hu et al. 2012 patient medical records are composed of big amounts of data regarding circumstances of patients along with treatment records. To develop the quality of care delivery together with minimizing medical costs can be provided by using sources of healthcare analysis. The providers are interested in hot spotting which is the process of determining heavy users of the systems in definite time intervals together with their patterns of usage, thus intervention programs can be used. Also, the process of determining anomalous usage cases is known as anomaly detection.

According to Hu et al. (2012) patient healthcare resource utilization patterns are composed of allocation of the appropriateness, medical requirements and resource planning. To be able to provide better patient care delivery, this type of analysis gains more importance. Patient conditions about treatments and procedures are gathered for patient medical records. To develop care delivery, observational data is used in utilization analysis with various ways and hot spotting is one of them. Also, the other one is anomaly detection.

Sammon et al. (2009) proposed in their work a Patient Data Analysis Information System (PDA-IS) for Geriatric Medicine and its initial end user evaluation. The PDA-IS is composed of patient data records that are appropriate for the Consultant Physician in Geriatric Medicine. The system propose many utilities and advantages for consultant physicians about gathering patient data.

According to Sammon et al. (2009) with the presented system, better quality clinical patient data can be stored and processed, thus a consultant physician in geriatric medicine can make more accurate decisions. So, healthcare delivery quality will be developed. Medical documentation focuses on contributing to the convenient medical care of every patient. In the presented work, data model and a User Interface (UI) are focused on to provide an integrated data capture and analysis because the work is based on providing the requirements of consultant physicians.

In the work of Mohanty et al. (2013) big data associates patients, researchers, providers and healthcare constituents and payers. By the effect of globalization and mobility, healthcare improves and changes. Patients request information about their healthcare situations and options, thus they have idea about their medical care.

According to Mohanty et al. (2013) traditional patient data includes medical history, clinical trials, patient demographics, drug effectiveness index and diagnostic. Today, if patient data can be collected over telematics and social media channels, then huge amounts of precious data is gained in addition to traditional patient data. Thus, patient treatments would be improved and costs would be reduced.

In the work of Feinleib (2014) Big Data is explained with volume, velocity and variety. For instance, patient data is combined with medical research. The great increase in the variety and amount of data is amazing. Also, collected and stored data by the utilized systems are incredibly growing. In addition to data collected by doctor's record charts and health questionnaires, digitally stored data will be used. Digital images from devices like iPhones, iPads and other medical imaging systems, for instance ultrasound devices and x-ray machines will be collected as healthcare data. The main aim of collecting, processing and storing patient data is to provide best patient care, health maintenance and self monitoring in the future. Also, better patient privacy will be provided by collecting data digitally. Today, more data can be captured and processed with lower prices. Because, as prices come down, consumption goes up.

Machine Generated and Sensor Data

The authors of Støa et al. (2008) and Jugulum (2014) discuss in their research that wireless sensor networks are an improving technology. During the last twenty years, WSNs gained great evolution in specific topics. One of the most attention attracting problem is handling limited capacities which is based on battery power restrictions and physical size limitations of the devices, thus energy efficiency improvement is considered and worked on. Furthermore, wireless sensors can be positioned in every place, thus they are mostly utilized in patient monitoring. The sensor technology have developed because medical knowledge cannot be used in the sensors. In the network, the sensors gather data and transfer them to a front-end to be processed.

According to Kirci et al. (2014) in computer and health sectors, gathering the health data of patients with wireless sensor methods and transmitting them to a remote center is a remarkable topic. Together with the improvements in communication and information, constructing portable, wireless, remote health monitoring systems becomes easier and cheaper. With these systems, monitoring of patients out of the hospital, informing related people and institutions at emergency situations is ensured. And these systems are used for providing long term recording for diagnosis of definite illnesses, thus the life standards of patients are improved.

Kirci et al. (2014) discuss in the research that generally, wireless sensor networks (WSNs) are utilized to define body temperature, body pressure, heart pulses and actvity rates of people at many applications. By the help of the sensors, huge amounts of data can be gathered easily and important results can be gained for medical systems. In addition to this, the rise in the number of smartphone users effects mobile application usage. So, it can be said that it is vital to use sensors with smartphones especially in health applications with the inexpensive, light and easy usage specialities. Equipping patients with wireless and wearable sensors eases gathering data for physiological states of patients.

Kirci et al. (2014) showed in the work that building a monitoring system which is connected with medical services will be a cheap and efficient application for both patients and doctors. In this system, smartphones will be used together with the sensors that have increasing usage rates. A safe and quick communication will be ensured between the patient and medical service. The system is composed of two parts: hardware part, software part, for instance. The design of the data collecting sensor nodes will be constructed in the hardware part and the integration of the hardware part is ensured by programing codes in the software part.

In the work of Kirci et al. (2014) the paper focused on gathering the heart beat rates of the patients whose health information need to be constantly monitored with a wearable sensor system and delivering this information to a center over a network gateway device. Owing to such a system, the progress of the patients' freedom of movement is assured with real time, long term monitoring. This will be helpful for aggregating real time informations in the patients' own habitat particularly for the patients who require frequent cardio monitoring.

FUTURE RESEARCH WORK AND DIRECTIONS

According to Feinleib (2014) the healthcare and big data own big potential to develop healthcare and minimize healthcare costs because of data gathering ability together with new applications and low cost cloud services for visualization, exploration. Furthermore, with new applications, it is obvious that, large amounts of health data can be collected over cheap devices.

5 Healthcare applications of Hadoop and Big data (2015) showed in the work that in healthcare, big data is utilized to improve the life quality of people with improving profits and curing diseases. But, the considerable amount of health care data is in printed form, thus the digitization of health care data attracts more attention. Because, big data can help in disease surveillance, health management and many other data management functions in healthcare industry.

Feinleib (2014) discuss in the research that in healthcare, large amounts of data are produced with DNA testing, imaging technologies and electronic health records (EHRs). Gathering and storing such huge amounts of data ensures both a challenge and an opportunity for healthcare providers. Novel and open systems collaborated with digitized patient data ensure perceptions that cause medical advances. The inventions and improvements in technology for analyzing data in EHRs and academic research with such as IBM's Watson computer will lead to ensure doctors with better data for making decisions about various illness treatments like cancer treatments. Besides, latest analysis, works and improvements will provide more perceptions as well. A smart system may warn a doctor about novel treatments and up to date data relevant to her particular area. Also, a medical analytics software may provide individual and private suggestions with utilizing the collected big data about other patients who own alike health profiles and health problems.

According to Byrne (2013) in the year of 2015, the estimated amount of patient data in a hospital was nearly 665 terabytes which is composed of 150 MB occupying 3D MRIs, 120 MB occupying mammograms, 1 GB occupying 3D CT scans and many other data types. Furthermore, every year, medical image archives rise between the amounts of 20% and 40%. But today, most of the gathered data molders in silos because of not utilizing them efficiently. When big data techniques and applications will be used efficiently, the gathered data will be evaluated. And the process and the navigation of data will be easier, thus most of the repeated tests and treatments will be prevented.

Feinleib (2014) discuss in the work that in the future, various patient data will be gathered and stored digitally. The collected data will include health questionnaires, doctor's record on charts and medical imaging system images: x-ray machines and ultrasound devices. Thus, better and more effective patient maintenance will be provided in the future because of having the ability to have more self monitoring and restrictive health care, and more information to work with for big data. Valuable data have to be collected for healthcare providers and individuals, not every kind of data. Also, patient privacy have to be considered while collecting data.

According to Feinleib (2014) Big Data develops both patient health and the environments in which we live. Lately, smart cities attract great attention because of their effective organization ability for growth. Smart cities gather, process and channel data to provide best decisions at the municipal level with utilizing technology. To improve the life standards of people, make their life easier and cheap, big data including technologies are more lucky because of the enormous opportunities that are provided by big data itself.

EON reality (2016) showed in the work that lately, virtual, service based businesses are emerged with presenting the novel virtual reality technologies and interactive 3D concepts. In medical education, virtual reality provides the best platform for modeling complex concepts when compared to two-dimensional teaching platforms. With interactive mirror, you can discover how your internal organs work with full skeleton tracking. With holographic 3D projection, the illusion of life size, 3 dimensional interactive images can be generated. Also, with Icatcher, interaction is provided between users and complete virtual environments.

According to Feinleib (2014) Big Data Applications (BDAs) will provide us to determine which data to share together with assisting us to realize the hidden implications of sharing personal data. BDAs will improve our lives with assisting us better understand information, to find the correct customers and to attend them efficiently. Also, they may provide self driving cars that drive according to the driver's commutes. It is obvious that, the Big Data will provide many innovations in the next years.

According to Stubbs (2014) Big data provides novelty that includes evolution and revolution together. To be able to perform them, various operating models should be used by organizations. According to the work of Maxson (2013) the future of Big Data will be arranged by utilizing inherent patterns and intuitive methods like genetic algorithms.

CONCLUSION

The authors of Raghupathi&Raghupathi (2014), Burghard (2012), Dembosky (2012), Feldman et al. (2012) and Fernandes et al. (2012) discuss in their research that the healthcare industry produces massive amounts of daily data mostly caused by patient record keeping and storing. In the backwards, the data was kept as hard copies. It leads to huge amounts of paper dissipation and paper works but today it is geting more challenging to keep large amounts of data thus digitization of these data is emerged. In addition to the large volume of healthcare industry data, it also owns many different types of data that should be processed as quickly as possible. The data in healthcare industry includes clinical data that arrives from clinical decision support systems. The considered data includes: patient data in electronic patient records (EPRs), physician's written notes and prescriptions, laboratory data, medical imaging data, pharmacy data and insurance data. In addition to this, machine generated and sensor data that is received with monitoring vital signs of patients belong to healthcare data type. To process this type of massive data, associations, patterns and trends need to be discovered within the data so it will be easier to improve care, improve medical quality, save lives, lower costs and produce better informed decisions.

The authors of Raghupathi&Raghupathi (2014), Burghard (2012), Dembosky (2012), Feldman et al. (2012) and Fernandes et al. (2012) discuss in their work that by examining and surveying the big data together with conceiving the associations and patterns will supply healthcare providers to propose insightful, better treatments and diagnoses together with high quality care for patients at lower costs. Also, with big data, patient characteristic changes can be examined to determine which one of the patients would benefit from preventative care. Cost effective treatments can be discovered for patients privately to identify predictive events at broad scale disease profiling. It can be utilized and prevention initiatives can be supported. And, to collect and synthesize patient clinical data sets on medical procedures will ensure vital and critical data for pharmaceutical companies that will produce better and important products for patients.

REFERENCES

Bhargava, H. K., & Mishra, A. N. (2011). Electronic medical records and physician productivity: Evidence from panel data analysis. *Management Science*, *60*(10), 2543–2562. doi:10.1287/mnsc.2014.1934

Branco, M. de O. (2009). *Distributed data management for large scale applications* (Doctoral Thesis). University of Southampton. Retrieved on May 11, 2016 from http://eprints.soton.ac.uk/72283/

Burghard, C. (2012). Big data and analytics key to accountable care success. *IDC Health Insights*, 1-9. Retrieved on May 10, 2016 from http://www-01.ibm.com/common/ssi/cgi-bin/ssialias?htmlfid=IML14338USEN&appname=skmwww

Byrne, E. (2013). Scientists save healthcare (But they are not from med school). *Forbes/tech*. Retrieved on May 23, 2016 from http://www.forbes.com/sites/netapp/2013/04/17/healthcare-big-data/#18dd12b3553f

Chaouchi, H., & Laurent-Maknavicius, M. (2009). *Wireless and Mobile Networks Security*. Hoboken, NJ: John Wiley & Sons. Retrieved on May 16, 2016 from http://eu.wiley.com/WileyCDA/WileyTitle/productCd-1848211171.html

CMS.gov. (2016). *Centers for Medicare & Medicaid Services*. Retrieved on May 14, 2016 from https://www.cms.gov/Medicare/Quality-Initiatives-Patient-Assessment Instruments/QualityInitiativesGenInfo/Health-Insurance-Marketplace-Quality-Initiatives.html

Coulouris, G., Dollimore, J., Kindberg, T., & Blair, G. (2005). *Distributed systems: Concepts and design*. Boston: Addison-Wesley, Pearson Education. Retrieved on May 14, 2016 from https://azmuri.files.wordpress.com/2013/09/george-coulouris-distributed-systems-concepts-and-design-5th-edition.pdf

Davies, J. (2012). *Understanding IPv6* (3rd ed.). Sebastopol, CA: O'Reilly Media. Retrieved on May 15, 2016 from http://www.amazon.com/Understanding-IPv6-3rd-Joseph-Davies/dp/0735659141

Dean, J. (2014). *Big data, data mining, and machine learning*. Hoboken, NJ: John Wiley & Sons. Retrieved on May 14, 2016 from http://eu.wiley.com/WileyCDA/WileyTitle/productCd-1118618041.html

Dembosky, A. (2012). Data prescription for better healthcare. *Financial Times*, p. 19. Retrieved on May 05, 2016 from http://www.ft.com/intl/cms/s/2/55cbca5a-4333-11e2-aa8f00144feabdc0.html#axzz2W9cuwajK

EON Reality. (2016). Retrieved on May 23, 2016 from http://www.eonreality.com/about-eon/

Feinleib, D. (2014). *Big data bootcamp*. New York, NY: Springer Science+Business Media, Apress. Retrieved on May 06, 2016 from http://www.apress.com/9781484200414

Feldman, B., Martin, E. M., & Skotnes, T. (2012). *Big data in healthcare hype and hope*. Dr. Bonnie 360. Retrieved on May 03, 2016 from http://www.west-info.eu/files/big-data-in-healthcare.pdf

Fernandes, L., O'Connor, M., & Weaver, V. (2012). Big data, bigger outcomes: Healthcare is embracing the big data movement, hoping to revolutionize HIM by distilling vast collection of data for specific analysis. *Journal of American Health Information Management Association*, *83*(10), 38–42. PMID:23061351

Healthcare applications of Hadoop and Big data. (2015). Retrieved on May 23, 2016 from https://www.dezyre.com/article/5-healthcare-applications-of-hadoop-and-big-data/85

Hu, J., Wang, F., Sun, J., Sorrentino, R., & Ebadollahi, S. (2012). A healthcare utilization analysis framework for hot spotting and contextual anomaly detection. *AMIA ... Annual Symposium Proceedings - AMIA Symposium. AMIA Symposium*, *360*(9). PMID:23304306

Jugulum, R. (2014). *Competing with high quality data: concepts, tools, and techniques for building a successful approach to data quality*. Hoboken, NJ: John Wiley & Sons, Inc. Retrieved on May 10, 2016 from http://eu.wiley.com/WileyCDA/WileyTitle/productCd-1118342321.html

Kenny, P. (2014). *Better business decisions from data-statistical analysis for professional success*. New York, NY: Springer Science+Business Media, Apress. Retrieved on May 1, 2016 from http://www.apress.com/9781484201855

Kirci, P., Kurt, G., & Ömercikoğlu, M. (2014). *Remote monitoring of heart pulses with smart phone*. Joint international symposium on 44th international conference on computers & industrial engineering-CIE44 & 9th international symposium on intelligent manufacturing and service systems- IMSS'14, İstanbul, Türkiye. Retrieved on April 22, 2016 from http://www.imss14-cie44.org/

Kwiatkowska, M., Atkins, M. S., Ayas, N. T., & Ryan, C. F. (2007). Knowledge-based data analysis: First step toward the creation of clinical prediction rules using a new typicality measure. *IEEE Transactions on Information Technology in Biomedicine*, *11*(6), 651–660. http://ieeexplore.ieee.org/xpl/articleDetails.jsp?arnumber=4358291&queryText=Knowledge-Based%20Data%20Analysis:%20First%20Step%20Toward%20the%20Creation%20of%20Clinical%20Prediction%20Rules%20Using%20a%20New%20Typicality%20Measure&newsearch=true Retrieved on May 12, 2016

Leskovec, J., Rajaraman, A., & Ullman, J. D. (2012). *Mining of massive datasets*. Cambridge, UK: Cambridge University Press. Retrieved on May 10, 2016 from http://infolab.stanford.edu/~ullman/mmds/book.pdf

Maxson, M. (2013). *The future of big data is quasi-structured*. Retrieved on March 3, 2016, from Chewy Chunks: http://chewychunks.wordpress.com/2013/03/23/future-of-big-data-structure/

Mayer-Schönberger, V., & Cukier, K. (2013). *Big Data: A revolution that will transform how we live, work and think*. London: John Murray (Publishers). Retrieved on March 22, 2016 from https://www.amazon.com/Big-Data-Revolution-Transform-Think-ebook/dp/B009N08NKW

Mohammed, E. A., Far, B. H., & Naugler, C. (2014). Applications of the MapReduce programming framework to clinical big data analysis: Current landscape and future trends. *BioData Mining*, *7*(22). PMID:25383096

Mohanty, S., Jagadeesh, M., & Srivatsa, H. (2013). *Big data imperatives*. New York, NY: Springer Science+Business Media, Apress. Retrieved on April 22, 2016 from http://www.apress.com/9781430248729

Obaidat, M. S., Denko, M., & Woungang, I. (2011). *Pervasive computing and Networking*. West Sussex, UK: John Wiley & Sons. Retrieved on May 20, 2016 from http://onlinelibrary.wiley.com/doi/10.1002/9781119970422.ch1/summary

Raghupathi, W., & Raghupathi, V. (2014). Big data analytics in healthcare: promise and Potential. *Health Information Science and Systems*, *2*(3). Retrieved on May 12, 2016 from http://hissjournal.biomedcentral.com/articles/10.1186/2047-2501-2-3

Sammon, D., O'Connor, K. A., & Leo, J. (2009). The Patient Data Analysis Information System: Addressing Data and Information Quality Issues. *The Electronic Journal Information Systems Evaluation, 12*(1), 95–108. Retrieved on May 1, 2016 from www.ejise.com/issue/download.html?idArticle=639

Shuman, S. (2000). Structure, mechanism, and evolution of the mRNA capping apparatus. *Progress in Nucleic Acid Research and Molecular Biology, 66,* 1–40. doi:10.1016/S0079-6603(00)66025-7 PMID:11051760

Støa, S., Lindeberg, M., & Goebel, V. (2008). Online analysis of myocardial ischemia from medical sensor data streams with esper. *First International Symposium on Applied Sciences on Biomedical and Communication Technologies, ISABEL '08.* Retrieved on May 6, 2016 from http://ieeexplore.ieee.org/xpl/articleDetails.jsp?tp=&arnumber=4712572

Stubbs, E. (2014). *Big data, big innovation-enabling competitive differentiation through business analytics.* Hoboken, NJ: John Wiley & Sons. Retrieved on May 8, 2016 from http://eu.wiley.com/WileyCDA/WileyTitle/productCd-111872464X.html

Warden, P. (2011). *Big data glossary.* Sebastopol, CA: O'Reilly Media, Inc. Retrieved on May 8, 2016 from http://shop.oreilly.com/product/0636920022466.do#

Zhou, X., Liu, B., Wang, Y., Zhang, R., Li, P., Chen, S., . . . Zhang, H. (2008). Building Clinical Data Warehouse for Traditional Chinese Medicine Knowledge Discovery. *International Conference on BioMedical Engineering and Informatics, 1,* 615-620. Retrieved on May 8, 2016 from http://ieeexplore.ieee.org/xpl/login.jsp?tp=&arnumber=4548743&url=http%3A%2F%2Fieeexplore.ieee.org%2Fxpls%2Fabs_all.jsp%3Farnumber%3D4548743

ADDITIONAL READING

Cios, K. J. (Ed.). (2001). *Medical data mining and knowledge discovery*, Medical Data Mining and Knowledge Discovery, Germany: Springer-Verlag Heidelberg, 1–20. Retrieved on May 7, 2016 from http://www.springer.com/gp/book/9783790813401

Colantonio, S., Esposito, M., Martinelli, M., Pietro, G. D., & Salvetti, O. (2012). A knowledge editing service for multisource data management in remote health monitoring. *IEEE Transactions on Information Technology in Biomedicine, 16*(6), 1096–1104. doi:10.1109/TITB.2012.2215622 PMID:22949084

Connolly, S., & Wooledge, S. (2016). *Harnessing the value of big data analytics.* Teradata. Hortonworks. Big data analytics. Retrieved on May 08, 2016 from http://hortonworks.com/wp-content/uploads/2012/06/WP_HadoopDataAnalytics_Final-12.pdf

Datta, M. (2013). *How big data will lower costs and advance personalized medicine. datafication could change healthcare.*GEN Exclusives, Tech. Rep. Retrieved on May 12, 2016 from http://www.genengnews.com/insight-and-intelligence/how-big-data-will-lower-costs-and-advance-personalized-medicine/77899962/

Georga, E. I., Protopappas, V. C., Bellos, C. V., Potsika, V. T., Fotiadis, D. I., Arvaniti, E., & Makriyiannis, D. (2014). *Development of a smart environment for diabetes data analysis and new knowledge mining.* EAI 4th International Conference on Wireless Mobile Communication and Healthcare (Mobihealth), 112-115. Retrieved on May 05, 2016 from http://ieeexplore.ieee.org/xpl/login.jsp?tp=&arnumber=70 15922&url=http%3A%2F%2Fieeexplore.ieee.org%2Fxpls%2Fabs_all.jsp%3Farnumber%3D7015922

Groves, P., Kayyali, B., Knott, D., & Kuiken, S. V. (2013). *The big data revolution in healthcare. Accelerating value and innovation.* New York, NY. McKinsey&Company. Retrieved on May 12, 2016 from www.mckinsey.com/

Heng, W., Chuanliang, Y., Yingzi, L., Yuping, Z., Yang, L., Siliang, W., . . . Haoyang, F. (2011). *Construction of semantic analysis system for traditional chinese medicine unstructured medical records.* IEEE International Conference on Bioinformatics and Biomedicine Workshops, Pg 823-828. Retrieved on May 09, 2016 from http://ieeexplore.ieee.org/search/searchresult.jsp?newsearch=true&queryTex t=Construction%20of%20Semantic%20Analysis%20System%20for%20Traditional%20Chinese%20 Medicine%20Unstructured%20Medical%20Records

Jadhav, A. S., Andrews, D., Fiksdal, A., Kumbamu, A., McCormick, J. B., Misitano, A., ... Pathak, J. (2014). Comparative analysis of online health queries originating from personal computers and smart devices on a consumer health information portal. *Journal of Medical Internet Research, 16*(7), e160. doi:10.2196/jmir.3186 PMID:25000537

Jadhav, A. S., Sheth, A. P., & Pathak, J. (2014). *Online information searching for cardiovascular diseases: an analysis of mayo clinic search query logs. american medical informatics association annual symposium.* Dayton, OH: Knoesis Publications. Retrieved on May 1, 2016 from http://corescholar. libraries.wright.edu/knoesis/539

Kańtoch, E., Augustyniak, P., Markiewicz, M., & Prusak, D. (2014). *Monitoring activities of daily living based on wearable wireless body sensor network.* 36th Annual International Conference of the IEEE Engineering in Medicine and Biology Society, IEEE Publisher, 586-589. Retrieved on May 12, 2016 from http://ieeexplore.ieee.org/xpl/articleDetails.jsp?arnumber=6943659&newsearch=true&queryTe xt=Monitoring%20activities%20of%20daily%20living%20based%20on%20wearable%20wireless%20 body%20sensor%20network

Kirci, P., Alan, U., Bıyık, V., & Samak, Z. (2015). *Healthcare navigation system.* Science and Information Conference (SAI), pg 406-409, London, U.K.: IEEE Publisher. Retrieved on May 12, 2016 from http://ieeexplore.ieee.org/xpl/articleDetails.jsp?arnumber=7237174&newsearch=true&queryText=He althcare%20Navigation%20System

Kirci, P., & Ünal, P. (2016). *Personalization of mobile health applications for remote health monitoring.* International Workshop on Personalization in Persuasive Technology, Salzburg, Austria,1582, 120-125. Retrieved on May 12, 2016 from http://ceur-ws.org/Vol-1582/10Kirci.pdf

Kusiak, A., Kern, J. A., Kernstine, K. H., & Tseng, B. T. L. (Eds.). (2000). Autonomous decision-making: A data mining approach, *IEEE Transactions on Information Technology in Biomedicine*, 4(4): 274–284, IEEE Publisher. Retrieved on May 12, 2016 from http://ieeexplore.ieee.org/xpl/articleDetails. jsp?arnumber=897059&queryText=Autonomous%20decision-making:%20A%20data%20mining%20 approach&newsearch=true

Kwiatkowska, M., & McMillan, L. (2010). *A semiotic approach to data in medical decision making*. IEEE International Conference on Fuzzy Systems (FUZZ), 1-8, Barcelona, Spain: IEEE Publisher. Retrieved on May 12, 2016 from http://ieeexplore.ieee.org/xpl/articleDetails.jsp?arnumber=5584301&newsearch= true&queryText=A%20semiotic%20approach%20to%20data%20in%20medical%20decision%20making

Lim, J., Kim, I. K., Bae, S., & Lee, S. H. (2014). *System proposal and CRS model design applying personal Information protection for big data analysis*. International Conference on Big Data and Smart Computing (BIGCOMP), Bangkok, Thailand, 231-234.Retrieved on May 12, 2016 from http://ieeexplore. ieee.org/xpl/articleDetails.jsp?tp=&arnumber=6741442

Liu, H., Hou, X. Q., Hu, G., Li, J., & Ding, Y. Q. (2009). Development of an EHR system for sharing - a semantic perspective. Medical Informatics in a United and Healthy Europe. *Study Health Technology Information*. 150: 113-117. Retrieved on May 10, 2016 from http://ebooks.iospress.nl/publication/12617

Madsen, L. B. (2014). *Data driven health care: How Analytics and BI are transforming the industry*. Hoboken, New Jersey: John Wiley & Sons, Inc. Retrieved on May 11, 2016 from http://onlinelibrary. wiley.com/book/10.1002/9781119205012

Manyika, J., Chui, M., Brown, B., Buhin, J., Dobbs, R., Roxburgh, C., & Byers, A. H. (2011). *Big Data: The next frontier for innovation, competition, and productivity*. New York City, NY, USA: McKinsey Global Institute, McKinsey & Company. Retrieved on May 11, 2016 from http://www.mckinsey.com/~/ media/McKinsey/Business%20Functions/Business%20Technology/Our%20Insights/Big%20data%20 The%20next%20frontier%20for%20innovation/MGI_big_data_full_report.ashx

Myatt, G. J., & Johnson, W. P. (2014). *Making sense of data.a practical guide to exploratory data analysis and data mining*. Hoboken, New Jersey: John Wiley & Sons, Inc. Retrieved on May 12, 2016 from http://onlinelibrary.wiley.com/doi/10.1002/9781118422007.ch2/summary

Naumann, T. (2013). *Distributed systems for clinical data analysis*. White paper. Intel distribution for apache hadoop software. Healthcare big data analytics. Retrieved on May 08, 2016 from http://www. intel.com/content/dam/www/public/us/en/documents/white-papers/big-data-hadoop-clinical-analysis-paper.pdf

Owens, D. K., & Sox, H. C. (Eds.). (2001). *Medical decision-making: Probabilistic medical reasoning*. Medical Informatics: Computer Applications in Health Care and Biomedicine, 2nd ed., E. H. Shortliffe and L.E. Perreault, Eds. New York City, NY: Springer New York, pp. 76–131. Retrieved on May 12, 2016 from http://link.springer.com/chapter/10.1007%2F978-0-387-21721-5_3

Panahiazar, M., Taslimitehrani, V., Jadhav, A., & Pathak, J. (2014). *Empowering personalized medicine with big data and semantic web technology: promises, challenges, and use cases.* IEEE International Conference on Big Data. 790-795. Retrieved on May 10, 2016 from http://ieeexplore.ieee.org/xpl/articleDetails.jsp?arnumber=7004307&newsearch=true&queryText=Empowering%20Personalized%20 Medicine%20with%20Big%20Data%20and%20Semantic%20Web%20Technology:%20Promises

Reyes, A. J. O., García, A. O., & Mué, Y. L. (2014). System for processing and analysis of information using clustering technique. *IEEE Latin America Transactions*, 12(2): 364-371, IEEE Publisher. Retrieved on May 12, 2016 from http://ieeexplore.ieee.org/search/searchresult.jsp?newsearch=true&queryText= System%20for%20Processing%20and%20Analysis%20of%20Information%20Using%20Clustering%20 Technique

Siddiqa, A., Niazi, M., Mustafa, F., Bokhari, H., Hussain, A., Akram, N., . . . Iqbal, S. (2009). *A new hybrid agent-based modeling & simulation decision support system for breast cancer data analysis.* International Conference on Information and Communication Technologies, ICICT '09, Karachi, Pakistan, pp 134-139,IEEE Publisher. Retrieved on May 11, 2016 from http://ieeexplore.ieee.org/xpl/articleDetails.jsp?arnumber=5267202&queryText=A%20New%20Hybrid%20AgentBased%20Modeling%20. AND.%20Simulation%20Decision%20Support%20System%20for%20Breast%20Cancer%20Data%20 Analysis&newsearch=true

Tripathy, A. K., Joshi, N., Kale, H., Durando, M., & Carvalho, L. (2015). *Detection of adverse drug events through data mining techniques.* 2015 International Conference on Technologies for Sustainable Development (ICTSD-2015), Mumbai, India, pp 1-6, IEEE Publisher. Retrieved on May 12, 2016 from http://ieeexplore.ieee.org/xpl/articleDetails.jsp?arnumber=7095897&newsearch=true&queryText=Det ection%20of%20Adverse%20Drug%20Events%20through%20Data%20Mining%20Techniques

Wang, J., Cui, M., Zhao, Y., & Mao, T. (2011). *To establish judgment model of chinese medicine efficacy based on subsequent visit medical records of asthma among adults.* International Symposium on IT in Medicine and Education (ITME). 1: 523-526. Retrieved on May 10, 2016 from http://ieeexplore.ieee.org/ xpl/login.jsp?tp=&arnumber=6130891&url=http%3A%2F%2Fieeexplore.ieee.org%2Fxpls%2Fabs_all. jsp%3Farnumber%3D6130891

Webb, J., & O'Brien, T. (2013). *Big data now, 2013 Edition.* Sebastopol, CA, U.S.A.: O'Reilly Media,Inc. Retrieved on May 12, 2016 from http://www.oreilly.com/data/free/bigdatanow2013.csp

Wilson, J., & Bock, A. (2012). *The benefit of using both claims data and electronic medical record data in health care analysis.* White paper. Optum. Retrieved on May 08, 2016 from https://www.optum. com/content/dam/optum/resources/whitePapers/Benefits-of-using-both-claims-and-EMR-data-in-HC-analysis-WhitePaper-ACS.pdf

Zhu, K., Lou, Z., Zhou, J., Ballester, N. A., Kong, N., & Parikh, P. (2015). Predicting 30-day hospital readmission with publicly available administrative database: A conditional logistic regression modeling approach. *Methods of Information in Medicine*, *54*(6), 560–567. doi:10.3414/ME14-02-0017 PMID:26548400

Zikopoulos, P. C., Eaton, C., DeRoos, D., Deutsch, T., & Lapis, G. (2012). *Understanding big data – analytics for enterprise class hadoop and streaming data.* New York City, NY: McGraw-Hill: Aspen Institute. Retrieved on May 12, 2016 from http://public.dhe.ibm.com/common/ssi/ecm/im/en/iml14296u-sen/IML14296USEN.PDF

KEY TERMS AND DEFINITIONS

Aggregation: The state by which particulars are collected based on a classification.

Algorithm: A finite series of deterministic or random elements including steps that provide a desired outcome.

Analytics: A data driven, manual analysis and optimization models including process that creates insight.

Big Data: A term presenting to datasets that own big amounts of data (volume), various data (variety), and rising speed of generation (velocity).

Data Cleansing: To specify, remove or correct incorrect data.

Data Management Process: The process of considering source data, performing some operations on it and transmit it to a predefined location.

Data Warehouse: A group of data from different sources organized to present useful guidance to an organization's decision makers. A shared repository of data.

Network: More than one subnets connected with routers.

Sensor Data: Machine produced data.

Structured Data: Data that adapts to a predefined structure.

Structured Query Language (SQL): Used to store data to and retrieve data from relational databases.

The Internet of Things (IoT): Objects that are recognizable, locatable and controllable over the Internet.

Tools: The main building stone through which many assets are developed.

Unstructured Data: Data that cannot adapt to a predefined structure.

Value: The real worth of an outcome to an individual.

Visualization: Provides display of acquired data within graphical form.

Volume, Variety, and Velocity: Three Vs, they are three commonly utilized specification of Big Data.

This research was previously published in the Handbook of Research on Promoting Business Process Improvement Through Inventory Control Techniques; pages 559-582, copyright year 2018 by Business Science Reference (an imprint of IGI Global).

Chapter 22

Evolution of Big Data in Medical Imaging Modalities to Extract Features Using Region Growing Segmentation, GLCM, and Discrete Wavelet Transform

Yogesh Kumar Gupta
ⓘ https://orcid.org/0000-0002-4572-178X
Banasthali Vidyapith, India

ABSTRACT

Big data refers to the massive amount of data from sundry sources (gregarious media, healthcare, different sensor, etc.) with very high velocity. Due to expeditious growth, the multimedia or image data has rapidly incremented due to the expansion of convivial networking, surveillance cameras, satellite images, and medical images. Healthcare is the most promising area where big data can be applied to make a vicissitude in human life. The process for analyzing the intricate data is mundanely concerned with the disclosing of hidden patterns. In healthcare fields capturing the visual context of any medical images, extraction is a well introduced word in digital image processing. The motive of this research is to present a detailed overview of big data in healthcare and processing of non-invasive medical images with the avail of feature extraction techniques such as region growing segmentation, GLCM, and discrete wavelet transform.

INTRODUCTION

In this digital, the astronomically immense data is a very critical quandary because of the tremendous amount of data engendered in routine life from sundry sources such as online transaction, e-mails, research journals and articles, convivial media sites (Facebook, Twitter, WhatsApp etc.) and web forums, different sensor's data composed from sundry sources such as healthcare science or medical data,

DOI: 10.4018/978-1-6684-3662-2.ch022

environmental organizations, meteorological department, business strategically data, trading market, company data being engendered daily life in different format such as structured, semi-structured and unstructured with a great velocity is customarily referred to as sizably voluminous Data (Singh, 2016). Data can be engendered on web in sundry forms like texts, audios, videos, images, texture or gregarious media posts data etc. This tremendous data is no more time stable in environment; rather it is updated according to time at rapid celerity. So that put an immensely colossal number of critical challenges on sizably voluminous data processing and storage. As an outcome, the conventional database computation implements and algorithms as well as data storage and management techniques has not able to deal with these data (Altera, 2016). Thus the astronomically immense data need to describe sundry innovative storage and processing implements (such as Hadoop, MapReduce, NoSQL database, HPCC and Apache Hive etc.) to acquire, store, distribute, handle and analyze. The process for analyzing the perplexed data mundanely concerned with the disclosing the hidden patterns. Big data involves sizably voluminous distributed file systems in commodity hardware for storing, which should be more flexible, fault toler-ant, scalable and reliable (Singh, 2016).

This digitized era needs to process the images for the manipulation of image properties. As immensely colossal data comes with the flood of intricate and digitize data so as to manage this data, there is need to have a discussion in an optimistic manner which describes its valuable and valid positive aspects. Healthcare industry conventionally has engendering astronomically immense amounts of data. As au-thors ken that historically the data stored in hard copies but nowadays there is a rapid digitization of this massive amount of stored data. The immensely colossal data analysis holds a broad accumulation of medical and healthcare applications such as public health management, clinical assessment and disease scrutiny. Big data analytics in healthcare has the puissance to decrement the costs of treatment, amend care, preserve lives and additionally ameliorate the quality of life.

From the commencement of evolution to 2003, only 5 Exabyte's of information has engendered, cur-rently by 2012 the authors engender that equipollent amount in just two days, if authors consider data of digital macrocosm that will cultivate to 2.72 Zeta bytes and by 2015 that will twice over every two years to reach 8 Zeta bytes (Tamilselvan, 2015).

According to the report given by McKinney Ecumenical Institute, it is considered that the healthcare sector could engender more than $300 billion value per year, if US healthcare organizations were to utilize immensely colossal data resourcefully and prosperously (Lodha, 2014). Big data in Healthcare is irresistible on account of its broadly expounded aspects termed as degree, verities of data and its pace .i.e. rate at which data is engendered (Archenaa, 2015). The electronic healthcare data includes medical imaging engendered through minimal and non-invasive medical imaging modalities techniques such as PET-Scan, CT-Scan, X-ray, MRI, Ultrasound etc., diagnostic reports, pharmacy information for health indemnification, medical research journals, and laboratory experiment values, implants and surgery test results, medication information etc. which is prone to avail the organizations to build a 360° view of each and every patient. The pace of Electronic Care Records (ECR) implementation exponentially increases in inpatient and outpatient aspects. To enhance the amelioration in outcomes, reduction of costs and excel-lence of care, this digitization of healthcare informatics is opening tremendous promising possibilities to avail the payers, stakeholders and providers (Gupta, 2016). All the healthcare organizations are required to turn into data driven area to survive in the period of immense transformation.

The motive of this research is to elaborate astronomically immense data in healthcare with processing of medical images with the avail of region growing segmentation technique and sizably voluminous data analytical implements and techniques. The chapter is withal fixating on sundry non-invasive medical imaging modalities such as PET-Scan, Ultrasound, MRI, CT-Scan and X-Ray. On the other hand for capturing the visual context of any medical image, extraction is well introduced word in the digital image processing. The purport of our chapter is to recognize the ROI from the medical images utilizing feature extraction Technique by applying it with the astronomically immense data processing Implements which provides the pertinent results in the favor of healthcare organizations.

Seven Stacks of Big Data

More and more data format in multimedia such as unstructured, structured and semi-structured data are the dimensions that make the healthcare data more challenging (Lodha, 2014). Size of big data is primary attribute to define but immensely colossal data isn't just about data volume. Sizably voluminous data can be defined by following characteristics (7Vs).

Volume: - (Quantity of data in terabytes to zetabytes) Health cognate data engendered and accumulated perpetually and engender unthinkable amount of data (Raghupathi, 2014). Incipient form of data for e.g., biometric sensor readings, 3D imaging and genomics are growing rapidly (Thabet, 2015).

Velocity: - (Pace of data generation) Authentic time data growing at very high rate (Kumari, 2015). Traditionally healthcare is static (Thabet, 2015). Constant rate of incipient data engenderment presents incipient challenges in data amassment, storage, analysis, modeling and data distribution (Lodha, 2014).

Value: - It refers to the process of finding obnubilated values from astronomically immense amount of data sets (Gupta, 2016).

Veracity: - (Meaningfulness) it refers to the 'data assurance' and 'data trust' (Thabet, 2015). Veracity is the goal of data analytics because healthcare data is highly unstructured and has the total concern with life and death, so data quality and correctness is the main issue.

Figure 1. Big Data Characteristics (Soni, 2016)

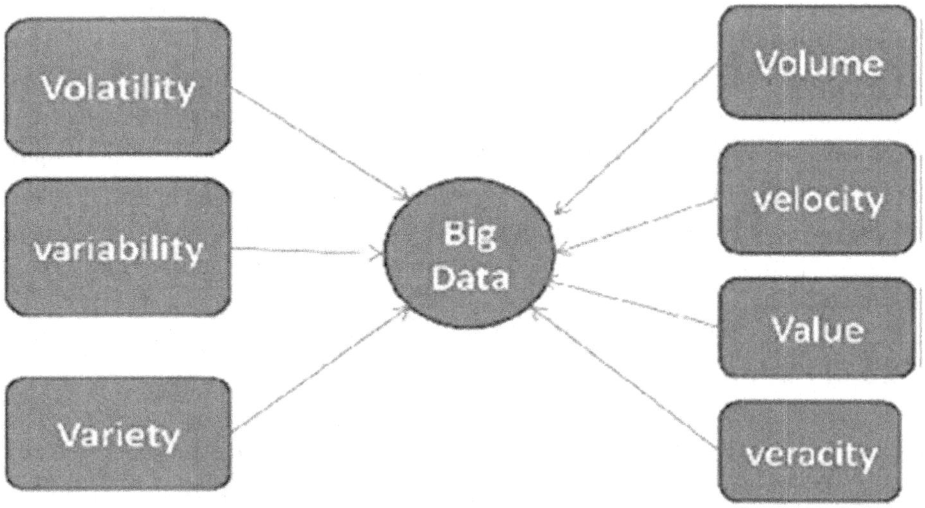

Variety: - (Multiplicity in data formats) refers to the intricacy and heterogeneity of healthcare data (Kumari, 2015). Healthcare data increases due to the digitization of subsisting data and from incipient engendered data (Thabet, 2015).

Variability: - Designates intricacy or the data whose meaning is fluctuating and variation in data flow rates.

Volatility: - It refers to the data validity and longitivity designates how long data will be subsidiary for us and it is additionally paramount to ken when the data is no longer felicitous for processing and analysis (Ammari, 2008).

Big Data Processing Tools

In authentic meaning, authors can summed up the analytics implements that facilitate users to frequently and expeditiously analyze sizably voluminous amount of data in authentic time and which provides a better framework for data mining techniques and infrastructures. Such analytic implements i.e. Hadoop, expounded briefly here along with the concept of MapReduce and HDFS incorporate into sundry phases of decision making processes for efficient analytics. In evolutionary astronomically immense data environment, the analytics of big data has been entered in a form of well-relished culture where MapReduce model is responsible for efficient analysis and for storing the approaching data; HDFS is utilized as storage layer.

Hadoop

There is an immensely colossal desideratum of immensely colossal data processing because it holds lots of sumptuous information. Computing capacity of traditional system would not copacetic to achieve the task in given time frame. The traditional RDBMS database storage capacity is in GB and it takes hours to days to process on astronomically immense data and engendering report. Processing gigabytes to petabytes data by utilizing mundane RDBMS system is very arduous and infeasible. There is hardware inhibition and lots of challenges authors are facing with traditional RDBMS system that is storage, processing, variety of data, and size of data. These challenges will solved by the hadoop. It reduces latency by moving the MapReduce code over the networks to clusters situated at another place and commence processing of cluster data.

Hadoop is java inscribed, Apache open source distributed framework that stores astronomically substantial amount of sundry type of data by unstable structures and utilizing single programming model, this framework sanctions running distributed processing applications on clusters of computers (Gupta, 2016). Hadoop solves the immensely colossal data quandary; it is a platform having gargantuan processing capability that can handle number of tasks and jobs. Until now the data that was arduous to analyze and manage, for this purport hadoop recommends a tremendous deal of facility in enabling enterprises to tie together the big data.

Architecture of Hadoop

Hadoop is applied to process high amount of data in any structure. It is utilized for distributed storage and analysis in authentic time on a single machine. MapReduce programming layer is a parallel processing model on which framework of Hadoop relays and HDFS is used for storing the data (Saraladevi, 2015). YARN framework and prevalent utilities are two additional aspects of the framework where YARN is utilized for resource management and job scheduling. And apart from that Hadoop Mundane contains some utilities and java libraries subsidiary for other components of framework.

Hadoop offers two major layers for processing large data in an efficient manner:

1)   Hadoop Distributed File System (HDFS) as storage layer
2)   MapReduce as processing layer

Figure 2. Hadoop Architecture (Kumar, 2015)

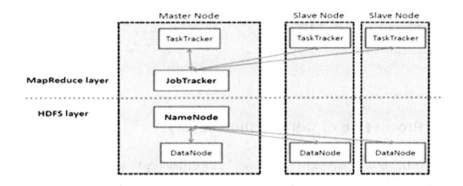

HDFS (Distributed and Storage Layer)

It is a portable java predicated dispersed file system that gives more reliability, scalability and which is highly fault tolerant than subsisting file system to store prodigiously and sizably voluminous files in streaming access patterns redundantly. It is predicated on Google File System (GFS) and optimized or designed to run on commodity cluster hardware (Priyanka, 2014). HDFS adopts the replication of data across the scattered nodes in order to achieve the fault tolerance i.e. it is highly resilient.

It follows the concept of master-slave architecture. A single Hadoop cluster is a coalescence of one NameNode as a MasterNode and numeral of DataNodes as SlaveNodes. NameNode is responsible to store the metadata like: denomination, locations of each and every block address, file attributes and replicas etc. whereas the authentically data is stored in the DataNodes, i.e. divided astronomically immense files which are in the form blocks or chunks, stored in DataNodes. It is considered that each chunk of data is replicated over other server node.

Big Data is not the quandary of managing the intricate data, while it's the quandary of managing it efficiently with minimum cost and in consequential manner. After having the analysis over the stored medical images the ROI corresponding to the images can be achieved that is proven auxiliary for some disease prognostication in a human body.

Figure 3. HDFS Architecture with Load Balancing (Das, 2013)

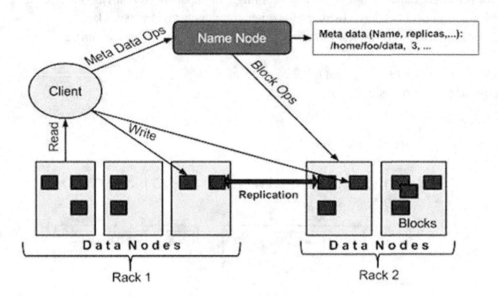

Map Reduce (Processing or Computation Layer)

It is a programming framework engendered by Google for distributed and parallel processing of massive amount of data by utilizing the concept of divide and surmount. It is incentivized by two terms "Map" and "Reduce" (performed by designated functions: Mapper and Reducer) which are utilized for processing by acclimating the concept of divide and surmount method (Manojbhai, 2016). The quandaries of big data are broken down into minuscule units of work and processed in a parallel way. Parallel processing is obligatory to achieve scalable solutions of sizably voluminous data quandary. It's a parallel computing framework that has been widely utilized for astronomically immense scale image narration and analysis (Kumar, 2015).

Conceptual Representation of MapReduce Programming Model

a. Representation of Input Data as a <K, V> pair output
b. Map: <K, V> pair → multi-set of <K, V> pairs, defined by user and easy to parallelize
c. Shuffle and Sort: Aggregate all <K, V> pairs with the same key.
d. Reduce: <K, multi-set (V)> → <K, multi-set (V)>, defined by user and easy to parallelize

Above steps are repeated for number of times until final result will come.

Non-Invasive Medical Imaging Modality

There are two types of medical imaging modalities Invasive and Non-Invasive. In invasive modalities need to do some surgical operation but in non-invasive there is no need to do the surgical operation. In this chapter authors used only Non-invasive medical imaging modalities such as USG, CT-Scan, X-Ray, MRI, PET-Scan etc.

Figure 4. MapReduce Parallel Processing Model

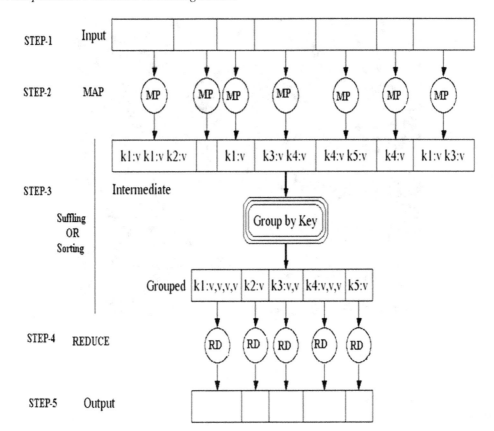

Ultra-Sonography

Ultrasound imaging is very efficient medical imaging technique to ascertain the blood circulation in heart and in blood vessels and to check the development of baby inside a mother's uterus (Kasban, 2015). Ultrasound medical imaging uses high frequency sound pulses in the range of megahertz and their echoes to engender medical images (Desai, 2016). Nowadays ultrasound technology is yarely present, inexpensive for the treatment of endometriomas, bladder lesions, rectovaginal septum and ovarian endometriosis (Hsu, 2010). Ultrasound has the three major area of application Obstetrics and Gynaecology, Cardiology and Urology as acclimated to detect intra and extra luminal abnormalities, observing fatal health, checking the sex of the baby, view inside the heart to apperceive the eccentric patterns, quantifying the blood circulation in major blood vessels or heart, finding kidney stones and cancer respectively (Lodha, 2014). As authors ken that ultrasound is energy so it can cause two major quandaries; first is: it enables increase of temperature and second is: ultrasound release gases which dissolved in the blood or tissues and it composes bubbles when gases go out (Soni, 2016).

Figure 5. Detection of Fetus (Haralampieva, 2014)

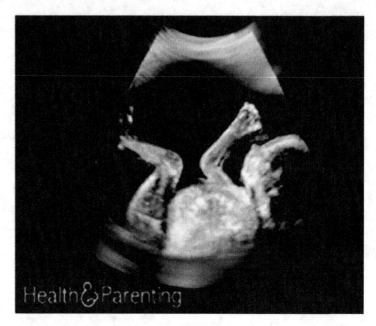

X-Ray Imaging

X-Ray is a type of high energy electromagnetic waves which can perforate many body components at varying levels such as portly, bones, tumours and other body components can absorb x-rays at different calibres, which will reflected in the x-ray image. X-ray attenuation is work more efficiently in bones rather than soft tissues. X-ray consists of many medical applications such as chiropractic and dental. Radiographs are habituated to view the kineticism of body components and subsidiary for blood vessels of heart and encephalon enables to take the internal structure of stomach, intestines and lungs, detect fracture in bones etc. Mammography is utilized to detect the breast cancer and Hysterosalpingogram is utilized for uterus and Fallopian tubes (Desai, 2016).

Due to the utilization of relatively high calibre of radiations people suffer from many quandaries such as skin reddening, hair loss, tissue effects such as cataracts and additionally increase chances to have cancer later in life (Yogamangalam, 2013).

Positron Emission Tomography (PET)

It is a radionuclide and very sensitive molecular technique, make utilization of short life isotopes, they have half-lives from 2 to 20 minutes for e.g. 15O, 13N and 11C (Smitha, 2011).

As compared to other technologies PET can tell, how the human body is functioning rather than, how it looks, it is finding very utilizable from medical perspective. PET-Scan is generally used to detect encephalon disorders, cancer, central nervous, heart quandaries and body system abnormalities and view the abnormalities at the cellular level. PET shows the medicos how the cancer is metabolizes, whether it is spreading to incipient areas and shows how the tumour is responding to chemotherapy (Smitha, 2011). PET has minimal health risks as compared to the salutary results in diagnosing solemn quanda-

Figure 6. Chest Internal Structure (Yogamangalam, 2013)

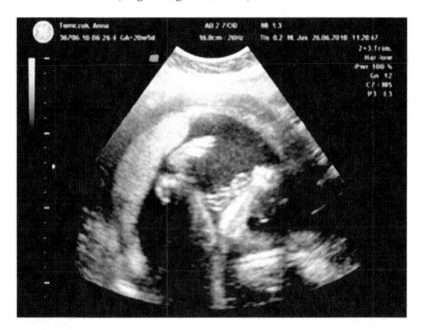

ries. However, radiations are not considered to be utilizable in fetus development and not for enceinte ladies, (Desai, 2016).

Big Data is a congregation of sizably voluminous datasets containing array of data types, which may be in Kilobytes, Gigabytes, Megabytes, Terabytes, Petabytes, Exabytes and Zetabytes engendered from sundry sources such as gregarious media, stock market, medical science, satellite data etc with very high velocity (Singh, 2013). The astronomically immense data referred to the enamours flock of structured, unstructured and semi-structured data which may be analysed for getting consequential information, pattern, trends and sodality especially cognate to human demeanour and interaction that intonates the business on a day to day substructure (Archenaa, 2015)

LITERATURE REVIEW

Since 2011 it has been considered that the interest area regarding immensely colossal data has been exponentially incremented which has been reviewed over here.

(Gandomi et al. 2014) "Beyond the Hype: Big data concepts, methods and analytics", a consolidated picture of immensely colossal data is given in this paper by integrating definitions from academics and practitioners. Utilization of analytics methods and implement techniques for unstructured data are the primary focus of this paper to gain valuable and valid insights form intricate data. To leverage sizably voluminous amount of heterogeneous data in audio, video and text formats, the fundamental desideratum of developing efficient and opportune analytical methods are tinted in this paper by the researchers. For structured immensely colossal data, the desideratum to devise emerging implements and methods for predictive analysis is withal reinforced by them. (Saraladevi, 2015) "Big Data and Hadoop – A Study in Security Perspective", suggested some approaches which concerns with the security issues occurs

Figure 7. PET-Scan of Brain (Smitha, 2011)

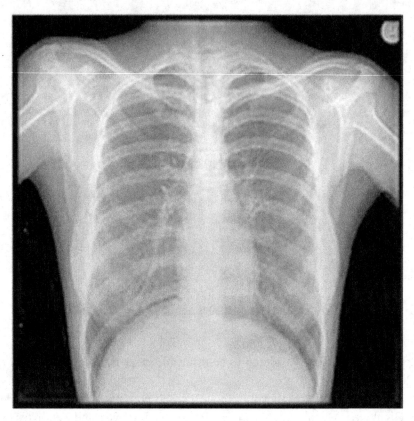

in Hadoop environment. Researchers mainly fixated on issue raised in Hadoop bottom layer i.e. HDFS which is more sensitive to the hazard of data spoofing, unauthorized access and dispensable exposure. They proposed some innovative approaches such as Kerberos, Bull Ocular Perceiver Algorithm and NameNode approach used to handle with these security aspects where Kerberos uses TGT concept for providing better security, the algorithm proves data centric security as well as the NameNode facilitated by the NNSE (Name Node Security Enhance) holding the Bull Ocular perceiver algorithm replicates the NameNode for the purport of decrementing the server crashes. (Peter, 2014) "Leveraging Big Data Analytics and Hadoop in Developing India's Healthcare Services", revealed the rewards of sizably voluminous data analytics and one such implement for the same purport i.e. Hadoop. By considering the immensely colossal data quandary in developing countries like India, this paper provides the centric impact on Hadoop platform to provide the accommodations of healthcare for each person in order to have finest cost. As healthcare field is infected by many challenges such as to process the medical images, here Hadoop is the merely hope used to pilling up these images from external or internal sources and mine the valuable information as a precise diagnostics results utilizing HIPI interface which elaborate the accomplishment of medical image processing. (Chen, 2013) "The Impact of Big Data on the Healthcare Information Systems", expounded impact of Astronomically Immense Data in the terms of healthcare informatics systems, by having exploring discussion on possibly considered issues. According to this paper patient care and genomics analytics, are mainly impacted applications by the immensely colossal Data in Healthcare Informatics, elsewhere the NoSQL and Haddop are considered as a future algorithm for the sizably voluminous data analytics. This paper withal fixated on the security, privacy and the ethical issues emerged from astronomically immense data. (Lavanya, 2016) describe a clear vision of HDFS, Hadoop and MapReduce. HDFS and MapReduce are widely accepted tools in many areas such as health, financial service sector, cyber security, defense, and telecommunication etc. (Gagana, 2016) the paper mainly focuses on security of healthcare data by introducing healthcare system architecture. Security of healthcare data is very important concern to discover knowledgeable information from it. Along with the Hadoop components paper also provides components of the healthcare system architecture: authentication module, EMR, information sharing by using encryption and decryption, HL7 clinical document architecture. There is a need of security of personal health record system against attackers. Because of privacy and security big data analytics become more difficult. Still the authors can use proper tools that can provide promising results in healthcare industry. According to the report of (Altera, 2016) "Altera Corporation in Medical Imaging Implementation using FPGAs" baby boomers are continuously looking for new and emerging therapies such as minimal invasive and non-invasive medical image modalities such as CT scan, X-ray, Ultrasound, MRI, and PET-scan etc., to treat and detect the ordinary diseases (Brain and Heart related ailments). To meet the patients requirements these modalities techniques are measured as a crucial drivers as the advancements of analytical imaging area. The Altera FPGA provides the flexible multicore CPU system named as DSP horsepower, on which the superior algorithms works and gives elevated performance, together with developments tools of great level and some IP implementation libraries. (Patel, 2016) mainly focused on the potential solution of big data Problem scenario that comes in existence while the implementation of Electronic Health Records (EHR) systems, which now exceed the capabilities of traditional database systems. This implementing probable solution of big data offers to bind this heterogeneity datasets, to extract the meaningful and valuable information's. This paper also has some discussion over its challenges, opportunities and applicable technological advancement tools for healthcare data analytics in order to improve quality of life and outcomes. (Chandel, 2012) Compares different algorithms of image segmentation techniques and implement them with their parameter value using MATLAB and select the best optimal result using the subjective approach of performance evaluation. (Kumari, 2015) describe the edge detection techniques such as region based, threshold based and clustering for segmentation of medical images. In this paper authors focuses on the clustering based segmentation and discuss the limitation of these techniques, for future they need a novel integrated method which helps to preserve smoothing and improve accuracy in procedure of segmentation. (Ravi, 2015) discuss to compare different methods of segmentation such as k-means, region growing and counter method on the basis of energy. (Smitha, 2011) describe the importance of image data classification techniques of medical images. They discuss texture classification techniques (Wavelet and Fourier Transformation), neural network technique (Bayesian Decision Theory) including supervised, unsupervised and some data mining techniques. (Kumar, 2015a) Describe the watermarking protocol based on DWT. Authors uses watermarked images that inserted into high frequency sub-bands of DWT. Thereafter authors applied principal component analysis for the selecting maximum energy blocks. (Kumar, 2015b), Talking about the buyer and seller rights on the behalf of the Buyer-Seller Watermarking protocol utilizing the Discrete Cosine Transform (DCT) and Discrete Wavelet Transform (DWT). Authors also describe the comparison between DCT and DWT on the behalf of some parameters. Authors show the result on the behalf of Peak Signal to Noise Ratio (PSNR), MSE and SF of watermarking images. (Kumar, 2014, 2017, 2018, 2019a, 2019b) and (Singh, 2018), proposed different watermarking protocol to provide secure and private transaction between the communicating parties by using cloud. (Gupta, 2017a, 2017b, 2019, 2020), (Dubay, 2017) and (Maheshwari, 2018),

Proposed different features extraction and edge detection techniques from the non-invasive medical Imaging Modalities in the evolutionary of big data Analytics

Research Gap:- After going through the exhaustive literature survey, it can be said that some researchers worked for the analysis of various kinds of images such as satellite images, ballistic images, Aqua satellite images, remote sensing images but nobody has worked on medical images using a big data analytical tools. So, this is the new emerging area for the researcher. Our purpose is to extract features from non-invasive medical imaging modalities using Region Growing Segmentation Technique, GLCM and Discrete Wavelet Transform in the evolutionary of Big Data Environment.

RESEARCH METHODOLOGY

In the proposed system, work is divided into two phases – theoretical and practical. Theoretical phase of our work involves the studying and understanding the aspects cognate to non-invasive medical imaging modalities, astronomically immense data, sundry storing and processing implements and techniques such as Hadoop, HDFS and MapReduce, that process substantial data on a cluster of commodity hardware whereas the practical phase involves the coding of proposed system utilizing MATLAB R2013a. It additionally, make a multinode cluster for storing and processing the substantial amount of medical imaging data utilizing Hadoop- 2.6.0 on Ubantu-14.04 and hardware: Intel® core™ i3-3210 CPU 540 @3.07 GHz, 500GB HDD, 4.00 GB RAM.

Process Model of Proposed Work

To execute our proposed idea here is process model given below which is to be followed considerably providing the acquired results.

Figure 8. Process Model of Proposed work

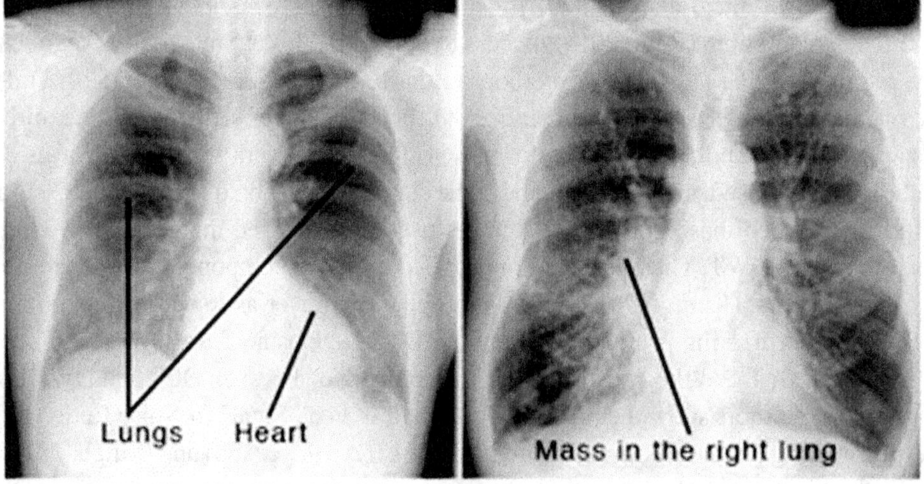

Proposed Method for Image Processing

Image processing is a method of extracting useful information from an image and the outcome of analysis is a mathematical data rather than an image. It involves the subsequent steps such as Acquisition of input images, Preprocessing on acquired images, Segmentation and Feature Extraction on preprocessed images, image classification on the behalf of features, and finally the image Evaluation on the behalf of predefined parameters. After the image processing, apply the data analytical tools to extract the useful information's or hidden patterns available in images, that assist the radiologists for making the decision and diagnose the disease properly.

Acquisition of Specific Medical Images

The initial step is to acquire the raw data i.e. different kinds of medical images from the secondary source i.e. internet. For this research, authors acquired 3000 of medical images in different modalities such MRI, PET-Scan, CT-Scan, X-ray and USG. The samples of several medical imaging modalities are shown in the below figure.

Figure 9. Various Non-Invasive Medical Imaging Modalities

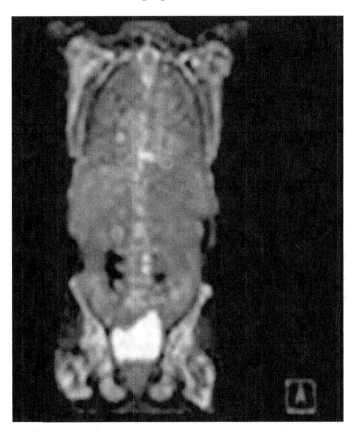

Preprocessing of Medical Images

Preprocessing of Medical Images is an important phase for the success of succeeding steps. It eliminates noises from the image, detects the edges, equalization the frequency level and is also used for inputting the images in to MATLAB environment. There is some list of techniques which is used by the proposed system for preprocessing are:-

a)   Equalization of frequency level i.e. Histogram
b)   Mapping of images from colored to grayscale
c)   Morphological operations

Equalization of Histogram

It represents the gray level frequency of the image in the form of graph. Basically histogram equalization are used to equalize the gray level frequency of the image, meanwhile it enhance the image intensities and contrast. In this chapter authors used CLAHE (Contrast Adaptive Histogram Equalization) technique that is proposed by Karel Zuiderveld and used to enhance the contrast of various Images. Predefined function for the CLAHE is-

MATLAB: R= adapthisteq (I)
Imhist (R) – Shows the histogram of Equalized Image
Imhist (I) – Shows the histogram of original image

Here I denote an input image and R is resultant equalized image.

It can be seen in both figures 10 and 11 that, the contrast of resultant histogram equalized images are much better than the input images, because the frequency level of histogram equalized image is much higher than the original image, which is beneficial for subsequent steps.

Mapping of Images From Colored to GrayScale

This is the most important step of image preprocessing because it is used to convert RGB or colored image into grayscale image to reduce the complexity for subsequent steps that shown in figure below. RGB image contain three plane such as Red, Green and Blue while grayscale image contain only one plane. This mapping reduces the data to be maintained at one third. This data reduction results help in faster processing of algorithm. So, this is an essential step before doing any further processing.

Where RGB is the colored image which is used for converting into grayscale and GS is the resultant image.

Morphological Operations

It is used for regions sharpening and to fill the gaps of image as shown in figure below. There are four types of morphological operations such as erosion, dilation, closing and opening. In our research morphological erosion is used. In erosion, every pixel which touches background pixel is converted into background pixel. After applying erosion operation the object becomes smaller. erosion is represented Mathematically as-

$(A\Theta B)(x) = \{x \in X, x=a+b: a \in A, b \in B\}$

Where A is the matrix of binary image and B is mask

MATLAB: SE = strel ('disk', 2, 0)
F = imerode (InputImage, SE)
BEI = InputImage-F

Where SE is a structuring element created with the help of strel in-built function in which shape is like disk of radius 2. BEI shows the boundary extracted image.

Figure 10. Histogram of input and equalized CT-SCAN Image

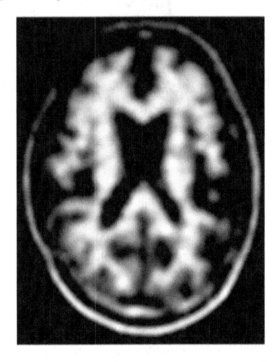

Image Segmentation: Region Splitting and Merging

Segmentation is most important step of image processing. It combines image pixels into multiple non-overlapping regions (set of pixels) that have same categories of attributes such as texture, color, intensity, range etc. Segmentation extracts only those features or parts of the image that require to be processed further. The selection of segmentation method is based on nature of the considered image and problem. Region based technique is also known as "similarity based segmentation" used to find out region directly.

Figure 11. Histogram of input and equalized MRI Image

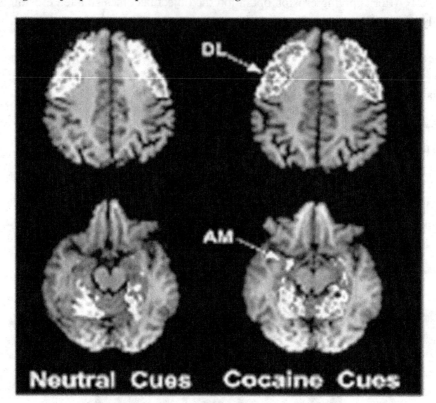

Algorithm

Step 1: Successively subdivide image into quadrant regions.
Step 2: Stop when all regions are homogeneous and obtain quad tree structure.
Step 3: At each level merge adjacent regions.
Step 4: Iterate until no further splitting/merging is possible.

Region Splitting and Merging Mathematical Model

To analyze medical images authors use this technique to identify the regions. Basically region growing technique is used to identify the edges from those images that are most noisy or unprocessed while other techniques are very difficult to identify region from the noisy images. Here authors use split and merge techniques to find out various image features such as- intensity, color, shape, texture etc. after that authors use feature vector database to store these image features and these stored image features will processed by using big data tools.

Feature Extraction Using GLCM and DWT

Feature of a medical images are the most prominent characteristic of the object that assist the radiologist to identify the cause of problem from that patient suffer. There are different types of features available in an image such as texture, color, shape, intensity and special location (Dubey, 2016). But the texture is the most important feature of an image that defines the nature of object. Feature extraction is the process of extracting most prominent or relevant features from the pre-processed image. Features are used for segmenting the images. Image segmentation can be done by two approaches: statistical and structural. The proposed research work uses statistical approach. There are several statistical techniques for measuring texture, shape an object, color of an object and special location of an object such as gray level co-occurrence matrix (GLCM), fractals, Gabor filters and wavelet transform. The proposed research work uses GLCM and wavelet transform with daubechies level four (db4). GLCM captures numerical feature values using partial relationship among neighborhood pixels features. These numerical features values are used for further comparing and classifying features. The wavelet transforms which are useful for defining the spatial or localized information's of the imaging data. Using GLCM and Wavelet transform authors can extract different types of features such as Max, Min, Mean, Median, Standard deviation, Variance, Skewness, Kurtosis, Shape, Contrast, Correlation, Energy, Homogeneity, Entropy, Colors(red, green, blue), Intensity value, Pixel density etc. Some features are calculated using GLCM and remaining are calculated using wavelet transform with the help of inbuilt function available in MATLAB R13a for a given image.

Figure 12. Result of RGB to Grayscale converted Image

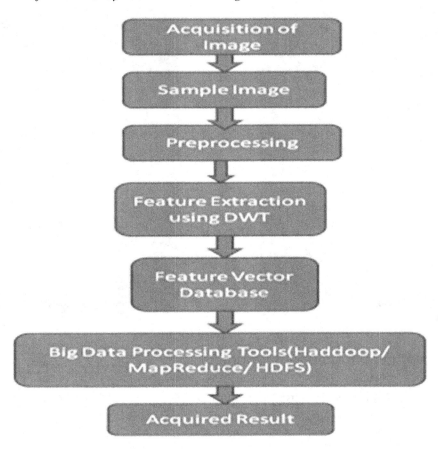

MATLAB function for GLCM:

  glcm = graycomatrix (image, 'Offset')

Where, offset is used to measure features from four different directions 00, 450, 900, 1350 and having offset value 0 1, -1 1, -1 0, -1 -1 respectively.

MATLAB function for Wavelet Transform:

  [cA, cH, cV, cD] = dwt2 (image,'db4')

Where, image is a variable used as an input image and 'db4' is a Daubechies wavelet up to 4 level decomposition and the image are decompose into 4 separate sub-bands named as HH (diagonal details), LL (which provides approximation image detail), HL (horizontal details), and LH (vertical details). These sub-bands also known as cD cA, cH, and cV subsequently, where only LL sub-band is used for next level decomposition as it retains most details.

Figure 13. Boundary Extracted Image

Figure 14. Region Splitting and merging algorithms process

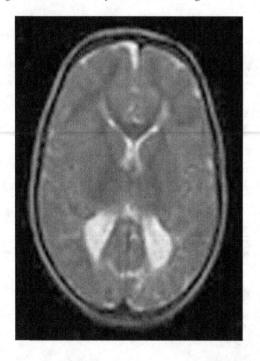

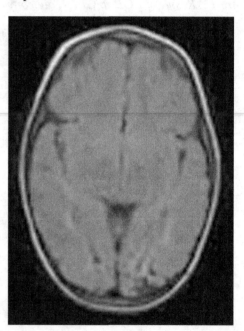

Proposed Feature Extraction Algorithm

The following steps are involved in proposed algorithm of feature extraction using Discrete Wavelet Transform:

Step 1: Load the input sample image.

Step 2: Use preprocessing step on loaded images which converts the RGB image into grayscale image.

Step 3: The grayscale image data are decomposed into 4 sub-bands using one level Discrete Wavelet Transform which provides low and high frequency coefficient vector.

Step 4: Create and display both the approximation and detail sub-bands from the 1 – level decomposition.

Step 5: Apply inverse wavelet transform over the retrieved coefficients to reconstruct image.

Step 6: 2nd level decomposition takes place to extract the local information by decomposing the approximation band from the step 4 into further sub-bands using Daubechies wavelet.

Step 7: Recreate and display both level 2 approximation and level 1 & 2 detail sub-bands.

Step 8: Display the resulted coefficients from where the entire detail band coefficient are chosen for analyzing and processing.

Step 9: Original image is reconstructed from the inverse transform.

Step 10: Features are extracted in MATLAB environment.

Step 11: The extracted features are then stored and analyzed by analytical tools.

After the extraction of features from the medical images authors create a feature vector database to store these image features that will processed further by big data analytical tools.

EXPERIMENTAL RESULTS AND DISCUSSION

The proposed work uses 3000 different types of non-invasive medical images, but here authors are going to show the results of 4 sample images as shown in figure 16.

Figure 15. Offset to measure features from four different directions (Dubay, 2017)

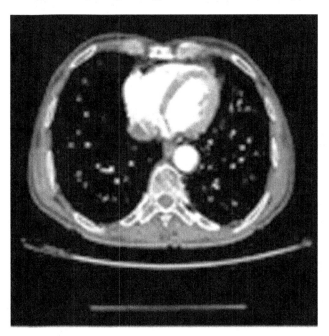

Figure 16. Four Input Sample of Non-Invasive Medical Images

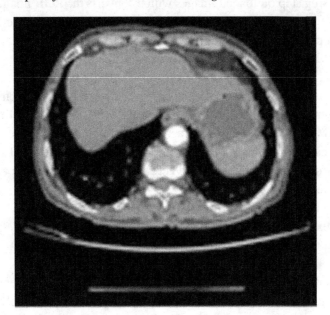

Here authors have performed the 2D- DWT over some medical images out of which only 4 resultant images are shown below which provides the intensity based features.

Here a1, a2, a3 and a4 are approximated image up to 4 levels and s is original image (Figure 17).

Here a1, a2, a3 and a4 are approximated image up to 4 levels and s is original image (Figure 18).

Here a1, a2, a3 and a4 are approximated image up to 4 levels and s is original image (Figure 19).

Here a1, a2, a3 and a4 are approximated image up to 4 levels and s is original image (Figure 20).

In this proposed work the input image decomposed up to four levels and then the best optimized approximated image that holds high intensity values is chosen. The intensity level of each pixel is shown in the histogram of figures 17 (d), 18 (d), 19 (d) and 20 (d), where a1, a2, a3 and a4 are approximated images up to 4 levels and s is original image. Outcome of the histogram is that the approximated image at level 4 (a4) has the highest intensity values than the other histogram level such as a1, a2 and a3. Decomposition up to four levels gives better or optimized resultant image that holds high intensity value and entire detail band coefficient of pixels of images that is used for further processing.

Extracted Feature in MATLAB Environment

The extracted features from the 4 sample medical images using region growing and splitting segmentation, GLCM and Discrete Wavelet transform as shown in Table 1.

After the extraction process, these extracted features are stored in the database first. The storage is to be done in feature vector database which are then used for the classification. Good separation of features in any image is to be achieved by SVM (Support Vector System) which is widest used classification system. Finally the classified images are to be processed using Big Data Tools to get the relevant information out of the stored and processed data.

Figure 17. Shows resultant Approximated image of CT-Scan

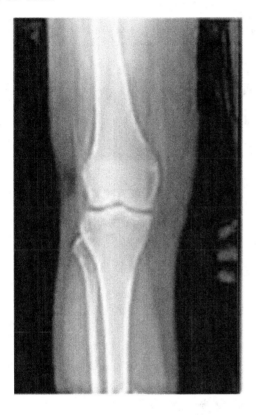

Figure 18. Shows resultant Approximated image of MRI

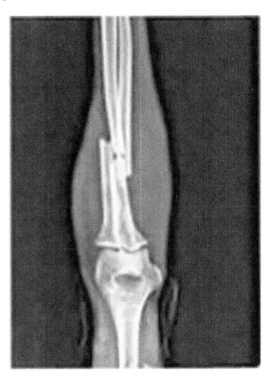

Figure 19. Shows resultant Approximated image of Brain MRI

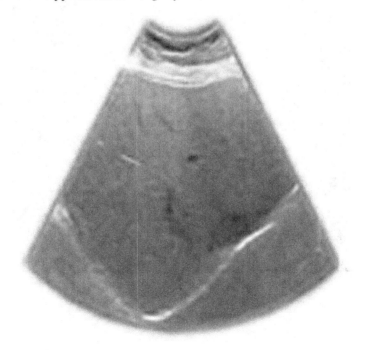

Figure 20. Shows resultant Approximated image of USG

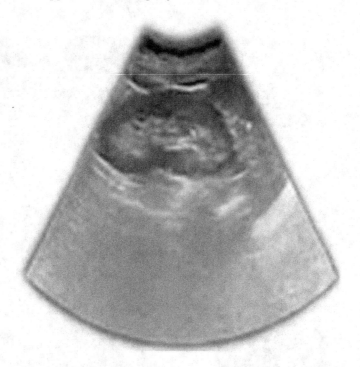

Figure 21. Extracted features using proposed work in MATLAB environment

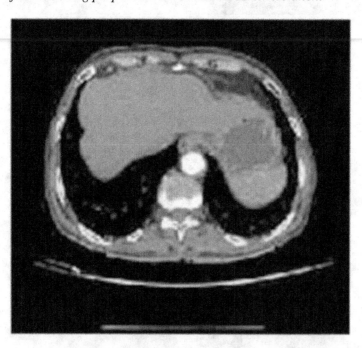

Figure 22. Extracted features using proposed work in MATLAB environment

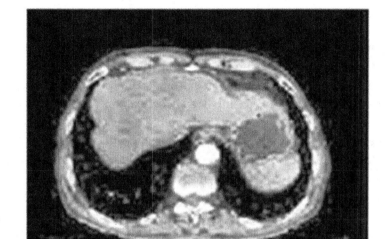

Table 1. Extracted features from the medical Images

Feature No.	Feature Name	Feature Value			
		Image1	Image2	Image3	Image4
1	Maximum	182.4	201.08	234.82	235.44
2	Minimum	2.0203	0.0221	1.88	0.69
3	Mean	230.82	286.55	296.4	636.30
4	Median	84.01	74.65	364.36	239.64
5	Std_deviation	446.92	446.66	963.55	690.05
6	Variance	353960	408660	971450	567250
7	Skewness	1.02	2.25	0.57	2.7
8	Kurtosis	2.94	9.04	2.09	11.09
9	Shape	12.38	14.04	16.34	15.78
10	Entropy	0.4489	0.3373	0.3955	0.3373
11	intensity_val	125.3469	113.83	134.48	92.69
12	pixel_density	0.0032	0.0034	0.0032	0.0035

CONCLUSION

The availability of data and their analytics are disconnected. The big data period is about the creation of potential information through the use of efficient analytic techniques rather than not to just collecting and storing the data. Authors conclude this chapter by providing a brief overview on how the big data analytics has a great impact on healthcare industry. Big data contains a sheer volume of data and it is a complex ecosystem that carries data of various characteristics (7 pillars of big data) as variability, velocity, variety, volatility, volume, veracity and value. Big data analytics has exposed outstanding outcomes in various application domains such as business, healthcare, IT industries etc. Healthcare industry is one of the most popular industries which have big implication of big data and its analysis. Authors extract the meaningful information from the medical images by using big data analytics tool and technologies and authors used methods to remove the unwanted region from the images and find out the interested region of the image. By processing medical images it is very beneficial for the doctors to diagnose disease of the patient. In future there will be more advancement in big data analytic technologies and processes, authors dream the healthcare cost will reduce considerably and will see much healthier public as compared to now. The future healthcare will be like god gifted. To make a change in human life, Healthcare is the most promising area where big data analytics can be applied. Healthcare industry usually has generating vast amounts of data exponentially. By having the primitive Review on the Big Data, now authors have adequate awareness about the Big Data Problem. To select the potential, it is mandatory to utilize the high performance solution in image processing. In this chapter authors presented a standard review over some feature extraction techniques such as, region growing and splitting segmentation, GLCM and Discrete Wavelet transform. However authors found that performing these feature extraction techniques over the specific non-invasive medical images that provides superior results. Big Data Analytics in Healthcare is defined by applying many advanced and leveraged analytical techniques on cluster of datasets for the purpose of getting more and more relevant data for the best decision making by the healthcare organizations. The objective of our work is to solve this drastic problem occurred in the concept of Big Data healthcare management by detecting the region of interest in the medical images collected from the diagnostic centers, clinics, medical centers.

Future Scope

In medical science, storing and processing of huge amount of medical images in a limited period of time is very difficult, they takes more time to process it and most of the time it seem as impractically because medical imaging data grow rapidly at very high speed. Features are the most important aspect in medical imaging. So our model assists the radiologist to extract the image features in a most prominent way and process it using big data analytical tools in a distributed environment. So this will be the big evolution in medical science. The researchers works in future on Medical image processing can go into frontier areas with the help of robots, for the detection of ROI and Non-ROI regions and CADBD (computer aided diagnosis with big data) can be used in the future research for better prediction of the diseases.

REFERENCES

Abubakar, F. M. (2013). Study of Image Segmentation using Thresholding Technique on a Noisy Image. *International Journal of Science and Research, 2*(1).

Altera. (2016). Medical Imaging Implementation using FPGAs (White Paper). Altera.

Ammari, H. (2008). *An International to Mathematics of Engineering Biomedical Imaging*. Springer-Verlag Berlin Heidelberg.

Archenaa, J. & Mary Anita, E. A. (2015). A Survey of Big Data Analytics in Healthcare and Government. Proceeding of Computer Science, 50, 408-413. doi: 10;1016/j.procs.15.04.021

Belle, A., Thiagarajan, R., Soroushmehr, R. S. M., Navaidi, F., Beard, A. D., & Najarian, K. (2015). Big Data Analytics in Healthcare. *BioMed Research International*, *2015*, 1–16. doi:10.1155/2015/370194 PubMed

Chandel, G. S., Kumar, R., Khare, D., & Verma, S. (2012). Analysis of Image Segmentation Algorithms Using MATLAB. *IJEIR*, *1*(1), 51–55.

Chandrakala, M., & Devi, P. D. (2016). Threshold Based Segmentation Using Block Processing. *International Journal of Innovative Research in Computer and Communication Engineering*, *4*. Advance online publication. doi:10.15680/IJIRCC.2016.0401050

Chen, L. K., & Lee, H. (2013). The Impact of Big Data on Healthcare Information Systems. *Transaction of the International Conference on Healthcare Information Technology Advancement*, 2(9).

Das, T. K., & Kumar, P. M. (2013). Big data Analytics: A Framework for unstructured Data Analytics. *IACSIT International Journal of Engineering and Technology*, ●●●, 5.

Desai, D. M., & Rajamenakshi, R. (2016). Large Scale Image Feature Extraction from Medical Image Analysis. *International Journal of Advanced Engineering Research and Science*, *3*(1).

Dubay, S., & Gupta, Y. K. (2017). Computational Comparison of Various Existing Edge Detection Techniques for Medical Images. *International Journal of Computers and Applications*, *16*(1), 185–193.

Dubay, S., Gupta, Y. K., & Soni, D. (2017). Role of Big Data in Healthcare with Non- Invasive and Minimal-Invasive Medical Imaging Modality. *International Journal of Innovative Research in Computer and Communication Engineering*, *5*(3), 5322–5331.

Dubey, S., Gupta, Y. K., & Soni, D. (2016). Comparative Study of Various Segmentation Techniques with their Effective Parameters. *International Journal of Innovative Research in Computer and Communication Engineering*, *4*(10).

Feldman, B., Martin, E. M., & Skotnes, T. (2012). *Big Data in Healthcare Hype and Hope. Dr Bonnie 360*. Business Dvelopment for Digital Health.

Gagana, H. S., & Thipperswamy, K. (2016). Healthcare System with Big Data Analytics: A Survey. International Journal of modern Computer Science and Application, 4.

Gagana, H. S. & Thipperswamy, K. (2016). Healthcare System with Big Data Analytics: A Survey. International Journal of modern Computer Science and Application, 4.

Gupta, Y. K. (2017a). A Novel Approach with Various Existing Edge Detection Techniques for Medical Imaging Modalities. *Journal of Advanced Computing and Communication Technologies*, *5*(3).

Gupta, Y. K. (2019). Empirical Aspect to Extract Hidden Features from Unattended Portion of Neuroimaging Modalities for Early Detection of Diseases. In International Conference Advanced Informatics for Computing Research (ICAICR). Communications in Computer and Information Science (CCIS). DOI: 10.1007/978-981-15-0108-1_21

Gupta, Y. K. (2020). Aspect of Big Data in Medical Imaging to Extract the Hidden Information Using HIPI in HDFS Environment. In *Advancement of Machine Intelligence in Interactive Medical Image Analysis. Algorithms for Intelligent Systems (AIS)* (pp. 19–40). Springer., doi:10.1007/978-981-15-1100-4_2

Gupta, Y. K., & Jha, C. K. (2016). Study of big data with medical imaging communication. International Conference on Communication Systems. CRC-press (Tylor &Fransis group), 6(1), 443-445. doi:10.1201/9781315364094-178

Gupta, Y. K., & Jha, C. K. (2016). A Review on the Study of Big Data with Comparison of Various Storage and Computing Tools and Their Relatives Capabilities. International Journal of Innovations in Engineering and Technology, 7.

Gupta, Y. K., & Maheshwari, A. (2017b). Comparative Study of Various Image Processing Tools with BigData Images in Parallel Environment. *International Journal on Future Revolution in Computer Science & Communication Engineering*, 3(11), 532–536.

Haralampieva, D. G., Ametamey. S. M., Sulser, T. & Eberli, D. (2014). Non-Invasive Modalities for Clinical Investigation in Regenerative Medicine. Intech Open Science| Open Minds. doi:10.5772/59356

Hsu, A. L., Khachikyan, I., & Stratton, P. (2010). Invasive and Non-Invasive Methods for the Diagnosis of Endometriosis. NIH Pubic Access Author Manuscript., 53(2), 413–419. doi: PubMed doi:10.1097/GRF.0b013e31db7ce8

Kasban, H., El-Bendary, M. A., & Salma, D. H. (2015). A Comparative Study of Medical Imaging Techniques. *International Journal of Information Science and Information Science and Intelligent Systems*, 4(2), 37–58.

Kumar, A. (2018). A Review on Implementation of Digital Image Watermarking Techniques Using LSB and DWT. Third International Conference on Information and Communication Technology for Sustainable Development (ICT4SD 2018).

Kumar, A. (2019). Design of Secure Image Fusion Technique Using Cloud for Privacy-Preserving and Copyright Protection. *International Journal of Cloud Applications and Computing*, 9(3), 22–36. doi:10.4018/IJCAC.2019070102

Kumar, A., Ghrera, S. P., & Tyagi, V. (2014). Implementation of wavelet based modified buyer-seller watermarking protocol. *WSEAS Trans. Signal Process*, 10, 212–220.

Kumar, A., Ghrera, S. P., & Tyagi, V. (2015a). A comparison of buyer-seller watermarking protocol (BSWP) based on discrete cosine transform (DCT) and discrete wavelet transform (DWT). Emerging ICT For Bridging The Future-Proceedings of The 49th Annual Convention Of The Computer Society Of India (CSI), 1, 401–408.

Kumar, A., Ghrera, S. P., & Tyagi, V. (2015b). Modified Buyer Seller Wa-termarking Protocol based on Discrete Wavelet Transform and Principal Component Analysis. *Indian Journal of Science and Technology*, 8(35), 1–9.

Kumar, A., Ghrera, S. P., & Tyagi, V. (2017). An ID-based Secure and Flexible Buyer-seller Watermarking Protocol for Copyright Protection. *Pertanika Journal of Science & Technology*, 25(1).

Kumar, A., & Shailaja Rani, P. B. (2019). Digital Image Forgery Detection Techniques: A Comprehensive Review. IEEE 3rd International Conference on Electronics and Communication and Aerospace Technology.

Kumari, R. & Sharma, N. (2015). A Study on the Different Image Segmentation Technique. International Journal of Engineering and Innovative Technology, 4.

Lavanya, S., Vikram, N. R., & Revathi, M. A. (2016). Systematic Big Data Study using HDFS and Map Reduce. International Journal of Advanced Research in Biology, Engineering, Science and Technology, 2.

Lodha, R., Jain, H. & Kurup, L. (2014). Big Data Challenges: Data Analytics Perspective. International Journal of Current Engineering and Technology.

Maheshwari, A., & Gupta, Y. K. (2018). Empirical Aspect of Big Data to Enhance Medical Images Using HIPI. Proceedings of the Second International Conference on Intelligent Computing and Control Systems (ICICCS), 215-220. doi:10.1109/ICCONS.2018.8663053

Manikannan, A., & SenthilMurugan, J. (2015). A Comparative Study about Region Based and Model Based using Segmentation Techniques. International Journal Innovative Research in Computer and Communication Engineering, 3(3).

Manojbhai, D. D., & Rajamenakshi, R. (2016). Large Scale Image Feature Extraction from the Medical Image Analysis. *International Journal of Advanced Engineering Research and Science*, *3*(1).

Naveenkumar, N. (2014). A Survey on Appliance and Secure In Big Data. *International Journal for Innovative Research in Science & Technology*, *1*(6).

Patel, S., & Patel, A. (2016). A Big Data Revolution in Healthcare Sector: Opportunities, Challenges and Technological Advancements. *International Journal of Information Sciences and Techniques*, *6*(1/2), 6216. doi:10.5121/ijist.2016.6216

Peter Augustine, D. (2014). Leveraging Big Data Analytics and Hadoop in Developing India's Healthcare Services. *International Journal of Computers and Applications*, •••, 89.

Priyanka, K., & Kulennavar, N. (2014). A Survey on Big Data Analytics in Healthcare. *International Journal of Computer Science and Information Technologies*, *5*(4).

Raghupathi, W., & Raghupathi, V. (2014). Big Data Analytics in Health: Promise and Potential. Health Information Science and Systems, 2(1), 3. doi:10.1186/2047-2501-2-3 PubMed

Ravi, M., & Basavaprasad, B. (2015). *A Comparative Study on Segmentation Methods for Medical Imaging*. Academic Press.

Sambasivarao, Ch., & Naganjaneyulu, V. (2014). An Efficient Boundary Detection and Image Segmentation Method Based on Perceptual Organization. *International Journal of Computer Trends and Technology*, •••, 7.

Saraladevi, B., Pazhaniraja, N., Victer Paul, P., Salem Basha, M. S., & Dhvachelvan, P. (2015). Big Data and Hadoop – A Study in Security Perspective. 2nd International Symposium on Big Data and Cloud Computing. Procedia Computer Science. doi:10.1016/j.procs.2015.04.091

Singh, P., & Chadha, S. R. (2013). A Novel Approach to Image Segmentation. *International Journal of Advanced Research in Computer Science and Software Engineering, 3*.

Singh, P., Kumar, A., & Kumar, M. (2018). RSA using Montgomery Powering Ladder on Dual Core. *Third International Conference on Information and Communication Technology for Sustainable Development (ICT4SD).*

Singh, P., & Singh, A. (2016). A Study on Image Segmentation Techniques. *International Journal of Recent Trends in Engineering & Research, 2*.

Smitha, P., Shaji, L., & Mini, M. G. (2011). A review of medical image classification techniques. *International conference on VLSI, Communication & Intrumrnataiom*, 34-38.

Soni, D., & Gupta, Y. K. (2017). Quantitative Approach to Extract Features from the Medical Images Using 2D-DWT. *International Journal of Computers and Applications, 16*(1), 149–157.

Soni, D., Gupta, Y. K., & Dubay, S. (2016). Empirical Study of DWT and FFT techniques to extract Intensity based features from the Images. *International Research Journal of Engineering and Technology, 3*(10), 437–443.

Tamilselvan, K. S., Murugesan, G., & Kandasamy, K. (2015). A Novel Image Segmentation Algorithm for Clinical CT Images using Wavelet Transform, Curvelet Transform and Multiple Kernel FCM. *Applied Mathematical Sciences, 9*, 2351–2362.

Thabet, N., & Soomro, T. R. (2015). Big Data Challenges. *Journal of Computer Engineering & Information Technology, 4*(3). Advance online publication. doi:10.4172/2324-9307.1000135

Thakur, A., & Madhusudan, K. (2016). Image Segmentation: A Comparative Study. *International Journal of Advances in Computer Science and Technology, 5*(6).

Vivekananth, P., & Baptist, L. J. A. (2015). An Analysis of Big Data Analytics Techniques. *International Journal of Engineering and Management Research, 5*(5).

Yogamangalam, R., & Karthikeyan, B. (2013). Segmentation Techniques Comparison in Image Processing. *IACSIT International Journal of Engineering and Technology*, ●●●, 5.

This research was previously published in Advancements in Security and Privacy Initiatives for Multimedia Images; pages 41-78, copyright year 2021 by Information Science Reference (an imprint of IGI Global).

Chapter 23
A Framework for Effective Data Analytics for Tourism Sector:
Big Data Approach

Sapna Sinha
Amity Institute of Information Technology, Noida, India

Vishal Bhatnagar
Department of Computer Science and Engineering, Ambedkar Institute of Advanced Communication Technologies and Research, New Delhi, India

Abhay Bansal
Amity School of Engineering and Information Technology, Noida, India

ABSTRACT

From BRICS nations, India is the second largest tourism market after China in Asia. Technological revolution has added new dimensions to the way technologies being used in all the sectors. Also, the use of electronic gadgets leaves trail of data, which is very huge in size, this data (Big Data) is exploited by every sector for providing better services and gaining competitive edge. This trend grabbed the attention of researchers and industry for development of more optimized tools and techniques. There are many general frameworks proposed by industry and researchers for implementation of Big Data in industry but, there is no framework proposed for tourism sector. In this paper, the authors propose unified IT infrastructure framework named as tAdvisor for effective data analytics using Big Data Analytics approach for increasing productivity in tourism sector. Various challenges and issues related with the implementation of Big Data Analytics is also discussed in the paper.

DOI: 10.4018/978-1-6684-3662-2.ch023

1. INTRODUCTION

Tourism sector plays very important role in the social and economic growth of any country. Tourism is contributing around 10% to worldwide GDP. Tourism sector has 6.3% share in GDP of India in 2015 and generated about 22 million jobs. In 2014 foreign exchange earnings from tourism was 20236 million US$ and earning from domestic tourist visit was 1281.95 million. For the convenience of international tourists, the government has started facility of E-tourist Visa for citizens of 113 countries at 16 airports. E-Visa is the electronic visa applied online and generated online. According to stats provided by Ministry of Tourism in year 2014 total 39046 E-Visa was issued from various airports and 22286 visas was issued in the month of January to August in year 2015.

Technologies like Internet, Mobile has changed the marketing strategy and function of the different sectors. Tourism sector is also using technology for product development, marketing, distribution and training, but there is a technological gap between tourism industry and the technology industry. To bridge this gap Online Travel Agents (OTA) came into existence. It has also observed that business operators and workforce within industry do not have sufficient knowledge, tools, and /or strategy to utilize technology correctly. This sector has now started embarrassing 3rd T, i.e. Travel, Tourism, Technology. Technology can be used in all the dimensions of tourism for gaining competitive edge and providing 360 degree services to customer. With the advancement of technology and 24X7 availability, customers are also demanding 24X7 services.

According to Moor, Moor's Law: as the impact of technological revolution grows in the society, there will be rise in ethical problem (Moor, 2005, p. 117). Advanced technology provides novel methods to use them, which does not hold well defined ethical policies. Tourism is one of such sector which is using technology in various modes. With the use of these technologies, ethical issues are also increasing. The new term Technoethics came into existence which refers to dealing with the ethical issues due to use of technology. According to (Johnson, 1985), the need of Technoethics will be disappearing once technology matures.

Tourism is defined as "Travel and stay of a non-resident". It is ranked ahead of all other categories of international trade. Tourism has three major components:

1. **Attraction:** Man made or Natural tourist sites.
2. **Accommodation:** Hotels, Lodges or place of stay during visit.
3. **Transport:** Mode of transportation to tourist sites and back to permanent habitat.

Mobile technology and Internet has added new dimensions to the sector, now Tourists need detailed information for each place they intend to visit like: Geographical information, landscape, climate, accommodation and dining options, shopping facility, accessibility and availability of transport, social and cultural information of the place, activity and entertainment facilities, best season to visit, quality of services and price of stay including exchange rates. It has been observed that during their visit tourists carry electronic gadgets for their ease like: Mobile Phones, Laptop, Digital Camera's, Internet accessibility etc. These gadgets leave a trail of data which can be used by this sector for increased productivity and better services. (Vidyullata Shekhar Jadhav et al., 2011) has given layered structure of tourism industry, Figure 1 shows the layered organization of tourism sector, authors have proposed new underlying layer of unified IT infrastructure framework tAdvisor which will provide support to all the components of tourism sector. tAdvisor is the name given by author to the proposed framework, it is a framework which ensures use of technology ethically.

The paper is structured as follows: Section 2 discusses literature survey and motivation behind creation of this paper, Section 3 describes research methodology adopted, Sector 4 focuses on basics of big data analytics, Section 5 describes introduction of tourism sector and conglomeration of it with big data analytics. Section 6 discusses various challenges associated with implementation of big data analytics in tourism sector, Section 7 discusses architecture of the proposed framework, and Section 8 provides an empirical case study for the implementation of proposed framework in tourism sector. Section 9 focuses on advantages and disadvantages associated with implementation of proposed framework and finally paper concludes with Section 10 on conclusion and suggested future work.

Figure 1. Layered organization of tourism structure

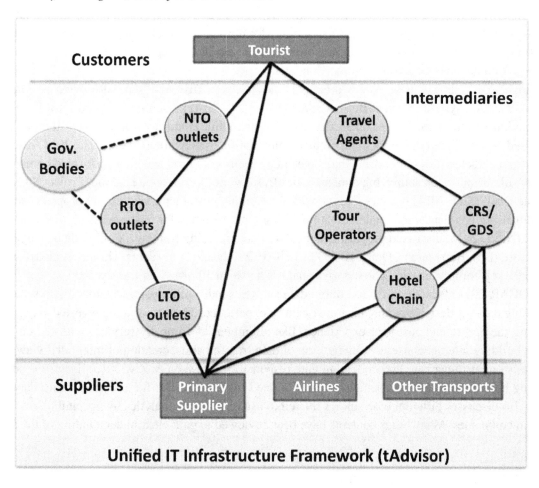

2. LITERATURE SURVEY AND MOTIVATION

Big Data Analytics is getting lot of attention these days. Customers are leaving trails of data during their travel related to activities performed by them from initial searching of the destination, planning of the trip, reservations made, services used and the posts posted on social networking site (Baggio, 2016). The Potential of this data can be exploited by collecting relevant data and analyzing it to get solution of the many real-life problems (Xiang, 2015). Novelty of the field, tools and technology for Big Data Analytics is still in evolutionary phase. Almost every sector is analyzing the potential of Big Data Analytics to get value out of it and to gain competitive advantages over their competitors.

Available literature on the framework architecture of big data analytics is reviewed and it has been observed that, most of them focuses on general architecture of big data analytics. Very few architecture frameworks are proposed for the specific domain. Domains like Banking and Healthcare have got few frameworks to implement big data analytics whereas frameworks for other domains are yet to be proposed. There are various issues related to defining Big Data framework, namely: Infrastructure, Data Structure, Data Models, Life Cycle Management, security issues, analysis requirements and suggestions to address challenges associated with Big Data (Demchenko, 2013).

(Sanders, 2013) presented layered model of analytics adoption model for health care sector but there is no framework is available for tourism sector. (Raghupathi, 2014) also discussed use of big data analytics in healthcare sector and presents methodology for the same. Framework flexAnalytics to enhance scalability and flexibility to eliminate the bottleneck caused due to gap between computation and I/O capacity for data analysis is proposed by (Zou, 2014).

(Singh, 2014) showed how open source tools like Hadoop, Hive and Mahout provides scalable intrusion detection system to detect Bot-net attack. (Youssef, 2014) presented framework for Healthcare Information System (HIS's) based on big data analytics in mobile cloud environment. (Ousterhout, 2015) discussed performance bottleneck in distributed computation framework. (Chandarana, 2014) discussed important characteristics of big data, challenges in its implementation and also performed comparative analysis of various open source big data analytics framework like, Apache Hadoop, Project Storm and Apache Drill. (Sun, 2014) presented framework for banking customer analytics and proposed solution for addressing challenges for implementation of big data analytics for customer analytics in banking sector. (NIST, 2015) discussed proposal received till date regarding framework of big data analytics by, Microsoft, IBM, Bob Marcus, Oracle, PIVOTAL, SAP, 9Sight and LexisNexis. This paper also discusses structure, key components and comparative analysis between all proposed frameworks.

(SOCAP, 2014) focuses on the use of big data analytics in hospitality, travel and tourism sector, the use of big data for designing more customer centric experience. The author has suggested six steps for building the end-to-end customer experience, like alignment of company services with the customer needs, building internal consensus, integration of data from all silos, creation of integrated view, more emphasis on customer care and collecting data responsibly. (Dawson & Ziv, 2013) discussed benefits of using big data in travel companies, challenges need to be addressed for adoption of big data. This paper also discusses different case studies related to use of big data analytics by hospitality, travel and tourism companies. Many blogs contents have been reviewed to gain clear understanding of the sector.

3. RESEARCH METHODOLOGY

Authors have conducted study for understanding the need of big data analytics in the tourism sector. The study led us to design a framework for big data analytics specific for the tourism sector, although many general frameworks are proposed by many organizations or authors. Frameworks for the specific domains are still not available. Authors have also attended many workshop and refresher courses to gain insight about the domain and technology. The research strategy adopted is as follows:

1. Importance of framework for big data analytics for the domain was felt after studying various literature and discussions.
2. Importance of big data analytics for effective data analytics for tourism domain is realized after studying literature and discussions.
3. Information related to big data analytics and tourism sector is collected through informal interview, discussions, conferences, seminars and workshops. This let to idea of using big data analytics in tourism sector.
4. A framework was proposed for effective data analytics for tourism sector, because the need was felt for the domain specific framework.

4. BIG DATA ANALYTICS: AN INTRODUCTION

Due to advancement of communication technology, data are collected from different types of sources like, sensors, mobile phones, web server logs, social networking sites. The data having characteristics of 5V's, Described as follows:

1. **Volume:** It signifies size and scale of the data; it should be in petabyte of zettabyte.
2. **Velocity:** It signifies frequency of the data, because real time streaming data is also the part of big data.
3. **Veracity:** It signifies trustworthiness and authenticity of the data.
4. **Variety:** It signifies format of the data, big data constitute of structured, semi-structured and unstructured data.
5. **Value:** It is a new dimension added (www.datatechnocrats.com/tag/big-data/), signifying extraction of knowledge out of big data.

Complexity, is another characteristics added by Gartner, represent complex format of the data.

Using pattern matching, Data Mining and Natural Language Processing techniques, big data is analyzed and results are used for effective decision making based on facts rather than intuition (see Figure 2).

5. TOURISM SECTOR: AN INTRODUCTION

Tourism is the one of the sector, which is generating huge amount of data every second. Right from booking reservations to posts on social media leave trails of data, using which organizations of tourism sector can design their services and become customer-centric organization. Advanced analytics can be used to understand their customers, to get end-to-end vision and info driven strategy. United Nations World Tourism Organization (UNWTO's) provides technical assistance to all the member countries to help them in develop and to promote tourism industry.

Figure 2. Characteristics of Big Data (www.datatechnocrats.com/tag/big-data/)

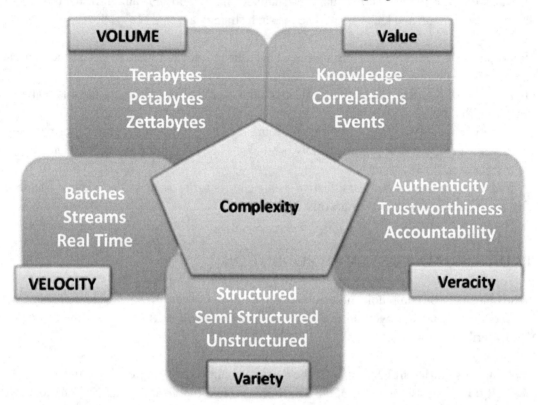

Big data analytics has potential of offering services based on customer budget, liking and disliking. Options for locations, dining, restaurants, nightclubs, resorts or hotels can be recommended before customer look for the options themselves. Opinions or reviews shared by customers on websites and blogs can be analyzed for accurate recommendations. Till now this is a dream but very soon it will turn into reality, once these organizations are able to exploit full potential of the Big Data. TravelAdvisors, TripTogether.com, Makemytrip.com and Yelp are the few websites that offers its user to rate suppliers, share reviews and offer comments about experiences, but they lack context in which opinion is made. Trustworthiness of these websites are also having question mark.

Customers of tourism sector is not loyal, they keep on switching from one company to another as per their convenience. Due to this, it is very difficult for the companies to retain their customers. Price elasticity is the biggest challenge for this sector. Initially online tourism portals came into existence as a threat to conventional tourism companies. Later on, these online companies have started their own Travel Boutiques to work in conventional mode. These tourism companies are moving towards Vertical Integration from Horizontal Integration. That is, now tourism is not the only component to which these companies are dealing, they started dealing in Ticketing, Hotels, Car Rentals, Travel Insurance, and Overseas Health Insurance too.

5.1. Conglomeration of Big Data Analytics and Tourism Sector

Big Data Analytics can help companies of tourism sector to streamline their operations and turning their organization into customer-centric-organization. Customer-centric processes will help companies to increase in customer retention. Customer needs fast and efficient services, for this they compromise with price.

6. CHALLENGES IN THE IMPLEMENTATION OF BIG DATA ANALYTICS IN TOURISM SECTOR

For embracing big data analytics, the tourism sector has to address various challenges associated to it. The main big data challenges are:

1. The data is fragmented and spread across multiple functions and units. For making effective decisions all these data from different silos are needed to be combined into a single data warehouse using a single set of algorithms. The proposed framework allows to integrated data from all silos in central data warehouse.
2. This sector has variety of data, both in structured and unstructured format. Monitoring, gathering, and analyzing unstructured data spread across various social networking sites and corporate servers is another major challenge. It is very difficult to integrate unstructured data with internal operational/transaction database systems. Data from heterogeneous sources can integrated using this framework.
3. Business and Technological alignment is the main issue, because Big Data ecosystem should coexist with the existing Hardware, Software and Databases. Big data often implemented on Hadoop, an open source platform based on MapReduce framework for distributed processing and storage. Databases used are both columnar and vertical; new scripting languages are needed like Python, Pig and Hive. This architecture should support processing data-appliances and in-memory analytics. A statistical processing tool like SAS, SPSS or R programs is also the need. The proposed framework allows use of different types of statistical processing tools.
4. Dealing with unstructured data, because it is available on distributed online transaction environment (DOLTP) using the "NoSQL." As the proposed framework allows processing of unstructured data extracted from web, NoSQL is used for querying it.
5. Shortage of skills means shortage of people having knowledge of data management, programming and lack of analytical skills to analyze the data and understanding of business processes. Data Scientists are the new brigade of workforce, which will be in demand in times to come.

In this paper, authors propose a framework to address challenges related to implementation of big data analytics in tourism sector. tAdvisor framework architecture uses layered approach (Figure 3) for the implementation of big data analytics in tourism sector. The following section describes architecture of tAdvisor framework to analyze customer behavior through text analytics in key business scenarios.

Figure 3. Layered Architecture of tAdvisor Framework

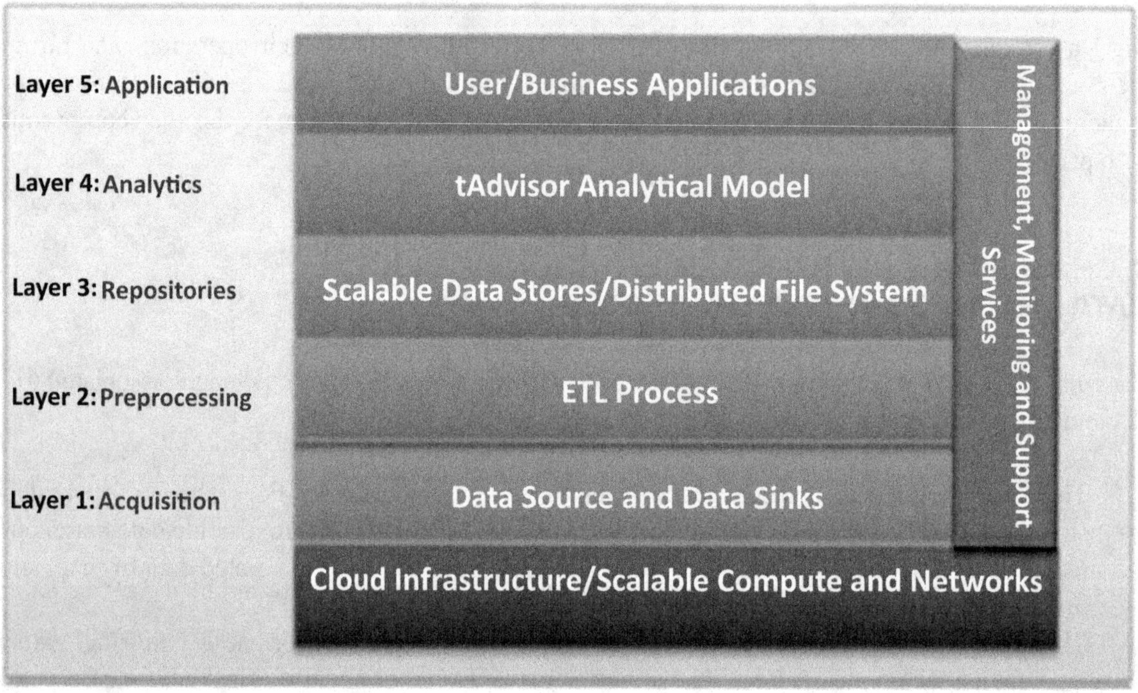

7. FRAMEWORK OF tADVISOR: PROPOSED SOLUTION

The architecture of tAdvisor framework is divided into horizontal and vertical layers. There are five layers defined horizontally along with one vertical layer. Cloud Infrastructure and networks layer is the base layer which provides hardware support and storage services to other layers. The horizontal layer on the top, takes services of layer below it and vertical layer provides services to all the horizontal layers. The first horizontal layer is Data Acquisition, second layer is Pre-processing, third layer is Repositories, fourth layer is Analytics and fifth layer is Application. tAdvisor will provide deeper customer insight to handle their needs from tourism industry.

The description of layers defined in the framework (Figure 4) is as follows:

7.1. Acquisition

Due to vertical integration, data is available in structured format in different silos of the sector. Data Federation software is also playing important role in for pointing locations where data can be found, like train schedule, capacity, etc. Data from this link is of structured format. Further, the increase in unstructured data has generated more complexity. Some unstructured data are organized internally by the organization like booking request and feedback received via emails, Call records, Videos, advertisements, notices, brochures etc. and some are available externally from social media data from Facebook, Twitter, Instagram, Blogs etc. These unstructured data cannot be stored in relational databases where data is stored in table in the form of rows and columns. They are stored in files and need special procedure to give structure to this unstructured data.

Figure 4. Framework of tAdvisor

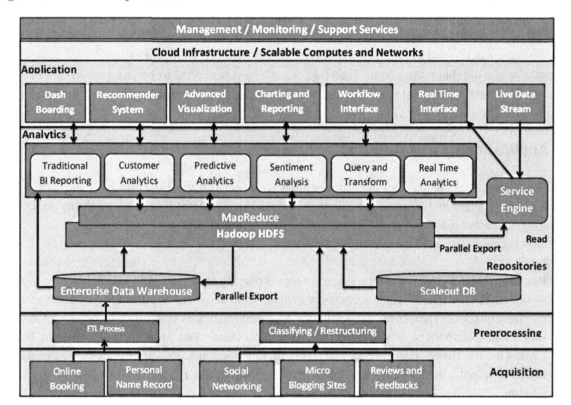

7.2. Preprocessing

In this phase anomalies, noise and incompleteness of structured data is removed and data is cleaned for storage in the databases. Whereas, treatment of unstructured data is different in this phase. Research is going on for finding best solution to give structure to unstructured data. The method to be adopted is outside the scope of this paper.

7.3. Repositories

This layer will contain enterprise data warehouse where data will come from transactional / operational database. Traditional data warehouse can be maintained locally or on cloud infrastructure too. Hadoop Distributed File System (HDFS) is used to store both structured and unstructured data. HDFS will provide underlying distributed storage clusters and other Hadoop technologies like, MapReduce provides interface to divide task into subtasks. Most of the available technologies related to big data analytics, wrap around Hadoop platform. CouchDB and MangoDB are the other available option. Hadoop-as-a-Service is also available to avail on demand Hadoop on cloud platform. Other proprietary solutions like IBM BigInsight can also be used.

7.4. Analytics

tAdvisor will have different analytical model for different business processes. The available techniques of data mining can be used to mine useful pattern and information. To deal with large scale data, single processor is not suitable to handle it. Therefore, parallelism is needed to be enforced in one or other form. For this, artificial neural networks and machine learning algorithm can be used for optimizing time and performance.

7.5. Applications

Big Data Analytics can help sector in customer analytics to convert itself in customer-centric organization. It can be applied in different applications associated to the sector like, trend analysis, prediction, marketing, customer retention, cross-selling and Fake Review Detection.

Following process can be integrated in tAdvisor:

1. **Recommender System:** Recommender system is playing important role in tourism too. Modern recommender system is using context-awareness, semantics and another approach for accurate recommendations. Hybrid Recommendation System which uses traditional approaches Content-Based and Collaborative approach in combination to create context awareness, Semantic Based, Cross-Domain Based, Peer-to-Peer and Cross-lingual approach. Recommender system using any of this approach can be used to recommend destinations, hotels, flights and travelling modes to the tourists.

2. **Customer Analytics:** k-means clustering algorithm can be used to identify the customer. Probable customers can be used for placing them in appropriate cluster and for customer segmentations. After that customers in the identified cluster can be targeted and better services can be designed as per their needs, so that more and more customer retention can be achieved.

3. **Customer Network Identification:** The customers who has already availed the services must be having friend and relatives in their social circle. This network can be analyzed and connections can be knocked to identify the probable customers. Many network analysis tools are available like iPoint, NetMiner, Keyhub, Sentinel Visualizer and many more tools along with open source tools are available in the market. The probability of visiting to same place where friends and relatives had already visited is always more due genuine feedback received from them.

4. **Better Customized Product:** Based on the feedback and booking analysis, better customized products can be designed for gaining high customer satisfaction. This will also help in customer acquisition.

In all these processes, Big Data Analytics can be used and all the processes defined above along with other processes can be optimized and utilized effectively.

For proving effectiveness of proposed framework empirical case study is presented which is based on discussions and direct observation. Validation of the proposed framework is in process.

8. AN EMPIRICAL CASE STUDY

Let us take a company from tourism sector. The company want to optimize their services and to become customer-centric organization. The company deals in other verticals of tourism sector like, hospitality, ticketing, travel and travel insurance too. They found that their customers keep on changing company for buying tickets, tour packages etc. The IT consultant of the company suggested company to adopt big data analytics. The clustering can help company to segment its customer. Sentiment analysis can be done on the posts, reviews and feedback received from social network sites and friends can be approached with appropriate recommendations. Based on the locations, liking and disliking of the customers, nearest eating joints, tourist places can be suggested. Frequent customers can be given loyalty bonus to ensure increase in customer retention. Tour packages can be designed in the budget of customer with other alternatives to choose from.

Adoption of big data analytics by hospitality, travel and tourism sectors like: Swiss International Airlines, Air-France –KLM, Lufthansa, Frontier Airlines proved very beneficial to their adopters. These companies are using big data analytics in some process and were able to generate more revenue out of it Oliver et al., (2014). These companies are not able exploit big data in full extent due to lack of unified framework. Figure 5 shows the processes flow of tAdvisor.

Figure 5. Process Flow of tAdvisor

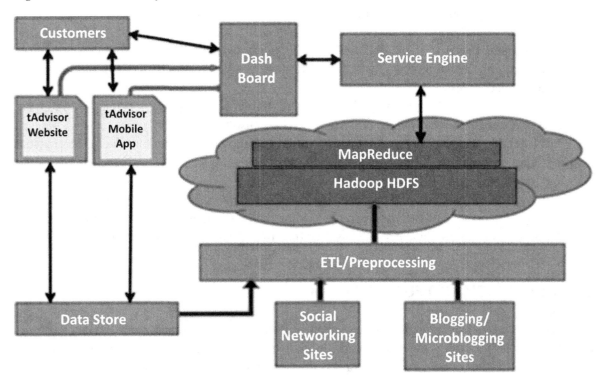

9. ADVANTAGES AND LIMITATIONS OF PROPOSED FRAMEWORK

The advantage of application of proposed framework of tAdvisor in the tourism sector is:

- **Holistic View of Customer:** tAdvisor will help in analyzing holistic view of a customer. Complete customer profile can be created.
- **Better Product Design:** Based on customer profiles, better customized products can be designed, to gain more and more customer satisfaction.
- **Increased Customer Retention:** Better customer satisfaction will lead to increase customer retention.
- **Cross-Selling:** Better service, timely identification of probable customers and reaching them on time will help in customer acquisition from other companies.
- **Improved Services:** Location based services; spatial analytics can help company to deliver services, where it is required, by recommending locations, restaurants and hotels.
- **Improved Champaign Strategy:** Once company becomes aware of customer liking and disliking they can design their Champaign accordingly. Right customer can be approached at right time with right offer.
- **Better Loyalty Points Calculation:** Loyalty points calculation will help companies to increase sense of belongingness to show their concern to their frequent customers.

The limitation of application of framework of tAdvisor is described as follows:

- **Security and Privacy:** Using data mining tools to discover information about customer. Data repositories are maintained on cloud, therefore there is always issue of security and privacy of customer data exists.
- **Infrastructure and Skills:** Cost of infrastructure will be high, if setup is maintained in-house. Cost of acquiring human skills to perform analytics is also high.
- **Not Effective Usage of Derived Information:** Formulation of problem for which data analytics is itself a problem. The information derived may not be used effectively due to lack of knowledge and proper strategy.
- **Automation of Process:** Manual intervention is required for generation of analytics reports. Automatic generation of analytics report is lacking, therefore when to generate report is dependent on the need only. Real Time Analytics is used only to provide location based and spatial services.

10. CONCLUSION AND FUTURE WORK

In this paper, authors have proposed framework of tAdvisor for implementation of Big Data Analytics in tourism sector. tAdvisor is the name authors have given to proposed solution. tAdvisor aims to integrated data from heterogeneous sources, transformed and stored in database, like Hadoop Distributed File System (HDFS). This framework can be implemented centrally to which all the stakeholders can subscribe and get common data/Information and can frame strategy to provide cost effective quality services throughout the country. The main task will be integration of data from different sources and preparation of tAdvisor analytical model. This paper contains only the framework of the proposed solution, suitable algorithms, methods and techniques are yet to be analyzed and verified.

REFERENCES

Akerkar, R. (2012). Big Data & Tourism (TMRF Report 11-2012, White Paper).

Baggio, R. (2016). Big Data, Business Intelligence and Tourism: a brief analysis of the literature. *Paper presented at the IFITTtalk@Östersund: Big Data & Business Intelligence in the Travel & Tourism Domain*, Östersund, SE, April 11-12.

Teradata.com. (2016, September 12). Big Data Reference Architecture. Retrieved from http://thinkbig.teradata.com/leading_big_data_technologies/big-data-reference-architecture/

Bunge, M. (1977). Towards a technoethics. *The Monist, 60*(1), 96–107. doi:10.5840/monist197760134

Chandarana, P., & Vijayalakshmi, M. (2014, April). Big Data analytics frameworks. In *Proceedings of the 2014 International Conference on Circuits, Systems, Communication and Information Technology Applications (CSCITA)* (pp. 430-434). IEEE. 10.1109/CSCITA.2014.6839299

Davenport, T. H. (2013). At the Big Data Crossroads: turning towards a smarter travel experience. Amadeus IT Group.

Dawson K., & Ziv, D. (2012, April 25). A Conversation on the Role of Big Data in Marketing and Customer Service. CRM.

Demchenko, Y., Ngo, C., & Membrey, P. (2013). Architecture framework and components for the big data ecosystem. *Journal of System and Network Engineering*.

Jadhav, V. S., & Shivaji, D. M. (2011). Information technology in Tourism. *International Journal of Computer Science and Information Technologies, 2*(6), 2822–2825.

Johnson, D. (1985). *Computer ethics*. NJ: Prentice-Hall.

Moor, J. H. (2005). Why we need better ethics for emerging technologies. *Ethics and Information Technology, 7*(3), 111–119. doi:10.100710676-006-0008-0

NIST. (2014). Draft NIST Big Data Interoperability Framework (Vol. 5). White Paper Survey.

Oliver, V., Garcia, E., Solana, A., Gonzalez, R., Pelaez, M. V., & Tome, M. J. (2014). Big Data And Tourism: New Indicators for Tourism Management (White Paper).

Ousterhout, K., Rasti, R., Ratnasamy, S., Shenker, S., & Chun, B. G., & ICSI, V. (2015, May). Making sense of performance in data analytics frameworks. In *Proceedings of the 12th USENIX Symposium on Networked Systems Design and Implementation (NSDI)*, Oakland, CA (pp. 293-307).

Raghupathi, W., & Raghupathi, V. (2014). Big data analytics in healthcare: Promise and potential. *Health Information Science and Systems, 2*(1), 3. doi:10.1186/2047-2501-2-3 PMID:25825667

Sanders, D., Burton, D. A., & Protti, D. (2013). The Healthcare Analytics Adoption Model: A Framework and Roadmap.

Singh, K., Guntuku, S. C., Thakur, A., & Hota, C. (2014). Big Data Analytics framework for Peer-to-Peer Botnet detection using Random Forests. *Inform. Sci.*, *278*, 488–497. doi:10.1016/j.ins.2014.03.066

Sinha, S., & Bhatnagar, V. (2012). Big Data Analytics: Need of the New Era. *Proceedings of FOBE '12*.

SOCAP International. (2013). Now Arriving: Big Data in the Hospitality, Travel and Tourism Sector. Retrieved from www.socap.org

Sun, N., Morris, J. G., Xu, J., Zhu, X., & Xie, M. (2014). iCARE: A framework for big data-based banking customer analytics. *IBM Journal of Research and Development*, *58*(5/6), 4–1. doi:10.1147/JRD.2014.2337118

Taylor, M. (2011). It's Time for Big Data to Improve the Customer Experience. Outlook Report.

Xiang, Z., Schwartz, Z., Gerdes, J. H. Jr, & Uysal, M. (2015). What can big data and text analytics tell us about hotel guest experience and satisfaction? *International Journal of Hospitality Management*, *44*, 120–130. doi:10.1016/j.ijhm.2014.10.013

Youssef, A. E. (2014). A framework for secure healthcare systems based on Big data analytics in mobile cloud computing environments. *Int. J. Ambient Syst. Appl.*, *2*(2), 1–11.

Zou, H., Yu, Y., Tang, W., & Chen, H. W. M. (2014). Flexanalytics: A flexible data analytics framework for big data applications with I/O performance improvement. *Big Data Research*, *1*, 4–13. doi:10.1016/j.bdr.2014.07.001

This research was previously published in the International Journal of Grid and High Performance Computing (IJGHPC), 9(4); pages 92-104, copyright year 2017 by IGI Publishing (an imprint of IGI Global).

Index

C

I

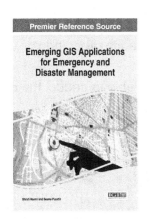

Printed in the United States
by Baker & Taylor Publisher Services